Wizards and Sorcerers

Wizards and Sorcerers

FROM ABRACADABRA TO ZOROASTER

TOM OGDEN

Facts On File, Inc.

Wizards and Sorcerers: From Abracadabra to Zoroaster

Copyright © 1997 by Tom Ogden

Facts On File, Inc.
11 Penn Plaza
New York NY 10001

Library of Congress Cataloging-in-Publication Data
Ogden, Tom.
  Wizards and sorcerers : from abracadabra to Zoroaster / Tom Ogden.
    p.   cm.
  Includes index.
  ISBN 0-8160-3151-7 (alk. paper).
    1. Magic—Encyclopedias. 2. Magic—History. 3. Occultism—
Encyclopedias. 4. Occultism—History. I. Title.
BF1588.043 1997
1334'3'03—dc21 96-52305

Facts On File books are available at special discounts when purchased in bulk quantities for
businesses, associations, institutions or sales promotions. Please call our Special Sales Department
in New York at (212) 967-8800 or (800) 322-8755.

You can find Facts On File on the World Wide Web at **http://www.factsonfile.com**

Text design and layout by Grace Ferrara
Cover design by Mark Safran

Printed in the United States of America

VB FOF 10 9 8 7 6 5 4 3 2 1

This book is printed on acid-free paper.

For Mom,

Who Watched Every Card Trick

And Ed Cashmore,

Who Started Me on the road to Wizardry

CONTENTS

INTRODUCTION

Like most writers in the fantasy field, I have been interested in the occult almost all my life. But my involvement in wizardry has been more than casual curiosity: For the past twenty years, my touring as a professional magician has taken me, quite literally, around the world, giving me the opportunity to visit the sites of ancient Grecian oracles, stand in awe before towering temple walls covered with Egyptian hieroglyphics and witness firsthand the mysteries of African shamans and Indian fakirs.

Perhaps due to the innate human desire to explain the unexplainable and to explore the unknown and the unknowable, interest in fantasy and sorcery is stronger than ever. Unfortunately, in everyday usage and even in most occult literature, such words as *wizard, shaman, enchantress/enchanter, witch doctor, voodoo doctor, medicine man, sorcerer/sorceress, magician, witch/warlock* and *necromancer* are used interchangeably, making it difficult to define or delineate terms.

Also, different fields of study have their own prejudicial definitions. Some African anthropologists, for example, define *witches* as those born with an inner gift of magic and *sorcerers* as those who, by studying their craft, use herbal potions or rely on representational magic. In Western tradition, however, the distinctions are drawn by the ways in which the arcane knowledge was gained (e.g., through study or selling one's soul) or the intent of the magic (e.g., black vs. white magic).

Classifications changed throughout history. For example, in medieval times, a king might have retained the services of a court wizard but would never have admitted to harboring a court sorcerer. The former—a combination alchemist, astrologer, magical entertainer and adviser—would have been beneficial to the court; the latter would have been perceived as an evil force, possibly harmful to the king himself.

Therefore, for the purposes of this book, it was necessary that I make my own distinctions, especially among the terms *wizard, witch* and *sorcerer*. Based on my judgment of the most-commonly agreed-upon definitions, I have made the following generalized differentiations throughout *Wizards and Sorcerers*:

Wizards are magicians, from the first priests who used trickery to entrance their congregations through the alchemists to modern-day cabalists. Generally, they seek wisdom and mystic truths and practice "white magic," based on experimentation and gained through apprenticeship, oral tradition, folklore or the study of arcane writings. Their work tends to be beneficent, or at least benign, particularly to their patrons.

Sorcerers are the practitioners of black magic and dark spells, who can call up the spirits of the dead and the Underworld. Above all, sorcerers seek unlimited knowledge, with a lust for power, control and mastery of the universe. They wish to use their powers to make them, in essence, gods. For some, the knowledge gained through the intense study of occult books and secret tracts is sufficient. For others, the cabalistic learning is used to summon up demons and spirits to do their bidding. Often a pact is signed with the Devil in exchange for earthly omnipotence and omniscience. Sorcerers do not worship Satan nor work on his behalf; instead, they seek to dominate and to control the powers of evil in an attempt to become divine themselves.

By this definition, witches are not sorceresses, at least not in the classic sense, because they obtain their powers by making pacts with and selling their souls to the Devil. In return, Satan teaches the witch her craft, provides her with a familiar spirit to communicate with his demons and celebrates with her at sabbats. Rather than seeking to become as powerful as the Devil herself, the witch worships his evil divinity. They are, therefore, obedient to him and use their hellish arts to serve their master on earth. Thus, enchantresses such as Circe and Morgan le Fay, who are often misnamed witches because of their gender, are more closely related to wizards than to sorcerers. In *Wizards and Sorcerers*, the word *witch* is used in its colloquial connotation rather than as a practitioner of the *religion* of witchcraft, or *wicca*.

Although many occult words are masculine in form, it should be noted that members of both sexes have been represented among the ranks of wizards, witches, sorcerers and enchanters. In fact, in many cultures the occult figures are predominantly women.

Some words do offer a gender choice (e.g., *sorcerer/sorceress*); others do not (*wizard*). With apologies for the English language, therefore, unless an entry calls for a specific gender, the accepted male noun and pronoun forms are usually employed. Unfortunately, politically-correct substitutes for many legitimate words (such as "humankind" for "mankind") are often pretentious, if not incorrect. One major exception is *warlock*, a word used only in Western countries to denote a male witch. The latter, more inclusive word is generally used throughout this book.

Occult texts are filled with unorthodox spellings and capitalizations, especially of jargon and alchemical terms. Where *Wizards and Sorcerers* varies from standard English, I have tried to follow the most common or accepted form in the original sources.

Wizards and Sorcerers is a historical overview of enchantment, magic and the occult. While the emphasis is on individuals, both fictional and real, I have covered relevant jargon and items from related supernatural fields of study, as well as relevant aspects of popular culture, such as films, theater and comics. In an effort to be *in*clusive rather than *ex*clusive, I have also entered some of the more popular supernatural characters (e.g., Og the leprechaun in *Finian's Rainbow* and the Blue Fairy from *Pinocchio*) who are creatures endowed with magic. I have chosen, however, not to emphasize such contemporary concepts as neopaganism, the "New Age" and Satanism.

Most, if not all, of the contemporary names and images in fantasy (including but not limited to comics, board and video games, toys and action figures) are protected by their respective creators, manufacturers or publishers under copyright and/or trademark. Mention in this compendium should in no way be inferred to allow their improper use.

There are many people who must be thanked for their assistance in the writing of this book: Jefferson Beeker (Saban Entertainment), Ian D. and Ann Campbell (San Diego Opera), Noel Lei Hayashi (La Mirada Theatre for the Performing Arts), Michael Kurland, Max Maven, Tom McLaughlin (TSR, Inc.), Marcia Newberger (Warren Cowan & Associates), Albert Ogden, Francisco Perez, Brian Rubin (La Jolla Playhouse), George and Nina Schindler, Chris Shorb (Third Planet), Michele D. Tell (MGM Grand), Brenda Thanepohn (Excalibur Hotel/Casino), Dottie Walters and Lilly Walters for supplying research materials and support; Eugene Burger and Jeff McBride, themselves New Age wizards; Gary M. Krebs for bringing me the project; my book agent Sharon Jarvis; and my editors Randy Ladenheim-Gil, Anne Baxter and Susan Schwartz.

Aaron's rod   Aaron's rod was the staff through which God demonstrated his blessing on the tribe of Aaron.

Aaron was the brother of MOSES, whose story is told in the Book of Exodus in the Bible's Old Testament. Ordained a priest by the Lord, Aaron assists Moses in his attempt to gain freedom for the Israelites. He performs the first of Jehovah's miracles before Pharaoh by changing Moses' staff into a snake.

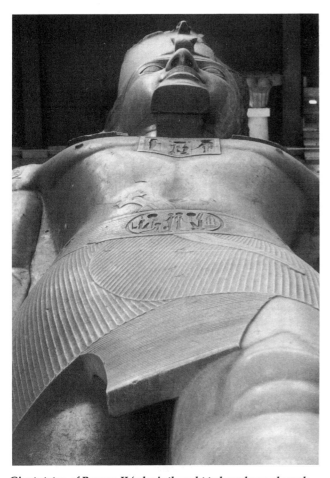

Giant statue of Ramses II (who is thought to have been pharaoh during the time of Moses, Aaron and the Exodus) discovered in Memphis, Egypt's capital during the Old Kingdom.   (Photo by author)

The staff known as Aaron's rod and its final disposition are both fully described in the Bible (17 Numbers). The Lord instructs Moses to gather a rod or staff from the head of each of the 12 tribes of Israel and to place them into the "tabernacle of the congregation." Moses is specifically told to have Aaron's name inscribed on the house of Levi's rod. God promises that he will show the quarreling tribes which one he has ordained as his favorite by making that house's rod bloom. The next day it is discovered that, miraculously, "the rod of Aaron for the house of Levi had sprouted and put forth buds, and produced blossoms, and it bore ripe almonds." The Lord told Moses to "Put back the rod of Aaron . . . to be kept as a sign for the rebels." Thus, Aaron's rod became a sacred relic, housed within the tabernacle. According to some traditions, Aaron's rod was actually placed inside the Ark of the Covenant next to the stone tablets inscribed with the Ten Commandments.

A Jewish legend claims that Aaron's rod was actually made on the sixth day of the Creation. Adam and Eve then carried it with them out of the Garden of Eden, and the staff passed down through the ages until reaching Aaron's hands. A Christian legend purports that Aaron's rod was carved from the Tree of Knowledge in Eden. Eventually the staff passed into Judas's hands and finally became the beam of Christ's cross. Both tales are apocryphal and not found in the Bible. (See also DIVINING ROD; WAND.)

Abaris   See PYTHAGORAS.

ablanathanalba   Literally translated as "Thou art a father to us," *Ablanathanalba* acted as a magic word to Egyptian GNOSTICS of the second century A.D. Comparable in power to the later CHARM *ABRACADABRA*, *Ablanathanalba* was often inscribed on AMULETs and TALISMANs. Like many cabalistic magic words, *Ablanathanalba* was thought to possess part of its potency because it read the same forwards and backwards. (See also ABRAXAS.)

abracadabra   The most common of all magic words, *abracadabra* was used to conjure in medieval times and probably had its origin centuries earlier.

Some theologians suggest that the word *abracadabra* is actually an acronym made up of the Hebrew letters for the Holy Trinity—Ab (Father), Ben (Son) and Ruach Acadsch (Holy

Spirit). Other authorities contend that *abracadabra* is a corruption of the GNOSTIC word *ABRAXAS*, possibly meaning "Hurt me not."

Ancient Jewish physicians had an unusual cure for fevers, which included a CHARM inscribed with a palindrome-like pattern of words. First, the mystic SPELL was scrawled on a small piece of parchment:

Ab Abr Abra Abrak Abraka
Abrakal Abrakala Abrakal
Abraka Abrak Abra Abr Ab

And the people called unto Moses and Moses prayed to God and the fire abated. May healing come from heaven from all kinds of fever and consumption—heat to N son of N.

Amen Amen Amen. Selah Selah Selah.

Then, the paper was hung around the neck of the sufferer, who was not to look at the writing for a full day. Through SYMPATHETIC MAGIC the "heat" of the fever (i.e., the patient's temperature) would lessen as the "fire abated."

Some theorists suggest that *abracadabra* comes from an ancient Aramaic phrase, *abhadda kedhabhra*, which means "disappear like this word," or from the Hebrew phrase, *abreq adhabra*, meaning "hurl your thunderbolt unto death."

The first extant record of the word written as *abracadabra* is in the works of Quintus Serenus Sammonicus (also seen as Samonicus), who may also have coined the word. A doctor who traveled with the Roman Emperor Severus to England in A.D. 208, Sammonicus used a "shrinking formula" in a poem as a cure for tertian fever. *ABRACADABRA* was to be written in a diminishing triangle on a piece of paper:

```
A B R A C A D A B R A
 A B R A C A D A B R
  A B R A C A D A B
   A B R A C A D A
    A B R A C A D
     A B R A C A
      A B R A C
       A B R A
        A B R
         A B
          A
```

Centuries later, occultist Eliphas LEVI would refer to this configuration as the "magic triangle" and try to associate it with the TAROT and the KABALLAH.

According to Sammonicus, once the paper was so-inscribed, it should be tied around the sufferer's neck with flax. After nine days, the paper was removed and thrown backwards over the shoulder and into a stream running toward the east. As the written words dissolved, it was believed, so too would the fever disappear.

The word *abracadabra* has been a part of folkloric medicine up to modern times. In his 1722 *Journal of the Plague Year*, Daniel Defoe wrote that many superstitious people thought that the disease was caused by an evil SPIRIT inhabiting the victim. They believed the demon could be dispossessed with "certain words or figures, as particularly the word 'Abracadabra' formed in a triangle or pyramid."

Only a little over a century later, famous American circus entrepreneur P.T. Barnum observed that many German peasants believed that writing *abracadabra* on a piece of paper and carrying it with them would protect them from cuts and wounds. Many also thought that throwing the paper into a house fire would instantly extinguish the flames.

Increase Mather of SALEM WITCHCRAFT–trial fame, denounced *abracadabra* as a "hobgoblin word" with no special powers, but modern-day WARLOCK Aleister CROWLEY wrote that the word, whose true spelling he felt should be *abrahadabra*, was a true magical word with incredible secret powers. Today, the word *abracadabra* has passed into the vernacular, losing the sting of mysticism and being relegated to the PATTER of the magical entertainer. (See also ABLANATHALBA; HOCUS POCUS.)

Abraham the Jew See *SACRED MAGIC OF ABRAMELIN THE MAGE, THE BOOK OF THE.*

Abramelin See *SACRED MAGIC OF ABRAMELIN THE MAGE, THE BOOK OF THE.*

Abraxas A GNOSTIC god whose name appeared on magical CHARMS beginning around the second century A.D., Abraxas (also seen as Abrasax) was named by Basilides, a Christian philosopher and teacher in Alexandria, Egypt, around A.D. 120 to A.D. 140.

The god's connection to magic probably has its basis in NUMEROLOGY: When the numbers corresponding to the Greek alphabet letters for *Abraxas* are added, they total 365, the

The snake-footed demon Abraxas, whose name is often associated with *abracadabra*. (Collin de Plancey, *Dictionnaire Infernal*, 1863)

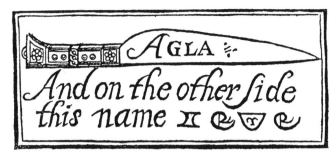

"The fashion or forme of the conjuring knife, with the names ther-on to be graven or written" as a charm invoking God's protection during cabalistic rituals. (Reginald Scot, *The Discoverie of Witchcraft*, 1584)

number of days in a solar cycle. Also, it was believed that in the SPIRIT hierarchy, Abraxas had 365 demigods who dwelt on 365 levels, the lowest of which was Earth. The seven letters of *Abraxas* also may have coincided with the seven planets known at the time.

The literal translation of *Abraxas* is "hurt me not." Inscribing the word on a rock or jewel made that object a particularly powerful charm or TALISMAN. Modern occultists speculate that *Abraxas* may be the root from which the contemporary magical word *ABRACADABRA* is derived. (See also ABLANATHALBA; ASTROLOGY.)

Acrasia In Book II of Spenser's The *FAERIE QUEENE*, Acrasia is revealed to be an enchantress. She has powers similar to CIRCE in Homer's The *ODYSSEY*, including the ability to turn men into swine. She lives in her forested Bower of Bliss, where she is confronted and captured by Sir Guyon.

Like everyone depicted in the work, Acrasia is an allegorical character; she represents Intemperance.

African magic See SHAMAN; VOODOO; WITCH DOCTOR.

AGLA A cabalistic word used by sorcerers to evoke demons, *AGLA* is made up of the first four Hebrew letters of the phrase *Aieth Gadol Leolam Adonai* ("God will be great forever").

Sorcerers, eager to have demons at their beck and call but wary of the horrors of Hell, often invoked angels with the word to help them secure the allegiance (and proscribe the evil) of the devilish fiends.

agrippa An agrippa was a specific style of GRIMOIRE, shaped like a human being. Its letters and characters were written in black ink or purple paper, and the manuscript purportedly smelled of smoke and sulphur. They were probably named for the infamous occultist Cornelius AGRIPPA.

The first agrippas were allegedly owned exclusively by priests and were always hidden in a room set aside for that purpose.

Agrippa, Heinrich (seen as Henry) Cornelius (1486–1535) Born Henricus (or Heinrich) Cornelis in Nettesheim, a town just outside Cologne, Germany, Agrippa was thought by many of his contemporaries to be a sorcerer

and a trafficker with the Devil. He is most remembered, however, for his occult writings in which he claimed that magic was the true path to God.

Early in his life, he changed his name, modifying *Cornelis* into the Latinized form *Cornelius*. He called himself *Agrippa* after the Roman founder of Cologne.

Agrippa traveled endlessly throughout Europe, often in the company of two large dogs, thought by many to be his FAMILIARS. He worked variously as a court astrologer, alchemist, faith healer, doctor, lawyer and political agent (at different times, for both the pope *and* the Holy Roman Emperor). His career was erratic, making him the toast of royalty at one moment and an inmate in jail (including a year of confinement in debtors prison in Brussels) the next.

Details of his life remain sketchy. What *is* known is that Agrippa amassed as many enemies as admirers, with both groups attributing acts of BLACK MAGIC to him. GOETHE is said to have partially based his character Faust on Agrippa, and the poet used many of the occultist's alleged demonic encounters in his play, *FAUST*.

In 1529, Agrippa published a three-volume treatise, DE OCCULTA PHILOSOPHIA (or *Occult Philosophy*), probably written in (or no later than) 1529 but possibly as early as 1510 during a trip to England. Agrippa wrote it after reading the STEGANOGRAPHIA of his mentor Johannes TRITHEMIUS, and its influence is clear.

Heinrich Cornelius Agrippa. (J. Schliebe, *Das Kloster*, 1846)

To his credit, before releasing the manuscript publicly, Agrippa took the first draft of his *Occult Philosophy* to Trithemius for his approval. The work, which discussed human relations to the natural universe and to God through the soul and through magic, in essence was Agrippa's attempt to combine the mystical teachings of the KABALLAH, his Christian faith and the logic of Neoplatonism.

Agrippa explored a then-popular notion: People are miniature versions of God, made in his image; the universe, or macrocosm, taken as a whole, is God; therefore, people are miniature copies, or microcosms, of the universe. Further, because people have souls, the universe and everything that exists must have a soul or some form of SPIRIT. Agrippa's foes, of course, interpreted this as his defense of WITCHCRAFT and communion with demons.

Occult Philosophy was published in Cologne in 1533 and first appeared in English in 1651, with a translation by John French (1616?–1657?). French, an army doctor, was also a mystic, having written a 1651 book on ALCHEMY entitled *The Art of Distillation*. In 1657, Robert TURNER announced his plans to make a new translation, but he died before being able to do so.

In 1530, Agrippa published *De incertitudine et vanitate scientiarum et artium*, or *De Vanitate Scientiarum*. In it, he examined all the known arts and sciences of the time, concluding that they were not really beneficial to humanity: The only reliable truth was in the word of God.

Also frequently attributed to Agrippa is the *Fourth Book of Occult Philosophy*. His authorship is uncertain because the *Fourth Book*, originally published in Latin at Marburg, did not appear until 1559, almost a quarter-century after Agrippa's death. *Of Geomancy*, also attributed (without date) to Agrippa, was one of five additional manuscripts bound with the *Fourth Book* when they were first translated into English and published by Turner in 1655.

In 1535, Agrippa's adversaries succeeded in having him imprisoned and tortured in Grenoble, France. Shattered physically, Agrippa died only a few weeks after his release. (See also ASTROLOGY.)

Ahmed, Prince Prince Ahmed is a character in "Prince Ahmed and the Fairy Peri-Banou," one of the stories of the *ARABIAN NIGHTS*. In the tale, three sons of a king are in love with the ruler's niece, Princess Nur-al-Nihar. According to the king, the brother who brings the princess the most magical gift can have her hand in marriage.

Although none of the princes were themselves wizards, each found a magical wonder as a present: Hussein, the oldest, returned with a flying carpet; Ali, the middle brother, brought back a telescope that could see into the future; Ahmed, the youngest, discovered an apple that could cure any illness.

When the brothers met to compare their gifts, the telescope revealed that the princess was dying. They flew to her side on the carpet, and the apple cured her. Because the brothers were all involved with the princess's recovery, the king could not declare a winner from among them. Therefore, an archery match was arranged to determine the outcome. Ahmed's arrow flew too far to be measured, so he lost the princess's hand. While searching for his arrow, however, he met the fairy Peri-Banou and fell in love with and married her.

Aix-en-Provence nuns See GAUFRIDI, FATHER LOUIS.

Akasa See ALCHEMY; ALKAHEST.

Aladdin See "ALADDIN AND THE WONDERFUL LAMP"; *ARABIAN NIGHTS*; FILMS, *ALADDIN*; JINN.

"Aladdin and the Wonderful Lamp" In the popular Oriental tale, Aladdin is the poor son of a Chinese tailor. An evil Moorish sorcerer convinces him to retrieve a magical lamp from a deep cave. Aladdin, discovering its powers, keeps the lamp.

Using the wishes granted by rubbing the lamp, he becomes rich, marries the Sultan's daughter Bedr-el-Budur and builds her a beautiful palace.

The wizard, masquerading as a traveling merchant, is able to obtain the enchanted lamp by switching "new lamps for old." He magically steals Aladdin's bride and flies her and the palace to Africa.

Aladdin follows the sorcerer, kills him, recovers the lamp and returns the palace and the princess to China.

Although commonly believed to be part of the *ARABIAN NIGHTS*, the story of "Aladdin and the Wonderful Lamp" is not found in any original manuscript of the book. (See also ALADDIN.)

Alchemist, The Considered by many to be the best play of Ben(jamin) Jonson (1572–1637), *The Alchemist* was first performed by the King's Men in 1610 and was published two years later.

The comedy tells the adventures of a number of satirically named characters. Face is, a servant placed in charge of a Blackfriars (London) home when his master, Lovewit, leaves town during an outbreak of the plague. With his friend, Subtle, a pseudoalchemist and bogus astrologer, and Subtle's mate Dol Common, Face sets up shop for Subtle's trade.

Subtle offers a miraculous panacea for each patron. Sir Epicure Mammon, an overweight knight, and Ananias and Tribulation Wholesome, two zealous Puritans, are offered the PHILOSOPHER'S STONE so that they can change any metal into gold. To improve his luck, Dapper, a clerk and inveterate gambler, asks for a magical CHARM (supposedly given to Subtle by his aunt, the Queen of Fairy) to improve his luck. Drugger, a tobacconist, learns a magical method to improve business. Kastril wants his widowed sister, the Dame Pliant, to marry a rich man.

The trio's operation is almost exposed when another con artist tries to upset the scam. The whole affair comes to an abrupt end when Lovewit returns. Subtle and Dol disappear; to assuage his master, Face convinces Lovewit to marry Dame Pliant. (See also ALCHEMY.)

alchemy A precursor to the modern field of chemistry, alchemy first came to Europe from the Arabic world, where it was called *al-kimia*. The word was Latinized into *alchemy*; the name for its practitioner, an *alchemist*. The words formed the basis for the modern terms *chemist* and *chemistry*.

To most people, the word *alchemy* conjures up images of a medieval scientist and his search for the PHILOSOPHER'S

STONE, the magic substance that could change any base metal into gold.

This was indeed one of the goals of the alchemist, but his true aspirations ran much deeper. Just as, through scientific means, he attempted to "perfect" metal to its purest form (i.e., gold), so too did the alchemist wish, through mystical means, to perfect himself and his soul. It was believed that the quest for the Philosopher's Stone itself would help transform the alchemist's soul into its purest (or, metaphorically, "golden") form.

Many of the experiments and discoveries were kept secret through oral tradition, passing from mentor to apprentice. Written knowledge often remained hidden because it was clothed in symbolism and purposely obscure language.

There were many reasons for this secrecy. Scholars during this period, especially those who proposed scientific theory at odds with accepted church doctrine, often found themselves accused of heresy and SORCERY because they appeared to be questioning the authority of the church.

In addition, many of the chemical experiments and alchemic procedures were dangerous, sometimes causing explosions or releasing toxic gases. The cryptic writings kept out the uninitiated and merely curious. Years of study, accompanied by prayers to God for guidance, were thought to be necessary for a true understanding of the alchemic manuscripts. This had to be followed by years of practical experience in mixing chemicals and laboratory work, all the time searching for new revelations in the art. Unfortunately, few early manuscripts remain, and those that do exist are full of cabalistic symbolism rather than straightforward text.

It is thought that the type of alchemy practiced in Europe and Great Britain during the Middle Ages began in Egypt in the last few centuries before the birth of JESUS Christ, with most of the basic alchemical beliefs being established by A.D. 400. From its beginnings, alchemy was a blend of practical metalworking and mystical beliefs, such as those of HERMES TRISMEGISTUS, whose name gave rise to alchemy's being known as the hermetic art. The desire to produce gold was also central to alchemy. Metallurgy was an established trade in Egypt by the time of the pharaohs, and there were many different names for various kinds and blends of gold. A papyrus manuscript, written in Greek around A.D. 300 and discovered in Thebes, gives a method for changing the color of metal to make it look like gold or silver. The text also says that the new metals would fool expert goldsmiths.

Several theories exist concerning the alchemists' belief that a Philosopher's Stone could be produced. One hypothesis concerns the belief in "first matter"—that everything in nature, including man, was formed from one primary material. By eliminating a substance's extraneous attributes and reducing it to its fundamental first matter, the alchemist thought that he would be able to rebuild it to his liking by adding the appropriate qualities.

The process of breaking down a metal to its first matter or base ELEMENT ended in a state called *nigredo*, which was thought to be symbolic of death or decomposing. During the procedure, the alchemist also passes into a state of psychic *nigredo*. Thus, the purification or rebuilding of the metals was simply a physical manifestation of one's own psychological purging, cleansing, refining and rejuvenation. The alchemists equated this entire process with the cycle of death and rebirth in nature but, more importantly, it also corresponded with the Crucifixion, death and Resurrection of Jesus Christ. It must be remembered that any of the alchemist's beliefs was wrapped up in his personal search for the soul's perfection through prayer and God's guidance.

Alchemists believed that *all* objects had a vital magical force within them. Thus, when a piece of wood was burned, the ash was the log's dead body, or corpse, and the smoke was the "soul" escaping into the heavens.

This thought had much in common with the theory conceived by ancient Greek philosophers and scientists, accepted well into the 17th century, that all matter is made up of some combination of four primary ELEMENTS—Earth, Air, Fire and Water—tempered by two of four "qualities"—dry, wet, hot and cold.

If the qualities changed, however, the state of the Element would change. Water, for instance, was thought to be, in its natural state, cold and wet; but if it became hot and wet, it changed into Air. The Elemental theory even named the processes that effected the changes: drying, liquefying, heating and cooling. Alchemists reasoned that if altering physical qualities in the basic Elements made observable changes, then altering the qualities of a more complex material (such as lead) might transform it into yet another complex object (such as gold).

Another alchemical theory corresponded each of the seven most-base metals with one of the seven planetary orbs known at the time: gold (Sun), silver (Moon), mercury (Mercury), copper (Venus), iron (Mars), tin (Jupiter) and lead (Saturn). It was believed that metals were alive and had a desire to grow to their highest state but were blocked by outside natural forces. Alchemists attempted to use their arcane abilities to help a base metal rise up through the planetary chain until it reached its purest end—gold.

Through the Enlightenment of the 18th century, many otherwise rational scientists clung to their alchemic beliefs and studies. For example, Sir Isaac Newton (1642–1727), the great mathematician, was brought up in hermetic thinking and wrote more than 2 million words on the subject of alchemy.

Other celebrated alchemists include CAGLIOSTRO, Raymond LULLY, SAINT-GERMAIN and Michael SCOT. But for every famous alchemist, there are many dozens of unknown and semiknown names in the annals of occult literature:

Francis Anthony: 17th-century pseudophysician, claimed to have distilled gold into a "universal remedy" for healing

Arnold of Villanova: 13th-century physician, wandered Europe and Africa, alleged to have achieved transmutation of metals and the evocation of demons

Elias Ashmole: 17th century, English

Johann Conrad Barchusen: 18th-century author on alchemy

J. Joachim Becher: 18th-century German chemist/alchemist

David Beuther: 17th century, alleged to have been successful at transmutation of metals; though jailed for his silence, he refused to give up his formulas; once released, he committed suicide by poison rather than reveal his secrets

Mark Antony Bragadini: 16th-century Italian, beheaded for claiming to have had Satanic assistance in transmuting metals into gold.

J.C. Chymierastes: 18th century

Osvaldus Crollius: 17th-century disciple of PARACELSUS

Nicholas Flamel: 16th century, French

Hu-Jum-Sin: Chinese occultist

Isaac of Holland: 15th century

Heinrich Khunrath: 16th-century German physician

Mary the Jewess: fourth century, associated with the alchemic element known as bain-marie

Pietro Mora: 17th-century sorcerer/Satanist/astrologer

George Ripley: 15th-century English occultist, purportedly successful at alchemical transmutation.

While attempting to find the Philosopher's Stone, the ELIXIR OF LIFE or some other metaphysical gold mine, many alchemists *instead* made practical, important discoveries that added to the evolving field of chemistry:

Brant (fl. c.1692): Of Hamburg, discovered phosphorus

Johann Friedrich Boetticher (1682–1719): The first European to produce porcelain

Johann Rudolf Glauber (1604–1668): Discovered sodium sulfate (Glauber salt), which many felt was the Philosopher's Stone

Raymond Lully: Prepared bicarbonate of potassium

Albertus MAGNUS: developed caustic potash; also described chemical composition of cinnabar, ceruse and minium

Theophrastus PARACELSUS: Described zinc and is credited as the first to prepare and use chemical compounds

Giambattista della Porta (1541–1615): Discovered tin oxide

Basil Valentine (fl. 15th century): Discovered sulphuric ether and hydrochloric acid

Jean Baptiste van Helmont (1577–1644): Discovered a third state of matter: gas

Blaise Vigener (1523–1596): Discovered benzoid acid

Although alchemy is thought of as an ancient and lost art, science or belief, the search for a scientific method to change base metals into gold exists even today. In fact, the documentation of molecular changes, especially in the field of nuclear physics, has only made the job of con artists posing as modern-day alchemists easier.

Alcina   A minor character appearing in two romantic, Italian epic poems, *ORLANDO INNAMORATO* and *ORLANDO FURIOSO*, Alcina is portrayed as an enchantress who tends a magical garden. Alcina has the ability to transform her prisoners/lovers, who include Rogero and Astolfo, into animals, trees or rocks. (See also CIRCE.)

Alexander the Paphlagonian (fl. second century A.D.)
Born in Abonotica, Alexander was a successful and famous wizard who installed an ORACLE in his own temple and whose prophetess was profitably consulted for more than 20 years. Among the oracle's powerful patrons was Emperor Marcus Aurelius.

"Alice Brand"   A tale found in the fourth canto of *The Lady of the Lake* (1810), "Alice Brand" was written by Sir Walter Scott (1771–1832). In the ballad, Urgan is kidnapped by the king of the elves and is transformed into a dwarf. Alice Brand, an enchantress, changes him back into "the fairest knight" and discovers that he is her long-lost brother.

alkahest   In the study of ALCHEMY, the alkahest is the divine force or power that underlies and allows any magical procedure. It has also been referred to as the "universal solvent."

The alkahest has the ability to "reduce" all physical matter, including the human body, to its basic elements or essence. Applied to the human body, this allows a practiced alchemist to rise above physical limitations and reach the apex of the spiritual being, or Higher Self. It was likewise believed that if an alkahest were applied to base metals, they would transmute into their truest and purest form, which, of course, would be gold.

All Hallow's Eve   See HALLOWEEN.

alphabet   Although the earliest-discovered forms of writings (cave drawings) go back to around 20,000 B.C., the first true "alphabets" were pictographic, in which a drawing represented an object. Next came ideographic writings, in which a drawing or symbol represented not only a thing but an idea or concept as well. Cuneiform is thought to be the world's first known writing system; French-Canadian archeologist Denise Schmandt-Besserat sets its beginnings at c.3200 B.C.

Indeed, pictographs and ideographs factor greatly in the concept of *Representational IMITATIVE MAGIC*, in which the essence or SPIRIT of the creature was captured in the drawing of it. The symbol not only represents the thing; it is the thing itself.

One of the first forms of writing, develop in at least 2600 B.C., was the Egyptian pictures and inscriptions used to decorate tombs and to keep records. The uneducated and superstitious masses believed that the ability to understand and manipulate these etchings was god-given and that those who could read and write possessed secret, mystical powers.

Ancient Greeks visiting Egypt called the inscriptions *hieroglyphics*, meaning "sacred carving" (from *hieros*, meaning "sacred" and *glyphe*, meaning "carving"). Plutarch rightly recognized them to be some sort of alphabet when he called them *ta hieroglyphika grammata* (literally, "the sacred carving letters").

This new ability to preserve history seems so miraculous that even Egyptians referred to their writings as the speech of the gods. In hieroglyphics, symbols were used to represent not just letters, but objects, full words or just parts of words. Their meaning remained lost in antiquity until their relatively recent interpretation by Jean-François Champollion (1790–1832) following the 1799 discovery of the Rosetta Stone near Rosetta (about 40 miles outside Alexandria), Egypt. This rock fragment, found by a soldier in Napoleon's invasion force, contains a passage inscribed in three different alphabets—Egyptian hieroglyphics, demotic (an alternate, modified form of hieroglyphics) and Greek, a known language. The Rosetta Stone, now located in London's British

"The Misterious Characters of Letters . . . call'd the Theban Alphabet." [sic] (Francis Barrett, *The Magus*)

Museum, became the key to deciphering all of the spectacular engravings that chronicled Egypt's glorious past.

Scholars agree that most of the modern alphabets seem to be based on one developed somewhere near Syria and Palestine between 1750–1500 B.C. This alphabet was phonetic; symbols represented certain sounds that could be mixed in different combinations to form words.

A type of alphabet widely used in northern Europe and Scandinavia in the first centuries after Christ was the RUNES, carved letters that were also believed to carry strong magic. The word *runes* means "secret" or "mystery," and the characters were used to mark and adorn such important items as swords and gravestones.

Ogham, or Ogam, was an early alphabet of Britain and Ireland. Consisting of 20 upright and diagonal lines and dots, the writing can be found on ancient stone and wood carvings.

The mystical belief that God spoke in Hebrew gave rise to the KABALLAH, an arcane belief in the magical importance of and power inherent in the Hebrew alphabet's 22 letters.

If, as the cabalists believed, the alphabet has a basis in divinity, it is understandable that magicians, especially sorcerers whose aim was power through knowledge, made careful study of its possible uses. Individual letters and words were strung together in carefully constructed CHARMs to effect everything from curing (or causing) disease to summoning Satan.

Because only the educated had an understanding of the alphabet and letters, and because common belief had it that magic words and SPELLs could be used to cause harm or summon demons, any learned person who was an original thinker and was not dominated by church doctrine was suspected of being a wizard, a witch or a sorcerer.

In 1581, John DEE, working with Edward KELLY, produced an entirely new set of 21 characters which they called the ANGELIC ALPHABET. Supposedly revealed to them by heavenly hosts, the new ENOCHIAN alphabet and its resultant words were used to create the proper supplications and prayers to invoke the angels.

The entire concept of magic words has its roots in the belief in the sacred power of script. The derivation of the most magical of words ABRACADABRA can best be understood in a cabalistic context. The trust in the power of letters and the alphabet gave rise to two other occult systems of thought, both of which still have strong adherents today: the theories of CORRESPONDENCES and NUMEROLOGY.

Correspondences is a system of classification based on the letters by which an object or thing is named; by understanding an item's correspondences, the sorcerer could control the object or its owner. Numerology assigns numerical values to the letters of the alphabet; any object's or person's name can be transformed into a collection of numbers that can be added and reduced to a single digit. By understanding the characteristics assigned to each number, a wizard can control any person whose name has been analyzed.

Alrunes In German and Scandinavian mythology, Alrunes were sorceresses (sometimes seen as female demons) noted for their ability at shape-shifting (i.e., transforming into other creatures or beings). According to legend, the Alrunes were the mothers of the Asian Huns. At one time, small statues of the Alrunes were common in northern European homes. The icons were said to be able to cry if unattended or to make prophecies by moving their heads.

amulet An amulet, from the Latin *amuletum*, is any object, natural or manufactured, believed to be endowed with supernatural powers, allowing it to bring good luck or fend off evil SPIRITS. Although the words are often used interchangeably, an amulet differs greatly from a TALISMAN because a talisman must be imbued with its mystic forces from an outside source.

One type of amulet is known as a FETISH, a natural object thought to have a SPIRIT residing within giving it its power. In Africa, tribal names for fetishes include *ju-ju, gri-gri, wong, mkissi* and *biang*. A fetish might be made from the wood of a particular tree thought to be sacred, such as the DRUIDS' did hazelwood and oak.

Gemstones were considered magical and used as fetishes because of their purity and rarity, traits believed to be shared with the deities. Separated and appraised by their different densities and colors, precious stones used as amulets were thought to provide specific destinies: rubies, the color of blood, preserved good health; sapphires manifested calm and piety, and they also protected against and healed snakebite; topaz worked against liquid (consumed) poisons; pearls cured headaches. Embedding magical stones into an amulet was thought to increase its potency.

The second form of amulet is the CHARM, a natural or manufactured object that receives its powers from the inscription of a message or arcane characters. (See RUNES.)

Often the amulet was small enough to be worn or otherwise carried. The good-luck charm and the charm bracelet (a piece of modern jewelry especially popular in 1950s United States) have their origins in ancient, transportable amulets.

Classic Western literature abounds in examples of amulet usage: Frequently, a RING is seen to possess magical powers; in *Sir GAWAIN AND THE GREEN KNIGHT*, for example, a girdle (or belt) protects the wearer.

Belief in the power of amulets certainly did not flourish only among "uncivilized" cultures or end in the Middle Ages; crystals were used in ancient times for healing and for focusing one's cosmic energies, but belief in crystal therapy is still held by millions. The psychic and physical curative powers of crystals, especially when worn or carried (as pocket crystals) is a major tenet of so-called New Age thinking.

Whether the positive benefits obtained from the use of amulets is god-given or self-induced is open for speculation and is a continuing debate in occult, religious and scientific communities. Psychologists and experts in motivational techniques have long touted the often unaccountable effects of the "power of positive thinking." If there is true conviction by the owner that an amulet will be a protection from harm or can cause good fortune, perhaps that is enough to effect results.

angelic alphabet   On March 10, 1582, Edward KELLY began a seven-year relationship with the occultist/physician John DEE in the doctor's quest to talk with angels. Kelly convinced Dee on his first trial that he was able to contact the archangel Uriel, and as Kelly acted as a conduit and human mouthpiece for the divine words, Dee hurriedly acted as scribe. Dee kept his writings in what became a five-part record book or diary which he called *Liber Mysteriorum* (*The Book of Mysteries*) (1581–1583).

Just over two weeks into their angelic encounters, on March 26, Kelly made a startling announcement: He presented 21 roughly drawn, mysterious symbols that, he claimed, had been revealed to him as the true ALPHABET of the angels, used to make up the words of the heavenly hosts. Kelly assigned a name, pronunciation and Latin-letter equivalent to each character, with four pairs of Latin letters *C/K, G/J, I/Y* and *U/V* each representing a single angelic sign. Dee duly recorded the alphabet in his *Fifth Book of Mysteries*. Because of its association with the angels, the new group of cyphers is often referred to by mystics as the ENOCHIAN alphabet.

According to Dee, the angelic letters, exquisitely drawn, appeared on May 6, 1583, in "light yellow cullor" [sic] on a page of the *Liber Mysteriorum*. Kelly apparently traced over the symbols, and the yellow faded away, leaving a black outline for each letter. Although Dee immediately accepted this manifestation as genuine, a skeptic might have noted that color-changing and vanishing inks were a staple of the Elizabethan magician's repertoire.

Regardless, between March 29 and April 6, 1583, using this angelic alphabet, Kelly received and dictated while Dee transcribed the first part of an angelic book which they called *Liber Logaeth*. Also called *The Book of Enoch, Liber Mysteriorum Sextus et Sanctus* or *The Book of the Speech of God*, this section supplied proper invocations to summon the angels along with several MAGIC SQUARES of 49 x 49 boxes of letters and occasionally numbers. The meanings and uses of the cryptic squares—if they were ever revealed to the men—were not recorded in the manuscript.

The angels, through Kelly, ordered that the book must be completed within 40 days (coincidentally a number of Judeo-Christian significance); and it was finished with a day to spare on May 6, 1583. Sometimes, Kelly would receive his images letter by letter, sometimes a full word at a time (which Dee was forced to transcribe phonetically).

According to Kelly, the angels demanded that the book be rewritten, replacing any Latin letters with the angelic equivalents, and that the pages be bound in silver. The latter seems never to have been accomplished. Dee apologized on August 16, 1584: "God he knoweth, and the Heavens, that I did the best I could, to have had the book silvered."

The *Liber Logaeth* gave the tools and laid the foundation for all of Dee's remaining angelic manuscripts. Between April 13 and July 13, 1584, in Cracow, Poland, the angels "delivered" three more volumes of invocations, or "keys," to summon them.

The *48 Claves Angelicae* (or *48 Angelic Keys*) (1584) was received letter by letter, backwards, reportedly to prevent accidentally calling the angels while transcribing the prayer. At about the same time, Kelly also gave the English rendering of the text (which modern scholars have celebrated for its poetic beauty). The book consists of 18 lesser invocations followed by a main key. This "19th call" could be addressed to any of the 30 heavenly levels of spirits (or "airs"), thus raising the total number of possible keys to 48.

This final invocation linked the *48 Angelic Keys* to the sorcerer's next work, *Liber Scientiae Auxilii et Victoriae Terrestris* (*The Book of Knowledge, Help and Earthly Victory*) (1585). This complicated latter work detailed the 30 concentric circular layers of airs or "aethers" surrounding the earth, with each level ruled over by a "prince of the air." *The Book of Knowledge . . .* also delineated 91 regions of the Earth (first, as ordained by God; then as decided by Man) divided into four quarters. In addition to identifying 12 angel kings ruling over 30 orders and their 12 tribes of Israel, a manuscript illustration of Jerusalem symbolically depicted the dispersal of the 12 tribes throughout the world by indicating their positions in different sections of the ancient city.

The third angelic manuscript, first revealed to Kelly in a heavenly vision on June 20, 1584, and in continuing "actions" through July 1584, was *A Book of Supplications and Invocations*. Received in Latin rather than in the angelic alphabet, the actual first inscription date of the manuscript is uncertain. This tract gives a series of prayers to summon the many angels who rule over Earth's four quarters named in *The Book of Knowledge*. Proper use of the invocations centered around the correct interpretation and use of four large letter-filled magic squares. (Dee later "reformed" these squares on April 20, 1587, according to instructions from the angel Raphael.)

In addition to these three angelic manuscripts, Dee also continued his personal diaries, working on *Liber Mysteriorum*, Books VII–XVIII from 1583 through 1587.

After Dee's death, the majority of his manuscripts were lost. In 1662, they were rediscovered, concealed in a hidden drawer of a trunk which had come into the possession of (Robert?) Jones, the owner of a confectionery store. Although he had no idea who had created the cryptic writings or what they meant, Jones kept the tracts at his Lombard Street, London, home until his death in 1664.

Although the cabinet holding the papers was destroyed in the Great London Fire two years later, the manuscripts were mostly unharmed. The widow Jones took her remaining possessions, including the mysterious writings, to a new home in Moon Fields. She remarried; with her consent, on August 10, 1672, her new husband Thomas Wale traded the strange script to a friend, Elias Ashmole, in exchange for a book the latter had written about the Institution of the Garter.

Ashmole, an occultist, was familiar with the works and immediately recognized them to be the only extant copies of the missing Dee manuscripts: *Libri Mysteriorum I–V; 48 Angelic Keys; The Book of Knowledge . . . ; A Book of Supplications . . .* and *De Heptarchia Mystica* (*The Mysteries of the Sevenfold Kingdom,* an early and incomplete work).

animals   Since the beginning of time, beasts from the animal kingdom have played a major role in sorcery and enchantment.

In one of Judeo-Christian religion's earliest stories, for example, Adam and Eve received their forbidden fruit from Satan in serpentine form. Perhaps not coincidentally, MOSES and Aaron produced a miracle from God by transforming AARON'S ROD into a snake.

Early stargazers devised ASTROLOGY as a way to help explain humanity's creation and destiny. The astrological ZODIAC contains seven animals, and people born under an animal's sign are supposed to share that creature's characteristics. For instance, those born under Leo the lion (traditionally July 23 to August 23), are purported to be bold, strong and towering, a "king of beasts." Other animals have been associated in occult writings with different planets, such as the dove with Venus.

Animals played a major part in the ancient arts of prophecy known as augury, DIVINATION by the observation of birds, and hepatoscopy, fortune-telling by the examination of a sacrificial animal's entrails. Wizards and seers looked for signs in various parts of the animals, but the liver was usually considered the most telling organ. Other important entrails for hepatoscopy included the stomach, spleen, kidneys, lungs and heart.

In 44 C.E. Spurinna Vestricius, Julius Caesar's haruspex (a specialist in an advanced form of Roman hepatoscopy known as haruspicy, from the Latin *haruga,* meaning "sacrifice" and *specire,* meaning "examine") was displeased with a slain bull's entrails. The incident was fictionalized by SHAKESPEARE in his tragedy *Julius Caesar*: When the conqueror asks "What say the augurers?" [sic], a servant relates that

> They would not have you to stir forth today.
> Plucking the entrails of an offering forth,
> They could not find a heart within the beast.
> (II, ii, 38–39)

SPIRITS and demons were thought to be able to take animal form or to possess an animal when entering the corporal world. A witch's FAMILIAR, it was believed, usually appeared as a crow, a cat or a mouse; Satan often appeared at the SABBATS as a half-human / half-goat.

Finally, enchantresses such as CIRCE and ALCINA were especially fond of turning their human prey into such animals as swine. Even the beneficent wizard MERLIN transformed people into animals: For ARTHUR's early education, Merlin turned him into various beasts to learn their wisdom and special skills. Conversely, animals have also been turned into human form at the whim of enchantresses, such as the Fairy Godmother's turning mice into valets in the Disney FILM version of *CINDERELLA*.

Apollonius of Tyana (fl. first century A.D.)   A Greek philosopher and sorcerer, Apollonius traveled the known world (as far east as India) in search of mystic truths. A teacher as well as practitioner of the occult, he was notorious for his evocation of demons. Along with SOLOMON, Apollonius was credited with the development of the ARS NOTORIA.

Apollonius's fame was so great and his acts considered so miraculous that Asia Minor temples were dedicated to his worship. In Rome, he was accused and tried for divination. Legends about Apollonius grew, and by the Middle Ages occultists sometimes referred to him as the archmagician.

In 1600, Simon FORMAN rediscovered the *Ars Notoria,* published as part of a two-volume book *De Arte Memoratus,* written by "Apollonius Niger." According to Robert TURNER, who translated a Latin manuscript of the *Ars Notoria* in 1657, Apollonius had titled his work *The Golden Flowers.*

Apuleius (fl. second century A.D.)   A Roman philosopher and wizard, Apuleius was accused and put on trial for

Apollonius of Tyana. (Jacques Boissard, *De Divinatione et Magicis*)

obtaining a wife through magic. He passionately and successfully defended himself in a public speech, a record of which still exists today. Of interest to modern mystics, he describes his occult practices and invocation techniques in detail.

Apuleius also authored a novel, *Metamorphoses*. Sometimes called *The Golden Ass*, the book depicts magical rituals and casting of SPELLS, all woven within the plot. Among the enchantresses mentioned by Apuleius are Meroë of Thessali, Oenothea (a priestess-sorceress) and Pamphile.

Aquarius See ASTROLOGY; HOROSCOPE; ZODIAC.

Aquinas, St. Thomas (c.1225–1274) The Dominican friar Thomas Aquinas, from Aquino in southern Italy, was one of the Catholic Church's great theologians. As a philosopher, he was greatly influenced by Aristotle and was known as Doctor Angelicus (angelic doctor).

Aquinas's writings were often cited as justification for the punishment of WITCHCRAFT and sorcery in medieval Europe. In 1223, Pope Gregory IX had placed the INQUISITION in the hands of the Dominicans; as member of their sect, Aquinas helped to shape their convictions.

Aquinas felt that all heretics should be burned at the stake. While Aquinas doubted that anyone made an actual written pact in blood with Satan, he taught, that by doing the Devil's work, witches were necessarily heretics. In his *Sententiae*, Aquinas professed that "Magicians perform miracles through personal contracts made with demons."

Within the pages of two monumental works, *Quaestiones Quodlibetales* and *Summa Theologica*, Aquinas detailed phenomena or activities of witches, including

1. *Metamorphosis.* Just as CIRCE was able to turn people into swine, so too are the Devil and his disciples able to change people into beasts. Aquinas believed that such transformations were illusionary rather than factual.
2. *Transvection.* Albertus MAGNUS had postulated that JESUS Christ had been carried on Satan's shoulders, flying from a mountaintop and over the holy lands, as the Devil tempted him in the wilderness. Aquinas accepted this assumption and extrapolated it to a sorcerer's having the seeming ability to fly by riding on the back of an invisible demon.
3. *Tempests.* Aquinas affirmed that, through the use of BLACK MAGIC, wizards and sorcerers could raise storms and produce other destructive acts of nature; he offered specific CHARMS against their occurrence.
4. *EVIL EYE.* Old crones and hags, Aquinas felt, were particularly apt to be in the Devil's service; they could control their victims, especially children, through fascination (i.e., the use of the "evil eye.")
5. *Unnatural sex.* Aquinas had no doubt that witches had sexual relations with the Devil, especially at their group meetings, or SABBATS; he also believed in the possibility of conception through sexual contact with an INCUBUS or SUCCUBUS.
6. *LIGATURE.* Aquinas concluded that Satan was responsible for most instances of impotence, writing "The Catholic faith maintains that they can do harm by their operations and impede carnal copulation."

While anathema to cabalists and occultists, Aquinas's treatises were accepted by witch hunters and clergy alike and laid the foundation for such later works on demonology as the *MALLEUS MALEFICARUM* of Krämer and Sprenger.

Arabian Nights Also known as the *Arabian Nights Entertainments* and *The Thousand and One Nights*, the *Arabian Nights* is a series of stories originally written in Arabic, although their sources are also Indian and Persian. The tales are populated with magical creatures, such as the JINN.

The tales are all set within the framework of one Persian story, *Hazar Afsanah* (*A Thousand Tales*) which gives the entire collection its name. An Arab sultan executes a series of wives the morning after consummating marriage with each. One wife, Scheherazade, saves her life by promising to tell the ruler a new tale each day.

"ALADDIN AND THE WONDERFUL LAMP," whose genie grants the lamp's owner three wishes, is perhaps the best-known story; however, it was not a part of the original manuscript of the *Arabian Nights*.

The first Western renderings of the tales were by Antoine Galland (1646–1715), whose French translations appeared between 1704 and 1717. Although incomplete and vulgarized, English versions appeared in 1705–1708 and 1839–1841 (the latter by E.W. Lane). The first true English translation was made in 1882–1884 by John Payne (1842–1916). The most faithful and most-remembered early rendition was made in between 1885 and 1888 by Sir Richard Burton.

In the Walt Disney animated FILM *Aladdin*, the story's hero vies with Jaffar, the sorcerer and evil vizier, for the hand of the daughter of the caliph. In the original *Arabian Nights* tale, the caliph's name is Harūn ar-Rashīd, and the vizier is named Ja'far al-Rashīd, or Jaffar the Barmecide. The word *Barmecide*, a princely surname taken from another *Arabian Nights* tale, referred to any fakir or trickster who offered items of false or dubious value. (See also AHMED, PRINCE.)

Archimago In Book I of Spenser's *The FAERIE QUEENE*, Archimago, a powerful wizard, fools Una by transforming himself to resemble the Redcrosse Knight (representing St. George, the patron saint of England). Just as Una and the Knight are metaphors for Truth and the Anglican Church, respectively, Archimago symbolizes Hypocrisy. The true knight defeats the magician and places him in a dungeon.

The use of enchantment continues as the knight is led astray by Duessa (the Roman Catholic Church). He loses his power when he drinks from a bewitched stream and is made a prisoner of the giant Orgoglio (Pride). Eventually he is rescued by then-Prince ARTHUR, who kills the ogre, and the knight is cleansed and reunited with Una.

In Book II, Archimago escapes the knight's imprisonment. Seeking revenge, with the help of Braggadochio, he sets out to attack Sir Guyon.

Ariel An "airy" and magical SPIRIT, Ariel is the supernatural aide of PROSPERO in William SHAKESPEARE's play *The TEMPEST*. Until Prospero gained control of Ariel, the spirit was enslaved by the "damn'd witch Sycorax."

Aries See ASTROLOGY; HOROSCOPE; ZODIAC.

Ars Notoria First popularized during the Middle Ages, the *Ars Notoria* detailed occult methods by which a wizard could purportedly obtain instant awareness *and* total recall of all the known arts and sciences. Although attributed to both APOLLONIUS OF TYANA and SOLOMON, the actual author(s) and inspiration of the *Ars Notoria* are unknown.

In the system, every division of learning was represented by a set of cabalistic seals and ciphers called *notae*. Merely by meditating on the appropriate signs and symbols while chanting the correct angelic invocations, the wizard gained immediate access to and understanding of the corresponding knowledge.

Despite its noble aims, the *Ars Notoria* was condemned as heresy by many Christian philosophers, especially Thomas AQUINAS, because of its supposed "short-cut" methods to the mind of God and its reliance on the aid of demons to gain infinite wisdom.

The wizards of Elizabethan England were well versed in the *Ars Notoria*. Robert FLUDD located a manuscript copy in Toulouse, France, during his tours on the Continent between 1600 and 1605. John DEE had two copies in his immense library of the occult on his Mortlake estate. In 1600, Simon FORMAN indicated in his personal diary that he "wrote out the two bockes of 'De Arte Memoratus' of Apollonius Niger, drawen with gould, of the seven liberal sciences." In 1634, William LILLY attempted to locate hidden treasure in the Westminster Abbey cloisters by following what he perceived as instructions in a Latin manuscript *Ars Notoria*.

Modern mystics are perhaps most familiar with Robert Turner's 1657 translation of a 16th-century Latin copy of the *Ars Notoria* (designated today as the Ashmole MSS 5151). A prayer from the Turner translation illustrates the intent of this "magical art of memory" as well as the method for achieving it:

> Glorify thy Holy and unspeakable Name this day in my heart, and strengthen my intellectual understanding; increase my memory, and confirm my eloquence; make my tongue ready, quick, and perfect in thy Sciences and Scriptures, that by thy power given unto me, and thy wisdom taught in my heart, I may praise thee, and know and understand thy Holy Name.

Turner sold his translation through his regular booksellers, and a new American edition of the work was printed in Seattle in 1987. The *Ars Notoria* has fallen into considerable disrepute due to its unfortunate compilation and publication with several demonic manuscripts by an unnamed occultist as part of the *LEMEGETON: THE LESSER KEY OF SOLOMON*. The *Ars Notoria* is not part of all the extant manuscripts of the *Lemegeton*, and its original inclusion predates Turner's translation.

Artephius (f. 12th century A.D.) According to legend, the sorcerer Artephius lived to be more than a thousand years old. He achieved this remarkable accomplishment, it is said, through the assistance of demons. The mystic gave his recipe for near-immortality in his book *The Art of Prolonging Life*, which he purportedly wrote when he was 1,025 years old.

Arthame See MAGIC CIRCLE.

Arthour and of Merlin, Of A 9,938-line poem in rhyming couplets, from the late 13th century, *Of Arthour and of Merlin* is contained within the anonymous Auchinleck manuscript. It was mostly likely written in Kent in Great Britain, but it owes its source to France and the Merlin section of the VULGATE CYCLE.

Although the first third of the epic deals with the adventures of Merlin and King ARTHUR, the remainder of the work deals with warfare.

Arthur, King The many myths surrounding King Arthur have some basis in fact in a warrior named Artorius who was a Briton general around A.D. 450. Romanized by the Empire's years of occupation, Artorius continued to defend the Britons against the marauding Saxons.

The first mention of a historical Arthur seems to be in the *Historia Britonum* (*History of the Britons*), written (or possibly only revised) by Nennius (fl. c.830) in the early 9th century. A blend of fact and legend as well as of earlier written texts (including those of Gildas and possibly Bede), Nennius's document was of great importance. Although the 33 surviving manuscripts of Nennius vary slightly, they place Arthur's ascension in the 5th or 6th century and describe 12 battles, including the battle of Mount Badon, in which Arthur is not a king but the *dux bellorum*, or war chief. An early text, Gildas's *Book of Complaints* (c.540) mentions Mount Badon as the site of a great battle, but not one specifically associated with Arthur.

The 10th-century *Annales Cambriae* (or *Cambrian Annals*) lists the Mount Badon battle as having occurred in 518 and the battle of Camlan, where Modred (seen as "Medraut") died and Arthur was fatally wounded, in 539. Arthur is also mentioned in the 10th-century *The Spoils of Annwn* and two 12th-century Welsh works, the *Black Book of Carmarthen* and *Kilhwch and Olwen* (also seen as *Culhwch and Olwen*, c.1100). Among the exploits described in the last of these is Arthur's fight with an enchantress, the "Black Witch, daughter of the White Witch, from the head of the Valley of Frief in the uplands of Hell."

Over the centuries, the Arthurian legend has been embellished by various authors, traveling minstrels and bards. At some points, the subsidiary characters took on as much or more importance in the tales as Arthur himself.

Among the most important written reckonings have been those of GEOFFREY OF MONMOUTH, Wace, LAȝAMON, the VULGATE CYCLE authors and Sir Thomas MALORY. *The IDYLLS OF THE KING* by Alfred Lord Tennyson is a poetic compilation or synthesis of all the former versions and has been the source of most modern adaptations of the tale in literature and FILMS.

The bare-bones outline of the well-known Arthurian legend, as it is generally told today, is that MERLIN disguised Uther Pendragon to resemble the Duke of Cornwall so that he could sneak into the bedchamber of Igraine, the duke's wife, at Tintagel Castle in Cornwall, Wales. A son, Arthur, was conceived. Following the duke's death, Pendragon and Igraine married. Arthur was made a ward of Sir Ector and was tutored in his early years by Merlin, whose unorthodox teaching methods included transforming the lad into various ANIMALS to see and learn of the world through nature's eyes. After pulling a sword, EXCALIBUR, out of an anvillike stone, Arthur was proclaimed the rightful king of all of Britain. He married Guinevere and set up a court at CAMELOT where he met with the Knights of the Round Table. He introduced the

King Arthur. (Daniel Beard illustration from the first edition of Mark Twain's *A Connecticut Yankee in King Arthur's Court*)

concept of chivalry, and among the knights' many exploits was the quest for the Holy Grail. On one of Arthur's trips out of the country, he was betrayed by his nephew (or, according to some versions of the myth, his illegitimate son) Modred. In a final battle, the usurper was killed and Arthur was mortally wounded. The king was taken by three fairies to Avalon, from which, it is said, he will return when Britain is in its greatest peril.

Scholars continue to debate whether there was an actual historical Arthur even as they look for archaeological proof of his existence. Glastonbury, located in the marshy countryside of Somerset, England, has received a great deal of attention as one of the traditional sites for the Isle of Avalon and the home of the LADY OF THE LAKE.

The Glastonbury abbey, dating before the 10th century, was purportedly founded by and was the burial place of Joseph of Arimathea, the leader of 12 apostles who were sent to Britain by St. Philip. Legend had it that at the time of Joseph's death, his staff (see WAND) was driven into the ground, only to bloom as the Glastonbury Thorn. Near the end of the 14th century, John of Glastonbury announced that the disciple's bones had been discovered in the abbey.

In 1191, however, the monks of the cathedral had already claimed to have discovered Arthur's oak coffin buried 16 feet in the earth. They displayed an iron cross said to have been found in the 500-year old casket, engraved "Here lies buried the renowned King Arthur with Guineveré his second wife in the Isle of Avalon." (Giraldus Cambrensis sets this discovery in the 1180s.) King Henry II agreed with the contention of an unidentified "certain Breton poet" that Glastonbury was, indeed, Avalon, but opponents suggested that Henry himself circulated the story and engineered the discovery to prevent any claims to his throne by a "resurrected" Arthur.

The Arthurian legend has been the basis for innumerable stories, novels, films, TELEVISION programs and plays (see MUSICAL THEATER). Among these are *King Arthur*, a 1691 OPERA (Henry Purcell, 1659–1695, music; John Dryden, 1631–1700, libretto); the movies *The Sword in the Stone* and *Excalibur*; Lerner and Loewe's musical play *Camelot*; novels such as Mark Twain's *A* CONNECTICUT YANKEE IN KING ARTHUR'S COURT, T.H. White's *The* ONCE AND FUTURE KING, John Steinbeck's *The Acts of King Arthur and His Noble Knights* (1976), Marion Bradley's *The Mists of Avalon* (published 1983 and recounting the legends from the point of views of the female characters), Deepak Chopra's *The Return of Merlin* (a 1995 metaphysical account of two English school lads falling back through a "web of time" to Arthur's Camelot) and Mary Stewart's "Merlin Trilogy," *The* CRYSTAL CAVE, *The Hollow Hills*, and *The Last Enchantment*.

Assyrian magic The practice of sorcery and demonology among the wizard-priests of the ancient Assyrians is legendary, but it was first confirmed when R. Campbell Thompson, among others, succeeded in translating the cuneiform writing on several tablets from the period. While the tablets have been dated by their mention of the ruler Assurbanipal, it is now conjectured that the bulk of the magical minutia is repeated from other sources six or seven thousand years older. One of the few sorcerers mentioned by name in any of the tablets is Tarmoendas.

More than a quarter of the works in the library of seventh century B.C. King Ashurbanipal of Nineveh deal with ASTROLOGY and DIVINATION. The Nineveh tablets, as they are known, were excavated in the mid-1800s by Austen Henry Layard and others. More than 20,000 additional cuneiform tablets were found in the archives of the destroyed palace of Lamgi-Mari, the Amorite king of Mari, in the mid-1930s by French archaeologist André Parrot. Many of the writings were "handbooks" for divination, the interpretation of omens and the practice of magic.

Archaeologists generally divide Assyrian-Babylonian culture into four periods: Old Assyrian and Old Babylonian (200–1600 B.C.), Middle Assyrian (1600–1000 B.C.), Neo-Assyrian (1000–605 B.C.) and Neo-Babylonian (605–539 B.C.)

Assyria was formed from the dominion north of the Tigris River that had been established by the descendants of Noah's grandson Canaan (see CHAM-ZOROASTER) and was a mighty nation by 900 B.C. Sargan II, the King of Assyria, conquered Israel in 721 B.C., and the mystical beliefs of the Hebrews accompanied the 27,290 Jews who were exiled to Media. In

612 B.C., Media and Babylonia conquered Assyria. Consequently, in 539 B.C., Cyrus of Persia overthrew both Media and Babylonia and allowed the Jewish expatriates to return to Israel and Jerusalem. Throughout the centuries, the practice of sorcery spread freely among the cultures.

The Assyrians believed that sickness and worldly evil could be caused by malevolent SPIRITS of the dead who returned to haunt the earth, but more frequently the pain and problems were effected by demons or creatures that were half-demon/half-human (such as Namtaru, who caused plagues, and LILITH, also seen as Lilû, Lîlitu or Ardat Lilî). To counteract a demon's deeds, it had to be exorcised by name; so the cuneiform tablets catalogued the known (or supposed) fiendish forces tormenting humanity.

In addition to being able to name the specific monster inflicting harm, the wizard also needed to know the "words of power" for identification and to invoke the aid of a benevolent deity or angel. To aid in the SPELL, the magician also often used a CHARM, a wax or clay figurine (or hair or nail clippings) of the intended victim.

Assyrian society recognized two types of wizards. The common magician was adept at SYMPATHETIC MAGIC and could produce love charms and TALISMANS against sinister forces. The sorcerer, on the other hand, dealt in demonology and NECROMANCY and was recognized as a "raiser of the departed spirit." He was capable of "laying a ghost" (i.e., exorcise) by removing the "hand of the ghost" from the afflicted.

Many magical beliefs and practices of the Assyrians, supported by cuneiform verses, have survived into modern times: the existence of haunted houses (as in the archaic text "O thou that dwelleth in ruins, get thee to thy ruins . . ."); the ritual use of "holy water" ("When I sprinkle the water of Ea on the sick man . . ."); the power of the number seven ("By the seven gates of the earth mayst thou be exorcised" and "Seven evil demons of oppression, seven in heaven and seven on earth"); fear of the EVIL EYE ("The roving evil eye hath looked on the neighborhood and vanished afar"); and the placement of a talisman over the door ("Fleabane [pyrethrum] on the lintel of the door I have hung, St. John's wort, caper and wheat ears, On the latch I have hung . . ."). This last practice, a clay charm against Bel, the evil god of the Underworld, can be compared to the posting of the Jewish MAZUZAH, the hanging of a horseshoe over entrances or the crosses of St. John's wort still seen today over doorways in the Landes district of France. (See also ALPHABET; CHALDEANS; CONTAGIOUS MAGIC; VOODOO DOLL.)

astrology   A method of DIVINATION in which the movements of celestial bodies are charted to ascertain their influence on human life, astrology is called an art by some, a science by others and a sham by detractors. Astrology has probably been the most frequently used method of fortune-telling throughout history, and it has served as one of the most important tools for wizards, sorcerers and seers.

Arabic astrologers and magi studying the heavens. (Macrobius, *In Somnium Sciponis*, 1513)

The basis for an astrological forecast is the exact time of birth, which places a person under the influence of a specific portion of the heavens and its ZODIAC sign. The planetary positions are drawn up on a chart known as a HOROSCOPE, which individualizes generalized characteristics shared by all people born "under" a particular sign.

Some form of astrology was practiced at the time of the pharaohs: one early Greek papyrus (now in the British Museum) speaks of astrology as a craft that "the ancient Egyptians with their laborious devotion to the art had discovered and handed down to posterity." (See EGYPTIAN MAGIC.)

The modern form of astrology was codified in Babylon before the time of JESUS. It was translated into Greek (approximately between 150 B.C. and A.D. 350), Arabic (10th century) and Latin (12th century). The belief was spread by the invention of the printing press, and by the mid-15th century both astrology and astronomy were accepted as scientific studies.

Even some theologians embraced astrology, asserting that it was a revelation inspired from heaven. After all, they contended, Genesis 1:14 in the Old Testament of the Bible stated "And God said, Let there be lights in the firmament of the heaven . . .; and let them be for signs, and for seasons . . .". It was argued that the scripture definitely distinguishes between the use of stars for dividing the "seasons" (i.e., calendar dates) and for ascertaining "signs" (i.e., signals). Because time is irrelevant in the mind of God, it followed that these signs, if properly analyzed and understood, could be a key to knowing the past, the present *and* the future. Astrologers and philosophers debated whether the stars were indicators of coming events (due to precognition of God) or whether (due to God's omnipotence) his stars actually caused those events to occur.

Because the zodiac is based on an earth-centered solar system, interest in astrology waned with discoveries by such scientists as Copernicus and Galileo in the 17th century. While the practice of astrology was all but forgotten in Europe in the 18th century, interest in England kept the art alive. Western curiosity in the occult during the late 19th and early 20th centuries spurred a major revival among followers, and consultations by such reliable thinkers as psychologist Dr. C.G. Jung seemed to give astrology credibility.

Today, naysayers maintain that astrology is not only based on a false vision of planetary motion but also on a sky that is significantly different than it was when the system was devised thousands of years ago. Believers in astrology are quick to point out too many coincidences and fulfilled predictions for astrology to be anything but authentic and reliable.

augury   See DIVINATION.

Baba Yaga A witch in Russian folklore, Baba Yaga lived in a hut that stood on gigantic chicken legs with dog heels and was surrounded by a circle of human heads impaled on spikes. The house, located in the "thrice tenth kingdom," was so small that she could spread her legs from one side of the single-roomed hut to the other.

Also called the "bony-legged one," Baba Yaga was notorious for eating human bones, especially those of children. Visitors to her hut were often greeted with the shout, "Fie! Fie! I smell a Russian bone!" As she flew through the air in her large iron CAULDRON, she would sweep away her trail with her broom. Supposedly she had two or three sisters who were also named Baba Yaga.

She is known by Western audiences primarily through *Pictures at an Exhibition*, a musical composition by Modest Mussorgsky (also seen as Mussorgsky) (1839–1881). In 1874, Victor Hartmann, a noted Russian architect and painter and the composer's friend, died. Vladimir Stasoff, fine-arts department director of the Imperial Library and Mussorgsky's mentor, arranged a memorial show of Hartmann's work. Affected by what he saw, the composer quickly penned ten short piano pieces in honor of the artist.

Completed in 1879 and published in 1886 (five years after Mussorgsky's death), the collected works have become known as *Pictures at an Exhibition*. The ninth "picture," inspired by Hartmann's portrayal of Baba Yaga in the form of a clock, is entitled "The Little Hut on Chicken's Legs." *Pictures at an Exhibition* is most often heard today in the 1922 Maurice Ravel orchestration commissioned by Serge Koussevitzky.

Bacon, Francis (1561–1626) Born in London, England, Francis Bacon, first baron Verulam and viscount St. Albans, was educated at Cambridge and quickly advanced through ministerial ranks as a political favorite, first of Queen Elizabeth I, then later of James I. His political career ended in 1621 when he admitted having taken bribes. He was censured by the House of Commons and endured a brief imprisonment in the Tower of London.

While his writing styles and subjects varied, it was in his *Novum Organum* (1620) that he argued against the then-prevalent preoccupation with mysticism. Unlike the contemporary diatribe against witchcraft by James I (DE-MONOLOGIE), Bacon argued that the use of the scientific method was the only way to discover the "true directions concerning the interpretation of nature."

According to Bacon, only the scientific classification of natural phenomena is possible; knowledge cannot be gained by occult means. Although Bacon believed that scientific laws could only be arrived at through direct observation, the object of his trials was the same as that of the sorcerer: power over nature and knowledge of its secrets. Bacon, however, dismissed any belief in the supernatural or use of SORCERY to command sway over natural forces.

Bacon, Roger (1210/1214–after 1292) Considered by many to have been a sorcerer, Roger Bacon was undoubtedly one of the best educated and greatest thinkers of the Middle Ages. Known as Doctor Mirabilis (i.e., wonderful teacher), he probably received his doctorate in Paris after studies at Oxford. His work in ALCHEMY and chemistry, combined with his use of multiple languages and abilities in physics, logic and mathematics, was his downfall, however. His nontheological studies made him suspect, and he was thought by many to be a heretic and possibly a witch.

In actual fact, while his philosophical writings, including *Opus Majus*, do have mystical leanings, Bacon was a practical scientist: He invented one of the first sets of eyeglasses and designed a type of early telescope. He also spoke openly against superstition and BLACK MAGIC, including the use of SPELLS and INCANTATIONS to invoke SPIRITS.

Nevertheless, Bacon was jailed in Paris for 10 years (c.1257 to 1267) at the behest of a group of fervent Franciscans and then again later for heresy (c.1278–1292). He is assumed to have died later and been buried at Oxford.

An incident in which Bacon purportedly summoned up Satan was sensationalized in an anonymous pamphlet *The famous historie of Fryar Bacon*. This tract served as the basis for a play entitled *The Honorable Historie of FRIER BACON, AND FRIER BONGAY* by Robert Greene.

ballet Like OPERA, FILM and MUSICAL THEATER, ballet has for centuries used folkloric tales as the source for some of its greatest stories. Ballet, an ephemeral and ethereal art, is especially well suited to present tales both mystic and mysterious. Magical beings, including wizards and sorcerers, have been featured in many of the most popular ballets still in today's standard repertoires, and some of the better-known examples follow:

Carmen   The ballet *Carmen* was arranged in five scenes to the music of George Bizet. A new libretto by Roland Petit closely followed that of the original Bizet OPERA, including the GYPSY fortune-telling scene. The ballet was choreographed by Petit and premiered at the Ballets de Paris at the Prince's Theatre in London on February 21, 1949. Later ballet interpretations of the Bizet opera include Alberto Alonso's 1967 production for the Bolshoi Ballet and John Cranko's 1971 staging for the Stuttgart Ballet.

Cinderella   Composed in three acts by Serge Prokofiev, the ballet *Cinderella* was first produced by Rostislave Zakharov at the Bolshoi Theatre in Moscow in 1945. Better known today than the original Russian staging is the Frederick Ashton–choreographed production because his *Cinderella* is recognized as the first English full-length classical ballet. Ashton's *Cinderella* was first performed by the Sadler's Wells Ballet at the Royal Opera House, Covent Garden, in London on December 23, 1948. Both productions closely follow the original fairy tale by the BROTHERS GRIMM. (See also CINDERELLA; FILMS, *CINDERELLA*; TELEVISION, *CINDERELLA*.)

Firebird, The   Composed by Igor Stravinsky (1882–1971), *The Firebird* premiered at the Paris Opéra on June 25, 1910, performed by Diaghilev's Ballets Russes. Choreographed by Michel Fokine, *The Firebird* was an immediate success, catapulting Stravinsky to fame. Although there have been many new productions of *The Firebird* since its debut, the best known is that choreographed by George Balanchine (with designs by Marc Chagall) for the New York City Ballet in 1949.

The story is based on an old Russian folktale about the young Tsarevich (i.e., son of the Tsar) named Ivan, a fairy (the Firebird) and a sorcerer, the green-taloned ogre Kastchei.

Deep in the forest at night, Ivan spies the shimmering Firebird picking golden apples from a silver tree and captures her. Begging to be released, she trades one of her magical feathers (which can be used as a WAND to summon her) in exchange for her freedom.

The next morning, Ivan awakens in front of Kastchei's enchanted castle. He follows 13 beautiful ladies, whom he assumes to be princesses, into the castle. To the hellish tolling of bells, Kastchei's fiendish courtiers arrive, followed by the sorcerer himself.

Kastchei attempts to turn the Tsarevich into stone, as he has so many knights before him, but Ivan quickly waves the mystic plume. The Firebird instantly appears and uses her powers to hurl the monstrous denizens into a frenzied dance. They collapse from exhaustion, and the Firebird casts them into a deep sleep.

With the Firebird's help, Ivan Tsarevich uncovers a hidden chest. Inside is a gigantic egg that, he learns, contains Kastchei's wicked soul. Ivan shatters it, and the evil sorcerer dies. As Kastchei vanishes, the castle and all its infernal inhabitants also evaporate.

The next morning, Ivan discovers that the stone statues have been transformed back into living knights and the princesses have been released from Kastchei's magic SPELL. He takes the most beautiful princess as his bride.

Midsummer Night's Dream, A   In two acts, choreographed by George Balanchine to the music of Felix Mendelssohn, *A MIDSUMMER NIGHT'S DREAM* was first performed by the New York City Ballet at the City Center, New York, on January 17, 1962. A revised version by Balanchine premiered at the State Theater at Lincoln Center on January 16, 1981.

The first act is a succinct retelling of the entire SHAKESPEARE play. The whole second act of *A Midsummer Night's Dream* is a dance in celebration of the marriages of the young lovers.

Nutcracker, The   In 1891, Peter Ilich Tchaikovsky (1840–1893) was commissioned by the Imperial Opera at the Maryinsky Theatre in St. Petersburg to produce a ballet. He composed a one-act curtain-raiser, *Iolanthe*, and the more ambitious, two-act *The Nutcracker*, based on the Alexandre Dumas *père* adaptation of E.T.A. Hoffmann's story, *The Nutcracker and the Mouse-King*. The libretto was outlined by Marius Petipa, who was to have choreographed, but due to his illness, his assistant Lev Ivanov provided the choreography. The ballet made its debut on December 17, 1892.

A six-selection suite of the ballet music had its concert debut in March 1892. *The Nutcracker Suite* has become one of the world's most beloved orchestral compositions and is probably better known than the ballet from which it was derived.

The ballet narrative begins in the home of Dr. Stahlbaum and his wife, who are giving a Christmas party. The curious and mysterious Herr Drosselmeyer arrives and gives mechanical toys to all of the children, including the doctor's young daughter Clara and son Fritz. Clara is given also a nutcracker by Drosselmeyer.

Perhaps Drosselmeyer is a bit magical, perhaps even a wizard—the truth is never revealed—but that night, Clara awakens to discover that the wooden owl decorating the family's grandfather clock has transformed into Drosselmeyer. The nutcracker and the toy soldiers have come to life and are fought by mice, led by the Mouse King. Clara ends the battle by throwing her slipper at the Mouse King, killing him. The toy nutcracker transforms into a handsome prince, and they begin a magical trip. In Act Two, Clara and the prince arrive at the court of the Sugar Plum Fairy, and there are dances in the girl's honor.

George Balanchine altered the libretto for his American production which premiered at the City Center, New York, on February 2, 1954. Yet another revision, with new choreography by Balanchine, debuted at the State Theater at Lincoln Center on December 11, 1964; Balanchine soon made *The Nutcracker* a Christmas tradition at the New York City Ballet.

In 1986, a FILM version, *The Nutcracker: The Movie*, was released, capturing the Pacific Northwest Ballet's version of the classic.

Petrushka   Composed by Igor Stravinsky between August 1910 and May 26, 1911, *Petrushka* is one of the most famous of all Russian ballets. Like many of Stravinsky's works, it is imbued with mystical qualities and characters.

Petrushka, in four scenes, premiered at the Théâtre du Châtelet in Paris on June 13, 1911, with choreography by Michel Fokine.

The ballet is set in St. Petersburg in 1830 during the last three days of a carnival. The scene opens to the holiday revelers in Admiralty Square. Two drummers draw the crowd's attention to a small puppet theater. The master of the theater, an old wizard called the Charlatan, performs a few tricks and then introduces his magical, animated puppets: Petrushka, a Blackamoor and a Ballerina. Petrushka mimes his love for the Ballerina, but the Blackamoor thrashes him. A frenzied Russian dance ends their performance.

The next scene opens on a tiny, empty room. The door is thrown open, and Petrushka is pushed in. He sees a portrait of the mystical Charlatan on the wall, and he quivers. He tries to escape, but his attempts are futile. Soon, the Charlatan tosses the Ballerina into the room, but, much to Petrushka's despair, his excitement at seeing the Ballerina drives her away.

In contrast to Petrushka's room, the Blackamoor lives in well-furnished luxury. The Ballerina enters his quarters, and the Blackamoor courts her. Petrushka is added to the scene by the Charlatan; his intrusion angers the Blackamoor, who drives him away.

The final scene is back in Admiralty Square in front of the puppet booth. Petrushka runs through the curtain, chased by the jealous and seething Blackamoor. The Blackamoor pulls out his scimitar and strikes Petrushka, who dies. The Blackamoor and the Ballerina slip away. The authorities arrive, but the Charlatan shows them that no murder has been committed: Petrushka is only a puppet, filled with straw and sawdust. The onlookers disperse, and the wizard drags his broken puppet back toward the theater. Mysteriously, Petrushka's SPIRIT appears over the puppet theater, taunting and threatening the wizard. Terrified, the Charlatan drops the puppet and flees as Petrushka's ghost slumps forward.

Sleeping Beauty, The   Composed in a prologue and three acts by Peter Ilich Tchaikovsky and choreographed by Marius Petipa, *The Sleeping Beauty* has a libretto by I. A. Vsevolozhsy based on the classic fairy-tale. It premiered at the Maryinsky Theatre in St. Petersburg on January 15, 1890.

In the Prologue, the fairy godmothers of Princess Aurora, led by the Lilac Fairy, arrive at the baby's christening to bestow their gifts. Carabosse, the wicked fairy, storms in. Furious for having been excluded from the guest list, she lays a CURSE on the baby: Aurora will prick her finger and die. The Lilac Fairy cannot break but is able to amend the SPELL. Rather than die, Aurora will fall asleep for 100 years and then be awakened by the kiss of a prince.

In Act One, Aurora is celebrating her 20th birthday. An old hag arrives to give her a present—a spindle. Aurora looks at it with curiosity because her father the King had all pointed objects in the kingdom destroyed years before. Aurora pricks her finger and starts to swoon. The crone reveals that she is, in fact, Carabosse in disguise. The Lilac Fairy arrives and commands that Aurora be taken inside. As the Lilac Fairy waves her WAND, everyone in the castle falls asleep and an enchanted forest begins to grow.

As Act Two opens, a century has gone by. Prince Désiré, unaware of the magic spell, is hunting near the mysterious forest. The Lilac Fairy, the prince's fairy godmother, arrives. She transports him by a mystic boat to the castle, where the prince finds Aurora and awakens her with a kiss. Suddenly, all of the castle's inhabitants wake up; and King Florestan XXIV gives the prince his daughter's hand in marriage. The ballet ends with a third act wedding celebration. (See also FILMS, SLEEPING BEAUTY.)

Swan Lake   In 1875, the Bolshoi Theatre commissioned Peter Ilich Tchaikovsky to compose *Swan Lake*, but choreographer Julius Reisinger and the orchestra conductor considered the completed work to be "too symphonic" with very little plot. During rehearsals, many of the musical pieces were replaced by compositions from other scores, and the premiere in 1877 was a disaster. Another attempt to stage *Swan Lake* for the Bolshoi was made in 1880, and it was revived in 1882, but neither production was remarkable or memorable.

On March 1, 1894, Act II was restaged at the Maryinski Theatre in St. Petersburg as a memorial performance to the composer. With its new production, the beauty and power of *Swan Lake* proved to be irresistible; so the work was given a full production, premiering on January 27, 1895, with choreography by Marius Petipa.

In the Prologue, Prince Siegfried is celebrating his 21st birthday. He is given a crossbow by his mother, and she reminds him that he must soon marry. Siegfried and his friends leave on a hunt for swans.

In Act One, the prince is alone by the lake. He sees a swan land and then transform into a beautiful girl, Odette. He promises her that he will not hurt her, so she tells him her sad tale. She has been enchanted by the sorcerer Von Rothbart, and Swan Lake is filled with her mother's tears. She, like all of the royal ladies, can only appear as maidens at night; by day, they are graceful swans. The CURSE, Odette explains, can be lifted only if a man truly falls in love with her and is forever faithful.

Siegfried makes a vow of love. Suddenly, a giant owl (Von Rothbart in disguise) descends. The prince aims his crossbow, but Odette stops him. If Von Rothbart is killed, the SPELL will never be broken. The swan maidens appear. Siegfried's companions arrive, but he prevents them from firing at the swans. After the hunters leave, Siegfried and Odette declare their love. Dawn approaches. The maidens, including Odette, transform back into swans and depart.

As the third act begins, Siegfried is entertaining six prospective fiancées at a court ball. Von Rothbart appears with his daughter, Odile (the Black Swan), disguised as Odette. The true Odette appears at the window, but the sorcerer casts a spell so that no one can see her.

Thinking Odile to be Odette, the prince declares his desire to marry her. Von Rothbart demands that the prince also pledge to be ever faithful to her, and Siegfried swears. Von Rothbart and Odile reveal the truth; horrified the prince races to his true beloved.

In the final act, Odette plans to kill herself. A storm brews over Swan Lake. Prince Siegfried arrives, but Odette explains that it is too late: now she can only be released from the sorcerer's curse through death. Von Rothbart enters, claiming Odette for his own. Odette plunges into the water, and Siegfried, sacrificing his own life for the sake of his love, follows. Together, they drown in Swan Lake. This act of pure love destroys Von Rothbart, who dies. In a final vision, Odette and Siegfried are seen rising to the heavens.

Sylphide, La   *La Sylphide*, with music by Schneitzhoeffer and choreography by Filippo Taglioni, premiered at the Paris Opéra ballet on March 12, 1832, with Taglioni's daughter Marie in the title role.

Two years later, Danish choreographer August Bournonville took his 15-year-old pupil Lucile Grahn to Paris to attend one of the prima ballerina's performances of *La Sylphide*. Bouronville decided that with modifications in the ballet's libretto, the role of the Sylph would be ideal for his student, with whom he was in love.

The original Schneitzhoeffer score, with its expensive performance rights, was replaced. Composed in two acts by Herman Løvenskjold to a libretto by Adolphe Nourrit, the new production of *La Sylphide* premiered with the Royal Danish Ballet at the Royal Theatre, Copenhagen, on November 28, 1836.

Although the work has had stagings by more recent choreographers, the Bouronville version, which became a standard piece in the Royal Danish Ballet, is the one which is most often seen today.

James, a young farmer, is haunted by the vision of a beautiful sylph in his dreams. He is engaged to be married; during a party for his fiancée Effie, a rival farmer named Gurn arrives to proclaim his love for the bride-to-be.

Madge, a sorceress and seer, appears, offering to tell fortunes. She reads the palms of two girls (see PALMISTRY) and then prophesies that Effie will marry Gurn. The witch is chased out of the house by James, so she lays a CURSE on him.

James, alone, is approached by the sylph, who has entered through the window. As she declares her love for him, a noise startles them. Gurn sees James hide the stranger beneath a cloth; when he whisks it away, however, no one is there.

The sylph appears at the wedding and steals James's wedding RING. She BEWITCHes him, and James follows her. The ballet's first act ends in panic and despair as Gurn brings the news of James's desertion.

Madge and her cronies meet in the dark of night and ready a mysterious scarf by dipping it in her CAULDRON. The cronies vanish as the sun rises.

A group of sylphs appear at dawn in a forest glade, and James's lover shows him her realm. Although she will not let him touch her, James pursues her. Gurn arrives, followed by Effie and her mother. Madge prods Gurn into proposing to Effie; and the girl, thinking her groom to be gone forever, accepts.

All but Madge depart. The witch gives James the enchanted scarf, telling him it will bind the sylph to him. He shows the scarf to the sylph, and she adores it. He ties it around her arms, as Madge told him to do. Immediately, the sylph's wings fall off. She gives James back his wedding ring and dies. Madge spies James as he first sees the wedding of Effie and Gurn and then the sylph ascending into the heavens. Overcome, James falls dead, and Madge celebrates his doom.

bao   Used by Hehe tribe WITCH DOCTORs in what is today Tanzania, a bao is a small paddle-shaped board, approximately three inches wide and eight inches long, with a groove carved along the entire length of one side. The groove is filled with water, and a small piece of wood is floated within.

As the witch doctor chants an INCANTATION, he tilts the board back and forth, causing the bobbing wood to drift within the groove. Questions are called out; as long as the wood float continues to slide, the response to the query is "no." Eventually, however, the water will dry, and the question that is being asked when the small bit of wood sticks to the paddle receives a "yes" answer.

A similar procedure, known as *Diwa* and using two wooden paddles, is performed by the Pagibeti tribe of Zaire. (See also EKWELE; HAKATA; SORTILEGE.)

barong dance   See RANGDA.

Beauty and the Beast   The most common version of the fairy tale *Beauty and the Beast* comes from the French adaptation by Madame LePrince de Beaumont from Madame de Villeneuve's work, the *Contes marins*. The original story, along with many other European folk stories, was most probably introduced in the nouvella *Piacevoli Notti* (*Pleasure Nights*), written in two parts (1550 and 1553) by the Italian author Giovan Francesco Straparola (c.1480–after 1577).

An enchantress, seeking to test the kindness of the realm's handsome prince, disguises herself as an old hag. When the prince is inhospitable to her, she transforms him into the hideous Beast. The SPELL can only be broken if he is able to win the love of a lady.

Beauty (*la Belle*), the youngest of several daughters of a traveling merchant, asks the merchant to bring her back a rose. On his return home, he unwittingly picks the flower from the Beast's garden. The Beast threatens to kill the father, but Beauty agrees to go to live with the monster if he will release her father. Although unable to return to her home, Beauty is able to see it by gazing into a magic mirror. She finally falls in love with the Beast. When she agrees to marry him, the Beast changes back into a prince.

A black-and-white FILM version of the story, *La Belle et la bête*, written and directed by Jean Cocteau (1889–1963) and based on the Beaumont adaptation, was released in 1946. Running 96 minutes (87 minutes in its U.S. release) and produced by Discina and André Paulvé, the film received critical kudos for its art direction and cinematography. Its stars included Jean Marais, Josette Day, Mila Parély, Marcel André, Nane Germon and Michel Auclair.

A loose adaptation of *Beauty and the Beast* set in modern-day Manhattan appeared on CBS TELEVISION from September 25, 1987 through August 4, 1990. Assistant D.A. Catherine Chandler (Linda Hamilton) was saved by a lionlike man-beast (Ron Perlman) who lives in the tunnels beneath the streets of New York City, and they fall in love. In the series's final season, she bears him a son before being murdered.

In 1991, Walt Disney studios, in co-production with Buena Vista, Silver Screen Partners IV and Don Hahn released an 85-minute animation feature film of *Beauty and the Beast*. The movie was written by Linda Woolverton, directed by Gary Trousdale and Kirk Wise and features the songs of Alan Menken and Howard Ashman (lyrics), with the voices of Paige O'Hara (Belle), Robby Benson (Beast), Jerry Orbach (Lumiere), Angela Lansbury (Mrs. Potts) and David Ogden Stiers (Cogsworth). In this adaptation of the classic tale, Beast's servants are also bewitched. Their only hope for being restored to human form is for Beast to break the curse before an enchanted rose withers and loses all of its petals.

Disney's *Beauty and the Beast*, costing a reported $28 million, earned $340 million in the first three years of release. The movie received five Academy Award nominations: Best Film; Best Score (Menken); and Best Song "Beauty and the Beast,"

"Belle" and "Be Our Guest" (all by Menken and Ashman). It won Oscars for Best Score as well as for the title song.

The movie received five Academy Award nominations (Best Film; Best Musical Score, Alan Menken; and three Best Songs, "Beauty and the Beast," "Belle" and "Be Our Guest") and won Oscars for Best Score as well as for the title song.

A Broadway musical adaptation of the Disney film opened at the Palace Theatre in New York City on April 18, 1994. The show boasted an additional six songs by Menken, a new collaborator in Tim Rice plus "Human Again," a Menken-Ashman song that had been written for but never used in the animated movie. Capitalized somewhere between the Disney-reported $11.9 million figure and a Broadway-rumored $20 million, it was the most expensive Broadway show up to that time.

Jim Steinmeyer and John Gaughn designed the many magical effects in the stage production, including the old hag's levitation and change into the beautiful enchantress, the prince's turning into the beast and the enchanted rose dropping its petals throughout the show. By far the most miraculous magic occurs at the play's conclusion when, in full view of the audience, Beast floats more than 20 feet into the air, spins like a gyroscope and visibly transforms back into the young, handsome prince.

Featured in the original Broadway cast were Wendy Oliver (Enchantress), Susan Egan (Belle), Terrence Mann (Beast), Burke Moses (Gaston), Tom Bosley (Maurice), Gary Beach (Lumiere) and Beth Fowler (Mrs. Potts), with the Prologue's voice-over narration by David Ogden Stiers.

The musical received nine Tony Award nominations, including Best Musical, Best Book for a Musical (Woolverton), Best Score (Menken, Ashman, Rice), Lead Actor in a Musical (Mann), Lead Actress in a Musical (Egan), Featured Actor in a Musical (Beach), Best Director of a Musical (Robert Jeff Roth) and Best Lighting (Natashia Katz); it won only for Best Costumes (Ann Hould-Ward).

On December 7, 1994, *La Belle et la Bête*, an OPERA for ensemble and film by minimalist composer Philip Glass, had its American premiere as part of the New Wave Festival in the Opera House at Brooklyn Academy of Music (BAM). The 90-minute piece is the second of a planned theatrical trilogy composed to accompany films of Jean Cocteau. Following performances in Europe, the production undertook a 35-city tour, including performances throughout the United States.

Betooverde Wereld, Die   See WORLD BEWITCHED, THE.

bewitch   The word *bewitch* derives from several different forms of the root *wicce* (*witrch*). In Old English, *wiccian* meant "to enchant"; the word appeared in Middle English as *bewicchen*.

The word was extant as *bewitch* by the 1700s when Increase Mather, the father of the famous witchcraft authority/priest Cotton MATHER wrote, "It is unlawful to entreat witches to heal bewitched persons because they cannot do this but by Satan." Ironically, many Hebrew scribes made the same accusation of JESUS, claiming that he called on Beelzebub to heal the sick by casting out demons.

black books   See GRIMOIRE.

Black Dwarf, The   A novel written in 1816 by Sir Walter Scott (1771–1832), *The Black Dwarf* tells the 18th-century story of a misshapen man who settles, almost as a hermit, in southern Scotland. Called Elshender the Recluse, or Elshie of the Mucklestanes, he is rumored by the local townsfolk to be a wizard, or at least to possess occult powers. (Historically, this type of accusation was commonly made against hags and the deformed.)

In the romantic story, the dwarf successfully thwarts the kidnapping of a young damsel and prevents the forced marriage of another. At the end of the book, he is revealed to be not a supernatural creature but a wealthy aristocrat who has gone into hiding because of his ugliness.

black magic   As opposed to WHITE MAGIC, black magic is that which is used for bad or evil purposes. NECROMANCY, using a VOODOO DOLL to cause injury and conversing with evil SPIRITS or demons are all examples of black magic.

Magic can be classified according to the wizard's or sorcerer's intention, but most magic is actually "neutral" until it is judged by the SPELL's recipient. For instance, the white magic that brings victory to one set of warriors would be considered black magic by the army on the other side of the battlefield.

Because of the antisocial and aberrant nature of black magic, those who practiced it were often accused of acts such as incest, homosexuality, pedophilia, necrophilia, transvestism or cannibalism. Conversely, those who practiced actions considered to be abnormal by their communities often found themselves accused of SORCERY or WITCHCRAFT. Enchantresses were often accused of bestiality: it was well known that they harbored animal FAMILIARS, and it was claimed that they kissed the "hindmost" part of the Devil when he appeared at their SABBATs in the form of a goat.

Black Mass   The Black Mass, used by sorcerers and also supposedly carried out at a witches' SABBAT, was purportedly a travesty (or satanic parody) of Catholic ritual. Reciting the Lord's Prayer backwards was also believed to be a standard part of the Black Mass. Other heretical acts alleged to be part of the Black Mass include desecration of the host wafer and the substitution of water or urine (especially that of a goat) for the wine.

In 1611, during his trial for sorcery, Father GAUFRIDI admitted to having conducted a Black Mass in which he made the sign of a cross backwards and released his congregation with the benediction, "Go, in the name of the Devil." Although such confessions were usually exhorted under torture by the INQUISITION, no evidence was ever found to support the wide-scale practice of the Black Mass.

The Marquise DE MONTESPAN, the mistress of the King Louis XIV of France, was infamous for participating in Black Masses. A priest had conducted demonic prayers on her behalf "that the Queen may be barren, that the King leave her bed and board." Still fearful of losing the king's attentions, in 1673, de Montespan arranged three more Black Masses in which she personally lay naked, taking the place of the altar. As part of the mass, the blood of a sacrificed child was used for the consecrated wine and was mixed with flour to prepare the holy host.

In his notorious novel *Justine* (1791), Comte Donatien Alphonse de Sade, known as the Marquis de Sade (1740–1814), described a similar service being conducted by friars:

> The monks made this virgin strip and lie down flat on her belly on a big table. They lit the holy candles and placed a statue of our Lady between her legs, and had the audacity to celebrate the most holy of our sacraments on the buttocks of this young girl.

The actual term *Black Mass* did not become common until the beginning of the 19th century; its first recorded mention in English is in 1896. Today, as when it evolved, the term is usually used in connection with Satanism and worship of the anti-Christ. (See also BLACK MAGIC.)

Blue Fairy, The   See FILMS, *PINOCCHIO*.

Bolingbroke, Roger (fl. 15th century A.D.)   Although by profession a magician for the public, the British entertainer Roger Bolingbroke was also accused for sorcery for his attempts to conjure demons and for casting HOROSCOPES.

He stood trial for using witchcraft in an effort to assassinate King Henry VI. Found guilty, Bolingbroke was hanged.

Book of Merlyn, The   First published in 1977 from a manuscript discovered among the author's collected papers at the University of Texas at Austin, *The Book of Merlyn* written by T.H. White was intended to be the fifth and final book of *The ONCE AND FUTURE KING*.

England was already at war with Germany by the time White began work on *The Candle in the Wind*, his fourth Arthurian book in 1941. Within two months, White conceived the contents for a fifth, concluding section of the saga, *The Book of Merlyn*. On December 6, 1940, he expressed his ideas in a letter to L.J. Potts, his former tutor at the University of Cambridge:

> After [*The Candle in the Wind*] I am going to add a new 5th volume, in which ARTHUR rejoins Merlyn underground (it turns out to be the badger's sett [sic] of Vol. I) and the animals come back again, mainly ants and wild geese. . . . You see, I have suddenly discovered that (1) the central theme of [MALORY'S] Morte d'Arthur is to find an antidote to war, (2) that the best way to examine the politics of man is to observe him, with Aristotle, as a political animal.

The Book of Merlyn begins with the wizard returning from oblivion to meet his former student on the eve of Arthur's final battle. The king is old, tired and despondent, despite Merlyn's insistence that the legend of CAMELOT and the Round Table will live on. Merlyn compares man to beast and returns the king to his childhood lessons, learning of humanity through observation of the animals. They view the totalitarian ants, the freedom of the geese and the garrulous hedgehog. At times didactic, *The Book of Merlyn* conveys the wartime concerns and convictions of a world-weary author. Nevertheless, amid the often obvious rhetoric, Merlyn and Arthur are both sympathetically drawn. The book, ending with its caring, sensitive description of the deaths of Arthur, Launcelot and Guenever, would have been a perfect conclusion—and resolution—for *The Once and Future King*.

In November 1941, T.H. White sent the manuscripts of *The Candle in the Wind* and *The Book of Merlyn*, along with revisions to his first three Arthurian books (adding subtle antiwar themes to presage the final section), to his London publisher. White insisted that the five books be printed together in one volume, but the publisher cautioned that the scarcity and expense of paper would make that difficult, if not impossible. Then, the editor failed to supply White with the proof sheets he required for *The Book of Merlyn*.

The project was set aside. Perhaps by the time *The Once and Future King* was finally published in 1958, the necessity and urgency to present the messages found in *The Book of Merlyn* were not as important to the author as they had been in the depths of the war. For whatever reason, *The Once and Future King* appeared as a four-book volume. The publication of *The Book of Merlyn* would have to wait for another 19 years. (See also MERLIN.)

Book of the Dead, The Egyptian   The funereal texts of ancient Egypt at the times of the pharaohs are collectively known as *The Book of the Dead*. The title of its first section, translated as "Coming forth by day," is indicative of the complete text's true purpose: to act as a guide to the deceased while making his or her way through the sleeping death back into waking and rebirth. Its tenets served as the basis for all EGYPTIAN MAGIC and religious life and, as such, it has been one of the most influential manuscripts in history.

The Egyptian Book of the Dead is a compilation of rituals and SPELLs used by the wizard-priests of the Nile to facilitate this passage. In addition, the text reveals the planes of the invisible heavens as well as providing the wizard with the proper incantations to travel through them by astral projection and to return to the physical world.

Some occultists divide the spells found in *The Book of the Dead* into High Magic and Low Magic. The former were used for personal spiritual enlightenment and evolution, for priesthood initiation ceremonies and to journey through the cosmos. Low Magic, on the other hand, was chanted over the mummified body of the deceased to direct and inspire its recently released and noncorporeal SPIRIT on the beginning of its voyage to the Other World. Some Low Magic spells also dealt with the practical, day-to-day duties of the wizard-priest, such as chanting incantations to induce healing, love or prosperity.

The authorship and dates of the original texts which were compiled as *The Book of the Dead* remains unknown. Whole sections, however, were carved into pyramids as early as the fifth Dynasty and were used to decorate the interior of tombs and sarcophagi.

The most complete text on one papyrus was discovered in 1888 by Dr. E.A. Wallis Budge, then the purchasing agent of Egyptian antiquities for the British Museum. In a tomb near Luxor, he found what he later described as "the largest roll of papyrus I had ever seen, tied with a thick band of papyrus, and in a perfect state of preservation."

The Egyptian Book of the Dead, as it came to be known, had been written around 1500 B.C. for Ani, "Royal Scribe of Thebes, Overseer of the Granaries of the Lords of Abydos, and Scribe of the Offerings of the Lords of Thebes." The work, still in hieroglyphs, was published by the British Museum in 1890, but the transliteration and translation by Budge (who went on to become Keeper of the Assyrian and Egyptian Antiquities in

Rafting down the Martha Brae. (Photo by author)

the British Museum) did not appear until five years later. Although more recent scholarship questions many of Budge's original interpretations, it is still his remarkable translation and commentary that is best known to scholars and occultists today. (See also ALPHABET; EYE OF HORUS; ISIS; THOTH.)

Boron, Robert de (fl. late 12th–early 13th century) A French poet, Robert de Boron wrote a trilogy (*Joseph d'Ari-mathie, Merlin* and *Perceval*) based on the British legends surrounding the Holy Grail. In the last two works particularly, de Boron included the myths regarding King ARTHUR.

De Boron's *Merlin* survives only in part, a remnant of 502 lines. Composed around 1202 (according to P. Le Gentil in *Arthurian Literature in the Middle Ages*), a variation of the poem appears as a section of the influential VULGATE CYCLE. (See also *ARTHOUR AND OF MERLIN, OF*; MERLIN.)

Brae, Martha According to local legend, the mild, mean-dering Jamaican stream known as the Martha Brae River takes its name from a young Arawak Indian enchantress.

Spanish conquerors, hearing tales of a local gold mine, attempted to coerce its location from the maiden. Realizing the futility of her situation, she seemingly agreed and led the soldiers to a riverbank. Using her magical CHARMs, she caused the flowing waters to change direction, instantly and without warning, in their direction. Although the men were drowned and the sacred mine was saved from plunder, Martha Brae

sacrificed her life to guard the secret. It is said that her *duppy* (i.e., ghost) still protects the gateway to the mine.

The scenic beauty coupled with the myth of the Arawak maiden makes a slow-rafting expedition down the Martha Brae River, located about 30 miles east of Montego Bay, a popular and relaxing tourist attraction in Jamaica.

braucherei See HEX; POWWOW.

Broceliande See LADY OF THE LAKE, THE; MERLIN.

broomstick The belief that witches flew to their SABBATs on their brooms began in earnest in Europe during the Middle Ages. The lore's origin is unknown: the only certain connec-tion is that most of the people who used brooms in their housework were women, and witches were believed to almost always be female. Further it was thought that because the witch's journey began indoors, she would fly up the chimney on the broom.

It was widely assumed that witches were capable of flying (or transvection, as it is known), and 16th-century engravings show witches astride brooms, shovels, poles, pitchforks or demonic animals, often carrying their FAMILIARs, during their nocturnal travels. (Male sorcerers and WARLOCKs were most

One of the earliest illustrations in print depicting witches in flight. (Ulrich Molitor, *De Lamiis*, 1489. Cornell University Library collection)

Two witches ascend their hut's chimney, flying on their broomsticks to a sabbat. (16th century woodcut engraving)

often portrayed riding pitchforks, hence the tool's modern association with Satan).

By the beginning of the 17th century, illustrations and engravings of transvection almost always showed witches on broomsticks or animals. The witch straddled the broom, which carried a bundle of fagots behind it so that she could sweep her tracks from the sky.

The brooms were not known for their ease of riding or balance. New witches often fell off; also, the sound of church bells could knock witches off or prevent a broom from flying. Still, the broomsticks were thought to be swift. The artist Goya, who painted a famous series of old crones, satirically captioned one of his line drawings of witches "The broom . . . , besides being useful for sweeping, can . . . be changed into a mule that runs so fast that even the Devil cannot keep pace with it."

In preparation for their nocturnal journeys, some witches were thought to apply a "flying ointment" on either themselves or their brooms. One of the most common alchemic ingredients was aconite, which is a sedative to the lungs and heart. Modern scholars suggest that the ointment most probably contained hallucinatory chemicals that, once absorbed through the skin, gave the women the delusion that they were, in fact, flying. (See also FILM, THE SORCERER'S APPRENTICE.)

Brothers Grimm, The Jacob Ludwig Carl Grimm (1785–1863) and Wilhelm Carl Grimm (1786–1859), who wrote as the Brothers Grimm, are best known to American readers for their collection of German fairy tales, *Kinder- und Hausmärchen* (1812–1815). The volume included such classic fables as CINDERELLA and *Hänsel und Gretel* and has served as the source for innumerable stories, FILMS, OPERAS, plays and other works of art. The first English translation, published in 1823 as *German Popular Stories*, was by Edgar Taylor, with illustrations by George Cruikshank (1792–1878).

In addition to their folkloric interests, the brothers also pursued German mythology, philosophy and law. In 1852, they started the first German dictionary to trace the language's roots.

Brut *Brut*, a 32,241-verse poem written in Middle English by Laȝamon (fl. late 1100s), examines early British history, including the reign of King ARTHUR.

A priest from Ernley (Arley Regis in Worcestershire), Laȝamon used Wace's French translation of GEOFFREY OF MONMOUTH's work as his major reference, but some of the "factual" material found in *Brut* cannot be traced to known sources from Wace's time. For example, Laȝamon also places Arthur's final battle (where he was mortally wounded) at Camelford; but Laȝamon has Arthur being whisked away on a magic boat to Avalon where Argante (i.e., Morgan LE FAY) waits for him.

Laȝamon also expanded the Round Table myth, stating that it was specially crafted for Arthur, to seat 1,600 and was round to avoid any disputes as to seating the "head of the table."

Bungay, Thomas (fl. 1290s) A Franciscan friar, Bungay lectured on divinity at Oxford and Cambridge. As was common with scholars of his day, Bungay had the reputation of being a sorcerer. His supposed occult escapades with Roger BACON were chronicled in the booklet *The famous historie of Fryar Bacon* and Robert Greene's play *FRIER BACON, AND FRIER BONGAY*.

Busirane Found in Book III of *The FAERIE QUEENE* of Edmund Spenser, Busirane is known as the "vile Enchaunter." He captures Amoret on the day she was to marry Sir Scudamour and locks her in his castle.

Although nominally an enchanter or wizard, Busirane, like all of the characters in *The Faerie Queene*, is also symbolic. Representing unsanctioned or illegal love, he is defeated by Britomart (Chastity) and is compelled to release Amoret.

cabbala See KABBALAH.

caduceus The earliest caduceus, a type of WAND symbolizing power, was probably a forked olive branch, garnished with intertwining ribbons. At some point, its depiction changed to a short pole or staff encircled by two snakes, often with wings at its top end.

The wand held by HERMES (and, subsequently, Mercury, his Roman counterpart) was a caduceus. According to some versions of the myths surrounding this messenger of the Greek gods, Apollo gave Hermes the caduceus in exchange for his lyre.

To most mystics, the caduceus symbolized the merging of power (as portrayed by the phallic rod) with wisdom (the serpents). If it were not already associated with the wizard's WAND, the caduceus certainly became so when students of ALCHEMY adopted the symbol, seeing the entwined snakes as representing the union of opposites. Because the early alchemist also often effected cures, the caduceus eventually came to be the symbol of the modern-day magician/healer, the physician.

The tall ceremonial staff carried by a herald of a king's court is also called a caduceus.

Cagliostro, Count Alessandro (1745–1795) Born Giuseppe Balsamo in Sicily, the young mystic adopted the surname of his maternally related godmother, the Countess Cagliostro.

Cagliostro's "career" as an occultist and royal advisor began in 1766 when he moved to Malta (according to some, to avoid arrest for petty crimes). The Grand Master of the Order of the Knights of Malta became his mentor and shared his arcane knowledge of ALCHEMY and ROSICRUCIAN thinking with the impressionable lad. Ten years later, Cagliostro and his wife Lorenza Feliciani (some scholars identify her as Serafina) moved to London, where he was admitted to the Freemasons, a "secret society" whose rites embraced many teachings of the KABBALAH.

Cagliostro, an admitted alchemist, truly believed he was on the road to discovering the PHILOSOPHER'S STONE and spent countless hours in its pursuit. He acquired a reputation for DIVINATION when he correctly predicted three winning lottery numbers in a row. Before long, it was said that he could CONJURE up SPIRITS of the dead, concoct love potions, produce philtres for cures and use alchemy to manufacture diamonds.

Count Alessandro Cagliostro. (Paul, Christian, *Histoire de la magie*).

Cagliostro's quest as a philosopher, however, was the attempt to reconcile the beliefs of Freemasonry and his own occult experiences with what he deemed to be the magic and sorcery mentioned in the Bible. The true magic of the universe, he thought, could only be revealed by God, but the tools to gain the wisdom of God were in the hands of the alchemist.

His notoriety soon brought him many enemies. Cagliostro hastily left London (purportedly to avoid criminal charges for fraud) with letters of introduction from the Grand Lodge of England to all the Freemasonry lodges of Europe. During his travels, Cagliostro was received by royalty and is alleged to have consulted with the Comte de SAINT-GERMAIN, the court wizard of King Louis XV of France. By 1779, he had made his home in Mittau, a small town in Courland, Prussia, which was known for its resident occultists. While there, he deciphered an Egyptian rite from an arcane magical papyrus, allowing him to cause a hypnotized child to see visions of angels.

Cagliostro's search for the unknowable led to his establishment of a society for mystics which he named the Egyptian Lodge, with himself installed as Grand Kophta. All were invited to join. The only qualification for membership was belief in the soul's immortality.

Secret, magical rites were performed at the lodge, including seances to contact the seven "pure spirits." Often in their oracular experiments, a pure, young girl, called the Dove, would practice scrying (peering into an empty bottle by the flickering light of two flaming torches). If she happened to see an angel in the flask, the Dove would be conducted away from the table and behind a partition. There, in private, she enjoyed a heavenly "union" with the angel.

Cagliostro's fame as a healer grew. In 1780, the Zurich pastor Johann Kaspar Lavater wrote the count, asking, "In what precisely does your knowledge reside?" The cabalist succinctly replied, "*In verbis, herbis et lapidibus*" ("In words, herbs and stones").

Cagliostro's most notable cure was that of the French cardinal de Rohan's uncle, the marshal de Soubise. Acclaimed by the royalty of France and commended by Freemasons throughout Europe, Cagliostro seemed to live a charmed life.

That radically changed in 1785 when he suddenly found himself in the center of controversy and political intrigue. As had occurred previously in England, his infamy aroused jealousy, suspicion and hate. Chief among his antagonists were the physicians, who were clearly nonplused by his miraculous cures, and the Catholic Church. It was the French royalty that had so embraced him, however, that caused his fall from grace.

Cagliostro was falsely accused of stealing a diamond-and-pearl necklace that Cardinal de Rohan, in an attempt to receive the blessings of King Louis XVI, had sent to Queen Marie Antoinette. The real thief, the comtesse de Valois de La Motte, was eventually exposed. Despite his innocence and release from the Bastille, Cagliostro was nevertheless expelled from France. He returned to London where, in 1786, Cagliostro wrote an open *Letter to the French People*, denouncing the French rulers and predicting a revolutionary downfall of the Bastille.

He began a nomadic life throughout Europe, eventually heading to Rome in 1789. Pope Pius VI was well aware of the wonder-worker's reputation, and despite Cagliostro's endorsement from several bishops, the pope asked for an investigation by the Office of the INQUISITION.

The Inquisition charged Cagliostro with heresy, sacrilege, deception, exploitation, fraud, prevarication, conspiracy, drunkenness and sexual promiscuity. Cagliostro was tried, found guilty and sentenced to death. The pope intervened, mitigating the sentence to life imprisonment. Once the favorite of the courts of Europe, Cagliostro died in the dungeons under the fortress of San Leo, near Urbino, Italy, on August 6, 1795, reportedly strangled by his captor/torturer. His grave has never been found. (See also PAPACY, THE.)

Caliban A character in William SHAKESPEARE's The TEMPEST, Caliban is the true owner of the island usurped by PROSPERO. He is only part-human, the son of the enchantress SYCORAX and (possibly) Setebos, who is variously characterized as a Patagonian god or a demon. Although Caliban delivers some of the most moving, literate and poetic soliloquies in the play, he is described in the "Names of the Actors" in the First Folio as "a savage and deformed slave." Shakespeare most likely derived the name *Caliban* from *cannibal* or the *Carib* Indian tribe. Robert Browning published his poem "Caliban upon Setebos" as part of his *Dramatis Personae* collection in 1864. In the work, Caliban comes to understand Setebos's plan in the creation of the world.

Caliburn See EXCALIBUR.

Camelot The site for the legendary court of King ARTHUR, if it ever existed, has been associated with several areas of Great Britain and is a continuing subject for debate.

Chrétien DE TROYES, writing his *Lancelot* (c.1160–1180), was the first writer to name Camelot explicitly as the location of Arthur's castle. Writing 300 years later, Sir Thomas MALORY seemed to equate Camelot with the town of Winchester; yet he also describes it as being north of Carlisle. Other antiquarians feel that the Roman Camulodunum in Colchester was built over the original site of Camelot.

Most Arthurian writers and scholars mention the district of Somerset as the most likely location. Laʒamon thought that the town of Camelford was first founded as Camelot. John Selden (1584–1654) and Michael Drayton (1563–1631) positioned Camelot in South Cadbury, Somerset.

Modern historians are no more certain than their predecessors in pinpointing sites identified with King Arthur and the wizard MERLIN. In *Arthurian Tradition and Chrétien de Troyes* (1949), for example, R.S. Loomis proposes that the name *Camelot* is a combination of the names *Avallon*, the fabled field in which Arthur fought Modred, and *Caerlon*, an existing town in South Wales.

If Camelot was an actual place and not, as Tennyson wrote in his IDYLLS OF THE KING, merely symbolic "of the gradual growth of human beliefs and institutions and of the spiritual development of man," then archaeological excavations may point to the ruins of the Cadbury Castle in Somerset as the most likely location for Arthur's court.

The so-called castle is an 18-acre earthen fort dating from before the Roman occupation, set 500 feet on a hill overlooking the plains between the Vale of Avalon and the Glastonbury Tor. Cadbury Castle is near Queen's Camel (once named simply Camel) and the River Cam.

This is the site favored by John Leland (c.1503–1552), a historian writing in the time of King Henry VIII. He professed that residents throughout antiquity referred to the hill and its fort as Camalat, the court of King Arthur. To this day, local tradition calls the flat summit King Arthur's Palace and a well within the ramparts King Arthur's Well. Provincial folklore says that Arthur sleeps in a nearby cave and that, in midsummer, phantom Knights of the Round Table can be heard riding across the plains.

Regardless of Camelot's true location, or even whether the legends have a basis in fact, Camelot remains synonymous with all that is best in humanity: optimism, moral right, vitality, vision and hope for the future.

Cancer   See ASTROLOGY; HOROSCOPE; ZODIAC.

Canon Episcopi   Although magic and sorcery have existed throughout history, it was not until the 13th century that the Catholic Church embraced the belief that human beings actually made pacts with the Devil and acted as his servant on earth. Until that time, it was considered heresy to promote the existence of WITCHCRAFT.

The Canon Episcopi (also seen as Capitulum Episcopi) was one of the earliest church documents espousing this latter view. Its actual date is unknown. Regino of Prüm, abbot of Trevers, first revealed the existence of the proclamation in A.D. 906; for years it was wrongly attributed to the Council of Ancyra (A.D. 314). In the 12th century, the proclamation became canon law when it was made part of the *Corpus Juris Canonici* by Gratian of Bologna.

In essence, the canon suggested that all traffic with the Devil, including flying and transforming oneself into an animal, were delusionary, or at least illusionary. As proof, the canon asks,

> Who is there that is not led out of himself in dreams and nocturnal visions, and sees much when sleeping which he had never seen waking?
> . . . It is therefore to be publicly proclaimed to all, that whoever believes [in witchcraft] or similar things loses the faith . . . [and] . . . is beyond doubt an infidel.

Theologians such as Thomas AQUINAS questioned the church's doctrine, however. One of their arguments was that dreaming of demonic acts made one as guilty as if the act itself were performed. Also, they contended, the world had changed since the canon was first written: while witchcraft may not have existed at one time, it was now quite real.

In 1458, Nicholas Jacquier, a Dominican inquisitor, was one of the first to openly disavow the church's dogma on the existence of witchcraft. It was not was officially changed, however, until the Papal Bull of 1484, in which Innocent VIII directly reversed the church's earlier canon. (See also INQUISITION; PAPACY, THE.)

Canterbury Tales, The   Written by Geoffrey Chaucer (c.1343–1400) and compiled around 1387, *The Canterbury Tales* is an epic saga in prose and verse of 31 Christians on a religious pilgrimage to Canterbury Cathedral.

Although some of the stories are incomplete (as is the entire work if judged by the parameters set by the prologue), the characters in *The Canterbury Tales* tell more than two dozen stories that are variously amusing, ribald, romantic or moralistic. Several of them contain elements of the occult, ancient mythology, magical happenings or supernatural characters.

In the General Prologue, the travelers meet at Tabard Inn in Southwark, England, where the host suggests that each pilgrim tell four tales each, two on the way to and two while returning from the cathedral.

In the sixth story, known as "The Wife of Bath's Tale," a knight is asked by a ugly, old witch, "What do men most desire?" The enchantress promises to tell him the answer to the riddle (Sovereignty) if he marries her. The knight agrees, and as soon as they are wed, a SPELL is broken and the witch transforms back into her true self—a beautiful, young woman.

The next yarn, "The Friar's Tale," is based on a popular fable of Chaucer's time. A court summoner meets Satan, who is dressed as a yeoman, and they agree to become traveling companions. They hear a cart driver cursing his horse and commending it to the devil. The summoner asks the demon why he did not whisk away the horse, and Satan replies that the man did not really mean his curse, that it did not come "from the heart" (or *ex corde*, as the theme was known). On their travels, they meet an old peasant woman. When the summoner demands 12 cents from her, she commends *him* to Hell. Satan sweeps the summoner down to the Underworld with the explanation that the old woman's curse came "from the heart."

"The Squire's Tale" is the 11th, though incomplete, narrative. It begins to tell the story of Cambuscan, king of Tartary, who receives mystical gifts as birthday presents from the king of Arabia. Among them is a magic RING which allows the wearer to understand the speech of birds. With the AMULET on her finger, the king's daughter, Canace, hears from a female falcon a story of desertion by her lover, a tercelet. (This story was later reworked and completed by Edmund Spenser for his masterpiece, *The FAERIE QUEENE*.)

"The Franklin's Tale," the next told, concerns a married woman, Dorigen, who puts off a persistent pursuer by telling him that she will not consent to infidelity until he removes all the stones from the shores of Britanny. This he accomplishes with the help of a wizard, but the lover does not hold Dorigen to her word.

The 22nd story is "The Canon's Yeoman's Tale." The yeoman and his master, a clergyman who is a practitioner of ALCHEMY, join the company late in the pilgrimmage. The first 200 lines of the narrative tells of the alchemist's unsuccessful search for the PHILOSOPHER'S STONE in his quest to change base metals into gold. The remainder of the tale is that of a fraudulent alchemist who charges a priest for bogus lessons in the art of alchemy. (This tale, along with the general public distrust of fake alchemists of the period, may have inspired the later play of Ben Jonson, *The ALCHEMIST*.

The next tale (and second to last in the entire work) is "The Manciple's Tale." An enchanted white crow has the ability to speak and tells Phebus that he is a cuckold. Jealous and angry, Phebus kills his wife. So that the crow can no longer talk, Phebus pulls out the crow's white feathers and casts it "unto the devel." This fable, known from the time of Ovid (Publius Ovidius Naso, 43 B.C.–A.D. 18), supposedly explains why crows have only black feathers.

The 24th and final story in *The Canterbury Tales* is "The Parson's Tale," which deals primarily with the "seven deadly sins" (also personified in *The Faerie Queene*). As part of his tale, the parson explains the difference between *maleficarum* (BLACK MAGIC) and harmless CHARM (WHITE MAGIC):

> What say we of them that believe in DIVINATIONS, as by birds [augury], or of beasts, or by sort, by geomancy, by dreams [oneiromancy] . . . and such manner wretchedness? . . . All this is defended [i.e., forbidden] by God and by all Holy Church. Charms for wounds or malady of men, . . . it may be peradventure that God suffereth it, for folk should give the more faith and reverence to his name.

(See also MUSICAL THEATER, *Canterbury Tales*.)

Capricorn See ASTROLOGY; HOROSCOPE; ZODIAC.

cards, playing See CARTOMANCY; DIVINATION; TAROT CARDS.

cartomancy From the Italian word *carta* (meaning "card") and the Greek word *manteia* (meaning "divination"), cartomancy is fortune-telling using playing cards or a special TAROT deck.

The use of cards in wizardry and prophecy has given rise to the common expression "in the cards," meaning that something is fated or was bound to occur. Folklore has long associated the GYPSY fortune-teller with the art of cartomancy, and this practice has been variously portrayed in the arts. In an early scene from the Bizet OPERA *Carmen*, for example, three women use cards to divine their own futures.

The origins of playing cards and the tarot are unknown, although the tarot's creation is usually ascribed to Egypt. The first major reference to playing cards is in a 1392 accounting by Charles Poupart, treasurer to Charles VI of France, for payment "to Jacquemin Gringonneur, painter, for three packs of cards in gold and divers colors of several designs, to be laid before our said Lord the King for his diversion . . . LVI sous of Paris."

Although Gringonneur has, therefore, often been cited as the inventor of playing cards, there is a passing reference to similar cards in Germany as early as 1329, and playing cards were known in Belgium, Italy, Spain and France long before the end of the 14th century.

Casanova, Giacomo (1725–1798) Well known for his affairs of the heart, the Italian romantic was also a sorcerer, practiced in various forms of DIVINATION and the invocation of SPIRITs. An ardent adventurer and wanderer, Casanova followed clues which he "found" within the KABBALAH to seek hidden treasure.

When it was discovered that he owned a copy of *The KEY OF SOLOMON*, Casanova was charged with heresy by the Spanish INQUISITION.

cats In the times of the pharaohs of Egypt, the cat was held as a sacred creature; the goddess Bast was portrayed with a woman's body and a feline head. The deification of cats spilled over into ancient Roman times, where the goddess Diana could transform herself into a cat.

Several explanations have surfaced for the early worship of the cat. The first is practical: Cats protected the granaries and food-storage houses from infestation by rodents. Also, cats were thought to be natural enemies of snakes, the serpent being a traditional symbol of evil. Occultists associated cats with the moon because it was a night creature whose eyes

Honored as deities in ancient Egypt, cats were thought to be common companions to witches in the Middle Ages. In a famous English witchcraft trial in 1619, Margaret Flower admitted that she had tried to kill one of the earl of Rutland's children by rubbing some of the victim's clothing against her cat, Pusse.

According to legend and superstition, the black cat in particular is often associated with bad luck. Even in modern cultures, it is believed by many that black cats hold mystic powers. (Photo by author)

appear to wax and wane with a seeming ability to see in the dark. To some, this capacity gave rise to the belief that the cat was CLAIRVOYANT.

By the Middle Ages, however, early Christian thinkers damned the cat, concluding that if the beast was divine in a "pagan" religion, then it must actually be an instrument or personification of the Devil. During the years of WITCHCRAFT hysteria in Europe, many believed that women could transform themselves into cats. More prevalent was the belief that cats acted as the witch's FAMILIAR, liaison between the sorceress and Satan.

In the United States and Europe, it is the black cat that is most closely associated with the demonic; curiously, in today's England the white cat is considered to be evil. In Elizabethan times, in fact, the black cat symbolized benign magic. Instead, the gray or dark yellowish brown, or brindled, cat was thought to be the witch's familiar. To signal the portentous timing of their divinations, for example, the weird sisters of SHAKESPEARE's MACBETH announced that "Thrice the brinded [sic] cat hath mewed."

Throughout the centuries, the irrational phobia of felines has given rise of any number of superstitions surrounding the cat. Many are still believed today:

A cat on a ship or in a theater brings good luck.
A cat in the theater bodes success unless it walks onto stage
  during a performance.
Cats suck the breath out of sleeping babies.
Bad luck comes from a black cat crossing one's path, especially
  from left to right.

(See also PUSS IN BOOTS.)

caul On rare occasions, a portion of the amniotic sac remains draped, but unattached, over the child's head at birth. This sheer membrane, resembling a veil, is known as a caul.

To the ancients, everything surrounding the birth process was considered magical, so such a rare event as a newborn wearing a caul was cause for considerable excitement. Being born with a caul was a sign of good luck, for the child would be rewarded with a CHARMed life.

Thought to be endowed with strong mystic powers, cauls were sought out by enchantresses for use in their SPELLs. Also, because the tissue held the fluids that surrounded the floating fetus, carrying a caul was thought by sailors to act as a TALISMAN to protect them from drowning.

cauldron Taken from the Greek *krater*, a cauldron is a large, roundish vessel generally used for preparing or serving food. Its occult connotation, however, is that of an oversized, black pot in which witches brew their magical potions. A popular example of this image is that of the crone witch preparing a poisoned apple in Disney's animated FILM version of *The SLEEPING BEAUTY*. The most famous example in Western literature is the scene in SHAKESPEARE's *MACBETH* in which the three weird sisters chant the INCANTATION

Double, double, toil and trouble
Fire burn and cauldron bubble.

Witches were also believed to sometimes fly to SABBATs in their cauldrons rather than on BROOMSTICKs.

Among the ancient Celts, some cauldrons were believed to contain potions that could confer the gift of poetry. The cauldron was a sacred symbol of abundance and fertility, and certain cauldrons were thought to be inexhaustible. (A modern equivalent in the stage magician's repertoire is the "Lota Bowl," from which the pseudowizard pours endless quantities of water.)

A few legends, such as that of Bran the Blessed of Wales, tell of water from a cauldron resurrecting or regenerating life. Historically, however, the cauldron was more often utilized in religious human sacrifices. The Celts were known to use cauldrons and vats for ceremonial drownings, and the Cimbri (Celtic-Germanic) tribe would ritually slit and then suspend their human offering over cauldrons to collect the blood. About the same period, the Gauls made sacrifices to their war-god Teutates by sealing their mortal tributes in cauldrons and thereby smothering them. Remnants of actual cauldrons used in these types of rites have been found in the marshes and bogs of Gundestrup and Bra in Jutland, Denmark, and in a prehistoric royal grave at Vix, France.

Other Celtic myths involve magical cauldrons owned by the gods. Their vessels could provide an endless cornucopia of food or instantly produce beer. Immortality could be gained by drinking from drafts prepared in the cauldrons of Goibniu, the Celtic god of smiths and forges, or Mider, the Irish god-king. A Welsh myth tells of King ARTHUR's quest for the mystic cauldron of Pwyll, Lord of Annwfn.

Celtic Twilight, The Written by William Butler Yeats (1865–1939), *The Celtic Twilight* is an anthology of magical and mystic tales published in 1893. The stories all portray an ancestral Irish belief in fairies, leprechauns and other SPIRITS. The themes were all seen in Yeats's earlier work, *Fairy and Folk Tales of the Irish Peasantry* (1888), and continued in *The Secret Rose* (1897).

Celts See DRUIDS.

Cerridwen In Celtic mythology, Cerridwen (also seen as *Keridwen*) was the DRUID goddess of magic, DIVINATION and knowledge. Among her many powers, Cerridwen was able to transform herself into other forms and beasts.

Cerridwen was most often by her mighty CAULDRON, stirring a potion of herbs and sea foam. After a year and a day, the brew would coalesce into three drops which, when drunk, would impart wisdom and creativity.

Her story is told in the *Book of Taliesin*, written around A.D. 1275. Some of the songs and poetry found in the work are attributed to Taliesin, a sixth-century Welsh troubadour. According to the legend, Cerridwen's philtre, intended for her son Avaggdu, was drunk by Gwin, who had been left minding the cauldron. Furious, she tried to kill the boy for his theft, but, with his newfound wisdom and arcane powers, he was able to escape. He stayed one step ahead of Cerridwen, transforming himself into a series of ANIMALS. Finally, he changed himself into a speck of wheat and hid himself in a field of grain. Cerridwen changed into a hen and swallowed young Gwin. As a result, the enchantress bore a son, whom she

Two medieval witches add a cock and a serpent as ingredients to the potion brewing in their cauldron. (Ulrich Molitor, *De Lamiis*, 1489)

named Taliesin. She tied the boy in a leather bag and tossed it into the ocean. Taliesin was saved, however, by Gwyddno and Elphin, who hauled in the sack while fishing.

Chaldeans An ancient people of Mesopotamia, the Chaldeans ruled over Babylon for almost a century before being routed by the Persians in 589 B.C. While in power, the Chaldeans built great temples in the city of Ur, often referred as Ur of the Chaldees.

The Chaldeans were famous—perhaps infamous—for their abilities as wizards, prophets and astrologers (see ASTROLOGY). Intact magical tracts from the Chaldeans show a heavy mystical influence from Egyptian and Hebraic sources. Although most of their great magicians' specific deeds have not been passed down, many of their names are recorded: Apusorus of Media, Astrampsychos; Belephantes (who, according to Diodorus Siculus, a Sicilian historian, correctly predicted Alexander the Great's death in Babylon), Berosus (who, according to Roman encyclopedist Pliny the Elder, A.D. 23–79, was so skilled in astrology and prophecy that the Athenians erected a statue with a tongue of gold in his honor), Gobryas, Pamphilos (mentioned by Galen in his medical writings in the second century A.D.), Pazalas (who amassed a large collection of CHARMS and predictions), and Zaratus of Media. Also living in Babylonia with the Chaldeans were the sorcerers Arabantiphocus and Marmarus.

The most famous kings of the Chaldeans, Nebuchadnezzar and Belshazzar, figure prominently in the Book of Daniel in the Old Testament of the Bible. Nebuchadnezzar became ruler of Babylonia following his father's death in 605 B.C. After conquering and destroying Jerusalem in 586 B.C., he ordered that the most wise, handsome and skillful of the Israelites be brought back to Babylon to learn the "letters and language of the Chaldeans." Among them were Hananiah, Mishael and Azariah (whom the Chaldeans renamed Shadrach, Meshach and Abednego) and Daniel (called Belteshazzar), who had the God-inspired power to interpret dreams. When Nebuchadnezzar eventually interviewed the four men, he found them "in every matter of wisdom and understanding . . . ten times better than all the magicians and enchanters that were in all his kingdom."

In his second year as king, Nebuchadnezzar started to have a recurring nightmare, so he "commanded that the magicians, the enchanters, the sorcerers and the Chaldeans be summoned" to tell him what the troubling dreams meant. When they were unable to decipher them, Nebuchadnezzar ordered that all the nation's "wise men" (which included Daniel and his three companions) be slaughtered. Through the divine vision from his Lord, Daniel, an adept at oneiromancy, was able to interpret the dream to the king's complete satisfaction. The young prophet was made overseer of Babylon, a task he turned over to his three friends.

Nebuchadnezzar's veneration of the Israeli God was short-lived, however. When Shadrach, Meshach and Abednego refused to bow down to a golden idol of a heathen deity that had been erected by the ruler, they were ordered cast into a fiery furnace. An angel of the Lord appeared with them amid the flames and delivered them from harm. Once again, Nebuchadnezzar praised their God.

Returning to his pagan worship, Nebuchadnezzar experienced a new dream. Daniel, who had been made "chief of the magicians, enchanters, Chaldeans and astrologers," faithfully interpreted this dream as well: The king must honor the God of Jerusalem or be cast from power, go mad and eat grass among the ANIMALS in the field. The ruler did not heed the warning, and the prophecy came to pass. Before his death, Nebuchadnezzar was filled with the SPIRIT of the God of Daniel, and the Lord removed his CURSE.

Nebuchadnezzar was succeeded by his son, Belshazzar. During a royal feast, guests were startled to see the disembodied hand of a man magically appear, floating in the air. On the plaster wall of the palace's great banquet hall, the hand wrote the cryptic words *Mene mene tekel parsin* and then vanished. When King Belshazzar's wizards were unable to decipher the inscription, Daniel, who was still living under royal patronage, was summoned. Belshazzar told the prophet he would be "the third ruler" in his kingdom if he were able to "read the writing and make known . . . its interpretation." Eschewing the reward, Daniel nevertheless made this revelation: "*Mene*, God has numbered the days of your kingdom and brought it to an end; *tekel*, you have been weighed in the balances and found wanting; *peres*, your kingdom is divided and given to the Medes and Persians."

Indeed, the prophecy was fulfilled. That same evening, Belshazzar was assassinated, and Darius the Mede assumed the throne. His rule was followed by that of Cyrus the Persian.

It was during Darius's rule that Daniel was cast into a den of lions. When the den was unsealed, Daniel was found alive and unhurt. The prophet announced that an angel of the Lord had descended to close the mouths of the lions. (See also ASSYRIAN MAGIC.)

Cham-Zoroaster   According to legend, Cham-Zoroaster was the first wizard to flourish after the Great Flood, the deluge common to the ancient mythology of almost all world cultures.

The great magician had four sons, Cush, Mizraim, Phut and Canaan, who were also wizards. Cham-Zoroaster separated the world into four regions and set one son in control of the magic in each area—Africa, Egypt, the (Middle Eastern) deserts and Phoenicia.

Although Cham-Zoroaster's sons are not identified as wizards in Judeo-Christian biblical texts, compatriots with strikingly similar names can be found in the Book of Genesis in the Old Testament of the Bible. Ham, Noah's youngest son, had four sons—Cush, Egypt, Püt and Canaan.

After the flood, Noah became drunk on the wine from his year's harvest. He fell asleep, naked, in his tent. When Noah discovered that Ham had seen him unclothed, he laid a CURSE on Ham's son, Canaan. As the family eventually dispersed, Cush's kingdom included Babylon and Assyria, territories later renowned for their many sorcerers while they were under the rule of the CHALDEANS.

Although sharing a name, Cham-Zoroaster of fable was not related to ZOROASTER, or Zarathustra. (See ASSYRIAN MAGIC; MAGI.)

Chandu, the Magician   See FILMS, *CHANDU THE MAGICIAN*.

charm   From the French word *charme*, derived from the Latin root *carmen*, meaning "song," the word *charm* came to mean a recitation or chant. This gave rise to its interpretation as an INCANTATION (a sung or recited SPELL).

The distinction between a charm and a prayer is more implied than explicit: Both call to a higher, unseen power (often the Judeo-Christian god) for protection or assistance. Not all charms, however, were considered beneficent. In their book *MALLEUS MALEFICARUM*, authors Krämer and Sprenger list seven ways to tell the difference between a good and an evil charm:

A good charm (i.e., acceptable to the Church) contains no

1. Falsehood.
2. "Rituals" other than the sign of the Cross.
3. Mention of a pact with the Devil
4. Supplication to obscure beings or names
5. Biblical reference or phrases out of context
6. Reliance on any providence other than God, and
7. Unnatural way or writing, reciting or wearing the charm.

By the 16th century, the word *charm* was in common usage. It also came to be defined as any kind of AMULET, TALISMAN or other small object, carried or worn, that was believed to have magical powers (for example, to ward off evil or to bring good luck). If someone were already the victim of a CURSE, the proper countercharm would be sought to break the original spell.

The word still carries the meaning of an action taken to create a magical effect, as in "Music hath charms to sooth the savage beast." In its verb form, to charm is to take an action that is liable to enchant. Likewise, a charming person can entice, captivate or seem to hold power magically over another individual.

A contemporary Western usage of *charm*, devoid of its occult overtones, is that of any bauble or trinket that can be worn, usually on a chain or bracelet. First popularized in the 1860s, charm bracelets appeal more to sentimentality than superstition. (See also GLAMOUR.)

Childe Roland   According to an ancient Scottish ballad, Childe Roland was the son of King ARTHUR. When his sister, Burd Ellen, is kidnapped by fairies, he seeks out the aid of MERLIN. The wizard tells Roland how to find the castle of the king of Elfland, where he discovers his sister and rescues her.

Christabel   An unfinished poem by Samuel Taylor Coleridge (1772–1834) that was published in 1816, *Christabel* was conceived as a three-part saga. The beginning was written in 1797 at Nether Stowey, England; the second part, written at Keswick, was completed in 1800; the final section was planned but never begun, no doubt due to Coleridge's increasing sickness, depression and opium addiction.

Much of Coleridge's writing possessed mystic and metaphysical overtones, most clearly seen in the symbolism of *The Rime of the Ancient Mariner*. *Christabel*, too, is allegorical, revealing how pure energy might be redeemed through contact with a spirit of innocent love. Even the chaste heroine's name incorporates the metaphorical words *Christ* and *bel* (beautiful). In the ode, Christabel, a young virgin, is the daughter of Sir Leoline. She goes to an enchanted wood where she prays for her fiancé. In the glen she meets the beautiful but distressed Geraldine and takes her home. Once safely indoors, Geraldine says that she was fleeing five soldiers who had abducted her from the home of her father, Sir Roland of Vaux, who once was a friend of Sir Leoline.

To soothe her, Christabel invites the visitor into her bed for the night where, in the comfort of her embrace, the enchantress Geraldine bewitches her.

In the morning, Sir Leoline states his intention to renew his friendship with Geraldine's father and punish her kidnappers. Struggling to overcome Geraldine's spiritual and sexual SPELL, Christabel insists that her father cast out the vixen. The uncompleted poem ends as Sir Leoline, offended by his daughter's apparent lack of courtesy, turns to Geraldine.

Chronicles of Narnia, The Written by C(live) S(taples) Lewis (1898–1963), *The Chronicles of Narnia* is the collective name given to his series of seven children's books, all of which are set in part in the mythical land of Narnia. *The Lion, The Witch and The Wardrobe* was the first book to be published (in 1950), and it is still the best known. A prequel was eventually written, placing *The Lion, The Witch and The Wardrobe* as the second installment in the final series. The entire collection remains extremely popular, and today *The Chronicles of Narnia* are Lewis's best-known writings.

During the bombing of London in World War II, many children were evacuated to the countryside for their safety. Lewis observed that those placed in The Kilns, his home in Oxford, read very little; he concluded it was because of the poor quality of children's literature.

Thus, *The Lion, the Witch and the Wardrobe* was conceived as a pure escapist adventure story, designed to fire the young reader's imagination. All the Narnia books are imbued with Christian values, mostly in subtext. The central character, who appears in all seven books, is Aslan the Great Lion, king of beasts and creator of Narnia; but, as the son of the "Emperor across the Sea," he could be viewed allegorically as JESUS Christ, the son of God.

According to Lewis's own sequencing of *The Chronicles of Narnia* following the completion of the series, the books in order are as follows: *The Magician's Nephew; The Lion, the Witch and the Wardrobe; The Horse and His Boy; Prince Caspian; The Voyage of the "Dawn Treader"; The Silver Chair;* and *The Last Battle.* Although all of the works contain supernatural creatures and kingdoms, magic and sorcery predominate in the first two books as well as the fifth and sixth in the series.

The Magician's Nephew introduces Andrew Ketterley, a nasty amateur magician. On her deathbed, Ketterley's "fairy godmother," the eccentric Mrs. LeFay (who actually *did* have fairy blood in her), made him promise to destroy an ancient box that she had hidden for years. Instead, Ketterley kept the chest. After studying archaic magic, he used the box's contents, a mound of dry dust, to form several magical finger RINGs, some yellow, some green.

Digory Kirke, Ketterley's nephew, and his friend Polly Plummer put on their fingers yellow rings and are instantly transported to an enchanted dimension that Ketterley has named "the Other Place."

The children explore the ancient ruined kingdom of Charn. They strike an enchanted golden bell covered with RUNES, which awakens the evil Queen Jadis. Centuries before, she had destroyed her entire country with a CURSE; she had only escaped death by placing herself in suspended animation.

The young pair use the green magic rings to escape back to London, but by holding onto the children, Jadis manages to travel along.

Next, Polly and Digory magically transport themselves, Uncle Andrew, Jadis and a hansom driver and his horse out of London to another world, an empty void in darkness. Suddenly, they see Aslan, and they are present at the creation of Narnia. As the power of Good creeps across the land, the wicked Jadis flees.

Aslan challenges Digory to retrieve a golden apple from a distant land. Aslan transforms a horse into a winged stallion, and Digory and Polly fly off. They find the golden apple tree, and Digory, careful to obey the prohibition not to eat the forbidden fruit, pockets an apple.

Jadis, now a full witch, appears. She has eaten an apple and, while gaining strength and wisdom, has turned white as salt. She tries to persuade the boy to eat an apple as well, telling him that it will give him eternal youth, secret knowledge and power. Digory rejects the temptation, escapes the witch's snare and returns the apple to Narnia.

Aslan crowns the cabman and his wife (whom he has transported from London) as King Frank and Queen Helen, the first monarchs of Narnia. Aslan gives Digory an apple that will heal his mother's sickness and then sends him, along with Polly and a chagrined Uncle Andrew (who never tries his hand at magic again), back home.

Digory's mother eats the apple and begins a miraculous recovery. The children bury the apple core surrounded by the magic rings, and a giant tree grows on the spot. Digory's father, who had been working in India, inherits a fortune and returns home. They move to a gigantic house in the country.

Years later, when Digory Kirke is a middle-aged professor, a storm blows down the apple tree behind the old Ketterley house, which he now owns. He has part of the tree trunk made into a large wardrobe, which he places in his country mansion.

The Lion, the Witch and the Wardrobe tells the story of four children (from oldest to youngest) Peter, Susan, Edmund and Lucy Pevensie, who are relocated to the home of an old professor during the London blitz. (The professor is, in fact, the grown-up Digory Kirke.) While exploring the professor's enormous house, Lucy crawls into a giant wardrobe (which had been made from the wood of the enchanted apple tree) and, rather than hitting a back wall, finds herself in Narnia.

Lucy is befriended by a faun who explains that the White Witch (the former Queen Jadis) has taken control of Narnia and bewitched the entire land. The once splendid dominion is in a state of eternal winter, and the White Witch is able to turn any living creature into a statue with her magic WAND.

Lucy returns through the wardrobe to tell her siblings of her adventures, but they mockingly disbelieve her. Later while playing hide-and-seek, Edmund, too, falls through to Narnia. He encounters the White Witch personally; he eats her HEXed Turkish Delight candy, which brings him under her power. Wary of a prophecy that warns that her magic will be destroyed when the four thrones of Cair Paravel are occupied by the Sons of Adam and the Daughters of Eve (i.e., humans), the White Witch demands that Edmund return to his own world and bring back his siblings; secretly, she plans to kill them all.

The four children arrive in Narnia and are pursued by the White Witch. An unexpected spring thaw signals that Aslan (and his magic) has returned to Narnia! The battle of Good versus Evil, the destruction of the Witch and the death and resurrection of Aslan make up the rest of the story.

The four children are crowned kings and queens, and they grow old and wise in their rule, their youth in England long forgotten. One day, while on the hunt for a mystic white stag, they make their way through a forest and back through the wardrobe. They are surprised to discover they are once again children, back in the professor's house, only moments after they had originally gone through the back of the wardrobe. The kindly professor explains that they will one day get back to Narnia, but never again through the wardrobe.

In *The Voyage of the "Dawn Treader"*, Edmund and Lucy return to Narnia. While on a voyage to the end of the sea, one of their adventures brings them into direct contact with the great wizard Coriakan. They land upon "the island of the voices," which is populated with invisible creatures. The beings explain that they are the servants of a powerful wizard who "uglified" them as a punishment. They couldn't bear their appearance, so some of them sneaked into the wizard's den, opened his giant GRIMOIRE and cast a SPELL of invisibility upon themselves.

Because it was believed that only a girl or the wizard himself could reverse a spell, Lucy is forced to peek into the book of magic. Only Lucy's conscience, in the form of Aslan, stops her from trying some of the forbidden spells. She finds "a spell to make things hidden visible" and carefully intones it aloud.

Almost immediately, Aslan appears at the door with Coriakan, the wizard and ruler of the island. Coriakan explains that he would have reversed the enchantment earlier, but he thought the Dufflepuds (as the creatures called themselves) preferred being invisible.

As the seafarers prepare to depart, the kindly wizard magically repairs their ship, the *Dawn Treader*, and produces a map of their travels. Later on their voyage, the travelers learn that Coriakan was, in fact, a star from the heavens, sent to Earth as punishment for an unrevealed transgression.

In *The Silver Chair*, King Caspian's wife, her son Prince Rilian and their entourage ride into northern Narnia one spring day. Resting alone, the queen is bitten by a green serpent and dies. Prince Rilian vows to find and kill the serpent. Soon, he begins to see a repeated vision of a beautiful young woman dressed in a "garment as green as poison."

She turns out to be a sorceress, the "Lady of the Green Kirtle," who bewitches the prince and takes him to her subterranean kingdom, the Underland. To prevent his escape, the witch has the prince bound to a silver chair for the one hour a day in which he remembers his true identity.

Ten years later (by Narnian time; one year by the Earth calendar), Eustace Clarence Scrubb and his school friend Jill Pole are whisked to Narnia to rescue the prince. They set out with Puddleglum, an ever-pessimistic Narnian creature known as a Marsh-wiggle. After many adventures in the lands

of the giants, they are captured and taken to the Lady of the Green Kirtle's underground palace by her slaves, the Earthmen. They are greeted by her consort, the Black Knight.

Later, the children realize that the knight is actually the prince, and they free him from the silver chair. Clearheaded, the prince springs to his sword, destroys the silver chair and breaks the witch's SPELL.

Suddenly, the witch arrives. She tosses some green powder on the fire, which immediately fills the rooms with clouds of scented smoke, and she attempts to entrance them all with her singing. (See SIRENS.) Puddleglum, who has webbed feet, jumps onto the flame. The smoke disperses, clearing the prisoner's minds.

Not to be deterred, the witch transforms herself into a giant serpent and coils herself around the prince. Before she can squeeze him to death, he fatally stabs her with his sword. The prince realizes that the Lady of the Green Kirtle was the green serpent that killed his mother a decade before, and he finally feels avenged.

The death of the witch precipitates a fire, flood and earthquake—the destruction of Underland. The Earthmen, also released from the witch's CURSE, flee down a chasm back to the lower depths, and the four heroes escape to the Overland (Narnia).

C.S. Lewis was born on November 29, 1898, in Belfast, Ireland, the son of a Welsh solicitor. He received a scholarship to Oxford; early in his academic career, in 1925, he was made a Fellow and tutor in English literature at Magdalen College at Oxford University. He later became professor of medieval and ROMANCE LITERATURE at Cambridge University and was there until his death.

Lewis was best known for his literary criticism (the masterwork being *English Literature in the Sixteenth Century*) and many books on Christian ethics (including *Mere Christianity*, based on his 1951 BBC radio lecture series on right and wrong, and *The Screwtape Letters*, 1942). The nature of love was an underlying theme in almost all his writings, especially in his treatise *The Allegory of Love* and his four novels for adults (including *Till We Have Faces* and *The Four Loves*).

Influenced by J.R. TOLKIEN (see *The* HOBBIT; LORD OF THE RINGS, THE) and Charles WILLIAMS, Lewis also wrote three science fiction novels, beginning with *Out of the Silent Planet* in 1938. His science fiction works, like his Narnia books that followed, were laced with his moralist convictions, especially Christian thought.

For most of his life, Lewis was a confirmed bachelor. In the 1950s, after a long international correspondence and eventual meeting with Joy Davidman, an American, Lewis fell in love and was married. Lewis examined his reaction to her tragic early death to cancer in *A Grief Observed*.

The relationship of Lewis and Davidman was recorded in *Lenten Lands* by Douglas Greshman, the younger of her two sons from a previous marriage. William Nicholson also wrote an original television play, *Shadowlands*, based on their story and later adapted it for the stage and for film. (The name for the play was taken from the last chapter of *The Silver Chair*, the last of the Narnia books. Lewis metaphorically referred to the Narnian Shadow-Lands as the "real world" as seen from Aslan's Heaven, in the same sense that Plato characterized man's reality as mere shadows of the true universe surrounding him.)

Britain's BBC TELEVISION produced a six-hour adaptation of *The Chronicles of Narnia*, dramatized by Alan Seymour, which aired in the United States on PBS's "Wonderworks" in 1989 and 1990. A boxed-set of three titles (*The Lion, the Witch and the Wardrobe*; *Prince Caspian and the Voyage of the "Dawn Treader"* and *The Silver Chair*) was released on video in 1996.

Cinderella   The fairy-tale *Cinderella*, based on a French folk tale, was published by Charles Perrault (1628–1703), who used his son Pierre's name as his nom de plume. *Cinderella* was first translated into English by Robert Samber in 1729.

In the well-known story, Cinderella is kept as little more than a domestic slave to her stepmother and two stepsisters and is left behind as the others go to the royal ball. An enchantress, Cinderella's fairy godmother, appears. She produces a fancy gown and transforms a pumpkin and six mice into a carriage and horses. She warns Cinderella that the SPELL will disappear at midnight.

At the ball, the prince falls in love with the mysterious newcomer to his kingdom. Although Cinderella does flee by midnight, she loses one of her tiny glass slippers (*pantoufle de verre*, although some scholars believe this is a mistranslation and *verre* should be *vair*, or "fur").

With slipper in hand, the prince searches his kingdom for the missing damsel, declaring that he will marry whomever the slipper fits perfectly. The evil stepmother secretly cuts off the toes of one of her daughters and the heel of the other, trying to get the petite slipper to fit one of them. The slipper, of course, fits only Cinderella, who also proves herself by presenting the other slipper.

Variations on the Cinderella theme appear in several art forms, including BALLET, OPERA, FILM, TELEVISION and MUSICAL THEATER. Among the many adaptations of the Cinderella story are Gioacchino Rossini's 1817 opera *La Cenerentola* (although the Italian libretto by Jacopo Ferretti, based on the French libretto by Charles Guillaume Etinenne, has no fairy godmother figure), Walt Disney's animated film *Cinderella*, Lerner and Loewe's musical *My Fair Lady*, George Bernard Shaw's play *Pygmalion*, Jerry Lewis's film *Cinderfella*, Rodgers and Hammerstein's made-for-television musical *Cinderella* and characters in Stephen Sondheim and James Lapine's musical *Into the Woods*. (See also GUARDIAN ANGEL.)

Circaea   See CIRCE; ENCHANTER'S NIGHTSHADE.

Circe   Perhaps the most famous enchantress in ancient Greek mythology, Circe (also seen as Kirkê) was an enchantress encountered by Odysseus and his crew on their homeward trip from the Trojan War. As described in Homer's *The ODYSSEY*, Circe was a "child of the Ocean stream," the sister of Aiêtes and the daughter of Hêlios, "the light of mortals."

Following a disastrous run-in with giants that saw all of the ships of his fleet except his own being sunk, Odysseus and his fellow adventurers landed on the island of Aeaea (also seen as Aiaia). After resting for two full days and nights, Odysseus climbed a tall hill and spied smoke coming from a house hidden away in a forest. The fourth morning, he split his company into two groups, and the one commanded by

Eurylochus (also seen as Eurylokhos) set out in search of the dwelling.

In a clearing, they found a fine house made of polished stones. Surprised by mountain lions and wolves roaming loose about the abode, they were even more shocked to find the beasts quite tame and friendly to the point of jumping up on them like pet dogs welcoming their masters home.

The travelers heard beguiling singing from inside the house, and they called out. Circe, a beautiful long-haired enchantress, came to the shining doors and bade them enter.

Circe sat them comfortably and fed them a feast of cheese and barley. To drink, she provided amber honey mixed with Pramnian wine that was poisoned with drugs to make them forget their home of Ithaca. After all of the men had drunk the draught and could not resist, she touched each man with her WAND, transforming them into swine. Circe shooed them to her pigsty and gave them acorns, mast and cornel berries to eat. It was now obvious that the beasts of the jungle that surrounded her house were really men who had also been changed into ANIMALS.

Eurylochus, who had been suspicious and remained outdoors, rushed back to the ship with the bad news. Odysseus strapped on his bronze sword, took up his bow and sped to the enchantress's hall, anxious to engage Circe.

On the way, he was intercepted by Hermes (Mercury), the gods' messenger. He was disguised as a "boy whose lip was downy in the first bloom of manhood" and held a golden CADUCEUS.

To overcome Circe's spell, Hermes gave Odysseus a secret herb—*moly* (or *molë*), a magical white-flowered plant with a black root—that the gods had made fatiguing and painful for mortals to pick. Hermes warned that Circe would try to poison Odysseus's drink:

> Your cup with numbing drops of night
> and evil, stilled of all remorse,
> she will infuse to CHARM your sight;
> but this great herb with holy force
> will keep your mind and senses clear.

Secure in his ability to overcome the enchantress, Odysseus strode to Circe's door and called out her name. The temptress led him to a finely carved chair with silver studs and placed his feet up onto a footstool. She fixed the same poisoned brew that she had served his companions, but as instructed, Odysseus secretly added the moly before drinking it.

Circe tapped him with her wand and whispered the curse: "Down in the sty and snore among the rest!"

Protected by Hermes's herb, Odysseus drew his sword and leapt at Circe. Because no one had ever avoided her spell before, she realized he must be Odysseus, whose arrival had been foretold by Hermes. She immediately fell prostrate at the hero's feet. As Hermes had predicted, Circe offered herself to Odysseus, saying "we two shall mingle and make love upon our bed."

The willing Odysseus first invoked a promise from her that she would never hurt him. She consented and he "entered Circe's flawless bed of love." Circe's handmaidens, nymphs from the woods, prepared a sumptuous table and bath for Odysseus. After they bathed Odysseus and rubbed him with olive oil, they brought him food and drink. These Odysseus refused until Circe agreed to free his men.

Circe took up her wand, went into the pigsty and separated out Odysseus's BEWITCHed crew:

> She stoked them, each in turn, with some new charm;
> and then, behold! their bristles fell away,
> the coarse pelt grown upon them by her drug
> melted away, and they were men again.

Restored to human form, the men were younger, taller and more handsome than before. Taking pity on all of Odysseus's company, Circe gave them food, wine, comfort and rest.

When Odysseus finally told Circe of his plans to leave, she gave immediate consent but prophesied that he and his men were fated to head toward Ithaca by way of the Underworld, "the cold homes of Death and pale Persephone." There Odysseus could consult with the SPIRIT of the soothsayer TIRESIAS about the remainder of his voyage. Fearful and distressed, but determined, they left the island of Aeaea after a full year under Circe's sheltered care.

While in the Underworld, Ulysses saw the spirit of Elpênor, one of his crew who had died by an accidental fall from the roof of Circe's house. Because his body remained unburied, Elpênor made Ulysses vow that he would return to Aeaea, burn his neglected body in a funeral pyre and erect a cairn in his memory.

As promised, after their voyage through the Kingdom of the Dead, Ulysses and his men returned to Circe's island. The enchantress spent the night with Ulysses, telling him that she foresaw even greater threats to his safety as he continued his way homeward.

First, they must pass the island of the SIRENS, temptresses who could bewitch men to their deaths just by the sound of their voices. After that, the ship must pass between the twin threats of Scylla and Charybdis, a six-headed reptilian monster and a living whirlpool/water spout, respectively. Finally, she foretold of their landing on Thrinákia, an island populated by the 350 prize cattle of Apollo. She reinforced Tiresias's warning that they must not harm any of the herd.

At dawn, Circe left Ulysses forever, "taking her way like a great goddess up the island."

Clavicle, The, or Key of Solomon   See KABBALAH; KEY OF SOLOMON, THE.

Colchis   Inhabited since ancient times, Colchis was identified in Greek myths as a home of sorcerers. Its reputation as a comfortable abode for enchanters may stem, in part, from its swamplike terrain and semitropical climate along the eastern coast of the Black Sea. Also the home of MEDEA, Colchis was the resting place of the Golden Fleece, sought by Jason and the Argonauts.

Today, the region is called Kolkhida; it is situated along the Rioni River, in a triangular region South of the Caucasian Mountains within the Georgian state of the former Soviet Union. Its chief products are citrus fruits, tea, grain (especially maize) and linen.

comic books, wizards and sorcerers in   Wizards, sorcerers and other magical characters, whose supernatural exploits can be imaginatively illustrated, have always been a staple in comic-book literature, and authors and artists were quick to use earth legends as a basis for many of their characters and stories. Over the years, DC Comics and Marvel Comics, the two largest publishers of comic books, have had literally hundreds of such characters grace their pages; indeed, mystic beings are also just as popular with smaller, independent comic book producers.

The magical characters found in comic books can be roughly divided into several categories: wizards and sorcerers who gain their powers through study, characters who are empowered with magic by others, characters who are innately magical by nature and characters who derive their powers through an AMULET, a TALISMAN or other occult paraphernalia.

Gemworld   Occasionally, an entire mythology is built around a set of magical characters, such as those associated with Gemworld in DC Comics. Many of these characters, as well as much of the Gemworld mythos, were created for DC Comics by Dan Mishkin, Gary Cohn and Ernie Colon.

The Lords of Order (and Light) and the Lords of Chaos (and Destruction) (first appearing in *More Fun Comics*, #55) are the supernatural embodiment of Good and Evil, respectively. (This duality of good and evil) is found in religious thought from at least the time of ZOROASTER.) The Lords of Order and Chaos battle for supremacy constantly, and each side gains dominance in regular cycles. The Lords of Chaos are due to win supremacy at the end of Earth's 20th century, but the Lords of Order are fighting the natural order in an attempt to prevent humanity's destruction. Their war is fought in the other-dimensional universe known as Gemworld.

In Gemworld, all inhabitants live under one of 12 houses of sorcerers. (Although an entirely different mythology, this division compares to the 12 divisions of the ZODIAC.) Each house is named for a different gem; Gemworld is ruled by the House of Amethyst.

Amethyst (first appearing in *Legion of Super-Heroes*, February 1983) is the daughter of Lady Amethyst and Lord Amethyst. Her father was possessed by Pantagones, one of the Lords of Order, at the time of her conception; so she was born a Lord of Order as well as a sorceress.

To save her life during one of the wars, Amethyst was sent to 20th-century Earth by the enchantress Citrina. Even after returning to Gemworld, Amethyst frequently visited Earth. During a war to help save Earth from aliens, Amethyst was blinded and was helped back to Gemworld by Doctor Fate (*More Fun Comics*, #55).

Doctor Fate was, in fact, Kent Nelson, a human who could transform into a superhero sorcerer, one of the mightiest in the universe, whenever he put on a masked golden helmet supplied by Nabu the Wise. Nabu, one of the Lords of Order, wished to be an Earth human and by means of the helmet could transfer his magical "essence" into a human body. One of Dr. Fate's first adventures was to save Inza Cramer from the sorcerer Wotan. Nelson and Cramer married shortly thereafter, and they learned to merge together as Dr. Fate.

Nelson's body was destroyed by the extreme stress put on it as Dr. Fate, so Nabu temporarily transferred his SPIRIT into another human, Eric Strauss. Nabu placed Nelson's and his wife's souls into a magical amulet, but he later resurrected the couples' corporeal bodies so that they could once again work as Dr. Fate.

Back in her own universe, Amethyst learned to "see" by using her magical inner vision, so she stayed to rule Gemworld. Her final battle was against Child (*Amethyst*, 2nd series, issue #15), who was a Lord of Chaos, and the evil wizard Mordru (*Adventure Comics*, #369). Gemworld was victorious, but its cosmic fabric was torn; in the process Amethyst's "being" was merged with Gemworld itself.

After his unsuccessful battle with Amethyst, the evil wizard Child created a magical rocklike servant, Flaw. Child lost the battle for the mystical world of Druspa Tau, but he returned to fight the powerful sorcerer Mordru.

Originally known as Wrynn, the wicked supersorcerer Mordru was the son of Lord Topaz and Lady Turquoise of Gemworld. After losing a battle against Amethyst, Mordru was merged with Gemworld—in essence, his psyche was buried alive. When he escaped in the 30th century, Mordru recharged his occult powers and became the dictator of Zeroz, as Gemworld was then known.

Also a part of Gemworld legends is Mysa Nal (*Adventure Comics*, #350), born the daughter of Kiwa Nal, the High Seer of Naltar. The psychic Naltorians were originally residents of Zeroz, and the Sorcerers' Community drew Mysa Nal back there after the death of her mother. Fearing her expanding power there, Mordru trapped Mysa Nal's spirit inside the ancient sorceress Xola Aq. The Sorcerers' Community, thinking her to be the evil enchantress, banished her.

Imprisoned in the witch's body, who was by then known as "The Hag," Mysa Nal next came under the sinister influence of Evillo, the Dark Prince of Tartarus (*Adventure Comics*, #350). Prince Evillo was the despotic monarch of the sunless planet Tartarus, where he ruled with a combination of sorcery, hypnotism and mind-control. His band of thieves, the Devil's Dozen, included The Hag.

Nura, Mysa Nal's sister, discovered the truth and used her superior magic to free her sibling. As Mysa Nal's magical powers flourished, she took on an albino appearance and was given the sobriquet "The White Witch."

Still a tyrannical ruler of the Sorcerers' World (as Zeroz was also known), Mordru sought to conquer other planets, including Earth. He was beaten and psychically rehabilitated by the Sorcerers' Council of Teachers back on Zeroz. Spiritually cleansed, he married Mysa Nal.

Late in the 30th century, a monumental battle of sorcerers known as the Magic Wars annihilated Zeroz. The Sorcerers' Community was forced to relocate to the planet Tharn, but before long they were attacked by the superior-forced Khunds. Knowing that only Mordru had the military acumen to fend off the invaders, the Sorcerers' Community reactivated his magical powers and made him Supreme Teacher. Unfortunately, as his occult powers returned, so did his demonic corruption. After vanquishing the Khunds, Mordru turned on the Sorcerers' Community and set himself up as absolute dictator of Tharn. Mysa Nal was cast aside by Mordru. Her powers waned, she lost her albino appearance and she eventually left Tharn.

The Ancient One/Dr. Strange Marvel Comics also produced a series of interwoven stories full of wizards and sorcerers, many of whom visited Earth from other dimensions.

The Vishanti (*Marvel Premiere*, #5) is a collection of godlike, noncorporeal entities that has complete control over the powers of magic throughout the universe. It cannot take human form, but one of the many visages in which it has appeared was Agamotto. Agamotto, the first Sorcerer Supreme of the Earth dimension, produced the Orb of Agamotto (a form of CRYSTAL BALL), the Eye of Agamotto (an amulet which allows the Vishanti to accompany its wearer) and the Book of Vishanti (a GRIMOIRE of SPELLS, CHARMS and INCANTATIONS). In legendary Babylonia, the Ancient One received all three supernatural tokens.

The Ancient One (*Strange Tales*, Vol. 1, #111), a sorcerer, studied magic in Tibet with Kaluu (*Strange Tales*, Vol. 1, #147), a 500-year old sorcerer who had learned his craft in Kamar-Taj, Tibet. Kaluu turned to BLACK MAGIC, and the Ancient One became his foe. Defeated, Kaluu escaped capture and fled to the Raggadoor dimension.

The Ancient One's first apprentice was the barely humanoid Mister Jip (*Strange Tales*, Vol. 3, #11). Mister Jip also began to use his powers for evil and was dismissed by the Ancient One, but his black powers remain unabated. However, to stay alive he must take over other beings and add parts of their bodies to his own.

Eventually, the Ancient One found a true successor in Doctor Strange (*Strange Tales*, Vol. 1, #115). Stephen Vincent Strange apprenticed under the Ancient One in the Tibetan Himalayas and also made his own studies in sorcery. The Ancient One bequeathed to Dr. Strange the Orb and Eye of Agamotto and the spell-laden Book of Vishanti, making him the new Sorcerer Supreme of the Earth. He can draw on all the magical and psychic forces of Earth and other dimensions. Working for the powers of good, Dr. Strange has teamed on occasion with almost every magical superhero in the Marvel Comics canon.

Kaluu returned and battled the combined forces of the Ancient One and Dr. Strange. He was beaten and placed into suspended animation in another dimension. At the end of his life, the Ancient One asked Dr. Strange to will his essence into Eternity.

Kaluu escaped exile and became an ally of Dr. Strange by sharing his dark arts. In return, Kaluu was allowed to return to modern-day Earth.

Concurrent to these stories, Umar (*Strange Tales*, Vol. 1, #150), the evil enchantress and ruler of the Dark Dimension, was born in the Faltine Dimension as an energy being. Her (twin or possibly elder) brother is Dormammu (*Strange Tales*, #126), her daughter is Clea (*Strange Tales*, Vol. 1, #126) and she (Umar) has taken Baron Mordo (*Strange Tales*, #111) as her lover.

Dormammu was born in (and later banished from) the Faltine Dimension. A powerful sorcerer/warrior who had both magical and telepathic powers, Dormammu was at one time the conqueror/lord of the Dark Dimension. His main adversaries throughout the ages have been the Ancient One and Doctor Strange (*Strange Tales*, #110).

Clea was instructed in magic by Doctor Strange; they married following Clea's battle of magic against her mother. Recognizing that Dormammu was their real threat, however,

Clea, Dr. Strange and Umar teamed with Baron Mordo to defeat him. Clea and Dr. Strange moved to New York, and Umar returned as queen of the Dark Dimension.

Born in Transylvania, Baron Mordo was a rogue sorcerer and was exiled by his former mentor, the Ancient One.

Voodoo and witchcraft Tales of VOODOO inspired Marvel Comics to create an interrelated cast of characters that range from Haitian vodun priests to other-dimension witches and sorcerers. Brother Voodoo (Marvel, *Strange Tales*, Vol. 1, #169), the former Jericho Drumm, learned *vodun* (Haitian voodoo) from Papa Jambo and graduated as a *houngan*, or voodoo priest. Drumm uses an amulet as a focal point to enter a trance and as Brother Voodoo is able to call on the *loa* (voodoo gods) and the spirit of his murdered brother.

Black Talon (Marvel, *Strange Tales*, Vol. 1, #173) was also involved in voodoo, having inherited the black magic powers of his mother, the voodoo queen Mama Limbo, and could create ZOMBIES. Though his chief opponent was Brother Voodoo, he was clubbed to death by his followers. Since then, a second Black Talon has emerged.

The stories of several other magical Marvel Comics characters, although peripherally connected to these mystic tales of voodoo, form their own mythos. Scarlet Witch (Marvel, *X-Men*, #4), one of the major enemies of the second Black Talon, is the superhero alterego of Wanda Maximoff. Born in Transia, Europe, and predisposed to magic, the Scarlet Witch studied sorcery under Agatha Harkness (*Fantastic Four*, #94). Even so, her powers are only effective about 80 percent of the time.

Agatha Harkness, who practices WHITE MAGIC, is a fountainhead of occult knowledge and is accompanied by Ebony, her CAT FAMILIAR. Her son was Nicholas Scratch (*Fantastic Four*, #185), a sorcerer and the master of New Salem, Colorado, a secret community of witches and WARLOCKS. The town tried and executed Harkness, but she rose from the dead. Scratch was eventually banished by his peers to the Dark Realm; later, New Salem and all its inhabitants were destroyed.

Mephisto (*Surfer*, Vol. 1, #3) is the monarch of an other-dimension realm of the dead. The infernal region was popularly misconceived to be Hades, which gave rise to Mephisto's name. It is unsure whether Mephisto is a demon or some other form of supernatural creature, but he has total knowledge of the magical arts and almost unlimited power of over their use. As in the legends of *FAUST*, Mephisto cannot exert his will over others without their prior consent. One of his conquests, for instance, was Baron Mordo.

Another of Mephisto's protégés was Master Pandemonium (*West Coast Avengers*, Vol. 2, #4), who was born Martin Preston. An actor-turned-CEO of a film studio, Preston was transformed into an archvillain by Mephisto. A master of black magic, Master Pandemonium was empowered by the Rakasha, a host of demons that Mephisto sent to dwell within him. For a time, he had a birdlike familiar that lived inside his powerful Amulet of Azmodeus.

Master Pandemonium had a hole carved in his chest in the shape of a pentagram, an inverted five-point star (see PENTA-CLE). Told by Mephisto that this was the home of five fragments of his scattered essence, Master Pandemonium began to search to retrieve the missing sections.

Master Pandemonium discovered that the Scarlet Witch's two children were, in fact, two of the pieces. He kidnapped them and placed them in his chest. Master Pandemonium did not know, however, that the children were, in actuality, supernatural entities formed from demonic portions of Mephisto. When Master Pandemonium located and absorbed the last three sections of the pentagram, he imploded into a black hole.

Mephisto had two children with a human, Victoria Wingate (now deceased): a son Hellstorm (*Marvel Spotlight*, Vol. 1, #12) and a daughter Satana (*Vampire Tales*, #2). Hellstorm has a large pentagram birthmark in the middle of his chest. Although a master demonologist, Hellstorm uses his powers for good and is an archenemy of his father. Satana, on the other hand, relishes in the black magic taught her by her father. She has a cat named Exiter as a familiar and also carries a demon, Basilisk, with her. Satana is a SUCCUBUS, and she needs to drain energy from mortals to live.

One of the Scarlet Witch's greatest enemies is Chton (*Marvel Chillers*, #1). A co-ruler of Earth in prehistory, Chton was banished to another dimension. There, he collected and assimilated the Darkhold, the collected cabalistic wisdom and black magic of the Elder Gods of Earth. On the few instances that he has been able to capture a human host body to reenter the Earth dimension, Chton has teamed with fellow sorcerers such as Modred the Mystic (*Marvel Chillers*, #1).

Modred the Mystic is totally unrelated to the Modred/Mordred of Arthurian myth. Though human, Modred was "possessed" by Chton in sixth-century London. The demon gained control of him when Modred, in an attempt to master all occult wisdom, studied the Darkhold, the grimoire of ancient, forbidden knowledge which had been collected by Chton. Modred fell into a state of suspended animation, but he (and, therefore Chton) were awakened in the 20th century by a team of archaeologists. One of Modred's chief foes in modern-day England is Captain Britain (Marvel, *Captain Britain*, Vol. #1).

Captain Britain was the son of James Braddock, a resident of the Otherworld dimension. Merlin (*Black Knight Comics*, #1) enhanced Braddock, Jr.'s latent mystic powers. As Captain Britain, he drew his magic from an enchanted costume, an amulet of right and a star-sceptre.

Arthurian legend The Merlin comic book character who helped Captain Britain is one of several Marvel Comics characters based on the English legends of King ARTHUR, Morgan LE-FAY and MERLIN.

Marvel's Morgan le Fay (*Spider-Woman*, #2) was born in Tintagel Castle in sixth-century England. Half-human, half-fairy, Morgan le Fay learned her craft from Merlin; when she turned to black magic. he became her enemy. She is able to transport her astral form to 20th-century Earth, where her adversaries include Doctor Strange and the Black Knight (*Avengers*, #47); Chton has also occasionally been her partner-in-crime.

Merlin was born in sixth-century Wales, purportedly the son of a demon; a prophet, he became the court wizard at King Arthur's CAMELOT. He was said to own the largest library of occult books and magic paraphernalia in the ancient world.

Merlin was ensnared by the faerie-enchantress NIMUË Although trapped deep within a secret cave, he is able to project his spirit to the outside world, where he continues to be an astral adviser to the Black Knight.

The Black Knight, the alter ego of American Dane Whitman, became a mystic-hero crime fighter after being visited by the spirit of an ancestor, Sir Percy of Scandia. His chief weapon is the Ebony Sword, which was forged and endowed with magic by Merlin.

Mythology-based characters   The backgrounds of comic-book wizard and sorcerer characters have a direct basis in occult and fantasy literature. In Marvel Comics, for example, Doctor Druid (*Amazing Adventures*, Vol. 1, #1) and Dredmund Druid (*Strange Tales*, Vol. 1, #144) are both based on the DRUIDS of Celtic and early British mythology. Sphinx (*Nova*, #6) is versed in EGYPTIAN MAGIC and took part in the confrontation with MOSES in the court of Ramses II; Centurious (*Ghost Rider*, Vol. 2, #74) became a master of ALCHEMY and the ELEMENTS studied in pharaonic Egypt. Talisman (*Alpha Flight*, #5) and Black Crow (*Captain America*, #290) practice NATIVE AMERICAN MAGIC.

In DC Comics, Circe (*Wonder Woman*, 1st series, #305) has a direct counterpart in the enchantress CIRCE found in *The* ODYSSEY. Green Lantern (*Showcase*, #22) receives his powers from a magical RING. Each member of the trio known as Three Witches (*The Witching Hour*, #1) represents one of the three guises in which witches are thought to appear: a beautiful young maiden, a mother figure and an ugly hag. They are eternal and have appeared many times throughout history in such guises as the Fates, the Furies, the three aspects of HECATE and, of course, the three weird sisters in SHAKESPEARE'S *MACBETH*.

There are dozens more characters with magical and supernatural powers found in DC Comics, Marvel Comics and the independent comic-book publishers. Some of the more important mystic figures from DC Comics include Anton Arcane (*Swamp Thing*, 1st series, #2), Blue Devil (*Fury of Firestorm*, #24), Roderick Burgess (*Sandman*, 2nd series), John Constantine (*Saga of the Swamp Thing*, #37), Dr. Alchemy (*Showcase*, #13), Dove (*Hawk & Dove*, #1), Etrigan (*The Demon*, 1st series, #1), Felix Faust (*Justice League of America*, #10), Hawk (*Hawk & Dove*, #1), Highfather (*The New Gods*, 1st series, #1), Tim Hunter (*The Books of Magic*, #1), Abra Kadabra (*Flash*, #128), Kestrel (*Hawk & Dove*, #1), Klarion the Witch-Boy (*The Demon*, 1st series, #7), Kono (*Legion of Super-Heroes*, 2nd series, #2), Matthew the Raven (*The Sandman*, 2nd series, #11), Mister E (*Secrets of Haunted House*, #31), Jack O'Lantern (*DC Comics Presents*, #46), Phantom Stranger (*Phantom Stranger*, 1st series, #1), Power Girl (*All-Star Comics*, #58), Spectre (*More Fun Comics*, #52), Silver Sorceress (*Justice League of America*, #87), Temptress (*Mister E*, #1), Vixen (*Action Comics*, #521), Wild Huntsman (*DC Comics Presents*, #46) and Wotan (*More Fun Comics*, #55).

Other magical characters in Marvel Comics include Absorbing Man (*Journey Into Mystery*, #114), Arabian Knight (*Incredible Hulk*, #257), Balor (*Avengers*, #225), Belasco (*Ka-Zar the Savage*, #11), Black Queen (*New Mutants*, #9), Bloodaxe (*Marvel, Thor*, #449), Ulysses Bloodstone (*Marvel Presents*, #1), Brothers Grimm (*Iron Man*, #187), Bulldozer (*Defenders*, #17), Chondu the Mystic (*Tales of Suspense*), Destroyer (*Journey Into Mystery*, #118), Dakihm (*Adventure Into Fear*, #14), Darkhawk (*Darkhawk*, #1), Demogoblin (*Web of Spider-Man*, #86), Diablo

(*Fantastic Four*, #30), Dreamqueen (*Alpha Flight*, #56), D'Spayre (*Marvel Team-Up*, #68), Earth-Lord (*Thor*, #395), Feron (*Excalibur*, #48), Forge (*X-Men*, #184), Gargoyle (*Defenders*, #94), Ghost Rider (*Ghost Rider*, Vol. 2, #1), Hobgoblin (I, *Amazing Spider-Man*, #18; II, *Amazing Spider-Man*, #289), Karnilla (*Journey Into Mystery*, #107), Hannibal King (*Tomb of Dracula*, Vol. 1, #25), Lilith (*Ghost Rider*, Vol. 3, #28), Llan the Sorcerer (*Alpha Flight*, #71), Magik (*Uncanny X-Men*, #160), Malekith (*Thor*, #344), Mangog (*Thor*, #154), Moonglow (I, *Squadron Supreme*, #10; II, *Defenders*, #112), Mysterio (*Amazing Spider-Man*, #13), N'Astirh (*X-Factor*, #32), Null the Living Darkness (*Defenders*, #103), Piledriver (*Defenders*, #17), Puck (*Alpha Flight*, #1), Puppet Master (*Fantastic Four*, #8), Rintrah (*Doctor Strange*, Vol. 2, #80), Satannish (*Doctor Strange*, Vol. 1, #74), Shroud (*Super-Villain Team-Up*, #5), Silver Dagger (*Doctor Strange*, Vol. 2, #1), Sise-Neg (*Marvel Premiere*, #13), Surtur (*Journey Into Mystery*, #97), Talon (*Guardians of the Galaxy*, #18), Thanos (*Iron Man*, #55), Thor (*Thor*, #19), Thunderstrike (*Thor*, #459), Tigra (*Giant-Size Creatures*, #1), Trump (*Daredevil*, #203), Tyrannus (*Incredible Hulk*, Vol. 1, #5), Werewolf (*Marvel Spotlight*, #2), White Tiger (*Deadly Hands of Kung-Fu*, #19), Wizard (*Strange Tales*, #102), Yandroth (*Strange Tales*, Vol. 1, #164), Yellow Claw (*Captain America*, #164), Zaladane (*Astonishing Tales*, #3), Zatanna (*Hawkman*, #4) and Zuras (*Eternals*, Vol. 1, #15).

(See also MANDRAKE THE MAGICIAN; SUPERMAN; WIZARD OF ID, THE.)

Compendium Maleficarum   Written by Francesco-Maria Guazzo (also seen as Guaccio or Guazzi), a 17th-century Italian friar, the *Compendium Maleficarum* (*Handbook of Witches*) recounted many of the practices of contemporary witches and sorcerers.

Guazzo was attached to the Brethern of St. Ambrose ad Nemus and St. Barnabas in Milan, and he compiled his work at the request of the Bishop of Milan. The book relied almost exclusively on previously published tracts about WITCHCRAFT, especially those of Martin Antoine DEL RIO and Nicholas REMY. The *Compendium Maleficarum* referenced 322 different authorities and sources and as such was considered one of the standard witchcraft encyclopedias of its time.

Connecticut Yankee in King Arthur's Court, A   Written by Mark Twain (Samuel Langhorne Clemens, 1835–1910) and first printed by the American Publishing Company in Hartford, Connecticut, in 1889, *A Connecticut Yankee in King Arthur's Court* is a fantasy tale in which a 19th-century New England resident, Hank Morgan, is propelled back to the CAMELOT of King ARTHUR in the year A.D. 528. The king's court quickly deserts MERLIN when this new, seemingly more powerful, wizard comes to town. As in all of Twain's writing, much of his satiric observation centered around the people's gullibility and their rapid desertion of the proven in favor of novelty.

Mark Twain visited England for the first time in 1872 and was familiar with Warwick Castle and many of the other historical sites mentioned in his book. He most likely first became acquainted with Sir Thomas MALORY'S *LE MORTE D'ARTHUR* when he was given a copy by his friend George Washington Cable, probably in fall 1884.

"It was a noble effect." The newcomer escapes burning at the stake and proves his magical powers by correctly "predicting" a solar eclipse. (Daniel Beard illustration, *A Connecticut Yankee in King Arthur's Court*)

Mark Twain draws a vivid portrait of Merlin, unlike any other description of the wizard elsewhere in literature. While Merlin is painted, to a large degree, as the villain of the novel, he is also treated sympathetically by Twain. Merlin is described as "a very old and white-bearded man, clothed in a flowing black gown . . . standing . . . upon unsteady legs, and feebly swaying his ancient head and surveying the company with his watering and wandering eye." He was, after all, the court wizard, admired and feared by one and all, only to find his reputation and position threatened by a stranger with unknown powers and purpose.

By today's standards, Merlin's attempts to cast spells are unintentionally comical, but they are probably a fairly accurate representation of a medieval wizard's ministrations when trying to impress onlookers:

> He drew an imaginary circle on the stones of the roof, and burnt a pinch of powder in it which sent up a small cloud of aromatic smoke, whereat everybody fell back, and began to cross themselves and get uncomfortable. Then he began to mutter and make passes in the air with his hands. He worked himself up slowly and gradually into a sort of frenzy, and got to thrashing around his arms like the sails of a windmill.

A Connecticut Yankee in King Arthur's Court begins as a narrative, a personal anecdote written by Twain. While touring Warwick Castle in England, he meets a mysterious stranger. That night, back in his hotel, Twain is reading Malory's *Le Morte D'Arthur* when there is a knock at the door. The stranger whom Twain had met earlier that day enters and tells an incredible tale.

He is Hank Morgan, a Connecticut craftsman and machine worker, especially skilled in blacksmithy and explosives. In a fight, he explains, he was hit on the head with a crowbar and awoke in Camelot.

The stranger tells Twain that he has written down all of his adventures and hands Twain a yellowed manuscript. The stranger goes into the next room to sleep, and Twain begins to read the peculiar tale.

Captured by Sir Kay, the time traveler is taken to Arthur's court, where he is displayed before the Round Table and sentenced to death. Recalling that a solar eclipse is to take place two days hence, the stranger announces that he is a mightier wizard than Merlin, whom he had seen at the sentencing, and will blot out the sun forever if he is not released. When the catastrophic eclipse occurs, the Yankee is released.

To prove his power, the stranger destroys Merlin's tower with a great blast, having surreptitiously impregnated it with gunpowder (which was unknown in Britain at the time). As a result, the newcomer is proclaimed to be the realm's most powerful sorcerer, much to the chagrin and humiliation of Merlin. The Yankee is made the right-hand minister and advisor to the king; before long, he has received the nickname, The Boss.

The Boss quickly solidifies his standing as the most powerful wizard in the land. He, of course, has an unfair advantage over Merlin: He knows the future, he knows science and technology and he knows human psychology.

He secretly sets up schools and factories for the working class, winning a loyal and dedicated staff. Among them is Sir Kay's page, Clarence. Soon The Boss has established an underground newspaper and a telephone system.

The Boss is forced to make a quest against three ogres who have imprisoned 45 virgins—damsels in distress—for 26 years. Along the way to the monsters' castle, he meets the enchantress Morgan LE FAY:

> She was held in awe by the whole realm, for she had made everybody believe she was a great sorceress. All her ways were wicked, all her instincts devillish [sic].

While she posed as menacing, she was actually frightened by rumors of The Boss's tremendous powers. Before taking his leave of Le Fay, The Boss tricks her into allowing him to release all the prisoners from her dungeons.

One of The Boss's biggest tests comes when he is called upon to restart a sacred fountain's flow of water. The abbot admonishes The Boss, "And see thou do it with enchantments that be holy, for the Church will not endure that work in her cause be done by devil's magic." Although he knows he can fix the well, The Boss does not want to intervene until Merlin, who has been muttering enchantments over the dry fountain, admits defeat. "Merlin is a very good magician in a small way," The Boss concedes, "and has quite a neat provincial reputation." Once again, The Boss succeeds where Merlin has failed to produce.

Shortly thereafter, an itinerant magician, a wanderer from the East, appears at Camelot. "His dress was the extreme of the fantastic; as showy and foolish as the sort of thing an Indian medicine man wears. He was mowing, and mumbling, and gesticulating, and drawing mystical figures in the air and on the floor—the regular thing, you know." The magician's specialty was being able to tell what anyone was doing anywhere on the face of the Earth. The courtiers were astounded that the wizard knew, for instance, exactly what the emperor of the East was doing at that very moment.

The Boss challenges the magician to say what he is doing with the hand he has kept behind his back. The charlatan answers that he can only divine the nobility's actions. The Boss learns the whereabouts of the king, who was away from court, by calling ahead on one of his hidden telephones. When The Boss correctly prophesies when the king will return to Camelot, the court once again proclaims him to be the greater wizard.

The Boss is challenged to a duel by a member of Arthur's Round Table, but during the joust the knight is unseated by The Boss, who uses a new, seemingly magical weapon: a lasso. The Boss is challenged by yet another knight, but the vengeful Merlin steals the lariat by sleight of hand. Nevertheless, The Boss accepts the joust and wins the tourney by shooting the knight with a concealed pistol. His victory in a subsequent battle against the combined force of 500 knights destroys the age of chivalry and knight errantry.

The remainder of the book describes the knights' collective war against The Boss, set against the story of Arthur, Guenever and Mordred. After the final battle, The Boss and his followers are holed up in their headquarters in Merlin's Cave.

After King Arthur proclaims him to be a stronger wizard than Merlin, the Yankee takes the nickname "The Boss." (Daniel Beard illustration, *A Connecticut Yankee in King Arthur's Court*)

On a foray to check the enemy's forces, The Boss is stabbed. An old crone makes her way to the cave and offers to help tend him. Clarence awakens to discover her making "curious passes in the air about The Boss's head and face" and then sneaking away. Clarence challenges her, and she throws off her disguise, shouting

> Ye were conquerors; ye are conquered! These others are perishing—you also. Ye shall all die in this place—everyone—except *him*. He sleepeth, now—and shall sleep thirteen centuries. I am Merlin!

In jubilation, Merlin leans backward in a triumphant laugh. He accidentally touches one of the electrified wires that had been strung to defend the cave and is instantly electrocuted.

In the book's final chapter, Twain, in his hotel, sets down the manuscript. He goes into the next room to find the stranger lying on the bed, muttering unintelligibly. Before becoming coherent, the stranger dies.

contagious magic   A form of SYMPATHETIC MAGIC, contagious magic is that which allows the wizard or sorcerer to affect a person by the magical manipulation of some object that has come in contact with that person. According to Sir James George Frazer, who coined the term *contagious magic* in *The GOLDEN BOUGH*, things once in contact continue to affect each other (the "Law of Contact"). Although the SPELL is strongest if the item was part of the person's body (e.g., fingernail clippings, hair), it is not absolutely necessary.

Most tribal societies fear the destructive capabilities of contagious magic to some degree, and so even a person's name is carefully guarded. For example, the true name of Pocahontas, the Native American princess, was Matoaka (pronounced *Mah-to-kay)*, but her people believed that knowledge of her real name could give their enemies power over her. She was given a spoken name—*Pocahontas*, meaning "full of mischief and joy." (See FILMS, *Pocahontas*.)

Although the practice of contagious magic is often used to harm an enemy, especially in VOODOO ritual, it can also be used for good purposes such as healing. Francis Bacon (1561–1626), for instance, wrote in "The Old Wives' Tale" that "It is constantly received and avouched, that the anointing of the weapon which maketh the wound will heal the wound itself."

Contagious magic is particularly popular because it can be performed in secret and over great distances. Truly effective contagious magic will work without the knowledge of the recipient or victim of the HEX. (See also IMITATIVE MAGIC.)

Coriakin   See *CHRONICLES OF NARNIA, THE.*

correspondences   The occult theory known as the Law of Correspondences was the classification system of interrelations by which all things in the universe, physical and supernatural, were categorized by wizards and sorcerers to facilitate their use during magic.

Since the beginning of time, humans have been trying to make sense of the world around them. The Law of Correspondences was one such attempt, based on the presumption that the universe is ordered and that each piece of the puzzle is part of a whole. The strands, or links, that hold the parts together are the correspondences. If magic is the attempt by humans to control their world by either natural or supernatural means, then understanding and being able to manipulate these correspondences would be essential toward mastery over one's own universe.

The days of the week, for example, corresponded to particular planets and their respective gods. Sunday was associated with the sun; the sun, of course, corresponds to the color yellow and to the metal gold. Thus, if the wizard were casting a SPELL to obtain wealth, the incantation's effectiveness might be improved by performing the ritual on a Sunday, using ceremonial instruments made of gold. The wizard might wear a yellow robe, light yellow candles or utilize a rooster (which crows at the dawning sun) during the rites.

In all the cabalistic arts, such as ASTROLOGY, ALCHEMY and angelic communication, enlightened wizards were cognizant of all the planetary influences within the cosmos. Thus, a chart could be drawn of correspondences (some now archaic and arcane, others seemingly logical) among the known planets, metals, colors and days of the week:

PLANET	METAL	COLOR	DAY
Sun	Gold	Yellow	Sunday
Moon	Silver	White	Monday
Mercury	Quicksilver	Grey	Tuesday
Venus	Copper	Green	Wednesday
Mars	Iron	Red	Thursday
Jupiter	Tin	Blue	Friday
Saturn	Lead	Black	Saturday

Further correspondences were made with the supposed ten *sefiroth*, or aspects of God, and the 22 upward paths that connect the *sefiroth* on the divine tree of life. Cabalist correspondences can be found to each of the 22 letters of the Hebrew ALPHABET and the 22 Major Arcana of TAROT CARDS. (See also ELEMENTS.)

Countess Kathleen, The A verse play by William Butler Yeats (1865–1939), *The Countess Kathleen* was published in 1892. It was based on one of his own short stories, first published in 1888 as part of his *Fairy and Folk Tales of the Irish Peasantry*. *The Countess Kathleen* was first performed in Dublin in 1899 at the Irish Literary Theatre, which was cofounded by Yeats and was the forerunner of the Abbey Theatre. It marked the beginning of a new interest in Irish literature often referred to as the Irish Revival.

In the play, set in Ireland during a famine, people are selling their souls to the Devil in exchange for food. To prevent kindly Countess Kathleen O'Shea from helping the hungry peasantry, the Devil reduces her to poverty and starvation as well. Eventually, she too agrees to sell her soul but sets her price so high that she is able to provide her neighbors with enough money to buy provisions. Because she has sacrificed herself for others, she is absolved at the end of the play. (See also *CELTIC TWILIGHT, THE*.)

coven A coven is a small group of witches, traditionally 13 in number, that meets for ceremonial rituals and revelry.

The source of the word *coven* is uncertain, but it is most likely derived from the same root as *convene*. Several forms of the word can be found. In *The* CANTERBURY TALES, Chaucer refers to a gathering of 13 people as a "covent." The original meaning of *convent* was either a religious gathering or the place in which it was held.

During the 1662 WITCHCRAFT trial of Isobel Gowdie in Auldearne, Scotland, she referred to her own local assembly of witches as a *covine*. In his LETTERS ON DEMONOLOGY AND WITCHCRAFT (1830), Sir Walter Scott described a "covine tree" as a regular meeting place for lords and their guests in front of the castle.

Montague Summers (1880–1948), a British author on witchcraft and demonology, coined the word *coventicles* (from the Latin *coventus*, meaning "assembly" or "coming together") and preferred its use to *coven*. Still other variants of the word include *covey*, *coeven* and *curving*.

Crowley, Aleister (1875–1947) Born Edward Alexander Crowley, the son of a Scottish brewer and preacher, Aleister Crowley was an occult author (both prose and poetry) and a self-described witch and sorcerer. At various times, Crowley claimed to be the reincarnation of Pope Alexander VI, Edward KELLY, CAGLIOSTRO, Eliphas LEVI (who had died the day Crowley was born) and Ankh-f-n-Khonsu, an Egyptian wizard-priest of the 26th Dynasty.

He entered Trinity College at Cambridge and, in 1898, published his first book of poetry, *Aceldama, A Place to Bury Strangers in. A Philosophical Poem. By a Gentleman of the University of Cambridge*.

Crowley, who had always been interested in the occult, was greatly influenced by A. E. WAITE's *The Book of Black Magic and of Pacts*. He sought out the author, who told Crowley of the Great White Brotherhood of mystics; on November 18, 1898, Crowley joined the London chapter of the Hermetic ORDER OF THE GOLDEN DAWN, which was the First or Outer Order of the Brotherhood.

Crowley soon left Trinity College without graduating, moved to London, renamed himself Count Vladimir and threw himself into his cabalistic studies. He advanced through the ranks of the Great White Brotherhood and into the Second Order, also known as the Order of the Red Rose and the Golden Cross.

Argumentative and egotistical, Crowley fought regularly with S.L. MacGregor MATHERS, the head of the Order of the Golden Dawn. Eventually, Crowley was forced out of the order, but in the process, Crowley's machinations had caused such divisions in the order that it soon disbanded. It was said that Mathers, himself a sorcerer, attacked his foe with an army of Elementals (see ELEMENTS).

Crowley left before entering the Third Order of the Great White Brotherhood, the *Argentum Astrum* (or Silver Star), known simply as A.A.

Crowley married Rose Kelly in 1903, with whom he had one child. A medium, Rose Kelly was able to contact Crowley's Holy GUARDIAN ANGEL, or True Self, a SPIRIT named Aiwass. On three consecutive days in April 1904, from noon until 1 P.M., Aiwass, through Crowley's wife, dictated *The Book of the Law*. This occult revelation is noted for its deliverance of "The Law of Thelema": "Do what thou whilt shall be the whole of the law." The law states that one should do what one must—not, as the law is commonly misinterpreted, whatever one wishes to do.

For four years, beginning in 1915, Crowley lived in the United States. In 1920, he moved to Sicily, where he founded the Abbey of Thelema as a retreat for mystics.

Crowley maintained a number of mistresses, or scarlet women as he called them, the most notable being Leah Hirsig, whom he named the Ape of Thoth. In 1921, during a ritual ceremony with Hirsig, Crowley claimed to have reached Ipissimus. Hirsig found that this achievement changed Crowley's temperament, however, and she soon found him unbearable. Crowley replaced her with a new scarlet woman, Dorothy Olsen.

In 1922, he became the director of the *Ordo Templi Orientis*, but the scandalous reports of his actions there led to his deportation from Italy the following year. Crowley traveled to France, Tunisia and Germany. He remarried in 1929 in Leipzig to Maria Ferrari de Miramar.

After years of financial insecurity and declining health, exacerbated by heroin addiction and heavy drinking, Crowley died in Hastings, England. His own "Hymn to Pan" was recited at part of his funeral services held in a Brighton crematorium chapel, and his disciples performed a BLACK MASS over his grave.

His numerous cabalistic writings include contributions (from 1909 to 1913) to *The Equinox*, an occult journal he founded, and articles in other magazines devoted to arcana. Books include *The Kabbalah Unveiled*, *The Diary of a Drug Fiend*, *The Stratagem* (collected short stories), *The Equinox of the Gods* (promoting *The Book of the Law* as the basis for a new religion), *Moonchild* (1929, based on his attempts to have a "magical child" with his scarlet women) and two volumes of a proposed six-volume "autohagiography" *The Confessions of Aleister Crowley*. His best known literary works are *Magick in Theory and Practice* (published in Paris in 1929, still in print and considered to be one of the most informative books ever written on ceremonial magic) and *The Book of Thoth* (an examination and interpretation of the TAROT).

Crowley is said to be the model for the protagonist of *The Magician*, a little-known work by W. Somerset Maugham (1874–1965). *The Great Beast* is the title of the best-known biography of Crowley, written by John Symonds. With the assistance of Kenneth Grant, Symonds also collected and edited Crowley's remaining autobiographical manuscripts, publishing them in one volume in 1969.

Crucible, The   Written by Arthur Miller (1915–) and opening at the Martin Beck Theatre in New York City on January 22, 1953, *The Crucible* is a fairly straightforward retelling of the WITCHCRAFT trials in the small village of Salem in the Massachusetts Bay Colony in 1692. Although the play was (for the most part) historically factual, events were condensed and heightened for dramatic purposes.

Featured in the original cast were Arthur Kennedy (John Proctor), Beatrice Straight (Elizabeth "Goody" Proctor), E. G. Marshall (Reverend John Hall), Jean Adair (Rebecca Nurse) and Jacqueline Andre (Tituba, the Parris's slave whose stories of Barbados sorcery helped start the witchcraft hysteria). While possessing its own dramatic integrity, the play can be viewed allegorically: It was penned in the midst of the hysteria

caused by the McCarthy hearings on un-American activities, which ran for approximately 10 years between 1948–1958, concentrated between February 9, 1950, when McCarthy declared that the State Department was overrun with communists, to 1954.

Miller himself was called before the House Committee on Un-American Activities in 1956. Refusing to cooperate or "name names" of suspected communists, Miller was cited for contempt by Congress. By the time, the courts reversed the ruling two years later, the McCarthy-led "witch hunt" was over.

In his collection *The Theater Essays of Arthur Miller*, the playwright told how he first conceived *The Crucible*: "When the McCarthy era came along, I remembered these stories and . . . I used to say, you know, McCarthy is actually saying certain lines that I recall the witch-hunters saying in Salem. So I started going back, not with the idea of writing a play, but to refresh my own mind because it was getting eerie." It was while watching Salem tourists casually passing documents and exhibits that he decided that he had to "tell them the significance of those relics."

The Crucible clearly alluded to the McCarthy hearings, but the work also carries more universal themes and warnings, such as the danger of ordinary people being swept up in and overwhelmed by extraordinary events, the ease with which people can betray each other, the extremities to which one will go for self-preservation and the nobility and / or foolishness of dying for one's beliefs.

During its initial run, the critics condemned the play as unemotional and cerebral. Others considered it didactic and little more than a political statement. It closed after a short run of a just few months to small audiences. Nevertheless, its importance was soon recognized, and it received four Tony Awards: Play; Author, Drama (Miller); Producer, Drama (Kermit Bloomgarden); and Supporting or Featured Actress, Drama (Beatrice Straight).

Just five years later, after the end of the McCarthy hearings, *The Crucible* was revived Off-Broadway, and the same critics were almost universal in their praise of the piece. Although the reviewers lauded the improvements in the script, Miller had not changed a word. "When McCarthyism was around," explained Miller in his collection, *The Theater Essays of Arthur Miller*, the press was "quite simply in fear of the theme of the play, which was witch-hunting. In [1958] they were not afraid of it, and they began to look at the play."

The first major Broadway revival of *The Crucible* appeared at the Belasco Theatre in 1991 as the first production of The National Actors Theatre.

A French / East German FILM version of *The Crucible*, also released as *The Witches of Salem*, was produced in 1957, with a screenplay adaptation by Jean-Paul Sartre and starring Simone Signoret and Yves Montand. The first American film version of *The Crucible*, with screenplay by Arthur Miller, was released by 20th Century Fox on November 27, 1996. The production was directed by Nicholas Hytner and starred Winona Ryder (Abigail Williams), Daniel Day-Lewis (John Proctor) and Joan Allen (Elizabeth Proctor). The film received two Academy Award nominations: Performance by an actress in a supporting role (Allen) and screenplay based on material previously produced or published (Miller).

Arthur Miller was born in New York in 1915 and matriculated at the University of Michigan from 1934 to 1938. His first notable play, which earned him a Drama Critics Circle Award, was *All My Sons* (1947). His drama, *Death of a Salesman*, which followed two years later, received the Pulitzer Prize and the Drama Critics Circle Award.

After *The Crucible* came several more significant plays by Miller, including *A View from the Bridge* (1955), *After the Fall* (1964) and *The Price* (1968). Other plays include *A Memory of Two Mondays, Incident at Vichy, The American Clock, The Archbishop's Ceiling, Danger: Memory, Two Way Mirror* and *The Ride Down Mt. Morgan* (1991). His most recent work produced on Broadway was *Broken Glass* (1994).

Miller's screenplays for film include *The Misfits* (1961), which starred his then-wife Marilyn Monroe; *Playing for Time* (made-for-TV movie, starring Vanessa Redgrave); and *Everybody Wins* (1990). Books include *In Russia, Chinese Encounters, Salesman in Beijing* and his autobiography *Timebends*.

crystal ball   A crystal ball, made of clear quartz crystal, is thought by wizards and occultists to have strong mystical powers. As with many gemstones, magic is thought to be inherent in the makeup of the crystal itself. The fact that the crystal is pure, unclouded and spherical (like earth) only makes the magic more potent.

Technically, consulting a crystal ball or, indeed, gazing at any reflective surface such as water or glass is known as scrying, a popular form of DIVINATION throughout history. A crystal ball is popularly thought to be a favorite tool of the GYPSY soothsayer, as well as one for modern fortune-tellers. Rather than actually transmitting a vision, the oracular orb is supposed to act as a focal point for concentration.

The size of the ball is unimportant. Some occultists prefer one that can be cupped neatly in the palm of the hand. A larger crystal ball is usually mounted on a small, ornamental stand in the center of a draped table.

Today, true crystal balls are exceptionally rare. Most crystal balls in use are actually made of leaded glass, blown into the shape of a sphere.

Perhaps the best-known image of a crystal ball occurs in the FILM version of L. Frank Baum's masterpiece *The WIZARD OF OZ*. Early in the tale, while still in Kansas, the itinerant fortune-teller Dr. Marvel claims to be able to "see all and know all" about Dorothy by gazing into his crystal ball. A charlatan, Dr. Marvel effects the ruse by rummaging through Dorothy's basket of personal possessions for hints of her past while the girl's eyes are obediently closed "in concentration." By a remarkable demonstration of "second sight," the seer is able to visualize Dorothy's Auntie Em pleading for her to come home. Later, in Oz, at the castle of the Wicked Witch of the West, the evil sorceress taunts Dorothy by showing her the image of her Auntie Em, crying, in a gigantic crystal ball.

A magical effect utilizing a pseudo-crystal ball can be seen in the Haunted Mansion attraction found in the Disney theme parks. As patrons circle around a seance room, a seemingly living disembodied head is seen inside a large glass ball sitting on a table.

Crystal Cave, The   First in a trilogy of fictional novels based on the legends of MERLIN and King ARTHUR, *The Crystal Cave* was written by (Florence Elinor) Mary Stewart (1916–) between February 1968 and February 1970. The title of the book (as well as that of the second book in the series) refers to the catacombs in which the enchantress NIMÜE imprisons Merlin for eternity. The books are narrated by Merlin, still trapped within the hollow hills, as reminiscences.

Stewart used the accounts by GEOFFREY OF MONMOUTH and, to a lesser extent, those of Sir Thomas MALORY as the basis for her own mythology. She portrays Merlin as half-human, half-demon, the son of a devil and the daughter of the king of South Wales. As a result of his parentage, Merlin has some mystical powers, but he also behaves like a man. He is a true wizard and a seer skilled in DIVINATION; yet he accomplishes many of his remarkable achievements through advanced technologies.

The Crystal Cave, published in 1970, tells the life of Merlin from his conception to the birth of Arthur. King Vortigern of Britain is having difficulty building his fortress: the tower crumbles after each attempt to erect it. The king's wizards tell him that it must be sprinkled with the sacrificial blood of a boy who never had a father. Vortigern hears rumors of Merlin's unusual conception and apprehends the boy and his mother. She tells the king how she was visited by a SPIRIT "in the shape of a handsome youth" who would "lay with me for some while in the shape of a man." Maugantius, the court soothsayer, admits to the king that such occurrences were well documented: Her nighttime visitor was undoubtedly one of the "spirits there be betwixt the moon and the earth, which we do call INCUBUS daemons." [sic]

Merlin challenges the court wizards' demands for his blood. He demontrates that the tower continues to fall because the masons are trying to build it over an underground lake. In the process of draining the pool, two dragons—one red, one white—are released, and they battle. The king asks Merlin to interpret the omen, and he foretells the coming of Vortigern's conqueror, Ambrosius.

Once crowned, Ambrosius erects a monument to commemorate his victory. Merlin uses his prescient understanding of steam power and leverage to move an ancient, circular ring of giant stones known as the Dance of Killare from Ireland to Stonehenge. After Ambrosius's death and burial within the mystic circle, Merlin predicts that Uther Pendragon, Ambrosius's brother, will assume the throne. He also prophesies that Pendragon will have a son "of surpassing mighty dominion, whose power shall extend over all the realms."

The following year during his coronation banquet, King Uther falls in love with Ygraine, the faithful wife of Gorlois, the Duke of Cornwall. Gorlois, aware and jealous of Uther's attention to his wife, hastily departs. While Uther's forces engage Gorlois and his army in battle, the king seeks a way to enter the seemingly impenetrable castle of Tintagel, where Gorlois has placed Ygraine. Merlin magically disguises the monarch to resemble Gorlois, so Uther is admitted without difficulty into the stronghold of his enemy. Thinking him to be her husband, Ygraine makes love to Uther, conceiving Arthur.

Gorlois is killed in combat that very night, and the deception is discovered by Ygraine. Nevertheless, Uther and Ygraine marry. Immediately upon his birth, Arthur is secreted out of Tintagel and delivered to Merlin.

The Hollow Hills was written between November 1970 and November 1972 and was published in 1973. The novel picks up Merlin's story the morning after Arthur's birth. Merlin takes the baby to Sir Ector, has the boy christened and leaves him to be raised as the knight's foster son. Fifteen years later, Uther, though fatally ill, defeats the Saxons in battle. Just before his death and at Merlin's insistence, the king acknowledges Arthur as his true son. Uther Pendragon is buried next to his brother within the ring of Stonehenge.

Arthur's whereabouts are unknown, however, so the nobles demand a miraculous sign for proof of identity. Merlin fashions a sword and embeds it in an altar shaped like an anvil. He places the stone in a London churchyard, with these words inscribed in gold on the sword's blade:

> Whoso pulleth out this sword of this stone and anvil, is rightwise king born of all England.

On a tournament day, Arthur acts as squire for Sir Kay, his foster brother. Kay has forgotten his sword, and Arthur is sent back to the inn where they are lodging to find it. The tavern is locked, but Arthur sees the sword in the stone. Unaware of the sword's significance (and the impossibility of removing it), he hastily and easily withdraws the blade and takes it Sir Kay.

The sword is recognized, but Arthur must prove and reprove to the jealous and suspicious aristocracy that only he can pull the sword from the stone. The nobility capitulate when the common people rally and demand Arthur as their king, despite his youth. Finally, Merlin discloses that Arthur is not the bastard son of Uther Pendragon and an adulterous Ygraine: The boy was, in fact, conceived three hours after the death of Gorlois, duke of Cornwall.

The Last Enchantment, written between 1975 and 1979 (when it was published), completes the trilogy. Arthur, newly crowned king, begins a series of wars against his country's foes, stopping only upon the insistence of Merlin. Arthur tells Merlin that he wishes to marry Guinevere, but Merlin advises against it. He prophesies an inevitable passion between the queen and Sir Lancelot, but Arthur ignores the wizard. The king marries Guinevere, and as part of her dowry King Arthur receives the Round Table from her father, King Leodegrance.

Arthur had already conceived a bastard son Mordred with his half-sister, Morgause (an enchantress and the wife of King Lot). Merlin told Arthur that Mordred would one day destroy his realm. To make sure that Mordred perished, the king set adrift at sea all the children of the kingdom born about the same time as his son. Mordred survived, however, but he does not meet his father until he is 14 years old.

Guinevere, already secretly in love with Lancelot, marries Arthur. In her husband's absence, the queen is kidnapped by King Meleagant, but she is rescued by Lancelot, who also avenges Arthur by slaying Meleagant.

Merlin falls obsessively in love with Nimuë, the LADY OF THE LAKE. Foreseeing his own fate and unable to prevent it despite his magical powers, Merlin informs Arthur that he will soon be imprisoned alive for eternity in a cavern beneath the earth. He instructs the king to hold his sword Caliburn (as the author Stewart calls EXCALIBUR throughout) close to him because it is destined to be stolen by a lady whom he trusts.

The wizard follows Nimuë to Brittany, where they meet King Ban, his wife Elaine and their young boy Galahad. Merlin foretells of the boy's greatness. They move on to Cornwall, where Merlin reveals a cave that can be sealed with a gigantic boulder. The sorceress bewitches Merlin and traps him in the underground catacombs. Later, while seeking a magical healing herb, Sir Bagdemagus discovers Merlin, but he is unable to move the massive stone to free him.

Arthur's sword is stolen by Morgan LE FAY, the king's ambitious sister (who is also an enchantress). She gives the sword to Sir Accolon to fight the king. One of le Fay's attendants returns Caliburn to Arthur, but it is a counterfeit. Knowing of Morgan le Fay's treason, Nimuë appears at the subsequent battle between Accolon and Arthur. Arthur's false sword quickly breaks, but he eventually captures Caliburn and defeats Sir Accolon. The knight reveals le Fay's role in the treachery, and he is forgiven by Arthur. Nimuë, the Lady in the Lake, replaces Merlin as King Arthur's counselor, protector and friend.

A fourth book based on the Arthurian myths, *The Wicked Day*, was written by Stewart between 1980 and 1983 (published in the latter year). Merlin is barely mentioned and does not appear as an active character in the novel; in fact, the Prologue opens with the words "Merlin is dead!" The tale completes the saga of Arthur's reign from the perspective of the witch-queen Morgause and Mordred.

Mary Stewart was born in Sunderland, County Durham, England. She received her B.A. in English and Literature from Durham University and later received an M.A. In 1945, she married Sir Frederick Stewart, who was made chairman of the Geology Department at Edinburgh University and a fellow of the Royal Society.

In 1954, Mary Stewart's *Madam, Will You Talk*? was published, the first of her more than 15 novels. She was elected fellow of the Royal Society of Arts in 1968. Three years later, she received the Frederick Niven award from Scottish Chapter of the International PEN Association for her first Arthurian novel, *The Crystal Cave*. Although successful books followed, Mary Stewart is undoubtedly best known for her Merlin trilogy.

crystals   See AMULET; CRYSTAL BALL.

curse   A curse is any declaration or desire—oral, written or enacted—that some misfortune will befall another person or object. The word *curse* is also used to mean the action of making the malefaction; the actual utterance, INCANTATION or repetition of the HEX is known as cursing.

Curses set in rhyme are thought to be especially effective. Rhyme not only makes a curse easier to remember, but it also makes the curse more difficult for the victim to forget! A rhythmic meter also assists during the incantation of the spell.

Almost all curses implicitly entreat the intervention or assistance of a supernatural force or deity to effect the injury. Cursing, then, has always been an inherent part of most major world religions, although frequently the prophets or god(s) proscribed against them.

Swearing also involves an oath or promise of some action in return for the assistance of a supernatural being or deity, but a swear is a curse only if its intent is to cause harm to another party.

Especially notorious is the infamous "mummy's curse," popularized in early horror FILMS. Ancient hieroglyphics in the tombs of the Valley of the Kings in Luxor, Egypt, warned would-be grave robbers not to disturb the remains of the pharaohs. The ancient Egyptian curses were noted for their flowery language and the imaginative ways in which the offender would suffer.

Perhaps the best-known Egyptian curse is the inscription on the walls of King Tutankhamen's tomb: "Death shall come on swift wings to him who disturbs the sleep of pharaoh." Legend has it that it was this curse that caused the sudden death of so many adventurers connected with the search for King Tut's tomb (including Lord Carnarvon, who financed the operation but died from a mosquito bite almost immediately after the tomb was opened).

The ancient Jews fleeing on the Exodus had been raised with the Egyptian tradition of cursing. Indeed, MOSES wrote several instances in which Yahweh himself had engaged in the practice, including:

The Lord said in his heart, "I will never again curse the ground because of man. . . ." (Genesis 8:21)

and

Now the Lord said to Abram, ". . . And I will bless those that bless you, and him who curses you I will curse." (Genesis 12:3)

Nevertheless, the Third Commandment, received by MOSES on Mount Sinai, specifically forbade swearing on the name of the Lord or invoking his name for a curse: "Thou shalt not take the name of the Lord thy God in vain." (Exodus 20:7)

Though JESUS implored his followers to "Love your enemies and pray for those who curse you" (Matthew 5:44), he personally used his power to curse. In an incident reported only in the Gospel of St. Matthew (21:18–21) of the Bible, Christ intones a curse against a barren fruit tree because he is hungry: "Let no fruit grown on thee henceforward forever."

In the Christian church, especially the Catholic Church, the ultimate curse is excommunication, being shunned forever from the mercy and grace of God.

Islam specifically forbids cursing anything, including man or beast, because Muhammad characterized the practice as the "eighth infirmity of the tongue." Because Allah bestows grace and mercy on everything, no Muslim can be cursed in his name. Even a non-believer should not be cursed: the heathen might one day convert to Islam, *and* cursing an infidel might prevent the infidel from embracing Islam. It *is* allowable, however, to curse an entire group of nonbelievers: Although an individual may convert, it is unlikely that *everyone* in a pagan group will embrace Islam. It is only truly "safe" to curse an individual after the person is dead (and therefore unable to receive Allah's favor and grace.)

This raises the valid question of when it is acceptable to invoke the name of one's God. Theologians could argue that there is often little difference between a curse and a prayer. Just as magic can be judged either as white or black, depending upon the point of view of the petitioner and the recipient, so too could one person's prayer (e.g., "God grant us victory in this battle") be perceived as another person's curse. Also, a supplicant's asking for "just punishment" to avenge evil already committed could be perceived by the victim as a curse or BLACK MAGIC.

The European GYPSY has long been accused of practicing prophecy, selling CHARMS and casting SPELLS. Ironically, legend has it that gypsies roam without end because they are themselves the victims of a curse.

Despite logical argument to the contrary, there is ample evidence that on many occasions, even in modern times, curses *do* have an effect on their intended victims. Psychologists proffer that the afflicted people convince themselves, through the power of suggestion, that they will suffer pain or injury. This, however, does not explain the instances in which victims do not know that a curse has been levied against them—which is often the case in VOODOO. Noted Satanist and *voudun* expert Anton La Vey explained the phenomenon, claiming, "If done properly, it is not necessary that your victim have any knowledge of our curse." (See also CURSE TABLET.)

curse tablet   Although a CURSE is usually spoken, a *written* curse is considered by some to be even more effective. Curse tablets were magical devices common in ancient Greece and Rome, especially during the fourth through third centuries B.C. They were frequently placed in sanctuaries dedicated to Demeter, a goddess of the Underworld. Most often made of lead, the small rectangular curse tablets usually measured no more than 2 or 3 inches on either side. The tablet would be inscribed with the name of the enemy and any specific HEX or magic words (frequently written backwards to increase the SPELL's power). The tablet would then be folded up and nailed to the temple wall or alter.

cycliomancy   See CRYSTAL BALL; DEE, JOHN; DIVINATION.

Dallben See FILMS, *THE BLACK CAULDRON.*

Damnation of Faust, The See OPERA.

Damn Yankees See MUSICAL THEATER.

Daniel See CHALDEANS; DIVINATION.

Dante, Alighieri See *DIVINE COMEDY, THE.*

Dedi (fl. 3700 B.C.?)   A magician in the time of the pharaohs, Dedi of Dedsnefru is the most famous wizard in all of EGYPTIAN MAGIC and one of the earliest in recorded history. Apocryphal sources date Dedi back to the time of Ramses II, but hieroglyphs place him at the court of Cheops (Khufu), the builder of the Great Pyramid.

Only two earlier wizard's names are recorded, that of Weba-āner and Jajamānekh, both the Ptah priest-magicians of the god Ptah.

All three wizards are mentioned in the famous Westcar Papyrus, written around 1700 B.C. and housed for years in the

The wizard Dedi performed before Cheops (Khufu), pharaoh and builder of the Great Pyramid (right) in Giza (outside Cairo), Egypt. (Photo by author)

Berlin State Museum (or, according to some sources, the Bode Museum in the former East Germany). The manuscript disappeared, but it is believed to be currently housed in a manuscript collection in the former Soviet Union.

Cheops followed Snefu onto the throne of Egypt. Prince Dedefhā, the youngest son of Cheops, told his father of an aged wizard named Dedi, supposedly 110 years old, living in Ded-Snefru. It was said that every day Dedi ate 500 loaves of bread and a full shoulder of beef and washed down them with 100 jars of beer. Legend had it, too, that Dedi knew the location of the secret chambers within the temple sanctuary dedicated to THOTH, the god of magic.

Sent by his father, Prince Dedefhā sailed south on the Nile with two ships to greet the great wizard. Dedi assured him that he had foreseen the approach of the royal entourage and that he was prepared to accompany the prince back to Memphis. Dedi traveled on the royal barge; the second boat carried his children and library of arcane papyri.

Cheops asked the wizard why they had never met. Dedi replied simply that he had never been invited to the court before. The wizard gave a performance for the pharaoh, passing a sword blade through the head of a bull calf. He decapitated and reattached the head of a live goose and repeated the miracle with a pelican. Dedi declined to perform this feat with a human prisoner, however, stating that it was forbidden to practice such sorcery on "the noble herd." (A version of the decapitation trick using a goose is explained in Reginald Scot's The DISCOVERIE OF WITCHCRAFT.)

Dee, John (1527–1608) Perhaps the most influential wizard of Elizabethan England, John Dee was born on July 13, 1527. He was the son of Roland Dee, who was employed as the head of the royal kitchen and master carver at the king's table at the court of Henry VIII and Joanna. Dee graduated from Chelmsford Grammar School in 1542 and moved on to St. John's College in Cambridge. A notable student, Dee received his bachelor of arts in 1544, was named a fellow in 1545 and later became one of founding fellows of Trinity College.

Dee became interested in the occult, especially the arts of ALCHEMY and ASTROLOGY and the secrets hidden in the KABBALAH. He gained a reputation as a wizard during his days at Cambridge when he employed little-known magicians' methods to enchance local theatrical productions. The stage effects, such as making people appear, disappear or fly, were unexplainable by the uneducated audience, giving rise to the belief that he evoked demonic SPIRITS to do his bidding.

In 1547, Dee took the first of many trips to the Continent. He returned briefly to pursue a master's degree at Cambridge but cut his matriculation short to continue his studies in Belgium. By this time, Dee was receiving royal patronage from King Edward VI, and, upon his return to England in 1551, Dee gave up his annual annuity to be named rector of Upton-on-Severn.

Unfortunately, Edward's rule was short-lived, and following the king's death in 1553, Mary Tudor took the throne. The ultraconservative Catholic queen had Dee imprisoned in June 1555 on charges of treason (for using enchantment to harm the queen) and "lewd and vain practices of calculating [i.e., preparing HOROSCOPES] or conjuring." The accusation of treason, of using enchantment to harm the queen, was quickly dropped, but Dee was forced to plead his case against the accusation of WITCHCRAFT before Bishop Bonner. An effective and persuasive speaker on religious canon, Dee eventually succeeded in having the allegations of heresy dismissed. On November 17, 1588, "Bloody Mary" died, freeing Dee and other mystics to renew their studies of the occult without fear of prosecution. In fact, to ascertain the most favorable day for her coronation, Elizabeth I consulted Dee on her horoscope.

As Dee's reputation as an astrologer and magus grew, foreign rulers beckoned him to their courts, but Dee chose to remain in England.

In 1570 Dee moved to Mortlake in Richmond-upon-Thames at the estate passed on to him by his late mother. There, he amassed a library of almost 3,000 books and an additional 1,000 manuscripts. As Dee's fame grew, the most illustrious minds of the age flocked to Mortlake to study and for contemplation. Queen Elizabeth herself visited the library on March 10, 1575.

It is thought that at some point Dee entered the queen's service, if not as a government agent or spy, then at least as an intelligencer of foreign affairs. Dee certainly had international interests; in fact, he is sometimes credited with originating the term British Empire.

Dee had a deep curiosity of codes and ciphering systems, shown by his exhilaration upon acquiring a copy of the STENOGRAPHIA of Johannes TRITHEMIUS, which reportedly contained a coding system hidden within the four "books" of the manuscript. Some scholars have suggested that the Enochian ALPHABET that Dee later produced was in reality a code he used to transmit state secrets.

Dee believed that the true cabalistic path to revealed wisdom involved high or angelic magic, which invoked the heavenly hosts to intercede on his behalf. His search of an angelic advisor was begun in earnest once he settled in at Mortlake. He employed crystals, mirrors and prayer in his attempts to communicate with angels, following rules set down by Cornelius AGRIPPA in the mystic's work, Occult Philosophy (DE OCCULTA PHILOSOPHIA). (A speculum, or magic mirror, that once belonged to Dee is now part of the British Museum collection.)

Dee soon discovered he had no talents as a medium, so he worked with a succession of supposed seers, hoping to act as a transcriber of the clairvoyants' revelations. There were still no tangible results.

On March 10, 1582, Dee's life became inextricably linked with that of Edward KELLY. Edward Talbot, as he was then known, sought out Mortlake and was told by Dee of the latter's quest. Dee produced a stone in a frame; he had been told that aliqui angeli boni (i.e., some good angels) were "answerable to it." Talbot offered to attempt to make contact through the stone. Almost immediately, Kelly became (in modern terminology) a channeler for the archangel Uriel. Uriel told Dee, through Talbot, that the stone could also be used to summon the angels Michael and Raphael and went on to discuss Dee's book SOYGA.

Dee hired Talbot. Five months later, the young medium inexplicably changed his surname to Kelly; from that time on Dee always referred to him as E.K. in his diaries.

The pair continued their "actions," as Dee called their angelic contacts; before long they had communicated with a whole host of the heavenly legions. As the spirits spoke through Kelly, Dee recorded every word.

One of the angels' first commandments was that Dee construct several magical instruments with which to summon them. Chief among them was a sort of altar to be called the Holy Table (or Table of Practice.) Made of 7/10-inch thick wood, the center of the table top measured 36" x 35 7/8". The slab fit upon a 2-feet-8-inch-square frame supported by four 2-feet-7 ½-inch-long legs. Dee was also instructed to create seven tin TALISMANS, the Seven Ensigns of Creation, but the angels later told him to paint the seven emblems onto the Holy Table with blue lines and red lettering. Other characters were added in gold. (After Dee's death, the Holy Table made its way into the collection of Sir John Cotton, but it was probably destroyed when the Cottonian Library burned in 1731. A 17th-century replica of the original, but in marble, can be found in the Oxford Museum of the History of Science.)

Completing the shrine was the Sigillum Dei Aemeth (or Sign of Truth), a 9-inch diameter wax PENTACLE, which was placed upon the Holy Table and covered with a red silk tablecloth. On top that, in a golden frame, rested a new crystal (replacing Dee's original scrying or focusing stone.)

The other essential instruments demanded by the angels for their invocation were a paper breastplate called the Lamine (also seen as the true Lamyne) and a magic gold RING inscribed with the word PELE ("He who works wonders" in Hebraic.) Because Dee refers to the ring only once in his diaries, however, it is possible that it was never produced.

On March 26 1582, the hosts delivered (through Kelly) a new 21-character ANGELIC ALPHABET. The Enochian alphabet recorded by Dee was the basis for most of his divinely delivered manuscripts, including the *Liber Logareth* (also known as *The Book of Enoch*) and the *48 Angelic Keys* (1584). These keys were to be used by Dee, Kelly and future wizards as prayers and supplications to summon the divine spirits. (See ENOCHIAN MAGIC.)

In 1583, Dee and Kelly set out on a tour of the Continent. Dee returned to England in 1589, but Kelly chose to remain in Europe, where he died in 1595. Dee gave a full report of his time with Kelly in Cracow and Prague, including the angelic and demonic invocations they performed there, in *A True and Faithful Relation of what passed for Many Years between Dr. John Dee . . . and Some Spirts*, published posthumously in 1659. Although Dee remained interested in the occult after their separation, he never actively engaged in the pursuit of angels again.

In 1595, Dee was appointed warden of Christ's College, Manchester; as part of his duties over the next decade, Dee was often called upon as a consultant in cases of suspected witchcraft. In addition to his personal experiments, he was able to draw upon the studies and writings of such authors as Johannes WIERUS and Reginald SCOT.

Queen Elizabeth I, Dee's protector and patron, died in 1603. James I, who followed her onto the throne, was less friendly to students and practitioners of the occult arts. (See DEMONOLOGIE.) Poor, old and in bad health, Dee retired to Mortlake, where he died in 1608. He is buried near his Richmond-upon-Thames home at the church of St. Mary the Virgin.

Deformed Transformed, The

This play by Lord Byron was published incomplete in 1824. It tells a variation of the FAUST legend in which the Devil approaches his victim unbidden.

Count Arnold, a hunchback, is confronted by the Devil, who parades before him the SPIRITS of several great men of history, including Caesar. The demon offers to change the monster's body to match any one of them. Arnold agrees to the temptation and is transformed into the body of Achilles. The Devil assumes Arnold's old misshapen form and acts as his servant as their adventures begin.

As the drama continues, the pair find themselves at the destruction of Rome in 1527. Arnold/Achilles boldly enters the fray and is heroically triumphant as the extant portion of the play ends.

Delphi, the oracle of Apollo at

In ancient Greece, most temples to Apollo, many of which housed an ORACLE, had been established in still earlier times, with the worship being transferred from pre-Hellenic deities to Apollo.

The site of the most famous of all the oracles, Delphi, was, according to one legend accidentally discovered by Coretas, a shepherd. Nearing fumes emanating from a natural cave or crevice on the hillside, Coretas was transported into an ecstatic state, speaking nonsensical sentences. Those who heard the words, while not understanding their meaning, concluded that they must be divine.

The oracular seat (or sit), like all such temples, became female-centered. Even the word *Delphi* derives from *Delphyne*, a serpent associated with an ancient mother goddess, also known as Delphyne, because her body was half-snake. A still-earlier form of the word was *delphys*, meaning "womb."

Originally, Delphi was serviced by a clairvoyant priestess dedicated to the worship of the earth goddess Gaia, the "mother of all life." It was at Delphi that Gaia had placed the sacred stone known as the *omphalos*, or "navel stone of the Earth"; the shrine, built underground in a beehive shape, was ruled by Gaia and her female snake Python (also seen as Tython). The great serpent had been created by Hera, Zeus's wife, after a great flood out of the mud and sludge at Delphi, located at the foot of Mount Parnassus.

The origin of the *omphalos* has its own mythology. Chronos, Gaia's husband, devoured all of their children to defy an ancient prophecy that one of his offspring would usurp him. To allow their son Zeus to survive, Gaia wrapped a rock in swaddling clothes and presented it to Chronos as the baby. Chronos promptly swallowed the rock, believing it to be Zeus. When Zeus returned as an adult and overthrew his father, Chronos was forced to disgorge the *omphalos* along with all of Zeus's previously ingested siblings.

According to pre-Hellenic myths, the first humans were created by Gaia, who grew six men and six women from her body. As the humans came to realize their mortality, they feared their uncertain future. Gaia sent her oracle to Delphi to give them some clues to comprehend Infinity, sending up vapors from her essence through a crack in the rocks at Delphi. A priestess, entranced by the fumes, heard and understood these messages and recounted them to the oracle's supplicants.

As often happens, the mythological timetable of events becomes somewhat jumbled. Exactly when the oracle was shifted from the worship of Gaia to Apollo is uncertain, but it occurred during the Hellenistic period as the entire mythological cosmology of the Greeks moved from a female hierarchy to a male-dominated one. The concept of the Apollo figure (later adopted by the Doric Greeks) seems to have come from Asia via Asia Minor. His connection with divination may come from his resemblance to Apulunas, an Anatolian Hittite god of fine arts with the ability to prophesy. To prove his power over the oracle at Delphi, Apollo slew Python, in most stories by using his arrows of sunlight.

The Apollonian oracle was always a woman. She sat on a small tripod in an inner recess of the temple, having prepared herself with ablutions and breathing heavy perfumed—possibly hallucinogenic—smoke and chewing special herbs. The oracle entered a trancelike state from which she would give obscure and barely discernable utterances. This mishmash of words was then transformed by the priests of the temple into the definitive pronouncement, often in the form of verse. It was the duty of the patron, who had probably paid a large sum for the privilege of hearing from the oracle, to discern the true meaning of the reading.

This was not a simple matter. Answers were always paradoxical or ambiguous, often misleading and always subject to interpretation. King Croesus, the ruler of most of Asia Minor, for example, was told by the oracle of Apollo at Delphi that if he attacked the Persians, a mighty empire would be destroyed. Indeed, it was: Croesus lost the war and his throne.

Oracles were often consulted for prophecies regarding the outcome of upcoming battles. One prince consulted the oracle at Delphi regarding his future. The oracle proclaimed, "You shall go shall return never you shall perish by the war." The prince understood the oracle to say, "You shall go, shall return, never you shall perish by the war." In fact, his doom was forecast by the true meaning of the oracle: "You shall go, shall return never, you shall perish by the war."

At first, the oracle spoke only one day a year: the seventh day of the "birth month" of Apollo. Her words were in such demand, however, that additional dates for soothsaying were added. Eventually, for a large enough sacrifice and offering to Apollo (i.e., for the right price), any supplicant could have the future foretold on request.

Today, the word *Delphic* is used to mean any statement or reply that can be interpreted in different ways or is deliberately ambiguous.

Del Rio, Martin Antoine (1551–1608)

Although Del Rio wrote at least 15 books of ecclesiastical commentary, he is remembered for *Disquisitonum Magicarum Libri Sex*, one of the 16th century's most important works on demonology.

Del Rio was born into a wealthy household in Antwerp, Belgium. He was well educated and was able to read Hebrew, CHALDEAN and five modern languages. In 1570, he published a study of Seneca and five years later was appointed vice-chancellor and attorney general for Brabant. He left secular life to join the Jesuits in 1580. He traveled extensively among Europe's Jesuit orders and he died in Brussels.

Disquisitonum . . . was written around 1596 and was published in Louvain in 1599. By 1747, it had gone through 20 editions, including a 1611 translation into French.

The book declared the certainty of witches in the world and called for their swift and sure punishment. It examined WITCH-CRAFT in six major subdivisions:

1. magic, both natural and artificial, and ALCHEMY
2. BLACK MAGIC, the SABBAT, the INCUBUS and apparitions
3. evil (*maleficia*) and evil SPIRITS
4. DIVINATION, both superstitious and heretical, prophecy and "ordeals" (e.g., SWIMMING)
5. guidelines for the judges at witchcraft trials
6. the Catholic confessor and ways to fight evil, both natural (e.g., gemstones) and supernatural (e.g., AMULETS or exorcism).

Just as Del Rio was greatly influenced by the *MALLEUS MALEFICARM* and other earlier writings, so too did his massive volume influence later authors, such as Guazzo (*COMPENDIUM MALEFICARUM*).

Demonologie

Personally handwritten by King James VI of Scotland (1566–1625) and published in the fall of 1597, *Demonologie* asserted that WITCHCRAFT truly existed in the world. Further, it defended the practice of hunting witches, enchantresses, wizards, sorcerers, magicians and seers for prosecution—*and* persecution. The full title of the work (Hanover edition, 1604) was *Dæmonologia, hoc est adversus incantationem sive magiam institutio, auctore serenissimo potentissimoque principe Dn. Jacobo, Deo gratia Angliæ, Scotiæ, Hyberniæ ac Franciæ Rege, fidei defensore*.

The book was written in three parts in the form of a conversation between two fictitious men, Philomathus and Epistemon. Philomathus supposedly represented the philosophical thinker and Epistemon the church view; however the latter character was, in fact, speaking for the conservative and fervently religious king. A typical exchange follows:

Philomathus: What affliction, think you, is deserved of these Sorcerers and Magician?
Epistemon: Witches and Magicians also must be delivered to the pain of death, in this following the commandment of the Law of the Lord, the law civil and imperial, and the law particular, lastly, of all Christian peoples, whosoever they be.
Philomathus: What manner of death must they be punished withal?
Epistemon: The death by flames of fire is that most often laid upon. But it is a thing indifferent. . . .

Almost certainly as a result of the publication of *Demonologie*, a witchcraft hysteria swept through the town of Aberdeen, Scotland. Before the craziness had ended, 24 men and women had been burned for practicing sorcery. Among the many accusations that resulted in the victims' arrests were dancing with Satan, causing LIGATURE, making love CHARMS, casting the EVIL EYE, producing night sweats and turning milk sour.

As James I, king of England from 1603–1625, the ruler continued his belief in and suppression of sorcery in Britain.

de Montespan, Madame Françoise-Athénaïs de Pardaillan (1641–1707)

In order to ensure the love of Louis XIV of France, Madame de Montespan, the king's mistress, turned to sorcery and BLACK MAGIC. She was assisted in her pursuits by Catherine La Voisin (a French enchantress and fortune-teller, who provided love potions to de Montespan), Lesage (an alchemist) and Guibourg (an abbé), among others.

Together, they reportedly conducted satanic rites, which sometimes included sexual orgies and child sacrifice. Charged with trying to poison Louis XIV, Madame de Montespan escaped through private influence. (See ALCHEMY; PAPACY, THE.)

De Occulta Philosophia   Published in three volumes in 1531, *De Occulta Philosophia libri tres*, or *Occult Philosophy*, is the best known and major work of the reputed sorcerer, Heinrich Cornelius AGRIPPA. Written in 1510, probably in England, the treatise discusses mankind's relationship to God and the universe.

Agrippa first posits a then-popular line of reasoning: Man is a miniature of God, having been created in his image; the universe, or macrocosm, taken as a whole, is God; therefore, Man is a miniature, or microcosm, of the universe. Conversely, just as man has a soul, so must every part of or thing in the universe, with each component adding a part to the total or universal soul. This would explain the seemingly magical properties of such inanimate objects as magnets and medicinal plants, as well as natural and celestial curiosities.

It is at this point that Agrippa breaks with the accepted philosophical thought of his contemporaries. In examining the soul's connection with the body, God and the universe, especially with respect to religion, arts and the sciences, including ASTROLOGY, Agrippa concluded that the means to understanding their correlation was through magic and NECROMANCY (i.e., calling up SPIRITS of the dead). Further, only select members of a special initiate—Agrippa founded several such secret societies during his lifetime—could be privy to this hidden magical knowledge. Agrippa's text has been interpreted to suggest that if there is a piece of magic in each of us and in all things, then by understanding and controlling this power it might be possible for a sorcerer to become a god.

deosil   When casting a SPELL, the wizard traditionally waved his hand(s) or arm(s) in a deosil direction (i.e., clockwise in a circle or from left to right.) The term comes from the Irish *deiseal*, meaning "turning to the right" or "holy round" and was associated with the path of the sun through the sky. Moving in the deosil direction was thought to create a positive or good force, so it was always used in WHITE MAGIC.

Because he appealed to angelic powers, the enchanter also drew his MAGIC CIRCLE in the deosil direction. Circular deosil dances were often performed in rural areas to celebrate plentiful harvests and the coming of spring. (See also WIDDERSHINS.)

de Troyes, Chrétien (fl. 1160s)   Chrétien de Troyes wrote a series of poems based on the stories of King ARTHUR that added to the lore of the king of the Britons. A French poet, he lived at the court of the countess of Champagne in Troyes in the 1160s. As in later French versions of the fables, Arthur became a secondary character in the tales as the exploits of the knights—and especially their quests and chivalrous deeds—were expounded. As opposed to the tone of GEOFFREY OF MONMOUTH's writings, Chrétien's poems were much more surreal in nature, full of magic, miraculous deeds and supernatural beings, including wizards and evil sorcerers.

Significantly, it was Chrétien who first added the sexual betrayal of Arthur by Guinevere and Lancelot to the legend.

Devil and Daniel Webster, The   Originally a short story published in 1937 by Stephen Vincent Benét (1898–1943), *The Devil and Daniel Webster* tells the tale of a debate between the famous orator and Satan over the demon's demand for New Hampshire farmer Jabez Stone's soul. Despite the Devil's claim, Webster is victorious in his logical arguments.

Benét, born in Pennsylvania and educated at Yale, was celebrated for his verse with American themes, including his 1928 Pulitzer Prize–winning poem *John Brown's Body*. He also supplied the libretto for a folk OPERA based on *The Devil and Devil Webster* in 1939. (See FILM, *ALL THAT MONEY CAN BUY*.)

Devil is an Ass, The   Written by Ben Jonson (1572/3–1637), this comic play was first acted by the King's Men in 1616 and was published in 1631. The story involves the troubles of Fitzdottrel, a landowner, who succumbs to the temptations of Meercraft, a swindler, who steals Fitzdottrel's estate by promising him the title of duke of Drowndland. Fitzdottrel discovers his error, and in an attempt to have the sales contracts nullified, he claims that he was BEWITCHed! Eventually, he admits otherwise. In the denouement, it is revealed that Wittipol and Manly, who had been attempting unsuccessfully to make Fitzdottrel a cuckold, have protected the title to his estate.

A subplot involves Pug, a demon, who takes human form and becomes Fitzdottrel's manservant. His intent is to spread evil, but his mortal counterparts outdo him. Pug winds up in Newgate Prison before going back to Hell.

Parts of *The Devil is an Ass* are purportedly founded on the true story of the "Leicester Boy," a 17th-century boy named John Smith (b. 1602 or 1603), the son of Sir Roger Smith of Husbands Bosworth, Leicestershire. Feigning fits and seizures, he pretended to be under demonic possession. His charges of sorcery resulted in the hanging of nine innocent women and the death of one more in prison.

His fraud was eventually exposed by King James I in 1616. The king was a noted demonologist (see DEMONOLOGIE) and, while passing through Leicester, heard of the remarkable boy. He examined the young lad personally and was suspicious. Within a few weeks, the servants of the archbishop abbot of Canterbury discovered the truth, and the king was immediately notified. A new trial resulted in the release of the five women who remained in jail as a result of the boy's deception.

Sergeant Crew and the gullible town magistrate, Sir Humphrey Crew, who had been completely taken in by the boy's hysterics, provided the basis for much of the satire in the Johnson play. In fact, it provided the comedy's title by telling how "a boy of thirteen year old made [the devil] an ass. . . ."

Devil's mark   A Devil's mark was any blemish on the skin, such as a mole, callus, corn, bunion, wart, birthmark, scar, tattoo or bruise or the reddish skin discoloration known as nevus. The Devil's mark was supposedly the spot where Satan had touched the initiate, leaving the blemish as a sort of brand of ownership on the new sorceress.

Judges, priests of the INQUISITION and witch-hunters sought tangible proof that an accused witch had made a pact with

Discolored or insensitive spots on a witch's body were called Devil's marks. They were purportedly produced at the point where Satan touched an initiate, which caused the lack of feeling. (Guazzo, *Compendium Maleficarum*)

Satan. Just such evidence was a Devil's mark (*stigmata diaboli*), sometimes called the Devil's seal (*sigillum diaboli*).

The discovery of a Devil's mark can be found in the records of almost every WITCHCRAFT trial. Under examination, for example, three Devil's marks were found on Father GAUFRIDI, and at his 1611 trial he confessed, "These marks were made as a sign that I shall be a good and faithful servant to the Devil all my life long."

An English addition to demonic lore was the witch's mark, which was any bump or protuberance on the body, especially supernumerary, or extra, breasts (*polymastia*) or nipples (*polythelia*). These were thought to be the spots at which the witch's FAMILIAR or the Devil himself sucked. Eventually, the witch's mark was classified as just one type of Devil's mark.

Supposedly, the proof that a blemish was a Devil's mark was its insensitivity and the inability to draw blood from it, although these characteristics true of most warts. Witch-hunters swore by the validity of the marks and the right to look for them. Cotton MATHER, the colonial cleric who was present at the SALEM witchcraft trials, argued

> Why should not witch marks be searched for? The properties, the qualities of those marks are described by divers weighty writers. I never saw any of those marks, but it is doubtless not impossible for a surgeon, when he sees them, to say what are magical.

It was, of course, to the witch-hunter's benefit to find a Devil's mark. When no blemish could be easily located, all of the accused witch's body hair would be shaved off, often publicly, and the body, especially the genitalia, were minutely examined. In his *COMPENDIUM MALEFICARUM*, Guazzo relates that

> When Claudia Bogarta was about to be tormented, she was shaved to the skin, as the custom is, so that a scar was revealed on the top of her bare brow. The inquisitor then suspecting the truth, namely, that it was a mark made by the devil's claw, which had before been covered by her hair, ordered a pin to be thrust deep into it.

Soon, witch hunters claimed that because the Devil knew that his disciples could be identified by visible blemishes, he also stamped them with *invisible* Devil's marks. Although the imprints were unable to be seen, there was an easy test to locate them: As everyone knew, Devil's marks were insensitive to pain. Therefore, by PRICKING an accused witch with a pin, lancet or dagger until such a spot was eventually found, the witch-hunter was almost always successful. Not uncommonly, the examination itself caused injury or death to the accused.

Devils of Loudon, The   See GRANDIER, FATHER URBAIN.

Dipsas   See *ENDIMION, THE MAN IN THE MOONE*.

Discoverie of Witchcraft, The   Published in 1584 by Reginald Scot (sometimes seen as Scott) (1538?–1599), *The Discoverie of Witchcraft* was an attempt to stop the imprisonment and execution of people unjustly condemned for WITCHCRAFT.

Scot was born into a monied family in Kent and matriculated at Oxford University, but he left before earning a degree. He led the life of a country gentleman, entering the civil service briefly and then representing New Romney in Parliament for 1588–1589. In 1574, Scot published *A perfite platforme of a hoppe garden* (*The Hop Garden*). He married twice before his death in 1599.

In the 16th century, the accusation of witchcraft was a simple way to eliminate an enemy or remove the old, infirm, mentally handicapped or eccentric. Scot, wishing to disprove the existence of sorcery and BLACK MAGIC, used the word *Discoverie* in the title of his book on witchcraft to mean an "explanation" or "exposure."

His views were certainly not popular, and Scot apparently self-published *The Discoverie of Witchcraft*. It was never officially entered into the Stationer's Register, and only a printer's name (not a publisher's) appears at the end of the book.

Scot's arguments pointed out the duplicity of witch-hunters and other accusers and questioned their motives and believability. The book is divided into 16 "booke"s [sic], a total of 259 chapters. The tone throughout is alternately skeptical and scornful and is aimed at casual readers rather than judicial authorities.

Thus, as part of his "discoverie," Scot attempts to show that entertainment and sleight-of-hand are frequently mistaken for bewitchment and demonic arts. He exposes many of the secrets and methods of medieval mountebanks, including more than a dozen popular conjuring routines of the time, as well as the art of juggling. The magic tricks are described in varied amounts of detail, but of a manuscript of more than 200,000 words, only 10,000 or so words deal with the entertainer's art.

Scot was not a conjuror himself, nor was he adept at legerdemain. To research the topic, Scot struck up a friendship with John Cauteres, a French magician living and performing in London, who shared some of the tricks of the trade. It is unlikely that Cauteres, who worked for gratuities in pubs and taverns and at markets and fairs, knew that Scot was planning to reveal his guarded secrets to the lay public. Regardless of the illusions' exposure, many of these same effects are still used by performing magicians today.

Although hardly a magic book in the modern sense of a how-to for entertainers, *The Discoverie of Witchcraft* was only the second (extant) book in Western literature to expose the methods of the conjurer. The first was Jean Prévost's *La Premiére Partie des Subtiles et Plaisantes Inventions*, published in France in January 1584, just months before the release of Scot's work. The Prévost book was filled with table tricks, puzzles and cunning stunts, with no allusion whatsoever to wizardry, sorcery or witchcraft.

The Discoverie of Witchcraft is the only magic book known to have been condemned and destroyed by royal decree. Upon assuming the English throne in 1603, James I (see DEMONOLO-GIE) ordered all copies of Scot's treatise to be burned, so extant original editions are exceedingly rare. Despite the denunciation of the book, it stood as an important testament against the witch-hunt frenzy of its time. Believed to have been used as a resource by Thomas Middleton for his play *The* WITCH and by SHAKESPEARE for the witches's scenes in *MACBETH* (and possibly the magical themes of *The* TEMPEST), *The Discoverie of Witchcraft* also served as a foundation for most of what was written in English for the entertainer-conjuror for the next 200 years.

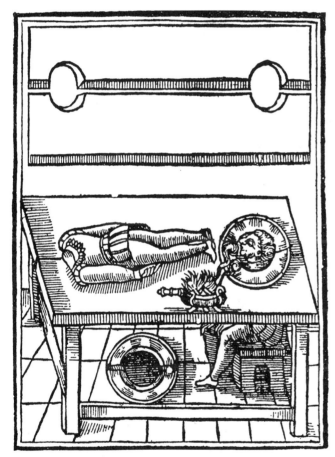

Reginald Scot's explanation for magically decapitating and restoring the head of a man ("To cutoff ones head, and to laie it in a platter, which the jugglers call the decollation of John Baptist"). Although similar in effect to Dedi's famous act with livestock, the Egyptian wizard had declined to execute the stunt with a member of the "noble herd." (Reginald Scot, *The Discoverie of Witchcraft*)

divination Since early times, people have sought to master and control their natural surroundings, giving rise to the birth of magic. Inherent in the practice of natural magic is the belief that all objects, animate and inanimate, have some force or SPIRIT whose powers and energies could be tapped.

The energies within natural objects, however, were *supernatural*, or divine. Because the deities were thought to be omniscient (and therefore prescient), it was thought that the essences within such objects could be consulted to reveal the future.

Not all prophets and psychics were wizards; yet almost all wizards and sorcerers were expected to be seers. Their methods of divination varied, but the most common for a wizard was scrying (i.e., focusing on a CRYSTAL BALL, a gemstone, a flat surface of water, or some other shiny surface).

Geomancy (interpretation of designs formed from tossed wood sticks or bone) and NUMEROLOGY (reducing the name of an object or person to its mystic meaning through a letter/number equivalency code) were popular with occultists, like John DEE, who were interested in ciphers and codes. A few, like the prophet Daniel, interpreted dreams (oneiromancy).

Over the centuries, anything and everything has been consulted in an attempt to foretell the future. The following list is just a few of the many forms of divination:

NAME	DIVINATION BY CONSULTING OR READING...
Aeromancy	air and sky
Aleuromancy	responses to possible questions baked into dough and then selected randomly to answer queries; the modern fortune cookie is a offshoot of this practice
Alomancy	salt
Alphitomancy	cakes that are digestible if party is innocent
Anthropomancy	human sacrifice
Apanthomancy	random meetings with animals; supertitions about black CATS may be a vestige of this
Arithmany	(also Arithmonmancy) NUMEROLOGY
Astragyromancy	numbered or lettered dice
Augury	flight of birds (from the Latin *avis*, meaning "bird" and *garrire*, meaning "to chatter")
Austromancy	wind
Axiomancy	the vibration of an axe or hatchet
Belomancy	throwing or balancing arrows
Bibliomancy	books
Botanomancy	burning leaves and tree branches
Capnomancy	rising smoke from a fire
CARTOMANCY	playing cards
Catoptromancy	moonlight reflected in a mirrored surface
Causimomancy	the ability of objects to burn
Cephalomancy	the skull (or head) of a goat or donkey
Ceraunoscopy	thunder and lightning
Ceroscopy	globules formed by pouring hot wax into water
Chiromancy	The hand (especially the palm, i.e., PALMISTRY)
Cleromancy	small, sometimes marked objects (other than dice) that are tossed
Clidomancy	(also Cleidomancy) a swinging key on a cord
Coscinomancy	a swinging sieve on a cord
Critomancy	barley cakes
Cromniomancy	onion sprouts
Cyclomancy	shiny surfaces, a form of scrying
Dactylomancy	a swinging ring on a string

Daphnomancy	the crackling of laurel wood in a fire
Demonomancy	demons
Dendromancy	oak or mistletoe
Geloscopy	laughter
Genethlialogy	the stars at the time of birth
Graphology	handwriting
Gyromancy	words spelled by touching letters in a circle after spinning around until dizzy
Halomancy	salt
Hepatoscopy	animal entrails, especially the livers
Hippomancy	stomping and whinnying of horses
Hydromancy	water, including the color, tides and ripples
Ichyomancy	fish
Lampadomancy	lights, flares, any source of illumination
Lecanomancy	a basin of water
Libranomancy	incense
Lithomancy	interpreting the colors of gemstones
Margaritomancy	pearls, which bounced to prove guilt
Metagnomy	remembrances while in a hypnotic trance
Meteoromancy	meteors
Metoposcopy	lines on the forehead
Molybdomancy	the sputtering and hissing of molten lead
Myomancy	the noise and damage from rats and mice
Oculomancy	eyes
Olinomancy	wine
Onomancy	names, especially personal names of people
Onychomancy	fingernails (in the light of day)
Oomantia	(also Ooscopy) eggs
Ophiomancy	snakes
Orniscopy	(also Ornithomancy) the flight of birds (from the Greek *ornis*, meaning "bird")
Ovomancy	eggs
Pegomancy	a babbling brook, spring or fountain
Pessomancy	pebbles
Phrenology	the shape of the head
Physiognomy	facial (and to a lesser extent, bodily) features
Psychography	writing
Pyromancy	(also Pyroscopy) fire, after throwing specially prepared powders into the flames
Rhabdomancy	a WAND, staff or stick, the precursor of the DOWSING and DIVINING ROD.
Rhapsodomancy	a random verse or stanza of poetry
Sciomancy	SPIRIT messages
Sideromancy	burning straw on flat iron, interpreting the curling shapes, smoke and fire
Spodomancy	cinders or soot
Stichomancy	random passages from a book of prose
Stolisomancy	the way a person dresses
Sycomancy	drying leaves that have had messages inscribed; good omens remain damp longest. (A more modern variation is balling wish papers and placing them in a strainer above steam. The first slip of paper to unroll will be answered first.)
Tephramancy	ashes, especially of tree bark
Tiromancy	cheese
Xylomancy	pieces of wood, by shape, size, flammability.

(See also NOSTRADAMUS; TIRESIAS.)

Divine Comedy, The The *Divine Comedy* (or *Divina Commedia*), the metaphysical masterpiece by DANTE Alighieri (1265–1321), was begun possibly as early as 1307, although some scholars place the date at 1314 or even later. Dante completed the work just before he died. It is divided into three independent sections, *Inferno*, *Purgatory* (*Purgatorio*) and *Paradise* (*Paradiso*), written in *terza rima* (nine line stanza, rhymed

in the scheme aba-bcb-cdc, with each line consisting of 11 syllables.)

In *The Inferno* section of the ode, sectioned by cantos, the ancient Roman poet Virgil (Publicus Vergilius Maro, 70–19 B.C.) is sent to be the author's guide down through the nine conical circles of hell. Dante chose the character of Virgil because, in his day, many considered the learned Roman poet to have been a magician and a prophet. (See GRECO-ROMAN MAGIC).

Sorcerers (which include seers, prophets and fortune-tellers) are cast into the fourth bowge (or level) of the eighth circle of hell. As the punishment, the sorcerers have their heads twisted round toward their backs, with their eyes constantly filled with tears. They face backward because they attempted to look too far forward into the future, the provence only of God, and their eyes are filled with tears so that they are almost blinded and unable to see even beyond themselves.

When Dante sees the twisted and contorted sorcerers, he begins to cry. Virgil reprimands him for showing compassion, saying "Here pity, or here piety, must die. . . ." We must be willing, Virgil suggests, to accept God's judgment. Dante's reaction to the sorcerers' plight was unusual in that he expressed no outward remorse for any of the other torments. This has been interpreted by some scholars as Dante's inability to "see" (or comprehend) the divine Word of God.

Virgil identifies several of the transgressors. Among the many sorcerers are TIRESIAS (the Greek prophet whom Ulysses met in the Underworld, chronicled in *The ODYSSEY*), his daughter Manto and Amphiaraus, one of the notorious "Seven Against Thebes" who foretold the circumstances of his own death.

Finally, Dante is met by the giants, one of which lifts him down to the ninth circle, the bottommost level of Hell. Opposite to traditional Christian thinking, Dante's pit is ice cold, not fire and brimstone. It is the Lake of Cocytus, in which traitors are frozen. In section xxxii, 61–2 of *The Divine Comedy*, Modred (see ARTHUR, KING) is indicated as the archetypical traitor.

divining rod Rhabdomancy, an archaic form of DIVINATION, is performed by the special handling of a small stick or sticks, usually made of wood. The short pole has come to be known, colloquially, as a divining rod or a DOWSING rod.

Some occultists have interpreted certain verses in the Bible as evidence of the ancient use of divining rods. They include the mention of AARON'S ROD in 17 Numbers and the "rod of the wicked" in Psalms 125:3. Hosea 4:12 says, "My people inquire of a thing of wood, and their staff gives them oracles" (Revised Standard Version).

Because no further descriptions are given in these Scriptures, it is impossible to tell how similar the use of these rods was to the contemporary divining rod. What is certain is that the WAND or staff has been an important symbol in wizardry since early times, at least as far back as the beginnings of EGYPTIAN MAGIC.

Although the origin of the shape of the divining rod is unknown, the forked stick was the norm by the Middle Ages in Europe. Hazelwood was the preferred material to make a divining rod; according to some wizards, the wood itself possessed special magical powers. It was discovered, how-

In medieval times, the divining rod was frequently employed to search for hidden metallic ores. (Georg Agricola, *De Re metallita*, Basel, 1571).

ever, that in the correct hands all woods (and sometimes metal) seemed to work equally well.

The concept of the *dowser* did not evolve until the 15th century among miners in the Harz Mountains of Germany. The forked design of the divining rod was the one most often illustrated by the 16th century when the first books on the subject appeared. Sebastian Münster's *Cosmographia universalis* and Georg Agricola's *De Re metallica*, published in Basel in 1544 and 1571, respectively, and S.E. Löhneyss's *Bericht vom Bergkwerck*, published in Zellerfeldt in 1617, all discussed the use of the divining rods in the exploration for coal and ore mines.

All three books were illustrated with diviners using pointed sticks in the shape of a Y, with one branch of the V section in each hand and the single point outward. When the diviner stood over a desirable spot, the tip of the rod would quiver, twist or point downward. Some believed that the miraculous movement was caused by the sensitivity of the diviner; others by some invisible force emanating

from the hidden deposit; still others felt it was the work of "Elemental" SPIRITS (see ELEMENTS).

The first recorded use of the divining rod in France was not until 1692 when Jacques Aymar of Dauphiné demonstrated its capabilities. His all-purpose divining rod was able to locate mines, water, buried treasure, thieves and murderers.

The classic (sometimes called the French) method of its use was perfectly described in Abbé de Vallemont's work, *La Physique occult ou traité de la baguette divinatoire* (published in Paris, 1725, and The Hague, 1762):

> A forked branch of hazel, or filbert, must be taken, a foot and a half long, as thick as a finger, and not more than a year old, as far as may be. The two limbs of the fork are held in the two hands, without gripping too tight, the back of the hand being toward the ground. The point goes foremost, and the rod lies horizontally. Then the diviner walks gently over the places where it is believed there is water, minerals, or hidden money. He must not tread roughly, or he will disperse the cloud of vapors and exhalations which rise from the spot where these things are and which impregnate the rod and cause it to slant.

Known as rhabdomancy, the use of a divining rod was a popular method of locating sites to dig mines. (Sebastian Münster, *Cosmographia universalis*, Basel, 1544)

A diviner named Sire Roger advocated using a forked rod with the single length lain across the back of the hand, horizontal to the ground. He instructed, "You must balance it as exactly as possible . . .; then walk gently, and when you pass across a watercourse the rod will turn."

A forked diving rod was not always used. At the end of the 18th century, Père Kircher explained that a popular method in Germany at the time involved finding a

> shoot of hazel quite straight and free from knots, cutting it into two parts of almost equal length, scooping a little hollow in the end of one length, and cutting the other to a point so that the end of one part may fit into the end of the other. The diviner will then carry the shoot thus joined before him, holding it between the two forefingers. . . . When he passes over springs of water or metalliferous veins these two wands will move and bend.

Yet another method for dowsing was described by the Abbé de Vallemont. Rather than prepare forked rods, the diviners would

> take a long shoot of hazel, or of any other wood, quite smooth and straight like an ordinary walking-stick; they hold the two ends of it in their hands, bending it a little and carrying in horizontally, and then the moment they pass above a spring of water the stick twists and the curve turns toward the ground.

A pendulum or plumb bob (any weight at the end of a free-moving string) has also been used quite successfully. Another unusual configuration is the L-shaped dowsing rod. The dowser holds an L-shaped piece of wood or metal in each hand, similar to the handling of a handgun. The horizontal lengths of the rods are pointed straight forward, parallel to the ground and to each other. When the two rods cross, the dowser has found his mark.

Diwa   See BAO.

Doctor Faustus   Titled in its entirety *The Tragicall Historie of the Life and Death of Doctor Faustus, Doctor Faustus* (as the work is more commonly known) is a masterpiece of Elizabethan playwrighting by Christopher Marlowe (1564–1593). Christopher Marlowe was born on February 6, 1564, the son of a prosperous shoemaker in Canterbury, England. Following graduation from King's School there in 1581, he entered Corpus Christi College in Cambridge, receiving a B.A. in 1584 and his M.A. in 1587. Because he had matriculated under a scholarship provided by Archbishop Parker, it was assumed that Marlowe would enter the clergy, but instead he became enamored of the theater. Shortly after graduation from Cambridge, Marlowe moved to London, soon becoming a playwright.

Known for consorting with rowdy company and shady characters, Marlowe frequently fell afoul of the law. In 1589, he was briefly detained in Newgate Prison after witnessing a fatal sword fight between acquaintances. Three years later, the constable of Shoreditch issued a warrant forcing him to keep the peace.

During the spring of 1593, he was investigated by the Privy Council for atheism and blasphemy, having been charged by his former roommate, the author Thomas Kyd (1558–1594). The Privy Council issued a warrant for Marlowe's arrest on May 18. They searched the home of Thomas Walsingham in Kent where Marlowe had been staying, in part to avoid the plague which was on the rampage in London. Before Marlowe could be arrested, however, he was murdered on May 30 during a brawl in Eleanor Bull's tavern in Deptford. Marlowe was buried on June 1, 1593, in the St. Nicholas churchyard in Deptford.

Marlowe is remembered today as a playwright whose career and talent were cut short before fully blossoming. His first major play, *Tamburlaine the Great*, had been produced and critically acclaimed in 1587. His other major works followed: *The Famous Tragedy of the Rich Jew of Malta* (1589), *Edward the Second* (c. 1592), *The Massacre at Paris* (1593), *Dido, Queen of Carthage* (completed by Thomas Nashe, 1594), translations of Lucan's *Pharsalia* and Ovid's *Amores* and a poem, *Hero and Leander*, which he paraphrased into heroic couplets and which was incomplete at the time of his death. Of course, in 1588 (or as many scholars of the Elizabethan period contend, in 1590), there was *Doctor Faustus*.

One paradox to dating the writing of the play is that *Doctor Faustus* has as its most direct source the German FAUSTBUCH, which was not translated into English until 1592. Appearing so soon after the publication of the *Faustbuch*, *Doctor Faustus* was probably the first time the FAUST legend appeared in play form; it was certainly the first Faust drama written in English. Its first authenticated performance was by the Lord Admiral's Men in 1594. The role of Doctor Faustus was created by Edward Alleyn (1566–1626), the leading player of the company. With partner Philip Henslowe (c.1550–1616), Alleyn built the Fortune Theatre, Cripplegate (London) in which *Doctor Faustus* premiered.

Although Stationer Thomas Bushell entered a notice for the publication of "A book called the play of *Doctor Faustus*" in the Stationers' Register in 1601, the earliest known quarto of *Doctor Faustus* was published in 1604. The 1604 text of the play had allusions that could not have been written by Marlowe because the events referred to occurred after his death. Also, several scenes involving clowns were almost certainly not by Marlowe; these were possibly the work of William Byrd (1543–1623) but more probably Samuel Rowley (d. c.1633), whom Henslowe had commissioned to make additions to the script in 1602. (It is difficult to judge the extent of Rowley's contibution to *Doctor Faustus*. Also an actor in the Admiral's Company, Rowley wrote several plays for Henslowe, but the only work that survives in its entirety is an 1603 historical play about Henry VIII entitled *When you see me, You know me*.)

The 1604 edition was reprinted in 1609 and 1611, and in 1616 a new, enlarged version with even more changes was published. Originally written in a combination of blank verse and prose, the 1616 edition is known as the B-text. After reprints in 1619, 1620, 1624, 1628, 1631 and 1663, it was almost impossible to tell exactly which passages had originally been Marlowe's.

The play generally follows the story as presented in the English translation of the *Faustbuch*, but Marlowe changed Faustus's character from that of a simple magician dabbling in BLACK MAGIC to a power-hungry sorcerer, well-versed in NECROMANCY.

After an opening scene in which a chorus sets the stage for the drama, Faust expresses his contempt for a career in philosophy, medicine, law or divinity. Instead, claiming that "a sound magician is a mighty god," he seeks the knowledge and power of the sorcerer:

> These metaphysics of magicians
> And necromantic books are heavenly:
> Lines, circles, signs, letters and characters—
> Ay, these are those that Faustus most desires.
> O what a world of profit and delight,
> Of power, of honor, of omnipotence
> Is promised to the studious artisan!

A Good Angel and an Evil Angel appear to Faustus, the first imploring him to repent and the latter to follow his heart. Later, two students of black magic, Valdes and Cornelius, arrive to help Faustus on his road to ruin by loaning him books filled with the secret incantations. Alone that evening, Faustus draws a MAGIC CIRCLE and conjures up a devil who, after changing his shape at Faustus's command, returns as Mephistophilis [sic]. The sorcerer demands that Mephistophilis do his bidding, but the demon demurs. He admits that Faustus's "conjuring speeches" did draw his attention, but he serves only Lucifer.

Faustus offers to give up his soul to Lucifer after 24 years of Mephistophilis attending on him and following his every command. The demon returns to hell to convey the offer to Lucifer.

The Good and Evil Angels return to battle for Faustus, but the demon reappears to announce that Lucifer has agreed to the bargain. Mephistophilis demands that the pact be signed by Faustus in his own blood.

As soon as the contract is signed, lesser devils arrive, dressing Faustus in "crowns and rich apparel." Mephistophilis begins to reveal to Faust the secrets of astronomy and cosmology and of heaven, Earth and hell. To continue his quest for infinite knowledge, Faustus demands three GRIMOIRES—one containing "all spells and incantations . . . [to] . . . raise up spirits," a second showing "all characters and planets of the heavens . . . [to] . . . know their motions and dispositions," and finally one to "see all plants, herbs, and trees that grow upon the earth."

At one point, Faustus wishes to repent, but the Evil Angel declares that God would not forgive him and that if Faustus renounces his pact, he will be torn apart by devils. This dire announcement is confirmed by the appearance of Beelzebub and Lucifer himself.

The bulk of the drama is a series of vignettes that take place over Faustus's remaining years on Earth. In one scene, Faustus is introduced to SPIRITS personifying the seven deadly sins. Later, Faustus, invisible, taunts the pope and his holy court of cardinals.

In a comic scene, Robin the Ostler steals one of Faustus's conjuring books with the plan to "search some circles for my own use," such as causing "all the maidens in our parish dance at my pleasure stark naked before me." His adven-

The title page from the first edition of Christopher Marlowe's play *The Tragicall Historie of the Life and Death of Doctor Faustus*.

tures are thwarted when he and his friend realize that neither one can read.

In another scene, Faustus is welcomed to the court of the emperor, who asks the doctor to provide a demonstration of his magic by raising Alexander the Great and his paramour from the dead. Faustus explains that he can produce only their spirits. A knight of the court is skeptical, saying that if Faustus is able to produce the two spirits, then the goddess Diana could transform him into a stag. The spirits appear, and the emperor checks a mole on the paramour's neck to prove to himself that they are real. When the spirits depart, it is discovered that the doubting knight has sprouted horns. (In Elizabethan theater, this held a double, ribald meaning: it inferred that the knight was a cuckold as well as being enchanted.) Faustus, made indignant by the knight's disbelief, had caused the transformation. The emperor intervenes on the knight's behalf, and Faustus restores the man's countenance.

Near the end of the play, Faustus sells his steed to a horse dealer, warning him not to take the animal into running water. The trader, thinking that the horse possessed some secret power, wades him into a deep pond, and the enchanted horse promptly disappears. He attacks Faustus but is frightened off when he accidentally pulls the sorcerer's leg off. Mephistophilis has, of course, arranged the surprise as a prank and restores the magician's limb.

At a party for the duchess of Vanholt, Faustus has Mephistophilis, who remains invisible to the guests, produce out-of-season grapes. He makes the spirit of Helen of Troy appear briefly for three scholars. After they depart, an old, holy man entreats Faustus to repent. Instead, Faustus calls up Helen once more to become his mistress. The play's most famous line is spoken by Faustus who, overwhelmed by Helen's beauty exclaims, "Was this the face that launched a thousand ships?"

In the final scene of the play, Dr Faustus reveals his pact with Lucifer to the three scholars. They retreat to save themselves, offering to pray for his soul. As the time to give up his soul approaches, Faustus describes his sorrow, terror and anguish. He laments having entered into the bargain as the devils carry him away to hell. (See also FAUSTUS, JOHANNES.)

Doctrine of Signatures

Since ancient times, people have used plants for medicinal purposes. The selection of specific herbs, saps or plant parts to effect cures evolved into what is commonly called FOLK MEDICINE.

It was not enough for metaphysical thinkers of the 16th and 17th centuries to know that a particular plant could bring about a cure: they sought to find the cosmic reason *why* that particular plant was effective. They found their answer in the Doctrine of Signatures, a belief popularized by the German wizard and magus PARACELSUS.

The Doctrine of Signatures held that almost every plant bore a signature, the telltale indication of how it could be used medicinally. The concept was succinctly explained by Robert TURNER in his book *Botanologia*: "God hath imprinted upon the Plants, Herbs and Flowers, as it were in Hieroglyphicks [sic], the very Signature of their Vertues."

The signature could appear in many forms. A plant or root might aid the part of the human body that it resembles; for example, a wrinkled walnut looks like a brain. The color of the plant might be a key factor—a red plant for a rash or a yellow plant for liver ailments. If the plant resembled an animal, it might be effective as an antidote to its venomous bite. Plants that bore no obvious signature were not necessarily useless: metaphysicians were encouraged to experiment and to record their own successful uses.

The doctrine became much more complex when the occult physician also took into account the laws of ASTROLOGY. Plants, parts of the body and diseases were all matched to—and therefore regulated by—a heavenly body (i.e., one of the five known planets, the sun or the moon) plus a sign of the ZODIAC. Thus, a disease caused by the influence of one planet could be cured by an herb whose planet is in opposition to it. Conversely, if the wizard were more adept at SYMPATHETIC MAGIC, he might cure a disease with a plant ruled by the same planet. Indeed, whole chapters (as well as part of the subtitle) of Turner's first book, *Mikrokosmos*, promise to teach "the cure of wounds . . . the sicknesses attributed to the twelve Signes and Planets, with their Natures."

Besides Turner, two other major 16th- and 17th-century British herbalists, John Gerard (1545–1612) and Nicholas Culpeper (1616–1654), professed belief in the Doctrine of Signatures. Culpeper published his herbal-remedy book, *The English Physician Enlarged, with 369 Medicines made of English Herbs* in 1653. Turner's *Botanologia. The British Physician; or, The Nature and Vertues of English Plants*—a title obviously modeled after Culpeper's own—did not appear until 1664.

Turner identified different curative plants and signatures from those of Culpeper, and he accused the rival author, who had died of tuberculosis ten years earlier, of quackery. Culpeper's book, however, was written in a more down-to-earth, understandable style than Turner's and always remained the more popular. (See also POWWOW; WHITE MAGIC.)

Dolorous Stroke, The

In the Book II of Malory's *Le MORTE D'ARTHUR*, Balyn (Balin Le Savage) uses his mighty sword to kill King Pellam. The death blow, referred to as the Dolorous Stroke, results in the ruin of three kingdoms, including the death of all of the subjects in Pellam's castle.

MERLIN predicts that the devastation of the area, known as the Waste Land, will not end until Sir Galahad finds the Holy Grail. The wizard also sees these events as a metaphor for the coming fall of CAMELOT and King ARTHUR. (T.S. Eliot used this part of the legend as a foundation for his poem *The Waste Land*, first published in 1922 in *The Criterion*.)

In another part of Malory's tale, Balyn kills the LADY OF THE LAKE because the supernatural nymph requests his head in exchange for giving the sword EXCALIBUR to King Arthur.

Don Quixote

Written in two parts by Miguel de Cervantes Saavedra (1547–1616), *Don Quixote* tells the story of Alonso Quixano, who fantasizes that he is a knight errant, Don Quixote de la Mancha. The first section of the novel (published in 1605) contains the best-known elements of the story: Quixote's travels with his "squire" Sancho Panza, Quixote's being dubbed a knight by an innkeeper, his idealization of the peasant girl Aldonza Lorenzo as the lady Dulcinea del Toboso and his jousting the windmills. Also in Part One, Quixote mistakes the brass shaving basin that a passing barber is wearing on his head to be the golden helmet of Mambrino, mentioned in the mystical ORLANDO FURIOSO.

Although this section was intended to be complete in itself, shortly after it was published, a writer working under the pseudonym of Alonso Fernandez de Avellaneda wrote a sequel to the tale. This prompted Cervantes to continue the knight's story himself, and *his* second part of Quixote's adventures was published in 1615.

Two incidents regarding the belief in enchantment take place in the second half of *Don Quixote*. While searching for Dulcinea, Quixote and Sancho chance upon a farm girl who looks similar to Aldonza. Sancho persuades Quixote that this is the same Dulcinea. She only resembles a rough commoner, Sancho claims, because she has been bewitched by an evil enchanter.

Later in the story, Quixote and Sancho are guests of a duke and duchess, who play numerous pranks on the pair. The duchess decides to have sport with Sancho, promising him the possibility of holding the governorship of his own island, Barataria. The royal couple has one of their servants dress up like the wizard MERLIN, and the imposter tells Sancho that the peasant girl he discovered along the road really *is* Dulcinea under enchantment. To break the spell, Sancho must whip himself with 3,300 lashes on his naked buttocks.

Sancho knows that he made up the story himself, but the duchess manages to convince him that the girl is indeed the spellbound princess and suggests that he will never get his island to rule until he breaks the CURSE. Sancho delivers five strokes to his bare buttocks and promises to give the remaining 3,295 on another day.

Shortly thereafter, Quixote is beaten in battle by the Knight of the Full Moon (a university student named Samson Carrasco in disguise), and, broken and cured of his insanity, the weary Alonso Quixano returns home, where he soon dies.

Don Quixote de la Mancha was first translated into English by Thomas Shelton (fl. 1612–1620) in 1616, and a new translation by Peter Anthony Motteux (1660–1718) appeared between 1700 and 1703. The now-standard J.M. Cohen edition did not appear until 1950. The book has spawned numerable plays and films, only some of which touch on the mystical elements in the book. Perhaps the best-known adaptation is the 1965 Broadway musical *Man of la Mancha* (See MUSICAL THEATER).

dowsing   A form of DIVINATION, dowsing is the use of a DIVINING ROD to locate something underground. In North America, the term generally refers to its use in the search for water. It is said to work because some invisible force pulls, pushes or exerts pressure on the dowsing rod. People thought to be extraordinarily sensitive to these powers, who hold the rods and are directed by them, are called dowsers.

Colloquially, a dowser is also known as a water witch. The stereotype of a backwoods bearded man wearing rumpled clothing trying to locate water by holding a forked wooden branch out in front of him is a part of American folklore.

Dowsers are most often asked to seek sunken water and wells; however an adept dowser can also locate precious ores, buried treasure, prehistoric ruins or lost items. Dowsers have also occasionally been called in by legal authorities to find evidence from or the deceased victims of crime. Most dowsers feel that, although they must concentrate on the item to be located, if they sought the object(s) on a conscious level, they would never be successful.

The first branches of the Society of Dowsers were located in England and Europe. The American Society of Dowsers has its headquarters located in Danville, Vermont, with chapters in most states; their 35th annual national convention was held in summer 1995.

dowsing rod   See DIVINATION; DIVINING ROD; DOWSING; WAND.

Dragon rouge, Le   *Le Dragon rouge, ou l'art de commander les esprits, célestes, áriens, terrestres, infernaux,* a GRIMOIRE of demonic magic, was published by Offray in Avignon, France. The anonymous book, which promises control over SPIRITs, angels, humans and demons, purportedly dates to 1522, but it was actually written about 300 years later.

The book is full of cabalistic symbols and seals that must be recreated by the sorcerer on parchment "made with the skin of a kid." *Le Dragon rouge* promises that by faithfully following its rituals, the *karcist* (or operator who initiates the invocations) will receive satanic treasure. The tract tells how to prepare a pact, written in blood, with Lucifer. *Le Dragon rouge* also suggests a prayer to God that might assist the truly contrite and repentant sorcerer in reneging on a demonic pledge: "Inspire me, O great God, with the sentiments necessary for enabling me to escape the claws of the Demon and of all evil spirits!"

Draupnir   A magic RING. Draupnir was owned by Odin, a legendary Germanic god. The ring was destroyed when Odin set it on Balder's funeral pyre.

In the myth, Draupnir was also the name of a dwarf, who may have been the smith who forged the ring.

"draw(ing) down the moon"   See GRECO-ROMAN MAGIC; MEDEA.

Druids   The Druids were a religious priesthood, with its first practitioners possibly dating back as far as 3000–5000 B.C. Although legend says that Hu Gadarn, the head of the Cymry (or brotherhood) coalesced the varied beliefs into the Druidic system, more credible scholars suggests that Aedd Mawr instituted the order under a codified system much more recently, around 1000 B.C.

The name *Druid* might come from *drus*, a Greek word for the oak tree (and also connoting knowledge), from the latin *druides,* or from *drui* or *druvid,* Irish words for learning.

The Celts, moving from Gaul to Britain and Ireland, were assimilated into the already established cultures. At their zenith, priests of the Celtic Druidic order stretched from Ireland to northwest Turkey and from southern Germany to Spain and Italy. They are remembered today mostly for their sacred, often mysterious megaliths such as Stonehenge.

The stone circles and the large single "standing stones" were erected as an essential part of their ceremonies. Although pagan, Druids believed in one universal source for all wisdom and that mankind's energy stemmed from the sun. Awen, the name given this divine force, was most accessible at the high holidays of the Druid faith—the annual solstices and equinoxes, known as the four Albans. For the rites, the stones in the ring were arranged to allow the sun's rays to pass between them and onto a rock, known as the stone of speech, in the center of the circle. By standing in the shaft of light, Druidic priests believed that they could communicate with Awen and gain divine wisdom.

The Druids were literate, ordained their head priest through election, punished sinners and believed in an afterlife. They sometimes practiced blood sacrifices and foretold the future by interpreting the death agonies of their offerings. Augury, DIVINATION by observing the flight of birds, was also used. Although most of the Druidic brotherhood resided in Britain, the priests met annually one a year in Gaul.

The tree as a symbol of fertility was central to Druid belief. As a result, the WAND was also important to their wizard-priests, representing their power over the earthly ELEMENTS. Through magic, priests could purportedly silence thunder or change a human into an animal, such a pig, bird or, most often, a swan.

The priestly hierarchy of the Druids had seven levels or degrees, each being allowed to carry a specific type of wand. Members of the top echelon, that of the *ollamb*, or healer, bore a golden wand. The second degree carried a silver wand, and all of the other levels carried wands made of bronze.

Different kinds of wands were used by different Druidic societies and for different rituals, but the ceremonial wands were always made of wood. The Irish and Scots used hazel, hawthorne or yew, but the Welsh, Cornish and French Breton Druids made their wands from only yew. Wands used in death rites were most often made of cypress or willow. The wands were carved with a knife sprinkled with blood at sunrise or sunset to capture the optimum energy from the sun.

Julius Caesar gave the first written description of the Druids in his work, *Gallic Wars*, Book 6:

> The Druids preside in matters of religion . . . and interpret the will of the gods. They have the direction and education of youth. . . . In almost all controversies . . . the decision is left to them . . . The Druids never go to war, are exempted from taxes and military service. . . . They teach likewise many things relating to the stars and their motions, the magnitude of the world and our earth, the nature of things and the power and prerogatives of the immortal gods.

Julius Caesar also noted that their rites were often carried out in groves of oak because the trees (and their acorns) were considered sacred. The mistletoe that grew on and encircled the oak trees was also considered to be magical; it was often removed and worn as an AMULET or used as a CHARM.

Other Roman historians offered additional insights to the Druids of the time. Pliny claimed they practiced FOLK MEDICINE and sorcery. He also described their dressing in white robes, sacrificing bulls and cutting the holy mistletoe with sickles made of gold. Strabo also mentions the gold, made into bracelets, and calls the Druids soothsayers.

The Druids were considered a threat to the Roman Empire since at least the time of Caesar Augustus. According to Tacitus, the last of the sacred Druid oak groves was cut down at Mona, Anglessey, in A.D. 61. While the Druids were driven underground, at least in England and Wales, their ceremonies continued throughout Britain. After the conversion of the British Isles to Christianity, many of the Druidic practices were adopted in the Culdees' rites.

Interest in the Druids was rekindled in the mid-18th century primarily by William Stukeley (1687–1765), a medical doctor, law student and expert in ancient artifacts. In his writings he asserted that the Druids were similar to Christians in the belief of a Holy Trinity but that they practiced human sacrifices. In his books, Stukeley also connected the Druids with Stonehenge (*Stonehenge: a temple restor'd to the British druids*, 1740) and the monolithic circle at Avebury (*Abury*, 1743). Almost all of his assertions, however, especially those regarding human sacrifice and the use of Stonehenge as a temple, have since been discredited.

dukun   See MEDICINE MAN.

"Dungeons & Dragons"   Created in the mid-1970s by Gary Gygax of Lake Geneva, Wisconsin, with input and feedback from several friends and fellow enthusiasts, "Dungeons & Dragons" (or "D&D," as it is also known) is perhaps the most famous and popular role-playing fantasy war game is existence. In the game, players adopt a role, such as that of a Wizard, and manipulate the character's powers for strategic advantage.

In 1969, Gygax and Jeff Perren created "Chainmail," a game which recreated medieval wars in miniature. Two years later, at GENCON 4, a games convention, Gygax met Dave Arneson, who the year before had invented another medieval war game in which the fighters entered a castle through a maze of underground sewers and, on the way, encountered fantasy creatures such as dragons. Gygax had already added supernatural characters to "Chainmail," so he was immediately attracted to Arneson's game. They joined forces to create a new medieval war game with the working title, "The Fantasy Game."

Gygax was unable to interest any game publisher or manufacturer in "The Fantasy Game," so in 1973, with a $1,000 investment by partner Don Kaye, Gygax self-published a new war game set during the English Civil War, titled "Cavaliers and Roundheads." They named their partnership Tactical Studies Rules, taken from an area gaming club, the Lake Geneva Tactical Studies Association.

A new investor, Brian Blume, joined the partnership in 1974, with financing to publish 1,000 sets of "Dungeons & Dragons," a name suggested by Gygax's wife Mary to replace the generic-sounding "The Fantasy Game." The games were assembled in and distributed from Kaye's dining room and front porch, and the first thousand were sold within a year.

At only 37 years of age, Kaye died of a heart attack in 1975. His widow, who inherited Kaye's share of the partnership, was not interested in gaming, so Tactical Studies Rules was dissolved. In July of that same year, Gygax and Blume formed a corporation TSR Hobbies, Inc., to pursue the future of "Dungeons & Dragons" along with other fantasy war games.

The corporate headquarters moved to Gygax's basement and dining room. Within the year, they released "Dungeon!," a family board-game version of "Dungeons & Dragons," plus two supplements to the original "Dungeons & Dragons."

In 1976, TSR opened The Dungeon Hobby Shop; in August, TSR hosted the GENCON game fair, where the first "Dungeons & Dragons" open tournament was held. Two new supplements for "Dungeons and Dragons" appeared—"Eldritch Wizardry" and "Gods, Demigods, and Heroes."

It soon became apparent that rules had to be clarified and codified for both Dungeon Masters and players, especially because the game was reaching an increasingly younger audience. J. Eric Holmes rewrote the rule book for the first "Dungeons & Dragons Basic Set" in 1977. Also to assist players, "Dungeon Geomorphs" (three-dimensional dungeon and cavern maps) and "Monster and Treasure Assortments" were released. More than 350 new monsters were suggested for play in TSR's *Monster Manual*. Kevin Blume, Brian's brother, joined the company, heading the financial department. Finally, 1977 saw a change from TSR's lizard-man logo (which had been adopted two years earlier) into a WAND-wielding wizard.

The first major rethinking of "Dungeons and Dragons" occurred in 1978. The original "Dungeons & Dragons" game, now often called "Basic D&D," is played without a board or pieces, using only a pen, paper, dice and memory and creative visualization to plan strategies and execute maneuvers. The game is overseen by a Dungeon Master, who creates the setting or atmosphere in which the battles will take place. Although usually played in a fantasy earthen medieval world, Dungeon Masters have been known to set the wars in another dimension, an alternate universe or even outer space.

Players create a character to their own liking, but they generally fall into one of four categories. The Fighters are the soldiers. Thieves, in addition to their ability to steal, can adopt any furtive role, such as a scout or spy. Clerics are known for their healing SPELLS. Their power is received from some higher spiritual authority, which will change according to the milieu set by the Dungeon Master. For example, if the game is played in the time of King ARTHUR and MERLIN, it would most likely be the Christian God, but placed among the DRUIDS or ancient Greece, the superior SPIRIT would be a pagan deity. Wizards are, perhaps, the most powerful characters because their enchantments use the magic found in all of Nature as the basis for their spells. More often good than evil, Wizards generally perform WHITE MAGIC; their art is more closely aligned with ALCHEMY than with WITCHCRAFT.

The drawback to "Basic D&D" is that, while the game is relatively simple, it is also open-ended, meaning that a game could take days or even weeks to complete. Often, new rules had to created on the spot to resolve unique problems.

In 1978, "Advanced Dungeons & Dragons" was inaugurated with more-thorough and -detailed rules. The *Players Handbook* included methods to create heroes, along with dozens of spells for use by both wizards and clerics.

By 1979, fantasy war gamers had begun to enact live action "Dungeons & Dragons" battles, both indoors as well as on open fields. That year, an avid player named James Dallas Egbert III, a college student in Lansing, Michigan, disappeared. A detective's speculation that the boy may have accidentally died in the steam tunnels beneath campus while playing a live-action "Dungeons & Dragons" game drew international attention. The fact that he turned up (after an extended visit with a friend off-campus and *not* having played "Dungeons & Dragons") was not as extensively reported.

Sales for "Dungeons & Dragons" became astronomical and continued to climb through the early 1980s. On September 17, 1983, the *Dungeons & Dragons* cartoon series first aired on television. A Dragonlance series started the next year proved to be a publishing bonanza in novels, calendars, computer games and other ancillary markets.

Critics expressed concerned over the cultlike obsession of some of the games' fans. Conversely, enthusiasts pointed out that "Dungeons & Dragons" promotes creativity, mental acuity, memory, concentration, commitment, attention to detail and friendly competition, as well as tactical, design and strategy-planning skills.

In 1986, Kevin and Brian Blume sold their shares in the company to a new investor, Lorraine Williams, and by year's end, Gary Gygax, the creator of "Dungeons & Dragons," had also left TSR.

TSR, Inc., continued, however, and in 1989 *The Complete Wizard's Handbook* was published along with other manuals. Two years later, a streamlined version of "Dungeons & Dragons" was launched, aimed at a new generation of complete beginner gamer. TSR also released authorized collector trading cards for the first time in its history.

In 1994, TSR released a fantasy role-playing game, "Spellfire: Master the Magic," using collectible trading cards that pictured characters and settings from its own "Advanced Dungeons & Dragons." (That same year, Wizards of the Coast, Inc., released Richard Garfield's rival fantasy trading-card game, "MAGIC: THE GATHERING.")

By 1996, two decades after the creation of "Dungeons & Dragons," TSR was truly diversified: a major publisher of fantasy and science-fiction books, magazines, board games, military strategy games, video and computer games and fantasy role-playing adventure/war games. Nevertheless, TSR, Inc., was still best known for its most popular and influential fantasy game, "Dungeons & Dragons."

In spring 1997, TSR, Inc., was acquired by Wizards of the Coast, Inc.

dunking (ducking) See SWIMMING; HOPKINS, MATTHEW.

Egyptian magic   It has been suggested that the roots of most, if not all, of the Western concepts of magic can be traced back to the beliefs and practices of ancient Egypt. While it is uncertain when those practices began, hieroglyphic records show that magic was common among the wizard-priests by the Fourth Dynasty.

Egyptian magic was inseparable from its religion, which taught that all natural and supernatural phenomena, including magic, were gifts from the gods. Their close association is shown by the fact that, while there are several words in ancient Egyptian religious manuscripts that can be translated into English as *magic*, there is no single word that simply means "religion."

According to the *Coffin Texts* of *The Egyptian* BOOK OF THE DEAD, one of the first actions of the creator deity was the invention of magic in the form of his eldest son Heka. Other gods, especially ISIS, HORUS and THOTH, were also granted *heka* (sometimes seen as *hīke*), or magical power. In time, humans were entrusted with the use of magic; thus, magic was seen as a form of prayer to the gods. It was supposedly by tapping into the *heka* of the gods that the priests were able to produce their magical effects.

In the ancient Egyptian religious texts, the word *heka*, meaning "magic," was used interchangeably with the name of the deity Heka. In the Coptic New Testament, the word *heka* was translated as the Greek word *mageia* which, of course, was the root of the English word *magic*.

The word *akhu* was also frequently used to mean "magic," but its power could only be used after death. The Egyptian word *ro*, which appears consistently throughout the *Book of the Dead*, means "mouth," but it was also used to mean a "speech," a SPELL or an INCANTATION.

Language played an essential part in Egyptian magic because words (given by the gods) were used to form prayers, spells and incantations. Thoughts, words and actions were considered to be different aspects of the magical operation in *heka*, and they were deemed to be equally effective. The hieroglyphic ALPHABET, after all, was a gift from the gods; so whether a spell was written or spoken, it had the same divine power.

Words of power could be spoken over any object, such as a waxen or clay figure, to place a deity's power within it. Miniature soldiers and servants carved from stone, wood or clay (known as *shabti*) were placed in a tomb in the belief that

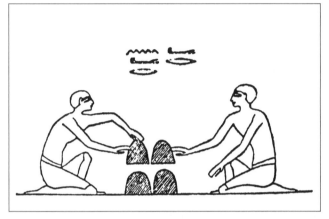

In ancient Egypt, the uninitiated thought hieroglyphics were magical symbols. (Photo by author)

they would come to life, grow, and attend to their master in the next world.

Given this belief, words played a central role in image magic, a form of IMITATIVE MAGIC in which the written or spoken language represents the magical action which the wizard-priest hoped to produce.

Image magic could also take a concrete form: *heka* could be placed into a *cippus* (an engraved stone stella), an AMULET or a TALISMAN. Often small ones were worn as jewelry. To protect a person's corpse, magical amulets were wrapped within the cloths of the mummy, the most important being the heart SCARAB, which was placed on the breast of the deceased. Such amulets were often made of nephrite, a green stone. Green was the color of rebirth: Osiris's face was usually depicted as green, and the Egyptian word for *green* also meant "to flourish."

Magic also extended to the paraphernalia used in ritual, especially in funereal rites, and many of the objects used by the wizard-priests were thought to hold *heka* within them. Perhaps the most important ceremony during mummification was the Opening of the Mouth ritual, in which the wizard-priest struck the mouth of the deceased or his image on the mummy case with a small hammerlike chisel while intoning, "I open your mouth with the adze (or iron) which split open the mouths of the gods." This rite supposedly returned the power of speech to the deceased so that he could defend himself to the gods when he is being judged in the next world.

In addition to word and image magic, three other types of magic were important in ancient Egypt: magic by consumption, magic by licking and magic by encirclement. The first two forms were thought to be effective because, being oral in nature, they were related to *ro* (the mouth/magical spells) and speech. The concept of *magic by consumption* suggested that, if the supplicant were illiterate and therefore unable to understand the incantations written in hieroglyphs, the spell could be inscribed on papyrus and ingested, either in solid form or after being dissolved in liquid. Similarly, it was believed that water poured over *cippi* absorbed their magic, which could then be received by drinking the liquid. Saliva, intimately connected with the mouth, was thought to have healing powers, and licking and spitting were believed to be very curative.

Finally, it was thought that evil forces could be trapped by encircling (*phkher*) them, and during a magical ritual an area might be circled many times to protect it. The word *pekhert* (the root of the English word *prescription*) was used to describe the ability to defend oneself against harmful or malevolent forces by encirclement. The act itself evolved centuries later into the wizard or sorcerer's drawing a MAGIC CIRCLE to protect himself from demonic SPIRITs.

The purpose of magic, of course, was to gain power over the forces of nature and to control the actions of the gods so that they would intercede on the supplicant's behalf.

Modern occultists sometimes divide Egyptian magic and its spells into Low Magic and High Magic. Low Magic, or *ua*, was used to cause changes in or effect the material world; High Magic, or *hekau*, was more spiritual in nature and aimed at personal self-fulfillment.

Low Magic included everyday, practical spells, such as healings and cures, performing protective rituals for mother and child at birth and the creation of amulets or talismans. It was believed that illness and disease could be caused by evil spirits afflicting the mind or body, so if a lay doctor's medicines were not entirely successful, a priest-magician (especially one known as a lector priest) was often called upon to effect the cure by Low Magic. Two popular methods of psychic healing were by ritual incantation (to the appropriate god) and by interpreting dreams from regular or drug-induced sleep. The drugs themselves were considered magical, or at least to contain magical qualities.

The penultimate duty of the wizard-priests was to ensure a safe, comfortable and successful passage of the deceased through the Afterlife to the Next World. Their techniques included the proper preparation of the deceased's mummy and the use of the correct burial rituals and incantations as prescribed by *The Egyptian Book of the Dead*. Some occultists define the process of mummification as Low Magic because many of the rites performed over the body were intended to help preserve the physical corpse.

By the use of High Magic, wizards sought to control the events in one's own life and to prepare for one's eventual rebirth. This was done through a series of rituals aimed at spiritual purification.

At this point, the distinction between Low Magic and High Magic becomes vague because both aim toward the ultimate goal of the rebirth, or reunification, of the corporal body with the two aspects of the astral spirit known as the *ka* (vital essence) and the *ba* (SPIRIT or personality). This could only be obtained by defending oneself successfully before Osiris and the Council of the Gods at the Day of Judgment, in a ceremony known as the Weighing of the Heart. If the deceased were found wanting, he was delivered to Ammit, the Swallower of the Dead. Egyptians did not believe in a heaven and hell: There was either an Afterlife or an end of existence.

Some of the names and stories of wizards and sorcerers from ancient Egypt have been passed down to us: Arnuphis (who lived in the second century A.D.), Imhetep (magician-priest in Memphis), Lotapes (a pharaoh's court magician), Tchatcha-em-ankh (a wizard-priest from the fourth century B.C., whose recorded feats include having raised the water level of a lake) and the priests of Sekhnet.

The Westcar Papyrus mentions the wizards Weba-aner (also seen as Abā-āner), a royal dignitary during the rule of Keb-ka (c.3830 B.C.), Jajamanekh and DEDI.

Weba-aner was able to transform a small, waxen image of a crocodile into a 12-feet long living creature at the court of King Nebka. The crocodile grabbed the lover of Weba-aner's wife, pulled him into the water and drowned him. The wizard then calmly transformed the beast back into wax.

In the time of the Pharaoh Snefru, the wizard Jajamanekh was called upon to retrieve a turquoise hair ornament accidentally dropped into a lake by one of the courtesans. Jajamanekh cast a spell that lifted one half of the lake up and onto the other half. He walked out onto the dry bed of the lake, retrieved the bauble and then restored the lake to its natural state.

Dedi was the most renowned of the three wizards. Some legends place Dedi at the palace of Ramses II, but more likely he attended Cheops, the builder of the Great Pyramid.

The legendary Setnau Khā-em-uast, a prince during the Ptolemaic period (fourth century B.C.), kept a huge library of magic scrolls and papyri, but he sought a fabled book which he claimed "was written by Thoth himself, and in it there are two formulas." The first would BEWITCH all heaven and earth and reveal all the creatures of the earth and the sea to the wizard. Chanting the other would "enable a man, if he be in the tomb, to take the form which he had upon earth."

With his brother, Setnau traveled to Memphis, where the book was buried in the tomb of Ptah-nefer-ka. Uttering a strong spell, Setnau cracked the earth open and descended to the graves of Ptah-nefer-ha, his wife and his son. Although the shadows pleaded with Setnau not to take their book of spells, he won it by defeating Ptah-nefer-ka in a game of draughts. Clasping the book to his breast, Setnau ascended into the heavens.

Many pharaohs were themselves wizards, or at least acutely interested in the occult arts. Ramses III, who ruled c.1200 B.C., was known to keep magic manuscripts in his royal library. Hui, an official in his service, bewitched small statues made to resemble treasonous soldiers and other enemies of the pharaoh. Hui received divine power by using spells found in the library's magical tracts and, by performing sympathetic magic on the tiny figurines, was able to do "horrible things and all the wickedness which his heart could imagine."

According to legend, Nectanebo II, who ruled 360–343 B.C. and was the last Egyptian-born pharaoh, was the most infamous ruler-wizard. He was versed in ASTROLOGY and could induce dreams by saturating a diminutive figure of the sleeper

The salamander, one of the four Elementals, represented Fire. (Michael Majer, *Scrutinium Chymicum*, 1687)

with a secret herbal brew. Through his powers of DIVINATION, he was purportedly able to elude enemies who might have threatened his life.

Perhaps Nectanebo II was most infamous for his ability to "rule all kings by his magical power" through his use of waxen images. Employing an ebony magic WAND, he would bring to life miniature replicas of his naval fleet and of his foe's ships as they floated on a basin of Nile River water. As the enemy's model ships sank to the bottom of the bowl, sympathetically so too did their actual vessels miles away on the open sea.

According to Egyptian tradition, Iannes and Iambres were among the wizards attached to the court of Ramses II who did magical battle against MOSES and Aaron (see AARON'S ROD). Arabic legend adds the names Sadur and Ghadur to the

pharaoh's magical forces. One of Ramses II's own sons, Khamuas, was also skilled in sorcery. (See also EYE OF HORUS; HERMES TRISMEGITUS.)

Egyptian Secrets   See HEX.

ekwele   A chain containing eight curved discs made of tortoise shell regularly attached along its length, an ekwele is used for fortune-telling by the WITCH DOCTORs of the Yoruba tribe of West Africa.

The witch doctor grasps the chain at its center. As he slowly lowers the chain to the ground, the shell discs spin. By interpreting the sequence of concave and convex shells, the seer is able to make his reading. (See also BAO; HAKATA; SORTILEGE.)

Elements   The Western occult belief that all things in the universe are made up of combinations of four basic Elements—Air, Earth, Fire and Water—is credited to Empedocles, the Sicilian philosopher, who lived in the fifth century B.C.

The theory was advanced by Plato and Aristotle, and it was accepted as scientific fact well into the 17th century. As such, the Elements stood side by side with the four HUMOURS postulated by Hippocrates in the study of medicine.

The concept of the Elements was quickly adopted by the leaders in the emerging field of ALCHEMY. The fact that matter was made up of combinations and permutations of just four Elements formed the foundation for the belief that metals could be merely transmuted from one into another—such as lead into gold.

Each Element was thought to exist in its own respective state: Air (gas), Earth (solid), Water (liquid) and Fire (energy or electricity). Air and Fire were thought to be positive, active, and masculine; Earth and Water were thought to be negative, passive and feminine. Additional characteristics and CORRESPONDENCES include:

Air   The east; the WAND; intelligence; sociability; frivolity; the color yellow; the metal silver.

Earth   The north; the PENTACLE; fertility; quiet; patience; the color green; the metal gold.

Fire   The south; the sword; courage; jealousy; the color orange; the metal gold.

Water   The west; the chalice or CAULDRON; emotional and receptive nature; sensitivity; the color blue; the metal silver.

In the ancient world, the entire universe was thought to be populated with SPIRITS, and it was just a small step from belief in the Elements to the identification of the supernatural beings, called Elementals, from which they received their powers. Lesser sprites and spirits from nature were also associated with each of the four Elements, but the primary elementals associated with the four Elements were sylphs (Air), gnomes (Earth), salamanders (Fire) and undines (Water). This connection between Elements and Elementals was probably conceived, or at least first promoted, by the neoplatonists, who added their own mystic and spiritual (often demonic) interpretations to the teachings of Plato.

The alchemist most closely associated with the doctrine of the Elementals was PARACELSUS. In fact, Paracelsus coined the word *gnome*. The wizard thought that humans were made up of three basic parts, the divine spirit (God), the astral body (soul) and the visible body. While humans needed all three components to exist, Elementals could exist in as few as one of these aspects.

Elementals, Paracelsus believed, were neither human nor spirit, but something in between. They were mortal, needed food and sleep, could procreate and had language and reason; what they lacked was a soul. In fact, Paracelsus believed, were it not for the divine spark of God within them, humans would be Elementals.

In Asia and the East, the occult world delineated five differing Elements and elementals: Earth, Fire (represented by the red bird), Metal (the white tiger), Water (the dark warrior, a creature that was part-tortoise, part-serpent) and Wood (the green dragon).   (See JINN; ZODIAC.)

elixir   According to Middle Eastern alchemists, an elixir was a hypothetical material that could turn worthless metals into gold. In later centuries, European alchemists more often called this transmuting reagent the PHILOSOPHER'S STONE.

The word *elixir* comes from the Arabic *al-iksir*, meaning "the dry powder." In time, *al-iksir* was Latinized to its present form *elixir*, meaning any type of magic potion. Discovering a youth-enhancing *elixir vitae*, or "ELIXIR OF LIFE," became one of the never-ending quests of alchemists.

To this day, the word *elixir* connotes a substance with mysterious or occult attributes and consequences.   (See ALCHEMY.)

Elixir of Life   Latinized from the Arabic, an ELIXIR was any agent that according to ancient alchemists and occultists, could transmute base metals into gold. Although "changing lead into gold" is the best-known quest of ALCHEMY, the science was really based on spiritual and metaphysical transformation. Just as the PHILOSOPHER'S STONE would purify base metals, so too the arcane knowledge obtained in the study of alchemy would perfect its student toward divine wisdom and understanding. This complete comprehension of life's mysteries would allow the alchemist to be master over all of life's obstacles, including sickness and aging.

Hence, the search for an *elixir vitae*, or " elixir of life," that could cure any disease became one of the never-ending quests of alchemists. The belief that such a universal remedy must exist was based on the principle that all illnesses had the same fundamental cause: an imbalance of the body's ELEMENTS or HUMOURS. Also, it was commonly believed that diseases were caused by some sort of imperfection or impurity (i.e., sin) of the body. Obviously, an elixir that could equalize and stabilize the Humours or neutralize any imperfections in body or spirit would be able to heal a patient of any affliction.

By extension, it was believed that the Elixir of Life could stop aging, prolong life and postpone death. In some versions of the FAUST legend, the sorcerer tried to brew a rejuvenating philtre (see DOCTOR FAUSTUS). So tantalizing was the elixir that the soldier/explorer Ponce de León unsuccessfully searched the swamplands of Florida in the New World for the fabled Fountain of Youth.

Some occultists believed that the Philosopher's Stone alone would act as an Elixir of Life; some believed that the formula for the Elixir of Life must include at least some powder from the Philosopher's Stone as an ingredient. Still others maintained that any number of mystic stones could also be used to concoct it.

Among the many alchemists who claimed to have discovered the Elixir of Life was PARACELSUS. In *De Tinctura Physicorum* (*On the Tincture of the Physicians*, published in 1570 and attributed to Paracelsus) such a tonic is described:

This is the tincture by which some of the first physicians in Egypt, and afterwards up till out times, have lived for 150 years. The lives of many of them lasted for some centuries, as history clearly teaches, although this does not seem to be true to anybody: because its force is so miraculous, that it is able to enlighten the body . . . and to strengthen him to such a degree that he will remain free of all diseases and, although afflicted by old age, will appear as it had been in his youth. Therefore the *tinctura physicorum* is a universal remedy which devours all sicknesses like a fire devouring wood. Its quantity is tiny, but its force is mighty.

Paracelsus's apprentices also referred to a similar philtre, *tinctura philosophorum* or "philosopher's tincture," that could cause the "resurrection and regeneration of nature."

Although the days of alchemy are long gone, the search for the Elixir of Life are not.

enchanter's nightshade   Enchanter's nightshade is the common name of *Circaea*, a flowering plant of the genus *Onagraceae* (the willow-herbs). There are ten species of *Circaea*, all with oval leaves, pointed at one end, paired opposite the stem.

The genus was named for CIRCE, although there is no clear connection to the mythical enchantress. Additionally, the plant has no reputation for use in SORCERY, magic SPELLs or even FOLK MEDICINE. It has been suggested, however, that the plant's habitat—shadowy, dank forests—helped contribute to its name.

Of more use to the sorcerer was the common nightshade, which is unrelated to enchanter's nightshade. Nightshade (belonging to the *Solanaceae* genus)—and especially dwale (also called deadly nightshade)—is poisonous, which made it an extremely valuable ingredient in some secret potions and philtres.

Endimion, The Man in the Moone [sic]   *Endimion* was one of a series of plays written by John Lyly (1554?–1606) to be performed solely by boy actors for court audiences. First published in 1591, the allegorical tale concerns a mortal, Endimion, who deserts Tellus (the earth) because he is hopelessly in love with Cynthia (the moon). The jealous and spurned Tellus asks a sorceress named Dipsas to casts a SPELL on Endimion, placing him in a deep sleep for 40 years. Cynthia kisses the entranced Endimion, waking him from his slumber.

Some courtesans saw this play as a metaphor for the attentions of Leicester (Endimion) by Elizabeth I (Cynthia) and Mary Queen of Scots (Tellus).

Enochian magic   Enochian magic is wizardry accomplished through the intervention or assistance of angels and angelic forces. The ANGELIC ALPHABET revealed to John DEE and Edward KELLY has formed the basis for its invocations. The pair of mystics disclosed their Enochian ALPHABET, along with the angelic actions which led to its revelation, in their treatise *Liber Logaeth* (also called *The Book of Enoch*).

In addition to angelic communication, Enochian magic professed that many levels of consciousness, called *aethyrs*, exist and that by using the proper techniques, the wizard could send out his astral body to travel through these planes.

Although introduced earlier, the word *Enochian* came into popular use among modern occultists around the beginning of the 20th century. The ORDER OF THE GOLDEN DAWN accepted the principles of Enochian magic, and its practice was vigorously endorsed by Aleister CROWLEY.

In 1978, Dr. Donald C. Laycock offered *The Complete Enochian Dictionary* (Askin Publications, London) as a scholarly examination of Dee's methods and results. Gerald Schueler's more recent books, *Enochian Magic—A Practical Manual* and

An Advanced Guide to Enochian Magick (Llewellyn Publications, Minnesota, 1987), discuss both angelic magic and the angelic alphabet.

Cabalists still debate whether Enochian speech is a true, angelically inspired language, a code (perhaps for political purposes) or just a nonsense dialect concocted by a conniving Kelly. Although Laycock notes that the Enochian tongue seems to follow the idiomatic rules of the English language, he admits "strangest of all is that we still do not know whether [Enochian] is a natural language or an invented language —or whether it is, perhaps, the language of the angels."

Ephesus   A major port and center for learning at the time of JESUS Christ, Ephesus was located in a bay on the Mediterranean coast of Turkey at the mouth of the Kaystros River. According to ancient historians, Ephesus was founded around 3000 B.C.

Natural phenomena, including fire, earthquakes and the silting of the river and bay, forced Ephesus to relocate many times. According to Greek legend, around the 10th century B.C., Androclos (the son of King Kodros of Athens, who had evaded the Doric invasion of Greece) sought to reposition Ephesus. Androclos consulted the oracle of Apollo at DELPHI to find the most propitious spot, and he received the typically cryptic response, "The new site of the city will be shown by a fish, and a wild boar will take you there."

As a hub for trade and a crossroads of world culture and civilization, Ephesus was also a religious center, reflecting, in succession, each of its dominant societies. During its Greek period, Ephesus became known for its worship of Artemis, the Greek goddess of chastity and hunting. (See HECATE.)

Ephesus was also the home of one of the Seven Wonders of the Ancient World, the glorious Artemision (also known as the Temple of Artemis), which was started around the seventh century B.C. and completed in 430 B.C.

By the first century A.D., Ephesus was firmly established as a colony of Rome, and the Temple of Artemis was converted to honor the parallel Roman goddess, Diana. The temple was destroyed by invading Goths in A.D. 262. Little is left of the magnificent temple, located in what is today the town of Selçuk. Some of the marble was used to build the nearby Basilica of St. John and the Isa Bey Mosque; many of its columns were incorporated into St. Sophia in Istanbul.

Like most major cosmopolitan centers, Ephesus was a haven for progressive and nontraditional thinking. Belief in magic was no exception, and the practice of sorcery abounded. It was in part Ephesus's reputation as a pagan center that drew the apostle Paul to preach there.

Among the sorcerers living there were seven sons of a Jewish high priest named Sceva. They attempted to emulate the apostle Paul's success at healing, but, according to Acts 19:15–16 of the New Testament of the Bible, when they attempted an exorcism the evil SPIRIT rebuked them, saying, "Jesus I know, and Paul I know; but who are you?" The demon overpowered the men "so that they fled out of that house naked and wounded."

When the incident became known, all of the residents of Ephesus—including the wizards—were afraid and held Paul and his Lord, in awe. After their conversion to Christianity, the magicians publicly destroyed their cabalistic texts: "And

Ruins of the great library of Celsus, located in Ephesus, in modern-day Turkey. Built in A.D. **117, the edifice contained papyrus copies of many of the known occult and magical manuscripts of its time.** (Photo by author)

a number of those who practiced magic arts brought their books together and burned them in the sight of all; and they counted the value of them and found it came to fifty thousand pieces of silver" (Acts 19:19).

Certainly, hundreds of magic texts were in the hands of the many wizards who had flocked to Ephesus. The full extent of the loss to the study of the occult sciences will never be known.

Ephesus later became the site of one of the most magnificent libraries of its age and the third largest in the ancient world (after those in Alexandria, Egypt, and Pergamum, Turkey). The building was originally constructed by the consul Gaius Julius Aquila in A.D. 117 as a *heroum* (i.e., the tomb of a hero), celebrating Celsus Polemaeanus, the father of the governor of the province. The facade of the two-story structure was decorated with four female statues representing destiny, intelligence, knowledge and wisdom. Inside the building, the walls contained niches to hold more than 2,000 papyrus scrolls; a unique system of double walls behind the recesses allowed flowing air to control the humidity, thus helping to maintain the manuscripts' condition.

Whether any magical treatises were among the Roman documents is unknown. It is said that Marc Anthony, for the love of Cleopatra, transferred the bulk of the library's manuscripts to Alexandria, Egypt. Those scrolls, of course, were later destroyed in the great fire that engulfed that city. Any scrolls that might have remained behind in Ephesus were lost in the city's plunder by the Goths.

Eventually, an outbreak of disease (possibly malaria) coupled with the complete silting and subsequent change of the Kaystros River's course, led to abandonment of Ephesus. The once mighty city is now only well-preserved ruins, a shadow of its former splendor.

Eutropa See PALMERIN OF ENGLAND.

evil eye The belief in being CURSEd by the glare of an evil eye, or simply "the eye," is perhaps as old as humanity itself. The fear of "being eyed" still thrives in even the most civilized countries, especially in southern Europe and in the Middle East. There is a word or phrase for the evil eye in almost every language, for example, *mauvais oeil* (French), *mal occhio* or *la iettatura* (Italian), *böser Blick* (German), *kine-ahora* (Yiddish) and *glamour* (Scottish, introduced into the English tongue by Sir Walter Scott; See GLAMOUR.) It is also sometimes referred to as the black glance or, in Ireland, the eye of Balor.

Concepts of the eye also vary from culture to culture. In the Mediterranean regions, for example, the eye (or *mati*) is not necessarily linked to an act of sorcery or magic (*mayia*). In fact, the eye can be cast accidentally, secretly or without deliberate malice.

Many believe that the eye is the result of jealousy or resentment provoked by a friend or acquaintance casting an admiring glance on a person, or on his or her family or possessions. Supposedly, those people (or items) most in jeopardy of being adversely affected by being eyed are those of special beauty or rarity, such as a newborn baby. Also in special danger are blue-eyed people—an attribute that the Greeks identify with the Turkish people, and, of course, valued livestock are always at risk.

The evil eye is mentioned in at least two of the New Testament gospels. Among the evil thoughts that proceed "out of the heart of man" listed by JESUS were "thefts, covetousness, wickedness, deceit, lasciviousness, an evil eye, blasphemy, pride, foolishness" (Mark 7:22). He teaches in the Gospel of St. Matthew that "If thine eye be evil, thy whole body shall be full of darkness." Some occult scholars believe that Christ himself used the evil eye when he cursed a barren fig tree (Mark 11:12–14)

Because it was believed that the most wicked of humans served Satan, surely anyone practicing the evil eye was a sorcerer or a witch. The *MALLEUS MALEFICARUM*, for example, states that "There are witches who can BEWITCH their judges by a mere look or glance from their eyes."

Practicing the evil eye is frequently referred to as fascination, from the Latin word *fascinum*, which means "bewitching" or "enchanting." A famous early book on the power of fascination was the 1675 *Tractatus de Fascinatione* by Johannes Christian Fromann. DEL RIO, a demonologist writing in 1599 recorded, "Fascination is a power derived from a pact with the Devil, who, when the so-called fasinator looks at another with an evil intent . . . he infects with evil the person at whom he looks."

A TALISMAN or AMULET, such as a string of glass beads, most often colored blue, can be worn to protect against fascination. Painting a blue eyeball on or near the item to be protected is also effective. Christian icons such as crosses or an image of the Madonna and child are thought to be powerful weapons against the evil eye. Interestingly, the word *fascinum* can also refer to a countercharm to the evil eye, especially if it is phallic shaped.

If true believers catch themselves being eyed, they will unfailingly develop adverse reactions, possibly including sickness or even death. If the HEX is discovered in time, the victim can negate its effects by the use of an appropriate counter SPELL, the INCANTATION of magic words or by pointing a forked piece of coral at the evildoer. In India, the afflicted person will break the curse by having an old woman wrap sugar, pepper and rice in a piece of muslin, circle the bundle around the victim five times and then burn it.

Sometimes, having been eyed is not suspected until *after* something unfortunate happens (e.g., livestock dies, a hand develops palsy, churned milk never hardens into cheese). Only then will victims begin to guess who might have wished them harm. This distrust of one's neighbors alone is often enough to promote the superstitious belief in the evil eye. Those suspected of being likely to cast the evil eye are frequently the outsiders or the loners, the mentally infirm or the physically deformed in the community. Unfortunately, it is but a short jump from the belief that someone has given the evil eye to an accusation of WITCHCRAFT.

One of the most famous literary descriptions of the evil eye appears in Mark Twain's *The Adventures of Tom Sawyer*. Huckleberry Finn tells Sawyer how his father was enchanted by the evil eye of Mother Hopkins:

> She witched pap. Pap says so his own self. He come along one day, and he see she was witching him, so he took up a rock, and if she hadn't doged, he'd a got her. Well that very night he rolled off'n a shed where' he was a laying drunk, and broke his arm. . . . Pap says when they keep looking at you right stiddy, they're a witching you. Specially if they mumble. Becuz when they mumble they're saying the Lord's Prayer back-ards.

(See also VOODOO.)

Excalibur   Called Caliburn in the early Geoffrey of Monmouth version of the Arthurian legend, Excalibur was the mighty sword of King ARTHUR. The name might also be related to that of a famous Irish sword Caladbolg, which literally means "battle-sword." Sir Thomas MALORY says that *Excalibur* means "cut steel."

In some versions of the tale, Arthur was proclaimed king when he withdrew the sword from a stone, where it had been imbedded by MERLIN.

In Malory's *Le MORT D'ARTHUR*, however, King Arthur received Excalibur from the LADY OF THE LAKE. Arthur saved Merlin from an assault by three scoundrels, and the wizard accompanied the king as he rode to confront King Pellinore, a robust and skillful knight who was unlawfully challenging everyone he passed. Although Arthur fought bravely, Pellinore was stronger. He broke Arthur's sword and wounded the king, knocking him unconscious. As Pellinore was about to administer a death blow to Arthur, Merlin cast a SPELL that placed the knight into a deep sleep. Merlin took Arthur to a mystic hermit, who healed the king.

The wizard led King Arthur to an enchanted lake, where the king saw a hand sticking out of the water and holding the sword Excalibur. The mysterious Lady of the Lake appeared and offered the king the sword, complete with a jeweled scabbard, in exchange for the promise of a favor in the future. The king agreed and gladly received Excalibur, but Merlin advised Arthur that, extraordinary as the sword was, the scabbard was more precious: As long as Arthur wore the scabbard, he would not bleed!

When Arthur was mortally wounded in his fight against Mordred, he sent Sir Bedevere to throw the sword and scabbard back into the lake. As it flew across the surface, a hand reached out from the depths, caught Excalibur and disappeared back into the water.   (See also FILMS, *EXCALIBUR; SWORD IN THE STONE, THE; FAERIE QUEENE, THE.*)

Eye of Horus   In ancient EGYPTIAN MAGIC, the Eye of HORUS was depicted as a single, decorated eye and was used as one of the most powerful CHARMS against sinister forces. The Eye of Horus was considered to be particularly effective as protection against the EVIL EYE. Its representation is seen on artifacts, manuscripts and jewelry as well as tomb, temple and pyramid paintings from every Dynastic period.

A hieroglyph painting inside one of the pyramids of Unas, the last king of the Fifth Dynasty (c.3333 B.C.) reads:

The two Eyes of Horus include the white and the black. You must acquire them in order for you to be initiated. May they be focused on you.

More frequently, however, the single Eye of Horus is depicted as a right eye (variously called the *utchat, uchat* or *udjat*, and also occasionally called the white eye), representing the sun. The left eye (though seldom rendered in hieroglyphs) is known as the *mehit* or black eye and represents the moon.

The magical power of the Eye of Horus has its basis in the mythology of the pantheon of Egyptian gods. Horus, portrayed as a falcon-headed man, was the son of ISIS (mother) and Osiris (father). Horus constantly warred with his wicked uncle Set, who had murdered Horus's father. In one battle, Horus castrated Set; in another, Set ripped out the eye of Horus and, according to some sources, ate it.

THOTH, the god of magic and a great healer, restored Horus's eye. As a result, the emblematic Eye of Horus came to represent live-giving forces and resurrection and was soon adopted as an important funereal AMULET.

Over the centuries, the gods' familial relationships changed as the legends evolved. At some point, the Horus and Osiris myths merged so that Horus became identified with the living pharaoh, and Osiris came to represent the pharaoh while in death.

Horus, seen as part bird, was the sky god; so the Horus myths necessarily became intertwined with those of Ra (also seen as Re), the sun god. The combined name of the two gods was Re-Horakhty (meaning "Re-Horus of the horizon"), and, as such, the Eye of Horus was used to denote one of the aspects or attributes of Ra.

Faerie Queene, The An epic made up of individual tales in verse by Edmund Spenser (c.1552–99), six books of *The Faerie Queene* were completed, the first three published in 1590 and the second three divisions six years later. Scholars suggest that the design may have been patterned after the ORLANDO FURIOSO.

Although the entire composition as planned was never achieved, Spenser stated in his introduction that the work when completed was to consist of 12 poems, each telling an adventure of one of the Faerie Queene's knights. Each knight would symbolize a virtue that would be reflected in the moral of his quest. Just as the knights were allegorical, so too were all of the characters in the stories, such as the Faerie Queene (who represented both Glory and Queen Elizabeth I) and Prince ARTHUR (Magnificence, meaning magnanimity and chivalry). Several of the most virtuous women in the poem, such as Britomart and Belphoebe, also probably referred to the queen.

The six existing odes are laced with mystical creatures and references to wizards and sorcery:

Book I. The Redcrosse Knight of Holiness (i.e., the Anglican Church) protects Una (the true faith) from ARCHIMAGO (Hypocrisy) and Duessa (dishonesty; the Catholic Church; Mary, Queen of Scots).

Book II. When Sir Guyon, the Knight of Temperance battles Pyrochles (Flames of Rage), the latter attempts suicide by drowning. He is saved and nursed to health by the wizard Archimago, only to be later slain by Prince Arthur.

Cymochles (Loose Living), the husband of the sorceress ACRASIA (Intemperance), thinking his brother Pyrochles dead, sets out to attack Sir Guyon, but Phaedria (Frivolity) stops him. Cymochles is later killed by Prince Arthur.

In this book (viii.20–21), the name of the sword that MERLIN has forged for Arthur is given as *Morddure* rather than the more commonly used EXCALIBUR.

After discovering but passing by without plunder the treasure cave of Mammon (Wealth), Sir Guyon defeats Acrasia. In the process, Gryll is transformed back into a man, having been enchanted, changed into a hog and set to roam in her Bower. Gryll's name has Plutarch (c.50–125) as a source: the Greek philosopher and biographer identified Gryllus as one of Odysseus's men who was changed into swine by CIRCE, as recounted in Homer's *The ODYSSEY*.

Also in Book II, a fraudulent and egotistic knight named Braggadochio (Boasting) is attended by his squire Trophee. Trophee, a trickster, is described as

wylie witted, and growne old
In cunning sleights and practick knavery. [sic]

They are both eventually unmasked and are thrown out of the castle.

Book III. Britomart, the female knight of Chastity, sees the reflection of Sir Artegall (Justice) in a magic mirror. She instantly falls in love with him, and they marry following her search for him.

Belphoebe, a female hunter also embodying Chastity, exiles Braggadochio. With an understanding of herbal FOLK MEDICINE, she nurses Timias, Prince Arthur's page, back to health. To thank her, Timias helps Belphoebe save her twin sister Amoret (Noble Grace) from Corlambo (Lust). Corlambo is later killed by Prince Arthur.

Book IV. Amoret marries Sir Scudamour, but on their wedding day she is stolen and jailed by the sorcerer BUSIRANE. Belphoebe, however, is able to rescue her sister. Timias falls in love with Amoret, but Belphoebe upbraids him—purportedly a thinly veiled reference to Queen Elizabeth's irritation over Sir Walter Ralegh's attentions to Elizabeth Throckmorton.

True Friendship is displayed by Cambell (also seen as Cambello) and Sir Triamond. Cambell offers to joust three brothers who are suitors for his sister Canacee. Only Triamond is undefeated, although he is wounded. Triamond's sister Cambrina intervenes, the men become best friends, Cambell marries Cambrina, and Triamond (healed by Canacee's magic RING) marries Canacee.

Book V. The adventures of Artegall, highly metaphorical of contemporary political and military events in the time of Spenser, are told.

Book VI. Sir Calidore, personifying Courtesy, travels the realm of the Faerie Queene. Included in the tale is his capture of the Blatant Beast. The monster, representing Envy and Denigration, eventually breaks its chains and is still loose in the world.

Two surviving sketches for Book VII, known as the Mutabilitie Cantos, suggest that the section was to have concerned the orderly procession of the seasons and of nature, including such allegorical characters as Jove, Titaness Mutabilitie and Constancie.

Fairy and Folk Tales of the Irish Peasantry See CELTIC TWILIGHT, THE; COUNTESS KATHLEEN, THE; YEATS, WILLIAM BUTLER.

Fairy Godmother See CINDERELLA; FILMS, CINDERELLA; GUARDIAN ANGEL.

Fairy Legends and Traditions in the South of Ireland

A forerunner of such works as William Butler YEATS's *The* CELTIC TWILIGHT and *Fairy and Folk Tales of the Irish Peasantry*, along with the whole Irish Revival movement, *Fairy Legends and Traditions in the South of Ireland* was published by Thomas Crofton Croker (1798–1854) and released in 1825 and 1828.

Croker is credited with being the first to collect traditional Irish legends, myths and tales as well-crafted stories, elevating them from oral folklore into a written national art form. Among his other books are *Researches in the South of Ireland* (1824), *Legends of the Lakes* (1829) and *Popular Songs of Ireland* (1839).

familiar A familiar is a demon that supposedly attends to and accompanies an enchantress or sorcerer, sometimes taking human form but more often appearing as a common animal, such as a CAT, dog, goat or lizard. The Devil assigns the familiar(s) to the witch to act as his liaison. Many times, the familiar actually carries out the witch's CURSEs.

Although the modern concept of the familiar is a largely English and Scottish contribution to WITCHCRAFT folklore, belief in such creatures long predated Reginald Scot's use of the term in his DISCOVERIE OF WITCHCRAFT (1584).

The term *familiar* may be derived from the phrase *familiar* SPIRIT, used in occult writings such as *The Clavicle or The* KEY OF SOLOMON. Solomon (the manuscript's purported author) explained that it was possible to employ specific invocations to "render the Angels familiar" (i.e., gain knowledge of and

The Devil, portrayed as a black man in clerical gown with a witch's hat, gives a familiar to one of his disciples. (John Ashton, *Chap-Books of the Eighteenth Century*, London, 1882)

control over them). "By the use of their seals and characters, render them familiar unto thee," was Solomon's charge.

The Key of Solomon was required reading not only for all cabalists and sorcerers, but also for all those who wished to oppose them. The PAPACY, for example, decreed that all sorcerers' invocations and conjurations were diabolical rather than angelic: therefore, the familiar spirits that they summoned were necessarily demonic. Likewise, a personal spiritual aide or familiar, in whatever form it assumed, was by definition a devil incarnate. The belief that familiars appeared as ordinary animals also made the job of the witch-hunters and the INQUISITION that much easier: a black cat, hoot owl or mouse surely could be found in the house or stables of anyone they wished to accuse.

Many notables were suspected of harboring familiars. AGRIPPA is alleged to have kept a black dog named Monsieur as a familiar. The familiar of the 15th-century French sorcerer Jehanneret Reynal-le-Boiteux was named Josaphat. The enemies of Oliver Cromwell (1599–1658) accused him of having a familiar named Grimoald. Other familiars named in occult literature were Phrin, Rapho, Robin and Zewuiel.

Fantasia Produced by Walt Disney and released in 1940, the inspired animation FILM *Fantasia* used classical music as the backdrop for its visuals. The 135-minute Technicolor film was supervised by Ben Sharpsteen and featured Leopold Stokowski conducting the Philadelphia Orchestra. Perhaps the best-remembered segment—and certainly the most closely visualized from its musical source—was Mickey Mouse portraying *The Sorcerer's Apprentice*.

The Sorcerer's Apprentice by the Parisian composer Paul Dukas (1865–1935) was first performed on May 17, 1897, and has remained his most popular piece. It had as its source a poem by the German poet Goethe (see FAUST) who, in turn, was inspired by an ancient legend. In his master's absence, the apprentice magician places the sorcerer's cap on his head and intones the magic words to animate a BROOMSTICK, commanding it to fetch water from a well to fill the sorcerer's bath. Unfortunately, the apprentice is unable to get the broom to stop, and soon the bath is overflowing. Panicked, the apprentice chops the broom with an ax. Both halves regenerate, and two brooms resume the chore. (In the Disney animated version, a single broom is multiplied into hundreds.) The cave is flooded, and the apprentice is almost drowned. Suddenly, the sorcerer returns. With a broad gesture, he makes the brooms stop and the water vanish, and his piercing glare and grumbling makes the sorcerer's apprentice hide his head in shame.

At least two other movies based on the legend of the sorcerer's apprentice predated *Fantasia*. In 1930, Hugo Reisenfeld and the Artcinema Association produced *The Wizard's Apprentice*. A few years later, the Compagnie Française des Films shot a version of *Der Zauberlehrling*, the Goethe work upon which Dukas based his composition. It is the Disney version, however, that will remain in the minds of moviegoers for ages to come.

One of the main reasons Walt Disney wanted to produce *Fantasia* was to update and reintroduce Mickey Mouse, who had appeared in a series of black-and-white animated cartoon shorts, to a new, wider movie audience. For Mickey's comeback, supervising animator Fred Moore and his associates made Mickey shorter, plumper and cuter (i.e., more lovable). Pupils were added to Mickey's eyes for the first time, and while still a humorous character, Mickey used less slapstick comedy in his actions.

For his role in *The Sorcerer's Apprentice*, Mickey Mouse was dressed in a loose red robe, with a corded belt bow-tied at the waist and long, brown slippers. (Moore revealed that the bouncy long hair of the athletic live-action model for Mickey gave him clues as to the motion of the apprentice's robe.) Perched on Mickey's head was his master's conical hat, decorated with a crescent moon, stars and other astronomical symbols.

The apprentice's master, the sorcerer, remained anonymous in the works by Goethe and Dukas, but he was given a name for *Fantasia*: Yen Sid (i.e., *Disney* spelled backwards). Nigel de Brulier, a silent-film star, became the live-action model from whose movements the animators created Yen Sid. The result is a frightening, yet fatherly figure, tall and bearded and dressed in a full-length blue robe with billowing sleeves.

The first piece of animation done for the entire film (and, therefore, for *The Sorcerer's Apprentice* as well) was the climactic segment in which Mickey dreams he is directing the movements of the stars and the planets. Rising, splashing water wakes him from his sleep. He realizes that the living broomsticks are out of control and that he must somehow stop them. Preston Blair did the live-action research and initial animation; Ugo D'Orsi inked in special water effects. None of the characters spoke, so no voice work was necessary for this segment.

Also depicted in *Fantasia* is *Night on Bald Mountain*, an 1867 tone poem composed by the Russian Modeste Petrovich Mussorgsky (also seen as Mussorsksy) (1839–1881). Originally entitled *St. John's Night on the Bare Mountain*, the work was inspired, at least in part, by Franz Liszt's *Totentanz* (*Dance of Death*) and Nikola Gogol's story "St. John's Eve." The orchestral composition impressively illustrates the Russian legend that each year on St. John's Eve, June 23, witches fly from all over the country for a SABBAT on the Bald Mountains near Kiev. There, they celebrate a BLACK MASS until dawn. (A similar German legend surrounding Walpurgis Night was the inspiration for the Act IV ballet music of Gounod's OPERA *FAUST*.

Mussorgsky actually composed *Night on Bald Mountain* on St. John's Eve 1867, and it remained one of his favorite pieces. Mussorgsky wrote:

> . . . the witches used to gather on this mountain, gossip, play tricks and await their chief—Satan. On his arrival they . . . formed a circle round the throne on which he sat in the form of a goat and sang his praise. When Satan was worked up into sufficient passion by the witches' praises, he gave the command for the sabbath in which he chose for himself the witches who caught his fancy.

Perhaps because of its subject matter, Mussorgsky had difficulty obtaining a performance of the work. He eventually revised it and placed it within his opera *Sorotchinsk Fair*. In 1881, after the composer's death, his friend Rimsky-Korsakov removed the selection, reorchestrated it and published it as *Night on the Bald Mountain*. It is this, the best-known and most popular version of the piece, that Disney used for *Fantasia*.

Essential to the success of the film's Bald Mountain segment was the creation of a nightmarish, horrifying Lord Demon. The terrifying Chernabog was created by Ukrainian animator Bill Tytla. He explained his inspiration in a 1976 John Canemaker article in *Cinéfantastique*:

> . . . for the devil on Bald Mountain . . . I did some reading about Mussorgsky. He talked about "Chorni-bok," the Black Art. Ukrainian folklore is based on "Chorni-bok."

According to the legend, the top of Bare Mountain, perched high above a sleeping village, is actually the back of the fiery demon Chernabog. On St. John's Eve, he awakens for a single night. Monstrous in size, Chernabog shrieks to the valley before, awakening the dead and summoning his hellish minions. Dancing skeletons, imps and ghouls, witches on broomsticks, fiends and phantoms, SPIRITS, specters and ghosts all attend him. They madly dance their dervishes, but at the first hint of dawn, Chernabog commands them to return back to their graves, tombs and sepulchers.

In *Fantasia*, the nighttime spectacle dissolves to a sunrise pilgrimage through the misty forest by torch-bearing Christians, who sing Schubert's "Ave Maria" (with new lyrics by poet Rachel Field). While many viewers appreciate the calming effect of the hymn after such a feverish scene, critics contended that their mismatched juxtaposition destroyed the full impact of both pieces, the pandemonium *and* the prayer.

Multiplane cameras, which give an illusion of three-dimensional depth to animation, were used for the first time in the making of *Fantasia*. Special Academy Awards for their unique achievement were bestowed upon both Disney and Stokowski. In 1990, prior to a home-video/laser-disc sale, the film was given a theatrical rerelease with a restored print and a new digital orchestral recording.

fascination   See EVIL EYE.

fata   From the Italian word for "FAIRY," a fata is a female occult figure first seen in Italian medieval literature. Although a supernatural creature, she is usually under the power of the demon Demogorgon.

The term *fata* is also sometimes used as a shortened form of *FATA MORGANA*, a mirage seen over water.

fata morgana   Originally, the term *fata morgana* meant a strange, shimmering mirage over water. They were first reported in the area of the Straits of Messina off Sicily or along the coastline of Calabria, Italy. *FATA* is the Italian word for "fairy." *Morgana* alludes to the Arthurian enchantress, Morgan LE FAY, who, according to the early Normans in England, lived in the Italian Straits.

Today the term *fata morgana* still usually refers to the SPIRIT or apparition of a female, but the phrase can also mean any illusionary image appearing on a watery surface (such as a lake or the sea) or in the air directly above it. The phrase is sometimes used more generally to mean any alluring, yet dangerous phenomenon.

Fata Morgana is also the name of a character in the epic poem *ORLANDO INNAMORATO*. *Fata Morgana* is the title of a 1924 American play by Ernst Vajda, produced by the Theatre Guild and starring Emily Stevens as Morgana, and a 1995 book (unrelated to the watery legends) by Lynn Stegner.

Faust   Begun by Johann Wolfgang von Goethe (1749–1832) around 1770 and completed before his death in 1832, this masterpiece of German drama was a lifelong work for Goethe and sets the legend of Johannes FAUSTUS in allegorical terms. Divided by the author into two parts, the first (12,111 lines) was published in 1808, and the second (with 7,499 lines in five acts) followed in 1832.

The original verses composed by Goethe, in essence the first draft of *Faust*, were completed in 1775 and are now known as the *Urfaust*. It detailed much of the story of Marguerite but lacked character motivation and resolution. Goethe added a few more scenes in 1788 and published the incomplete poem as *Faust. Ein Fragment* in 1790.

Following a 1794 meeting, Johann Christoph Friedrich von Schiller (1759–1805) urged Goethe to resume work on *Faust*. Although Part I was more or less completed by 1800–1801, Goethe always hoped to extend the narrative. He finally published Part I, which ended with the death of Faust's beloved Marguerite, in 1808.

As far back as 1797, Goethe had planned to write the more-metaphysical Part II of *Faust*, and he completed one scene, "Helena," in 1800. Two decades passed. Finally, goaded by his secretary Eckermann, Goethe started to work in earnest in 1825. He separately published *Helena. Classic-Romantic Phantasmagoria. Interlude to Faust* in 1827. Revised, this later became part of Act Three of Part II. Continuing composition in both directions from Faust's encounter with Helen of Troy, Goethe finished *Faust* in the summer of 1831. (The last section to be completed was part of Act Four.)

Knowing that Part II would be quite controversial (both artistically and ideologically), Goethe insisted that it not be printed until after his death. In 1832, *Faust, The Second Part of the Tragedy, in Five Acts*, was published.

In the Prologue to Part I, set in heaven, Mephistopheles challenges God that he can entice Faust into selling his soul. God agrees to the wager, confident in Faust's ability to ward off temptation.

Goethe's Faust is characterized much differently than Marlowe's DOCTOR FAUSTUS in the play of that name. As Goethe's play begins, Faust is seen less a power-mad sorcerer than a melancholy man who has given up on the world in which he lives. As in Marlowe, Faust is attended by his valet Wagner.

Mephistopheles appears in Faust's chambers. The Devil, ever smiling, is "clad like a traveling scholar . . . with a sword at his side and a feather in his hat." He offers to show Goethe "more [joy] than any man has ever seen before" in exchange for his soul. Mephistopheles asks him to sign the pact in blood ("Just write a line or two at least"), but Faust insists that his word is good.

They first travel to Auerbach's Tavern in Leipzig. (Auerbach's Keller, opened in 1525, actually exists and was a favorite drinking spot of university-student Goethe. The tavern remains open today as a restaurant and tourist attraction.) After an exchange of comic, rowdy songs with the inn's customers, Mephistopheles magically produces wine for them. They recognize him as a demon, and he quickly vanishes with Faust in arm.

In a "Witch's Kitchen," Mephistopheles shows Faust a vision of Marguerite in a magic mirror. He then asks the witch to give Faust a youth/love philtre. Faust is brought into a MAGIC CIRCLE. The witch intones an elaborate INCANTATION, and Faust drinks.

Faust passes Marguerite (variously called Margaret, Gretchen and Gretel) in the street and falls in love. Mephistopheles delivers Faust to her bedchamber, and the pair become lovers. To prevent their being disturbed, Faust gives the girl a sleeping potion (which he received from Mephistopheles) to put in her mother's bedtime drink.

Marguerite becomes pregnant; unwed, her reputation is ruined. Valentine, her brother, CURSES her and is killed in a sword fight with Faust. To prevent Faust's capture, Mephistopheles whisks him away to the Harz Mountains, where they experience the witches' SABBAT on Walpurgis Night.

Faust has a vision of Marguerite with a red line of blood around her neck. She has been imprisoned and condemned to die for killing her baby and poisoning her mother (who died from an overdose of sleeping potion). Faust demands that Mephistopheles take him to his lover.

Faust attempts to rescue Marguerite, but, guilt-ridden and repentant, she refuses to leave her cell. She recognizes Faust's companion as the Devil and prays to God for deliverance and salvation. Faust and Mephistopheles must flee at daybreak, but as they depart the Devil triumphantly proclaims, "She is condemned!" A heavenly voice corrects him: "Is saved!"

Part II of *Faust* is less plot oriented and more metaphorical. It, too, can be broken into two sections, the first part (originally intended as a separate poem) concerns Faust's confrontation of ideal Beauty, as personified by Helen of Troy (here named Helena). Mephistopheles calls up her SPIRIT from Hades, and Faust relentlessly pursues her. Eventually, she is parted from him, but not before they produce a son, Euphorion. The boy comes to represent poetry and the merging of classic and romantic thought, as embodied by Lord Byron, before he disappears in flames. The Devil offers to summon up more images of beauty; Faust will lose his soul only if he finds one so beautiful that he exclaims, "Stay, thou art so fair."

A series of diversions follow in which Mephistopheles tries to trick Faust into uttering the terrible oath. Several scenes in Goethe's *Faust* are later depicted by Marlowe, but they differ in detail and purpose. There is a section in both, for example, in which the sorcerer performs for the court at a ruler's palace. While Marlowe uses this part of the tale to show the might of Faustus's magic, Goethe employs it allegorically to point out the vanity and avarice of royalty. Goethe, for instance, does not give a specific name to the emperor, any of his minions or the commoners, perhaps in an attempt to suggest the universality of his themes.

Mephistopheles sits beside the emperor, who is more interested in an upcoming carnival than ruling the business affairs of his kingdom—which, according to the citizens, is in ruins. The Devil transforms himself into a jester, flatters the emperor and then offers money for the bankrupt country. Although the chancellor recognizes the evil in the outsiders, referring to them as "the black magician" and "the wizard and the fool [who] live hide in hide," he is ignored. A court astrologer, under the influence of Mephistopheles proclaims that untold amounts of gold will be discovered and mined. To prevent the emperor from demanding an immediate production of the gold, the demon has the astrologer insist that the carnival begin.

In the final acts, Four and Five, Faust recants his heathen worldliness. Secure in his belief that he is saved, he utters the dreaded words: "Ah, stay, thou art so fair." Faust immediately dies. Mephistopheles attempts to claim his soul, but God sends angels to carry the reclaimed sinner to heaven.

One of the best foreign translations of *Faust* was the Russian edition completed by Boris Pasternak (1890–1960) during Stalin's publication ban (1933–1943) of the Soviet author's original works. Among the many works that were directly inspired by Goethe's *Faust* were the OPERAS *The Damnation of Faust* (Berlioz) and *Faust* (Gounod).

Faustbuch   Appearing in German in Frankfort in 1587, *Faustbuch*, or *Faustbook*, was a volume of short stories about an evil sorcerer, loosely based on legends surrounding the life of Johannes FAUSTUS. Written from a conservative Protestant perspective, the tales were part myth and part morality tale.

The *Faustbuch* was clearly a product of its age. At the time of the *Faustbuch*'s publication, scientists and philosophers throughout Europe—men such as Galileo and Sir Walter Raleigh—were being rebuked by the church or charged with heresy for challenging the established theological views of creation and the universe. "Free thinkers" were especially suspect of being in league with the Devil. In addition to its anti–Roman Catholic rhetoric, *Faustbuch* was also entertaining and well written, making it a best-seller that was quickly translated into many languages.

Although the Faust legend would be the inspiration for countless works of literature even up to modern day, the *Faustbuch* itself was the most direct source for Christopher Marlowe's play *The Tragicall History of the Life and Death of Doctor Faustus*. Despite the obvious borrowing of themes and incidents by Marlowe, the correlation has puzzled Elizabethan-period scholars because DOCTOR FAUSTUS (as it was known) was thought to have been written in 1590, two years before the English translation of *Faustbuch*, published as *The historie of the damnable life, and deserved death of Doctor John Faustus*.

Faustus, Johannes (fl. 1480–1540)   The legend of FAUST, who sold his soul to the Devil in exchange for infinite knowledge, has some basis in a historical personage. Although little is known for certain about his background and life, Johannes (also seen as Johann) Faustus was infamous throughout middle Europe between 1480 and 1540 as a German scholar, an itinerant magician and possibly a doctor.

Those who were kindest thought him a harmless charlatan or street entertainer, performing with a trained dog and educated horse. Others less charitable considered him a con man and drunkard/vagrant. His enemies, or at least those in awe and/or fear of him, thought that he was a sorcerer. It was claimed that Faustus had studied BLACK MAGIC in Cracow, Poland, and began to practice NECROMANCY after damning his soul in a pact with the Devil. Faustus's dog and horse were said to be demons, or at the very least his FAMILIARS.

These last tales most captured the imagination of superstitious people of the times. Legends enumerating the purported feats of Faustus, or Faust as he because known, culminated in the publication of the FAUSTBUCH in 1587.

The first great adaptation of the legend into dramatic form was *The Tragicall History of the Life and Death of Doctor Faustus* (see DOCTOR FAUSTUS) by Christopher Marlowe. Probably the most influential poem concerning the Faust legend was the narrative poem FAUST by Goethe.

Musical works based, at least in part, on it include the following: the OPERAs *The Damnation of Faust* by Hector Berlioz, *Faust* by Charles Gounod and *Mefistofele* by Arrigo Boito; lesser operas by Spohr, Lutz, Brüggemann, Busoni and Louise Bertin; *Le petit Faust*, a popular operetta by Florimond Hervé; Schubert's version of Marguerite's "Spinning Song"; Franz Lizst's 1854 *Faust Symphony*, plus several additional songs; Richard Wagner's *Faust Overture*; and pieces by Schumann and Spontini.

Plays include Robert Greene's FRIER BACON, AND FRIER BONGAY; *The MERRY DEVIL OF EDMONTON; MELMOTH THE WANDERER* by C.R. Maturin; the allegory of *Peter Schlemihls* by Adelbert von Chamisso and *The COUNTESS KATHLEEN*, an 1892 play by William Butler YEATS; and *Doktor Faustus*, published in 1947 by Thomas Mann, which used the legend as a metaphor for Germany embracing Nazism, a theme he further explored two years later in his book *Die Entstehung des Doktor Faustus (The Genesis of Doctor Faustus)*.

In many variations of the tale, the Devil arrives unbidden and the confrontation and subsequent offer are not always the result of sorcery. Such is the case with Lord Byron's unfinished play *The DEFORMED TRANSFORMED* and the Broadway musical *Damn Yankees*. (See also FILMS; MUSICAL THEATER.)

Festus   Written in verse form by Philip James Bailey (1816–1902), *Festus* is a variation of Goethe's FAUST. After Satan receives permission from God to tempt Festus, the mortal is attended by both the Devil and his GUARDIAN ANGEL. Though supremely tempted, Festus is welcomed into the Elect Spirits after the Last Judgment.

After a short career as a trial lawyer at Lincoln's Inn, England, Bailey moved back home to Old Basset, near Nottingham, to begin work on his manuscript. *Festus* was begun in 1836 and first published three years later. An expanded edition arrived in 1845, followed in 1855 by a massive final edition (more than 40,000 lines) that included three previously published works of poetry (*The Angel World*, 1850; *The Mystic*, 1855; and *The Universal Hymn*, 1867).

fetish   See AMULET.

films   Since the invention of motion pictures, filmmakers have been intrigued with the medium's possibilities in the field of fantasy. In fact, one of the earliest "flicks," Georges Méliès's 1902 animation-and-live action *A Trip to the Moon* (also seen titled as *Voyage to the Moon*), was just such a flight of the imagination. In its most famous sequence, a bullet-shaped rocket ship hits the man in the moon in the right eye.

Today, "sword & sorcery" films are a vibrant subgenre of fantasy films, and with the seemingly endless possibilities of digital special effects, acts of wizardry and witchcraft can be shown on the screen as never before.

Hundreds of films, from action-adventure to animation, have featured occult themes and/or leading characters who were wizards, sorcerers, witches or enchanters. Thumbnail sketches of some of the more important films in the field follow.

Adventures of Sir Galahad　(Columbia; 1949) The holiest knight from the court of King ARTHUR goes on a quest to find EXCALIBUR. Galahad was played by George Reeves (who would later portray SUPERMAN on TELEVISION).

Aladdin　(Walt Disney; 1992) This animated feature is roughly based on parts of the tales of the *ARABIAN NIGHTS*. In faraway Agrabah, a street waif named Aladdin (voiced by Scott Weinger) falls in love at first sight with Princess Jasmine (Linda Larkin), much to the consternation of his pet monkey Abu (Frank Welker). Aladdin is sent to recover a mystical lamp from a deep cavern, where he is trapped. He rubs the lamp and out pops a big, blue, boisterous and bouncy genie (Robin Williams) (see JINN), eager to treat the boy to three wishes. Unfortunately, the evil Jafar (Jonathan Freeman) and his loud-mouthed parrot Iago (Gilbert Gottfried) stand in Aladdin's way to happiness.

Aladdin was the top box-office film of the year, and it won two Academy Awards: Best Score (Alan Menken) and Best Song, "A Whole New World" (Menken, Rim Rice).

The success of the film prompted Disney's first direct-to-video animated feature, the sequel *The Return of Jafar* (1994). A thief accidentally allows Jafar to escape from his magic lamp. Still an "all-powerful genie," he plans his vengeance against Aladdin, Jasmine and the genie (voiced by Don Castellaneta, replacing Robin Williams). In a third direct-to-video animated feature, *Aladdin and the King of Thieves* (1996), Aladdin and Jasmine marry following the prince's adventures with Ali Baba and the 40 Thieves. Williams returned to voice the genie.

In additional, Disney has released a home-video series entitled *Aladdin's Arabian Adventures*. An Aladdin cartoon series has also been produced for children's television.

The Alchemist　(Video Forum/Ideal Films; 1981) A man (Robert Ginty) is plagued by an ancient CURSE, which is lifted by an enchantress.

Alias Nick Beal　(Paramount; 1949) In a modern update of the FAUST legend, a stranger (Ray Milland) offers money and power to a politician.

All That Money Can Buy　(RKO; 1941) In this film based on the FAUST-inspired story *The* DEVIL AND DANIEL WEBSTER by Stephen Vincent Benét, Webster (Edward Arnold) defends a 19th-century New Hampshire farmer who signed a pact with the Devil, Mr. Scratch (Walter Huston). He then puts Satan on trial to win the man's freedom.

Angel Heart　(Tri-Star; 1987) Based on the novel *Falling Angel* by William Hjortsberg, this adaptation of the FAUST legend is set in New York in 1955. The signer of a pact wants to be let out of his agreement after being taken away by Satan (Robert De Niro). A private detective (Mickey Bourke) sets out on the trail of the "missing person," eventually following him into the pit of hell.

Arabian Adventure　(Badger Films, Great Britain; 1979) A prince wishes to marry the daughter of the ruler of Jadur, but the monarch first insists that the young man bring him a

In his pioneering film *Voyage to the Moon*, Georges Méliès shows the visual possibilities of the new medium.

magical rose. This adaptation of the *ARABIAN NIGHTS* tale includes a flying carpet and a genie (see JINN) in a bottle.

Arabian Knight　(1995; animated) Zigzag, an evil sorcerer, locks up Tack, a young cobbler's apprentice, in the royal dungeons. Princess Yum Yum, the king's daughter, meets Tack, and they fall in love. Zigzag asks for the princess's hand in marriage, but he is refused. His attacks to avenge his "honor" are thwarted by Tack and Princess Yum Yum.

Beastmaster　(EMI; 1982) In a cult sword-and-sorcery favorite, a king's baby is stolen by a sorceress. He is saved by a commoner, who unaware of the boy's noble birth, raises him and teaches him the martial arts he later uses to recapture his inheritance. Marc Singer played the title role in this and its two sequels (1991, 1995).

Beauty and the Beast　See BEAUTY AND THE BEAST.

Bedazzled　(TCF, Great Britain; 1967) A cook considers suicide but is talked out of it by Mr. Spiggott. More the FAUST legend than *It's a Wonderful Life*, Spiggott turns out to be the Devil, who offers the cook seven wishes in exchange for his immortal soul.

Bedknob and Broomsticks　(Walt Disney; 1971) *Bedknobs and Broomsticks* tells the story of three children and a befuddled witch (Angela Lansbury) who fight victoriously to stop an invasion of England in 1940. The many magical special effects include a battle scene with SPIRIT-infested suits of armor. Also, in lieu of using a BROOMSTICK, the enchantress and the children ride on a flying bedstead.

Bell, Book and Candle　(Columbia; 1958) Based on the comic stage play by John Van Druten, a publisher (James Stewart) becomes aware that his girlfriend (Kim Novak) is actually a witch.

Belle et la Bête, La　(Discina, France; 1946) Written and directed by Jean Cocteau from the original story by Madame LePrince de Beaumont, this remains the classic film against which all other adaptations of BEAUTY AND THE BEAST are judged.

Black Cat, The (Universal; 1934) Starring Boris Karloff and Bela Lugosi, *The Black Cat* involves a doctor seeking the death of a traitorous Austrian architect and satanist. The movie shows an amusing BLACK MASS scene.

Black Cauldron, The (Walt Disney Prods.; 1985; animated) As its premise, *The Black Cauldron*, based on *The Chronicles of Prydain* by Lloyd Alexander, tells of ancient times, when the gods buried an evil king, still alive, in a CAULDRON of molten iron. Anyone finding it would be able to raise an army of immortal, demonic warriors—the Cauldron Born—as his personal slaves.

In the mythical land of Prydain, Taran (voiced by Grant Bardsley), a young boy living with Dallben (Freddie Jones), an old wizard, takes care of Hen Wen, a pig that also happens to be an ORACLE. The source and extant of Dallben's powers is not revealed, but he consults an arcane GRIMOIRE entitled *The Book of Three*.

By scrying (see DIVINATION), Dallben perceives that the Horned King (John Hurt) is seeking Hen Wen to force it to locate the Black Cauldron. Taran flees with the pig, winds up being captured and jailed with Eilonway (Susan Sheridan), a princess and apprentice enchantress.

They escape with Fflam (Nigel Hawthorne), a minstrel who was also imprisoned. They are joined by Gurgi (John Byner), a hairy doglike creature and a friend of Taran. The boy finds a magical sword, and they soon arrive in the marshes of Mordu.

There, they spy the hut of the three witches of Morva, Orddu, Orgoch and Orwen (Eda Reiss Merin, Billie Hayes and Adele Malia-Morey, respectively). As they enter the cottage, hundreds of frogs (actually people who had been transformed by the witches) hop off to freedom. The party discovers that the room is filled with cauldrons.

The witches return. Orddu, the largest of the three hags, turns Fflam into a frog, but the SPELL is reversed by Orwen, who has taken quite a liking to him.

Taran boldly demands to be given the Black Cauldron. In a fury, the sorceresses animate their kitchen utensils to battle the heroes, but the implements are beaten back by the magical sword, which comes alive to fight off attack. As the suggestion of Orddu, the witches trade the Black Cauldron for the sword.

The Horned King and his men arrive and seize the Black Cauldron. Back at his castle, the king tosses in skeletons, which emerge alive as the Cauldron Born. To stop the cauldron, Gurgi jumps in.

The hellish corps of warriors vanishes, but the cauldron becomes a maelstromlike whirlpool. The Horned King is drawn in, and he, his castle and his henchmen are destroyed.

The witches of Morva return, hoping to win back the Black Cauldron. Knowing that its power for evil is gone, Taran agrees to release the cauldron; in exchange, the witches return Gurgi to them alive.

In the final scene, it's seen that, by scrying, the wizard Dallben, with Hen Wen at his side, has been watching the final events unfold.

Black Magic (Edward Small; 1949) Involved in political intrigue, CAGLIOSTRO (Orson Welles) plans to magically produce a twin of Marie Antoinette (Nancy Guild).

Black Sunday (Galatra/Jolly, Italy; 1960) A witch (Barbara Steele) is tortured and killed by being pressed and punctured in an Iron Maiden, but she returns from the grave to avenge her death.

Boom! (Universal/World Film Services/Moon Lake Productions; 1968) On a Mediterranean island, a fatally-ill millionairess (Elizabeth Taylor) takes a poet (Richard Burton) as her lover. He turns out to be the Angel of Death. Noel Coward portrays the Witch of Capri. The screenplay for the British film was written by Tennessee Williams, based on his play *The Milk Train Doesn't Stop Here Any More*.

Brass Bottle, The (U-I/Scarus; 1964) Based on the novel by F. Anstey. An architect (Tony Randall) buys a bottle in an antique shop, opens it and releases Fakrash, a pesky and unruly genie (Burl Ives) (see JINN). Frustrated and dispirited because the architect won't let him annihilate anybody, Fakrash transforms the father of his master's girlfriend (Barbara Eden) into a mule. Ironically, Barbara Eden soon went on to portray a "Jeannie" herself in television's *I Dream of Jeannie* (1965–70).

Camelot See MUSICAL THEATER, CAMELOT.

Captain Sinbad (King Brothers, U.S./Germany; 1963) Sinbad (Guy Williams) uses wizardry to upset the evil sultan of Baristan (Pedro Armendariz).

Care Bears Movie, The (Nelvana; 1985) In this animated feature, the Care Bears use their special brand of WHITE MAGIC to ward off a nasty SPIRIT.

Carmen Jones See OPERA, CARMEN.

Chandu the Magician (Fox; 1932) More a spiritualist medium than a wizard, Chandu (Edmund Lowe) fights a lunatic (Bela Lugosi) who threatens the world with a death ray. Several early serials were reedited into two feature sequels: *Chandu and the Magic Isle* and *The Return of Chandu*.

A popular radio serial based on the same character aired in the United States from 1932 to 1950. *Chandu, the Magician* followed the adventures of the American-born mystic Frank Chandler (portrayed by Gayne Whitman and later Tom Collins) as he fought evil as an agent for the U.S. federal government. Chandu received his magical wisdom and occult powers by training with a yogi in India.

Cinderella (Walt Disney; 1950) When Disney animated this classic PERRAULT fairy tale, all of the gruesome elements of the original CINDERELLA story (such as the wicked stepmother cutting off her daughter's heel to fit the slipper) were removed. Still, the basic and most magical elements remain: the maiden in ashes, a fairy godmother, the handsome prince and a happily-ever-after.

The Fairy Godmother (voiced by Verna Felton) who comes to Cinderella's rescue is a GUARDIAN ANGEL character. Disney animators portrayed her as a lovable granny type, a bit stout with a plump, dimpled face, white hair and wearing a hooded cloak. Cheery but absent-minded, she often misplaces her own magic WAND. Casting her SPELL with the magic words *bibbidy bobbidy boo*, she transforms a pumpkin into a carriage, mice into horses, the horse Major into a coachman and the dog Bruno into a footman. Of course, she also produces the glass slippers. Finally, she warns Cinderella (Ilene Woods) that the SPELL will only last until midnight, after which time everything will change back to what it once was.

City of the Dead (Vulcan, Great Britain; released in the United States as *Horror Hotel*; 1960) A witch (Patricia Jessel), thought to have been burned at the stake in Massachusetts at the beginning of the 18th century, is actually still alive and well and running a hotel. Unfortunately, many of the guests never get to check out: they become casualties of her revenge against humanity.

Conan the Barbarian (Dino de Laurentiis/Edward R. Pressman; 1981) Based on the character created by Robert E. Howard. In the Dark Ages, the warrior Conan (Arnold Schwarzenegger), armed with a magic sword, avenges his parents who were murdered by a savage tribe led by a occultist master.

Conan the Destroyer (Dino de Laurentiis; 1984) Conan (Arnold Schwarzenegger) returns. A wicked sorceress (Grace Jones) promises to resurrect Conan's recently-deceased lover from the grave if he succeeds at an impossible undertaking she has set for him. To accomplish his goal, Conan requires magic as well as might.

Connecticut Yankee, A (Fox; 1931) Two other versions of Mark Twain's classic *A CONNECTICUT YANKEE IN KING ARTHUR'S COURT* were filmed in 1929 (silent) and 1949 (sound). This was the first sound adaptation, with Will Rogers playing the Yankee who dreams himself back into the court of King ARTHUR, where he is mistaken for a wizard.

Connecticut Yankee in King Arthur's Court, A (Paramount; 1949) Although charming, this musical comedy adaptation takes great liberties with the Twain classic in order to serve as a star vehicle for Bing Crosby. Rodgers and Hammerstein (see MUSICAL THEATER, CINDERELLA declined to work on the film project, so Johnny Burke and Jimmy Van Heusen, contract composers for Paramount, were given the film.

Crucible, The See *CRUCIBLE, THE*; SALEM WITCHCRAFT TRIALS.

Cry of the Banshee (AIP, Great Britain; 1970) Set in the 16th century, a sorceress (Elisabeth Bergner) lays a CURSE on the local magistrate (Vincent Price). She CONJURES a demon who, in human guise, sets out to vanquish the judge.

Curse of the Crimson Altar (Tigon/AIP, Great Britain: also released as *The Crimson Cult*; 1968) Boris Karloff and Christopher Lee, two notable actors famous for their work in the horror genre, star in a story of satanism and WITCHCRAFT at an English country estate.

Damn Yankees (Warner; 1958) Adapted by George Abbott from on his own musical play based on the novel *The Year the Yankees Lost the Pennant* by Douglas Wallop, *Damn Yankees* featured music by Richard Adler and lyrics by Jerry Ross. In a faithful transfer to screen from the MUSICAL THEATER stage, *Damn Yankees* is a modern variation of the FAUST legend. A middle-aged fan of the Washington Senators trades his soul to the Devil, Mr. Applegate (Ray Walston), to recapture his youth and help the team win the pennant. To keep the young Joe (Tab Hunter) from exercising an escape clause, Applegate enlists the "finest homewrecker on [his] staff," Lola (Gwen Verdon).

Dark Crystal, The (Universal; 1982) Strange and vile creatures (portrayed by Jim Henson Muppets) steal a piece from the Dark Crystal in an occult attempt to seize control of the planet, but two children overcome their evil.

Dawn of the Dead (Target Int'l/Laurel Group/Dawn Assoc.; 1979) This cult camp horror classic from George A.

Romero shows carnivorous ZOMBIEs, their origin unknown, eating their way through America. The movie spawned three sequels: *Day of the Dead* (Laurel/United; 1985), *The Night of the Living Dead* (Image Ten; 1968) and *The Night of the Living Dead* (Columbia/21st Century/George A. Romero/Menahem Golan; 1990).

Day of Wrath (Palladium, Denmark; 1943) Based on the play *Anne Pedersdotter* by Hans Wiers Jenssen, *Day of Wrath* is set in a 17th-century village. An old crone, judged to be a witch by the local preacher, is burned at the stake. At her death, she lays a CURSE on the minister, who soon dies. His mother charges the pastor's wife, who is involved with another man, with the WITCHCRAFT slaying of her son.

Devil and Max Devlin, The (Walt Disney; 1981) A hateful and malicious building manager is run over by a bus. He winds up in hell, but the Devil, seeing FAUSTian potential in the new arrival, offers him a deal: his release in exchange for recruiting three souls in two months.

Devil and the Nun, The (Kadr, Poland; 1960) Based on a novel by Jaroslav Iwaszkiewicz and suggested by incidents of supposed demonic possessions at Loudon. (See GRANDIER, FATHER URBAIN.) A convent of sisters and a priest are overwhelmed by devils in the 17th century. Another priest, who tries to exorcise them, is accused of sorcery and is burned at the stake.

Devils, The (Warner/Russo, Great Britain; 1970) *Very* loosely adapted by Ken Russell from a play by John Whiting based on Aldous Huxley's book *The Devils of Loudon*, *The Devils* centers around a group of demon-possessed nuns in the 17th century. Their priest (Oliver Reed), accused as the cause of their affliction, is burned at the stake for WITCHCRAFT.

Devil's Rain, The (Rank/Sandy Howard; 1975) When residents of a western town begin to liquefy like "the devil's rain," WITCHCRAFT is suspected. The son of one of the dead fights the head of a satanic cult.

Disembodied, The (Allied Artists; 1957) A doctor and his wife are out in the jungle; little does he realize that she is secretly a VOODOO queen who wants to kill him!

Doctor Faustus (Columbia/Oxford University Screen Prods./Nassau Film/Venfilms, Great Britain; 1968) Based on the play *DOCTOR FAUSTUS* by Christopher Marlowe. FAUSTUS (Richard Burton) sells his soul to Mephistopheles (Andreas Teuber) in order to live a mortal life filled with ultimate wisdom, wealth, comfort and carnality. Elizabeth Taylor appears in a cameo role as Helen of Troy.

Dracula AD 1972 (Warner/Hammer, Great Britain; 1972) Dracula awakens in 20th-century Chelsea, England, among psychedelic, occultist teens fooling with WITCHCRAFT and BLACK MAGIC.

Dragonslayer (Walt Disney/Paramount; 1981) In mythical times in an unspecified land, a sorcerer's apprentice (Peter MacNichol) battles the usual sword-and-sorcery foes, armed with an occult AMULET from his tutor.

DuckTales: The Movie—Treasure of the Lost Lamp (Disney, Disney Movietoons; 1990; animated) Based on the *DuckTales* COMIC-BOOK series created by Carl Barks. Scrooge McDuck (voiced by Alan Young), accompanied by his three nephews and their friend Webbigail (Webby) Vanderquack—(all voiced by Russi Taylor), search for the lost riches of Collie Baba and his 40 Thieves. (See *ARABIAN NIGHTS*.) Unbeknownst to the adventurers, the weasel Dijon who accompanies them is in cahoots with the wicked wizard Merlock (Christopher Lloyd).

Merlock seeks a magic lamp hidden away with the treasure hoard. McDuck finds the seemingly worthless old oil lamp and gives it to Webby.

Back home in Duckburg, Webby polishes the "teapot" and inadvertently summons the genie (Rip Taylor). She and the nephews are each granted three wishes, but they foolishly (or at least frivolously) waste most of them immediately.

Merlock arrives in Duckburg, determined to find the lamp. Meanwhile, McDuck has found out about the genie and becomes the lamp's new owner. Through a farcical series of misadventures, Dijon obtains the lamp and, at the genie's urging, keeps it for himself.

Scrooge finds Dijon and seizes the lamp, but Merlock, in turn, grabs it from him. During a midair battle with McDuck for the lamp, Merlock's TALISMAN (the source for the sorcerer's power) falls from his neck. Merlock plummets downward, apparently to his death.

Scrooge, back in full possession of the lamp, wishes them all safely back to Duckburg. As his third and final wish, Scrooge McDuck wishes that the genie would become a real boy. (See also *Aladdin*, above; "ALADDIN AND THE WONDERFUL LAMP".)

Dunwich Horror, The (AIP; 1970) From the story by H.P. Lovecraft, a warlock tries to force his young girlfriend to take part in a satanic ritual.

Elvira, Mistress of the Dark (Entertainment/New World/NBC/Queen B; 1988) To act as a hostess of a TELEVISION show running old horror films, Cassandra Peterson created the character Elvira, a cross between Vampira (Mila Nurmi, who portrayed a similar role on television decades earlier) and Morticia Addams (of *The Addams Family* cartoon panels, television series [Carolyn Jones] and FILMs [Angelica Huston]). In the film, Elvira plays "herself" in a campy frolic heavily laced with sexual innuendo (much of which refers to the enormous size of her breasts, a comic bit carried over from the televised show). The thin plot revolves around the actress/witch discovering that she actually *does* have magical powers.

Escape to Witch Mountain (Walt Disney; 1974) Based on the novel by Alexander Key, a conniving millionaire businessman pursues two small children, apparently orphaned, who have incredible and unexplainable magical powers. They turn out not to be witches, as the movie's title might suggest, but space aliens!

Evil Dead, The (Palace/Renaissance; 1980, released 1983) Five teenagers, stuck in a cabin in the woods, find an ancient GRIMOIRE and, on a lark, attempt to conjure wood demons using the cabalistic SPELLs. Sequels, *Evil Dead 2: Dead by Dawn* and *Evil Dead 3*, were released in 1987 and 1989.

Excalibur (Warner/Orion; 1981) Lushly photographed and often graphically realistic as shot by cinematographer Alex Thomson, this is a visual retelling of the story of King ARTHUR (Nigel Terry), MERLIN (Nicol Williamson), Uther Pendragon, the LADY OF THE LAKE, MORGAN LE FAY (Helen Mirren), and, of course, the sword EXCALIBUR.

Face of Marble, The (Monogram; 1946) VOODOO is used to try to bring the dead back to life.

Fantasia See *FANTASIA*.

Faust (UFA Germany; 1926) Director F.W. Murnau's faithful movie adaptation of the classic *FAUST* legend of a man (Emil Jannings) who sells his soul to Satan, *Faust* is certainly the best of the silent versions and compares very favorably with many of the sound editions as well.

Finian's Rainbow (Warner/Seven Arts; 1968) Based on the 1947 musical play by E.Y. Harburg and Fred Saidy, with music by Burton Lane and lyrics by Harburg. Magic is the subtext of this story of an Irish leprechaun (Tommy Steele) whose pot of gold is discovered by Finian (Fred Astaire) and taken to the United States. (See MUSICAL THEATER, FINIAN'S RAINBOW.)

Fire and Ice (Fox/PSO; 1982) In an animated tale of evil versus good, Lord Neckron uses sorcery and BLACK MAGIC in his attempt to overthrow King Jarol.

Flash Gordon A comic-strip character created by Alex Raymond, Flash Gordon was the 25th-century alter-ego hero of a Yale graduate/polo player. In his first adventure, accompanied by his girlfriend Dale and the ever-prevent Doctor Zarkov, Flash Gordon flew to Mongo, where he fought the magical and maniacal Emperor Ming, who was planning to conquer and annihilate Earth. After several battles, Flash Gordon finally prevailed over Ming and his cohorts, and the superhero went on to combat other evil enemies, including the Mad Witch of Neptune.

In 1935, Flash Gordon was made into a radio series, starring Gale Gordon as Flash Gordon.

Universal Studios quickly released three black-and-white serials, all of which starred Buster Crabbe (Gordon) and Charles Middleton (Ming): *Flash Gordon* (1936), *Flash Gordon's Trip to Mars* (1938) and *Flash Gordon Conquers the Universe* (1940).

A TELEVISION series (1953–54, 39 half-hour syndicated shows) followed, starring Steve Holland as Flash Gordon.

In 1974, a soft-core pornographic parody of the character, *Flesh Gordon*, was theatrically released. Six years later, EMI/Famous/Starling of Great Britain released a big-budget *Flash Gordon* starring Sam J. Jones (Gordon), Max Von Sydow (Ming), Topol (Doctor Zarkov) and Melody Anderson (Dale).

Flight of the Dragon, The (Rankin/Bass; 1982) In this animated movie based on the book *The Flight of Dragons* by Peter Dickinson, a modern-day author (spoken by John Ritter) is mystically whisked back to a past of fantasy and legend where he is called upon to help save the "real" magic in the universe.

Four Skulls of Jonathan Drake, The (United Artists/Vogue; 1959) While exploring through the jungles of Ecuador, a family unexpectedly encounters a MEDICINE MAN/head hunter who lays a dreaded CURSE upon them.

Gawain and the Green Knight (United Artists/Sancrest, Great Britain; 1973) The tale of Sir Gawain is one of the many legends surrounding the court of King ARTHUR. Here, Gawain (Murray Head) is a seen as a mysterious, seemingly invincible knight who offers to prove his valor by fighting any of the men of the Round Table. (See *Sir GAWAIN AND THE GREEN KNIGHT*.)

Ghost Breakers, The (Paramount; 1940) Based on the comic play by Charles W. Goddard and Paul Dickey. A young woman (Paulette Goddard), inherits a castle on a plantation in the West Indies and soon discovers that it seems to be haunted by SPIRITS and ZOMBIES.

Starring Bob Hope, this was the third of four incarnations of the same story. It was shot in 1914 and 1922 and then as *Scared Stiff* with Dean Martin and Jerry Lewis in 1953.

Glass Slipper, The (MGM; 1954) The fairy tale of CINDER-ELLA was given the MGM musical movie treatment, with music and lyrics by Helen Deutsch and choreography by Roland Petit. It starred Leslie Caron (Cinderella) and Estelle Winwood (Fairy Godmother).

Golden Blade, The (U-I; 1953) In an ARABIAN NIGHTS-type tale, Harun (Rock Hudson) uses a magic sword to help him rescue the princess (Piper Laurie).

Golden Mistress, The (United Artists/RKO; 1954) Off Haiti, an American adventurer and his girlfriend seek sunken treasure from a native tribe. The film shows several graphic scenes of VOODOO rites.

Golem, The There were three early German films made with this identical title, in 1913, 1917 and 1920 (UFA). Critics consider the last of these to be the best of the early European film versions of the story. Two Czechoslovakian films were also made, in 1935/1936 (AB) and 1951. The former of these was rereleased in England under the title *The Legend of Prague*.

They all have the same story, based on an ancient Hebrew legend and carried on through the KABALLAH and writings on ALCHEMY. In Prague during the 16th century, an occultist rabbi constructs a monstrous man out of clay. Through magical INCANTATIONS, he brings the GOLEM to life so that it can defend the Jewish community against its enemies.

Gospel According to St. Matthew, The (Arco/Lux, Italy/France; 1964) Originally titled *Il Vangelo Secondo Matteo*, this story of the Messiah was shot in cinema-vérité or documentary style by film maker Pier Paolo Pasolini.

In recent years, respected British actor Alec McCowan has toured a solo stage production entitled *The Gospel According to St. Matthew* in which he recites and acts the complete text of the book from the New Testament.

Greatest Story Ever Told, The (United Artists/George Stevens, 1965) Slowly paced and reverential, *The Greatest Story Ever Told* is a film treatment of the life, death, resurrection and miracles of JESUS (with Max Von Sydow as the Christ).

Hawk the Slayer (ITC/Chips, Great Britain; 1980) Two brothers, one good, one evil, battle for an enchanted sword that gives them the power to fly.

Heavenly Body, The (MGM; 1943) Consulting the stars through ASTROLOGY, the wife of an astronomer (who gives more attention to the heavenly bodies than to the "heavenly body" of his spouse) meets a tall, dark, handsome stranger.

Henry the Rainmaker (Monogram; 1948) While running for mayor of a drought-stricken community, a candidate invites a RAINMAKER to the small town.

Hotel Haywire (Paramount; 1937) An astrologer flirts with a dentist's wife.

Houdini (Paramount; 1953) This fictionalized and romanticized version of the great Houdini starred Tony Curtis as the escape artist/magician and Janet Leigh as his wife Bess.

Hunchback of Notre Dame, The *See HUNCHBACK OF NOTRE DAME, THE*

I Married a Witch (United Artists/Cinema Guild/René Clair; 1942) In this romantic comedy based on the novel *The Passionate Witch* by Thorne Smith, a father (Cecil Kellaway) and daughter (Veronica Lake), both SALEM witches who had

been burned at the stake, return to harass a modern-day descendant (Fredric Morah) of their 17th-century inquisitor.

I Walked with a Zombie (RKO; 1943) In the Caribbean, a nurse (Frances Dee) is hired by a wealthy planter to attend his wife, thought to be suffering from a VOODOO CURSE.

Incredible Strange Creatures Who Stopped Living and Became Mixed-Up Zombies, The (Morgan Steckler Prods.; 1963) A GYPSY tells fortunes at a carnival. Unfortunately, she also conjures up demons and monsters that she must hide in her cabana.

Indian in the Cupboard, The (Paramount/Columbia; 1995) Based on the children's novel by Lynne Reid Banks. For his ninth birthday, Omri (Hal Scardino) receives a skateboard and helmet, a skeleton-warrior action figure and, from his best friend Patrick (Rishi Bhat), a Native American brave action figure. Omri's brother gives him what seems to be a "dud" present, a beat-up wooden cupboard that he found in an alley. The boy discovers that when he uses the special, magic key to open the cupboard, any toy which had been placed inside will come to life.

The Indian in the Cupboard, published in 1980, is the first of four books involving the enchanted cupboard and its miniature inhabitants. The remaining three in the series (to date) are *The Return of the Indian* (1986), *The Secret of the Indian* (1989) and *The Mystery of the Cupboard* (1993).

It's a Wonderful Life *See GUARDIAN ANGEL.*

Jason and the Argonauts (Columbia; 1963) Renowned for its classic special effects and stop-action animation by Ray Harryhausen, Jason (Todd Armstrong), future husband of MEDEA, meets a plethora of monsters on his voyage with the Argonauts to capture the Golden Fleece.

Jesus Christ Superstar (Universal; 1973) The film, based on the musical play by Andrew Lloyd Webber (music) and Tim Rice (lyrics), stars Ted Neeley (JESUS), Carl Anderson (Judas) and Yvonne Elliman (Mary Magdelene). A group of itinerant performers, busing across the desert, stop and musically enact the story of the last seven days of the ministry of Christ. André Previn won an Academy Award for his musical direction.

Joan of Arc *See JOAN OF ARC, ST.*

Joan the Woman *See JOAN OF ARC, ST.*

Journey Back to Oz (Norm Prescott and Lou Scheimer/Filmation; filmed 1964, but released 1974) In this animated feature, Dorothy (voiced by Liza Minnelli) is called back to Oz to help battle the sister of the Wicked Witch (voiced by Margaret Hamilton, who portrayed the Wicked Witch of the West in the classic 1939 MGM movie *The Wizard of Oz*). (See WIZARD OF OZ, THE).

Juliet of the Spirits (Federiz/Francoriz, Italy/Germany; 1965) Originally released in Europe as *Giulietta degli Spiriti*, the Federico Fellini film follows the fantasy life of a world-weary middle-aged woman (Giulietta Masina) who suddenly discovers that she has the power to summon SPIRITs. The phantoms provide her with a world of sensual and sexual satisfaction.

Kazaam (Touchstone Pictures; 1996) Shaquille O'Neal plays a genie who helps out a young boy in 20th-century America.

Kid in King Arthur's Court, A (Walt Disney; 1995) MER-LIN whisks Calvin Fuller (Thomas Ian Nicholas), a boy from modern-day Reseda, California, to the court of King ARTHUR to help save Britain. When the lad stops using the standard medieval methods of battle and applies his 20th-century know-how (including the introduction of roller blades), the round tables turn.

King of Kings   Two feature films with this title were made about the life and ministry (including recreations of several of the attributed miracles) of JESUS Christ.

The first, released by Pathé in 1927, directed by Cecil B. de Mille and starring H.B. Warner as Jesus, is deservedly considered a classic. The latter, released by MGM/Samuel Bronston in 1961, starred Jeffrey Hunter as the Christ.

Kismet   Three film versions of the this story from the ARABIAN NIGHTS, in which a good wizard defeats the evil vizier of Baghdad, bear this title. The first *Kismet*, based on the play by Edward Knoblock, was released by Warner Studios in 1930, starring Otis Skinner, Loretta Young and Sidney Blackmer. A 1944 remake by MGM starred Ronald Colman and Marlene Dietrich (in gold body make-up). When released to television, the movie was retitled *Oriental Dream*. Eleven years later, MGM released a *Kismet* based on the musical play by Charles Lederer and Luther Davis, which featured new lyrics to the music of Borodin. Directed by Vicente Minnelli, the film starred Howard Keel, Ann Blyth, Dolores Gray, Monte Woolley and Vic Damone. In 1967, a made-for-television adaptation starred José Ferrer and Barbara Eden. (See also MUSICAL THEATER, KISMET.)

Knights of the Round Table   (MGM; 1953) Lancelot (Robert Taylor) had been exiled for his romance with Queen Guinevere (Ava Gardner), but he comes back to England to assist ARTHUR (Mel Ferrer) in the king's final (unsuccessful) battle against Modred.

Ladyhawke   (Warner/Richard Donner and Lauren Schuler; 1985) A young boy (Matthew Broderick) and girl (Michelle Pfieffer), lovers in a mystical, mythical medieval time, are CURSEd by their magical transformation into a wolf and a hawk, respectively. The SPELL allows them to change back into human form but never at the same time.

Lancelot and Guinevere   (Emblem, Great Britain; 1963) Released in the United States as *Sword of Lancelot*, this tale of Lancelot's (Cornel Wilde) unconsummated love for Guinevere (Jean Wallace) has the queen entering a nunnery following the death of King ARTHUR (Brian Aherne).

Last Wave, The   (United Artists with Ayer/MacElroy/Derek Power, Australia; 1977) Unusual weather over Australia and strange dreams prompt a lawyer (Richard Chamberlain) to investigate Aboriginal prophecy about worldwide devastation by flood. The Peter Weir film is full of mystic overtones, SHAMANism and acts of DIVINATION.

Leaves from Satan's Book   (Nordisk, Denmark; 1919) From the novel *The Sorrows of Satan* by Marie Corelli. In anthology format, the film shows special events in the life of Satan, including his temptations of JESUS, the INQUISITION and the French and Russian Revolutions.

Lion King, The   (Walt Disney; 1994; animated) After the death of his father Mufasa (voiced by James Earl Jones), a lion cub named Simba (Jonathan Taylor-Thomas) must grow up to take his place as the rightful Lion King (Matthew Broderick) by taking back the throne from the usurper, his evil uncle Scar (Jeremy Irons).

Two mystic elements, appropriate to the African Seregenti where the film is set, recur throughout the movie. Rafiki (Robert Guillaume), a wise baboon with mystical powers, acts as a SHAMAN to the animal kingdom: He selects the proper time for Simba's presentation to the herds. He christens the prince, anointing him with proper ceremonial markings. Later, Rafiki's powers of DIVINATION (through austromancy, the reading of the wind) reveal to him that Simba, thought to have dead for many years, is actually still alive.

The other continuing motif is the belief in a SPIRIT world. Simba's father explains to his son that we are all a part of the "circle of life" and that he will always be with him. True to his word, when Simba is most in need of courage and resolve, Mufasa's spirit appears to him in a cloud of stars.

The Lion King won an Academy Awards for Best Song ("Can You Feel the Love Tonight,"—Elton John, music; Tim Rice, lyrics) and for Best Score (Hans Zimmer).

Little Mermaid, The   (Warner/Walt Disney/Silver Screen Partners IV; 1989) Based on the story by Hans Christian Andersen, the film featured a musical score by Alan Menken with songs by Menken (music) and Howard Ashman (lyrics). The film won two Academy Awards, for Best Score and for Best Song ("Under the Sea").

Ariel (voiced by Jodi Benson), the titular mermaid, falls in love with Prince Eric (Christopher Daniel Barnes), a human who has seen her but only remembers her haunting voice. Ursula (Pat Carroll), the Sea Witch, agrees to change the mermaid into a human girl in exchange for Ariel's voice. As part of the SPELL, the prince must fall in love with Ariel and kiss her within three days. Otherwise, Ursula will win Ariel's soul.

To spoil the plan, Ursula transforms herself into a human, the vivacious Vanessa who, using Ariel's voice (which she has trapped in her AMULET pendant), is able to bewitch the prince.

During an immediate wedding ceremony aboard the prince's ship, the witch's pendant is broken. Ariel regains her voice, and the prince snaps out of Ursula's spell and falls in love with Ariel. He kisses her, but it is too late. In triumph, Ursula grows to monstrous proportions, towering over the ship. Prince Eric kills her by spearing her with part of the ship's broken bow.

Ursula is certainly the slimiest of all the Disney villains. She is part-octopus, part-human, blue-skinned with a shock of white hair and blood red lipstick. She is comically broad and oily: Carroll called her "part Shakespearean actress, with all the flair, flamboyance and theatricality, and part used-car salesman with a touch of con artist."

Following the success of *The Little Mermaid*, a series of made direct-to-video animated films, featuring many of the same characters, was released under the collective title "Ariel's Undersea Adventures." (See also LITTLE MERMAID, THE; OPERA, RUSALKA.)

Live and Let Die   (United Artists/Eon; 1973) 007's adventures take him to New Orleans and the Caribbean, where James Bond (Roger Moore) is surrounded by practitioners of VOODOO. Bond's sleight-of-hand with TAROT CARDS is the first step in turning a captive ORACLE (Jane Seymour) away from her diabolical master (Yaphet Kotto).

Lord of Illusions   (United Artists; 1995) Harry D'Amour (Scott Bakula), a New York City private detective, is hired to investigate insurance fraud in Los Angeles. On

Venice Beach, he discovers a fortune-teller's shop that turns out to be a gateway to hell. Central to the plot is stage magician Philip Swann (Kevin J. O'Connor), who may or may not have died in an escape trick, and his widow Dorothea (Famke Janssen), both of whom were once controlled by a seemingly supernatural sorcerer named Nix (Daniel Von Bargen).

Lord of the Rings (United Artists/Fantasy; 1978; animated) Based on the LORD OF THE RINGS trilogy by J.R.R. TOLKIEN, a hobbit goes on a great adventure to destroy the RING of power and invisibility sought by the Dark Lord.

Lost City, The (Krellberg; 1934) A scientist charts the source of worldwide electrical storms to the Magnetic Mountain in central Africa. Once there, he encounters a wizard named Zolok, who has created the tempests.

Macbeth (Republic/Mercury; 1948) With a screenplay by Orson Welles based on SHAKESPEARE'S MACBETH, the entire film was shot in 21 days on inexpensive (some say cardboard) sets. Welles portrayed the tragic Scot with Jeanette Nolan as Lady Macbeth.

Magic Carpet, The (Sam Katzman/Columbia; 1951) In an ARABIAN NIGHTS–style tale, the caliph is overthrown. His son takes on a superhero alter-ego, the Scarlet Falcon, to battle for the throne.

Magic Sword, The (United Artists/Bert I. Gordon; 1962) Set in medieval times, a princess is captured by a wicked sorcerer. The son of a good witch sets off to save her with the help of the titular sword.

Magician, The (MGM; 1926) Based on the novel by Somerset Maugham. A neophyte wizard is unprepared for the destructive power of his occult INCANTATIONS and SPELLS when he uses them to win a young lady's affection.

Magician of Lublin, The (Geria-Golan-Globus, West Germany/Israel; 1979) Based on the novel by Isaac Bashevis Singer. In addition to having a voracious sexual appetite, a traveling wizard in 1901 believes that he really has the power to fly. (See SIMON.)

Magus, The (TCF/Blazer, Great Britain) Adapted by John Fowles from his novel. A British school teacher (Michael Caine) travels to a small Greek island where he comes up against an aged wizard (Anthony Quinn).

Maid of Salem (Paramount; 1937) In the midst of the 1692 SALEM WITCHCRAFT trials, one of the girls who had been denounced (Claudette Colbert) is rescued by her boyfriend (Fred MacMurray).

Mandrake the Magician (Columbia; 1939) The famous comic-strip character MANDRAKE THE MAGICIAN (Warren Hull) battles a gang leader known as The Wasp.

Manitou, The (Herman Weist/Melvin Simon; 1978) Based on the novel by Graham Masterton. A self-proclaimed spiritualist is in fact a charlatan, making him seemingly powerless when his girlfriend is possessed by the evil SPIRIT of an Indian who lived 400 years ago.

Manon des Sources (Films Marcel Pagnol, France; 1952) A quirky French girl (Jacqueline Pagnol) in the Provinces is accused of being a witch by villagers because she lives alone up in the hills, with only mountain goats for friends. Angered by their abuse, she stops up the stream providing water to the town.

Manon des Sources effectively shows the suspicion that townspeople had of the unknown. Marcel Pagnol adapted the screenplay into two novels, which he later filmed as a two-part movie. The individual sections, released in 1987, were titled *Jean de Florette 2* and *Manon des Sources* (in the United States, called *Manon of the Spring*).

Marguerite de la Nuit (SNEG/Gaumont Actualités/Cino del Duca, France/Italy; 1955) A man in his 80s falls in love with a young woman; so, like Faust, he trades his soul to the Devil. He regains his youth, but he accidentally causes the woman's death.

Mary Poppins (Walt Disney; 1964) Based on the popular series of Mary Poppins children's books by P.L. Travers.

In the time of Edwardian England, Mary Poppins (Julie Andrews) appears in the London sky (holding her opened umbrella as a sail) to act as nanny for a small boy and girl. By film's end, she has reunited the affections of the father and the children. The source for and extent of (enchantress) Poppins's powers is never revealed, but she is able to animate toys, bring her mirrored reflection to life, take others with her into chalk paintings on the pavement (where they interact with animated characters), plus other miraculous deeds.

Julie Andrews received a Best Actress Academy Award. The Sherman Brothers (Richard M., music; Robert B., lyrics) won the Oscar for Best Score as well as for Best Song ("Chim Chim Cheree").

Masque of Red Death, The (AIP/Alta Vista, Great Britain; 1964) Loosely based on the story by Edgar Allan Poe. An Italian prince (Vincent Price) in the Middle Ages is a satanist. Oblivious to the plague in the streets outside his villa, he holds a masked ball. Though not invited, Death is one of the visitors.

Medea (San Marco/Number One/Janus, Italy/France/West Germany; 1970) Based on the play by Euripides and directed by Pier Paolo Pasolini. When Jason returns home with the Golden Fleece, he brings along the sorceress MEDEA (Maria Callas) as his wife.

Men of Respect (Central City/Arthur Goldblatt; 1990) *Men of Respect* is SHAKESPEARE'S MACBETH in gangster clothing, complete with lines of dialogue lifted straight from the Elizabethan tragedy. A common hit man is told by a fortune-teller that he will become the Mafia Godfather. When he confides in his wife, she prods (and assists) him into fulfilling the prophecy.

Men of Two Worlds (GFD/Two Cities, Great Britain; 1946; released in the United States as *Witch Doctor* and also as *Kisenga, Man of Africa*). An area of Tanganyika is overcome with a plague, but the natives will only consult their WITCH DOCTOR for healing. An educated tribesman tries to help visiting doctors in their attempt to aid the local residents through modern medicine.

Mephisto Waltz, The (TCF/QM Prods.; 1971) A concert pianist (Curt Jurgens) is a student of satanism and the occult. At the moment he is about to die, the musician sends his SPIRIT into a writer (Alan Alda), taking possession of him.

Midsummer Night's Dream, A (Warner; 1935) Produced and directed by Max Reinhardt, based on his Broadway production of the SHAKESPEARE comedy, the film adaptation is both faithful to the original and yet magical in its own right. A young Mickey Rooney portrayed Puck. The film won the Academy Awards for Cinematography (Hal Mohr, Fred Jackman and Byron Haskin) and Best Editing (Ralph Dawson).

Almost 50 years later, Woody Allen filmed a modern variation on the theme: *A Midsummer Night's Sex Comedy* (Warner/Orion/Rollins-Joffe; 1982).

Monk, The Rank/Maya/Comacico/Peri/Tritone/Studio Films, France/Italy/West Germany; 1972) From the novel by M.G. Lewis, the film's original title was *Le Moine* before being dubbed for American audiences. A woman, posing as a monk, makes love to an abbot. Corrupted, the abbot falls further into sin and degradation, managing to avoid prosecution on Earth only by making a FAUSTian pact with Satan.

Monkey Business (TCF; 1952) A chimpanzee locked up in a laboratory full of chemicals and test tubes inadvertently brews an ELIXIR OF LIFE.

Monster Club, The (ITC/Chips, Great Britain; 1980) Based on stories by R. Chetwynd-Hayes. In an anthology-format satirical film, a vampire (Vincent Price) brings his new victim to his macabre fraternal club for witches, demons, et al. One by one, each member gets to tell a gruesome tale.

Monty Python and the Holy Grail (EMI/Python (Monty) Pictures/Michael White, Great Britain; 1975) Outrageous comic sight gags fill the screen and witty verbal jousts abound as King ARTHUR and his Knights of the Round Table go on quest for the Holy Grail.

Monty Python's Life of Brian (Hand Made Films, Great Britain; 1979) An ordinary man, living at the same time of JESUS Christ, is proclaimed the Messiah by the masses, much to his chagrin, and is eventually crucified.

Religious critics found the movie irreverent, even blasphemous, but at the beginning of the first millennium, there were many itinerant pseudoprophets in the Holy Land claiming to be the Messiah. Most made use of sorcery and illusions to convince the commoners of their divinity, so the film's premise of an unwilling citizen swept up in such events is not improbable.

Münchausen (UFA, Germany; 1943) *The Adventures of Baron Münchausen*, as the movie is also known, is set in the 1940s. The baron tells incredible tales that supposedly happened to his same-named ancestor. It is soon revealed, however, that the story-teller, is in fact the original baron. Due to a gift (or CURSE) from a wizard, the baron is able to live forever!

My Little Pony (Sunbow/Hasbro; 1986) This movie, with animation work executed in Japan, was co-produced by the makers of the popular My Little Pony line of children's toys. Ponyland must fight off Hydra, a wicked witch.

Necromancy (Cinerama; 1973) Produced, written and directed by Bert I. Gordon and starring Orson Welles, *Necromancy* tells of two people in a rural community dabbling with WITCHCRAFT, resulting in dire, unexpected consequences.

Night of the Demon (Columbia/Sabre, Great Britain; 1957; released in the United States as *Curse of the Demon*). Based on the story "Casting the Runes" by M.R. James. A satanist (Dana Andrews) CONJURES up an ancient, gargantuan devil to murder his foes.

976-EVIL (Medusa/Cinetel/Horrorscope, 1988) A teenager acquires hellish powers after he conjures a demon (by telephone).

Oh God! You Devil (Warner; 1984) *Oh God, You Devil!* was the second sequel to the clever *Oh, God!* George Burns played the double role of God and the Devil in a twist on the FAUST legend! A hard-working but unsuccessful musician decides to sell his soul for fame and fortune.

Perceval Le Gallois (Les Films du Losange/Barbet Schroeder/FR3/ARD/SSR/RAI/Gaumont, France; 1978) Based on an epic poem by Chrétien DE TROYES. A young man from Wales joins the Round Table to serve under ARTHUR. On his quests, he meets the legendary Fisher King.

Peter Pan (Walt Disney; 1953) The Disney animated classic was based on Sir James Barrie's play *Peter Pan* and his subsequent novelizations. The basic story is well known by young and old alike. Peter Pan, the boy who never grew up, and his fairy companion Tinkerbell take the Darling Children to visit Neverland (also seen as Never Never Land). They are able to fly there after being sprinkled by fairy dust. Once there, Wendy becomes a surrogate mother to Peter's band of Lost Boys. After adventures with pirates, led by Captain Hook, and Indians, Tinkerbell sprinkles the pirate ship with pixie dust, and all of the children, except Peter, return to grow up in London.

The biggest change in a character from stage to screen occurs to the magical fairy Tinkerbell. The fairy effect is always achieved in theatrical productions with a small spotlight, pinspot or laser. For the Disney film, Tinkerbell was drawn as a tiny but physically mature young woman, flirting one second and pouting or jealous in the next. Tinkerbell was animated by Marc Davis after live-action studies by actress Margaret Kerry. In the 1991 movie *Hook*, the passionate feelings Tinkerbell had for Peter were explored in the fairy's portrayal by actress Julia Roberts.

In the stage and musical play versions of *Peter Pan*, Tinkerbell almost dies by drinking poison intended for Peter. Her light starts to fade and threatens to go out. The only way Peter can save her is by encouraging the audience to "Clap! Clap, if you believe in fairies." The applause always rejuvenates the fairy, and her twinkle of light grows stronger than ever. The Disney film did not include Peter's direct plea to audience.

From the first *Walt Disney* TELEVISION shows (beginning with *Disneyland* on ABC in 1954), Tinkerbell has been associated with Sleeping Beauty's Castle at Disneyland as she swoops around the castle over the show's credits. A tap of her magic wand marked the beginning of the feature presentation.

Phantom Creeps, The (Universal; 1939) An evil scientist and creator of a monstrous robot, Dr. Zorka (Bela Lugosi) has the power to turn men into ZOMBIES and place them under his command.

Picture of Dorian Gray, The (MGM; 1945) Based on the novel by Oscar Wilde. This classic twist on the FAUST legend takes place in Victorian England, where a gentleman (Hurd Hatfield) stays eternally young. His ELIXIR OF LIFE is an oil portrait of himself, kept in his attic, in which the image in the portrait grows older. The plot is set in motion when Dorian verbalizes the pact, "If only the picture could change and I could be always what I am now. For that, I would give anything. Yes, there's nothing in the whole world I wouldn't give. I'd give my soul for that."

Pied Piper, The (Sagittarius/Goodtimes, Great Britain; 1971) Based on the poetic fable "THE PIED PIPER OF HAMELIN" and set in 1349, a wandering minstrel offers to rid the town of Hamelin of its rats. When the town council refuses to pay him, he leads the children away with his musical flute. While the piper is never identified as a wizard or sorcerer per se, certainly his magical powers of enchantment are crucial to the story.

Pinocchio   (Walt Disney, 1940) Screenplay based on the classic 1883 book (after its two years of serialization in a Roman newspaper) by Carlo Collodi (pen name of Carlo Lorenzini) (1826–1990). Arguably the best drawn of all the Disney animated features, *Pinocchio* won an Academy Award for its musical score and for the song "When You Wish Upon a Star" (music by Leigh Harline; lyrics by Ned Washington).

The Disney version of the story disregards many of the recurring magic themes and varying encounters with the Blue Fairy, who appears in several different mystical guises in the original book. Nevertheless, the film is still a work of enchantment. To satisfy wood-carver Geppetto's (voiced by Christian Rub) wish for a son, the Blue Fairy (Evelyn Venable) brings his puppet Pinocchio (Dickie Jones) to life. A series of misadventures follows in which Jiminy Cricket (who, in the book, is squashed early on by the doll) (Cliff Edwards) attempts to guide him into doing right. To assist him, the Blue Fairy places a SPELL on the boy: his nose grows whenever he tells a lie. At the film's end, the Blue Fairy rewards Pinocchio for his honesty, humility, repentance, bravery and devotion by transforming him into a real, human boy.

The Blue Fairy is not just a embodiment of good; she also has strong magic powers, bringing Pinocchio to life *twice* in the movie. It is she who appoints Jiminy Cricket as Pinocchio's conscience, and she acts as sort of GUARDIAN ANGEL to them both throughout the film.

Her time on screen is brief but memorable. She appears as a beautiful, blond woman in a blue-and-white diaphanous gown with giant gossamer wings. Despite the fact that she is a supernatural creature, she is drawn more realistically than any other character in the film. Her live-action model, after whom the animators created the Blue Fairy's movements and appearance, was Marjorie Babbitt (born Belcher, now Bell). Evelyn Venable recorded each of the Blue Fairy's lines several times, using many different inflections and intonations and allowed the sound editors to choose their favorites.

Plague of the Zombies, The   (Hammer, Great Britain; 1965) The owner of a tin mine in Cornwall uses VOODOO to raise the dead and then transforms them into ZOMBIE workers.

Pocahontas   (Walt Disney Pictures; 1995; animated) Although taking liberties with actual historical events, the Disney version of the tale of Pocahontas and John Smith gives some insight into NATIVE AMERICAN MAGIC and belief in SPIRITS.

The Powhatan tribe's belief in magic is evidenced by its MEDICINE MAN's (see also SHAMAN; WITCH DOCTOR) explanation of the British approach through the use of capnomancy (the interpretation of rising smoke) and pyromancy (reading omens in the flames after tossing special powders on the fire). (See DIVINATION.) Later, the wise man attempts (without much success) to heal the bullet wound of a brave using herbal FOLK MEDICINE.

Spirits abound in *Pocahontas*. As is often seen in tribal cultures, the people believe that all things, animate and inanimate, contain a spirit. Ancestor worship is also practiced. In *Pocahontas*, the two mystic concepts merge in the character of Grandmother Willow, the essence of the princess's grandmother returned as a tree spirit. Grandmother Willow also

practices oneiromancy, helping Pocahontas to understand the meaning of her dream about a spinning arrow.

Prospero's Books   (Palace/Allarts/Cinea/Camera One/ Penta/Elsevier Vendex/Film Four/VPRO/Canal Plus/ NHK, Netherlands/France/Italy; 1991). Based on the play *The TEMPEST* by William SHAKESPEARE. A visual and surrealistic extravaganza, the film's verse is spoken throughout solely by its narrator, portrayed by John Gielgud. The usurped Duke of Milan, a sorcerer, creates a sea storm to bring those who overthrew him to his remote island.

Pufnstuf   (Universal/Krofft; 1970) *Pufnstuf* uses the same blend of cartoonish costumes, acting and puppetry seen on the TELEVISION show on which the movie is based. A young boy (Jack Wild) and his enchanted, talking flute take an enchanted, talking boat across the sea to Living Island, where the enchanted, talking creatures are afraid of the witch who rules over them.

Queen of Spades, The   (ABP/World Screen Plays, Great Britain; 1948) From the novel by Alexander Pushkin, based on the FAUST legend. To learn an aged countess's (Dame Edith Evans) secret method for always winning at cards, a Russian officer signs a pact with the devil. When the army man confronts the noble, she dies, but her SPIRIT returns to haunt him.

Race with the Devil   (TCF/Saber/Maslansky; 1975) A group of innocent vacationers accidentally see a BLACK MASS taking place. As a result, they are stalked by the satanists, who wish to protect their secret society.

Rainmaker, The   See RAINMAKER.

Rainmakers, The   (RKO; 1935) Charlatans posing as RAINMAKERs try to defraud a group of midwestern farmers. The swindlers are chased cross-country to California, where, true to their nature, they get mixed up in a questionable irrigation project.

Raven, The   (AIP/Alta Vista; 1963) The nebulous plot leads up to a dramatic (and entertaining) magic duel to the death between the two 15th century sorcerers, portrayed by Vincent Price and Boris Karloff.

Return to Oz   See WIZARD OF OZ, THE.

Rosemary's Baby   (Paramount/William Castle, 1968) Screenplay by the film's director Roman Polanski, based on the 1967 novel by Ira Levin. A young actor (John Cassavetes) and his wife Rosemary (Mia Farrow) move into an apartment building next door to an elderly couple (Ruth Gordon and Sidney Blackmer), unaware that they are satanists (or "witches," as they call themselves) and leaders of a COVEN. After a seemingly hallucinatory sexual experience, Rosemary discovers she is pregnant and eventually gives birth to the Devil's son. Despite her initial intention to kill the monster, Rosemary decides to mother him.

Ruth Gordon won an Academy Award for her portrayal of a sorceress. Although no sequel was produced for theatrical release, the story was continued in a made-for-TELEVISION movie, *Look What Happened to Rosemary's Baby*.

Saadia   (MGM; 1953) From the novel *Echec au Destin* by Francis D'Autheville. A French physician, working near the Sahara of northern Africa, incurs the wrath of his rival, the local WITCH DOCTOR.

Serpent and the Rainbow, The   (UIP/Universal; 1987) From the novel by Wade Davis. A scientist, trying to find evidence of VOODOO in Haiti, discovers all that he desired and more.

Seven Faces of Dr. Lao   (Galaxy-Scarus/MGM; 1964) Based on the novel *The Circus of Dr. Lao* by Charles G. Finney. In a *tour de force* performance Tony Randall portrays seven characters (Dr. Lao / MERLIN the Magician / Pan / The Abominable Snowman / Medusa / The Giant Serpent / APOLLONIUS OF TYANA) when the old Western town of Abalone is visited by the Asian enchanter Dr. Lao and his circus.

Seventh Voyage of Sinbad, The   (Columbia/Morningside; 1958) With special effects by Ray Harryhausen. A wicked wizard has shrunk Sinbad's fiancée, and the SPELL can only be broken by the magic found in the egg of the mythical birdlike roc.

Shaggy Dog, The   (Walt Disney; 1959) From the novel *The Hound of Florence* by Felix Salten. With the help of a magic RING, a boy turns into a crime-fighting shaggy sheepdog. Seventeen years later, Disney put out a sequel, *The Shaggy DA* (1976) in which a promising lawyer puts on the ring and transforms into the still-shaggy, talking dog to fight crime and corruption.

Shout, The   (Rank/Recorded Picture, Great Britain; 1978) A possibly insane man, believing that the aboriginal SHAMAN was able to kill tribal enemies by shouting, decides to develop the same murderous skill. He befriends a young couple, moves in with them, and gradually takes over their lives.

Silent Flute, The   (Volare; 1978) The winner of a martial arts contest is selected to do battle against a wizard named Zetan.

Sinbad and the Eye of the Tiger   (Columbia/Andor, Great Britain; 1977) Special effects by Ray Harryhausen. An evil enchantress (Jane Seymour) places a curse on an entire town, and only Sinbad (Patrick Wayne) can break the SPELL.

Slipper and the Rose, The   (Paradine Co-Productions, Great Britain; 1976) The story of CINDERELLA is told in a live-action musical adaptation with music by Richard M. Sherman and lyrics by Robert B. Sherman. The film starred Richard Chamberlain (Prince), Gemma Craven (Cinderella) and Edith Evans (Fairy Godmother).

Sleeping Beauty, The   (Walt Disney; 1959) Based on *The SLEEPING BEAUTY* as written by Charles Perrault; starring the voices of Mary Costa (Sleeping Beauty/Briar Rose) and Eleanor Audley (Maleficent). In this animated adaptation of the age-old fairy tale, the christening of Aurora, the daughter of the 14th-century King Stefan and his queen, is attended by three good fairies, Flora (voiced by Verna Felton), Fauna (Barbara Jo Allen) and Merryweather (Barbara Luddy).

Suddenly, Maleficent arrives. Although also a fairy, in both actions and appearance Maleficent more closely resembles a sorceress. Angry that she was not invited, she lays a CURSE on the baby: the girl will prick her finger on a spinning wheel and die before her 16th birthday. Merryweather, who has not yet bestowed her gift, amends the curse so that, if Aurora is pricked, she will merely fall asleep until awakened by a true lover's kiss.

Sixteen years pass. Maleficent appears, hypnotizes Aurora, and leads her to her castle tower. There, the girl reaches out to Maleficent's spinning wheel, pricks her finger on the needle and falls asleep. The good fairies lay the girl in state in her father's castle and place everyone in the kingdom into a deep sleep as well.

Maleficent transforms herself into a fire-breathing dragon to ward off Prince Phillip (Bill Shirley), who is determined to awaken the sleeping beauty. He slays the dragon, slashes through a hedge of thorns to reach the enchanted castle, kisses the sleeping beauty and breaks the SPELL.

Snow White and the Seven Dwarfs   (Walt Disney; 1937) Based on the BROTHERS GRIMM fairy tale told in *Kinder- und Hausmärchen* (1812–1815). An evil witch-queen (voiced by Lucille La Verne) consults the Spirit of the Magic Mirror (Moroni Olsen) and discovers that Snow White (Adriana Caselotti) is more beautiful than she, in both body and soul. She orders a huntsman to take Snow White into the forest and kill her, but he takes pity at the last moment and lets the girl escape.

The queen learns from Spirit that Snow White is still alive and has been adopted into a family of seven dwarfs. In order to kill the girl the queen transforms herself into a crone witch and offers the girl a poisoned apple. Snow White innocently takes a bite from it and "dies;" the dwarfs lay her on a funeral bier. A handsome prince (Harry Stockwell), who had fallen in love with Snow White before she was banished, rides by, is overwhelmed and kisses her. The SPELL is broken, the witch is killed by lightning and they all live happily ever after.

The regally splendid Queen/Witch, once described by Walt Disney as "a mixture of Lady MACBETH and the Big Bad Wolf," was created by animator Art Babbitt. The Witch, animated by Norm Ferguson, was drawn as an ugly, bent old woman, dressed in a black robe with a pointed hood. The Spirit (or Slave), imprisoned within the Queen's Magic Mirror, was seen as a disembodied face resembling a classical Greek mask, a greenish-blue phantom floating in blackened glass.

The first full-length animated feature, Snow White was a milestone in film history. Walt Disney was given a special Academy Award for "a significant screen innovation." The Oscar shared its pedestal with seven miniature Oscarettes.

Something Wicked This Way Comes   (Walt Disney/Bryna; 1983) Screenplay by Ray Bradbury from his novella. A mysterious carnival appears, seemingly by magic, in the dead of night, in a small Illinois village. The town's citizens, especially two young boys, are entranced. It is left to the imagination to decide whether the carnival master (Jonathan Pryce) of Cooger & Dark's Pandemonium Shadow Show is a sorcerer or satanic.

Sorceress   (Triboro; 1994) A sorceress (Linda Blair) uses her BLACK MAGIC to CURSE the new girlfriend of her ex-lover.

Supergirl   (Cantharus/Ilya Salkind, 1984) A super power source from Krypton is seized by the evil enchantress (Faye Dunaway). Only Supergirl (Helen Slater) can save the day. (See SUPERMAN.)

Superman   See SUPERMAN.

Swan Princess, The   (Vest Entertainment; 1994) Based on the BALLET *Swan Lake*. This animated movie retells the classic Peter Ilich Tchaikovsky ballet with the addition of several forest animals and songs to make the story more accessible to children.

Sword and the Sorcerer, The   (Sorcerer Prods./Group One/Brandon Chase; 1982) A sword-and-sorcery film is which Prince Talon must free a kingdom from the rule of a wicked, despotic usurper who is backed by a powerful sorcerer.

Sword in the Stone, The (Walt Disney; 1963) Based on *The Sword in the Stone* (1939), collected into the novel *The ONCE AND FUTURE KING* by T.H. White.

Young Wart/ARTHUR visits his mentor, the befuddled wizard MERLIN (voiced by Karl Swenson), who lives in a cluttered forest cottage with his owl, Archimedes. Disney's Merlin is a true wizard, with a blue gown, pointed cap and an ankle-length beard; a short walking staff doubles as a magic WAND. He has great powers but is absent-minded. Much of his confusion comes from living "backwards in time."

Merlin gives the boy a lesson, transforming him into various animals to see the world through their eyes. At one point, they find themselves in the hut of the dizzy witch Madame Mim (Martha Wentworth). Far from looking like the stereotypical witch, the plump Mim wears a purple-and-red dress over pink bloomers and sports a mop of disheveled gray hair, a silly grin and a crazed look in her eyes.

The two enchanters engage in a giant magic contest. Merlin finally wins by changing himself into a germ and infecting the witch. The movie culminates in Arthur's being crowned king of Britain after pulling a sword out of an anvillike stone.

More wickedly feisty than truly evil, Madam Mim has been a continuing character in Disney comic books, where her frequent partner-in-witchcraft is MAGICA DE SPELL.

Sword of the Valiant (Cannon, Great Britain; 1984) A gritty rendering of the medieval legend of Gawain (Sean Connery) versus the magic-imbued Green Knight. (See *GAWAIN AND THE GREEN KNIGHT, SIR.*)

Tempest, The (Boyd's Company, Great Britain; 1980) Writer/director Derek Jarman adapts SHAKESPEARE's *The TEMPEST* into the punk era.

Tempest (Columbia; 1982) An architect (John Cassavetes) leaves his adulterous wife (Gena Rowlands) and travels with his daughter (Molly Ringwald) to a small Greek island. Their only aide is a feeble-minded shepherd (Raul Julia). While the similarities to SHAKESPEARE's *The TEMPEST* were intentional, the modernization eliminated the enchantment and supernatural elements of the original.

Ten Commandments, The This tale of the life of MOSES, the Exodus, God's deliverance of the stone tablets and the wanderings of the Israelites toward the Promised Land received two classic screen treatments, both directed by Cecil B. de Mille.

The Ten Commandments (Paramount/Famous Players-Laskey; 1923) Starring Theodore Roberts as Moses and Charles de Roche as Ramses, the film is in two parts. The first is the Moses tale, but the latter half, though a morality fable, is a 20th-century story unrelated to the biblical Exodus.

The Ten Commandments (Paramount/Cecil B. de Mille; 1956) This better known film version starred Charlton Heston as Moses and Yul Brynner as the pharaoh.

Thief of Baghdad, The Three films with this title were produced, separated by about 20 years.

The Thief of Bagdad [sic] (1924) The thief (Douglas Fairbanks) employs magic to usurp the wicked Caliph.

The Thief of Baghdad (London Films. Great Britain; 1940) In the most acclaimed of the same-named trio of movies, Abu (Sabu), a young waif and thief, helps a sultan (Morton Selten)

regain his throne from the wicked caliph (Conrad Veidt). The film received Academy Awards for Cinematography (Georges Périnal) and Art Direction (Vincent Korda).

The Thief of Baghdad (Titanus/Lus, Italy/France; 1960) Steve Reeves starred as the thief.

Thief of Damascus (Columbia/Sam Katzman; 1952) The tyrant of Damascus is overthrown by his army general, assisted by the skills and magic of Aladdin, Sinbad and Scheherezade. The film interpolated old footage taken directly from the 1948 feature *Joan of Arc*.

Throne of Blood (Toho, Japan; 1957) Originally titled *Kumonosu-Jo* by director Akira Kurosawa and based on SHAKESPEARE's *MACBETH*, the film tells of a samurai (Toshiro Mifune) who, after receiving a prophecy from a witch is goaded by his wife into assassinating his sovereign at Cobweb Castle.

Thunderstorm (Hemisphere/Binnie Barnes, Great Britain; 1955) A strange girl (Linda Christian), believed to be witch by her village, is set adrift in a small boat. She is subsequently rescued by a Spanish fisherman.

Time of the Gypsies (Enterprise/Forum Film/Sarajevo TV, Yugoslavia; 1989) Edited from a six-part made-for-TELEVISION series entitled *Dom Za Vesanje*. Although a young GYPSY girl has true occult powers, she must remain with her vagabond band of tramps and thieves. For his work on this film, Emir Kusturica was voted Best Director by the Cannes Film Festival.

Tomb of Ligeia, The (American International, Great Britain; 1964) Based on the story by Edgar Allan Poe. A Victorian occultist (Vincent Price) transforms his deceased wife (Elizabeth Shepherd) into a CAT and then back into a woman, the lovely Lady Rowena.

Trick or Treat (Walt Disney; 1952; animated short) *Treat or Treat* introduced the cheery, granny-type enchantress named Witch Hazel. A short, rotund crone, Witch Hazel is accompanied by her ever-present BROOMSTICK named Beelzebub, which has its own separate and distinct personality. Witch Hazel's voice was provided by June Foray.

Donald Duck plays a trick-or-trick gag on his nephews, Huey, Dewey and Louie, placing fireworks in their bags and dousing them with water. Witch Hazel comes to his door to complain: Beelzebub was frightened by the noise. Donald, thinking her face to be a mask, pulls at Witch Hazel's nose and then throws a bucket of water on her, too. Only after being treated so inconsiderately does Witch Hazel finally use her magic against Donald. She joins the nephews on their rounds, but with dawn approaching, Witch Hazel jumps on her broomstick and flies away.

Ulysses (Lux Film/Ponti-de Laurentiis, Italy; 1954) Based on *The ODYSSEY* by Homer. CURSEd by the goddess Cassandra to wander the Aegean on their voyage home from Troy, Ulysses (Kirk Douglas) and his men encounter the sorceress CIRCE, battle the Cyclops and evade the SIRENS, among other adventures.

Undead, The (Balboa Prods.; 1956) An occultist-hypnotist regresses a street prostitute to a past life where, in the Middle Ages, she is involved in sorcery.

Viking Queen, The (Warner/Hammer, Great Britain; 1967) The queen of the Iceni tries to placate the conquering Romans in the first century A.D. Unfortunately, the DRUID priests refuse to acquiesce so quietly.

Voodoo (Image Organization/Planet Productions Corp.; 1995). A college transfer student (Corey Feldman) joins a ZOMBIE fraternity.

War Lord, The (Universal/Court, 1965) Based on the play *The Lovers* by Leslie Stevens. The army officer (Charlton Heston) for the Duke of Normandy is sent out to persuade the DRUIDS to accept the nobleman's rule; their alternative is annihilation.

Warlock (Medusa/New World; 1988) A 17th-century witch (Julian Sands) and the witch-hunter (Richard E. Grant) who is chasing him are magically transported to 20th-century Los Angeles.

Watcher in the Woods, The (Walt Disney; 1980, withdrawn for editing; 1982 rerelease) Based on the novel by Engel Randall. An American girl travels with her father, a composer, to England. While wandering through the country and farmlands, she begins to experience seemingly occult phenomena, accentuated by her encounter with a wizened woman (Bette Davis) in the woods.

Wholly Moses (Columbia/David Begelman; 1908) Sharing the same premise as *Monty Python's Life of Brian* (see above), *Wholly Moses* is a misadventure of misidentification. A shepherd, overhearing (but not seeing) God speaking to MOSES, believes that he had been chosen as the leader of the Israelites.

Willie Wonka and the Chocolate Factory (David Wolper; 1971) A young boy wins a contest, allowing him to visit a chocolate factory. Unexpectedly, he falls into the clutches of an evil wizard.

Witchcraft (TCF/Lippert, Great Britain; 1964) An entire family of witches decide to decimate their foes by BLACK MAGIC.

Witchcraft through the Ages (Svensk Filmindustri, Sweden; 1922) Written and directed by Benjamin Christiansen, this silent black-and-white documentary-style film recreates centuries of arcane rites and persecution of witches.

Witches, The Two totally unrelated films with this same title were distributed by Warner Studios almost 25 years apart.

The Witches (Warner/Hammer, Great Britain; 1966) From the novel *The Devil's Own* by Peter Curtis. Released in the United States as *The Devil's Own*, the film shows the consequences when an English schoolteacher discovers WITCHCRAFT in a small rural community.

The Witches (Warner/Lorimar; 1990) From the novel by Roald Dahl. A coven of witches plots to poison all the children in England. Only one boy, who has been transformed into a mouse, knows the secret, and he has to convince his grandmother to help him stop the witches' scheme.

Witches of Eastwick, The Warner/Guber-Peters/Kennedy-Miller; 1987) Based on the novel by John Updike. On a lark, three Connecticut divorcees (Cher, Susan Sarandon and Michelle Pfeiffer) try their hand at sorcery, attempting to conjure up a love SPELL. Their invocation is answered, but not in the manner they expected. The Devil (Jack Nicholson) himself makes the call.

Witches of Salem, The (Borderie/CICC/DEFA/Pathé, France/East Germany; 1957) Screenplay by Jean-Paul Sartre based on the play *The CRUCIBLE* by Arthur Miller. Originally titled *Les Sorcières de Salem*, the European film, which stars Simone Signoret and Yves Montand, is faithful to the plot of its American source: accusations of WITCHCRAFT abound in 1692 SALEM, Massachusetts.

Witchfinder General (Tigon/American Int'l, Great Britain; 1968) From the novel by Ronald Bassett. Released in the United States as *The Conqueror Worm*, the movie is set in 1645. An unscrupulous, money-hungry lawyer (Vincent Price) takes up a second vocation—that of a witch-hunter.

Wizard of Oz, The See WIZARD OF OZ, THE.

Wiz, The See WIZARD OF OZ, THE

Woman Who Came Back, The (Republic; 1945) When a girl returns to her home town in New England, the residents try to make her believe she is a witch.

Wonderful World of the Brothers Grimm, The (MGM/Cinerama/George Pal; 1962) Three of the fairy tales written by the Brothers Grimm (including CINDERELLA) augment a biopic of the German writers.

Wonders of Aladdin, The (Embassy/Lux, Italy; 1961) Aladdin (Donald O'Connor) overcomes the wicked vizier who has taken over the throne and wins the hand of the princess, all with the assistance of his friendly genie.

Yaaba (Oasis/Les Films de l'Avinir/Thelma Film/Arcadia Films, Burkina Faso/France/Switzerland; 1989) In an African village, an aged crone, thought to be witch, has been banished from the community. This does not stop a little boy from becoming her friend.

Yeelen (Artificial Eye/Les Films Cissé/Souleymane Cissé, Mali; 1987) Despite the taboo of fratricide, a young man is convinced that he must kill his father, a sorcerer who practices BLACK MAGIC.

Several movies not listed have characters who are stage magicians (i.e., platform entertainers). While these characters are not wizards and sorcerers in the occult sense, students of legerdemain might also wish to review such films as *A-Haunting We Will Go* (featuring real-life illusionist Dante)(1942), *The Escape Artist* (1982), *Eternally Yours* (1939), *F for Fake* (1973), *Fingers at the Window* (1942), *The Geisha Boy* (1958), *Get to Know Your Rabbit* (1972), *Hugo the Hippo* (1975), *Lili* (1953), *The Mad Magician* (1954), *The Mask of Dijon* (1946), *Miracles for Sale* (1939), *New York Stories* (1989), *Phantom of Paris* (1931), *Siren of Bagdad* [sic] (1953), *The Spider* (1940), *The Strange Mr. Gregory* (1945), *Those Wonderful Movie Cranks* (1978), *Two on a Guillotine* (1965) and *West of Zanzibar* (1928).

Firebird, The *See* BALLET.

Fludd, Robert (1574–1637) A wizard, philosopher and physician in Elizabethan England, Robert Fludd was born in Milgate House, Bearsted, near Maidstone in Kent, the fifth son of Sir Thomas Fludd, the royal treasurer for the British armed services stationed in the Netherlands. Little is known of Robert Fludd's childhood until 1592 when he entered St. John College at Oxford. Four years later he received his Bachelor of Arts degree, and in 1598 he received his master's.

Fludd traveled the Continent for six years, mostly at his father's expense but occasionally tutoring in royal and prominent households. Coming back to continue studies in England, he earned his Doctorate in Medicine from Christ Church Oxford in 1605. Because his views on medical treatment often clashed with established custom, he did not immediately receive a fellowship from the Royal College of Physicians. In fact, he was forced to endure three grueling certification exams before finally being awarded a license to practice medicine in September 1609.

Fludd moved to London. Like his near-contemporary, Simon FORMAN, Fludd's practice was unorthodox, including the prescription and use of specially formulated secret potions. While unsettling to his colleagues, the cures were surprisingly successful.

Fludd believed that for all illnesses the mind and spirit must be treated before the body. His approach included diagnosis through ASTROLOGY and casting a patient's HOROSCOPE.

As the years progressed, Fludd became more and more involved in the occult, actively practicing ALCHEMY and cabalistic magic. He inexplicably took an enigmatic alias, *De Fluctibus*, meaning "of the waves, or Flood."

Just as AGRIPPA had examined the universe in his masterpiece *Occult Philosophy* (DE OCCULTA PHILOSOPHIA), Fludd contemplated the role of the divine cosmos in a 1617 two-volume work *Utriusque Cosmi . . . Historia* (*History of the Macrocosm and the Microcosm*). The first half dealt mainly with the nature of God, the heavens and humanity. The second volume surveyed various forms of DIVINATION, especially geomancy (a practice in which Fludd was particularly adept), PALMISTRY and astrology.

Fludd's most questionable investigations involved his quest for the mystic bloodstone, which had been described by PARACELSUS. In the course of his experimentation, Fludd was thought to have distilled blood and ripped the living head off a man's body. According to a contemporary Scottish physician named William Maxwell, Fludd also owned a human magnet: Made of the rotting flesh taken "from a body still warm, and from a man who has died a violent death," a human magnet supposedly had the ability to attract other bodily organs to it for their alchemic or ritual use.

Whether Fludd actually practiced BLACK MAGIC is uncertain, but he defended the art in two works, *Mosaical Philosophy* and *Summum Bonum*. He also wrote treatises defending the ROSICRUCIANS, most notably *Apologia Compendiaria Fraternitatem de Roseacroce* (1616).

Fludd died on July 8, 1637. He was buried in Holy Cross Church in Bearsted under a simple slab which he had designed. In August 1638, Thomas Fludd presented a sculpted bust of his uncle Robert to the church, where it still remains. Recognizing Fludd's dual life as physician and metaphysician, its inscription begins, "Sacred to the memory of Robert Fludd . . ., Doctor of both medicines."

folk medicine While folk medicine is often dismissed as superstitious nonsense and a collection of old wives' tales, its roots lie in primitive human attempts to combat sickness and disease through an understanding of his surroundings.

In many tribal societies, where the natives are unaware of biological causes, illness is still thought of in supernatural rather than scientific terms. In tribal Africa, for example, the MEDICINE MAN is responsible for the prevention and curing of disease. Over generations, these primitive doctors have learned the medicinal uses of herbs, leaves and roots. While it is acknowledged that the medicine man's potions are useful in healing, it is assumed that the sickness itself was probably caused by evil SPIRITS or WITCHCRAFT. Thus, the medicine man might also need to use a special TALISMAN or INCANTATION to fight off the malevolent forces. Therefore, it is the secret tonic derived from plants delivered in combination with the use of magical AMULETs and CHARMS—a form of psychological faith healing—that is the medicine man's crude form of folk medicine. Here, the medicine man is playing the role of magician, albeit one practicing WHITE MAGIC, as much as that of a doctor.

Throughout the centuries, even as established medical learning progressed, unconventional medical wisdom grew as well. Some of the unorthodox prescriptions actually worked—the result of generations of trial-and-error experiments on the treatment of common disorders with organic drugs. Occasionally, cures take place that cannot be attributed to the use of herbs or root derivatives. Author Martin Gardner suggests two reasons why this might occur:

1. The body is self-healing, and many illnesses pass through the system on their own; and
2. Many ailments have a psychological rather than a physical basis, often allowing "miracle cures" to occur.

Because many of these cures have happened under rather unusual circumstances, a whole litany of old-wives'-tale cures have emerged. For example, one of the most colorful methods of removing, or curing, warts is described by the title character in Mark Twain's *The Adventures of Tom Sawyer*:

> You got to go all by yourself, to the middle of the woods, where you know there's a spunk-water stump, and just as it's midnight you back up against the stump and jam your hand in and say:
> "Barley-corn, Barley-corn, injun-meal shorts,
> Spunk-water, spunk-water, swaller these warts."
> and then walk away quick, eleven steps, with your eyes shut, and then turn around three times and walk home without speaking to anybody. Because if you speak the charm's busted.

Huckleberry Finn recommends that, instead, the sufferer should draw blood from the wart, drop several drops on a bean and then bury the bean in a crossroads. It was believed that as the bean rotted, the wart would shrink and disappear. (This type of cure endorses the "law of similia" or "like cures like," a form of SYMPATHETIC MAGIC.)

Fin also gives perhaps the ultimate cure for warts:

> Why you take your cat and go and get in the graveyard 'long about midnight when somebody that was wicked has been buried; and when it's midnight a devil will come, or maybe two or three, but you can't see 'em, you can only hear something like the wind, or maybe hear 'em talk; and when they're taking that feller away, you heave your cat after 'em and say, "Devil follow corpse, cat follow devil, warts follow cat, I'm done with ye!" That'll fetch *any* wart.

In *The New Apocrypha*, John Sladek explains the appeal of folk medicine by comparing the use of orthodox versus "fringe" medicine:

ORTHODOX MEDICINE	FOLK MEDICINE
Uses synthetic/ compounded drugs	"Natural" remedies
Technical/difficult to understand	Simple/common sense

Simon Forman, the notorious 17th-century wizard, necromancer and astrologer.

Expensive	Inexpensively homemade
Uncaring physician	Sympathetic doctor
Treatment painful/ unpleasant	Cure is calm and relaxed
Cure uncertain	Cure guaranteed
Admits incurable cases	Never admits defeat
Failures reported	Failures seldom discussed

There is no doubt that folk medicine exists and is commonly practiced today, from mending a child's small scrape by "kissing it to make it better" to curing a cold by drinking a concoction of whiskey, honey and lemon. In a very real sense, the practitioners of folk medicine are our modern-day wizards and alchemists, using a blend of psychology, charms and secret herbal knowledge to effect seemingly magical cures.

Forman, Simon (1552–1611) Born December 30, 1552, in Quidhampton, Wiltshire, Simon Forman was a notorious practitioner of ASTROLOGY, NECROMANCY and the invocation and communication with SPIRITS. Like most wizards in the time of Elizabethan England, he was also adept at making CHARMS, TALISMANS and ELIXIRS, including love potions and poisons. At some point, Forman purportedly used waxen images (see VOODOO DOLL) to cast SPELLS among the courtiers of King James VI of Scotland (later James I of England, 1603–25).

In 1589 Forman moved to the Cripplegate section of London, and he set up shop as an astrologer and magician to support himself. Forman had only completed grammar school, but his working knowledge of Latin was enough to help convince an unsuspecting public that he could also practice medicine.

His work was visible enough to draw the unwelcome attention of the Royal College of Physicians and the Guild of Barber-Surgeons, both of which sought his censure. At one point he was fined and jailed for a year; after his release, he moved further away from his foes to the neighboring Lambeth district.

Despite his unorthodox treatments, which included diagnosis by casting HOROSCOPES, Forman seemed to be at least—and often times more—successful than his more learned medical colleagues. In fact, Forman was frequently more heroic, staying in London to treat victims of the plague (as best he could) while other doctors deserted the city. In 1603 Forman was eventually awarded a medical license from Cambridge University.

A man of enormous sexual desires, Forman had several mistresses in addition to his wife. Certainly he appreciated the countess of Somerset's reasons when she approached him about providing her with a potion that would cause her husband-by-arrangement, the earl of Essex, to be impotent. The philtre worked, and the countess was able to secure an annulment on the grounds that the marriage had never been, and never could be, consummated. She immediately turned her attentions to the earl of Somerset. To win his love, she utilized a waxen image provided by Forman, and she was finally wed to the earl in 1613.

On July 26, 1604, Forman met John DEE, who shared his fascination in ENOCHIAN MAGIC and the KABALLAH. Forman

Sir Thomas Overbury was the victim of poisoning by the Countess of Somerset, a client of the late Simon Forman, and the wizard's apprentice, Anne Turner.

remained a student of the arcane and ancient GRIMOIRES, such as *The KEY OF SOLOMON*, for the remainder of his life.

Simon Forman dropped dead on September 8, 1611, while rowing on the Thames River, near Puddle-dock. According to William LILLY, Forman had used astrology to predict correctly the exact hour of his own death. Forman left behind personal copies of numerous magical writings, from notes to full manuscripts, but it is unknown which he had actually used during his occult investigations. "Sweet Father Forman," a supposedly simple trader in common magical goods for household use, left a sizable estate for his time—1,200 pounds.

The resolution to the countess of Somerset story occurred after Forman's death. The earl's friend, Sir Thomas Overbury, was aware of the countess's magical schemes and complicity with Forman, but before he could warn the earl, he was jailed as a political prisoner in the Tower of London. The countess made a plan to poison Overbury while he was in the tower, but Forman, who could have provided the magical brew, was gone.

She convinced Mrs. Anne Turner, a former aide to Forman, to sneak poison into Overbury's food. Soon after the body of Overbury was discovered, Turner was charged with murder by use of BLACK MAGIC. Her statement implicated the countess and the earl, who were subsequently arrested as accomplices.

The trial was held in 1616. After hearing all of the evidence, which included testimony on the nefarious sorcery of Forman, Lord Chief Justice Sir Edward Coke declared that Forman had been Satan incarnate and that Anne Turner was his daughter. He found all three defendants guilty of murder. The countess and the earl had royal connections, of course, and they were eventually pardoned by King James. Mrs. Turner was not so fortunate and was executed at Tyburn. (See also ANGELIC ALPHABET; ANGELIC KEYS; KELLY, EDWARD; SYMPATHETIC MAGIC.)

fortune-telling See CARTOMANCY; CRYSTAL BALL; DIVINATION; GYPSY; TAROT CARDS.

48 Angelic Keys See ANGELIC ALPHABET; DEE, JOHN; KELLY, EDWARD.

Fourth Book of Occult Philosophy See AGRIPPA, HEINRICH CORNELIUS; TURNER, ROBERT.

Frier Bacon, and Frier Bongay, The Honorable Historie of Written by Robert Greene (1558–92) and first acted and published posthumously in 1594, the comic verse-and-prose play *Frier Bacon, and Frier Bongay* is a variation on the FAUST legend. It is also based on a pamphlet *The famous historie of Fryar Bacon*, which told the tales of real-life scholars Roger BACON (1210/1214–post 1292) and Thomas BUNGAY (fl. 1290s).

In the play, the two friars sculpt a head out of brass and, using sorcery, call up the Devil to teach them how to make the head speak. The Devil makes his pact but warns that the friars must be alert. The head will talk within a month, and "If they heard it not before it had done speaking, all their labour should be lost."

To preclude his missing the bust speaking any prophetic words, Bacon hovers over the head, night and day, for three weeks. Exhausted, he turns over the guard to Miles, a servant, and falls asleep. Almost immediately, the brass head intones two words: "Time is."

Miles, not wishing to disturb Bacon for such an insignificant message, allows him to sleep. The head drones: "Time was." One last time it speaks ("Time is past"), then falls to the floor and shatters. The crash awakens Bacon, who CURSES and punishes his servant.

As in many works based on the Faust theme, one of the scenes involves a demonstration of magical skills before royalty. In *Frier Bacon, and Frier Bongay*, the protagonists of the title and a German wizard each perform for the German emperor and the kings of England and Spain (Castile).

Gandalf See *HOBBIT, THE; LORD OF THE RINGS, THE;* TOLKIEN, J.R.R..

Gaufridi, Father Louis (1572–1611) Almost certainly *not* in league with the Devil, Father Louis Gaufridi was tried and executed for sorcery and WITCHCRAFT in 1611 because of accusations made against him by nuns in the Aix-en-Provence region of France.

At the age of 11, Madeleine de Demandolx de la Palud (1593–1670) was placed into the Ursuline convent at Aix, but she was soon returned to her parents. She was placed under the care of the parish priest of Accoules in Marseilles, Father Gaufridi.

Because Gaufridi already had a reputation of being far from celibate—in fact, he was very popular as a private counselor and confessor—Mother Superior of the Ursuline Convent Catherine de Gaumer became quite concerned about the priest's relationship with Madeleine. Her fears were well founded: when Madeleine joined the convent the next year, she confessed her sexual affairs with Gaufridi to de Gaumer.

At the age of 14, Madeleine began convulsing, seemingly in the throes of demonic possession. An exorcism was attempted by the Jesuit Father Romillon, but during the ordeal Madeleine accused Gaufridi of having had sex with her three years earlier, a charge Gaufridi promptly denied. Madeleine next denounced Gaufridi as being a witch and worshiping Satan.

By this time, the hysterics had spread to another sister, Louise Capeau. Before long, she claimed to be possessed by Astaroth, Beelzebub and Leviathan plus thousands of other demons.

The Flemish exorcist Father Domptius attempted to treat Capeau; it was during one of his sessions that one of the demons, through Capeau, CURSEd Gaufridi for Madeleine's condition. Gaufridi himself attempted an exorcism of Capeau, only to hear her further accuse him of sexual perversions and being a sorcerer.

Before long, eight nuns were condemning Gaufridi. Although a search of Gaufridi's living quarters produced no evidence of BLACK MAGIC being practiced by the priest, he was still under suspicion by the Grand Inquisitor Sebastian Michaelis.

In 1611, Gaufridi was imprisoned and tried in Aix. In court, both Madeleine and Capeau, in shrieks and hysteria, denounced Gaufridi as a wizard, of cannibalism and of being an agent of the Devil. Madeleine's testimony was considered all the more truthful when "DEVIL'S MARKs" were discovered on her body.

Three such marks were also found on Gaufridi's body. Under torture, he signed a confession that he had eaten babies and celebrated a BLACK MASS at a witches' SABBAT. Finally, the "actual" pact Gaufridi had made with Satan, signed by the priest with his own blood, was produced in court.

Although Gaufridi claimed his confession was coerced by torture, he was found guilty and sentenced to death by fire. First, he endured more torture—being roasted over a pile of slow-burning bushes. He made a new confession on April 20, 1611; 10 days later, he officially asked God's pardon, as required before execution.

Gaufridi suffered additional torture: first, he was hoisted upward by the ropes that tied his wrists together behind his back. Meanwhile, weights were attached to his feet and thumbscrews were also applied. A second torture, known as squassation, followed: After hanging for a period with even heavier weights connected to the legs, the rope was suddenly released and then stopped suddenly; the jerk dislocated every joint in the body. Still living, Gaufridi was dragged through the streets and then, mercifully, strangled before being publicly burned. Despite his sexual sins, Gaufridi almost certainly had virtually no guilt as a sorcerer; yet he paid the ultimate price for practicing witchcraft.

Madeleine miraculously recovered from possession, but she continued to be suspect by the INQUISITION. In 1642 she successfully defended herself against witchcraft, but 10 years later the Devil's marks reappeared and she was tried and sentenced to life imprisonment. She was finally released shortly before her death at the age of 77.

See also GRANDIER, FATHER URBAIN.

Gawain and the Green Knight, Sir Written anonymously (or by an author whose name is now lost) at the end of the 14th century (c.1375) in the northwest midlands of Britain, *Sir Gawain and the Green Knight* is a 2,530-1ine alliterative poem, composed in Middle English. The verses are separated into four sections, called fitts, two of which describe the power of a magical AMULET.

In Fitt I, King ARTHUR and his court await a predicted magical phenomenon to take place on New Year's Day. The Green Knight approaches and offers to allow any knight to behead him if he may return to decapitate that same knight the following year. Gawain accepts the challenge and beheads the foreign knight, who promptly picks up his head and departs from the stunned court.

In the second fitt, Gawain sets out on a mission on Christmas Eve of the following year. A lord allows him to stay in his castle while the lord hunts on the surrounding grounds on condition that each night the men exchange their plunder for the day.

The third fitt tells of the next three days in which the master hunts outside while Gawain entertains the lady of the castle. On the first day, Gawain receives one kiss; on the second day, two kisses; on the third day, he receives a magical belt, or girdle, which he is told will save his life. Gawain gladly swaps the first two days' kisses for the game that the lord has captured, but he keeps the girdle for his imminent meeting with the Green Knight.

In the final part of the poem, Gawain enters the chapel of the Green Knight and kneels. The Green Knight twice pretends to strike Gawain, and a third blow only makes a small cut on Sir Gawain's neck. The Green Knight reveals himself to be the lord of the castle and explains that while the girdle *did* save his life, the slash was sustained because Gawain was not completely honest in his dealings. When Sir Gawain tells this tale back at King Arthur's court, all of the knights adopt the wearing of a green girdle.

Gebir Written by W.S. Landor (1775–1864), the epic poem *Gebir* was published in seven volumes in 1798. Some of the poem originally appeared in Latin, and Landor later published the work in its entirety in Latin as *Gebirus.*

It tells the story of Gebir, a prince of Iberia, who sets out to conquer Egypt but falls in love with and marries Charoba, the queen. Dalica, the queen's nurse, arranges Gebir's murder, and a magic SPELL destroys the new city he is building. In a supernatural subplot, Gebir's brother Tamat, a shepherd, is safely whisked under the ocean by a nymph.

Gemini See ASTROLOGY; HOROSCOPE; ZODIAC.

genie or genii See "ALADDIN AND THE WONDERFUL LAMP;" FILM, *ALADDIN;* JINN; *KEY OF SOLOMON, THE.*

Geoffrey of Monmouth (c.1100–1154) More precisely named Gaufridus Monemutensis, Geoffrey was most probably a Benedictine monk at Monmouth. After studying at Oxford, he became archdeacon of Llandaff and, in 1152, bishop of St. Asaph.

His reputation rests on his literary masterpiece, the *Historia Regum Britanniae* (*History of the British Kings*), published about 1136. The work is a 1,900 year survey of the rulers of pre-Christian Britain, through the time of Brut, the country's first acknowledged "king," up to the rule of Cadwallader in A.D. 689. Much of the tome concentrates on the legends surrounding King ARTHUR and MERLIN; in fact, the fifth section of the book, *The Prophecies of Merlin,* was eventually published as a separate volume in 1603.

The *Historia* was translated into many different languages, including Anglo-Norman (by Geoffrei Gaimar, fl. c.1140, and Wace, in the mid-1100s), English (Laȝamon, in the late 1100s, and Robert of Gloucester, fl. 1260–1300) and French. Its French

editions precipitated in part the VULGATE CYCLE, which, in turn, heavily influenced Sir Thomas MALORY and subsequent writers on Merlin and the Arthurian myths.

Geoffrey claimed to have received his information from an early (but unsubstantiated) Welsh book given him by Walter Calenius (d. 1151), the archdeacon at Oxford. More probably, his work was a combination of ancient British legends, the writings of Bede (673–735) and Nennius (fl. c.830), plus his own fertile imagination. Although Geoffrey's *Historia* and its source were denounced as fiction from many quarters, including William of Newburgh (1136–98?) and Ranulf Higden (c.1280–1364), it remains a valuable account for its insight into the accepted traditions of early Britain and for its influence on later generations.

Because the modern conception of Arthur and the surrounding legends has as its most early directly traceable source the writings of Geoffrey of Monmouth, his *Historia* deserves some examination in detail, especially its differences with the writings of later authors. Foremost is its tone. Even though the work is populated with some supernatural creatures and Arthur and his knights are credited with several physically impossible deeds, the book is, for the most part, realistic rather than fantastic in style.

According to Geoffrey, Arthur's father is Utherpendragon (given by later authors as Uther Pendragon). Pendragon becomes king of the Britons and desires Ygerne (later seen as Ygaerne, Igerne or Igraine), the wife of Gorlois, the duke of Cornwall. Pendragon convinces Merlin to transform him into the duke's double so that he may enter Ygerne's bed. This union conceives Arthur. After Gorlois's death, Pendragon marries Ygerne.

Historically, no Uther Pendragon seems to have ever existed. Scholars suggest that Geoffrey formed the name from a bastardization of the Welsh *Arhur mab Uthr,* "Arthur the terrible" into "Arthur son of Uther." *Pendragon* means "chief dragon." *Uther* may be a variation of the Welsh word *uthr,* meaning "terrible."

Arthur is crowned king at Silchester at the age of 15 when Pendragon dies (and is buried at Stonehenge). Wielding his mighty sword Caliburn (named EXCALIBUR by later authors) and his shield Pridwen (the name of his ship in *The Spoils of Annwn*), Arthur fights the Saxons, wins a decisive victory at Somerset (an incident probably based on the battle of Mount Baden) and becomes ruler over all of Britain. He marries Guanhamara (Guinevere), a Roman noblewoman, and sets up his court at Caerleon. Arthur's half-sister Anna (identified in later writings as Morgawse and sometimes Morcades), the daughter of Igraine and Gorlois, marries King Lot of Lothian, king of Orkney. Anna and Lot have five sons: Gawain, Gaheris, Agravain (or Agravaine), Gareth and Modred. Geoffrey suggests that Modred is Arthur's son through an accidental (i.e., mistaken-identity) incestuous union with Morgawse and therefore only the half-brother of Gawain and the others. (Beginning with Malory and continuing at least through Tennyson, Modred's name is spelled *Mordred.*)

Arthur conquers all of the British Isles, Iceland, Norway, Denmark and, after nine years of fighting, France.

When Roman Emperor Lucius Hiberius demands tribute, Arthur declares war and travels across Europe, leaving Guanhamara and Modred in charge of the kingdom. After defeating the emperor's collected armies of 40,000, Arthur begins to descend on Rome.

According to Geoffrey of Monmouth, Lucius Hiberius's killer is unknown, but in Malory, Arthur himself kills him. In still other versions, the emperor is slain by Sir Gawain. Regardless, it is during his offense on Rome that Arthur hears of Modred's treason: With the queen and the nation's consent, he has taken Guanhamara as his lover and assumed the throne.

Arthur rushes back and slays Modred in battle in Cornwall by the river Camel (Geoffrey's translation of the battle of Camlann from the *Annales Cambriae*). In the fray, Modred succeeds in mortally wounding Arthur, and the king is carried to the island of Avalon, one of the Celtic Isles of the Blest, for rejuvenation. According to Geoffrey and others, *Avalon* meant the "Island of Apples." Avalon has also been named as the island ruled by Avalloc along with his daughters, including Morgan. Repentant, Guanhamara enters a nunnery.

geomancy   See DEE, JOHN; DIVINATION; TURNER, RICHARD.

Geraldine   See *CHRISTABEL*.

ghost   See SPIRIT.

glamour   Although today the words *glamour* (also written *glamor*) and *glamourous* have the innocent meaning of "bewitchingly beautiful," their original connotation was connected to the mysteries of ancient ALPHABETs.

In the times of the pharaohs, the Egyptian priests and scribes maintained their power, at least in part, by their seemingly supernatural ability to read and write in hieroglyphics. The written words of successive languages of other ancient lands also remained elusive and incredible to the uninitiated (i.e., the uneducated). The ability of the clergy, learned men and occultists of medieval Europe to communicate in a written Latin *grammar* seemed just as awesome to commoners as magic, or even WITCHCRAFT.

Through the natural evolution of language, *grammar* became *glamour*, still maintaining its aura of mystery. In time, the word's cabalistic sense was lost, so that today a glamourous woman is merely one who casts her SPELL over an appreciative male. Likewise, an unexplainable, almost mystical hold over another person is sometimes still referred to as a glamour.

Glinda, the Good Witch of the North   See *WIZARD OF OZ, THE*.

Glubbdubdrib   Visited by Gulliver in Part III, Chapter VII of *GULLIVER'S TRAVELS* by Jonathan Swift (1667–1745), Glubbdubdrib is the island of sorcerers.

Upon arrival, Gulliver meets the governor of Glubbdubdrib. Although the methods or source of the sorcerers' powers are not revealed to him, Gulliver is empowered to conjure up anyone from the dead.

Most interested in what he refers to as people of "pomp and magnificence," Gulliver first calls up famous political leaders, generals and rulers of the past—Alexander the Great, Hannibal, Caesar, Pompey and Brutus. Of them all, Gulliver is most impressed by Brutus, who seems to possess "virtue, bravery and firmness of mind."

Finally, Gulliver summons a series of political and historical heroes, "destroyers of tyrants and usurpers, and the restorers of liberty to oppressed and injured nations." Through his discussions with these great men of ancient times, Gulliver discovers some of the great hoaxes and lies in history.

Gnostics and Gnosticism   Gnosticism was a spiritual system, established around ancient Alexandria, Egypt, which incorporated the beliefs from the religions of Egypt, Babylonia and Persia, along with elements of the Judeo-Christian faith (including their cabalistic traditions). The Gnostics acquired their name from the Greek word *gnosis* (meaning "knowledge"): because of their quest for absolute, divine wisdom. At one end of the scale, the mind of the One Supreme Being was considered Ideal (and, therefore, perfect in its goodness); everything on earth was thought to be, at its core, evil. Although not an original tenet of Gnosticism, later adherents to the religion practiced magic and sorcery.

Employed as a CHARM in ancient Egypt, the word *Ablanathanalba* (thought to mean "Thou art a father to us") was used by the Gnostics as a magic word for conjuration.

Gnosticism embraced more than 70 different sects. The wizard Basilides was the founder of a group of Gnostics that lived in Alexandria in the second century A.D. Other sects included the Messalians of Armenia (whose influence moved westward toward the Balkans between the fourth and 11th centuries) and the Paulicians, who, in A.D. 872, also entered the Balkans. Together, the Messalians and the Paulicians shaped the Bogomils, who were in Bulgaria by A.D. 950 and in Bosnia, Italy and France by the 12th century.

Goetia   See *LEMEGETON: THE LESSER KEY OF SOLOMON*.

Golden Bough, The   Written by Scottish anthropologist Sir James George Frazer (1854–1941) and first published in two volumes in 1890, *The Golden Bough: A Study in Magic & Religion* is one of the most important and influential studies of comparative myth and magic in the past century. The now-standard single-volume abridged edition first appeared in 1922.

In *The Golden Bough*, Frazer suggested that civilizations evolve through belief systems, from the magical to the religious to the scientific. He defined mankind's attempt to control his environment through the ritual manipulation of similar objects as SYMPATHETIC MAGIC, based on a "Law of Sympathy." He delineated two forms of sympathetic magic: homeopathic magic (also called IMITATIVE MAGIC) and CONTAGIOUS MAGIC. Further, Frazer discussed the role of the priest-kings in ancient societies, tree SPIRITs and the magical control of the weather (see RAINMAKER).

Frazer was educated at the universities of Glasgow and Cambridge and was a fellow of Trinity College, Cambridge. In addition to *The Golden Bough*, for which he is best known, his other works include *Totemism and Exogamy* (1910) and *Folklore in the Old Testament* (1918).

golem   Many cultures have among their folklore a tale of the golem, a mud or clay statue being brought to life through magical evocation. In some versions of the story, the creature can speak, but in most the golem remains mute.

The first creator of a golem according to Jewish legend was Rabbi Elijah of Chelm (d. 1583). Better remembered because of the many stories that surrounded him was Judah Loew ben Bezaleel, the rabbi of Prague (c.1520–1609), who animated a red-clay figure through the INCANTATION of cabalistic invocations and writing *Emeth* (meaning "Life") on the statue's forehead. Eventually the figure was turned back into earth by removing the inscription.

According to another tale, Rabbi Loew would transform the golem back into clay every Friday at dusk because all creatures must rest on the Sabbath. He did this by erasing the words *Shem Hameforash* (the name of God) from the golem's forehead. One week, however, he was careless and the word *Shem* was not completely obliterated. Midway through the rabbi's service, the golem broke into the synagogue, scattering the congregation.

Jakob Grimm, of the BROTHERS GRIMM, told the story in his 1808 book *Journal for Hermits* of a man awakening his clay statue by writing *Emeth* on its forehead and reciting God's name. The creature was used as a servant but soon grew larger than its master. The word *Emeth* was changed to *Meth* (meaning "He is dead"), and the golem turned to dust.

In a variation of his own story, Grimm mentions one golem that grew too tall for the sorcerer to reach its forehead. He commanded the creature to remove its boots and bend forward, which it did. The golem's master erased the first letter *E*, the creature collapsed on top of him, and the man was crushed to death.

The Talmud uses the Hebrew word *golem* to refer to Adam's body immediately following creation, after he was formed by God but before he had received the "breath of life." It is also used to mean an uncultured, crude or uncouth man. *Golem* only appears once in the Old Testament of the Bible and is used to suggest an unborn human being, in essence an embryo or fetus (Psalm 139.6). The term later assumed the same meaning as the Greek word *hyle*, matter which has no definite or discernible form. When and how the word *golem* entered Jewish lore is unknown; today *golem* has come to mean any living being, especially one that is human, that has been created and animated by magic.

The concept of the golem passed into ALCHEMY, which sought to originate life in the form of a HOMUNCULUS, a being produced artificially through the liquefaction and mixture of precious metals. In many ways, the story of the golem is similar to that of Dr. Frankenstein and his creature or the animated BROOMSTICKS of *The Sorcerer's Apprentice* (see FANTASIA).

good fairies, the (Flora, Fauna and Merryweather)   See FILMS, *SLEEPING BEAUTY.*

Grand Grimoire, The   See GRIMOIRE.

Grandier, Father Urbain   Father Urbain Grandier was at the center of the last major WITCHCRAFT trial of the 17th century, which took place in Loudon, France. This sensational case accused Father Grandier with sorcery and the BEWITCHMENT of several of the sisters in the town's nunnery.

The handsome, young Father Grandier was appointed parish priest of St.-Pierre-du-Marché in Loudon in 1617. His amorous adventures with area women were infamous, and on June 2, 1630, he was charged with immorality before the bishop of Poitiers, one of his adversaries in the church hierarchy. Grandier was pronounced guilty, but his friend the Archbishop Sourdis of Bordeaux acquitted him.

Gaudier's foes were not content. Father Mignon, confessor to the nuns at the Ursuline convent in Loudon, convinced Mother Superior Jeanne des Anges (Madame de Béclier) and another nun to pretend to be possessed by demons. During exorcism by Father Mignon and his coconspirator, Father Pierre Barré, the nuns were to swear that they were bewitched by Grandier. The archbishop was not deceived, and he forbade Mignon and Barré from performing exorcisms.

Father Grandier had a major enemy, however, in Cardinal RICHELIEU (1585–1642), whose spiritual and secular power were consolidated under King Louis XIII. With Richelieu's tacit consent, the witchcraft plot was reactivated. Under instruction from the Franciscan Father Lactance, the Capuchin Father Tranquille and the Jesuit Father Surin, many of the nuns in the convent began to fall into hysterics, seemingly the victims of demonic possession. Several of Grandier's rejected mistresses also became afflicted, adding to the frenzy.

Their priest/confessors were careful to exorcise them in public, where all could hear the women accuse Grandier of sorcery. Grandier was forced to lead several exorcisms personally, which allowed the nuns to accuse him to his face. In all, Grandier was denounced by 60 witnesses. Finally, a blood-signed pact with the Devil in Grandier's hand was produced. (It is still extant in the Bibliothèque Nationale in Paris).

The INQUISITION insisted that Grandier's trial for heresy and WITCHCRAFT be held in a secular, not an ecclesiastical, court. Character witnesses for Grandier were not allowed to testify,

A 1627 woodcut portrait of Father Urbain Grandier, who was accused and found guilty of bewitching several of the nuns of Loudon.

As punishment for his supposed heresy, Grandier was burned alive at the stake, in Loudon in 1634. (Contemporary etching)

and others (including Grandier's brothers and a doctor who had diagnosed the nun's delirium as fraudulent) were forced to flee the country to save their lives. None of the repentant nuns (including the mother superior, who threatened to hang herself) were allowed to retract their accusations. A public meeting held in Grandier's defense was declared treasonous to the king.

On November 30, 1633, Father Grandier was convicted of sorcery, and on August 18, 1634, he was sentenced to death by Councillor of State Monsieur Jean de Laubardemont for "the crime of magic, witchcraft, and causing possession." Grander was "to have his body burned alive and therewith the pacts and magic characters now resting in the office of the Registrar." [sic]

Even under subsequent horrendous torture, a confession of sorcery was never obtained from Father Grandier. Father Lactance died from insanity within a month of Grandier's execution, and Father Tranquille died of madness within five years. In 1640, Father Barré was exiled from France for concocting additional false stories of demon possession. Many of the nuns continued their hysterics, however, and the town of Loudon and its notorious convent attracted curious visitors for years.

The historical events at the nunnery of Loudon were the basis for at least two popular literary pieces. *The Devils of Loudon*, written by Aldous Huxley (1894–1963) in 1952 examines sexual frenzy. Huxley's book, in turn, was the inspiration for *The Devils*, a 1961 dramatic adaptation by John Whiting (1917–1963). Two FILMS, *The Devil and the Nun* (1960) and *The Devils* (1970), were also based on the lurid tales of Loudon. See also GAUFRIDI, FATHER LOUIS.

Greco-Roman magic   Belief in magic and sorcery was prevalent, if not universal, in the times of ancient Greece and Rome, and its practice was frequently mentioned in the cultures' literature. Homer, for example, named the enchantress Agamede in his *The Iliad*; and *The ODYSSEY* secured the legend of CIRCE, who was able to transform men into swine.

Mentioned in the writings of Cicero (106–43 B.C.), Bacis was a sage and seer in ancient Boeotia. Demosthenes (c.383–322 B.C.), the famous Athenian orator and writer of prose, mentions Theodoris of Lemnos, a Greek enchantress who was sentenced to death for her use of sorcery. According to the Greek historian Herodotus (c.480–c.425 B.C.), Lemnos was infamous for the practice of WITCHCRAFT.

The legend of Glaukias and Chrysis, as told by Lucian of Samosata (A.D. c.125–c.200), involved one of the great love SPELLs of the ancient Greeks—"drawing down the moon." Glaukias, overcome with unrequited love for Chrysis, petitioned a sorcerer from Hypoborea to help him. The mystic invoked HECATE, the goddess of magic and queen of the Underworld, who lowered the moon to Earth. The lunar orb enchanted a clay figurine, which came to life (see GOLEM), hurried to Chrysis and filled her with love for Glaukias. Representations of drawing down the moon were painted on Grecian vases as early as 200 B.C.

Lucian of Samosata described two other love spells, both of which involved the use of waxen images. In the first method, a doll of wax, gum and tar was formed into the shape of a dog, about 6 inches long, and "words of power" were carved into the area of its ribs. The same CHARM was written on a horizontal clay tablet. The dog figurine was set on top of the tablet, and both were placed on a sacred tripod. The wizard then spoke the words aloud. If the dog barked, the supplicant's love would be requited; if the dog growled, the lover would never arrive. (Lucian did not record the meaning or consequences if the statue made no response.)

The second method was also image magic but bordered on NECROMANCY. The enchanter made two waxen statuettes: one of the woman he sought, sculpted in a kneeling position, and one of the god of war Ares, standing over her and holding a sword to her throat. The names of demons were inscribed on the arms and legs of the female figurine. Then, the sorcerer stabbed 13 bronze pins into the female doll. He chanted, "I pierce this (arm or leg) that she may think of me," while he jabbed a needle into each of the corresponding parts of the figure. (See VOODOO DOLL).

Next, both figurines were tied to a specially engraved metal tablet by a cord containing 365 knots. The items were taken to a cemetery and interred in the grave of someone who had died violently or young. After the sorcerer made a final petition-and-prayer to the god of the Underworld, the woman that the enchanter desired would fall in love with him.

Lucian also tells of his journey crossing the Euphrates river with the wizard Mithrobarzanes. In a thick forest on the far side, they sacrificed a sheep to the gods: "The magician, holding a lighted torch, cried out loudly, invoking all kinds of demons, the avengers, the furies, nocturnal Hecate and the lofty Proserpine, mixing up with his invocations certain barbarous and unintelligible polysyllables."

Like the prophet Daniel among the CHALDEANS, Artemidorus (fl. second century A.D.) was an expert in oneiromancy, the interpretation of dreams. His discourse on the subject, *De Somniorum Interpretatione Libri Quinque*, was translated into many languages and was read well into the 18th century.

Hermotimus, also known as Hermodorus of Clazomene, was an ancient Greek wizard, noted for his mastery of astral projection, the ability to will his soul or essence to depart from his body consciously and return whenever desired. On the island of Crete, the philosopher Epimenides was also suspected of practicing sorcery.

Grecian occultists took their magic with them when they emigrated to Alexandria, Egypt, where they founded a cult worship surrounding HERMES TRISMEGISTUS ("Hermes Thrice Greatest"), the glorious enchanter, astrologer and alchemist.

Perhaps the greatest sorceress of mythological times, whose story was dramatized by Euripides, was the witch-queen MEDEA, native of COLCHIS, a region renowned for its wizardry.

Throughout recent centuries, arcane Greek papyri that teach the occult arts have been discovered, and some are currently housed in the British Museum and in Leyden. They instruct the wizard in the production of love charms and magic finger RINGS (for success), inducing dreams, locating robbers, conferring with the gods and exorcising demons (by making the possessed person inhale sulphur and bitumen as the sorcerer exhorts the devil to depart).

The Greek author Melampus wrote two manuscripts on the art of DIVINATION. The wizard Osthanes is thought to have written the first manuscript on the medicinal use of magic. In the fourth century B.C., he was a mentor to Democritus, teaching him ALCHEMY.

Greece, of course, was famous for its ORACLEs, especially those dedicated to the service of Apollo. The most famous seer of the age was located in the temple at DELPHI, and the site became a pilgrimage for prominent and privileged citizens.

Since at least ancient Greece, superstition has said that anyone born veiled by a CAUL would be clairvoyant. Belief in the SPIRITS was universal. Fear of the EVIL EYE was prevalent: The sorcerer Diodorus of Catania, for example, was notorious for using it to control others. His infamous life came to an end when he was burned alive in an oven.

Magicians had begun to use the magic WAND, a descendant of the CADUCEUS carried by Hermes, messenger of the deities. Also among their treasured paraphernalia were ritual oil and incense lamps, keys, cymbals, a magic mirror or vessel of water (for divination), thread and human remains.

To cast spells over others, sorcerers were also using a rhombus, or "witch's wheel," which was spun to draw the victim's essence near. For long-distance bewitchment, a waxen figure or clay doll was frequently employed. CURSES were thought to be more powerful if written, especially if an occult ALPHABET were used. The words might be inscribed on a CURSE TABLET and then nailed to an altar or scribbled on a small piece of parchment which could be hidden, such as inside a hollow image of the prey.

Although NUMEROLOGY, in the modern sense, was not yet practiced, certain numbers were considered more magical than others. Also, ASTROLOGY did not play a very important role in Grecian magic until just before the time of conquest by the Romans.

The use of magic was established in Rome before its invasion of Greece. In fact, the Sabine and the Etruscan peoples were well known as wizards. The latter, in fact, were famed for their abilities as necromancers, RAINMAKERs and locating well water (see DIVINING ROD; DOWSING). Just as the Romans had absorbed and adapted the beliefs and practices of their other conquered lands, so too were they influenced by Grecian magic.

Dread of being caught by the evil eye was, if possible, even more of a concern in ancient Rome than in Greece. (In fact, although muted, the superstition lingers to this day in much of Italy.) To shield oneself, it was necessary to wear a protective AMULET. The most popular design was in the shape of a phallus, in gold, silver or bronze, and worn on a chain.

The first reference to magic in Roman writings appears to be in a legal tablet known as the Twelve Tables. One of the edicts expressly prohibits transplanting crops from one field to another by wizardry.

Love potions, sold mostly by the old wise women of the communities, were so popular that to curb their use, the early emperors proclaimed edicts calling them poisons. In actuality, the substances may very well have been toxic. Various recipes etched on extant magical papyri call for such ingredients as the blood of a pigeon, powdered snake skeleton, skin from the head of newborn colt, hair from the tail of a wolf, animal entrails and the granulated bone from the left side of a toad that had been devoured by ants!

Several Roman poets and authors mentioned enchanters in their writings. The poet Horace (65–8 B.C.) alluded to two nefarious Roman sorceresses, Sagana and Canidia (whose hair was braided with poisonous snakes).

Horace detailed Canidia's attempt to force a young man, Varus, to return her love for him. First, she mixed and set ablaze a poultice consisting of roots from a fig or a cypress tree grown over a tomb, eggs of a toad covered in blood, feathers

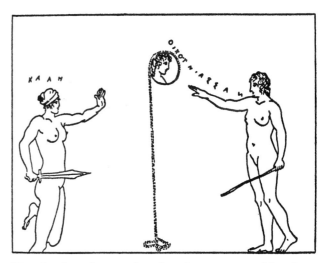

"Drawing down the moon" as a love charm was a specialty of enchantresses in ancient Greece. (Illustration from a Greek vase, c. 200 B.C.)

The frontispiece of a French edition, most likely from the 18th century, of *The Grimoire of Honorius*, one of two "black books" attributed to Pope Honorius III.

from an owl, herbs from the plains of Thessaly, fragrances from COLCHIS and jawbones ripped from a starving dog.

Meanwhile, one of Canidia's assistants "called down the moon (and the stars)." Another apprentice witch, described as having hair like the bristles of a boar or the quills of a hedgehog, ceremonially moistened the soil with water from Lake Avernus (considered to be an entrance to the Infernal Regions located at the center of the earth). A third aide dug a deep, narrow pit into which Varus was to be thrown naked so that only his head remained visible, until he professed his love for Canidia.

In his eighth *Eclogue*, Virgil (70–19 B.C.) described an enchantress weaving a love spell. First, a helper burned frankincense and vervain for fumigation. Then, the sorceress intoned an INCANTATION, "drawing down the moon." Reciting "Thus I bind the fillets of Venus," she wound a three-colored cord around a small image of the beloved while she circled a sacred altar.

Two figurines of the lover, one of wax and one of clay, were then set in front of a fire. If the wax melted before the clay

hardened, the heart of the one who was adored would also "melt" (by SYMPATHETIC MAGIC). If the clay hardened first, however, the lover's heart would turn to stone instead.

In his *Fourth* (or *Messianic*) *Eclogue*, Virgil wrote of the birth of a child who would restore a golden age. In the Middle Ages, many pointed to this as a prediction of the birth of JESUS Christ, and they proclaimed the poet a prophet and/or a wizard. So strong and prevalent was this mystic belief that it prompted Dante to select Virgil to be his guide on his fantasy journey through hell and purgatory in his masterpiece The DIVINE COMEDY.

Although it is now known that earlier writings existed, the manuscripts by Osthanes were credited by Pliny the Elder (A.D. 23–79) as being the first books to teach the magical arts. The occultist-author Osthanes traveled as an advisor with Xerxes during the warrior's campaign against Greece.

Pliny also related an accepted recipe for a gruesome charm of the time. A nest of live, newborn swallows was to be buried underground in a box. After several days, the box was exhumed and opened. A bird that had died with its beak closed could be used as an amulet to induce love; one that had died "as if gasping for breath" would drive a suitor away.

Ovid (43 B.C.–A.D. 17) makes note of Dipsias, a witch. The writer describes Dipsias's powers to fly, to raise the SPIRITS of the dead and to distill FOLK MEDICINE made from herbs.

In his epic work *Pharsalia*, the Roman poet Lucan (A.D. 39–65) tells the story of Erichtho, a sorceress who practices BLACK MAGIC and necromancy.

Tacitus (A.D. c.55–after 115), the greatest historian of Imperial Rome, records the work of Libro Drusus, also a necromancer, and Vellada, a priestess-prophetess (and, therefore, a suspected sorceress) practicing in what is today Germany.

In the fourth century A.D., the author Julius Firmicus Maternus, an authority on cabalistic magic and astrology, wrote an eight-volume book on occult subjects entitled *Mathesis*.

Quintus Serenus Sammonicus, a Roman physician in the third century A.D., was accused of using magical means to effect his cures. The wizard Julianus, also called Theurgus the Necromancer, purportedly ended the plague in ancient Rome through the use of a mystical invocation.

Rome numbered several emperors among its wizards and sorcerers. Salvius Julianus, a Roman Emperor from the second century A.D., was reputed to be a wizard. According to Pliny, Nero also attempted to learn black magic but was not very successful. His teacher, the sorcerer King Tyridates of Armenia, traveled to Rome by land rather than by sea because he

> thought it unlawful (as all magicians do) either to spit into the sea or otherwise to discharge into it from men's bodies what might pollute and defile that ELEMENT. He instructed Nero in the principles of Magic, yea and admitted him to sacred feasts and solemn suppers to initiate him into the profession; but all to no purpose, for Nero could never receive at his hands the skill of this Science.

Even emperors, however, were not immune to the magic of more powerful wizards. Roman Emperor Constantius was turned back from his siege of Ravenna by the overwhelming magic of the wizard Libanius. The sorcerer Ascletarion was ridiculed when he foretold that the body of Roman Emperor Domitian would be eaten by dogs. The prophecy did come true, however: Domitian did not die from an *attack* by hounds; *after* his death he was consumed by canines.

The myths of ancient Greece and Rome, along with stories of their magical practices, have passed into Western culture and still influence occult thinking today.

grimoire Also known as "black books," grimoires were the arcane and cabalistic sorcerers' handbooks written during the medieval ages. Though many grimoires were written anonymously, some were alleged to have been authored by such notaries as Alexander the Great or Hippocrates and passed down through the centuries. Others claimed to have been compiled by popes (see PAPACY) or occultists such as Albertus MAGNUS. The most famous grimoires were those attributed to SOLOMON.

All included specific, if almost incomprehensible, methods of invoking angels or demons or both for one's personal use. Often profusely illustrated with such designs as PENTACLES and MAGIC SQUARES, the grimoires explained mystic rites, rituals and ceremonies. Readers were warned to take the instructions literally and to follow the preparations and IN-CANTATIONS exactly as described. If they varied the procedures or were not serious in their task, the sorcerer risked failure or worse.

A list of the best-known grimoires follows:

The Almadel Arbatel

The Black Dragon (attributed to Pope Honorius III, giving seven rituals to invoke a different demon each day, starting with Lucifer on Monday, and following with Frimost, Astaroth, Silcharde, Bechard, Guland and Surgat, respectively)

The Black Hen (also known as *The Black Pullet*, and other similar titles, an early manuscript of BLACK MAGIC purportedly first published in Egypt in 1740, but more probably of late 18th-century Roman or other European origin)

The Book of Death

The Book of Raziel (purportedly based on *The Book of Signs*, which was attributed to Adam)

The Book of SACRED MAGIC OF ABRAMELIN THE MAGE

The Constitution of Honorius (attributed to 13th-century Pope Honorius III, first published in Rome in 1629 or 1670)

Enchiridion (attributed to Pope Leo III, who sent a copy to Charlemagne, A.D. 742–814; in return, the French ruler, crowned emperor of the West by Pope Leo II in A.D. 800, became the aged pope's protector)

The Grand Grimoire (purportedly edited by Antonio Venitiana del Rabina from a transcription of a work by Solomon; Part One of the black-magic grimoire teaches the evocation of the evil SPIRIT Lucifuge Rofocale by using a "blasting rod"; Part Two is the *Sanctum Regnum* or the "Rite for Making Pacts"; Eliphas LEVI used this disreputable grimoire as a major source for his writings.)

The Great and Powerful Sea Ghost (attributed to Johannes FAUSTUS)

Le Grimore (or *Black Book*, also attributed to Pope Honorius III)

Grimoirium Verum ("Translated from Hebrew by Plainagier, a Dominican Jesuit" and attributed to Alibeck the Egyptian and published in 1517; in actuality an 18th-century French work based on *The* KEY OF SOLOMON)

Hell's Coercion (also attributed to FAUSTUS)

Lemegeton: The Lesser Key of Solomon

Liber Pentaculorum

Liber Spirituum (*The Book of Spirits*)

Little Albert Oupnekhat (originally in Sanskrit, translated into Persian and then, in 1801, into Latin)

Red Book of Appin

Red Dragon

The Sage of the Pyramids

Sanctum Regum

Shemamphorus (also seen as *Shemhamphoras*, originally written in Hebrew)

The Sword of Moses (from the 10th century)

The Testament of Solomon (attributed to Solomon, written in Greek, describing the demonic assistance in the construction of Solomon's Temple; date of origin uncertain, seen as early as A.D. 100–400 and as late as the 10th century A.D.)

Tonalamatl (a Mexican "Book of Fate")

True Black Magic (or the *Secret of Secrets*, purportedly found in Solomon's tomb and translated from Hebrew by the Magus Iroe-Grgo in Rome in 1750)

Y-Kim (attributed to an anonymous wizard in China, from the fourth century B.C.)

Zekerboni (dated from the 17th century)

Grimoirium Verum See GRIMOIRE.

guardian angel The concept of *guardian* SPIRITS, intangible beings who look out for the welfare of humans, has its roots in tribal societies. The practice of ancestor worship, in fact, is based on the presumption that those who have come before us remain in our proximity after death and can be appealed to or invoked for their advice and assistance.

As part of ancient EGYPTIAN MAGIC and religion, priests and the laity often made sacrifice and devotion to the specific god who could protect or aid them. The panhellistic classic Greeks and Romans also assigned different interests to their gods and sought the attention of the proper deity for their needs.

It was well known that each Babylonian wizard had his own JINN at his disposal, giving rise to many of the tales of the *ARABIAN NIGHTS*. Even the great King SOLOMON was said to be able to summon genies at his command. In later centuries, students of the KABBALAH would cite *The* KEY OF SOLOMON as proof that such spiritual guardians and spectral servants exist.

Early Hebrew scholars accepted the concept of protective spirits but identified them as heavenly or angelic forces. By the time of the Elizabethan era in England, occultists such as John DEE and Edward KELLY had accepted these powers as guardian angels and were conducting experiments in angelic communication.

By the time of PERRAULT, the 17th-century French author of fairy tales, a vernacular equivalent to the Christian-grounded guardian angel emerged: the fairy godmother. This supernatural entity was thought to materialize in a warm, matronly human form, appearing at times of great need. The archetypal example, of course, is CINDERELLA's Fairy Godmother, whose magic transformed the "girl from the ashes" into the "belle of the ball" and ultimately helped make her a princess.

Guardian angels also appear as characters in FILMS (e.g. *It's A Wonderful Life*), OPERA (*Hansel und Gretel*) and TELEVISION (*Highway to Heaven, Touched by An Angel*). (See also NATIVE AMERICAN MAGIC; *SACRED MAGIC OF ABRAMELIN THE MAGE, THE BOOK OF THE*.)

Gulliver's Travels   *Gulliver's Travels* is an allegorical tale in which the author vents his political and sociological ideas for a better society. Written by the prolific Jonathan Swift (1667–1745) and published in 1726, the book was probably conceived at meetings with the Scriblerus Club (a group of fellow authors that met from January to July 1714 to satirize the current tastes of society), and Swift may have begun work on his *Travels* as early as 1720. It was one of his few writings that was not published anonymously and the only one for which he ever received any money (200 pounds).

The best-known incident in *Gulliver's Travels* involves the title character's contact with the miniature Lilliputians in Part I of the four-sectioned novel.

Part II describes Gulliver's experiences on Brobdingnag, where all the residents were as tall as church steeples.

The final section, by far the most biting, concerns the land of the Houyhnhnms, inhabited by creatures resembling horses that could reason and speak. Compared with dirty, slothful, vice-ridden humans, the horses seemed refreshingly clean and sober.

Of greatest significance to students of wizardry, however, is Part III, which was written last, in which Gulliver visits a variety of ancient and wise men. Chapter VII in particular tells of Gulliver's voyage to GLUBBDUBDRIB, the island of sorcerers, where he is given the ability to call up SPIRITs from the dead. Gulliver conjures up political and military figures, and mirroring the sentiments of Swift himself, Gulliver comments on their true qualities and historical importance.

Gwydion the Wizard   Gwydion was a valiant wizard of North Wales mentioned in *The Mabinogion* and in Celtic mythology. He was the son of Don, a Welsh goddess; he had a brother, Gofannon the Smith, and a sister, Arianrod (or Arianrhod). The lunar goddess of dawn and fertility, Arianrod was also the mistress of her brother Gwydion. Together, they had twin sons, Llew Llaw Gyffes and Dylan, the sea god.

In addition to having great magical powers, Gwydion was a master of science, logic and enlightenment, and he was an intermediary to Earth for gifts from the gods. (See HERMES.)

The impulsive Gwydion frequently used his magic improperly. The gods punished him for employing his enchantments against mortals and for stealing a herd of hog from Pryderi (the son of Pwyll, god of the Underworld). Ultimately, Gwydion the Wizard killed Pryderi.

Welsh folklore suggests that one of Gwydion's tricks might be the origin of the April Fool's Day tradition: He is said to have deceived Arianrod one April 1st by producing a large army, prompting his sister/lover to provide weapons for Llew Llaw Gyffes.

Another time, with the aid of Math, the god of wealth, Gwydion created a bride for his son Llew Law Gyffes. The beautiful girl, Blodeuwed, fell in love with another man, however, and as a result of her treason Llew Llaw Gyffes was murdered. According to Welsh mythology, Gwydion the Wizard tracks across the sky, with the Milky Way trailing behind him, as he looks for his late son.

gypsy   Today's gypsies are descended from the Rom, a tribal people from northern India who migrated to the Middle East and then on to Europe in the Middle Ages. Those who settled in France became known as Bohemians because they were supposed to have come from the central European region of Bohemia. The tribes that reached England (around 1450) were thought to have traveled from Egypt, hence their appellation as gypsians, or gypsies.

European gypsies have no fixed address, traveling from town to town as their providence draws (or chases) them. Legend has it that centuries ago, a gypsy king broke the taboo of marrying his sister, bringing upon his clan the dreaded "gypsy curse"

> May you wander over the face of the earth forever, never sleep twice in the same place, never drink water twice from the same well, and never cross the same river twice in a year.

Gypsies are clannish, have their own secretive customs and have their own language (a variant of Romany). As is the case with most itinerant groups, they are often met with suspicion and distrust. They are frequently accused of thievery, and their reputation as con artists has led to the abbreviation of the word *gypsy* into the derogatory slang term *gyp*.

Traditionally, gypsies, especially the women, are keenly adept at fortune-telling, especially by reading cards, tea leaves or palms and by consulting a CRYSTAL BALL. (See also CARTOMANCY; FILMS, *HUNCHBACK OF NOTRE DAME, TIME OF THE GYPSIES; HUNCHBACK OF NOTRE DAME, THE*; PALMISTRY; TAROT CARDS.)

hakata   Hakata are small pieces of ivory, wood or, quite often, bone used by African WITCH DOCTORS in their fortune-telling. To add to their mystical power, signs of the ZODIAC are sometimes carved into the hakata pieces.

The witch doctor tosses the bits onto the ground and, by interpreting the pattern in which they fall, he is able to make his prophecies. (See also BAO; EKWELE; SORTILEGE.)

Hakim   Also called Mocanna, the wizard Hakim was a legendary disciple of Muhammad. Among the many feats Hakim is alleged to have performed was turning night into day by producing a shining moon from a holy well. His end was just as dramatic: Supposedly, all but a lock of his hair dissolved when he stepped in a mystic bath that he had personally readied.

Halloween   Begun by the CELTS who crossed from France into Britain during the eighth and seventh centuries B.C., Halloween was originally a pagan harvest festival of Samhain celebrated on October 31. Giant bonfires were lit to scare away devils, witches and SPIRITS of the dead who were thought to return that night.

In the ninth century, the Christian church, new to Britain, clothed the ritual with Catholic trappings and named it "All Hallow's Eve" (*hallow* meaning "to make holy") to coincide with their All Saints Day (November 1) and All Souls Days (November 2).

Halloween was brought to the United States with the wave of Irish immigrants in the 19th century as a time for merrymaking and mischief, of "trick-or-treat."

Halloween is still traditionally linked with WITCHCRAFT, and witches are said to celebrate their most important SABBAT on that night.

hand of glory   The hand of glory, a dried human hand from a corpse, was an important instrument used during a sorcerer's necromantic ceremonies. It was usually kept in the wizard's home on the mantle over the fireplace. Witches kept theirs by the chimney through which they ascended to fly to SABBAT.

According to *Secrets merveilleux de la magie naturelle et cabalistique du Petit Albert*, a 1722 book published in Cologne, the hand of glory could be used "to stupefy those to whom it is displayed and render them motionless, in such a way that they can no more stir than if they were dead."

Secrets . . . du Petit Albert also explained that the sorcerer could nullify the effects of his hand of glory if stolen, or he could guard against another hand of glory brought into his house by another magus, by rubbing "the threshold or other parts of the house by which they may enter with an unguent composed of the gall of a black cat, the fat of a white hen, and the blood of a screech owl."

The book explains the method for the hand of glory's preparation:

> Take the right or left hand of a felon who is hanging from a gibbet beside a highway; wrap it in part of a funeral pall and so wrapped squeeze it well. Then put it into an earthenware vessel with zimat, nitre, salt, and long peppers, the whole well powdered. Leave it in this vessel for a fortnight, then take it out and expose it to full sunlight during the dog-days until it becomes quite dry. If the sun is not strong enough put it in an oven heated with fern and vervain. Next make a kind of candle with the fat of a gibbeted felon, virgin wax, sesame, and ponie, and use the Hand of Glory as a candlestick to hold this candle when lighted, and then those in every place into which you go with this baneful instrument shall remain motionless.

Modern scholars have attempted to recreate this recipe, but they are unsure of some of the necessary ingredients. *Zimat*, they surmise, might be a misspelling of *zimar*, meaning "verdigris," or it might be *zimax*, an Arabic sulphate of iron. *Ponie* is probably a colloquial Norman word for horse manure.

Harriot, Thomas (1560–1621)   Also seen as Thomas Hariot, the learned astronomer and mathematician was a tutor in the home of Sir Walter Ralegh (1554–1618) and accompanied the adventurer/poet on his 1585–86 trip to America. Although he was probably a practicing Christian, Harriot had the reputation of being an atheist and, like so many educated men of his generation, a sorcerer. Many critics also considered him to be the true force behind the nefarious SCHOOL OF NIGHT.

Heart of Man, The   See HEX.

Hecate   The first recorded reference to Hecate, the goddess of WITCHCRAFT and sorcery, was by the Greek poet Hesiod. In Greek and Roman mythology, the souls of the dead were said to attend Hecate as she traveled by night. It was believed that the most auspicious time for her invocation was at sunset or just before sunrise, during the new or full moon. Greek play-

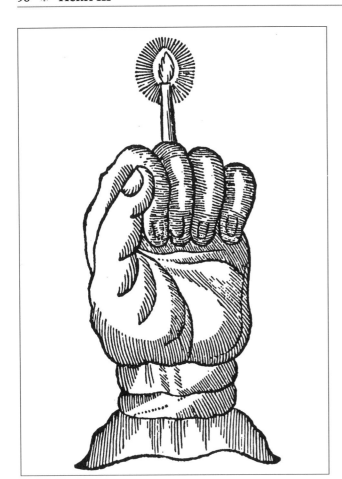

The hand of glory. (Petit Albert, *Secrets merveilleux de la magie naturelle et cabalistique du Petit Albert*)

wrights called her the Queen of the Ghost-World, and dogs began to wail in warning when she came near.

According to occult legend, Hecate performed satanic rituals and human sacrifice. Among the nefarious agents doing her evil bidding in the mortal world were Empusas, the Silent Watchers of the Night, Mormo and assorted female SPIRITS and demons.

She was considered a triple goddess because she could appear in any of three forms, with some statues representing her in all three roles: Artemis (the Huntress, on Earth), Selene (the Moon, in the Heavens) and Persephone (the Queen of the Underworld).

In ancient Greece, the remains of sacrifices, known as Hecate's suppers, were often left in her honor at crossroads, which were thought to be intensely magical sites. Occasionally, supplicants fashioned small wax or clay figures of the goddess. The writer Eusebius describes a small idol of Hecate made of the "root of rue" and powdered reptiles. Also, any use of the number three or any multiples of it was considered especially effective in conjuring Hecate.

Her name remained infamous through at least the time of Elizabethan England, as evidenced by this immortalization in SHAKESPEARE'S *MACBETH*:

> Now o'er the one half-world
> Nature seems dead, and wicked dreams abuse
> The curtain'd sleep. Witchcraft celebrates
> Pale Hecate's offerings. . . . (II, i, 49–52)

Henri III (1551–1589) Catherine de Médicis and her son, Henri III, king of France, were both suspected of sorcery during their lifetimes. It was claimed that Henri III conducted many a BLACK MASS at the Louvre and had sex with his FAMILIAR, Terragon.

Purportedly, Henri III learned his cabalistic techniques from a notorious magician Saint-Mégrin d'Espernon. The king is said to have performed his experiments at his palace at Vincennes in a tower called the Tour de Paris (or possibly in the opposing tower, the Tour du Diable). Whether the rumors of demonic invocation are true is uncertain, but after Henri III's death, the "dressed skin of a child" along with other strange occultist paraphernalia were discovered in the Vincennes castle.

A now-rare anonymous, satirical booklet, *Les Sorceleries de Henri de Valois*, described a few of the objects:

> There were lately found two silver-gilt satyrs four inches high, grasping each one a great club in his left hand and leaning thereupon, and in the right upholding a bowl of pure and very shining crystal. . . . In these bowls were unknown drugs which they had for oblations, and, what is most hateful in this matter, these satyrs were before a golden cross, in the middle whereof was inlaid wood of the True Cross of Our Lord Jesus Christ . . . Be it considered, furthermore, that the beasts turned their backsides toward the said True Cross.

Hepatoscopy See ANIMALS; DIVINATION.

Hermes The Greek messenger god Hermes was depicted wearing a winged helmet, with small wings on his ankles, and carrying a CADUCEUS. He was also the god of magic, and he frequently used his staff as a magic WAND to cast SPELLS. One of the most famous myths involving Hermes is detailed in *The ODYSSEY*: Hermes visits Odysseus on the island belonging to CIRCE, where he points out an herb that will prevent the hero from falling under the enchantress's power.

The Greeks drew close comparisons between Hermes and THOTH, the Egyptian god of magic and wisdom. Their inseparable association gave rise to the legend of HERMES TRISMEGITUS, the thrice-greatest Hermes, the legendary philosopher-priest-king and purported author of the HERMETICA.

Hermes was assimilated into the Roman pantheon as Mercury. An analogous figure appeared as a messenger to the gods Odin and Wotan in Norse and Teutonic mythology; in Celtic and Welsh legends, GWYDION THE WIZARD was known as the British Hermes.

Hermes Trismegistus Hermes Trismegistus was considered by many ancient cabalists to be the mythical Greco-Egyptian lord of ALCHEMY. As Grecians colonized Egypt, especially around the port city of Alexandria, the distinct identities of HERMES, the Greek messenger god and protector of magic, and THOTH, the Egyptian god of wisdom and magic, became inseparably intertwined. Thus, the thrice-greatest Hermes, as he was called, was considered an amalgam of both and superior to either.

Thought to be human or a demigod, Hermes Trismegistus was revered for his arcane knowledge. Thousands of occult texts were attributed to the mystic: Iamblichus (c.250–c.330 B.C.), a Syrian philosopher, claimed Hermes Trismegistus had written 20,000 manuscripts; Manetho (fl. 300 B.C.), an Egyptian priest and historian, credited him with 36,000.

The 42 surviving books attributed to Hermes Trismegistus are known as the HERMETICA. Fourteen of the short Greek texts were kept hidden for centuries by members of the Coptic church. A religious tract, *Poimandres, the Good Shepherd* reads similarly to the Gospel of St. John in the Bible. Others compare to writings of Jewish thinkers, another to Plato's *Timaeus*.

Though other writings attributed to Hermes Trismegistus mostly concern ASTROLOGY, early wizards insisted that the true secrets of alchemy were hidden within his parables. His most legendary magical writings, engraved on a tablet (or table) made of emerald, were supposedly found "in the hands of Hermes' mummy, in an obscure pit where his interred body lay" within the great pyramid of Giza. If it ever really existed, the emerald tablet of Hermes Trismegistus has long since disappeared.

Hermetica   The Hermetica is a collection of occult texts (42 in all, according to some sources), written sometime between the third century B.C. and the first century A.D. All are attributed to HERMES TRISMEGISTUS, the legendary wizard-priest and philosopher of ancient Egypt.

The works *may* have been written by one man who may or may not have been Hermes Trismegistus, but more likely they were written by a series of mystics and accumulated over the

Hermes Trismegistus. (Jacques Boissard, *De Divinatione et Magicus*)

years. According to Clement of Alexandria, 36 of the books contained the entire epistemology of the Egyptians up to that time. Of them, two dealt with music, four taught ASTROLOGY, six covered medicine, a group of 10 called the *Hieratic* delineated law and 10 more examined Egyptian sacred ritual and theology.

Unfortunately, most of the books of the Hermetica were destroyed during the burning of Alexandria and its famous library. Legend has it, however, that some complete papyri survived and are hidden deep in the desert, privy only to special initiates and members of secret cults.

Of the few known extant pieces of the Hermetica now housed in museums and libraries, all are written in the form of dialogues between Hermes Trismegistus and various Egyptian deities, including Imhotep, Ammon, ISIS, THOTH and HORUS. Much of the philosophy is similar to that of Greek thinkers of the era, especially Plato, Aristotle and the Stoics; as such, the Hermetica has some concepts in common with the concurrent writings of the GNOSTICS.

Perhaps the earliest of the Hermetic texts are those known as the *Corpus Hermeticum*, also called *The Divine Pyrander*. A collection of 17 fragments, it is an inexact translation from the first centuries A.D. of even earlier manuscripts. Still, they reveal many of the precepts of Hermes Trismegistus, how he was enlightened with divine wisdom and the ways in which he, in turn, passed on that knowledge.

The second of these books, *Poimandres* (or *The Vision*), details the Egyptian concept of the heavens and the evolution of the soul. The author takes a heavenly journey with a SPIRIT named Poimandres, who explains that the universe was separated into Darkness and Light. From the Light (or Mind) came man's reason (*Logos*, or logic). Man is made mortal, subject to Fate; yet a part of him remains immortal and spiritual. At first, man and woman coexisted in one body but they were separated in order to allow procreation. At death, the physical body is abandoned, and the spirit travels upward through the seven spheres of planets to the eighth sphere, where it is assimilated into the Godhead.

In the fifth century A.D., John Stobaeus amassed another collection of Hermetica fragments, and extracts of others were cited by Lactantius (A.D. c.300), Iamblichus (early fourth century) and Cyril of Alexandria (who quoted from one of 15 supposedly existing manuscripts in the early fifth century).

The entire text of the *Kore Kosmou* (meaning "daughter of the world" or "pupil of the world") has survived. It is a dialogue between Isis and Horus, and pieces of it can also be found in the compilation by Stobaeus. Another full manuscript is a Latin translation of the *Asclepius*, dating from around the third century. The writings of St. Augustine (d. between A.D. 604 and 609) concerning the *Asclepius* continued to influence thinking about the Hermetica up through the early 15th century.

Legend tells of the Emerald Tablet, also known as the Emerald Table, a gemstone that was inscribed (in Phoenician text) with all the wisdom and secrets of the ancient Egyptians. It was said to have been buried in the hands of Hermes Trismegistus and discovered by Sarah, the wife of Abraham. Others mystic say that APOLLONIUS OF TYANA found the tomb and the tablet.

Hex signs adorn a barn in the village of Yellow House in Berks County, Pennsylvania. (Photo by author)

By the end of the first millennium, several Arabic versions of the text from the Emerald Tablet had surfaced. The first Latin edition dates no later than A.D. 1200. Ironically, no two versions are alike, and none is completely comprehendible. All begin with the same words, however: "That which is above is like that which is below and that which is below is like that which is above, to achieve the wonders of the one thing." As observed by author Rosemary Ellen Guiley in *The Encyclopedia of Witches and Witchcraft*, "This is the foundation of astrology and ALCHEMY: that the microcosm of mankind and the earth is a reflection of the macrocosm of God and the heavens."

Hermetic Order of the Golden Dawn   See ORDER OF THE GOLDEN DAWN.

hex   The word *hex*, peculiar to the northeastern United States, is commonly used to mean either a CURSE or the witch who makes it. The tradition came to America, however, from medieval Europe.

The expression *hexerei* (BLACK MAGIC or WITCHCRAFT), as practiced by a hex (witch), originated in the 1600s among the German settlers of colonial Pennsylvania, especially Lancaster, Lebanon, Berks and surrounding counties. Due to a mispronunciation of their Deutsche ancestry, these immigrants erroneously became known as the Pennsylvania Dutch.

Two types of wizardry exists among the Pennsylvania Dutch, *braucherei* (WHITE MAGIC known as POWWOWwing) and, of course, hexerei. The powers of the hex come directly from the Devil and, as such, are considered to be evil.

If a person suspects that he or she has been *ferhext* (BE-WITCHed), the victim must seek out another witch, known as a hex doctor, to reverse the curse. Because the hex doctor has as much power as a fellow witch (they consult the same occult books), and perhaps even more, the hex doctor was as feared as the original sorcerer(ess) who cast the wicked SPELL.

The afflicted person does not have to believe in either God or the Devil for the hex doctor's magic to work. Being bewitched and showing up at the doctor's door is sufficient faith for magic to work. Receiving a cure does not obligate the victim's soul to the Devil, but it is expected that a proper gift will be given to the hex doctor. Usually the offering is quite generous to prevent the hex doctor from laying his own curse.

In order to become a hex (witch), the initiate must, in some way, renounce God and accept the Devil as one's master. Several methods have been recorded to summon Lucifer to make the pact, including boiling a black cat alive and tossing its remains in a creek. The novice could also draw a MAGIC CIRCLE on the kitchen floor with a piece of coal and step inside; Satan will make a DEVIL'S MARK on the witch's hand to signify his acceptance of the contract. Perhaps the most colorful method is standing on a dung heap in a cow stable and shouting the rhyme

Here I stand on a pile of manure
And do JESUS Christ abjure.

Pennsylvania Dutch hex (witches) are well known for their ability to cast the EVIL EYE, transform into animals (especially CATs), cause farm animals to become ill, steal milk from their neighbors' homes and prevent butter from churning. The most typical indications that an animal has been *ferhext* are hair loss, loss of appetite and restlessness. One of the most infamous (and common) ways in which a hex bewitches a cow is to conjure a ball of hair (known as a witch ball or hex-balla) into the bovine's stomach, thus decreasing its capacity for producing milk.

It is, of course, possible for the witch to lay a curse directly on another human being. The symptoms of the *ferhext* victim usually fall into one or more of four categories:

1. Incurable insomnia
2. Wasting away due to lack of appetite or an inability to keep down food
3. An uncomfortable or painful (though rarely fatal) physical sensation, feeling like a pin prick or choking
4. General and inescapable bad luck

By far, the first two manifestations are the most common and, unless remedied, are invariably lethal. Many precautions can be taken to ward off a hex, but the safeguards are kept as secretive as possible. After all, the witch or hex doctor must not know that the prey is protected; if so, the evildoer might be able to find an alternate spell.

A *hexa-foos*, a small five-pointed star, scribbled on a door frame or windowsill will prevent a witch from entering the building. A hex letter, a short oath against the witch, usually written in High German and hidden in the rafters of the barn, is also thought to be effective. Mercury sacks (small muslin bags filled with mercury) or "Deivel's-dreck" (bags filled with sanctified earth known as devil's dirt or *asafetida*) can be hung or nailed over stables and stalls to protect animals or cure those that are ailing. To prevent a hex from entering a house, it is only necessary to lay a BROOMSTICK across the threshold; the witch will be unable to cross or step over it.

One of the most popular TALISMANs against hexes is the Himmelsbrief, a letter which was supposedly written personally by God and dropped from the heavens. All of the Himmelsbriefs contain biblical commandments and teachings, pointing the way to righteousness. The most famous of these is the Magdeburg Brief; the original appeared in Magdeburg, Germany, in 1783, purportedly written in gold. A brief can be carried on the person or kept in the home for protection against harm.

Also widely seen in the Pennsylvania Dutch country is the book entitled *The Heart of Man: A Temple of God or the Habitation of Satan*. Its illustrations graphically depict the different journeys the eternal soul might take, depending whether the individual has chosen God or Satan as master.

Three works stand out as the most important hex books used among the Pennsylvania Dutch. By far the most popular in the l9th century, and still widely distributed today, is John George Hohman's thin volume, *The Long Lost Friend*. Hohman and his wife Catherine emigrated to the United States from Germany in 1802, settling near Reading, Pennsylvania, in

Berks County. A Roman Catholic, Hohman believed in miraculous cures through faith, but he failed in his own attempts as a powwower. He was also not a very successful farmer. In 1819, he began to collect many of the CHARMs, spells and herbal cures from area folklore to place into a book. Published the following year, *The Long Lost Friend* contains more than 180 spells and INCANTATIONs to cure illness and disease, both natural and supernatural, of both man and beast.

Egyptian Secrets, said to have been written by Albertus MAGNUS, has more than 500 spells of both white and black magic. The three-volume book first appeared in the Pennsylvania Dutch country around 1869, and its popularity and influence were immediate. *Egyptian Secrets* was written in Europe, not by the pen of a Pennsylvania Dutchman and almost certainly not by Magnus. The 13th-century occultist's name was held in such reverence, however, that many 19th-century hex books were attributed to him. For example, an 1839 reprint of *The Long Lost Friend*, published as *House Friend* in Montgomery County, Pennsylvania, bears Magnus's name rather than Hohman's as author. Otherwise, the two texts are identical.

Also containing some of the most effective and powerful hexerei against animals and man is the arcane GRIMOIRE known as the *6th and 7th Book of Moses*, but its acceptance and use has never been as great as that afforded *The Long Lost Friend* or *Egyptian Secrets*. The twin-volume work, bound as a single book, was written in German, possibly originating in Europe, and first appeared in the Pennsylvania Dutch County around 1870. The contents consist mainly of PENTACLEs, seals, signs and hieroglyphics, along with a final chapter explaining how to utilize the psalms of David for healing.

These grimoires were intended for the eyes of hex doctors and powwow doctors only. Because it is believed that all hexerei were written by Satan, it is feared that any noninitiate reading the arcane formulas would immediately become enslaved by the Devil. The only recourse to salvation would be to reread backwards the section of the book that had already been consulted, thereby undoing any harm it may have caused. Reading fast (i.e., reading too much of a hex book at one time to be able to read yourself out) is always a dangerous possibility.

However, merely owning the book or having it in one's possession is not considered unsafe; in fact, it is considered to be rather lucky. Added to later editions of *The Long Lost Friend* was the benediction

Whoever carries this book with him, is safe from all his enemies, visible or invisible; and whoever has this book with him, cannot die without the Holy Corpse of Jesus Christ, nor be drowned in any water, burn up in any fire, nor can any unjust sentence be passed upon him.

So Help Me.

Hexerei formulas and actions fall into one of four categories: AMULETS or talismans that protect against or prevent curses; spells to be cast against others; spells to break or undo other spells; and spells to increase personal power, fortune or abilities.

The colorful hex signs so commonly seen throughout southeastern Pennsylvania are often mistaken by visitors as being talismans against witchcraft. These geometrically patterned circles, usually painted on the side of a barn or a house, may be part of the Pennsylvania Dutch culture, but they have nothing to do with hexerei, and they have no power to protect the property or its inhabitants from a witch's hex. Rather, area residents recognize hex signs for their worth as traditional folk art and for their decorative value.

hieroglyphics See ALPHABET.

high magic See *BOOK OF THE DEAD, THE EGYPTIAN*; EGYPTIAN MAGIC.

Himmelsbrief See HEX.

Hobbit, The Written by J.R.R. TOLKIEN and published in 1937, *The Hobbit* remains one of the most celebrated books ever written in the fantasy genre. In the tale, the ultimate battle of Good versus Evil takes place in Middle-Earth, an other-world populated with supernatural characters, including five wizards.

The hero of *The Hobbit* is Bilbo Baggins, a furry humanoid animal known as a hobbit, who under the guidance of Gandalf the wizard, joins a company of dwarfs in their quest to retrieve a lost treasure guarded by Smaug the dragon on Lonely Mountain.

Gandalf the Grey, the good wizard, is perhaps the central character of *The Hobbit*, however, because he sets the chain of events in motion that results in Baggin's big adventure. Nevertheless, he remains a man of mystery. Gandalf is portrayed as an old man, wearing a blue robe and the stereotypical conical hat. He has bushy eyebrows that are so long that they protrude beyond the brim of his hat. A man of many moods, Gandalf is variously comical, pensive, childish, grouchy and petulant. Like all wizards, he is clever and clearly in touch with higher powers.

Gandalf gives Bilbo and his dwarf companions a treasure map and a key and sends them on their way. The party leaves the hobbit's shire and, after a long journey, reaches the Lonelands. Gandalf disappears, and trolls capture Bilbo and all but one of the dwarfs, their leader Thorin. Bilbo escapes, but he and Thorin are unable to save the other dwarfs. Gandalf returns and, using ventriloquism, starts a long, heated argument among the trolls. They quarrel past sunrise, and the light turns the trolls to stone.

Free, the party continues to Rivendell to meet Elrond. On the way, they hear the singing of hidden elves. Elrond explains the RUNES on the treasure map: the setting sun will point to the hidden keyhole "when the thrush knocks."

Gandalf points the adventurers on their way through the Misty Mountains, but a sudden storm forces them into a cave. There, they are captured by goblins and are carried into the depths of the earth. Gandalf appears and, wielding WAND and sword, kills the Grand Goblin. The dwarfs scramble out of the darkness, but Bilbo, knocked unconscious, is left behind.

Crawling along in the pitch black, Bilbo feels a small metal RING. Without thinking, he drops it in his pocket. He happens upon a small, slimy beast named Gollum, who plays a riddle game with Bilbo. The wager is Bilbo's life against Gollum's revealing the way out of the caverns. Bilbo wins, but the frustrated Gollum swears to kill the hobbit anyway. Gollum seeks his "precious," a ring that makes the wearer invisible so

that he can sneak up on sword-wielding Bilbo. The hobbit realizes that he has it in his pocket, slips it on and vanishes. Gollum runs up the tunnel that leads to the outside, thinking he is chasing Bilbo. Wisely, the hobbit follows and escapes.

As they flee, the treasure seekers are chased up trees by a pack of wolflike animals called Wargs. Gandalf appears and hurls magical flaming pine cones to chase them away. The Wargs scatter, but the fire sets the trees ablaze. Eagles arrive to carry off the dwarfs.

The next day, the birds drop them near the forest Mirkwood. Beorn, a shape-shifter who can transform from a man into a bear, learns that the dwarfs have killed his enemy, the Great Goblin, and supplies them for the next leg of their journey—the perilous transit through the Mirkwood Forest.

All sorts of evil omens meet them on their way. One dwarf plunges into a river and falls into a never-ending sleep. Bilbo and the dwarfs are captured by giant spiders, and by using Sting (his sword) and his magic ring, Bilbo frees himself and the others.

Next, all but Bilbo are captured by the Wood-elves. Bilbo invisibly sneaks into the elfin lair to rescue the dwarfs. They all hide in empty barrels and float downriver to Lake-town. There they discover their luck: despite the warnings of Gandalf and Beorn not to leave the path through Mirkwood Forest, the woods had become so dangerous that their only possible safe route was the one they had taken by water.

The party finally reaches Lonely Mountain. They hear a thrush dropping a nail onto a rock, and remembering the clue on their map, they hold the key up to the sun. Its shadow reveals the location of the secret keyhole to the dragon lair. Bilbo, whom the dwarfs think is an expert burglar, is sent in alone. He steals a golden cup from under the sleeping monster.

The winged creature awakens, discovers the missing goblet and flies out to find the robber. The dwarfs hide in the dragon's den while Bilbo, invisible, tries to outwit it. While playing a question-and-answer game with Smaug, Bilbo discovers a possibly vulnerable spot on the dragon which is not covered with iron scales.

Bilbo slips into the cave. Smaug, tired of the game and ready for revenge, seals up the den, trapping the dwarfs and the hobbit, and flies down to destroy Lake-town, whose human residents he feels are somehow responsible for the theft. A thrush descends and tells Bard, the town's most skillful archer, where to aim his arrow; Bard succeeds in killing the dragon.

The dwarfs unblock the entrance to the cave, but with no dragon to guard the treasure, the men of Lake-town and the elves of Mirkwood Forest decide to fight the dwarfs for the gold. All sides reject an attempt at peaceful diplomacy by Bilbo. Just as reinforcements arrive for the dwarfs, the goblins and the Wargs join the fray. The band of eagles ends the Battle of the Five Armies by dropping boulders on all of the forces, and a truce is drawn.

Gandalf has prophesied that Bilbo might really need his share of the captured treasure. Bilbo returns home to discover that he has been away so long that his house has been confiscated and his belongings are being auctioned!

Years later, Gandalf the Grey visits Bilbo once more, bringing him up to date on the humans and dwarfs at Lake-town.

As the adventure comes to a close, Gandalf implies that there was a greater power at work than any of them realized.

hocus pocus   Next to "ABRACADABRA," *hocus pocus* are the most common magic words spoken by today's stage magicians. Unlike the former term, which has a rather solid cabalistic background, the occult roots of *hocus pocus* are harder to trace.

One legend credits the phrase to Ochus Bochus, a Norse wizard and demon. Another possible, very credible origin is based on early magic's close alignment with religion. *Hocus pocus* may be a corruption of a phrase from the Catholic Latin mass: *hoc est enim corpus meum* ("This is indeed my body").

Thomas Ady, in his 1656 book *A Candle in the Dark; or a Treatise Concerning the Nature of Witches and Witchcraft*, claimed that the term was the stage name of a magician who was renowned for his use of the phrase in his PATTER:

> I will speake of one man . . . who called himself "The Kings Majesties most excellent Hocus Pocus," and so he was called, because that at the playing of every Tricke, he used to say, "Hocus pocus, tonus talontus, vade celeriter jubeo," a dark composure of words, to blinde the eyes of the beholders, to make his trick pass the more currantly without discovery.

Over the years, *hocus pocus* has come to mean any type of magic, trick, illusion or deception. *Hocus pocus* also connotes double-talk, unintelligible or incomprehensible babble or mumbo jumbo.

Hollow Hills, The   See ARTHUR, KING; *CRYSTAL CAVE, THE*.

homeopathic magic   See *GOLDEN BOUGH*, THE; IMITATIVE MAGIC; SYMPATHETIC MAGIC.

homunculus   As opposed to the GOLEM (a mud or clay statue brought to life by wizardry) or a ZOMBIE (a corpse reanimated by VOODOO), the homunculus, a manufactured human, was created using the arcane science of ALCHEMY.

The first recorded mention of a homunculus was by the Greek alchemist Zosimus (fl. third or fourth century A.D.), who had a vision of a human formed by the transmutation of metals, from copper to silver to gold to flesh. The catalyst for the reaction was burning the blood and bones of a dragon.

SIMON Magus was said to have created a homunculus using the SPIRIT of a dead boy and transforming it through the ELEMENTS of Air and Water, then into blood and finally into flesh. It was said that Simon could also revert the homunculus back into Air.

Arnold (also seen as Arnau) of Villanova (c. 1235–1312), a court physician, astrologer and alchemist, purportedly attempted to make a homunculus, although other sources suggest he was actually seeking an ELIXIR OF LIFE. Apparently, Borel, a court physician of Louis XIV and Robert FLUDD also tried to create life.

In 1775, John Ferdinand, count of Kufstein in the Tyrol, assisted by the Italian mystic Abbé Geloni, supposedly succeeded in producing 10 homunculi in bottles. Their experiments were recorded in the diary of the count's butler and then reported in a paper by Dr. Emil Besetzny in 1873.

Hopkins, the Witch Finder Generall, with two witches as they identify their familiars.   (Contemporary woodcut)

PARACELSUS left the best-known and most-detailed instructions on the alchemic generation of a homunculus. He directed that, first, a man's semen must be sealed in a glass container, "magnetized" and buried in horse manure for 40 days. Retrieved at the end of that period, the jar would contain a transparent but growing homunculus. The homunculus should be kept at the temperature of a mare's womb and fed daily with human blood. After 40 weeks, the creature will have grown into a perfectly developed child, only much smaller. Paracelsus ends his explanation with the admonition, "It may be raised and educated like any other child until it grows older and is able to look after itself."

Hopkins, Matthew (d. 1647)   Known as the Witch Finder Generall and the most infamous of all British witch-hunters, Matthew Hopkins was born the son of a Suffolk minister. For a time, he was a lawyer at Ipswich and then Manningtree in Sussex, but he wasn't very successful in either location.

With WITCHCRAFT hysteria in England having begun in earnest under King James I, Hopkins, with no ecclesiastical training or knowledge of demonology (beyond reading *DEMONOLOGIE* and a few smaller tracts on sorcery), declared himself an expert witch-hunter around March 1645. Given the Puritans' fervent fear of sorcery and the everyday jealousies, suspicions and hatreds in England at the time of the English Civil War (1642–1648), Hopkins found no shortage of clients or prey.

His first victim was a one-legged crone named Elizabeth Clarke who, after PRICKING, starvation, sleep deprivation and other tortures, implicated five others. Joined by John Stearne, an assistant witch-hunter, Hopkins managed to increase the number of those accused to at least 38. They were tried in Chelmsford, and, although the records are not complete, it is known that of those 38, 17 were hanged, six were found guilty but released, four died in jail and two were found innocent.

Witch-hunting was a lucrative profession. When the average worker earned sixpence a day, Hopkins was paid six pounds to find witches in Aldeburgh and 23 pounds to identify the witches of Stowmarket. It is estimated that in a two-year career, during which time at least 230 people were convicted and executed due to his accusations and testimony, Hopkins earned in excess of 1,000 pounds!

The first major public opposition to Hopkins was in April 1646 by John Gaule, a minister in Huntingdon. He published his *Select Cases of Conscience*, exposing Hopkins's methods, and the witch-hunter attempted to justify his practices in his 1647 pamphlet *The Discovery of Witches*.

As with any hysteria, the zeal waned and, with it, the demand for Hopkins's services. Eventually, Hopkins was forced to retire, and he retreated to his home in Manningtree in the summer of 1646. Stearne, concerned that the public outcry against Hopkins might endanger him, moved to Bury St. Edmunds.

No record of Matthew Hopkins exists after 1647. An apocryphal story claims that Hopkins himself was accused of witchcraft and was drowned or hanged. Most probably, he died of tuberculosis; there is a record of his burial at Mistley Church in 1647.

horoscope   A horoscope is a chart or map containing astronomical data that is used in ASTROLOGY. By diagramming an individual's exact date and time of birth and comparing it to the stellar and planetary positions, the astrologer can forecast the person's future and make specific recommendations regarding his or her future activities. These prophecies are based, in large part, upon the qualities of the sign of the ZODIAC (based on the position of the sun) under which the subject was born.

Early wizards were renowned for their ability as astrologers and at casting horoscopes. While the origin of casting horoscopes cannot be definitively ascertained, noted Egyptologist E.A. Wallis Budge claims that the practice began in the land of the pharaohs. Whether or not the horoscope, as we know it today, was devised there, at least some form of astrology was practiced in the royal courts and by the wizard-priests of ancient Egypt.

A true study of casting and analyzing individual horoscopes takes years of study, and dozens of books are available for the initiate. Obviously, the horoscope readings seen in newspapers and periodicals are generalized predictions for all people born under the zodiac, or sun signs. Personal horoscopes go into much more detail and need exact information about the subject.

Horus   See EGYPTIAN MAGIC; EYE OF HORUS; ISIS; THOTH.

House of the Seven Gables, The   Written by Nathaniel Hawthorne (1804–1864) and published in 1851, *The House of the Seven Gables* explores the moralist belief that sins of the fathers, (i.e., wickedness or wrongdoing by ancestors) must be repaid or atoned for by the descendants.

The tale begins as "old Wizard Maule" has been wrongly accused and tried for sorcery, allowing Colonel Pyncheon to seize his seven-peaked house and property. From the hanging scaffold, Maule levels a CURSE on Pyncheon: "God will give him blood to drink!"

The story, which involves several cousins of the Pyncheon family, picks up generations later. The spinster Hepzibah Pyncheon, the impoverished matriarch of the household, must open a shop to meet expenses. Clifford Pyncheon, who had been unjustly jailed by Judge Pyncheon, is released from prison but continues to be abused until the judge's sudden death. Holgrave, a descendant of the original Maule, aids and reforms Clifford and, in the process, falls in love with Phoebe, another Pyncheon cousin. When Holgrave and Phoebe marry, the ancient Maule curse disappears.

Hudibras   Perhaps influenced by the recently released DON QUIXOTE, Samuel Butler (1612–1680) wrote and released *Hudibras* in three parts between 1663 and 1678. The satirical poem tells the story of a Presbyterian knight accompanied by a squire through a series of misadventures. Among the people they meet on their quest is Sidrophel, a fraudulent astrologer.

Among the beliefs that Butler addresses and parodies through his characters are ALCHEMY, ASTROLOGY and WITCHCRAFT.

Humours   Most ancient and medieval philosophers, physicians and metaphysical thinkers (including wizards and alchemists) agreed that a person's individual nature and personality were governed by varying combinations of four internal liquids called Humours (from the Latin *humor*, meaning "moisture")—blood, choler, melancholy (or black choler) and phlegm.

The belief was espoused by the famous Greek physician Hippocrates and was introduced in Rome by Galen in the second century A.D.

Each of the Humours was associated with one of the four ELEMENTS, as they were expounded by Plato and Aristotle, and each caused a specific, natural temperament:

HUMOUR	ELEMENT	TEMPERAMENT
Blood	Air	Sanguine (Cheer and optimism)
Choler	Fire	Yellow bile
Melancholy	Earth	Black bile
Phlegm	Water	Phlegmatic (Apathy and sloth)

It was considered essential to keep the four Humours in perfect balance in order to maintain good health and an even disposition. An imbalance of the Humours resulted in peculiar or idiosyncratic behavior and disease. A person who was too sanguine (and, therefore, had too much blood) needed to be bled. An excess of phlegm caused colds. Too much choler produced jaundice. (The disease cholera was thought to be caused by too much yellow bile in the system.)

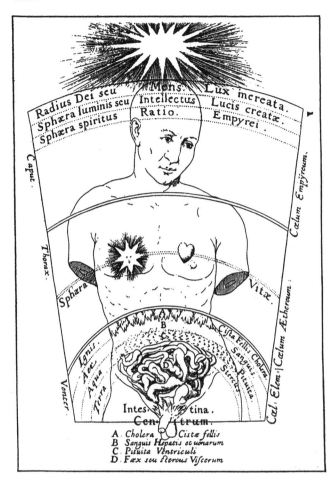

A cabalistic schematic of a man in relation to the cosmos and the influence of the Elements on the bodily Humours, depicted as being produced in the bowels. (Robert Fludd, *Utriusque cosmi historia*)

The belief's linguistic legacy is the modern word *humor*. Because an individual's quirkiness (i.e., unbalanced Humour) was often perceived as comical or ludicrous, the word *humor* took on the meaning of something that is witty or laughable.

Hunchback of Notre Dame, The
A masterpiece of RO-MANCE LITERATURE, *The Hunchback of Notre Dame* was written by Victor(-Marie) Hugo (1802–1885) and first published as *Notre-Dame de Paris* in March 1831 (with its first English translation by William Hazlitt the Younger appearing two years later). The novel, set in 15th-century Paris, tells the story of Quasimodo, a hideously ugly, deaf-mute hunchback and the bell-ringer of Notre Dame Cathedral, who is torn between his love for Esmeralda, a GYPSY dancer, and his loyalty to his protector, the archdeacon Claude Frollo.

The archdeacon Frollo had taken in Quasimodo when he was abandoned as a baby. Having developed a sorcerer's craving for absolute knowledge—as well as a lust for women—the once-righteous archdeacon has turned to AL-CHEMY and NECROMANCY.

Quasimodo is elected prince at the annual Festival of Fools because he has the ugliest face at the celebration. While he is paraded around the city, he sees La Esmeralda, called the Bohemian, and her trained goat Djali dancing. Because of the "Egyptian"'s BEWITCHing beauty and enchanting dance, some Parisians suspect her of WITCHCRAFT.

That night, Frollo and Quasimodo attempt to kidnap Esmeralda. Captain Phoebus de Châteaupeurs rescues Esmeralda, and she falls in love with him.

Quasimodo is brought before the courts and charged with keeping questionable company (with Esmeralda and Frollo, who were suspected of sorcery). Quasimodo is placed in a pillory, and only Esmeralda brings him water to drink. Esmeralda has Djali spell out Phoebus's name with lettered blocks beneath a balcony where Phoebus is courting a young lady. Jealous, the woman accuses Esmeralda—and the goat—of witchcraft.

Phoebus meets Esmeralda the following night. The archdeacon jumps from a hiding place and stabs Phoebus. Thought to be dead, Phoebus stays hidden to avoid involvement in Esmeralda's witchcraft trial.

Rumors of Esmeralda's killing Phoebus by sorcery spread. She is imprisoned and tried by the ecclesiastical court for witchcraft, and under torture she confesses. She is convicted and sentenced to ask for redemption on the steps of Notre Dame before being publicly hanged.

At Esmeralda's appearance before the archdeacon, Frollo offers to save her if she concedes to be his. She refuses. Quasimodo appears and whisks Esmeralda to sanctuary within the cathedral.

A mob gathers to force Esmeralda out, but Quasimodo fights them off. Esmeralda escapes with the help of the poet Pierre Gringoire, who leads her to a boat where the archdeacon is waiting. Esmeralda flees and hides in the cell of a madwoman who turns out to be her mother, from whom she had been stolen as a baby by the gypsies.

Esmeralda is captured, and the next morning, dressed in white, she is hanged. Quasimodo, brokenhearted and enraged by Frollo's triumphant laughter, throws the archdeacon from the bell tower. Quasimodo disappears.

Years later, the tomb of Montfaucon, a burial vault for criminals, is opened. The skeleton of a woman, still covered with scraps of white cloth, is embraced by that of a deformed man. "When those who found this skeleton attempted to disengage it from which it held in its grasp, it crumbed to dust."

FILM treatments of the story include *Esmeralda* (1906, French), *Notre-Dame de Paris* (1911, French), *The Darling of Paris* (1917, starring Theda Bara) and two classics entitled *The Hunchback of Notre Dame*. The first was a silent 1923 feature starring Lon Chaney as the bell-ringer; its 1939 remake starred Charles Laughton as the hunchback. In 1996, Disney released an animated version of *The Hunchback of Notre Dame* with Tom Hulce and Demi Moore voicing Quasimodo and Esmeralda respectively. Frollo's character was changed from that of archdeacon to minister of justice, and, except for his nominal accusation of witchcraft against Esmeralda, all mention of enchantment and sorcery were removed from the tale.

Iamblichus (A.D. c.250–c.330)   A Neoplatonic philosopher and author, Iamblichus was an expert on sorcery and its roots. His justification of occult studies, *The Mysteries of the Egyptians, Chaldeans, and Assyrians,* exists in manuscript form. (See ASSYRIAN MAGIC; CHALDEANS; EGYPTIAN MAGIC.)

Idylls of the King, The   Originally published between 1859 and 1885 as individual works, *The Idylls of the King,* is a collection of 12 related poems by Alfred, first Baron Tennyson (known as Alfred Lord Tennyson) (1809–1892) on the life and court of King ARTHUR, including the legend of MERLIN.

Tennyson, a rector's son, was educated at Trinity College and Cambridge and wrote his first poems as early as 1827. He was already an established poet by 1842 when his "Morte d'Arthur" appeared. It had been written in 1833 following the death of his close, young friend A(rthur) H(enry) Hallam (1811–1833).

The Arthurian legends, especially the writings of Sir Thomas MALORY and LAƷAMON, fascinated Tennyson, and he returned to the myths throughout his lifetime. In fact, many critics have characterized *The Idylls of the King* as a poetic distillation of all of the Arthurian writings up to that time.

In 1850 Tennyson was made poet laureate of Great Britain, but it was another five years before he began work on his first idyll, "Merlin and Vivien." "Enid," which followed shortly thereafter, was later separated into "Geraint and Enid" and "The Marriage of Geraint." In 1859, Tennyson published the first four of what would later be idylls: "Enid," "Vivien," "Elaine" and "Guinevere."

Ten years later four more idylls were published: "The Coming of Arthur," "The Holy Grail," "Pelleas and Ettarre" and "The Passing of Arthur." (His earlier poem "Morte d'Arthur" was made part of the verse of "The Passing of Arthur.") "The Last Tournament" appeared in the magazine *Contemporary Review* in 1871, as did "Gareth and Lynette" one year later. Although it had been written between 1872 and 1874, "Balin and Balan" was not printed until 1885. The Arthurian poems were all revised, compiled and published in their present order and form as *The Idylls of the King* in 1891. Tennyson died the following year, and he was buried in Westminster Abbey.

Although the poems have been criticized for their lack of realism and their unrestrained glorification of Arthur, *The Idylls of the King* enjoyed immense popularity during Tennyson's own lifetime, as they still do today.

Illusion, The   Written as *L'Illusion Comique* in 1636 by the French playwright Pierre Corneille (1606–1684), *The Illusion* tells the story of Pridamant of Avignon, a father who tries to learn the fate of the son he had exiled 15 years earlier. He travels to a mysterious cave to consult Alcandre, a wizard who can conjure up the past.

Alcandre shows the father visions of the son as a vagrant and drifter, a lover, a prisoner and then an escapee. To his horror, the father sees his son being fatally stabbed by a jealous husband. In the end, however, the wizard summons his magic to right all wrongs.

Credited with the creation of the French classical tragedy, Corneille wrote a total of 33 plays. He is best known for *Le Cid* (1637), along with *Horace* (1640), *Cinna* (1641) and *Polyeucte* (1643).

Tony Kushner authored a new translation, "freely adapted" from the early Corneille work. After productions in regional theaters, *The Illusion* had its New York premiere in January 1994 off-Broadway at the Classic Stage Company, with Rocco Sisto portraying the role of Alcandre.

imitative magic   Also known as homeopathic magic, imitative magic is based on the "Law of Similarity," which states that like produces like and an effect resembles its cause. Perhaps the best known example is the manipulation of a waxen image or a VOODOO DOLL to lay a CURSE. Likewise, by the use of imitative magic, the wizard or sorcerer could reproduce any action or effect, natural or supernatural, simply by simulating the original.

Imitative magic is a form of SYMPATHETIC MAGIC. This terminology was first recorded in Sir James George Frazer's study on magic and religion, *The GOLDEN BOUGH.*

incantation   An incantation is the recitation or chanting of a SPELL or other magic words. The often-repetitive, rhythmic and/or rhyming utterances are frequently preceded by elaborate rituals, such as the drawing of a MAGIC CIRCLE. The word *incantation* is used to describe either the words spoken or the entire process, from preparation for the rites through casting a spell or attempting to conjure a SPIRIT.

The ancient GRIMOIREs, or "black books" of cabalistic wisdom, were filled with incantations to evoke both angelic forces and demons. John DEE and Edward KELLY claimed to have

Dissatisfied with Pope Lucius II's earlier attempts to stop heretic teaching by the priests in the northern German churches, Pope Innocent III (who reigned from 1198 to 1216) created his own intense band of *inquisitores* who answered directly and only to His Holiness.

received an entire ANGELIC ALPHABET with which to contact the heavenly hosts.

The Grand Grimoire gives a detailed example of a BLACK MAGIC incantation to evoke a demon. The karcist (the wizard or sorcerer casting the spell) and his aides draw and enter the magic circle, light candles and "fumigate" the room with incenses. The specific prayer and incantation offered would vary depending which demonic force the wizard or sorcerer wished to evoke.

incubus In the Middle Ages, it was thought that a male demon known as an incubus (from the Latin *incubare* or *incubo*, meaning "to lie upon") traveled the night sky, attacking and/or sexually assaulting unprotected and unsuspecting women. At the very least, the incubus could cause bad dreams; more often, his sexual attack would leave the female victim bearing his child. The "spawn of Satan" would be born an enchantress.

The belief in the existence of incubi was most probably an attempt to excuse or explain away infidelities or births out of wedlock. After all, a woman could not be held accountable for an unwanted pregnancy if she had been inseminated by a

devil in her sleep, without her knowledge and certainly against her wishes.

The word *incubus* is in general usage today, without its occult connotation, meaning a person or thing that burdens or crushes another. (See SUCCUBUS).

Inferno, The See DIVINE COMEDY, THE.

Inquisition, The The persecution of WITCHCRAFT that culminated in the inhumanities executed by the Inquisition are directly linked to canon law and the PAPACY.

When Christianity became the official faith of the Roman Empire, its religious laws were largely adopted into civil law. It is known that by A.D. 430 the penalty of death for committing heresy was in place in the civil courts (although it was rarely carried out).

The Canon Episcopi of A.D. 906 was the first Catholic body to expressly forbid the use of witchcraft, but sorcery itself was not strictly defined as heresy. For centuries, the papacy did little to enforce its law against sorcery; in fact, many popes were themselves suspected of sorcery.

Pope Gregory IX, who reigned from 1227 to 1241, is often referred to as the Father of the Inquisition. He proclaimed that all inquisitors working on behalf of the church must be Dominicans. He charged them with rooting out both heresy and "unnatural magic" among the priesthood. In practice, the line between the two abominable sins frequently blurred, and soon sorcery was identified as heresy.

In Europe, the Inquisition's ultimate punishment for sorcery was being burned alive at the stake. Merciful inquisitors allowed condemned prisoners to be strangled to death before the fagots at their feet were lit.

In 1144, Pope Lucius II created the first ecclesiastical body of bishops to make *inquisitio* of, or investigate, priests who were rumored to be teaching doctrine other than strict canon. This first inquisitory group put a rule into place that would be used for centuries to come: the victims had to prove their own innocence to the church. If not, they would be turned over to civil officials, who would punish the accused or risk excommunication themselves.

The Vatican wasn't satisfied with the progress made by regional leaders in rooting out heresy, especially in the most civilized, wealthy and pleasure-seeking cities of northern and western Europe. Innocent III commissioned his own *inquisitores* who answered directly to him; their authority was made official in the bull of March 25, 1199.

In 1233, Pope Gregory IX issued a bull that declared that all *inquisitores* must be Dominicans. It also instructed the Dominican priest Conrad of Marburg to seek out possible heresy and the use of unnatural magic within the clergy in Germany. This was probably the first direct linkage of the two offenses by the papacy.

In two bulls to the Franciscans and Dominicans by Pope Alexander IV (dated 1258 and 1260), inquisitors were warned to be careful to distinguish between (or at least separate the charges of) witchcraft and heresy, but the caution was largely ignored. Many considered that sorcery, by its very nature,

entailed allegiance to Satan and was, therefore, evidence of heresy.

To ease the job of the inquisitors, Pope Innocent IV decreed in 1254 that accusers could remain anonymous, preventing victims from confronting their denouncers. Just three years later, he authorized and officially condoned torture as a method of eliciting confessions of heresy. (Later popes reconfirmed this ruling, and torture as a means to solicit testimony was sanctioned until Pope Pius VII rescinded the order in 1816.) A fine point: Once the victims admitted their crimes to their captors under torture, they were led away from the chamber and into another room to repeat the confessions to the inquisitors. That way it could be claimed the confessions were given without duress.

Although Alexander IV (in 1258) and John XXII (whose reign began in 1316) also issued bulls against the use of magic and sorcery, it was Pope John XXII who first defined them as heresy. On August 22, 1320, through Cardinal William Goudin at Avignon, he ordered the Inquisition at Carcassonne to brand all "magicians, sorcerers, and those who invoked demons or made waxen images or abused the sacraments" as heretics, allowing the church to take their property. In a 1318 bull, he had already allowed the trial and conviction of dead heretics, as well as the confiscation of the land bequeathed to their heirs. Pope John XXII was responsible for major witchcraft scourges in 1323, 1326, 1327 and 1331.

Almost every pope for the next two centuries issued some sort of antisorcery declaration, including Benedict XII (1334–42); Pope Innocent VI (who, around 1350, decreed that all copies of *Le Livre de Salomon,* which contained INCANTATIONs to invoke the Devil, be burned); Gregory XI (1370–78); Alexander V (1409–10); Martin V (1417–31); Eugenius IV (1431–47, whose fourth bull in 1437 warned of various guises that demons and evil SPIRITs might assume); Nicholas V (1447–55); Calixtus III (1455–58) and Pius II (1458–64).

Finally, in his bulls of 1473, 1478 and 1483, Sixtus IV ruled that witchcraft and BLACK MAGIC were a form of heresy. These declarations eased the Inquisitors' and witch-hunters' restrictions, allowing them to more easily accuse, condemn and punish their victims. At the turn of the century, Alexander VI became the first pope, in his bull of 1500, to mention the witches' SABBAT, the INCUBUS and transvection (i.e., flying).

Innocent VIII (whose papacy dated 1484–92) probably had the greatest impact of any pope on the Western world's pursuit and persecution of witchcraft as a specific heresy. His bull of (December 9) 1484, known as the *Summis desiderantes affectibus* ("Desiring with the most profound anxiety") was delivered in the first year of his papacy and reinforced his office's faith in the Inquisition. In addition, it strengthened the powers and authority of Heinrich Krämer, the prior of Cologne, and Jakob Sprenger, the Dominican inquisitor of

In England and colonial America, hanging was the preferred method of execution for witchcraft. Chelmsford was the site for several infamous witchcraft trials in England, and testimony from the witch-pricker Matthew Hopkins helped to hang many of the accused women. (Woodcut illustration from a 16th-century pamphlet illustrating the hanging of Joan Prentice, Joan Cony and Joan Upney in 1589 after the third major witchcraft trial held in Chelmsford.)

Torture was sanctioned for use in extracting confessions of heresy and witchcraft during the Inquisition. The confessions had to be repeated away from the instruments of torment so that the inquisitors could provide the court with testimony that was supposedly given freely and that had not been coerced under torture. (*Bambergische Halsgerichtsordnun,* 1508)

Cologne, the authors of *The MALLEUS MALEFICARUM,* to seek out and destroy witchcraft throughout Germany. The bull was reprinted in its entirety as an introduction to *The Hammer of Witches,* which, thanks to the recently invented printing press, spread the pope's words throughout Christendom.

Of course, once accused, a victim had almost no possibility of escaping death. The verdict was always rendered as "guilty" or "not proven" (rather than "innocent"). If found guilty, the accused was put to death. In either case, the victim's land was confiscated by the Inquisition.

Needless to say, this expropriation, often shared with Rome and sometimes with local secular officials, certainly made it advantageous for the church to accuse the well-to-do. In 1360, Inquisitor Eymeric bemoaned, "In our days there are no more rich heretics; it is a pity that so salutary an institution as ours should be so uncertain of its future."

Nevertheless, it was estimated that between 1450 and 1600, the Inquisition was responsible for burning 30,000 witches in Europe.

Isis, the goddess of Egyptian magic. (Modern stylized rendering on papyrus of a tomb painting and hieroglyph. Photo by author)

Isis In the religion of ancient Egypt, Isis was the supreme and most-worshipped goddess. The daughter of Seb and Nut, she was sister and mate of Osiris (who died and was reborn), and she was the mother of HORUS. Together, Isis, Osiris and Horus formed the focus of religious life. A moon goddess, Isis presided over the practice of the magic arts. She was represented as wearing a headdress bearing a disc between the horns of a cow.

Isis was assimilated into Greek and Roman worship and was variously associated with several of their pagan goddesses, most often HECATE, Demeter or Aphrodite, but also Bellona, Ceres, Cybele, Demeter, Diana and Juno. The cult worship of Isis flourished for eight millennia, from the fourth century B.C. to the fourth century A.D.. Isis had her own temples and festivals dedicated to her, and her priests were particularly noted for their skills at oneiromancy, the interpretation of dreams. (See also EGYPTIAN MAGIC; GRECO-ROMAN MAGIC.)

jalon arang See RANGDA.

Jesus (A.D. 0–A.D. c.32) According to the beliefs of his followers (today known as Christians), Jesus Christ is the human Son of God, born of Mary of Immaculate Concepcion. Because of his moral teachings, Jesus is accepted by all creeds as a great philosopher and rabbi. He is also credited with having performed many miracles throughout his short lifetime.

If indeed Jesus is the Christ, the savior and Messiah prophesied throughout the Old Testament of the Bible, his miracles are easily explained: He is that part of the Godhead (Father, Son and Holy Spirit) in human form; as God on Earth, his powers are endless.

If, on the other hand, as non-Christians believe, he was merely a great religious leader, his miracles, if they actually occurred, were simply magic used to illustrate his teachings. This confronts the historical charge that rather than being the Messiah, Jesus was a merely a clever wizard.

Religious skeptics point out that at the time of Jesus there were many false prophets and self-proclaimed messiahs, most of whom are credited in legend with having performed miraculous healings and other wonders. Perhaps the most famous wizard contemporaneous with Jesus was SIMON Magus (i.e., the magician Simon), who was best known for his supposed ability to fly.

Most of Jesus's miracles are described in the first four chapters of the New Testament of the Bible (the gospels According to St. Matthew, St. Mark, St. Luke and St. John). Most of the miracles fall into one of two broad categories—healings (many by exorcism) or demonstrations of control over nature.

Jesus disclosed his intention to perform the former "miracles" in one of his first sermons in a synagogue in Nazareth. As recorded in the Gospel of St. Luke 14:18, Jesus recited from the book of Esaias that "The Spirit of the Lord *is* upon me because he hath anointed me to preach the gospel to the poor he hath sent me to heal the brokenhearted, to preach deliverance to the captives, and recovering of sight to the blind."

The Gospel of St. Matthew 5:23–4 tells that "Jesus went about all Galilee . . . healing all manner of sickness and all manner of disease among the people. And his fame went throughout all Syria: and they brought unto him all sick people that were taken with divers [sic] diseases and torments, and those which were possessed with devils, and those which were lunatick [sic], and those that had the palsy; and he healed them."

Among the many sufferers mentioned in the gospels who were cured by the word or touch of Jesus were the deaf, dumb and blind and those with blood disease, fevers, palsy and the plague. He cured the lepers and the lame, restored the severed ear of a soldier in the garden of Gethsemane (Luke 22:50–51 and John 18:10), mended a withered hand and healed dropsy and speech impediments.

Three different instances are mentioned in the gospels in which Jesus brought the dead back to life—the daughter of a Jairus, a local religious ruler (Matthew 9:18–19, 23–25; 5 Mark; 8 Luke), the son of a widow from his funeral bier (7 Luke) and Lazarus, who was one of Christ's personal friends (11 John). 11 John is one of the most heart-wrenching chapters of the Bible. While calling Lazarus from his tomb in Bethany, Jesus in effect proclaimed his own divinity by saying "I am the resurrection, and the life: he that believeth in me, though he were dead, yet shall he live: And whosoever liveth and believeth in me shall never die" (John 11:25–26).

The details of Jesus's methods of effecting cures are recorded in only a few instances. In 7 Mark, Jesus cures a deaf person who also has a speech impediment: "And he took him aside from the multitude, and put his fingers into his ears, and he spit, and touched his tongue; And looking up to heaven, he sighed, and saith unto him, Ephphatha, that is, Be opened." In the curing of a blind man, recounted in Matthew 8:22–25, Jesus "took the blind man by the hand, and led him out of the town; and when he had spit on his eyes, and put his hands upon him, he asked him if he saw ought. And he looked up, and said, I see men as trees, walking. After that he put *his* hands again upon his eyes, and made him look up; and he was restored, and saw every man clearly." To heal another blind man, Jesus "spat on the ground, and made clay of the spittle, and he anointed the eyes of the blind man with the clay, And said unto him, Go wash in the pool of Siloam. . . . He went his way therefore, and washed, and came seeing." (John 9:6–7)

The command (some would say SPELL) given by Jesus to heal the cripple of 38 years at the pool of Bethesda in Jerusalem was merely "Rise, take up thy bed, and walk." (5 John)

Today, religious skeptics claim that many of these cures were achieved through a combination of FOLK MEDICINE and faith healing. Their belief is reinforced by the fact that in his hometown (where his former neighbors had known him since his childhood), Jesus was unable to perform many miracles. According to Matthew 12:58, "He did not many mighty works there"; and 6 Mark states that Jesus could "do no mighty work, save that he laid his hands upon a few sick folk." To the religious believer, however, Jesus was able to heal through his divine power and that of God his Father. His failure to effect cures in Galilee was caused by lack of faith of the locals.

Jesus cured many of the afflicted who were "possessed with devils" (1 Mark) by casting out demons or, as they were sometimes called, "unclean spirits" (Mark 1:23–6). That is to say, he performed exorcisms. He cured the mother-in-law of his disciple Simon Peter, for example, by "rebuking" her fever. One of Jesus's most unusual cures by exorcism was the casting out of an "unclean spirit" (5 Mark; or, according to 8 Luke, a "legion" of demons) from a wild man and into a herd of swine. Recorded in 9 Mark is the actual INCANTATION Jesus used to cast the demon out of the child whom the apostles could not cure: "*Thou* dumb and deaf spirit," Christ intones, "I charge thee, come out of him, and enter no more into him."

From almost the beginning of Jesus's ministry, the Pharisees and other leaders of the Jewish congregations saw a formidable threat in the growth of Jesus's following. They sought ways to discredit him. One of their most frequent tactics was to accuse Jesus of heresy for healing on the Sabbath.

He healed another man by forgiving his sin—a blasphemy, according the Jewish scribes in attendance because only God can forgive sin.

Before long, the scribes of Jerusalem accused him of BLACK MAGIC, saying "He hath Beelzebub, and by the prince of the devils casteth he out devils." Jesus countered with the argument "If a kingdom be divided against itself, that kingdom cannot stand." In other words, only God, not Satan, could or would cast out demons. The Pharisees and scribes demanded to see signs of Jesus's divinity, but he countered that only "an evil and adulterous generation seeketh after a sign." (Matthew 12:39)

Realizing that one man can only reach so many people personally, Jesus endowed his Apostles (recounted in Matthew 10:1, 6 Mark and 9 Luke) with the "power *against* unclean spirits, to cast them out, and to heal all manner of sickness and all manner of disease."

In 10 Luke, Jesus indoctrinates another 70 disciples (in addition to the original 12 Apostles), giving them the power to cure through his name. As recounted in 9 Mark, Jesus gave permission for all his followers, not just the original 12 Apostles, to heal in his name.

Jesus's description of the miracles that might be performed by true believers in his divinity laid the groundwork for the

The Church of the First Feeding in Tabgha, Israel, marks the traditional location for Jesus's first miracle, the multiplication of the loaves and fishes. A centuries-old floor mosaic by the rock altar depicts two fishes surrounding a basket filled with circular loaves of bread. (Photo by author)

modern Pentecostal Church: "And these signs shall follow them that believe; In my name shall they cast out devils; they shall speak with new tongues; They shall take up serpents; and if they drink any deadly thing, it shall not hurt them; they shall lay hands on the sick, and they shall recover."

Non-Christian skeptics have often suggested that the healings performed by the Apostles before the Crucifixion and after the Resurrection (described in *The Acts of the Apostles*) employed secret magical methods passed along by their teacher. Indeed, some occultists have proposed that, based on St. Mark 14: 50–52, a SABBAT-like meeting to initiate a new follower (who fled naked from the scene) was in progress when Jesus was surprised and arrested in the secluded gardens of Gethsemane.

The second major category of miracles performed by Jesus, his domination over the forces of nature, cannot be explained as psychological cures of ecstatics.

In the most famous example of Jesus's control over the winds and the sea, as told in 22–23 Matthew and 6 Mark, he walked from shore to the disciples' boat across the stormy waters of the Sea of Galilee. Further, he gave Peter the power, through faith, to also walk on water. This same, or another instance, is related in 6 John in which Jesus's disciples cross a troubled sea toward Capernaum and Jesus walks across the water out to their boat to calm them.

In an incident described in 8 Luke, Jesus falls asleep in the boat in which he and his Apostles are sailing. A sudden storm whips up and fills the boat with water. The disciples, fearing for their lives, wake their master, and Jesus "rebuked the wind and the raging of the water: and they ceased, and there was a calm." According to 4 Luke, his words to the sea were simple: "Peace, be still." This tale, or another in which "the wind ceased," is told in 22–23 Matthew.

Christian skeptics point out that both healings and demonstrations of mastery over storms and the sea were also being performed by acknowledged wizards concurrent with Jesus. Except for describing the Afterlife in heaven and prophesying his own death (16 Matthew) and Resurrection (9 Mark), however, Jesus did *not* practice DIVINATION, which was considered *de rigueur* for magicians of that era. Also, several of Jesus's miracles do not fall into the two broad categories of healings or the control of nature and have no counterpart in accounts of wizards and sorcerers practicing at the time of Jesus.

Mentioned only in the second chapter of the Gospel of St. John, Jesus's first miracle, performed at his mother's implied request, was turning six waterpots of water into fine wine at a wedding feast in Cana.

In another unique episode, this one in the Gospel of St. Mark (11), a hungry Jesus laid a CURSE on a fig tree because it was not bearing fruit (even though it was out of season to be doing so): "No man eat fruit of thee hereafter for ever [sic]." Within hours, the tree "withered away" and died.

An event that has no parallel in occult literature is the Transfiguration, described in 17 Matthew, 9 Mark and 9 Luke. Traditionally, Jesus performed this apparent proof of his divinity (although that was not his stated intention) for three of his disciples on the slopes of Mount Tabor. Jesus is "transfigured" (i.e., transformed) in front of his brother James as well as Peter and John: His face and garments glowed as bright as the sun, and Moses and Elias appeared beside him as a disem-bodied voice from the clouds pronounced, "This is my beloved Son, in whom I am well pleased; hear ye him."

In one of his most extraordinary manifestations, Jesus fed a multitude of more than 5,000 people gathered one evening at Tabgha along the shores of the Sea of Galilee. Matthew 14:15–21 tells how Jesus took only five loaves of bread and two fishes [sic], blessed the meager amount of food and then proceeded to break it into enough morsels to feed all those waiting to see and hear him preach. "And they that had eaten were about five thousand men, beside women and children," with food to spare. This event is also recounted in 6 Mark, 9 Luke and 6 John.

Jesus repeated the loaves and fishes miracle at Capernaum (recounted in 15 Matthew and 8 Mark), producing more than enough food to feed a crowd of 4,000 men plus women and children from seven loaves and a few little fishes.

Belief in Jesus's Resurrection, his escape from a sealed sepulchre three days after his Crucifixion and his Ascension into heaven is central to the faith of Christianity. To Christians, the Resurrection is the ultimate evidence that Jesus was the Son of God and not, as nay-sayers contend, merely a mortal wizard. For nonbelievers, the true explanations for the empty tomb range from the theft of the body by his disciples to Jesus's never having really died on the cross.

According to 24 Luke, after the Resurrection, Jesus first appeared to two men. They didn't recognize him, but as soon as they were able to identify him, Jesus vanished from their sight. Later, while the Apostles were discussing the rumors of Jesus's having risen from the dead, he appeared in their midst. He was able to be touched, and he ate with his men.

According to the Gospel of St. John, which gives the most detailed number of "sightings" after the Resurrection, Jesus first appeared to Mary Magdalene. He was not recognized by her until he called her name. Jesus did not allow her to touch him, however, because he explained that he was, in essence, still a SPIRIT, the Holy Ghost, having "not yet ascended to [his] Father." That same night, behind locked doors, he suddenly appeared among his Apostles. One of the disciples, Thomas, was not there, however, and he later doubted his fellow disciples' claim that Jesus had been there. Jesus materialized among them eight days later, again behind closed doors. He invited Thomas to "reach hither thy finger, and behold my hands; and reach hither thy hand, and thrust *it* into my side: and be not faithless, but believing."

One last time, Jesus appeared to the Apostles along the sea at Tiberias. At first unrecognized, he suggested to Simon Peter, who had caught no fish that day, that he might do well to cast his net off the right side of the boat. His instructions followed, the catch was phenomenal. (A similar occurrence had taken place before the Crucifixion. As told in 5 Luke, Jesus bid Simon Peter to cast out his fishing net. Despite Peter's protests that nothing had been caught that day, the nets returned two boats full of fish.) In Tiberias, Peter and the others recognized Jesus only when Jesus said, "It is the Lord," and they had one last meal together before the Ascension.

There is little argument that a historical Jesus lived and, as part of his ministry, performed feats which seemed miraculous, even by today's standards. In the end, the belief in those acts as having been performed through the power of God and the conviction in the divinity of Jesus comes down to a matter of faith.

jinn (djinn) In much of the pagan Arabic world, the jinn (also seen as *jinne, jinnee, genie* or *genii*) were considered to be malevolent, dark or hostile supernatural forces. Among the Muslims, or Mohammedan culture, it was thought that, although the jinn *could* be evil, they were more often good SPIRITS, closer in concept to that of the "GUARDIAN ANGEL." Although the jinn were independent sprites, wizards and sorcerers had INCANTATIONS and SPELLS to invoke and control them.

According to the KABALLAH, King SOLOMON was able to control the jinn, and, by using a magic RING, he forced them to build his great temple and palaces. In *The KEY OF SOLOMON*, the author explains that, while each wizard does have a personal jinn, he must go to great lengths to find the correct invocational tools to establish contact.

The nonoccultist image of the jinn is an all-powerful and magical supernatural being, performing at the beck and call of just one person, his "master."

See also "ALADDIN AND THE WONDERFUL LAMP"; FILM *ALADDIN*; Television, *I DREAM OF JEANNIE*.

Joan of Arc, St. (1412–1431) Born Jeanne Darc (also seen Jehanette or Jehanne Darc), the daughter of a farmer Jacques Darc, the warrior saint rose from illiteracy and obscurity to help fight for France's freedom from England during the reign of Charles VII. Claiming to be guided by the visionary voices of St. Michael, St. Catherine and St. Margaret, she fought at the battle of Orléans (gaining her the sobriquet of "The Maid of Orleans").

Her military career ended with her capture on May 23, 1430, while she was trying to end the siege of Compiègne by the Bastard of Wandomme. The French sovereign ignored overtures to ransom her release, so Pierre Cauchon, bishop of Beauvais, acting in the service of the English, obtained ecclesiastical jurisdiction over her. Although not formally charging her, the bishop was said to suspect her of sorcery and the invocation of devils.

In the course of Joan of Arc's preliminary hearing in Rouen Castle (which began February 21, 1431), 42 different priests questioned her on behalf of the INQUISITION. The official charge was not sorcery, but heresy. At her formal trial, or "trial in ordinary," which began on March 27, 70 indictments were leveled against her, in which she was charged with being a "sorceress, witch, diviner, pseudo-prophetess, invoker of evil SPIRITS, conjurer, superstitious, implicated in and given to the arts of magic." Testimony centered around her visions, her hearing angelic voices and dressing in men's clothing.

Eventually, on April 2, all counts of sorcery or WITCHCRAFT against her were dropped, leaving only 12 charges of various forms of heresy. Three days later, she was found guilty of heresy by the inquisitors of the Rouen Cathedral.

On May 24, 1431, she denied her visions and promised to obey the canon of the church. In exchange, her sentence of death would be commuted to life imprisonment. On May 28, Joan of Arc was pronounced a relapsed heretic, and she retracted her original confession. Two days later, she was excommunicated by the church. The bishop of Rouen ordered her executed, and she was burned alive at the stake on May 30, 1431.

Victorious in their war against the English, the French declared Joan of Arc innocent of all charges on June 16, 1456. On May 9, 1920, she was canonized as a saint of the Catholic church by Pope Benedict IX, and a month later, the French government declared May 30 as a national holiday in her honor.

Joan D'Arc has been the subject of countless literary works, including *La Pucelle* (*The Maid*) (1755) by Voltaire (1694–1778); *Die Jungfrau von Orleans* (*The Maid of Orleans*) (1801) by Johann Christoph Friedrich von Schiller (1759–1805); *Saint Joan* (1923, published 1924) by George Bernard Shaw (1856–1950); *L'Alouette* (1953) (translated in English as *The Lark*, 1955) by Jean Anouilh (b. 1910) and *Joan of Lorraine* by Maxwell Anderson (1888–1959). SHAKESPEARE also referred to "la Pucelle" in *Henry VI*.

She was also the heroine of at least two major films: *Joan the Woman* (1916, starring Geraldine Farrar) and *Joan of Arc* (1948, based on the Anderson play and starring Ingrid Bergman).

There have been at least three MUSICAL THEATER adaptations of the Joan of Arc story. *Jeanne*, music, book and lyrics by Shirlie Roden, was performed at London's Sadler's Wells Theatre in 1986 with Rebecca Storm in the title role. *Jeanne la Pucelle* (1997), with book and lyrics by Vincente de Tourdonnet and music by Peter Sipos, direction by Martin Charnin and starring Judith Berard as Joan, was performed on alternate evenings in English and French at the Place des Arts in Montreal, Quebec, Canada. On Broadway, *Goodtime Charley* (Palace Theatre, March 3, 1975) told the story of Joan of Arc (Ann Reinking) and the young French Dauphin (Joel Grey). The show garnered seven Tony nominations: Actor, Musical (Grey); Actress, Musical (Reinking); Actor, Supporting or Featured, Musical (Richard B. Shull); Actress, Supporting or Featured, Musical (Susan Browning); Scenic Designer (Rouben Ter-Arutunian); Costume Designer (Willa Kim); and Lighting Designer (Abe Feder).

jumbie Associated with VOODOO beliefs in the West Indies, a jumbie is a type of evil SPIRIT. Unlike a ZOMBIE, the jumbie has no corporeal substance and is not controlled by a human master.

Kabbalah Also seen as *Cabbala, Cabala, Cabalah, Kabbala* and *Kabala,* or in the Hebrew form *qabbalah,* the word *kabbalah* is based on a root *Kbl,* (in Hebrew *gibbel*) meaning "to receive." In essence, the Kabbalah is "received" (or revealed) wisdom.

The Kabbalah is not an individual book or even a specific compilation of doctrine, although certain texts are almost always considered cabalistic. The Kabbalah is the collected thought of ancient wizards and the never-ending interpretation of many of the occult writings from ALCHEMY, GRECO-ROMAN MAGIC, ASSYRIAN MAGIC, the CHALDEANS, Judeo-Christian mysticism (including books purportedly written by SOLOMON and Talmudic testaments), eastern influences (such as the precepts of ZOROASTER) and EGYPTIAN MAGIC.

Written between the 9th and 13th centuries in several distinct sections, the Kabbalah shows the way in which the supernatural interacts with the natural world and how the infinite universe interacts with the finite world. It also attempts to reveal the true, inner meanings of the ancient Jewish legends.

Even before the "creation" of the Kabbalah, Jewish tradition and lore was filled with mysticism. A Samaritan legend, for example, claims that the source of sorcery was a Book of Signs, which was delivered to Adam after the Fall. In Jewish mythology, the arcane text is known as the Book of Adam or the Book of Razel the latter title being the one most often mentioned in cabalistic texts.

The Book of Enoch suggests that sorcery was taught to humans by two fallen angels named Uzza and Azael. Azael was responsible not only for teaching women WITCHCRAFT but also for introducing the artifice of cosmetics and makeup!

Although wizardry and sorcery was forbidden in Jewish law, the practice was endured if the magician called upon angels to fight against the forces of evil. Thus, from the earliest Judeo-Christian ethics, there arose an artificial distinction between WHITE MAGIC and BLACK MAGIC.

Cabalistic legend suggests that MOSES, although elected by God as the deliverer of the Israelites, had already been trained in Egyptian magic in the court of Ramses II.

The Book of Tobit tells the story of the demon Ashmodæus falling in love with Sarah. Only by "fumigation" and the power of the angel Raphael was the "king of the powers of evil" cast out.

Numbered among the early Jewish wizards was Balaam, who taught sorcery and witchcraft to the daughters of Moab. Manasseh "observed times, used enchantments and witch-craft and dealt with a familiar SPIRIT and with wizards" (II Chronicles 33:6). Isaiah mentions wizards that "peep and mutter." Magicians among the Moabites and Medes who used DIVINING RODs or poles are noted in Hosea 4:12: "My people ask counsel at their stocks, and their staff declareth unto them." The apocryphal Nahum 3:4 refers to a "mistress of witchcrafts." In the Book of Samuel, the WITCH OF ENDOR is consulted by Saul. Perhaps the greatest Jewish mystic of Old Testament times was King Solomon. Probably more fiction than fact, Solomon is credited with writing, among many others tracts, two of the most famous magical GRIMOIREs, *The KEY OF SOLOMON* and *LEGEMETON: THE LESSER KEY OF SOLOMON.*

Not all ancient occult writings were relegated to the Kabal-lah. Scriptures of the Old Testament of the Bible are filled with mention (and usually prohibition) of witchcraft, sorcery, divination, soothsaying, NECROMANCY, ASTROLOGY, SPIRITS, FAMILIARs and the interpretation of dreams, for example:

You shall not permit a sorceress to live. (RSV)

or

Thou shalt not suffer a witch to live. (KJV)
(Exodus 22:18)

A man or woman that hath a familiar spirit or that is a wizard shall be stoned to death.
(Leviticus 20:27)

There shall not be found among you . . . any one who practices divination, a soothsayer, or an augur, or a sorcerer, or a charmer, or a medium, or a wizard, or a necromancer. For whoever does these things is an abomination to the Lord.
(Deuteronomy 18:10–13)

Fewer wizards and sorcerers are mentioned in the New Testament of the Bible. In Acts 13:6–8 there is mention of Bar-jesus, also known as Elymas ("a certain sorcerer, a false prophet, a Jew" on the Isle of Paphos). A medium was exorcised by Paul, who "brought her master much gain through her divination" (Acts 16:16), and there were multitudes of itinerant healers and so-called exorcists who emulated the acts of the Apostles. Paul also confronted the wizards of EPHESUS. Probably the best known sorcerer/mystic was SIMON (possibly a biblical reference to Simon Magus) who purportedly converted to Christianity and followed Philip after "wondering and beholding the miracles [Philip] wrought."

Scholars differ on the contents and the meaning of the Kabbalah, but it was an accumulation, or more accurately a distillation, of Jewish magical lore, up to time of its compilation. Because most of the secret traditions had been transmitted orally through generations, much of the occult thinking appeared in writing for the first time in the Kabbalah.

Among the tenets of the Kabbalah is that all peoples and religions are descended from one original race and set of beliefs. One cabalistic scholar, S(amuel) L(iddell) MacGregor MATHERS (1854–1918) explains it this way: God taught the Kabbalah to the angels, who passed it on to humans. From Adam through Noah, the hidden wisdom reached Abraham, who revealed it to the Egyptians. Moses's knowledge of Egyptian magic was refined by angels of the Lord during the 40 years of wandering in the desert, and Moses used his powers several times to forestall rioting by the Israelites. Moses taught the mysteries to the 70 elders of the collected tribes, and the secret formulas and rituals were eventually passed down to King David and his son, Solomon. All this time, the magical tradition was orally transmitted.

Beginning around the time of the second destruction of the temple of Jerusalem and continuing up to his death, Simon Ben Jochai is thought to have written down the many cabalistic myths. His son Rabbi Eleazar and Rabbi Abba collected the tracts and produced the *ZHR*, or *Sepher Ha Zohar* (meaning *Book of the Splendor*), considered by most occultists to be the most important part of the Kabbalah. (The *Zohar* introduced into Spain by Moses de Leon in the 13th century was alternately attributed by him to Simon Ben Jochai, a second-century rabbi.)

Among the several works making up the *Zohar* are the *House of Elohim* (which deals with angels, devils and spirits), *Asch Metzareph* (or *Purifying Fire*, a treatise on alchemy), the *Siphra Dtzenioutha* (*Concealed Book of Mystery*) and the *Midraschim* (commentaries on Old Testament scriptures). These books are believed to have been originally written in Chaldean or Hebrew because the name *Jehovah* is seen as *IHVH* (the TETRAGRAMMATON), a form also used by Jewish mystic writers.

According to the *Zohar*, the highest Holy of Holies ruled the heavens with Adni, his Queen. (Her sinless nature is thought by some scholars of comparative religion to have been transformed by Christian writers of the New Testament scriptures into the concept of the Virgin Mary.) Together IHVH and Adni opposed Samael Smal, who was Evil Incarnate as the Lord of the Devils, the Angel of Death.

In addition to the *Zohar*, the mystical manuscripts of the Kabbalah include the *Sepher Yezirah* (also seen as *Sefer Yetsirah* or *Sepher Jetzirah*, or *The Book of Creation* or *Formation*). Although its author is unknown, the *Sepher Yezirah* was probably written between the third and sixth centuries A.D. The book suggests that God created the world using a combination of the numbers one to ten and the 22 Hebrew letters. The ALPHABET was believed to have been divinely inspired and, therefore, part of the "body" of God.

Belief in, and the study of, the Kabbalah led to the development of other occult sciences. The *Sepher Yezirah*, for example, classified everything in the universe under one of the 22 Hebrew letters. Seven of the letters were connected to the seven days of the week and the seven known planets. Three remaining letters (mem, shin and aleph, known as the mother letters) represented either Earth-heaven-hell or air-fire-water. The 12 remaining letters of the Hebrew alphabet corresponded to the 12 ZODIAC signs used in ASTROLOGY, the 12 months of the year or 12 of the body's internal organs.

Such a classification system set the stage for the occult belief in CORRESPONDENCES, by which one object could represent another. This had important magical implications because the sorcerer could use magic power to control another individual without having to be in direct contact with the subject; he or she merely had to possess or control and an item which belonged to or corresponded to the intended victim. This eventually led to the practice of IMITATIVE, CONTAGIOUS and SYMPATHETIC MAGIC.

The cabalistic belief that biblical text can be translated into numbers to reveal hidden secrets almost certainly led to the development of NUMEROLOGY, a form of divination in which numbers are used to correspond to letters and words.

Kastchei   See BALLET, *FIREBIRD, THE.*

Kelly, Edward (1555–1595)   Although many of his exploits with John DEE have been documented, little certain is known of the early life of Edward Kelly (also seen as Kelley). According to Anthony à Wood's 1813 book *Anthenae Oxoniensis*, the mystic was born Edward Talbot in Worcester on August 1, 1555.

The son of an Irish apothecary, Talbot matriculated at Oxford. Talbot abruptly left Oxford under mysterious circumstances and moved to Lancaster. Already interested in the occult, Talbot and his friend Paul Waring tried to resurrect a corpse in the cemetery at Walton le Dale. According to a near-contemporary account, they disinterred a freshly buried man and "by their INCANTATIONS . . . made him to speak . . . strange predictions."

Talbot was found guilty of forgery while in Lancaster, and he was sentenced to the pillory. Unconfirmed legend has it that his ears were also cut off as punishment, but scholars suggest that this was not the case: Such an obvious brand would have deterred Dee, who traveled in high social circles and royal company, from accepting him as a partner.

Talbot wandered through Wales, and at some point he acquired the *Book of St Dunstan* [sic], a manuscript that taught the secrets of ALCHEMY, and two "powders of projection" which could, purportedly, transmute base metals into silver or gold.

Settling in London, Talbot took up work as the secretary to Thomas Allen, a noted magician. Whether Allen instructed Talbot in the arcane arts is unknown, but by the time he first met with Dee, Talbot was already well versed in magic and was still practicing NECROMANCY.

According to Dee, Kelley appeared at the door to his Mortlake home on March 10, 1582, "being willing and desyrous to see or show some thing of spirituall practise." [sic] After Talbot demonstrated his ability to receive visions of and speak for the Archangel Uriel, Dee placed the 26-year-old medium in his employ for 50 British pounds per year.

Just five months later, Talbot changed his surname to Kelly.

A brilliant collaboration of seven years followed in which a multitude of heavenly hosts, speaking through Kelly, dictated a new 21-letter ANGELIC ALPHABET. Kelly and Dee received further messages from the angels, perhaps the most

Edward Kelly. (Medieval portrait engraving)

important being a series of prayers and incantations to summon them. Dee dutifully recorded the invocations and titled the manuscript the *48 Angelic Keys*.

At some point, upon the order of the angel Michael, Kelly married. He chose Joan Cooper of Chipping Norton, but the couple were never really happy together. In 1584 Kelly set off on a tour of the Continent with Dee.

When Dee returned to England almost six years later, Kelly chose to stay behind in Prague. Before long, Kelly inveigled his way into the court of the Bohemian Emperor Rudolph II by promising to use his alchemic skills to produce gold for the ruler. When the gold failed to materialize, the emperor had the occultist locked first in the dungeon of the castle Zobeslau and then the castle Zerner. Dee prevailed upon his royal patron Queen Elizabeth to seek Kelly's freedom, but Emperor Rudolph stood firm. In November 1595, with no hope for pardon or release, Kelly tried to escape. He fell from a castle turret in the attempt and died shortly thereafter.

Dee's last mention of Kelly was entered matter-of-factly in his diary: "Nov. 25th, the newes that Sir Edward Kelly was slayne." [sic]

The question remains whether Kelly was a mere charlatan or whether he, in fact, was (or believed he was) able to speak with angels and transmute lead into gold. If his repetition of the angels' messages were a deliberate hoax, it means that Kelly possessed the near-genius capability to deliver cryptic utterances backwards *and* in cipher—all the while remembering his previous communications. As impossible of a feat as that may seem, the alternative—that he was actually speaking with angels—is even more fantastic to believe.

In addition to his work with Dee, Kelly authored three books on occult matters: *The Stone of the Philosophers, The Humid Way* and *The Theatre of Terrestrial Astronomy*.

Key of Solomon, The The occult book known variously as *The Clavicle or Key of Solomon, The Key of Solomon the King* (*Clavicula Salomonis*) and *The Worke of Solomon the Wise* is one of the most important occult writings in the history of magic. The INCANTATIONS and rites provide a direct link from the ancient EGYPTIAN MAGIC, up through the sorcery of the Babylonians, CHALDEANS and ASSYRIANS to almost all of the early ritualistic magic and ALCHEMY of the European wizards.

The authorship of the *Key of Solomon* has long been attributed to the biblical King SOLOMON. Besides the Judaic and Arabic traditions that Solomon was a practicing wizard, the Jewish / Roman historian Josephus (A.D. c.37–c.98) also recorded that the king had written and hidden tracts of forbidden magical wisdom. Throughout the centuries, poets and priests from the Middle East to as far away as India wrote about and embellished upon the story of Solomon, the archmagician.

The church seemed to accept the pagan allegations about Solomon. In an 11th-century Pentecost sermon, Leonitus of Constantinople asked, "Nonne Salomon dominatus dæmonum est?" ("Had not Solomon dominion over demons?") Gregentius, the archbishop of Taphar, declared that Solomon trapped his demons in earthen urns and buried them underground.

By the 13th century, several different occult manuscripts attributed to Solomon had appeared in the eastern Mediterranean-Cairo-Constantinople crescent. At the time, there was little reason to doubt their authenticity; after all, it was common knowledge in every Eurasian culture that King Solomon, by whatever power, had been conversant with demons and had recorded his SPELLS and TALISMANS before his death. When the "clavicles" made the jump from Byzantine Eurasia to the GRECO-ROMAN arena around A.D. 1200, occultists and clergy alike were apt to agree that they were actual Solomonic writings.

According to legend, one of the first Latin translations was executed by Pope Honorius III, believed to be a sorcerer, who assumed the PAPACY in 1216.

By the middle of the 13th century, Roger BACON had read several of the treatises, enough to insist that Solomon could not have written them. Solomon, Bacon contended, was too wise to have fallen in league with the Devil. TRITHEMIUS, in his *Antipalus maleficiorum* (published near the end of the 15th century), also judged the works to be non-Solomonic.

Although still rare, manuscript copies of *The Key of Solomon* became available throughout Europe of the 1500s. The first recorded *printed* edition of a *Key of Solomon* surfaced in Rome in 1629, making the work less difficult to acquire. Occultists and sorcerers continued to believe, however, that handwritten, parchment manuscripts were much more magical and that their use made the raising of demons much more effective.

The earliest extant copies of *The Clavicle or The Key of Solomon* date from the 16th century. Several Solomonic GRIMOIRES are housed at the Bibliothèque de l'Arsenal in Paris; the majority were part of a collection started by Antoine René de Voyer d'Argenson, marquis de Paulmy, a soldier, romantic and mystic. None of the Parisian copies are in Hebrew, the language in which the original tracts *should* have been written, but many do exist elsewhere. Still other versions of the manuscripts in a variety of languages (including French, German, and Italian) exist in libraries and collections throughout Europe.

The authoritative English translation of the work was by S.L. MacGregor MATHERS of London and was completed in October 1888. He worked from several differing codices of *The Key of Solomon* including some written in Hebrew that are housed in the British Museum.

The introductory comments found in the various manuscript copies provide differing accounts of *The Key of Solomon*'s origin. The oldest codex of *The Key of Solomon* dating from the 16th century and now in the British Museum collection was "translated into Latin from the Hebrew idiom." In them, Solomon tells his son Roboam how he preserved "the secret of secrets" in his book and that only *The Key of Solomon* could "open the knowledge and understanding of magical arts and sciences."

Solomon asks Roboam to hide *The Key of Solomon* in an ivory casket. After the king's death, the casket was placed, as requested, next to his corpse in the sepulchre so that it would not "fall into the hands of the wicked." The casket remained in the tomb until several "certain Babylonian Philosophers"

The frontispiece of a 17th edition of *The Key of Solomon*, perhaps the most important of all the grimoires.

decided to erect a more massive monument to Solomon. During excavation, they discovered the casket and opened it.

That night, the wisest of the men, Iohé Grevis (also seen as Iroe Grecis), prayed mightily to the Lord to explain the text's meaning. An angel of the Lord appeared and said that God had made the words indecipherable to prevent their being used for evil. He agreed to make them comprehendible if Iohé would promise that only those who were trustworthy would be told its secrets.

A slightly different version, certified by the Greek philosopher "Ptolomei" [sic.] (fl. second century A.D.) as containing "Secret of all Secrets to all crafts magicall of Nigromancy" [i.e., NECROMANCY], adds that the text was revealed to Solomon in his sleep by the angel Raziell.

Yet a third variant assures the reader that the book was not written by Solomon but given to him by Kamazan and Zazant, two wise men sent by Sameton, the prince of Babylon. *The Key of Solomon* was supposedly the first manuscript written after the fall of Adam, penned by the Chaldeans and then translated into Hebrew.

The Lansdowne manuscript, written in French and beautifully illustrated, purports to have been originally "translated from the Hebrew into the Latin language by the Rabbi Abognazar" (whose real name Mathers believed to be Aben Ezra). According to its text, near the end of his life, Solomon prepared a testament for his son Roboam. He engraved all the wisdom that he possessed on pieces of bark:

> PENTACLES were inscribed in Hebrew letters on plates of copper, so that they might be carefully preserved in the Temple. . . . This Testament was in ancient times translated from the Hebrew into . . . Latin . . . by Rabbi Abognazar [probably an aberration of *Aben Ezra*], who transported it with him into the town of Arles in Provence, where . . . the ancient Hebrew Clavicle . . . fell into the hands of the Archbishop of Arles, after the destruction of the Jews in that city; who, from the Latin, translated it into the vulgar tongue [i.e., French].

In his tract, Solomon explained that all things, celestial and terrestrial, are governed by angels. He promised to reveal to Roboam the "the names [of the angels] in order, their exercises and particular employments to which they are destined, together with the days over which they particularly preside." Solomon vowed that Roboam would be able to command the angels "provided that all [his] works only tend unto the honor of God."

Solomon explained that "there are different kinds of SPIRITS, according to the things over which they preside . . . some to regulate the motion of the Stars, others to inhabit the ELEMENTS, others to aid and direct men, and others again to sing continually the praises of the Lord."

Solomon told his son that "God hath destined to each one of us a Spirit, which watches over us and takes care of our preservation." (Today, we might call these spirits "GUARDIAN ANGELS"; Solomon called them the Genii (see JINN). The Genii were "Elementary" like humans; likewise, they existed under the same astrological rules. (See ASTROLOGY.) To best summon his Genii, the sorcerer had to discover which Elements the angel inhabited and which the two of them shared in sympathy. Solomon detailed that the wizard had to take into account the best day, hour, ruling planet, colors, metals, herbs, plants, animals (aquatic, aerial and terrestrial), incenses, seals, characters, divine letters and conjurations when invoking a spirit.

The text in the manuscripts and the order of its sections also varied. Most often a codex was separated into two books with several chapters each, some with subheadings. According to a prefatory note to readers found in four of the British Museum manuscripts, in the first book "thou mayest see and know how to avoid errors in Experiments, Operations, and in the Spirits themselves. In the second thou art taught in what manner Magical Arts may be reduced to the proposed object and end." In layman's terms, Book One lists general invocations and specific spells; Book Two gives technical advice, such as selecting the proper clothing, correct inks for drawing talismans and SIGILs and how to counsel assistants.

The reader is further advised that "Any Art or Operation . . . will not attain its end, unless the Master of the Art, or Exorcist, shall have this Work completely in his power, that is to say, unless he thoroughly understand it, for without this he will never attain the effect of any operation." For example, brandishing a pentacle and WAND to make a CURSE without invoking the appropriate SPIRIT or attempting to conjure before entering a MAGIC CIRCLE would not only be ineffective, but it might also possibly be dangerous to the wizard.

In the end, the primary purpose of learning the contents of *The Key of Solomon* was to communicate with or control angels. Even if the wizard or sorcerer wanted to conjure demons, he prayed for a heavenly angel to assist him. (The *LEMEGETON*, on the other hand, gave very direct means to summon demons, going to great lengths to enumerate the many devils.) Mathers was very aware of this thin line between WHITE and BLACK MAGIC. In the introduction to his translation of *The Key of Solomon*, for example, he strongly cautioned "Let him who, in spite of the warnings of this volume, determines to work evil, be assured that the evil will recoil on himself." (See also KABBALAH.)

Knights Templar   Founded between A.D. 1119 and 1188 by Hugh de Payens of Champagne, France, the Knights Templar (also known as the Order of the Temple) was a secret society of Christian warriors. Initially, their mission was to accompany and protect pilgrims traveling from Europe to Jerusalem and the Holy Lands.

In addition to their fortifications, the Knights Templar built churches, and they tended to locate them near grottoes or other allegedly "mystical" sites. Their white flag showed a crimson cross, but their emblem was a mysterious, four-pointed "claw-shaped cross." PENTAGRAMs, three-headed icons and other occultlike statuary were also used as ornamentation in their churches. Many of their later churches showed distinct Arabic influences in the architecture.

The knighthood was organized as a religious organization, thus avoiding taxation and civil laws. Although the individual knights took vows of poverty and chastity, the group, as a whole, accepted contributions to fund their temples and travels. Over the years, they amassed great tracts of land and sizable wealth. With their castles spread throughout Europe, they became the continent's first bankers.

Although the Knights Templar became an international organization, its power base remained in France. By the 14th century, the order was an object of envy from royalty, especially of King Philip IV of France (who owed them money), and the clergy, especially Pope Clement V. Philip was aware that if the Templars were convicted of heresy, their lands and fortunes would be subject to seizure by the state.

Rumors were spread that the Knights Templar had renounced their celibacy, practical homosexuality and took part in drunken orgies behind their cloistered walls. The derisive expression "to drink like a Templar" became commonplace. The Templars were further accused of WITCHCRAFT, sorcery and worshiping Baphomet (see LEVI, ELIPHAS), and their seal (two men riding horseback on one saddle) was said to be proof of their indulgence in homosexuality.

On October 13, 1307, Philip arrested and tortured the knight's leader, Grand Master Jacques de Molay, and 140 of his followers. A month later, on November 22, the pope issued a bull directing all countries to seize the knight's possessions.

In 1310, the trials of the Templars began in earnest. Many confessed under torture; those who didn't were burned at the stake on the king's orders. Finally, in 1312, King Philip of France succeeded in pressuring the pope to dissolve the society officially by Papal bull. Noble troops were given license to destroy the Templar's churches and castles. The pope directed that all land and monies that were confiscated should be turned over to the Hospitallers, another order of knights, but little of what was taken ever reached their organization.

De Molay was publicly burned at the stake in 1314 when he refused to confess to the charges made against him. In fact, he CURSEd both the king and the pope from the scaffold, saying that he would see them in judgment before God within a year. Indeed, both men did die within that period.

Because no great horde of gold or riches was ever found, speculation has continued to this day that the true treasures of the Knights Templar are yet to be discovered.

kris   A ritual Balinese knife identifiable by its wavy blade, the kris is considered to be a symbolic projection of the owner's soul. Said to have a life essence of its own, a kris is thought to be able to BEWITCH humans, to fly, to swim or to talk (often to signal its owner of impending peril). The magical strength of a kris can be increased by touching it to blood or the innards of snakes. Needless to say, one who possesses and can control the power of a kris is commonly suspected of being a sorcerer.

Although the mystical knives are still produced, the ancient skill of forging a true kris is a lost art. Those still existing from early times are highly revered. They are ceremoniously washed and purified and are usually held in their own shrines.

The kris's blade, called the pamor, is made of alternating layers of nickel and iron extracted from a meteorite. The hilt is prepared only after the pamor has been crafted as close to perfection as possible. Sculpted from wood, ivory, bone or metal, the handle is often inlaid or imbedded with semiprecious and precious gems. The sheath, or scabbard, usually carved from wood, is considered to have a mystical symbiosis with the pamor.

Lady of the Lake, The   A peripheral but recurrent figure in the Arthurian legends, the Lady of the Lake has been identified by different names.

In the version told by Thomas MALORY, the Lady of the Lake is referred to as the mysterious creature who bestows EXCALIBUR on King ARTHUR. In return she requests the head of Balyn, who promptly beheads her (causing him to be exiled from CAMELOT).

Malory identifies the Lady of the Lake as Nimiane (seen elsewhere as VIVIEN, Nymus and NIMUË or Nimue), the wife of Pelleas. The fact that Malory alludes to her as the "chief" lady seems to imply that there were several such mystic ladies. A powerful enchantress in love with MERLIN, she discovers all of the wizard's secrets. The Lady of the Lake uses them against Merlin to trap the magician forever in an airborne tower located in the midst of a forest of thorns in Broceliande. The mighty wizard remains ensnared there, fast asleep, although his voice can still occasionally be heard.

Also according to Malory, Nimiane traveled with the three queens who carried away the body of Arthur across the lake after his final and fatal battle with Modred. Earlier legends, however, have identified this Lady of the Lake as Morgan or even Morgan LE FAY.

Lalla Rookh   Written by Thomas Moore (1779–1852) and published in 1817, *Lalla Rookh* tells in prose the story of the Indian emperor's daughter on her way from Delhi to Kashmir to meet her intended husband, the king of Bucharia. On the way she is entertained by four tales, recited to her in verse by Feramorz, a poet. Lalla Rookh falls in love with the poet, but all ends happily when the young man is revealed to be the king in disguise.

The first three verse tales are "The Veiled Prophet of Khorassan," "Paradise and the Peri" and "The Fire-Worshippers." The fourth poem, "The Light of the Haram" [sic] tells of Nourmahal's arguing with her husband Selim. To win back his love, she consults an enchantress named Namouna, who teaches her a spellbinding song. (See SIRENS.) When Nourmahal sings the melody to her estranged husband, they are happily reunited.

Last Enchantment, The   See ARTHUR, KING; *CRYSTAL CAVE, THE*.

Law of Correspondences   See CORRESPONDENCES.

Lay of the Last Minstrel, The   The first great work by Sir Walter Scott (1771–1802), *The Lay of the Last Minstrel*, published in 1805, is a six-canto poem of irregular stanzas, with lines of seven to twelve syllables. Based on an ancient Scottish fable of Gilpen Horner, a goblin, the verses are filled with mystical happenings, occult references and impish creatures. The title refers to the narrator of the piece, a wandering minstrel.

In the tale set in the mid-1500s, Lady Branksome, seeking revenge for what she perceives as the wrongful death of her husband, mistakenly blames Lord Cranstoun (who wishes to marry her daughter Margaret). Branksome charges Sir William Deloraine with retrieving an ancient GRIMOIRE from the crypt of Michael SCOT in Melrose Abbey. She hopes the arcane manuscript will provide a secret means by which she may achieve her retribution on Cranstoun.

Despite the recovery of the book, Deloraine is wounded in combat by Cranstoun. The victor's page, an elf, magically transports Deloraine to Branksome Hall but, as a prank, steals away the lady's young son and gives him to her true enemy, the British Lord Dacre. Dacre, with Lord William Howard, plans to assault Branksome Hall, unaware that the Scottish army is on the way to defend it.

Meanwhile, the elf transforms Cranstoun to resemble the still-injured Deloraine, who is set to duel Sir Richard Musgrove for guardianship of the little boy. Cranstoun is triumphant, his visage is restored and Lady Branksome, in gratitude for the return of her son and the heir to the estate, grants the hand of her daughter in marriage to Cranstoun.

le Fay, Morgan   The queen of Avalon, the other-worldly "Isle of the Blest," Morgan le Fay runs throughout Arthurian legends and Celtic myths. Her role may derive from the early "Morrigan" mythology of Wales and Ireland; in fact, her name is also variously seen as Morgaine or Morgana. Morgan le Fay is most fully realized in Sir Thomas MALORY's *MORTE D'ARTHUR* as the sister of Morgawse and Elayne and the half-brother of Arthur (sharing a mother, Ygerne).

Certainly, le Fay and Arthur have a most unorthodox sibling relationship. At one point, she steals Arthur's scabbard and sword, EXCALIBUR, and sends them to her lover, Sir Accolon of Gaul. Her plan is to have Accolon kill Arthur with the king's own sword while she murders her husband. After-

Morgan le Fay (Daniel Beard, *A Connecticut Yankee in King Arthur's Court.*)

ward, the lovers would marry, and le Fay would use her magical powers to make Accolon the new king of Britain. During his duel with Arthur, however, Accolon drops Excalibur, which is quickly grabbed by its rightful owner. Accolon confesses his treason, but Arthur shows mercy and spares his life.

Morgan le Fay steals the sword once more, this time throwing it into the lake. She sends an enchanted robe to her brother, intending its poison to kill him. Sensing the treachery, Arthur makes Le Fay's messenger try on the robe so that he can admire it. The messenger drops dead, "being burnt to a coal." (In a similar Greek legend, the sorceress/queen MEDEA enchanted a robe so that it would burst into flames when worn.)

Morgan le Fay is also portrayed as despising Guinevere, as seen in *Sir GAWAIN AND THE GREEN KNIGHT*, where she attempts to scare the queen to death.

Despite this seeming hatred of le Fay for her stepbrother, she is in charge of the maidens who carry Arthur across the waters to Avalon to attempt to heal him of the mortal wound received from Modred. While Geoffrey of Monmouth identi-

fies this queen-leader as Argante rather than le Fay, later writers beginning with Giraldus Cambrensis (de Barri) (1146?–1220?) and the authors of the VULGATE CYCLE concur that the savior is Morgan.

Enchantresses and occult characters bearing the same or a similar name as Morgan le Fay are prominent in many other ancient stories. It is uncertain as to whether they all refer to the Arthurian le Fay. In *Ogier the Dane*, for example, Morgan allows Ogier to visit her on the Isle of Avalon. Ogier is more than 100 years old, but Morgan le Fay marries him after using a SPELL to make him young again.

In *ORLANDO FURIOSO*, le Fay is called Morgana and is a LADY OF THE LAKE, living at its bottom. She generously gives out gifts to those for whom she cares. In *ORLANDO INNAMORATO*, she is at first seen as the beneficent FATA MORGANA, "Lady Fortune," but she reverts to her evil ways later in the tale.

Leicester Boy See *DEVIL IS AN ASS, THE.*

Lemegeton: The Lesser Key of Solomon Compiled in the 17th century by an unknown cabalist, The *Lemegeton* is actually comprised of separate occult manuscripts attributed to (but almost certainly not written by) King SOLOMON. The five works most often included in (and usually considered as constituting) the *Lemegeton* are *Goetia: the Book of Evil Spirits*, *Theurgia-Goetia*, the *Pauline Art*, the *Art Almadel* and the ARS NOTORIA.

As evidence of its "recent" composition, Elizabethan-era wizards such as DEE, WIERUS and TRITHEMIUS had all heard of (and/or owned copies of) the individual tracts but not of the *Lemegeton*. A version of the *Goetia* formed a part of Wier's *De Praestigiis Daemonum* (1563), which was well known to Dee. The *Theurgia-Goetia* is a variation of the first section of Trithemius's *Steganographia* (1500).

The *Pauline Art* found in the *Lemegeton* is most probably a transcription from a 16th-century Latin manuscript now housed in the Bibliothèque Nationale in Paris. It was probably based, at least in part, on the system of prayer and invocation called the Pauline Art, which was supposedly revealed to the Apostle Paul and delivered to the Christian community at Corinth.

The *Art Almadel*, which delineates "Four Altitudes" surrounding the Earth and their respective SPIRITS, is part of a 15th-century manuscript housed in a Florence museum/library.

The "Sloane 3648" manuscript of the *Lemegeton* is probably a four-book transcription of a missing 1640/1641 tract, with a near-illegible copy of the 1657 Turner translation of the *Ars Notoria* added on. This most comprehensive *Lemegeton* also includes part of PARACELSUS's *Archidoxes Magicae* and AGRIPPA's *Occult Philosophy (DE OCCULTA PHILOSOPHIA)*.

Extant copies of the *Lemegeton* differ. Most notably, the *Ars Notoria*, the magical art of memory, is not a part of all the tracts. The "Sloane 2731" manuscript, for instance, begun on January 18, 1687, actually postdates "Sloane 3648" and used it as a source; yet the *Ars Notoria* is not included. Some scholars have suggested that it was omitted because Turner's translation was still readily available at book stalls. The discrepancies probably exist, as modern researcher/author Richard Turner suggests because the *Lemegeton* manuscripts were "compilations of early GRIMOIREs, adapted to suit the requirements of individual seventeenth-century magicians, rather than copies of a medieval comprehensive grimoire."

The church did not officially approve of *The Clavicle or The KEY OF SOLOMON* (which appealed to angelic forces), but neither did the church actively commit to its vilification. However, the *Lemegeton: The Lesser Keys of Solomon* was condemned by many Christian philosophers, especially Thomas AQUINAS, due to its encouragement of trafficking with demons and the explanation of methods for their invocation. The difference between the two works and the church's attitude toward them perfectly illustrates the varied perceptions of WHITE MAGIC (*The Key of Solomon*) and BLACK MAGIC (the *Lemegeton*).

Leo   See ASTROLOGY; HOROSCOPE; ZODIAC.

Letters on Demonology and Witchcraft   Written and published in 1830 by Sir Walter Scott (1771–1832), *Letters on Demonology and Witchcraft* was a literary essay discussing the existence of satanic practices. Despite a prolific career, he contributed no other writing to the occult field. His 1810 poem *The Lady Of The Lake* was unconnected to the Arthurian legends.

Born in Edinburgh, Scotland, the son of a writer, Scott matriculated in law but moved quickly from the bar to writing. He soon was a partner in a publishing house. He refused the honor of poet laureate in 1813 but accepted a barony in 1820. When his publishing firm entered bankruptcy, he took over the entire debt, which was eventually paid off after his death.

Levi, Eliphas (1810–1875)   A celebrated 19th-century French cabalist, Eliphas Levi (also seen as Eliphaz Lévi) was born in Paris, the son of a shoemaker.

Levi was educated at Roman Catholic schools, but he was not a particularly good student. In December 1835 he was ordained a deacon (Abbé Louis Constant), but he never took his vows to become a full priest.

About 1844, coincidental with his unhappy marriage to Noémi Cadiot who was 18 years his junior, Levi became strongly interested in the occult. He was inspired by the British occultist Francis BARRETT, the author of an 1801 book, *The MAGUS*, as well as by the writings of Cornelius AGRIPPA and Raymund LULLY. Levi was also most likely taught arcane mysteries by the Polish mathematician and mystic Hoëne-Wronski.

In 1854, Levi's marriage ended. He traveled to London, hoping for a new start by becoming a tutor of the supernatural. He was unable to speak English, however, which was definitely a hindrance. Also, he discovered that he was expected to perform demonstrations, if not "miracles." He did attempt one such ritual of ceremonial magic for a friend of his sponsor, Sir Edward Bulwer-Lytton (himself a respected occultist and the author of the 1842 mystic novel *Zanoni*). According to Levi's later book, *Transcendental Magic*, it was during this rite of NECROMANCY that he successfully conjured up the SPIRIT of APOLLONIUS.

Levi returned to Paris in August 1854 and, destitute, was aided by Adolphe Desbarolles (1801–1886). (Desbarolles's book *Les Mystères de la Main* was published posthumously in

Known for his illustrations, Eliphas Levi rendered the best-known drawing of Baphomet (or the Goat of Mendes), the satanic goat attended by witches at sabbats. In an effort to break up the Knights Templar, a powerful 13th- and 14th-century occult/military sect and secret society, King Philip IV of France accused them in 1307 of worshiping Baphomet, along with charges of heresy and homosexuality. No longer a symbol of witchcraft, Baphomet's image is still used by modern Satanists.

1869, and it proved to be the century's most significant work on PALMISTRY.) Soon Levi had a stable of students of the KABALLAH.

In May 1861 he returned to London where, by then, he was well known in occult societies. While there, he revealed that he had been studying the TAROT since 1835 and that he believed that all arcane knowledge was symbolically hidden in the pack. Levi was perhaps the first to note the possible correlation between the 22 cards of the Major Arcana and the 22 letters of the Hebrew ALPHABET.

After studying *The KEY OF SOLOMON*, Levi wrote his own *Dogme et Rituel de la Haute Magie* (*Doctrine and Ritual of High Magic*). One of the rites was an invocation of SOLOMON himself. Levi's translation of fragments from *The Key of Solomon* appeared his in *Philosophie Occulte*.

A.E. WAITE, an English scholar and mystic, claimed that Levi revealed the secret ceremonies of an association of occultists in the book and was, therefore, ousted from the order.

In his writings, Levi gave careful instructions for the sorcerer's preparation prior to performing demonic invocations. The steps included spiritual, psychic and physical cleansing by way of sleep deprivation, ritual bathing and abstinence from sex, alcohol and meat.

The last 15 years of Levi's life were fairly tranquil, pleasant and prosperous. He died in Paris at the age of 65. Some modern mystics claim that Levi was reincarnated as Aleister CROWLEY.

Three of Levi's most important writings are still in print in English editions: *The Key of the Mysteries*, translated and edited by Aleister Crowley; *Transcendental Magic*; and *Histoire de la Magie* (*The History of Magic*, possibly co-written with a pupil, Christian), the last two translated by Waite. (See also ABRACADABRA.)

Libra See ASTROLOGY; HOROSCOPE; ZODIAC.

Life of Robert the Devil, The A story in French verse and first published in English by Wynkyn de Worde in 1496, *The Life of Robert the Devil* is a fictional account of the life of Robert, the sixth duke of Normandy and the father of William the Conqueror. The historical Robert, duke of Normandy, was known for being vicious and brutal, perhaps the inspiration for the fictional work.

In the tale, a childless woman bids Satan to give her a son in return for the boy's soul. "Robert the Devil" grows to be wicked and cruel, but he eventually renounces Satan, repents and marries the daughter of the emperor. The repentance in the tale may be based on the fact the real Robert, duke of Normandy, died on religious pilgrimage to Jerusalem.

Thomas Lodge (1558–1625) later wrote a play based on the same story.

ligature Ligature, impotence caused by sorcery, was considered to be one of the most heinous of all CURSES. In his antiWITCHCRAFT tome *De le Démonomanie des sorciers* (*Demonomania of witches*, Paris, 1580), Jean Bodin (1529–1896) called ligature a "detestable impiety which merited the witch's death."

The sorcerer or enchantress could produce ligature on the victim by administering a philtre, but a much more common method was the tying of knots in a thread, cord, leather strip or cloth, which was then hidden. One sorceress revealed to Boldin that there were more than 50 ways different ways to tie the knots, depending in what way(s) (e.g., affecting urination, copulation or procreation) and for what duration the victim was intended to suffer.

In his *COMPENDIUM MALEFICARUM*, Guazzo compiled seven types and/or causes of ligature:

1. When one or both partners in a marriage are made "hateful" to the other
2. When a "bodily hindrance" or "phantasm" keeps the spouses physically separated
3. When the "vital spirit" does not flow, preventing "emission"
4. Infertility
5. When, despite desire, a man remains unaroused
6. When "certain natural drugs" prevent conception
7. When the female genitals shrink or close, or the male genitals "retract." (The *MALLEUS MALEFICARUM* had stated that a witch can push a man's genitals back into his abdomen, apparently a common HEX among German sorceresses of the 15th century.)

Belief in ligature existed long before the WITCHCRAFT hysteria of the Middle Ages: Virgil (70–19 B.C.) mentioned the "nine knots" that prevented sexual union in his *Eclogues*. Ligature was part of almost every Western culture's folklore: in ancient Rome, it was called (in Latin) *væcordia*; in Italy, *ghirlanda delle streghe*; in France, *aiguillette*.

Even Catholic scholar Thomas AQUINAS accepted the notion of ligature, asserting that "there are demons . . . that by their doings . . . can inflict injury on men and prevent carnal copulation." He did, however, make a distinction between *frigiditas*, where a man (*frigidus*) could not function sexually with any woman, and ligature, where a bewitched man (*maleficiatus*) could not perform with a specific woman. To stop the number of marriage annulments granted on the grounds of *impotentia ex maleficio*, the Catholic Church decreed in its *Corpus Juris Canonici* (A.D. c.1140) that

1. ligature could be caused by "malice."
2. ligature, like all things in the universe, exists only by God's permission.
3. ligature is brought about by the Devil, and therefore
4. an end of ligature can be achieved, with God's assistance, through prayer and abstinence.

The canon insisted that those afflicted by ligature should not turn to WHITE MAGIC or FOLK MEDICINE for a cure, but, of course, that command was largely ignored. Most often sought were herbal potions. Pliny suggested placing wolf-grease on the windowsills and lintels of the bedroom door to break the SPELL. Obviously, untying the knots of the aguillette or destroying it would be the most effective cure; the *Malleus Maleficarum* even suggests making a truce or settlement with the witch.

"Light of the Haram, The" See *LALLA ROOKH*.

Lilith According to Jewish Talmudic lore, Lilith was Adam's first wife, preceding Eve. She was also imaged on God and created from the dust (*adamah*) of the earth. Reckless and lustful, she was one of the wives of Sammael (or Satan) before being made human on Earth as Adam's mate. Because she came from the same source as Adam, she considered herself to be his equal and refused to be submissive and serve him.

Lilith left Eden to live in the sky, but Adam prayed for her to return. God sent three angels to capture her, but because Lilith refused to go back to Adam, God commanded that each day 100 of her children would die. As a result, Lilith swore revenge on all children. God, seeing that Adam was lonely, created a new wife, Eve, for him.

Some Jewish tradition contends that even after Adam was expelled from Eden, Lilith slept with him, giving birth to all evil SPIRITs. In Islamic lore, Lilith slept with Satan and bore the wicked JINN (or jinni).

A Lilith figure, sometimes with a different name, was part of the mythic traditions of ancient Babylon and, from at least 2300 BCE, of Sumeria. According to Sumerian belief, Lilith was sexually liberated and, in fact, quite earthy and darkly sensuous. She objected when Adam tried to force himself upon her sexually. Growing wings from her shoulders and ankles, Lilith flew out of Paradise and into the desert.

The Flying Goddess, as she was called, is also known as the Hand of Inanna and the Lady of the Beasts. All animals were divine to her, but the jackal, owl and raven were of particular sacred importance.

In ASSYRIAN MAGIC lore, Lilith is simply a female demon, portrayed with wings and wild, unkempt hair.

In later Western/European myths, Lilith was seen as a SUCCUBUS, a night demon who seduces men. She caused nocturnal emissions and gave birth to witches known as lilim. Because it was thought that Lilith kidnapped and murdered children, mothers protected them with AMULETS and CHARMS.

According to legend, because she avoided the Fall and disgrace in the Garden of Eden, Lilith remained immortal, and she is always portrayed as the ultimate temptress. Goethe introduced her in his play FAUST as

'Tis Lilith . . . Adam's first wife is she.
Beware the lure within her lovely tresses.

She has been seen in various incarnations throughout history, always an enchantress and a temptress who lures men to their graves. Some have associated her with the SIRENS who called to Ulysses's men in The ODYSSEY.

Perhaps the most poetic description of Lilith comes from Dante Gabriel Rossetti in his work *Body's Beauty*:

Of Adam's first wife, Lilith, it is told
(The witch he loved before the gift of Eve)
That, ere the snake's, her sweet tongue could deceive
And her enchanted hair was the first gold.
And still she sits, young while the earth is old,
And, subtly of herself contemplative,
Draws men to watch the bright web she can weave,
Till heart and body and life are in its hold.

By the 19th century, the symbol of Lilith as a seductress had entered mainstream literature. British fiction in particular frequently based a female character, who often bore her name, on the Lilith myth. Invariably, she was cold hearted as she snared a man, enticed him to fall in love and then broke his heart. If Lilith became a mother, she was a poor or evil one, and the children were often disfigured or abnormal.

Throughout the world, there are still legends today of a Lilith. She is recognized in the swamp regions of Mérida, Mexico, as a vixen who combs her long, yellow hair as she entices men into the marsh with her singing. Among the Indonesian cultures, especially those of Bali and the Iban tribes of Borneo, Lilith appears as a creature called the leyak. This evil female spirit is prone to haunt roadsides and pathways after dark, steal men away by her alluring appearance and then suck out their souls.

By the late 20th century, many feminist thinkers had adopted Lilith as a role model. Her demonic traits were ignored or reworked into such positive traits as strength, self-assuredness, self-reliance and independence.

Lilly, William (1602–1681) William Lilly was a notorious astrologer (see ASTROLOGY) and author of two books on the subject. Because he wrote under the pseudonym *Merlinus Anglicus*, he was often referred to as the English Merlin. Lilly was perhaps the most internationally recognized occultist of the middle 17th century.

In 1634 he tried unsuccessfully to locate a cache of riches supposedly hidden in Westminster Abbey by interpreting the symbols and Latin text of the ARS NOTORIA.

A contemporary of Richard TURNER, Lilly contributed introductory comments to at least one of the noted translator's works. In the 1655 *Astrologicall Opticks*, for example, Lilly stated that Turner "hath very well translated it and delivered the Astrologicall sense of every sentence judiciously." (See also FORMAN, SIMON.)

Lion, the Witch and the Wardrobe, The See CHRONICLES OF NARNIA, THE.

Lives of the Mayfair Witches A trilogy of WITCHCRAFT-themed books by Anne Rice, Lives of the Mayfair Witches is made up of *The Witching Hour* (1990), *Lasher* (1993) and *Taltos* (1994), three novels that center around the Mayfair family. Major characters include Rowan Mayfair (the witch-queen of her COVEN), Lasher (a demon SPIRIT who is made flesh), Ashlar (and his fellow supernatural beings, the Taltos), the Little People and the mystic scholars, the Talamasca. To research the atmosphere she wished to create for *The Witching Hour*, which is set in New Orleans, Rice read the novels of Henry James and Nathaniel Hawthorne (see HOUSE OF THE SEVEN GABLES, THE.)

Anne Rice is perhaps best known for her five best-selling novels that collectively make up the Vampire Chronicles: *Interview with the Vampire* (1977), *The Vampire Lestat* (1985), *The Queen of the Damned* (1988), *The Tale of the Body Thief* (1992) and *Memnoch the Devil* (1995).

Although the witchcraft and vampire series are distinctly separate, they do have in common the mystic realm that Anne Rice calls "the Dark Universe," a world populated by spirits, "discarnate entities, some evil, some good—who can interfere with mankind. . . . These spirits are a form of matter that we just can't measure and understand yet."

Anne Rice explains that "there is no magic per se" in the Dark Universe and that, in her books, "Witches play with fire when they play with spirits; they want what spirits know, but again and again they pay a hell of a price for it."

Anne Rice, born Howard Allen O'Brien in New Orleans on October 4, 1941, is the author of 16 books. In addition to the Lives of the Mayfair Witches and the Vampire Chronicles, she has written *The Mummy, or Ramses the Damned* (1989) plus two historical novels, *The Feast of All Saints* (1979) and *Cry to Heaven* (1982). Under the pseudonym A.N. Rocquelaure, she has written three erotic novels, *The Claiming of Sleeping Beauty*, *Beauty's Punishment* and *Beauty's Release*; as Anne Rampling, Anne Rice wrote *Exit to Eden* and *Belinda*.

Logistilla See ORLANDO FURIOSO.

Long Lost Friend, The See HEX.

Lord of the Rings, The Written by J.R.R. TOLKIEN, *The Lord of the Rings* is a trilogy (with each part being divided into two books) that continues the story of Middle-Earth undertaken in *The HOBBIT*. While having read *The Hobbit* is helpful for an understanding of *The Lord of the Rings*, it is not essential. A masterpiece of fantasy literature, the trilogy is inhabited by all sorts of magical and supernatural creatures, including wizards.

Tolkien began to write the trilogy in 1936 and had completed most of the work by 1949. The first volume, *The Fellowship of the Ring,* was published in 1954; the two subsequent volumes, *The Two Towers* and *The Return of the Ring,* were published in the next two years. The first American paperback edition of *The Lord of the Rings* appeared in 1965, and it acquired somewhat of a cult following among its mostly college and high school readers.

In the tale, Frodo Baggins, nephew of Bilbo Baggins (hero of *The Hobbit*), is visited by GANDALF the wizard to undertake a quest—the Ring of Power's final destruction.

The Ring of Power is central to Middle-Earth's history in the Third Age, and a knowledge of its background is necessary to understand the books' mythology. Long before the events in *The Lord of the Ring,* around 1500 in the Second Age, Erigion's smiths forged several lesser RINGS of power. Sauron himself forged the one ring that would unite and control them all.

Sauron is defeated during battle in Gondor. The warrior Isildur cut the ring from Sauron's finger, but it was later washed down the Anduin River. (It was eventually obtained by Gollum and then found by Bilbo Baggins in *The Hobbit.*)

In the year 2463 of the Third Age, the Wise (a body comprised of wizards, the High elves and other select, superior magical and supernatural entities) formed the White Council. Saruman was made the council head; the council's mission was to discover the wicked Sauron's actions and help drive him from Mordor.

In about 1100 of the Third Age, Saruman was one of the five Istari, or wizards, sent (most probably by the godlike Valar) to help Middle-Earth fight Sauron. The Valar are described as divine or angelic SPIRITS, and although never stated, the wizards were quite possibly the Valar in human form. Only three of the wizards are ever identified in *The Lord of the Rings*: Saruman the White, Gandalf the Grey and Radagast the Brown, who was noted for his friendship with the birds and the ANIMALS.

Like his fellow wizards, Saruman could give only limited assistance to the Middle-Earth beings, who had to fight and win their own war against Sauron. Saruman was seduced by his own desire to own the Ring of Power, however, and, about 300 years before the beginning of the *The Lord of the Rings*'s events, he installed himself in the ancient fortress of Isengard in the kingdom of Gondor.

As the epic tale begins, Gandalf approaches Frodo and commands him to destroy the ring, passed down to him by his Uncle Bilbo, before it is seized by Sauron. Ownership of the Ring of Power along with the lesser rings would make Sauron omnipotent. The Ring of Power alone, however, eventually corrupts its owner; even the *desire* to possess it corrupts! Thus, the Ring of Power cannot be used against Sauron because, in the process, the new owner would be contaminated. Also, the ring cannot be merely set aside because its gnawing, persuasive influence for evil cannot be ignored for long. The only alternative, as Gandalf demands, is that the ring be destroyed.

Three lesser magical rings are still in the hands of the elves. Sauron originally hoped to use the rings to control the elves, but, with Sauron's loss of the Ring of Power, the elves were able to use their rings to do much good, such as healing.

Frodo sets out for Mount Doom, where the Ring of Power must be dropped into the volcano to be destroyed. Meanwhile, Saruman, who believes that Gandalf knows the ring's location, invites the wizard to a secret meeting, purportedly to discuss how Saruman can assist in the continuing fight against Sauron.

Once Gandalf arrives, Saruman reveals his true purpose: He proposes that Gandalf help him obtain the ring, and then they can combine forces to dominate Middle-Earth. He even paints a lurid picture of their rule together: Powerful enemies would be endured, but weak allies would be destroyed.

Gandalf, appalled, refuses to unite with him in such evil, so Saruman imprisons him on a mountain top. Once Saruman has departed, Gandalf is rescued by Gwaihir the eagle.

Gandalf accompanies Frodo on his journey, and the wizard leads the party into the mines of Moria. Attacked and then chased through the mines by orcs (goblinlike creatures) and trolls, the company reaches the bridge of Khazad-dum. The bridge, spanning a bottomless chasm, must be crossed to reach the Great Gate, the mine's exit.

A hideous Balrog appears, and Gandalf stays behind to do battle as his friends cross to safety. Halfway across the bridge, he stops to face the Balrog and after an intense struggle, casts the Balrog over the edge. As he falls into the pit, however, the monster wraps his whip around the wizard's leg, and drags Gandalf along into the chasm, seemingly to his doom.

The wizard reappears among his friends, having passed through Death and been resurrected as Gandalf the White. He approaches Saruman one last time, begging him to give up his pursuit of the Ring of Power. Saruman refuses. Gandalf deposes him as White Council chief and removes his powers by magically breaking his WAND in two.

The War of the Ring erupts between Sauron and the forces of Middle-Earth. Against all odds and against a background of supernatural intrigue and shenanigans, Frodo reaches the volcano's crest. Gollum appears and bites off Frodo's finger, swallowing the ring. Unbalanced, Gollum plummets into the fiery depths. The ring is destroyed, and Sauron's armies are annihilated.

With the Ring of Power gone and Frodo's enterprise at an end, Gandalf informs the residents of Middle-Earth that they are now in charge of their own destiny. As Frodo departs for home, Saruman, now a beggar, appears. He rebuffs a sympathetic Gandalf and CURSEs them all.

Upon returning home, Frodo discovers that the hobbit Shire has been transformed into a police state. The might behind the dictator, a hobbit named Lotho, is the mysterious Sharkey. With his newfound courage and fighting skills, Frodo battles the traitors. Frodo and his men capture Sharkey, who turns out to be Saruman in disguise. Saruman betrays his henchman Wormtongue, who suddenly rises against his master and slits his throat. As the ex-wizard

A woodcut engraving by Raymund Lully depicting the 13 steps to obtain the wisdom and power of God. (Lully, *On the Ascent*)

dies, a human-shaped fog floats out from the body, faces west and disperses.

At the trilogy's end, Gandalf returns to convey Bilbo and Frodo Baggins to the Blessed Realm.

Loudon See GRANDIER, FATHER URBAIN.

low magic See *BOOK OF THE DEAD, THE EGYPTIAN*; EGYPTIAN MAGIC.

Lully, Raymund (1235–1315) There is little biographical detail surrounding the early life of the Spanish occultist Raymund (also seen as *Raymond*) Lully. A student of the KABALLAH and ALCHEMY, Lully claimed to have successfully changed worthless metal into gold. The product of this unique transmutation was named, in his honor, *aurum Raymundi*.

In 1657, Richard TURNER and an assistant (W.W.) translated an alchemical tract written in High German and Latin and credited to Lully. Turner titled Lully's work *Philosophical and Chymical Experiments of that famous Philosopher Raymond Lully; containing the right and due Composition of both Elixirs; the admirable and perfect way of making the great Stone of the Philosophers.* Turner bound it in a single volume along with his translation of a PARACELSUS piece, *Of the Chymical Transmutation, Genealogy, and Generation of Metals and Minerals.*

Mabinogion See MATH.

Macbeth Written by William SHAKESPEARE most probably in 1606 (when it was first performed at the Globe Theater), *Macbeth* is the tragic story of a prideful but superstitious military general who, with his ambitious wife, ascends to the throne of Scotland through assassination. Because of the many occult references and characters in the work, it is thought that the play may have been presented before King James I, the author of *DEMONOLOGIE*. James I was also possibly a descendant of Banquo, an important character in the play.

The drama, short by comparison to other Shakespeare works, was first published in the First Folio of 1623. Experts tend to agree that the existing text is adulterated with additions not by Shakespeare and contains at least two songs by Thomas Middleton (1580–1627). These additions have caused scholars to look closely at the similarities and differences between the three weird sisters in *Macbeth* and HECATE in Middleton's play *The WITCH*.

Although the inspiration for Shakespeare's *Macbeth* is uncertain, one possible source is *The Orygnale Cronykil* (written c.1420 but first published in 1795). Penned by Andrew Wyntoun (c.1350–c.1425), the *Cronykil* is a verse history of Scotland from prehistory to the time of James I, including the accounts of Macbeth, Macduff, Malcolm and the three witches.

Macbeth has obtained the notorious distinction of being the most "troubled" of Shakespeare's canon during rehearsal and performance, almost as though the CURSE of Macbeth extends to those actors and theaters that dare to perform it. Since its earliest productions, "accidents" seem to occur whenever the play is performed. Theatrical superstition forbids saying *Macbeth* inside of any theater, as if even saying the word aloud will draw calamity. Magical CHARMs to overcome the accidental saying of *Macbeth* include spinning three times in a circle and spitting.

At the play's opening, Macbeth and Banquo, two generals in King Duncan's army, have just won a battle against rebels. The play's tragic events are set in motion by their encounter with three witches, called the weird sisters.

The witches prophesy Macbeth's eventual rise to the Scottish crown, after his first being named thane of Cawdor. They further predict that Banquo's sons will be kings, although he himself will never rule. Almost immediately news arrives that, to reward the general's valor in battle, King Duncan has, indeed, made Macbeth the thane of Cawdor.

Macbeth relates the seemingly supernatural events to his wife, the power-hungry Lady Macbeth. Goaded by her, Macbeth murders Duncan when the king visits his castle. Duncan's sons, Malcolm and Donalbain, flee for their lives, allowing Macbeth to take the throne.

To ensure that the witches' prophecy regarding Banquo is never fulfilled, Macbeth orders two men to kill Banquo and his son, Fleance. Fleance, however, manages to elude his assailants.

Banquo's ghost returns to haunt Macbeth. In terror, Macbeth returns to the weird sisters for guidance. Having just met with Hecate, queen of the witches, the weird sisters brew a demonic potion as they chant

> Double, double toil and trouble;
> Fire burn and CAULDRON bubble.

The witches give Macbeth three predictions: Beware Macduff, the thane of Fife; none born of a woman can hurt Macbeth; and Macbeth shall rule until Birnam Wood comes to the castle Dunsinane. (This pronouncement follows in the ancient tradition that ORACLEs, such as the one located at DELPHI, give prophecy that is deliberately obscure and subject to interpretation.)

Because Macbeth takes the weird sisters' words literally, the last two prophecies seem impossible to materialize. Macbeth fears only Macduff, and when he hears that Macduff has joined forces with Malcolm in England, Macbeth and his army storm Macduff's castle and murders Macduff's wife and children. Afterward, a guilt-ridden Lady Macbeth goes mad and dies.

As the combined armies of Malcolm and Macduff approach Dunsinane, they pass through Birnam Wood. Each man cuts a branch and holds it in front of himself as camouflage. The forest of Birnam Wood seems to march toward Macbeth's castle, fulfilling the second prophecy. The third prediction comes true when, during his confrontation with Macbeth, Macduff reveals that he was delivered by caesarian section rather than by natural childbirth. Macbeth is killed by Macduff, and Malcolm becomes rightful king of Scotland.

Some scholars suggest that although their actions show them to be witches, the weird sisters may have been intended as metaphors to represent destiny, rather than as living creatures. Shakespeare's plays, they contend, were written when the English language was in constant flux, and study has suggested that the playwright's spelling for the *weird* sisters may have actually been *wyrd*, an Old English word for "fate." If so, the three weird sisters may, in fact, have represented the three Fates of ancient Greek mythology. Other occult references in *Macbeth* include augurs (see DIVINATION), Golgotha (literally "the Place of the Skull," the location of the crucifixion of JESUS) and graymalkin (a witch's FAMILIAR, in this case a gray cat).

The tale of Macbeth has been the basis for numerous other artistic works, including the 1847 Italian OPERA *Macbeth* by Giuseppe Verdi. In 1888, early in his career, Richard Strauss (1864–1949) wrote a music tone poem to accompany an 1890 German production of *Macbeth*. Also, during a decade-long publishing ban (1933–1943) of his own writings in the Soviet Union, Nobel Prize-winning author Boris Pasternak (1890–1960) made a distinguished translation of *Macbeth* into his native Russian.

Magi

The first record of the Magi can be dated to Persia at around 591 B.C., but they were at their greatest power and prestige when Cyrus established the Persian Empire. Most probably descendants of the Medians, the Magi set themselves apart from the Persians and further split their own sect into castes. Most of the priests followed the teachings of ZOROASTER.

The Magi were famous for healing and their practice of various forms of DIVINATION, which they performed in their temples. Although forbidding idolatry, the Magi believed in the divinity of the Cosmos, and, according to the Greek historian Herodotus (c.480–c.425 B.C.), they made supplications to all of the heavenly bodies, including Earth, Fire, Water and Winds. (See ELEMENTS.)

The Persian word *magus* (meaning "priest" and "fire worshiper") was adapted into Greek as *magos* (meaning a "wise one," "wizard" or "juggler.") Demonstrations, feats or traits "of a wizard" were said to be *magikos*, and it was this Greek root that was Westernized into *magic* and *magical*.

Because of their mystical abilities and learning, the Magi held sway over many political decisions. A state-sponsored suppression around 500 B.C. led to the Magi moving outward from Persia, westward to Greece and as far east as India (becoming the ancestors of today's Parsi community).

Although the Magi were serious stargazers, they did not practice ASTROLOGY in the modern sense of the word. They did believe, however, that events on Earth could be foreseen or revealed by signs in the heavens.

Many biblical scholars believe that the three "wise men from the East" who attended the newborn JESUS in Bethlehem (mentioned in the New Testament of the Bible; Matthew 2:1) were probably Persian Magi.

Their hypothesis is based on several factors: "Wise men" could refer to their being followers of Ahura-Mazda, the omniscient source of ultimate knowledge. They had obviously traveled some distance because Herod based his slaughtering of "all the children that were in Bethlehem, and in all the coasts thereof, from two years old and under" (Matthew 2:16) on the time that the wise men had been seeing and trailing the star. Finally, having followed "the star, which they saw in the east," (Matthew 2:9), the wise men were not only acutely aware of heavenly signs but had traveled from the Zoroastrian stronghold of Persia.

Those who doubt the Zoroastrian connection suggest that it was the *star* that was in the east and not the *wise men*. Also, the prophet Jesus was worshiped by the wise men, but the Zoroastrian Magi never proclaimed Jesus to be a deity or made him the major figure in their faith or a replacement for their own religion's founder.

It has been suggested by religious scholars, however, that the story of the Magi (whether an actual event or not) may have been included in the scriptures by the early Christian writers to suggest that all pagan deities and religions are inferior and subservient to Jesus and the new "true faith."

Magica de Spell

First appearing in 1961 as a Disney COMIC BOOK character, the sorceress Magica de Spell was created by artist Carl Barks. She joined the cast surrounding Scrooge McDuck in the animated *DuckTales* cartoons, which began on TELEVISION in the fall of 1987. Her European-accented voice is provided by June Foray.

In her efforts to irritate McDuck, Magica de Spell often teams up with Madam Mim, the enchantress who battled MERLIN in the Disney animated feature FILM *The Sword and the Stone*. Most of all, Magica de Spell hopes to capture McDuck's good luck CHARM: the first dime he ever earned!

magic circle

Although usually an actual circle, a magic circle is any geometric design or diagram drawn around a karcist (a person invoking a SPIRIT) prior to a magical operation, such as an INCANTATION or casting a SPELL. The purpose of the magic circle is to separate and protect the wizard or sorcerer from diabolic powers. Demons may enter the circle and join the sorcerer only at his request or command.

The magic circle is drawn with a ceremonial knife, the two most popular types being the arthame and the KRIS. Described in *The KEY OF SOLOMON* and other arcane texts, an arthame is usually quite ornate, decorated with RUNES or other cabalistic symbols on its handle and blade.

"This is the circle for the maister to sit in, and his fellowe or fellowes, at the first calling, sit in backe to backe, when he calleth the spirit." (Scot, *The Discoverie of Witchcraft*)

In his book *DISCOVERIE OF WITCHCRAFT*, Reginald Scot reveals the proper places for a wizard to draw his magic circle:

> As for the places of Magical Circles, they are to be chosen melancholy, doleful, dark and lonely; either in Woods or Deserts, or in a place where three ways meet, or amongst ruins of Castles, Abbeys, Monasteries, etc., or upon the Seashore when the Moon shines clear, or else in some large Parlor hung with black . . . , with doors and windows closely shut, and waxen candles lighted.

Many GRIMOIREs offer the proper or recommended technique for drawing the circle. The explanation given in *The Grand Grimoire* for drawing the magic circle and beginning a demonic evocation is one of the best and most complete:

> You will begin by making a circle with the goatskin, . . . nailing down the skin with four nails. Then you will take your blood stone and trace a triangle inside the circle, beginning with the direction of the east; and you will also trace with the blood stone the great A, the small E, the small A and the small J, along with the holy name of JESUS, between two crosses, to prevent the SPIRITS from attacking you.
>
> After which, the karcist will gather his assistants into the circle, each in his own place, . . . and he will enter it himself without fear, whatever sounds he may hear.

Any adornment or additional designs drawn in or around the magic circle must be done carefully so as not to offend the spirit to be invoked. All ritual instruments, including the knives, the colors of inks and fumigations (i.e., perfumes or incense), must be taken into account; and a HOROSCOPE should be cast to find the most fortuitus day and time to take the magic action.

Like the ELEMENTS and HUMOURS, each cardinal (or compass) point of the magic circle has its own CORRESPONDENCES:

North	Darkness; mystery; great power; the Element Earth; the PENTACLE; the colors black and gold.
South	The sun; energy; the Element Fire; the magic WAND; the colors blue and white.
East	Wisdom; light; the Element Air; the sword; the colors red and white.
West	Emotions; the female forces of creativity and fertility; the Element Water; the chalice; the colors red and gray.

magic mirror See BEAUTY AND THE BEAST; DEE, JOHN; DIVINATION; films, *MARY POPPINS, SNOW WHITE AND THE SEVEN DWARFS*; GRECO-ROMAN MAGIC; NOSTRADAMUS; PARACELSUS; SOLOMON.

magic square Magic squares, or *kameas*, were a traditional and important part of cabalistic magic. The magic square is a seal or PENTACLE, inscribed to effect magic. As such, it can also act as a form of TALISMAN.

Magic squares are seen throughout the writings of such occultists as ABANO, AGRIPPA, DEE and TRITHEMIUS. They were a standard part of magical GRIMOIREs, and the most important magic squares made up the bulk of Francis Barrett's *The MAGUS*.

Usually, a magic square is representative of a specific planet and its astrological sphere of influence. The square is subdivided into an equal number of rows and columns, with the same number of squares in each. If a NUMEROLOGY system is to be used, a number is placed in each smaller box, and each

line, summed horizontally or vertically, should add up the same number. One magic square that represents the planet Jupiter is

4	14	15	1
9	7	6	12
5	11	10	8
16	2	3	13

The wizard imposes a name (often an angel he wishes to invoke) on the magic square by substituting each letter of that name with its numerological value. A line is used to connect each of those numbers, in order, within the magic square, and that line and its design (considered to be a graphic representation of the name) is known as a sigil. The sigil can then be used to control the person or power with respect to that square's attributes. For example, the attribute of the planet Venus is love; thus, the sigil drawn on the magic square of Venus can be used as a love talisman.

The oldest known numerical magic square is that used to invoke the power and influence of Saturn:

4	9	2
3	5	7
8	1	6

The pentacle is drawn in three rows and columns because Saturn is in the third sephira, or level of the heavens in which God supposedly created the universe.

Occasionally, letters of the ALPHABET are used in place of numbers, in which case the words must read the same across as down. The most famous example of an alphabetical magic square is the pentacle for the planet Saturn, as seen in *The KEY OF SOLOMON*:

S	A	T	O	R
A	R	E	P	O
T	E	N	E	T
O	P	E	R	A
R	O	T	A	S

In conjunction with Saturn, the esoteric words within the magic square also have a meaning, forming a sentence: SATOR (The Creator), AREPO (slow-moving), TENET (maintains) OPERA (his creation) ROTAS (as vortices). The square is thought by some occultists to be an anagram of the Christian Paternoster. (See PATTER.)

Although this last magical square has been used indiscriminately as a powerful pentacle, it supposedly induces Saturn's negative energies of sorrow and restriction. *The SACRED MAGIC OF ABRAMELIN THE MAGE* offers an alternate magic square for the purposes of obtaining love and approval:

S	A	L	O	M
A	R	E	P	O
L	E	M	E	L
O	P	E	R	A
M	O	L	A	S

Here the words have an entirely different meaning: SALOM (Peace), AREPO (he distills), LEMEL (unto fullness), OPERA (upon the dry ground), MOLAS (into life, or quick motion).

It was thought that magic squares could be prepared for almost any purpose, from invoking a particular angel to acquiring gold or for healing. The astrologically correct time of day had to be observed when drawing the sigil, and to be most effective the magic square was engraved on the specific metal or parchment associated with that planetary sphere. The proper color of ink, perfumes for fumigation and other variables were taken into account as well. As with all ritual magic, the preparation and use of a magic square had to be preceded by the correct rites, including fasting, cleansing, purification and abstinence.

"Magic: The Gathering"

Created by Richard Garfield and produced by Wizards of the Coast, Inc., of Renton, Washington, "Magic: The Gathering" is a fantasy game using trading cards to represent mystical creatures and entities. Each player portrays a wizard, armed with a personally assembled deck of 40 illustrated cards. By casting SPELLS and calling on monsters to drive out all opposition, each wizard battles for domination over the plane of Dominia.

Garfield's first attempt at a fantasy game, "The Five Magics," was developed in 1982. Ten years later, Garfield and Mike Davis approached a new games manufacturer, Wizards of the Coast, headed by Peter Adkinson and James Hays, with a board game they had cocreated, but the company was looking for a game that required minimal equipment.

Garfield felt he was on the right track with a fantasy role-playing trading-card game and after two years of testplaying, released "Magic: The Gathering" in August 1994.

There are more than 4,000 different designs available from which the player can assemble a basic "Magic: The Gathering" deck, divided into land cards and SPELL cards. There are five different types of lands and magic, each represented by a particular color: black, blue, green, red and white. The remaining cards are divided into six different types of spells, some usable one time only and others that are permanent: Instants, Interrupts, Sorceries, Enchantments (including Enchant Worlds), Artifacts and Summons (Creatures).

By understanding the capabilities and limitations of each type of land card and spell card, each wizard can compile a strong working deck. Advance strategy consists of finding a balance of colors and lands, a proper proportion of spells to lands and combinations of lands and spells that attack well together.

During each of seven phases of play, each wizard has one or more options: to set a land into play, to make an attack or to cast a spell against the other wizard(s). At the end of each turn, the wizard heals any injured creatures and clears the effects of temporary spells. Wizards gain or lose "life" points by casting or being affected by spells, and any wizard with a "life" of zero or less at the end of a phase has been driven from the plane of Dominia (i.e., loses the game). To win the game the wizard must inflict 20 points of damage on the opposing wizard.

As opposed to play of the fantasy game "DUNGEONS AND DRAGONS" (in which battles can take hours or days), an entire game of "Magic: The Gathering" may take only minutes, depending upon the cards played.

Fifty million trading cards, in basic decks of 60 and "booster packs" of 15, were sold in the first six months of the game's release, and two billion were sold, according to Wizards of the Coast, by May 1997. In addition to the trading card game "Magic: The Gathering," there are already "Magic" tournaments and computer games (CD-ROM and on-line versions), plus four "Magic"-based novels and a *Pocket Players' Guide* in print. In 1997, Wizards of the Coast, Inc., acquired TSR, Inc., which manufactures "Dungeons and Dragons."

Magnus, Albertus (1206–1280)

The bishop of Ratisbon, Albertus Magnus was fascinated with the occult arts and sciences, especially ALCHEMY. His most famous pupil was St. Thomas AQUINAS.

Magnus purportedly succeeded at transmuting lead into gold by use of the PHILOSOPHER'S STONE and is also credited with being able to control the weather. He is said to have created an artificial human, but it was supposedly so talkative that Magnus finally destroyed it to stop the noise!

Albertus Magnus was a prolific author, writing several cabalistic tracts for aspiring alchemists. In his book *On Alchemy*, Magnus wrote "The alchemist must be silent and discreet. To no one should he reveal the results of his operations. . . . He shall live in loneliness, remote from men. His house should have two or three rooms consecrated entirely to his work."

His own best teacher, Magnus's true techniques were never revealed, and no one has ever duplicated his legendary feats.

Magnus, Simon   See SIMON.

Magus, The

Written by Francis Barrett and published in London in 1801, *The Magus, or Celestial Intelligencer; Being a Complete System of Occult Philosophy* was an attempt by the author to rekindle interest in the occult in 19th-century England. Despite its subject matter, the style of *The Magus* suggests that it was written for a refined, Christian readership.

The Magus is divided into chapters on natural magic (i.e., the inherent powers of gemstones, herbs and ANIMALS),

Francis Barrett, author of *The Magus* (1801).

ALCHEMY, TALISMANS, NUMEROLOGY, magnetism, the KABAL-LAH and ceremonial or ritual magic (mostly repeated from earlier GRIMOIRES). As if to prove the validity of his INCANTATIONS, Barrett claimed that he had "by only speaking a few words, and used some other things, caused terrible rains and claps of thunder."

The book depicts a large number of different styles for drawing the MAGIC CIRCLE. Barrett also illustrates invocational paraphernalia, including candles, torches, a magic WAND, a RING engraved with a PENTACLE, a dagger, a scrying crystal and the SEAL OF SOLOMON. *The Magus* is also well known for Barrett's drawings of various demons.

The book and its author's teachings had a major influence on the occult thinking and writings of Eliphas LEVI.

Maleficent   See FILMS, *SLEEPING BEAUTY*.

Malleus Maleficarum   Written and published in 1486 by two Dominican friars, Heinrich Krämer (or Kramer) (c.1430–1505) and James (or Jakob) Sprenger (1436 or 1438–95), the *Malleus Maleficarum* (*The Witch's Hammer* or *The Hammer of Witches*) is one of the earliest books on the subjects of WITCHCRAFT and demonology and, most probably, the most important and influential ever written. It was quickly acknowledged as the definitive textbook on how to discover and punish witches.

The *Malleus Maleficarum* was all the more authoritative because the authors' credentials were sanctioned by Pope

Innocent VIII. In his bull of 1484, the pope reasserted that witchcraft was a heresy, and he authorized Krämer and Sprenger to seek out and destroy witchcraft in northern Germany. Krämer and Sprenger wisely reprinted the papal bull in full as an introduction in their book.

The book's popularity was unrivaled throughout Europe. At least 13 editions appeared by 1520; another 16 or more were published between 1574 and 1669. Its acceptance and impact were weaker in England, partly because the first English translation did not appear until 1584. Also, the persecution of witches in England was more often based on their deeds rather than for their supposed heresy.

Between the time of its release and the 1678 publication of John Bunyan's *Pilgrim's Progress*, the book was second only to *The Holy Bible* in the number of copies sold. Needless to say, its influence on witch-hunters, members of the Inquisition and ecclesiastical and secular courts throughout the 15th, 16th and 17th centuries cannot be overstated.

The *Malleus Maleficarum* is composed of three parts. In each section, a proposition is raised and then proven through logic, debate or example. Throughout, the work is misogynistic, portraying women as being particularly weak and susceptible to the Devil's wiles: for example, the authors wrongly claim

Title page from the first edition of *Malleus Maleficarum*, the most influential antiwitchcraft book in history.

that the Latin word *femina* ("woman") is derived from *fe* (meaning "faith") and *minus* (meaning "less").

Part I of the *Malleus Maleficarum* examines the various evils that witches, in league with the Devil, perpetrate on humankind (albeit with God's permission). Part II discloses the methods witches use to CURSE and BEWITCH others, along with ways to break these SPELLs. The authors also emphasize the pact witches must sign in order to sell their souls to the Devil. The final section, Part III, deals with legalistic matters: how to obtain and record testimony, methods for interrogation (including torture) and for obtaining confessions, plus guidelines for sentencing.

Heinrich Krämer was born in Schlettstadt in Lower Alsace. At an early age, he was made a prior in the Dominican House located there. The church appointed him an inquisitor for the provinces of Bohemia, Moravia, Salzburg and Tyrol in 1474, but the discovery of the deceitful methods he used to "discover" witchcraft led to his dismissal and expulsion by the bishop of Brixen. Nevertheless, in 1485, he wrote a manuscript (later incorporated into the *Malleus Maleficarum*) that expounded his views on the heretical nature of witchcraft.

Born in Basel, James Sprenger was also a Dominican. Early in his career, Sprenger was a prior and regent of studies at the Cologne Convent. Later, he was made provincial of the province of Germany and dean of Cologne University. By 1486, when Krämer joined with Sprenger to co-author the *Malleus Maleficarum*, the two men were presiding as the prior and the inquisitor of Cologne, respectively. (See also INQUISITION, THE; PAPACY, THE.)

Malory, Sir Thomas (d. 1471)

Although few biographical details about him are known, Sir Thomas Malory is credited as the author of *Le MORTE D'ARTHUR*. It *is* known that the epic poem, largely an adapted translation of one (or more) French book(s), was written while its author was in prison. It was also known that Malory had been knighted at some point before 1442 and that sometime after 1450 he was charged with theft, assault and rape, possibly leading to imprisonment.

Using these few clues and a 15th-century manuscript by Malory, Vinaver, the editor of the now-definitive 1947 printing of the poem, concluded that Sir Thomas Malory of Newbold Revel, Warwickshire, England, indeed, must have been the author of the entire *Le Morte D'Arthur*.

Some scholars doubt that Malory could have written *Le Morte D'Arthur*. They contend that its author, in order to have access to the original source, would have had to have been jailed in France rather than in England during that period. (See *A CONNECTICUT YANKEE IN KING ARTHUR'S COURT*; ARTHUR, KING.)

mandrake

Since ancient times the plant commonly known as the mandrake has been thought to hold magical properties. It was a common ingredient in love philtres, and it was thought that CIRCE used mandrake roots to prepare her most powerful potions. Because of its inherent mystical qualities, dried mandrake, carried on the person, was thought by many occultists to be a powerful AMULET.

St. Hildegard described the mandrake in the Liber 1, "De Plantis" chapter of her comprehensive *Physica*:

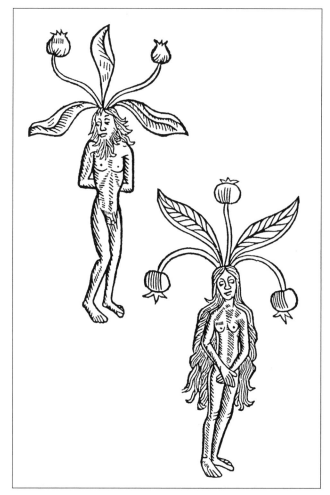

A fanciful medieval conception of male and female mandrake roots. (Johannes de Cuba, *Hortus Sanitatis*)

It is hot . . . something watery, and formed of the moistened earth wherewith Adam was created; hence is it that this herb, being made in man's likeness, ministers much more than other plants to the suggestion of the Devil; according to man's desire good or evil may be aroused at will, as was done aforetime with idols.

According to all mentions of the plant by medieval alchemic writers, the mandrake assumed one of two humanlike shapes, either female ("species feminæ hujus herbæ") or male ("species masculi hujus herbæ"). Johannes de Cuba went so far as to illustrate the plant roots in his book *Hortus Sanitatis* (original publication date uncertain, first translated into French around 1498 by A. Vérard in Paris).

Because of the plant roots' appearance, SYMPATHETIC MAGIC played a large role in their use. The mandrake was frequently employed for DIVINATION: many fortune-tellers believed that the miniature figures would nod or shake their heads to answer questions about the future. Some occultists asserted that FAMILIARs and demons lived in the roots.

It is uncertain whether the occult mandrake is the same plant mentioned in the story of Reuben and Leah in the Bible. In Genesis 30:14–15, Reuben gives his mother Leah several mandrakes, causing Rachel to become jealous. Some herbalists believe that the biblical mandrake was actually the *mandragora officinarum* or mandragore, a member of the potato family. Many cabalists identify the biblical mandrake as the dodaim, a plant related to the lily, amomum, helicabum and calathum. (Ancients considered dodaim to be the plant of Venus, able to produce fertility in women.)

It is also unclear whether the mandrake of today, *atropa mandragora*, is the same plant that was so meticulously studied and employed by early healers (especially those in Germany) and mystics.

Mandrake the Magician   Created by writer Lee Falk (1905–) and artist Phil Davis (1906–1964), the comic strip *Mandrake the Magician* first appeared as a daily cartoon, distributed by King Features Syndicate, on June 11, 1934, and in the Sunday newspapers on February 3, 1935.

Falk first conceived of the Mandrake character in 1924 when he was still an undergraduate at the University of Illinois. He named the character for the MANDRAKE root, a plant known for its occult connections and uses in FOLK MEDICINE.

Mandrake studied magic and illusionary arts under Luciphor in the mountains of Tibet. Back in the United States, he turned his talents to fighting crime. At first, Mandrake was portrayed as an actual wizard in the strip, with real magic and supernatural powers. Today, most of Mandrake's illusions are achieved through hypnosis, of which he is a master, and his magic skills are augmented by intelligence and cunning. Mandrake the Magician is pictured as a stereotypical night-club magician, with swallowtail tuxedo jacket, an opera hat and red-lined black cape.

Mandrake is assisted by Lothar, who abdicated his title as prince of the Federated Tribes in Africa to work with the magician. Immensely strong and wearing a fez and leopard-skin vest, Lothar was the first principal black character to appear in an adventure comic strip.

Foes of Mandrake have included aliens, tyrannical despots and sorcerers. The first to appear in the comic strip, and still occasionally seen, is The Cobra, the name taken by Mandrake's ex-mentor Luciphor after turning to villainy and BLACK MAGIC.

In 1939, a black-and-white movie serial (see FILMS) of *Mandrake the Magician* appeared. The *Mandrake* strips were repeatedly reprinted in book form, and there was also a series of *Mandrake* "Big Little Books." Today, *Mandrake the Magician* is still distributed to more than 200 newspapers worldwide and is translated into eight languages on six continents.

Lee Falk was born in St. Louis, Missouri, and has been a writer since his days in high school. Following his graduation from the University of Illinois, he became a copywriter for a St. Louis advertising agency, where he met his future collaborator, Phil Davis. Falk went on to write and produce for local radio before selling *Mandrake the Magician* to King Features in 1934. Just two years later, he created another still-popular strip, *The Phantom*, for the syndication house. At the Comics Conference in Lucca, Italy, in 1971, Lee Falk was honored for his work as a comic-strip author.

Phil Davis was also born in St. Louis, on March 4, 1906, and matriculated at the Washington University Art School. He was a commercial artist/draftsman for the telephone company, freelanced as a magazine illustrator and joined the advertising art staff of the *St. Louis Post-Dispatch* (in 1928) before meeting Falk in 1933. Davis served as the art director for Curtiss-Wright Aircraft during World War II, so his wife Martha, a talented fashion artist, began to assist in inking the strip. Davis drew the strip until his death on December 16, 1964, but in the later years, much of the work had actually been done by his wife. After Davis's death, Falk chose Fred Fredericks to take over the artwork.

Harold (Fred) Fredericks, Jr., was born in Atlantic City, New Jersey, on August 9, 1929, and studied at the Atlantic City Friends Schools. Fredericks also studied for three years at the School of Visual Arts in Manhattan, New York. From 1960 through 1965, Fredericks worked on COMIC BOOKS for Dell and Gold Key. Fredericks's artwork for *Mandrake the Magician* began to appear in April 1965. Since June 1965 Fredericks has been cosigning the strips with Falk.

Manfred   A play in verse by Lord (George Gordon) Byron (1788–1824), *Manfred* was published in 1817. Never fully pleased with the work, Byron did not want the drama ever to be performed, a request honored until after his death.

Manfred, a sorcerer, lives like a hermit in an Alpine castle. Shameful and full of guilt over his incestuous love for his sister Astarte, Manfred CONJURES SPIRITS. He hopes that they will punish him for his sin by casting him into a void of nothingness. When they refuse, he attempts suicide but is rescued by a hunter.

Manfred summons the Witch of the Alps who, sympathetic to his plea, takes him to the Hall of Arimanes in the Underworld. There, a spectral dream of Astarte promises him release from life on the following day.

When Manfred returns to his castle, an abbot attempts to absolve his guilt, but the sorcerer is still under diabolic influence. At the last minute, however, Manfred is able to break free from the demons' grasp and denounces the devils. As they disappear, Manfred dies.

Math   A wizard found in the classic Welsh epic poem *MABINOGION*, Math must use the powers of his magic WAND to prove the virginity of Lady Arianrhod.

This act, having the royal lady walk over the wand, no doubt had as its inspiration the old wedding custom or superstition of making the wedding couple step over a BROOMSTICK before they consummate their marriage.

Mather, Cotton (1663–1728)   A harsh "fire-and-brimstone" Presbyterian minister from Boston, Massachusetts, Cotton Mather is best remembered for his role as an authority on WITCHCRAFT during the notorious SALEM trials of 1692. Mather, more than anyone else, gave credence to the charges of demon possession in the small community.

The son of a preacher, Mather entered Harvard University at the age of 12 and assumed the pulpit of the North Church in Boston during his father's visit to England as a representative of the Massachusetts colony. It was during this period that Sir William Phips, the colony's governor, asked the Boston clergy its opinion of the occurrences at Salem, to which Mather wrote the collected minsters' reply. Mather was considered the authority, having written *Memorable Providences Relating to Witchcrafts and Possessions* in 1689.

Appointed by Phips, Mather attended the Salem trials as the official court recorder. Despite his reservations about some of the evidence in the trial, Mather did nothing to stop the village's hysteria. In fact, at the hanging of George Burroughs, he gave an impassioned plea for the assembled crowd to ignore the condemned witch's ability to recite the Lord's Prayer on the gallows. A prolific writer, Mather reflected on the trials in his book *On Witchcraft: Being the Wonders of the Invisible World* (1693).

Mather's reputation was sullied when, in 1696, Samuel Sewall (1652–1730), the presiding judge over the trials, publicly repented for the errors committed at Salem and, in part, blamed Mather for the enthusiastic prosecution of the accused witches. Robert Calef continued the attack on Mather in *Another Brand Pluckt Out of the Burning or More Wonders of the Invisible World* (written in 1696, published in London, 1700).

To defend himself, Mather justified his beliefs in *Magnalia Christi Americana* (1702), a very important ecclesiastical history of New England considered to be Mather's masterpiece. Public opinion had already turned against him, however. Mather's bid for the presidency of Harvard University was subsequently rejected on several occasions. In 1721, convinced that Harvard had become too liberal to accept his views, Mather convinced Elihu Yale, a London merchant, to found the Calvinist-leaning Yale University in New Haven, Connecticut.

Despite this important behind-the-scenes role in the foundation of Yale University, Mathers continued to be ridiculed, then largely ignored at the end of his life because of his role in the Salem trials.

Mathers, S.L. MacGregor (d. 1918)

One of the founders and the first leader (the Visible Head) of the ORDER OF THE GOLDEN DAWN, S.L. MacGregor Mathers was born Samuel Liddle Mathers. In addition to changing his name, he also took the titles Chavalier MacGregor and comte de Glenstrae.

Mathers married a clairvoyant, Moina Bergson, the sister of the Nobel Prize-winning author and philosopher Henri Bergson (1859–1941). Together, Mathers and his wife translated an arcane manuscript, uncovered by a London cleric in 1884. Brought to him by William Winn Wescott, the book dealt with the KABALLAH and the TAROT and Mathers published it as *Kabbalah Unveiled*.

Mathers claimed that his powers were conferred on him by "Hidden and Secret Chiefs." In this, he was not unlike Aleister CROWLEY, whom he brought into the Order of the Golden Dawn. To a large extent, it was the conflict between Mathers and Crowley, both strong willed and domineering men, that resulted in the break up of the order. In fact, when Mathers died in 1918, it was rumored that Crowley had caused his death through the use of BLACK MAGIC.

Although Mathers had been an early mentor of Crowley, the latter's fame and occult influence far exceeded his own. Mathers is most remembered as an editor and translator of several texts, the best known being *The KEY OF SOLOMON* and *The SACRED MAGIC OF ABRAMELIN THE MAGE*.

In the introduction to the 1938 edition to *Kabbalah Unveiled*, Mather's widow reminisced that the highest aim of the Order of the Golden Dawn had been to identify "the intelligent forces behind Nature, the Constitution of man and his relation to God" so that a person might learn to unite with "the Divine Man latent in himself."

mazuzah

The mazuzah posted beside the door frame of a Jewish household is a traditional TALISMAN that harkens back to the original Passover at the time of MOSES. The Lord warned that, as a final plague, he would pass from household to household, killing all the firstborn living creatures in the land of Egypt.

To protect their children from harm, the Jews were instructed to place blood from a sacrificial lamb "on the two doorposts and the lintel of the houses." The Lord promised, "When I see the blood, I will pass over you, and no plague shall fall upon you to destroy you, when I smite the land of Egypt." (Exodus 12:13)

This incident is commemorated and ritualized by the mazuzah, a small slim tablet usually made of wood and often inscribed with a Hebraic prayer or word(s). Upon approaching the door, the visitor kisses his fingertips and then touches the mazuzah, ensuring his continued blessing and protection by God.

Other cultures had similar practices. In ancient Babylon, for example, the wizard-priests produced a talisman that, when hung over a doorway, would prevent Bel, a god of the Underworld, from entering the house. A common modern superstition suggests that hanging a horseshoe over a door brings good luck. Some claim that the prongs of the shoe should face up (forming a "U" shape) to trap the good SPIRITS within; others feel the horseshoe could face down (an inverted "U") so that the bad spirits will fall out. (See ASSYRIAN MAGIC.)

Medea

A mighty yet tragic figure in Greek mythology, Medea was the daughter of Aeëtes, the ruler of COLCHIS. The region was known in ancient times as a center for magic, and Medea was one of its greatest sorceresses. Her powers enabled her to quell storms, make herself invisible and stay eternally youthful. One of her most famous SPELLS, supposedly native to the wizards of Thessaly, was a love enchantment known as calling or drawing down the moon.

Her craft included great knowledge of herbs and their effects, allowing her to make poisons, potions and salves for invulnerability. According to legend, while flying over Thessaly on her winged dragon, she accidentally dropped her box of CHARMS. Medea's most magical herbs sprouted from where it settled.

The story of Medea is inextricably linked with that of Jason (of the Argonauts) because she betrayed her family and country by leading the adventurer to the Golden Fleece and helping him steal it.

Years prior, Phrixus and Helle, the children of King Athamas of Boeotia, had escaped the wrath of their evil stepmother Ino. They saved their lives by flying away on an intelligent talking ram with wool of gold, given to them by HERMES. Helle accidentally fell from the ram's back and drowned in the sea; in her honor, that stretch of water was named the Hellespont (now called the Dardenelles in Turkey). Her brother Phrixus reached Colchis at the mouth of the River Phasis, where he sacrificed the ram to Zeus to thank him for his delivery. In return for his hospitality, Phrixus gave the Golden Fleece to King Aeëtes, who draped it on a tree and placed a dragon to guard it.

During this same period in Iolcus, Thessaly, Pelias overthrew his brother, King Aeson, while Jason (Aeson's son) was under the guardianship of the centaur Chiron. Once grown, Jason returned to the court of Pelias to demand a portion of his rightful inheritance.

Pelias, who had been warned by an ORACLE to "beware of the man who wears but one sandal" was nevertheless shocked when a stranger (Jason) appeared before him dressed in that manner. Hoping to rid himself of the menace, Pelias promised Jason his share of the kingdom if he captured the Golden Fleece.

Jason assembled a crew that included such famous warriors as Hercules. They set sail in the 50-oared *Argo*, which had been constructed with the help of the goddess Hera and Athena. To advise him during his travels, Jason carried along a branch from the oracular oak tree at Dodona.

After many adventures, Jason and his mighty crew reached Colchis. Rather than risk war, Aeëtes met them warmly and acceded to Jason's demand for the Fleece—*if* in exchange Jason would capture two wild, bronze-hoofed fire-breathing bulls, strap them to a plough and plant a field with dragon's teeth for the king.

During Jason's audience with Aeëtes, Medea fell in love with the Greek hero; so without her father's knowledge, the sorceress revealed to Jason the means to accomplish the impossible task. After Aeëtes reneged on his part of the bargain, Medea magically helped Jason overcome the dragon and steal the Golden Fleece. Medea slit the throat of her own brother, dismembered him and scattered his limbs on the path behind them as they fled. The horror of her act so shocked and overwhelmed those in pursuit that the Greeks managed to escape.

Medea returned with Jason to his home in Thessaly. Some myths say that during Jason's absence, Pelias had Aeson killed; others contend that Aeson was still alive when Jason returned and that Medea brewed a potion to restore him to full health and vigor. The witch-queen convinced the daughters of Pelias that she could devise an ELIXIR OF LIFE that would revitalize their father enough to fight Jason, but, as part of the spell, the women had to slice Pelias up into pieces and cook him in a CAULDRON. The daughters were thus deceived into performing patricide, and Jason and Medea moved on to Corinth.

There, the royal couple lived for ten years, and Medea bore Jason two sons. Jason, however, fell in love with Creusa (also seen as Glauce), the daughter of King Creon, and he deserted Medea. Pretending to accept the new situation gracefully and step aside, Medea prepared a majestic robe as a wedding gift for Creusa. When the bride put it on, however, the robe burst into flames.

Knowing the consequences of her treasonous actions, Medea murdered her two sons so that Jason would have no male heirs. According to some stories, she then committed suicide. Most myths say that she escaped Corinth, found shelter in Athens and married King Aegeus. When Aegeus's "lost" son Theseus revealed himself to his father, Medea became resentful. She concocted a brew, and, at the welcom-

ing banquet in his honor, she attempted to poison Theseus. Her plan discovered, Medea fled Athens with her children and returned in shame to her father at Colchis. This part of the Medea legend is related in Ovid's *Metamorphoses.*

The end was equally lamentable for Jason. Some legends say that, filled with ennui, he committed suicide. Others tell a less dramatic tale: as he relaxed beside the *Argo*, its main mast snapped, fell and crushed him.

Current scholarship suggests that a historical Jason actually did take a route up the Hellespont, possibly in search of treasure (which might have included a legendary golden fleece); more probable reasons for his voyage were conquest and colonization. It is thought by some that he settled, at least for a time, on the shores of the Black Sea near what is today Sozopol (once Apollonia, the oldest of the Greek colonies) in what is now southeastern Bulgaria.

The classic Greek drama *Medea* was written by Euripides (484–406 B.C.) and is one of his 17 surviving plays. He is noted for being the first dramatist to use a chorus to comment on the action of the play, to have heroes to speak in vernacular rather than formal Greek and to suggest that human suffering is not always caused by divine judgment.

Perhaps most noted in the 20th century for her portrayal of Medea both on stage and in FILM was Dame Judith Anderson, who won a Tony Award for her performance in 1948. A major revival in the 1981–82 Broadway season starred Zoe Caldwell, who also won a Tony Award for the role; in the same production, Anderson was nominated for Best Performance by a Featured Actress in a Play for her portrayal of the nurse. The most recent New York revival of *Medea* (1994) was an imported British production by the Almeida Theatre Company. Diana Rigg, who starred in the new Alistar Elliot translation of the classic, received the Tony Award for her performance.

Other works based on the Medea story include Seneca's tragedy *Medea*, plays by Franz Grillparzer and Jean Anouilh and an OPERA by Luigi Cherubini.

medicine man   The medicine man, like the African WITCH DOCTOR, is a sorcerer of sorts, depending upon a blend of FOLK MEDICINE and magic to effect cures. An analogous figure existed in parts of tribal Southeast Asia as well as in the Western Hemisphere, where the medicine man was a central figure in NATIVE AMERICAN MAGIC.

Many of the medicine man's remedies depend upon a knowledge of the drugs found naturally in or distilled from plants. While the entire community might know the common medicinal uses of some plants, effective herbal treatment of more esoteric ailments and diseases often remains secret and is passed down from one generation of medicine men to the next, from master to apprentice.

To instill a proper sense of awe for his wonder-working, the medicine man often carries a small leather bag containing his magical TALISMANs and tokens. Among different cultures, the "conjure bag" is known by such names as a *goofer bag, gris-gris, mojo bag, ouanga, trick bag, toby* and *wanga bag*. The AMULETs carried in the conjure bag—often mere clumps of feathers, bones or beads—are employed in conjunction with chanting SPELLs and the administration of potions. Although to the Western mind these CHARMs might be thought to be mere psychological placebos, their curative effects cannot be denied. As Roger Walsh observes in *The Spirit of Shamanism*, when medicine men heal, "some of the 'tricks' they use are regarded as essential parts of the healing process, done primarily for the benefit of the patient."

Thus, tribal medicines can be divided into two types: The first, tonics derived from plants and roots, are aligned with the common notion of folk medicine; the other cures, which combine odd ingredients with even stranger instructions for their use, seem closer to the practice of sorcery. Regardless of which type of medicine he utilizes, the medicine man succeeds as much through the patient's belief in his special powers and his use of psychology as he does through his secret magical knowledge or any understanding of science.

Among African tribes, the medicine man takes a large role in the initiation rite of circumcision. Although it is the tribal elders who conduct the rite-of-passage ceremonies on the boys (at some point between the ages of 10 and 17) and many girls, it is the medicine man who actually performs the circumcision. Because it is inextricably linked to the coming-of-age ritual, the act of circumcision is considered to be a spiritual act. Unfortunately, mutilation, disease and/or death often result from the use of unsanitary knives or botched surgery.

As in many cultures, the Melanu tribe of Malaysia believes that sickness is caused by the SPIRITS, and they have enumerated more than 40 malevolent ones. The *dukun*, or medicine man, is an expert in herbs and magical charms, which allows him to prescribe the correct medicine to assuage the demons. Not just accomplished in folk medicine, the *dukun* is considered to be an intermediary between the spirits and the real

"The Flyer," a medicine man of the Algonquian tribe of Native Americans, illustrated by John White. His dance portrays the myth that the bird is the intermediary between the heavens and the earth. The medicine man has attached to his head a dried bird that symbolically assists in his spiritual flight, and at his side is an otter-skin bag filled with magic charms. (Author's collection)

world and, as such, often tends to both the physical and the religious needs of the community.

If the medicine man's herbal cures do not work and an illness continues, the *dukun* might carve an image of the spirit out of sago pith, the resultant totem being called a "blum." The *dukun* casts a spell over the blum, chews the traditional mixture of betelnut, sereh leaves and lime and then spits at the carving. This causes the evil spirit to leave the patient and move into the blum. As a sort of fixative, water is poured on the image and on the patient. Because the spirit will reside in the image for only three days, it is imperative that the blum be taken quickly to the spirit's original dwelling, whether it be the river or the jungle, and left behind. The sickness will stay with the blum and not return to the sufferer.

If these remedies are not effective, more elaborate healing ceremonies, such as the *berbayoh*, *baguda* or the *berayun* are required. During such rites, a blum may also be used.

As with their African and Asian counterparts, the Native American medicine men use herbal remedies combined with a belief in spiritual intervention. As the importance of Native American civilizations is being reexamined by historians, cultural anthropologists and sociologists, the role and contributions of the tribal medicine man are also being reviewed and corrected. While authoritative works as recent as the 1970s dismissed the practices of the Native American medicine man as charlatanism, recent, more enlightened books, such as Eugene Burger and Robert E. Neale's *Magic and Meaning*, examine the use of ceremonial magic by the medicine man as a means to increase the efficacy of his cures.

Among some of the Native American tribes, the medicine man was chosen in early childhood based on observed eccentric or unusual behavior. Among the Algonquians, for instance, the boy might have fallen into epileptic seizures, seen visions or shown an inclination toward homosexuality. The boy would be taken to an experienced medicine man to serve a sort of apprenticeship. After years of study, and if his peculiar skills remained with him after adolescence, the neophyte was permitted to enter the elect rank of the medicine man.

The medicine man acted as a SHAMAN, and his "between-two-worlds" nature can be seen in "The Flyer," a painting by John White, whose artwork depicted many early Native American subjects. The medicine man is portrayed in a dance, wearing an embalmed bird as his headdress and amulets on his belt. The dance seems to simulate flight, representing the medicine man's ability to receive and carry messages between the earth and the heavenly spirits above.

Melissa See *ORLANDO FURIOSO*.

Melmoth the Wanderer Written by C(harles) R(obert) Maturin (1782–1824) and published in 1820, *Melmoth the Wanderer* is a classic example of the Gothic school of literature, based on the story of Johannes FAUSTUS.

Melmoth uses sorcery to trade his eternal soul for an extended life on earth. Finally realizing the implications of his agreement, Melmoth attempts to persuade various people to take over his part of the bargain. In exchange, Melmoth offers to free them of their misery. The sufferers include Moncada (being tortured by the INQUISITION), Walberg (watching his

Merlin. (Photo courtesy of Excalibur Hotel/Casino)

children waste away from starvation) and Stanton (inescapably locked away with a madman). None are foolish enough to accept Melmoth's deal.

Merlin   Merlin, perhaps the most famous wizard in history, was the magical mentor and tutor of King ARTHUR. There is some evidence that an historical Merlin actually existed: An apocryphal tale describes a traveling troubadour and seer named Myrddhin who was born in Wales or Britain around the end of the fifth century. He was credited with composing several poems before becoming the court bard to King Arthur, and his rhyming prophecies in his poems may have resulted in his reputation as a wizard. Myrddhin later lost his sanity and died on a riverbank following a clash between the Britons and the Romans at the battle of Arthuret (Arfderydd) in A.D. 573.

There are so many myths regarding Merlin that they often intertwine. A wizard character resembling Merlin first appeared by the name *Ambrosius* in the writings of Nennius. Like Myrddhin before and Merlin after him, Ambrosius was a prophet and an interpreter of omens. One of the most famous incidents surrounding Ambrosius, also found in the stories about Myrddhin and Merlin, involved King Vortigern.

Vortigern, the legendary fifth-century monarch whose wartime alliances helped result in the Anglo-Saxon domination of Britain, met Ambrosius and was amazed by the wizard's predictions of the future. While building castle fortifications, Vortigern's men released two dragons. The red

dragon slew the white dragon, which Ambrosius correctly interpreted to mean that the Britons would win their impending battle against the Saxons. Merlin's part in the tale was over by the time Vortigern was later burnt alive in the tower of his castle in Wales.

According to Geoffrey of Monmouth's *Historia Regum Britanniae*, the clairvoyant and magical figure Merlin interacted with several kings of Britain. In Book Eight of his history, Geoffrey told of Merlin's magically transforming Uther Pendragon to resemble Ygraine's husband so that he could enter her bedchamber. Arthur was conceived during that deception. It was also in this book that the Latinized name *Merlin* is first seen. According to Geoffrey, Stonehenge was created by rocks that Merlin magically transported from Naas, Ireland, to England; the author/historian also reiterated the Vortigern encounter from Nennius.

In fact, the writings of Nennius served as the major source for the embroidered and detailed Merlin story that Geoffrey of Monmouth told at length in another major literary work, *Vita Merlini* (c.1150). Merlin was born the illegitimate, hirsute son of a fair damsel and a demon and was named for his maternal grandfather. Merlin was strong willed and gifted with great intelligence. Like his father, Merlin was adept at DIVINATION. He became involved in conjuring and casting magic SPELLS, but he performed WHITE MAGIC rather than sorcery. Because he was baptized (by Blaise), Merlin escaped the clutches of Satan.

As the court magician for Pendragon, Merlin guided and instructed young Arthur, finally revealing to the boy his noble ancestry.

About the time Arthur was growing into adulthood, Merlin was charmed by the enchantress NIMUË (also seen as Nimiane or Vivien and often referred to as the LADY OF THE LAKE). She used her powers to imprison Merlin in a forest of thornbushes where

Mark Twain portrayed Merlin as a cantankerous and ineffectual wizard, given more to ritual ceremony and pomposity than to alchemical science. (Daniel Beard, *A Connecticut Yankee in King Arthur's Court.*)

he still sleeps; in other versions of the story, she trapped him for a time in a rock. Arthurian myths place the legendary Tomb of Merlin in Broceliande, a wooded area near Brittany. As research for his historical ode *Roman de Rou* (1160–1174) the poet Wace (c.1100–after 1174) traveled to Brecheliant in Brittany, but he was unable to find the wizard's grave.

In Robert de BORON's *Mort Artu*, part of the 13th-century VULGATE CYCLE, there is yet another version of Merlin's death. After the ascension of Arthur, Merlin retreated to his *esplumeoir* in Grail Castle. He willingly instructed Morgan LE FAY but fell in love with Nimiane. He revealed his secrets as well to Nimiane, and the wicked enchantress used her new powers to force Merlin into the Forest of Broceliande, from which he never escaped.

Modern thought is that Merlin is a composite of the early occultists and scientists practicing ALCHEMY. So advanced in thought and methods was Merlin that the uneducated or superstitious had only one explanation for his powers: wizardry. If he had not been under the protectorate of Arthur, Merlin quite possibly would have been tried for witchcraft.

Merlin has been the subject of or a principal character in countless works of art from ancient manuscripts to fantasy literature and COMIC BOOKS, from paintings and MUSICAL THEATER to FILMS. In addition to those books already mentioned, there are the classic writings of Wace, *Merlin* and *Suite de Merlin* (*Huth Merlin*) in the Vulgate cycle, Laȝamon's BRUT, MALORY's *Le MORTE D'ARTHUR*, Spenser's *The FAERIE QUEENE* (III, iii), the 13th-century poem *Of ARTHOUR AND OF MERLIN*, Alfred Lord Tennyson's *IDYLLS OF THE KING*, a 1917 narrative poem by Edward Arlington Robinson, the English romantic novel *Merlin*, C.S. Lewis's *That Hideous Strength* (1946), Mark Twain's *A CONNECTICUT YANKEE IN KING ARTHUR'S COURT* and the modern trilogy on the Arthurian legend by Mary Stuart (*The CRYSTAL CAVE*, *The Hollow Hills* and *The Last Enchantment*). Films include *Excalibur* and *The Sword and the Stone*, and Broadway musicals include *Merlin* and *Camelot*.

"Merlin and Vivien"

"Merlin and Vivien" is one of the tales in the *IDYLLS OF THE KING* by Alfred Lord Tennyson (1809–1892). Originally published as "Vivien" in 1859, the idyll received its current name in 1870.

VIVIEN, a powerful enchantress, in an act of vengeance against King ARTHUR woos his aged mentor MERLIN and traps him in an oak tree for eternity.

Merlock

See FILMS, *DUCKTALES: THE MOVIE—TREASURE OF THE LOST LAMP*.

Merry Devil of Edmonton, The

Published anonymously in 1608, this comic play undoubtedly had as its inspiration Christopher MARLOWE's *DOCTOR FAUSTUS*, which was first presented in 1594 and published in 1604. As the play's prologue opens, time has run out for Peter Fabel, a sorcerer who has sold his soul to the Devil. When the demon appears to take Fabel to the pit of hell, the magician successfully binds the fiend to an enchanted chair. The Devil must let Fabel out of his pact in order to be released.

The remainder of the romantic play deals with Sir and Mrs. Arthur Clarke trying to separate their daughter Millicent from her beau, Raymond Mounchensey. With the magical help of Fabel, the young pair elope. (See ROMANCE LITERATURE.)

Midsummer Night's Dream, A

One of the earliest comedies of William SHAKESPEARE, written around 1595 or 1596 and first published in 1600, *A Midsummer Night's Dream* is filled with magical events caused by the supernatural creatures who live in the enchanted forest where much of the play's action is set.

The play concerns four mismatched lovers who meet in the woods to sort out their romantic affairs. A farcical subplot develops as Bottom and a motley lot of coarse fellow-laborers enter the same woods to practice a play they hope to present at the duke's wedding. Chief among the sprites are Oberon and Titania, king and queen of the fairies, who quarrel over Puck, a mischievous changeling, whom both want for a page.

Magical effects seen in the play include Puck's transformation of Bottom's head into that of an ass. Oberon also sends the young lovers into a deep sleep using the INCANTATION

The iron tongue of midnight hath told twelve;
Lovers, to bed; 'tis almost fairy time. (V, i, 372)

Most of the misadventures in the play are precipitated by a love potion that is derived from a flower's juice and is used by both Oberon and Puck. The potion accidentally causes the wrong people to fall in love, most comically Titania with the donkey-headed Bottom. Eventually, Oberon breaks the SPELLS caused by the love philtre.

The play has inspired other artistic works, including two FILM treatments, a 1935 black-and-white version by Warner Bros. Studio and the 1982 loose adaptation written and directed by Woody Allen entitled *A Midsummer Night's Sex Comedy*.

The most popular and enduring compositions of Felix Mendelssohn (-Bartholdy) (1809–47) were his incidental pieces for a production of *A Midsummer Night's Dream*. The famous overture was first written as a piano duet in 1826, and some of the additional 13 pieces utilized themes from it. The scherzo, the nocturne and the well-known (and now traditional) wedding march were first heard during an 1843 Berlin production of the Shakespeare play.

Mighty Morphin Power Rangers

Produced by Saban Entertainment (Haim Saban and Shuki Levy, executive producers), *Mighty Morphin Power Rangers* premiered on the Fox Children's Network on August 28, 1993. Haim Saban, while working in Japan in the 1980s, discovered *Zyu Rangers*, a live-action children's show featuring costumed characters. He bought the rights, dubbed scenes into English, added new scenes with American actors and (combining the popular fads of dinosaurs, transformation/transformer toys and martial arts) created *Mighty Morphin Power Rangers*.

The classic good-versus-evil stories feature the Power Rangers, the superhero alter-egos of six teenagers from Angel Grove who fight Rita Repulsa (portrayed in the first and early second season footage by Soga Machiko, later by Carla Perez, but with voice-over throughout by Barbara Goodson), the masked Lord Zedd (voiced by Robert Axelrod) and their minions in their attempts to conquer the Earth. In the *Zyu Ranger* series, Rita Repulsa was known as Bandra. No early footage exists of Rita Repulsa and Lord Zedd together in the same shot, however, because the character of Zedd is a Saban creation.

Thousands of years ago, Zordon (acted and voiced by David Fielding for the first 20 episodes, succeeded by Bob Manahan), a moral and great sage, battled Rita Repulsa, a wicked sorceress, who sought to control the universe. Zordon won, imprisoning Rita Repulsa in an intergalactic recycling bin, but her powers were still strong enough to trap Zordon in an interdimensional time warp.

In modern times, two lunar astronauts uncovered the trash container and opened it, releasing the Empress of Evil to begin her attack on Earth.

Unable to enter our dimension, Zordon instructed Alpha Five, his robot assistant in the California desert, to assemble a band of young Earth heroes (the Power Rangers) to conduct the campaign against Rita Repulsa.

Alpha Five selected five exceptional teenagers and trained them in martial arts and hand-to-hand combat. They also received special skills from the magic Power Coins, produced by the mysterious Ninjor. Each Power Ranger was distinguished by a specifically colored costume and accessories. The original members of the squad were Jason, the Red Ranger, (portrayed by Austin St. John), Zack, the Black Ranger (Walter Jones), Kimberly, the Pink Ranger (Amy Jo Johnson), Billy, the Blue Ranger (David Yost) and Trini, the Yellow Ranger (Thuy Trang). They transformed from teenagers into Power Rangers with the call, "It's Morphin Time!"

Each Ranger was armed with a unique weapon and a giant warring vehicle called a Dinozoid (or Zord, for short) that resembled a creature from the days of ancient dinosaurs and

The sorceress Rita Repulsa, nemesis of the Mighty Morphin Power Rangers, with her leader, Lord Zedd. (Photo courtesy of Saban Entertainment)

could be called upon when the Rangers were overpowered. The Rangers also drew upon the SPIRITS of these different ANIMALS for their immense powers.

At first, the Rangers unified their hand weapons into a single, stronger weapon when it was necessary; in time, they learned that their Zords could also be merged together to form the mighty Megazord.

During the first season of TELEVISION episodes, Rita Repulsa bewitched a new teenager in town named Tommy (Jason David Frank) and transformed him into her own weapon for wickedness, the Green Ranger. Rita Repulsa controlled the Green Ranger through the Sword of Darkness she had given him; he also had his own Zord to combat the Power Rangers. Jason managed to destroy the sword, freeing Tommy, who then joined the Power Rangers team.

In the second season, Lord Zedd, Rita Repulsa's boss, appeared. He was furious that the enchantress had not destroyed the Rangers. Zedd banished Rita Repulsa back to the dumpster and proceeded to make war against the Rangers personally. To help him achieve his vile ends, he created several outrageous creatures as henchmen, first the Pirantishead, followed by Primator, Octophantom and Saliguana.

Jason, Trini and Zack left to attend a Teen Peace Conference in Switzerland, and they were replaced by three new Angel Grove teenagers (and actors): Rocky, the Red Ranger (Steve Cardenas), Aisha, the Yellow Ranger (Karan Ashley) and Adam, the Black Ranger (Johnny Yong Bosch). From the Rangers received new, more potent Zords (the Thunderzords) whose spirits acted as their power sources. Tommy emerged as the Rangers' leader, the new White Ranger. At season's end, Rita Repulsa cast a SPELL on Lord Zedd, causing him to fall in love with her. They married and swore to combine their energies to eliminate the Power Rangers.

The 1995 season opened with a new villain entering the fold, Rita's long-lost brother Rito. Resembling a massive skeleton, Rito brought the newlyweds several Tenga Warrior eggs, which hatched into ravenlike monsters. The Tenga Warriors replaced the Putty Patrol, the gang of clay creatures created by Rita Repulsa and Finster (voiced by Robert Axelrod), Lord Zedd's aide; and the malevolent "birds" smashed the Zords and removed the Rangers' powers.

After traveling across the Desert of Despair, the Power Rangers located Ninjor, who was able to endow them with new Zords (the Ninjazords) and strengths. Once again, the Zords were able to combine together to form a single, more powerful fighting unit, the Megafalconzord. Also, Tommy received an enchanted white sabre, Saba.

Mighty Morphin Power Rangers is a worldwide phenomenon, ranking number one in almost every market where it is broadcast, both domestically and overseas. (Initially, Toei Co. of Japan co-produced with Saban Entertainment an Asian-market edition of *Mighty Morphin Power Rangers* with Japanese actors portraying the teenagers.)

The Rangers have a series of books and direct-to-video movies as well as a full line of action figures and other merchandising from bed sheets to lunch boxes. The Power Rangers attract enormous crowds at personal appearances, and, in 1995, *The Mighty Morphin Power Rangers Live*, a musical stage spectacular featuring the Rangers made a 76-city American tour. *Mighty Morphin Power Rangers: The Movie*, the first full-length FILM featuring the Rangers, was released by Twentieth Century Fox on June 30, 1995, with Julia Cortez portraying Rita Repulsa. In *Turbo: A Power Rangers Movie* (1997), the Rangers fight Divatox, a space pirate bent on conquering the universe. In the process, they rescue Lerigot, a gentle, friendly wizard from another world.

Mim, Madam See FILMS, *THE SWORD AND THE STONE;* MAGICA DE SPELL.

Mr. Mistoffolees Quaxo, otherwise known as Mr. Mistoffolees, is "the original conjuring cat," one of the most colorful felines depicted in *Old Possum's Book of Practical Cats.* Originally written in letters to his godchildren by T.S. Eliot (1888–1915), the poems were collected and published in October 1939. Eliot was a lover of cats, and the title for his collection of poems comes from *Possum,* his nickname among his friends.

Mr. Mistoffolees is so-called because of his cleverness and his talent for deception. Like a magician, he seems to be able to make cutlery or a bit of cork disappear. Mr. Mistoffolees is adept at tricks with playing cards and dice, and his voice often seems to come from one place while he is somewhere else entirely. He proclaims that his greatest achievements as a magician was to produce "seven kittens right out of a hat."

The poems in *Old Possum's Book of Practical Cats,* along with other unpublished fragments provided by Eliot's widow, were set to music by Andrew Lloyd Webber and was fashioned into *CATS.* An international sensation, *CATS* premiered in London's New London Theatre in 1981. *CATS* opened at the Winter Garden Theatre on Broadway on October 7, 1982; in the role of Mr. Mistoffolees was Timothy Scott, who performed magic tricks while singing his feature song. *CATS* received seven 1983 Tony Awards: Musical, Book of a Musical (Eliot), Score (music, Webber; lyrics, Eliot), Direction (Trevor Nunn), Actress (Featured Role—Musical) (Betty Buckley), Costume Design (John Napier) and Lighting Design (David Hersey). (See also MUSICAL THEATER.)

Monastery, The A novel written by Sir Walter Scott (1771–1832) and published in 1820, *The Monastery* tells the story of two brothers, Halbert and Edward, sons of an inhabitant of the monastery of Kennaquhair, in Scotland. They vie for the hand of Mary Avenel, and Halbert eventually marries her. Hopelessly resigned to a life without his love, Edward enters the monastic order.

As with most ROMANCE LITERATURE, occult elements are woven throughout the story. Foremost is the character of the White Lady of Avenel, an enchantress or possibly a SPIRIT. Among her several miracles, she brings Sir Piercie Shafton back to life after Halbert kills him in a duel.

Monk, The Written by M(atthew) G(regory) Lewis (1775–1818), published in 1796, and originally titled *Ambrosio, or The Monk,* this is a sexually charged novel containing occult and religious themes.

Ambrosio, the leader of the Catholic Capuchin monks in Madrid, has a carnal affair with Matilda, a promiscuous girl who is in league with the Devil. She had been able to enter the monastery disguised as a young boy wishing to become a novice.

Having fallen from grace, Ambrosio seduces another of his flock by using SORCERY and killing those who obstruct him. Finally, he murders the girl to prevent her from betraying him. Ambrosio's crime is discovered; he is tortured by the Spanish INQUISITION and sentenced to die. Ambrosio meets Satan and pleads for absolution or mercy, but the monk is cast into the fiery pits of hell.

Morgaine See ARTHUR, KING; LADY OF THE LAKE, THE; LE FAY, MORGAN.

Morgana See LADY OF THE LAKE; *ORLANDO FURIOSO;* LE FAY, MORGAN; ARTHUR, KING; FATA MORGANA.

Morgan le Fay See LE FAY, MORGAN.

Mort Artu See VULGATE CYCLE, THE.

Morte Arthur, Le Known as the "Stanzaic Morte Arthur," *Le Morte Arthur* is a 14th-century narrative poem from the Northwest Midlands of Great Britain. Composed in eight-line rhyming verses, only one manuscript exists of the 3,834-line epic. Along with the alliterative *MORTE ARTHURE* and several French sources from the same period, the stanzaic version served as the inspiration for the final two sections (or Works) of MALORY's *Le MORTE D'ARTHUR.* Stories include the illicit affair between Launcelot and Guinevere, the romance between Launcelot and the Maid of Astolat, the final battles of ARTHUR and his delivery, near death, to Avalon.

Morte Arthure Known as the alliterative version, *Morte Arthure* is a 14th-century, 4,346-line poem in alliterative Middle English verse. Scholars consider it to be the best-constructed and most-effective epic poem of its period.

Its importance lies in its being the probable source for much of the writing by Wace on King ARTHUR. It was definitely the inspiration for the encounter of Arthur and Lucius in the first section of *Le MORTE D'ARTHUR* by MALORY. In fact, *Morte Arthure*'s narratives of the young Arthur, his European quests and his final confrontation with Modred almost directly parallel the storylines of the first, second and eighth sections, or Works, in Malory.

Morte D'Arthur Written by Alfred Lord Tennyson in 1833 and 1834, *Morte d'Arthur* was published in 1842. An expanded version with 198 additional lines (with 169 added at the beginning and 29 to the end of the original poem) was renamed "The Passing of Arthur" and became one of the *IDYLLS OF THE KING. Morte D'Arthur* was the first work based on Arthurian legend completed by Tennyson, and its story begins immediately after the king's final and mortal battle with Modred.

Morte D'Arthur, Le Completed in 1470 by Sir Thomas MALORY and first published in 21 "books" by William Caxton (c.1422–1491) in 1485, *Le Morte D'Arthur* is an epic poem that tells the history of King ARTHUR and his court, including the mystical figures of MERLIN and Morgan LE FAY.

In 1934, W.F. Oakeshott located in Winchester College Library a manuscript by Malory from the same time as Caxton's imprint but divided into 8 sections rather than the editor's 21. This prompted a new and now-standard edition of *Le Morte D'Arthur*: The resultant 1947 Vinaver three-volume edition follows the Malory manuscript and is segmented into eight separate sections, or Works, each telling a part of the Arthurian legend.

Based at least in part upon the French VULGATE CYCLE, Malory composed his verse in his native English but titled it in the more exotic-sounding French. Malory himself consistently credited a French book as his inspiration, but scholars have speculated that there may have been many additional sources. They also continue to debate whether *Le Morte D'Arthur* should be considered one complete book or eight individual works, although tradition favors the former view.

The Vinaver divisions and the text's probable sources are as follows:

Work 1. The Tale of Arthur and Lucius, based on MORTE ARTHURE.

Work 2. The Book of King Arthur, based on the *Suite du Merlin*, itself derived from the Vulgate Cycle.

Work 3. The Tale of Sir Launcelot du Lac, based on two sections of *Launcelot* in the Vulgate Cycle. Within this Work, Launcelot and Elaine (the daughter of King Pelles), enchanted, meet and conceive Galahad.

Work 4. The Tale of Sir Gareth of Orkney, basis unknown.

Work 5. The Tale of Tristram de Lyones, possibly a translation of a lost French work about Tristan. (See OPERA, *TRISTAN UND ISOLDE*.)

Work 6. The Quest for the Holy Grail, based on *Queste del Saint Graal* from the Vulgate Cycle. The purity and godliness of Galahad (whose name means "the Haute Prince") allow him to undertake the Siege Perilous, or Quest for the Holy Grail. After the Grail is revealed to him, Galahad, enraptured, dies.

Work 7. The Tale of Launcelot du Lac and Gwynevere (commonly seen as Guinevere), based on MORT ARTU in the Vulgate Cycle and *Le* MORTE ARTHUR.

Work 8. The Death of Arthur, based on *Mort Artu* in the Vulgate Cycle and *Le Morte Arthur*.

Le Mort D'Arthur, sometimes seen simply as *Mort D'Arthur*, is probably the most lyrical expression of the fable and certainly the most read and influential up until the time of Tennyson's *The IDYLLS OF THE KING*.

In Malory's version of the traditional legend, Merlin assisted Uther Pendragon in disguising himself as the Duke of Cornwall so that he could make adulterous love to the duke's wife Igraine. The site was Tintagel, a castle on the northern coastline of Cornwall (in later years the home of King Mark of Cornwall). Arthur was conceived. Thirteen days later, Pendragon and Igraine married. Merlin took the infant Arthur and gave him to Sir Ector to be raised. Pendragon died two years later.

As a boy, Arthur was made the page of Sir Kay, Ector's own son (and, therefore, Arthur's foster brother). According to the Merlin myths, Sir Kay was surly to Arthur because Kay was breast-fed by a nursemaid while Arthur was nursed by Kay's mother.

Malory's poem also detailed the myth of the sword in the stone. With no heir apparent to Uther Pendragon, Merlin conceived of a plan of worthiness among the contenders to the throne. He produced

> a great stone four square, like unto a marble stone; and in midst thereof was like an anvil of steel a foot on high, and therein stuck a fair sword naked by the point, and letters there were written in gold about the sword that said thus: Whoso pulleth out the sword of this stone and anvil, is rightwise king born of all England.

Many knights took the challenge, but no one was able to pull out the sword. But, Arthur, unaware of the SPELL and quickly needing to replace a sword for Kay, nonchalantly removed the blade. Once crowned, Merlin acknowledged the boy's royal blood and revealed his true heritage.

The sword in the stone was *not* Excalibur; Arthur received that weapon on a visit to a mysterious lake with Merlin. As Arthur watched in awe, an arm thrust out from beneath the surface of the water bearing a great sword. The weapon Excalibur belonged to the LADY OF THE LAKE; she made it her gift to Arthur as a sign of his future greatness.

According to Malory's tale, Arthur unknowingly committed adultery with his aunt Queen Morgawse, who was sister to Igraine and wife to King Lot. Merlin was furious and predicted that the incestuous act would result, years later, in Arthur's death and the dissolution of his court. Morgawse bore Arthur a bastard son, Modred, whom Arthur unsuccessfully tried to drown.

After King Lot's death, Morgawse and her lover Sir Lamorak de Galis were discovered in bed by her sons. Dishonored, the men killed Lamorak, and Gaheris slew his mother.

Later, as king, Arthur married Gwynevere, the daughter of King Lodegreaunce (commonly seen as Lodegran) of Camelerde (today's Cornwall). As a wedding gift, Lodegran gave Arthur the Round Table, which had originally been owned by Uther Pendragon. Lodegran also provided the service of 100 knights. Malory painted a colorful history and importance for the Round Table, making it a symbol of unity and might: 150 knights could sit around the table in equality!

As in the French stories by such writers as Chrétien DE TROYES, the majority of the Works of *Le Morte D'Arthur* placed Arthur into the background while the knights' exploits were explored. The stories are full of magic and are populated with wizards and sorcerers.

In one, for instance, Merlin fell in love with the sorceress Nyneve (also seen as Nimiane, NIMUË or VIVIEN), and after seducing him into revealing his magical SPELLS, she used her newfound wisdom and power to imprison the wizard for all eternity in an enchanted, secret cave in Cornwall.

In another tale, Arthur came under the power of an evil witch in the Forest Perilous of North Wales. He was finally saved by his knights who cut off the enchantress's head. Likewise, Sir Bors was enticed to a bewitched castle of SIRENS, but when he made the Sign of the Cross they vanished into thin air. Sir Launcelot was enchanted when he made love to Elaine, King Pelles's daughter, which resulted in the conception of Sir Galahad.

Work Five of *Morte D'Arthur* tells of Iseult's magical healing of Tristram's wound from a poisoned arrow. Although she was betrothed in a marriage-by-arrangement to King Mark,

Iseult fell in love with Tristram, a passion intensified by a love philtre that the couple shared. Tristram was eventually murdered, stabbed in the back, by King Mark.

Morgan LE FAY also figures prominently in Malory's version of the Arthurian legend. A sorceress, le Fay was Arthur's half-sister. She married King Uryens of Gore, and they had a son, Sir Uwayne. She took a lover, Sir Accolon; together they planned to murder both Arthur and Uryens and then take the throne for themselves. Nyneve, with the aid of Sir Uwayne, managed to stop them. Le Fay also captured and attempted to seduce other members of the Round Table, including Sir Lancelot and Sir Tristram.

It is in the final book of Malory's *Le Morte D'Arthur* that the story is significantly changed from the events in the earlier chronicles of GEOFFREY OF MONMOUTH. Arthur ignored the love affair of Guinevere and Lancelot because he knew that to reveal the treason publicly would cause the end of the Round Table. Modred, with Agravaine's assistance, forced its disclosure. During the resulting melee, Lancelot killed Agravaine and escaped, followed by many of the knights who were his friends. Those remaining loyal to Arthur pursued Lancelot to France, where they met in battle.

While Arthur was out of the country, Modred seized the throne and unsuccessfully attempted to seduce Guinevere. Hearing of this new betrayal, Arthur returned to England and fought Modred's armies. Arthur killed Modred personally with a spear, but in the process, he, too, was mortally wounded.

As he lay dying, Arthur ordered Bedivere, one of his most trusted knights, to throw Excalibur back into the lake from whence it came: "There came an arm and an hand above the water and met it, and caught it, and . . . then vanished away the hand with the sword in the water."

Bedivere then carried his king to the edge of the lake, where a barge with three hooded queens aboard waited to whisk Arthur off to Avalon, the land of immortal heroes. As tradition dictated, Malory also placed the site of the lake in Glastonbury.

For Malory, the Arthurian legend ends with a Christlike theme of resurrection, with the promise that Arthur would one day return. Arthur's tomb was engraved *Hic jacet Arthurus rex quondam rexque futurus*: "Here lies Arthur, the once and future king."

Moses   Called by Jehovah in the book of Exodus of the Old Testament of the Bible to lead his fellow Jews to freedom from Egypt, Moses presented a number of miracles before the pharaoh's court. Because the Egyptians did not share in Moses's religious beliefs, certainly he was perceived by the pharaoh and his court as a wizard. In fact, according to an ancient Samaritan legend, the Egyptian wizard Palti had predicted the birth of Moses to the pharaoh.

To effect his miracles and prove his power, God transformed Moses's staff into a form of magic WAND.

> The Lord said to [Moses], "What is that in your hand?" He said, "A rod." And he said, "Cast it on the ground." So he cast it on the ground, and it became a serpent; and Moses fled from it. But the Lord said to Moses, "Put out your hand, and take it by the tail'"—so he put out his hand and caught it, and it became a rod in his hand. (Exodus 4:2–4)

The Lord further commissioned Moses that when he and his brother Aaron went before the pharaoh, "You shall take in your hand this rod, with which you shall do the signs." Moses was empowered to transform and restore his hand from healthy to leprous skin and to change water from the Nile into blood as signs to the pharaoh of his Lord's omnipotence.

What transpired was a confrontation—some would say a competition—between Moses and Aaron and the court magicians (whose names, according to the aforementioned Samaritan myth, were Jannes and Jambres).

> So Moses and Aaron went to Pharaoh and did as the Lord commanded; Aaron cast down his rod before Pharaoh and his servants, and it became a serpent. Then Pharaoh summoned the wise men and the sorcerers; and they also, the magicians of Egypt, did the same by their secret arts. For every man cast down his rod, and they became serpents. But AARON'S ROD swallowed up their rods. (Exodus 7: 10–12)

A curious tale from the time of Muhammad corroborates the story of Aaron's rod changing into a snake. However, it adds that the serpent then held the pharaoh's throne in the air and proclaimed, "If it please Allah, I could swallow up not only the throne with thee and all that are here present but even thy palace and all that it contains without anyone seeing the slightest change in me."

The transformation of Aaron's rod into a serpent did not convince the pharaoh to release the Israelites from bondage. According to the Old Testament, in later confrontations with the pharaoh and his wizards, Moses used the rod (and the power of God) to effect the plagues as commanded by the Lord:

> "Take your rod and stretch out your hand over the waters of Egypt, over their rivers, their canals, and their ponds, and all their pools of water, that they may become blood."
> "Stretch out your hand with your rod over the rivers, over the canals, and over the pools, and cause frogs to come upon the land of Egypt."
> "Stretch out your rod and strike the dust of the earth, that it may become gnats throughout all the land of Egypt."

This last plague was a turning point because, while the court sorcerers could seemingly change water to blood and make frogs appear, they could not produce gnats. After the production of several more miracles, during which the use of the wand (rod) was not explicitly mentioned, Moses "stretched forth his rod toward heaven; and the Lord sent thunder and hail, and fire ran down to the earth." Then "Moses stretched forth his rod over the land of Egypt . . . and when it was morning the east wind had brought the locusts" which destroyed all the nation's crops.

The plague that finally convinced the pharaoh to release the Israelites was the Passover, in which God caused "all the firstborn in the land of Egypt [to] die, from the firstborn of Pharaoh that sitteth upon his throne, even unto the firstborn of the maidservant." (See MAZUZAH.)

According to popular tradition, this pharaoh who released the Israelites was Ramses II, but current scholarship suggests that it was most probably Merenpthah (also written Memptah), one of Ramses II's sons.

Perhaps the greatest miracle performed by Moses was parting the Red Sea during the Exodus itself. The Lord commanded, "Lift up your rod, and stretch out your hand over the sea and divide it, that the people of Israel may go on dry ground through the sea."

During the 40 years of wandering in the wilderness, Moses continued to use the "rod of God," as he called it. At one point, he produced "manna from Heaven" to feed the multitudes. Another time, when no water was available, the Lord instructed Moses to "take in your hand the rod with which you struck the Nile. . . . Strike the rock, and water shall come out of it, that the people may drink."

According to one legend, the staff of Moses is buried along with other religious RELICs within the base of the Burnt Column, also known as the banded column Gemberlitas, in Istanbul. The column was originally erected as part of a temple to Apollo in Rome, but it was moved to then-Constantinople by Emperor Constantine I (A.D. 306–337).

Throughout the story of the Exodus, Moses and Aaron are portrayed as miracle workers, and they were, perhaps, seen as wizards by their own people. Indeed, because Moses personally accepted his people's blessing for producing water from the rock (instead of properly crediting God to them), the Lord later denied Moses entrance to the Promised Land.

musical theater From *The Black Crook* to MERLIN, magic, fairy tales and fables along with legends of wizardry, WITCH-CRAFT and the occult have been a part of the world's musical theater. Some of the more interesting American and British examples of the last 150 years are described, listed alphabetically. Theaters and opening dates of the initial Broadway run (if available) are listed in parentheses, and actors who originated important roles are also identified.

A Connecticut Yankee (Vanderbilt Theatre; November 3, 1927) With a score by Richard Rodgers (music) and Lorenz Hart (lyrics) and a book by Herbert Fields, A *Connecticut Yankee*, was adapted from the Mark Twain novel A CONNECTICUT YANKEE IN KING ARTHU'S COURT.

When Martin (William Gaxton) flirts with a young lady at his bachelor party, he is hit over the head with a champagne bottle by his fiancée Fay Morgan (Nana Bryant). He wakes up in CAMELOT, surrounded by his buddies, who are now knights of the Round Table. Confused and frightened by Martin's sudden appearance, locals plan to burn him at the stake. By correctly predicting a conveniently remembered solar eclipse, however, Martin seems to perform mighty magic, and he is released as a powerful, though friendly sorcerer. Soon he is using 20th-century know-how to modernize Camelot, much to the chagrin of his nemesis, Morgan LE FAY (Bryant) and Merlin (William Norris). After comic catastrophes, Martin awakens back in his Hartford hotel room in the 20th century, recovering from a headache. (See also FILMS, *CONNECTICUT YANKEE, A*, and *CONNECTICUT YANKEE IN KING ARTHUR'S COURT, A*.)

A Hero Is Born (Adelphi; October 1, 1937) Produced by the Theatre Guild of the WPA Federal Theatre Project, *A Hero Is Born* was adapted by Theresa Helburn from an Andrew Lang fairy tale. The score was by Lehman Engel, and there were almost 100 people in the cast.

The fairy kingdom gives Prince Prigio of Pantouflia (Ben Starkie) a cache of gifts at his christening, but his mother, a bitter and practical woman, hides the magical presents. Years later, he finds the many gifts, which include a flying carpet and two hats, one that grants wishes and another that makes him invisible when it is worn. The presents also help him learn humility and win the hand of Princess Rosalind (Drue Leyton).

Aladdin, Jr. (Broadway Theatre; April 8, 1895) Aladdin (with Anna Boyd performing a male role, as in British pantomime tradition) battles the villainous Abanazar (Henry Norman) across the face of the earth, from Peking to an Egyptian palace, and into the depths of a magic cave.

Beauty and the Beast   See BEAUTY AND THE BEAST.

Black Crook, The (Niblo's Garden; September 12, 1866) Considered by many to be the first true American musical, *The Black Crook* merged two dissimilar shows, a Charles M. Barras melodrama based on the FAUST legend, with music by Thomas Baker, and a French ballet imported by Henry C. Jarrett and Harry Palmer. The ballet troupe augmented the regular cast, portraying SPIRITs, sprites and demons.

Hertzog (C.H. Morton), known as the Black Crook, must capture a soul each year at midnight on New Year's Eve. Without revealing his ulterior motive, Hertzog frees an unjustly imprisoned painter named Rudolf, also seen as Rodolphe (G.C. Boniface) and offers him a pot of gold. While searching for the riches, Rudolf rescues a dove, which turns out to be Stalacta (Annie Kemp Bowler), the enchanted queen of the Golden Realm. She saves him from the Devil's snare and unites him with his lover, Amina (Rose Morton).

The popular production spawned several national tours, and Broadway revivals (or New York stops on road tours) were seen in 1869, 1871, 1873, 1879, 1881, 1884, 1889 and 1903.

Camelot (Majestic Theatre; December 3, 1960) *Camelot*, by the team of Alan Jay Lerner (book, lyrics) and Frederick Loewe (music), was based on the T.H. White novel *The ONCE AND FUTURE KING*, which included part of the legend of MERLIN.

As the play opens, Guenevere (Julie Andrews), the reluctant bride-to-be, is approaching by carriage. A sheepish King ARTHUR (Richard Burton) has climbed a tree to catch a glimpse of her. Merlyn (David Hurst), described in the *dramatis personae* as "a rococo figure of a man, with a huge pointed hat; flowing, heavily embroidered robes; and the legendary apparel of wisdom—a long white beard," comes looking for Arthur.

Merlyn finds Wart, as he has nicknamed Arthur in boyhood, and tells him to come down. Arthur complains to his mentor, friend and advisor that he has never been taught about love and marriage. Arthur asks if Guenevere is beautiful. Merlyn says he doesn't know, but Arthur reminds the wizard that he can see into the future. Finally, Merlyn assures the king that she is beautiful.

Merlyn informs Arthur that soon he will be leaving CAMELOT forever. He is destined to be BEWITCHed by the sorceress NIMUË, who will rob Merlyn of his magical powers and seal him in a cave for hundreds of years. Indeed, almost immediately after Arthur and Guenevere meet, Merlyn is called by the nymph and spirited away.

The play jumps forward five years. The kingdom is safe, chivalry is in vogue and the Round Table is in place. Lancelot (Robert Goulet) appears on the scene and is invited to Camelot by Arthur. At a subsequent joust, Sir Lionel is lanced by Lancelot. Lancelot kneels beside the dead knight, takes his hand and prays, and Sir Lionel is resurrected from the dead.

The queen's heart is lost to Lancelot, and as Act One ends, Arthur prays that Guenevere and Lancelot have the strength to keep them faithful to their respective vows.

Act Two opens with Lancelot and the queen declaring their love for one another. Modred (Roddy McDowall) appears before Arthur, announcing that he now knows he is the king's bastard son. Before he was king, Arthur had "bewitched" and seduced the wife of King Lot, conceiving Modred. Arthur offers Modred a place at the Round Table, but, once alone, Modred vows its doom.

Modred conjures up his aunt, the enchantress Morgan LE FAY (M'el Dowd) who lives in an invisible castle with her courtiers. Le Fay does not wish to harm Arthur, but in exchange for chocolates from Modred, le Fay agrees to play a prank on her brother Arthur. She uses her sorcery to imprison the king overnight within an invisible wall in the forest, unaware that it is part of Modred's plan to allow Lancelot and Guenevere to spend a night alone together.

The lovers succumb to temptation. Arthur's knights, having been warned by Modred, surprise the lovers. Lancelot escapes, but Arthur is forced to condemn the captive queen to be burned at the stake for treason.

In a daring sunrise raid, Lancelot rescues Guenevere. Although Arthur is happy for her deliverance, he knows that war will be the outcome. On the morning of the battle, Arthur, Lancelot and Guenevere have a clandestine meeting at which the king learns that his wife has entered a nunnery. Though both men are loathe to fight, they know that, to satisfy their respective supporters, they must.

In a final scene, King Arthur knights a young boy, commands him to hurry far from the battlefield and to carry on the legend of Camelot.

Camelot received four Tony Awards (Burton, Actor in a Musical; Franz Allers, Conductor and Musical Director; Oliver Smith, Scenic Design, Musical; Adrian, and Tony Duquette Costume Designer, Musical). For many, the optimism of "one brief shining moment" of Camelot also became a metaphor for the Kennedy years in the White House.

In 1967, a FILM version of *Camelot* was released by Warner Studios starring Vanessa Redgrave as Guenevere and Richard Harris as Arthur. As in the play, MERLYN is seen only briefly to set the plot in motion. An Academy Award was won by Richard H. Kline for cinematography.

Burton returned as Arthur in New York revivals of *Camelot* in 1976 and 1980; Richard Harris played the role in a 1981 tour and New York revival; and Robert Goulet assumed the role in a 1994 revival.

Canterbury Tales   The musical based on Chaucer's famous CANTERBURY TALES premiered at the Phoenix Theatre in London on March 21, 1968. With music by Richard Hill and John Hawkins and lyrics by Nevill Coghill, the show's libretto by Coghill and Martin Starkie was based on Coghill's own adaptation of the Chaucer poem. The libretto featured four of the bawdiest tales: "The Miller's Tale," "The Merchant's Tale," "The Steward's Tale" and "The Wife of Bath's Tale."

The short-lived Broadway edition opened at the Eugene O'Neill Theatre on February 3, 1969. *Canterbury Tales* received one Tony Award (for Costume Design, Louden Sainthill).

Carmen Jones   See OPERA, CARMEN.

Carnival   (Imperial Theatre; April 13, 1961) *Carnival* was an adaptation of the FILM *Lili*, the tale of an orphaned girl who finds a home in a traveling French circus. In fact, *Carnival* was the first Broadway musical adapted from a film musical. The original movie had been written by Helen Deutsch from a story by Paul Gallico. With a score by Bob Merrill (music and lyrics), *Carnival* changed the show's emphasis from dance (for the film's star, Leslie Caron) to song.

Lili (Anna Maria Alberghetti) begins work for a seemingly cruel, lame puppeteer Paul Berthalet (Jerry Orbach) and his assistant Jacquot (Pierre Olaf). Almost immediately, Lili becomes infatuated with the flamboyant magician Marco the Magnificent (James Mitchell). Marco's lover and assistant Rosalie (Kaye Ballard) puts an end to the affair before it really begins. Marco has an outrageous solo, the flashy "With a Sword and a Rose and a Cape," and a circus-performance production number "Magic, Magic," in which he uses volunteers (actually actors positioned in the audience) in his routines. Later, a comic duet ("Always, Always You") is sung as Marco, wielding swords, stabs the wicker box in which Rosalie is sitting. At the musical's end, Lili discovers she really loves Paul, the shy puppeteer.

In a tie, Anna Maria Alberghetti shared that season's Tony Award for Actress (Musical) with Diahann Carroll (*No Strings*). Will Steven Armstrong also won for his scenic design.

Chin-Chin   (Globe; October 20, 1914) With the unique comic talents of Dave Montgomery and Fred Stone in the cast (see *The Wizard of Oz* and *The Lady and the Slipper*, listed below), the success of the whimsical musical *Chin-Chin* was almost guaranteed.

Widow Twankey (Zelma Rawlston), the aunt of Aladdin (Douglas Stevenson), owns "a golden lamp that looks like brass." See FILM, ALADDIN; "ALADDIN AND THE WONDERFUL LAMP;" ARABIAN NIGHTS. The evil Abanazar (Charles T. Aldrich), knowing its power, wants to buy it for his toy shop and then resell it to Cornelius Bond (R.E. Graham), a wealthy American. Bond's daughter Violet (Helen Falconer) and Aladdin fall in love, but the father forbids their marriage: Aladdin is too poor. Stone and Montgomery (as Chin Hop Hi and Chin Hop Lo, respectively) come to the rescue. They instruct Aladdin to rub the lamp, and, instantly, Aladdin is wealthy enough to claim Violet Bond's hand.

In Act Two, Abanazar steals the lamp. Oddly, he whisks everyone first to a Dutch circus and then to a Parisian park. The silly plot device was designed to allow Montgomery and Stone to dress in a number of ludicrous costumes, from clowns to gendarmes.

Chris and the Wonderful Lamp   (Victoria Theatre; January 1, 1900) This Broadway show was the only musical with a score written expressly for children by the March King, John Philip Sousa. Its libretto was penned by Glen MacDonough, who would later write several children's pieces with Victor Herbert.

Chris Wagstaff (Edna Wallace Hopper, in a British pantomime-tradition "pants role") buys Aladdin's magical lamp. He and his girlfriend Fanny (Ethel Irene) skip school, and with the help of the Genie (Jerome Sykes), they all visit Aladdin (Emile Beaupre) in the enchanted, celestial land of Etheria. Aladdin falls in love with Fanny, and he takes back the lamp so that she will not leave him. She succeeds in rubbing the lamp, however; the Genie appears, and the children safely return home. (See FILM, *ALADDIN*; "ALADDIN AND THE WONDERFUL LAMP"; *ARABIAN NIGHTS*; JINN.)

Damn Yankees (46th St. Theatre; May 5, 1955) Adapted by George Abbott and (John) Douglass Wallop from the latter's novel *The Year the Yankees Lost the Pennant*, *Damn Yankees* is the FAUST legend in a baseball uniform. The musical featured a score by Richard Adler and Jerry Ross and was produced by Hal Prince, Frederick Brisson and Robert E. Griffith, directed by Abbott and choreographed by Bob Fosse.

Middle-aged Joe Boyd (Robert Shafer), watching his beloved Washington Senators lose another game to the Yankees, mutters that he would trade his soul to see his team win. A dapper Devil named Applegate (Ray Walston) suddenly appears and offers to accept the bargain. Boyd agrees to the pact, but only if he has an escape clause. Instantly, Boyd is transformed into the young, virile Joe Hardy (Stephen Douglass). After a tryout with the Senator's Coach Van Buren (Russ Brown), Joe makes the team.

Fearful that Joe may "welch" on the deal, Applegate sends in Lola (Gwen Verdon), an old crone in disguise who centuries before had sold her soul for beauty. Her mission is to win Hardy's love and allegiance.

Lola falls for Joe but, recognizing his true love for his wife, helps him escape his pact. While Joe is on the field in the final play of the pennant race against the Yankees, Applegate, in a fit of temper, changes him back into an old man in front of everyone in the stadium. Boyd still manages to hit a home run to win the game and the pennant but quickly "disappears" in the jubilant crowd. Joe returns to his wife and ignores Applegate's attempts to woo him back as the curtain falls.

Damn Yankees received ten Tony Awards: Musical; Abbott and Wallop, Authors (Musical); Gwen Verdon, Actress (Musical); Ray Walston, Actor (Musical); Russ Brown, Supporting Actor (Musical); Brisson, Griffith and Prince, Producers (Musical); Adler and Ross, Composer and Lyricist; Hal Hastings, Conductor and Musical Director; Fosse, Choreography and Harry Green, electrician and sound man, Stage Technician.

A 1958 FILM version starred Verdon and Walston recreating their roles and Tab Hunter as Joe Hardy, and an abbreviated made-for-television version followed.

The first major New York revival of *Damn Yankees* opened at the Marquis Theatre on March 3, 1994, starring Bebe Neuwirth as Lola, Victor Garber as Applegate, Dick Latessa as Van Buren and Jarrod Emick (who won a Tony Award for his performance) as Shoeless Joe Hardy.

At the time of the show's opening, George Abbott was 102 years old and had acted as a consultant and adviser to director Jack O'Brien during rewrites. The revival ran through the end of 1995, closed for two months and then reopened with Jerry Lewis, in his Broadway debut, assuming the role of Applegate.

EFX More extravaganza than conventional musical theater, *EFX* opened in mid-1995 at the MGM Grand Hotel, Casino and Theme Park in Las Vegas, Nevada. The multimedia spectacle, featuring a cast of 70, utilizes magic, music, dance, pyrotechnics and special theatrical effects.

The EFX Master (Michael Crawford, succeeded by David Cassidy) guides the audience through the nine-act (plus finale) production, portraying four characters (MERLIN, P.T. Barnum, Harry Houdini and H.G. Wells) along the way.

Other characters in the extravaganza include the Master of Magic (Jeffrey Polk), the Master of the SPIRIT World (Kevin Koelbl), the Master of Time (Rick Stockwell) and the Master of Laughter (Stewart Daylida).

In Act III, Merlin begins to instruct Young ARTHUR (Lisa Geist) when the enchantress Morgana (Tina Walsh-Pooley) appears. A duel between the wonder workers follows, ending in Morgana's defeat and entrapment.

In Act VI, Houdini, aided by his wife Bess (Walsh-Pooley) recreates a classical spirit seance and performs a number of traditional stage tricks, including a variation of the classic trunk escape.

The stage illusions for *EFX* were created by David Mendoza, an internationally recognized designer and builder of magic.

Faust *Faust* had its world premiere opening (after a week of preview performances) at the La Jolla Playhouse in La Jolla, California, on September 24, 1995. Music, lyrics and libretto are by pop composer Randy Newman, who began work on *Faust* in the mid-1980s. Under the direction of Michael Greif, Ken Page portrayed the Lord, David Garrison was the Devil, Bellamy Young was Margaret and Kurt Deutsch was Henry FAUST, a self-centered and callous youth who makes a pact with Satan.

In Newman's version of the legend, Faust is a secondary character. The Devil makes a wager with the Lord that he can win the soul of a random human being. If the Devil wins, he can return to heaven; if he loses, the Lord will have the mortal's soul for eternity. They agree to put Henry Faust, a Notre Dame University student, to the test.

Faust is egotistical and too lazy to even sign the Devil's pact to which he agrees. Faust falls in love with Margaret, the most beautiful girl in South Bend, Indiana, and the Devil is smitten with her best friend, the worldly Martha.

So that he can be alone to have sex with Margaret, Faust poisons his lover's mother and then kills her brother Valentine, who has discovered their rendezvous. Faust and the Devil quickly leave town; they hide out for a year in a cabin on the shore of Lake Superior near Duluth, Minnesota.

Back in South Bend, Margaret has Faust's child, and, mad with guilt and grief, she drowns the baby. She is arrested, tried, found guilty of murder and sentenced to death at the Indiana State Prison in Michigan City. Impressed that the angels take her into heaven even before she is dead, Faust begs for forgiveness from the Lord. He receives salvation, much to the chagrin of the Devil.

Faust up to Date (Broadway Theatre; December 10, 1889) Members of London's Gaiety Theatre were imported for this production which took great liberties with the FAUST legend. The show's lead, Florence St. John (Marguerite) was too sick to perform at the opening but, according to first-nighters, male audience members still enjoyed the "frank display of the lower limbs" of the obligatory female chorus.

Faustus; or, The Demon of the Dragonfels (Broadway Theatre; January 13, 1851) Considered a spectacle rather than a musical drama, this show tells the story of the king of Naples who sells his soul to the Devil. A shipwreck transforms into the carnival in Venice, followed by a finale described in the program as "the intrusion of Venetians seeking redress against the base Seducer! Wizard!! Murderer!!!"

Finian's Rainbow (46th Street Theatre; January 10, 1947) A popular hit, *Finian's Rainbow* had songs by Burton Lane (music) and E.Y. Harburg (lyrics) and a book by Harburg and Fred Saidy (book and additional lyrics).

Finian McLonergan (Albert Sharpe) has stolen a pot of gold from the leprechauns of Glocca Morra, Ireland. He flees to the United States with his daughter Sharon (Ella Logan) in tow. Unbeknownst to them, the leprechaun Og (David Wayne) follows them, hoping to recover the treasure.

McLonergan believes that if the gold is planted at Fort Knox, it will grow and multiply, just like the wealth of the United States itself. The trio make it as far as Rainbow Valley, Missitucky, where Sharon falls in love with a local union organizer, Woody Mahoney (Donald Richards). Og has also fallen in love—with Sharon—and he is becoming more and more human the longer he is away from Ireland.

When Sharon hears the Missitucky Senator Billboard Rawkins (Robert Pitkin) make racial slurs, she muses that if he were black he could understand things from a different point of view. Unfortunately, she has made the wish next to the enchanted pot, and her wish comes true. Og manages to reverse the spell. He also heals the mute dancer Susan Mahoney (Anita Alvarez) and, realizing that his unrequited love for Sharon is hopeless, turns his attentions to Susan.

Finian's Rainbow won Tony Awards for Supporting Actor in a Musical (Wayne) and Choreographer (Michael Kidd).

City Center, noted for its seasons of New York revivals, had three major productions of *Finian's Rainbow* (1955, 1960 and 1967) prior to the 1968 Warner FILM version, directed by Francis Ford Coppola and starring Fred Astaire, Petula Clark and Tommy Steele (as Og).

Flahooley (Broadhurst; May 14, 1951) E.Y. Harburg and Fred Saidy (book and lyrics) attempted to recapture the whimsy of their popular *Finian's Rainbow*, but despite charming music by Sammy Fain and the vocal contributions of Barbara Cook and Yma Sumac, the show was not a success. The basic plot involves the creation of a doll that laughs, a genie (see JINN) similar to Og the leprechaun (from *Finian's Rainbow,*) Arab spies and political reactionaries.

Gingerbread Man, The (Liberty Theatre; December 25, 1905) *The Gingerbread Man* by Frederic Ranken and A. Baldwin Sloane was billed as a "Fairyesque" and spun a tale about the king of BonBon Land (Eddie Redway), who is afraid of being eaten. He is so tasty because he had been turned into a gingerbread man by the evil wizard Machevavelius. Santa and Mrs. Claus appear on a sleigh and magically transform the king back into a human.

Goodtime Charley See JOAN OF ARC, ST.

Home Sweet Homer (Palace Theatre; January 4, 1976) Based on Homer's *The ODYSSEY, Home Sweet Homer* starred Yul Brenner as Odysseus, Joan Diener as Penelope and Russ Thacker as Telemachus. Despite a 10-month pre-Broadway tour, the musical's many problems were never solved, and the show quickly closed in New York.

Idol's Eye, The (Broadway; October 25, 1897) Frank Daniels, the star of *The Wizard of the Nile* (see below), commissioned Victor Herbert and Harry B. Smith to create another show for him. The result was *The Idol's Eye.*

In India, Jamie McSniffy (Alf C. Whelan), a Scottish kleptomaniac, has just stolen the ruby eye of a jungle idol. The mystical eye has a SPELL attached, making everyone fall in love with its owner. Abel Conn (Daniels) lands in a hot-air balloon and discovers a duplicate ruby; only this one has a CURSE: it causes everyone to hate its possessor! The magical stones are switched back and forth, a pair of young lovers get caught in the comic chaos and, of course, they all live happily ever after.

Into the Woods (Martin Beck Theatre; November 5, 1987) *Into the Woods* featured music and lyrics by Stephen Sondheim and a book by James Lapine, who also directed. The team created a new fairy tale ("The Baker and His Wife") and interwove its two characters with the well-known tales of "Jack and the Beanstalk," "Little Red Riding Hood," "CINDERELLA," "Rapunzel" and, to a lesser extent, "The SLEEPING BEAUTY" and "Snow White."

Set in motion by a Narrator (Tom Aldredge), the musical starts with Cinderella (Kim Crosby) making preparations for her stepsisters Florinda (Lay McClelland) and Lucinda (Lauren Mitchell) to go to the ball of the prince (Robert Westenberg). In the process, she consults the SPIRIT of her deceased mother (Merle Louise), who resides in a giant tree in the woods. Meanwhile, Jack (Ben Wright) is sent to the market by his mother (Barbara Bryne) to try to sell their aged cow. Little Red Ridinghood (Danielle Ferland) drops in on the baker (Chip Zien) and his wife (Joanna Gleason) to get treats for her grandmother (Louise) and then warily sets off into the wolf (Westenberg)-infested woods.

Suddenly, the ugly witch (Bernadette Peters) appears, telling the baker and his wife that they are barren because of a CURSE she had leveled on his father for stealing magic beans from her garden. She also reveals that the baker had a sister, but does not divulge that it is Rapunzel (Pamela Winslow), whom she has adopted as her own child and has hidden in a tower. The witch offers to lift the curse if, within three days, the baker and his wife can bring her a cow as white as milk, a cape as red as blood, strands of hair as yellow as corn and a slipper as pure as gold.

Eventually, the baker and his wife obtain the items from the other characters. The witch feeds the cape, slipper and "hair" (corn husk substituting for Rapunzel's tresses) to the cow and drinks the resultant milk. In a flash, her ugliness melts into beauty, but as part of the transformation, the witch loses her magical powers.

Act Two examines the consequences of having wishes come true. The wife of the giant that Jack has killed descends the beanstalk for revenge. Frustrated by the human follies that cause several of their own deaths, the witch explains that she represents the unknown and ominous specter that people blame when reality intrudes on their complacency. She calls to her mother to take her away, and the witch disappears in a puff of smoke.

Left alone, the baker, Cinderella, Jack and Little Red Ridinghood devise a plan and succeed in killing the giantess. Together, they begin to rebuild their lives.

Into the Woods captured Tony Awards for Score, Book and Leading Actress in a Musical (Gleason). A national tour of *Into the Woods* followed, starring Cleo Laine as the witch and Charlotte Rae as Jack's mother.

"It's A Bird It's A Plane It's Superman" See SUPERMAN.

Jeanne See JOAN OF ARC, ST.

Jeanne la Pucelle See JOAN OF ARC, ST.

Jesus Christ Superstar (Mark Hellinger Theatre; October 12, 1971) Expanded from the song "Superstar" into an entire rock-opera concept album for Decca Records by Andrew Lloyd Webber (music) and Tim Rice (lyrics), *Jesus Christ Superstar* tells the story of the last days and passion of JESUS.

The success of the LP led to a concert tour and it was first staged as a theatrical piece by director Tom O'Horgan, who is also credited with the Broadway production's book. The cast included Jeff Fenholt (Jesus), Yvonne Elliman (Mary Magdalene), Ben Vereen (Judas) and Barry Dennen (Pontius Pilate).

Although the libretto of *Jesus Christ Superstar* focuses on the last week of Jesus's life, many of his miracles and healings are enacted or referenced in the musical. At least four of Christ's miracles are mentioned in "King Herod's Song" alone: healing cripples, raising from the dead, walking on water and the feeding of the multitudes.

In 1973, the FILM version of *Superstar* was released, starring Ted Neeley (Jesus), Carl Anderson (Judas), Josh Mostel (King Herod) and, from the Broadway cast, Elliman (Mary Magdalene) and Dennen (Pilate).

Jesus Christ Superstar was revived at the Longacre Theatre on November 23, 1977. Several national tours have been mounted, many of which have starred Neeley and Anderson reprising their film roles for the stage.

Kismet (Ziegfeld; December 3, 1953) The musical *Kismet* (described as "A Musical ARABIAN NIGHT"), with a book by Charles Lederer and Luther Davis based on the 1911 Edward Knoblock play, featured songs with lyrics by Robert Wright and George Forrest set to melodies by Alexander Borodin. *Kismet* originated in Los Angeles as part of Edwin Lester's Los Angeles Civic Light Opera Association season.

Hajj (Alfred Drake), a poet and beggar, is magically transformed into the emir of Baghdad for one day. His daughter Marsinah (Doretta Morrow) marries a handsome gardener, really the Caliph (Richard Kiley) in disguise. Hajj battles the evil Wazir of Police (Henry Calvin), who drowns; then Hajj marries the Wazir's widow Lalume (Joan Diener).

Kismet won six Tony Awards: Musical; Author(s), Musical (Lederer and Davis); Producer, Musical (Lederer); Composer (Borodin); Actor, Musical (Drake); and Musical Conductor (Louis Adrian). Other awards included the Outer Circle Critics Award for Best Musical, the Donaldson Awards for Drake and for Lemuel Ayers (Costumes) and the Variety Drama Critics' Poll for Drake's performance.

This was not the first adaptation of the Knoblock play. Produced in New York and opening on December 25, 1911, a nonmusical *Kismet* starred Otis Skinner as Hajj. Three FILM versions and a made-for-TELEVISION adaptation followed in 1930, 1944, 1955 and 1967, respectively.

Lady of the Slipper, The (Globe; October 28, 1912) This adaptation of the well-known CINDERELLA story featured a score by Victor Herbert and Elsie Janis as Cinderella. Comic actors Dave Montgomery and Fred Stone portrayed country bumpkins (not dissimilar from their WIZARD OF OZ characters), which replaced the fairy godmother's role. They made sure that Cinderella got to the ball and that Crown Prince Maximilian (Douglas Stevenson) later found her.

Magic Ring, The (Liberty; October 1, 1923) Zelda Sears (book) and Harold Levey (score) wrote *The Magic Ring* as a star vehicle for Mitzi (stage name of Mitzi Hajos). A poor, female organ-grinder finds a magic RING, which provides her with riches and romance.

Magic Show, The (Cort Theatre; May 28, 1974) *The Magic Show* starred newcomer Doug Henning, a young Canadian magician who had been scouted in Toronto while fronting for a rock-and-roll band. The musical's creators conceived and designed the show, writing the book (Bob Randall) and music and lyrics (Stephen Schwartz) around the illusions and talents of their discovery.

A young illusionist (Henning) gets his chance to perform at The Passaic Top Hat nightclub in New Jersey at the expense of an older and traditional but passé magician (David Ogden Stiers).

Schwartz opens the show with a rousing chorus number full of magic, reminiscent of his "Magic to Do" number in *Pippin* (see below).

The national touring company was headed by Peter De Paula, and the show was also later produced in Australia. A highly adapted FILM version of *The Magic Show* was produced for and aired on Canadian TELEVISION, but it was never released theatrically. Because Henning would not prepare a prompt book to teach the secrets of the show's illusions, *The Magic Show* has never been released for performance by regional, local or school theaters.

Man of La Mancha (Anta Washington Square Theatre; November 22, 1965) *Man of La Mancha*, a highly stylized retelling of Cervantes's famous novel, DON QUIXOTE, quietly opened in New York City at a temporary Greenwich Village theater adjacent to New York University. In early 1968, the show finally moved midtown to the Martin Beck Theatre.

For the New York production, book-writer Dale Wasserman adapted and expanded his own TELEVISION play *I, Don Quixote*. Although it significantly compressed the plot of the novel, *Man of la Mancha* nonetheless retained the essence of the tale, that of a nobleman so overwhelmed by reading books on the Age of Chivalry that he goes mad and thinks himself to be a knight. The medieval belief in the power of magic is seen in Quixote's reaction to "The Enchanter," also called the "Knight of the Mirrors."

The musical's unusual one-act format is that of a play-within-a-play. Cervantes, imprisoned in a dungeon for heresy and awaiting trial by the Spanish INQUISITION, enacts his novel *Don Quixote* using fellow inmates as characters. The show's leads included Richard Kiley (Cervantes/Quixote, in his most famous role), Irving Jacobson (Sancho Panza), Joan Diener (Aldonza/Dulcinea) and Jon Cypher (Dr. Carrasco/Enchanter).

Despite its downtown opening, *Man of La Mancha* was clearly a Broadway-style production, and the ANTA Theatre qualified it as such for Tony Award consideration. It won five: Musical, Director (Albert Marre), Composer and Lyricist (Mitch Leigh and Joe Darion, respectively), Actor (Kiley) and Scenic Design (Howard Bay).

In 1972, a New York revival starring Kiley appeared at the Vivian Beaumont Theatre at Lincoln Center. Kiley continued to appear both regionally and/or on the road with *Man of La Mancha*; as part of a national tour, the show opened (with Kiley) at the Palace Theatre on September 15, 1977. A major revival opened on Broadway in 1991 with Raul Julia (Cervantes), Sheena Easton (Aldonza) and Tony Martinez (Sancho). During its New York run at the Marquis Theatre, Easton was succeeded by the original Dulcinea, Joan Diener.

Man of Magic (Piccadilly Theatre, London; 1965 or 1966) Produced by Harold Fielding, directed by Peter Ebert, with music by Milfred Wylam and lyrics and book by John Morley and Aubrey Cash, choreography by Norman Maen and escapology and magic by Dill-Russell, *Man of Magic* was "suggested" by the life of Erich Weiss, known to his audiences as Harry Houdini. Stuart Damon starred as Harry [sic] Weiss, and Judith Bruce portrayed his wife Bess.

Marguerite (Olympia; February 3, 1896) Oscar Hammerstein created and produced this variation on the FAUST story. Marguerite (Alice Rose) is already the wife of Faust (Thomas Evans Green), a painter. Mephisto (Adolph Dahm-Peterson) appears, and with a wave of his dragon-headed staff (see WAND), the Devil brings Faust's paintings to life. The show's plot was merely an excuse to present a series of elaborate "living pictures," a then-popular theatrical device wherein actors froze into a pose, usually recreating a famous painting or historical event.

Merlin (Mark Hellinger Theatre; February 13, 1983) After almost a decade-long absence, Doug Henning returned to Broadway in a book musical. Charles Reynolds, longtime consultant to Henning, designed the show's 30 major illusions.

An aged wizard (Edmund Lyndeck) tells a pre-Arthurian story of MERLIN (Henning). Also acting as a mentor to Merlin, the enchanter teaches him SPELLS.

Merlin must fight off the evil queen (Chita Rivera), who is attempting to place her son, the bumbling Prince Fergus (Nathan Lane), on the throne. She knows that unless she destroys Merlin, he will one day choose ARTHUR to be king. As the show's finale, there is a magician's duel-to-the-death between Merlin (with his WHITE MAGIC) and the queen (with her BLACK MAGIC). The victorious Merlin is free to prepare the means for the young Arthur (Christian Slater) to be crowned king.

According to Henning, who first conceived *Merlin* in 1976, "In his day, Merlin did *real* magic. He was an enlightened man who used 100 percent of his mind's potential rather than the 10 percent normal people use. Merlin was what we all could become if we just knew how to do it." As conceived by Henning, the young wizard in *Merlin* "has magic in the beginning, but he doesn't know how to use it. . . . Merlin's journey is from using selfish magic to gain his own ends to learning real magic and using it for the good of the world."

Mountebanks, The (Garden Theatre; January 11, 1893) Written by W.S. Gilbert (book and lyrics) and Alfred Cellier (music), *The Mountebanks* concerns a magic potion which makes "everyone who drinks it exactly what he pretends to be." The production was disappointing, but Lillian Russell's appearance in a leading role allowed the show to stay open for a month and half, plus tour.

110 in the Shade See RAINMAKER.

Pippin (Imperial Theatre; October 23, 1972) With a libretto by Roger O. Hirson and songs by Stephen Schwartz, *Pippin* tells the story of Pepin (spelled as Pippin) (John Rubinstein), the son of King Charlemagne, on his quest for happiness. Acting as a narrator for the magical journey is the Leading Player (Ben Vereen).

In an unforgettable opening scene, as directed and choreographed by Bob Fosse, white-gloved hands appear floating in a midair mist as the ephemeral chorus of "players" beckons Pippin (and the theatergoers). They have "Magic to Do." Stepping from the fog, the players promise "miracle plays to play" as they actually perform illusions, from appearing canes and flowers and color-changing scarves to a levitation of Pippin.

Pippin experiences the excesses of sex, war and violence, but at the show's end, he still feels unfulfilled. The Leading Player suggests one last grand illusion: committing suicide by immolation. Instead, Pippin marries the widow Catherine (Jill Clayburgh) and settles for the simple joys of domesticated life.

Pippin received 11 Tony Award nominations, winning five: Actor in a Musical (Vereen), Director (Fosse), Scenic Design (Tony Walton), Choreographer (Fosse) and Lighting Design (Jules Fisher).

A major revival of *Pippin*, directed by and starring Ben Vereen (once again as the Leading Player), toured the country and landed back on Broadway for a limited run in 1986.

Ragtime, The Musical (Ford Center for the Performing Arts; January 18, 1997) Based on the novel by E.L. Doctorow, *Ragtime, The Musical* had its world premiere in Toronto on December 8, 1996. A separate run in Los Angeles (opening June 15, 1997) also preceded the new production in New York. The $11.5 million show, produced by Garth Drabinsky's Livent Inc., featured a book by Terrence McNally, music by Stephen Flaherty and lyrics by Lynn Ahrens. Frank Galati directed, with musical staging by Graciela Daniele and illusions by consultant Franz Harary. *Ragtime, The Musical* interweaves the stories of three fictional families in turn-of-the-century New York. Among the historical characters depicted in the show is Harry Houdini (portrayed in the Canadian production by Jim Corti and in Los Angeles by Jason Graae). In the musical's first act, Houdini escapes from handcuffs and a locked trunk, and in Act Two, he sings a duet "I Have a Feeling" with the character Evelyn Nesbit, an early American sex symbol.

Rainmaker of Syria, The (Casino; September 25–October 12, 1893) With book and lyrics by Sydney Rosenfeld and music by Rudolph Aronson, *The Rainmaker* told of an Egyptian, Amosis (Mark Smith), who claimed to be a RAINMAKER. Understanding the cyclical aspect nature of nature, Amosis makes a correct forecast, and rain ends a long drought. As payment, King Thesaurus (Harry Davenport) offers him the hand of his unattractive daughter. Instead, Amosis surprises the pharaoh's court by asking to marry Hatchupoo (or Hatshepu) (Bertha Ricci), thought to be a prince but really a beautiful princess in disguise.

Sisterella A black adaptation of the CINDERELLA story, set in turn-of-the-century New York City, had its world premiere at the Pasadena Playhouse in Pasadena, California, after previews, on March 17, 1996. Pop star Michael Jackson served as one of executive producers of the show by composer/lyricist/librettist Larry Hart. The story surrounds Ella, a young $900-million heiress who is placed in an insane asylum by her wicked stepmother. Ella's lawyer and a transvestite fairy godmother come to her rescue.

Sisterella is not the first all-black musical version of the Cinderella tale: Previous productions have included *Cindy-*

Ella in London and *Cindy*, a 1978 American TELEVISION musical special.

Sorcerer, The (Broadway Theatre; February 21, 1879, and revived Bijou Theatre; October 16, 1882) A comic opera in two acts by W.S. Gilbert (book and lyrics) and Arthur Sullivan (music), *The Sorcerer* debuted at the Opera Comique, London, on November 17, 1877, and in a revised version at the Savoy Theatre on October 11, 1884, both with George Grossmith in the title role.

Alexis Poindextre is so thrilled about his engagement to Aline Sangazure that he decides to make a surprise gift to his village. He hires a London sorcerer, John Wellington Wells, of J.W. Wells & Co., Family Sorcerers, to slip a love philtre into the town's communal afternoon tea. The townsfolk drink the love draught and fall fast asleep.

In Act Two, the people awaken, only to fall in love with the first unmarried person each of them sees. Comic confusion and mismatchings result. Wells agrees to call off the spell but warns that someone who was involved in the INCANTATION must give up his life to the SPIRIT controlling the philtre's magic. Wells is elected. He disappears in a ball of red fire, and the spell is broken.

Three Wishes for Jamie (Mark Hellinger; March 21, 1952) This piece of fantasy was set at the end of the 19th century, with songs by Ralph Blane and a libretto by Charles O'Neal and Abe Burrows. Irishman Jamie McRuin (John Raitt) is given three wishes by a fairy. He asks to travel and to marry. Soon, McRuin finds himself on the way to the United States, where he meets and marries Maeve Harrigan (Anne Jeffreys) in Georgia. Jamie's third wish is to have a son. His wife cannot conceive, so they adopt a boy, who is mute. Magically, the boy receives the power of speech—but he only speaks Gaelic!

Treemonisha (Palace Theatre; October 21, 1975) Scott Joplin wrote this original ragtime opera in 1907, but it was never produced during his lifetime. Gunther Schuller reconstructed Joplin's orchestrations for *Treemonisha*, and the musical, conducted by Schuller, had its world premiere at the Houston Grand Opera before touring and moving to New York.

At the start of the musical, Treemonisha (Carmen Balthrop, alternating with Kathleen Battle) is 18. She had been discovered while still a baby by a barren black couple, Ned (Willard White) and Monisha (Betty Allen or Lorna Myers). They found her under a tree; hence, they named the girl Treemonisha. Knowing that they could not properly educate her, however, they gave the infant to a white family.

Now a young woman, Treemonisha is kidnapped by a VOODOO priest named Zodzetrick (Ben Harney) to prevent her from revealing his mystic secrets to others. Her friend Remus (Curtis Rayam), masquerading as a scarecrow, heads the hunt to free her. Treemonisha forgives Zodzetrick for his offense, and the villagers honor her as the head of their community.

Which Witch (Piccadilly Theatre; October 22, 1992) Commissioned as a concept piece for the Bergen International Festival in May 1987, *Which Witch* was written by Benedicte Adrian and Ingrid Bjornov (music) and Kit Hesketh-Harvey (lyrics), purportedly based on a story in MALLEUS MALEFICARUM as well as a manuscript by Ole A. Sorli.

Set in 1537, *Which Witch* tells the tale of a young Italian woman, Maria Vittoria (Adrian) who falls in love with the Bishop Daniel (Graham Bickley) from Germany. Their forbidden affair is aggravated by the bishop's possessive and jealous sister, Anna Regina. The story culminates with an executioner (Jahn Teigen) burning Maria at the stake.

Wiz, The See WIZARD OF OZ, THE.

Wizard of Oz, The See WIZARD OF OZ, THE.

Wizard of the Nile, The (Casino; November 4, 1895) Featuring the songs of Victor Herbert, the Harry B. Smith libretto of *The Wizard of the Nile* borrowed heavily from 1893's *The Rainmaker of Syria* (see above).

Egypt is experiencing a severe drought, and an itinerant wizard named Kibosh (Frank Daniels) produces rain. When Kibosh is unable to stop the downpour or the resulting floods, the pharaoh (Walter Allen) commands his minions to entomb the magician alive. Unfortunately, the ruler is sealed in with him! They escape, and the RAINMAKER is pardoned. A subplot involves the unconsummated love of the musician Ptarmigan (Edward Isham) and Cleopatra (Dorothy Morton): she decides to wait for Mark Antony.

Mxyzptlk, Mr. See SUPERMAN.

Namouna See *LALLA ROOKH*.

Narnia See *CHRONICLES OF NARNIA, THE*.

Native American Magic The tradition of spiritual and healing (i.e., physical) magic performed by the SHAMAN and the MEDICINE MAN of North American tribes paralleled that of similar civilizations throughout the world. Likewise, the mystics' functions in the societies also mirrored those of their counterparts in the Eastern and Southern Hemispheres.

The early European explorers, missionaries and pioneers recorded many instances of awesome illusions performed by these wizardlike figures. The soldiers of Mexican armies equated the tribal shamans of the Southwest with sorcerers, calling them by the Spanish word *brujo* (meaning "witch;" the feminine form is *bruja*). The Spanish used the term *curandero* (or the rarer feminine form *curandera*) for the medicine man who used magic to cure psychological ailments (see FOLK MEDICINE). The word *nahualli* (meaning "sorcerer") from the language of the Nahuatl tribe evolved into *nagual* among the Mexican Spaniards and was used to describe a "GUARDIAN ANGEL" or "power" received from the SPIRITS.

Medicine men and shamans along the St. Lawrence River were said to be able to raise or end storms (see RAINMAKER) and to make crops grow or fail. They could decapitate and restore humans (see DEDI), make drawings and clay figures come to life and make people instantly vanish from one loca-

A Seminole chief in colonial Florida consults his tribal shaman.

PHANTASMAGORIA,
THIS and every EVENING,
AT THE
LYCEUM, STRAND.

Sorcerers were notorious for raising spirits of the dead through necromancy. De Philipsthal, a British stage conjuror, took advantage of this belief in his advertising in 1803.

tion and reappear in another. Magical feats performed by the medicine men and shamans among other Native American tribes include rapidly growing corn- or beanstalks (Hopi, Pawnee, Zuni), transforming snowballs or white feathers into flintlike stones (Hidatsa, Mandan), animating clay images or dolls (Ojibwa), transforming oneself into a wolf (known as a skinwalker) (Navajo), catching bullets or being invulnerable to them (Ponca and Algonquian, respectively), producing snakes from woven baskets (Navajo) or from leather bags (Menomini) or transforming a bag into a snake (Ottawa).

A special skill seemingly shared by almost all medicine men and shamans, regardless of their tribe, was the power to escape from ropes or other bindings. Most frequently mentioned by observers, however, was their uncanny ability to make a distant, unoccupied tent or tents move or quiver—a phenomenon known as tent-shaking.

Before his conversion to Christianity in 1830, the shaman Was-chus-co, who lived on Mackinaw Island, Michigan, was locally famous for tent-shaking. For 10 days before an attempt at tent-shaking, Was-chus-co would fast to focus his mind and senses, and, once entranced, he often saw visions of faces and lights. He explained, "I possessed a power which I cannot explain or describe to you. . . . I held communication with supernatural beings, or thinking minds or spirits, which acted on my mind, or soul."

The ritual purpose of Native American magic has seldom, if ever, been examined. Early adventurers' journals never addressed its ceremonial function. Whether the medicine men and shamans achieved such magical feats through deception is moot but immaterial. Thus, as Eugene Burger, co-author of *Magic & Meaning* points out,

Shamans . . . are not entertainers at all—and those who witnessed their work were not audiences but, rather, *participants in mutual ritual action* wherein both moved into altered states of consciousness. Shamans were the *healers* of the community and also the repositories of an amazing amount of *knowledge*. Not only did they know the secret lore of plants, animals, spirits and precious stones, they also kept all of the tribe's shared mythology and collective wisdom.

necromancy   Today the word *necromancy* is used interchangeably with *magic*, albeit with an occult connotation. Originally, however, the term referred to a specific art: being able to call on the SPIRITs of the dead, especially to have them foretell the future. Summoning a spirit involved great preparations on the part of the sorcerer, often including fasting, secret rituals (including the drawing of MAGIC CIRCLE) and the recitation of esoteric INCANTATIONs.

Necromancy is a derivation of the Greek word *nekromantia*, which in turn came from the two roots *nekros* ("a dead person") and *manteia* ("divination"). Necromancy was considered to be an essential skill of all true wizards, sorcerers and fortune-tellers.

The practice of necromancy was almost commonplace among the alchemists. Usually, the secret rituals took place at night in the local cemetery. A famous 18th-century engraving by Ames, made from a drawing by Sibly, shows a successful necromantic churchyard ceremony being conducted in England by Edward KELLY and John DEE. The depiction is based on a supposedly true

Nostradamus in 1562, dressed in royal attire rather than the stereotypical wardrobe of a wizard.

incident from around 1582. A new rendering of the illustration was used as the frontispiece to Mathieu Giraldo's *Histoire curieuse et pittoresque des sorciers*, published in Paris in 1846.

Spain was considered the capital of necromancy during the Middle Ages. The nefarious craft was actually taught in Toledo, Seville and Salamanca, deep in caves outside the cities. As awareness of the practice grew, rumors started to circulate that witches were seen eating human flesh. Eventually, Queen Isabella, a fervent Catholic, sealed up the caverns.

The most famous recorded case of necromancy is that of Saul consulting the WITCH OF ENDOR, told in the book of 1 Samuel in the Old Testament of the Bible. Saul himself had outlawed sorcery among the Israelites. Nevertheless, the beleaguered king, seeking advice, sought out the enchantress and asked her to call up the prophet Samuel from his grave.

In more modern times, the desire to speak to the dead gave rise to Spiritualism. Practitioners believe that participants in a seance might be able to contact those on the "other side" through a medium. Methods to receive messages from the spirits have been as varied as they have been ingenious, but none has been proven to have established actual contact with the beyond.

Nibelungenlied   See *RING DES NIBELUNGEN, DER*.

Night on Bald Mountain   See *FANTASIA*.

Nimuë (Nimiane)   In most versions of the legends of King ARTHUR, Nimuë (also seen as Nimue and, especially in MALORY, Nimiane) is the LADY OF THE LAKE. A mighty enchantress, she learns the enchantments of MERLIN and uses them to entrance the wizard, placing him into a deep sleep for eternity. Nimuë imprisons Merlin in either a forest of thorns, a crystal cave or a rock, depending upon the storyteller.

Nimuë marries Sir Pelleas, the Noble Knight, after the death of his lover Ettarde. Another version of the knight's tale was published in 1869 as *Pelleas and Ettarre*, one of Tennyson's *IDYLLS OF THE KING*. (See also VIVIEN.)

Nostradamus (1503–1566)   Nostradamus, one of history's greatest and most enigmatic seers, was born Michel de Nostre-Dame. For many years, the French astrologer and physician put out an annual *Almanac*. In 1556, Nostradamus published *Centuries*, the infamous book that contained the majority of his prophecies. Near the end of his life (which he also purportedly predicted), Nostradamus was welcomed at the court of Catherine de Médicis (1519–89), where he continued his prognostications.

Nostradamus used scrying, one of the traditional techniques of the wizard, to receive his DIVINATIONs. He would build a triangle, or pyramid, out of three WANDs over a small bowl of water and then touch one or other wands or "branches," as he described them, to the water. The visions would reveal themselves as he peered into the ripples on the surface.

Centuries had its first English translation in 1672 and was eventually condemned by the pope in 1781. Yet its cult popularity continued underground, and around World War II, as 20th-century events seemed to mirror Nostradamus's ancient predictions, interest in his writings was awakened and began to grow.

In the wizard's magic mirror placed above the fireplace, Nostradamus reveals the succession of future kings to Catherine of France. He further prophesies the end of the French monarchy with Louis XIV.

The text, in French, was arranged in groups of 100 rhymed quatrains. They were enigmatic—vague at best—and, like the prophecies of the early ORACLES, could be interpreted to almost anyone's satisfaction. A popular phrase, "as good a prophet as Nostradamus," reflected this ambiguity.

Many of his predictions were reinterpreted time and again by successive generations. Thus, the phrases that supposedly foretold the French Revolution later were said to have prophesied World War II.

The Nostradamus verse "There will go from Mount Gaulfier and Aventine / One who from the hole will warn the army," for instance, supposedly predicts the invention of the hot-air balloon by Montgolfier. Napoleon's name purportedly appears as an anagram at the beginning of the phrase "Pau . nay . loron will be more fire than blood . . ."

The most notorious 20th-century figure said to have been predicted by the psychic was Adolf Hitler. Since Hitler's ascension in the 1930s, Nostradamus champions have pointed to those verses dealing with "Hister" as actually referring to the Nazi dictator.

For example, adherents such as Stewart Robb (*Prophecies on World Events by Nostradamus*, 1961) suggest that the following quatrain refers to Hister's invasion of Bulgaria:

> Liberty will not be recovered,
> A bold, black, base-born, iniquitous man will occupy it,
> When the material of the bridge is completed,
> The republic of Venice will be annoyed by Hister.

Detractors of these interpretations claim that the verses refer to the Hister River, a name for the Danube River at the time of Nostradamus, rather than to Hitler.

Among Nostradamus's other predictions were a British-American federation, a Golden Age starting around 1963, "a world of increasing Moslem might," Armageddon (beginning in 1973 and lasting up to the 1999 invasion) and a thousand years of peace.

In researcher L. Sprague de Camp's analysis of the 449 discernable predictions that can be deduced out of Nostradamus's writings, 18 had been proved false, only 41 could be interpreted as having come true and the other 390 could not be identified with anything that had yet occurred.

numerology Numerology, a system of identifying the characteristics of people according to the numerical equivalent of the letters in their names, has its source in several occult beliefs, including the works of the KABBALAH. The importance of numerology to wizards and sorcerers is that, if the system works, it gives enough insight into another person's attitudes and attributes that those wishing to do evil could use the knowledge to hurt or control others.

Although entire volumes have been filled on the theory of numerology, a brief examination is of interest. To find the numerical equivalent of a name, the letters are substituted by numbers according to the following chart:

1	2	3	4	5	6	7	8
A	B	C	D	E	U	O	F
I	K	G	M	H	V	Z	P
Q	R	L	T	N	W		
J		S			X		
Y							

Because there are only 22 letters in the Hebrew ALPHABET, Greek letters are used to fill in for the rest of the modern Western alphabet.

Next, a single number is assigned to each letter of the person's name. The numbers are totaled, and that sum is further reduced to a single digit. For instance:

J	O	H	N	D	O	E
1	7	5	5	4	7	5

Adds up to 34; 3 + 4 = 7

Therefore, the number 7 should provide the most information about the true character of a person of that name.

The following chart gives some of the supposed major characteristics of each of the nine magical digits:

ONE	TWO	THREE
Powerful	Quiet	Charming
Ambitious	Very sensitive	Talented
"God's number"	"The Devil's number"	Show-offs

FOUR	FIVE	SIX
Hard working	Clever	Peaceful
Cautious	Risk-taker	Reliable
Conventional	Sexually successful	Busybody

SEVEN	EIGHT	NINE
Scholarly	Successful	Visionary
Sardonic	Selfish	Energetic
Dignified	Hard driven	Emotional

It should be noted that numerology also allows for the analysis of words and dates, not just names.

Nutcracker, The See BALLET.

Nymus See LADY OF THE LAKE, THE; VIVIEN.

Oberon See *MIDSUMMER NIGHT'S DREAM, A.*

Occult Philosophy See AGRIPPA, HEINRICH, CORNELIUS; *DE OCCULTA PHILOSOPHIA*; TURNER, ROBERT.

Odyssey, The Attributed to the Greek poet Homer and written around the eighth century B.C., *The Odyssey* recounts Odysseus's attempt to return to his island home of Ithaca following nine years of battles at Troy (detailed in *The Iliad*, an earlier work also attributed to Homer). In the course of his travels, Odysseus meets and overcomes the magic and sorcery of several mythological and supernatural beings.

Early in the voyage, Odysseus's ships land on a small island just off the shore of the land of the Cyclops. The monstrous Polyphemos traps Odysseus and several of his crew in his cave. To escape, Odysseus and his companions drive a sharpened pole into the Cyclops's single eye, blinding him. As his ships depart, Odysseus reveals his true identity to the Cyclops, who then realized that the events had been prophesied:

> A wizard, grand and wondrous, lived here—TELEMOS,
> a son of Eurymos; great length of days
> he had in wizardry among the Cyclops,
> and these things he foretold for time to come:
> my great eye lost, and at Odysseus' hand.

Later, Odysseus sails on to the island of CIRCE, the enchantress. Odysseus overcomes her powerful magic—and her ability to turn his men into swine—with the help of HERMES, the god's messenger.

Odysseus's next trial is a visit to the Kingdom of the Dead, where he meets several SPIRITS and receives prophecy from the seer TIRESIAS. The sailors stop briefly back on Circe's island to conduct funeral rites for a lost crewman and then continue onward. They successfully avoid the temptations of the SIRENS.

The ships land on the island where Apollo's cattle graze, and they butcher one of the sacred animals, as foretold by Tiresias. As punishment, Zeus smashes Odysseus's boat with thunderbolts and gales. Odysseus alone washes ashore, and he is entranced by the nymph Calypso. After several years, the gods allow Odysseus to continue to Ithaca.

In the final chapters of the saga, Odysseus arrives home and slaughters all of the men who have been wooing his faithful wife Penelope during his absence. The goddess Athena arranges peace between the enraged townspeople and Odysseus. (See also FILMS, *ULYSSES*; *MUSICAL THEATER, HOME SWEET HOMER*; TELEVISION, *ODYSSEY, THE.*

Old Fortunatus A comic play by Thomas Dekker (1570?–1632?) published in 1600, *Old Fortunatus* is a retelling of a 1509 German tale and a 1553 play by Hans Sachs (1494–1576). A beggar, Fortunatus, is granted a favor from Fortune, and he chooses a magic purse of endless wealth. He also acquires the Soldan of Turkey's magical hat which will transport him anywhere in the world. Fortunatus does not, however, wish for good health, and Fortune ends his life. Andelocia, Fortunatus's son, also chooses to use the purse, and he, too, dies young.

Old Wives' Tale, The Written by George Peele (1556–1596) and published in 1595, *The Old Wives' Tale* was the first English play to satirize the romantic drama then in vogue. Sacrapant, a sorcerer, has BEWITCHed and imprisoned Delia. Her two brothers set out to rescue her but are also enchanted by Sacrapant. All three are saved by Eumenides, a knight, assisted by the ghost of Jack, whose funeral had been paid for by Eumenides. (See ROMANCE LITERATURE).

Once and Future King, The Four books (published in one volume) based on the legends of King ARTHUR and MERLIN, *The Once and Future King* was written by T(erence) H(anbury) White (1906–1964).

The Sword in the Stone, published separately in 1937, is in itself a classic and was included as the first book of the tetralogy. The book tells the story of Arthur's boyhood up to the time of his coronation. Merlin, as his tutor, advisor and friend, plays a major role throughout the saga.

The Witch in the Wood was published in 1940, and it was renamed *The Queen of Air and Darkness* when it became the second part of *The Once and Future King*. The book centers around Arthur's trials with Morgause, the queen of Orkney and wife of King Lot.

The Ill-Made Knight, published in 1941, had Sir Launcelot as its protagonist. It was later included as the third volume of the tetralogy.

The consummation of Launcelot's love affair with Queen Guenever and its aftermath, ending on the eve of Arthur's final battle with Mordred, does not occur until the fourth book. *The Candle in the Wind* was started in October 1939 and completed in 1941. Its narrative form follows the outline of a play White had already sketched on the subject.

Having decided that the true theme of MALORY's *Le MORTE D'ARTHUR* was the futility of war, White revised his first three Arthurian works, added *The Candle in the Wind* and his newly completed *The BOOK OF MERLYN* and sent them to his publisher in November 1941.

White insisted that *The Once and Future King* be printed as a single five-book volume, but because of a paper shortage during wartime England and other problems in negotiation the novel was not published until 1958. Even then, *The Once and Future King* appeared as a tetralogy, without *The Book of Merlyn*, which was published posthumously as a separate volume for the first time in 1977.

T.H. White was born in India, where his father was a member of the Indian Civil Service. His early education was at Cheltenham College, and he was a well-respected student at the University of Cambridge. When White was stricken with tuberculous in his second year, his dons provided the expenses for a sabbatical in Italy, during which White wrote his first novel, *They Winter Abroad*. White returned to Cambridge and graduated with First Class with Distinction honors. In 1932, with Cambridge's recommendation, White was made head of the English Department at Stowe School, where he stayed until the midsummer of 1936.

His career as an author soon began in earnest. Almost immediately, he published a popular diary of hunting and fishing stories under the title *England Have My Bones*, plus several detective stories and poetry. White's first major work was *The Sword in the Stone*. White's other books include *Masham's Repose* (1947), *The Goshawk* (1951) and *The Book of Beasts* (a 1954 translation from a 12th-century Latin work), plus an unfinished manuscript dating from 1938 entitled *Grief for the Grey Goose*, but none achieved the lasting popularity of his Arthurian masterpieces.

oneiromancy See CHALADEANS; DIVINATION.

opera For centuries, grand operas (most of them based on earlier stories and legends) have made use of wizard and sorcerer characters. The elements of magic, mysticism, SPELLS and enchantment have also pervaded the genre. The stories of some of the most enduring operas with occult themes or characters follow.

Alceste Composed in three acts by Christoph Willibald Gluck to an Italian libretto by Raniero da Calzabigi, *Alceste* (or *Alcestis*) is based on a tragic Greek myth originally dramatized by Euripides. The opera's first performance was in Vienna on December 26, 1767. Gluck revised his score and libretto (which was also translated into French) for its Paris premiere on April 23, 1776. Although the production was unsuccessful at the time, it is this version that is usually performed today.

Admetus, the king of Thessaly, is on his deathbed, and the city's populace pray to Apollo for his divine intervention. The ORACLE of Apollo, through her high priest, proclaims that Admetus can be cured, but the god requires someone else's life in exchange. Unable to conceive of existence without her husband, Queen Alcestis, alone with her thoughts, decides to trade her own life for his.

Alcestis descends to the Underworld. Hercules arrives in Thessaly. He vows to retrieve the queen, and Admestus follows. Apollo, impressed with the love between husband and wife as well as Hercules's unmatched friendship and devotion, returns the king and queen to life on earth and bestows immortality on Hercules.

Amahl and the Night Visitors Composed in one act with an English libretto by Gian Carlo Menotti (see *The Medium*, below), *Amahl and the Night Visitors* was the first opera commissioned by and written expressly for TELEVISION production. The opera first appeared live on NBC (from New York City) on Christmas Eve 1951, and the first New York stage production followed soon after on April 27, 1952.

The MAGI, Kaspar, Melchior and Balthazar, enroute to Bethlehem, stop at the home of a poor woman and her crippled son, Amahl, and ask for a night's lodging. They explain that they are on their way to see "the child" (who, of course, is JESUS).

Amahl and the neighbors entertain the kings and then all fall fast asleep. Tempted, Amahl's mother steals some of gold that the kings have brought for the newborn.

When the theft is discovered, Melchior comforts her by saying that the Christ child doesn't need the gold. "On love alone, he will build his kingdom." The mother returns the gold, and, impulsively, the boy offers his crutch, holding it at arm's length. "He walks!" they proclaim. A miracle healing has occurred, a heavenly reward for the boy's sacrifice, motherly devotion and selflessness. Amahl joins the kings on their caravan to Bethlehem to present his gift personally.

Bastien und Bastienne Composed in one act by Wolfgang Amadeus Mozart (at the age of 12) to a German libretto by F.W. Weiskern et al., *Bastien und Bastienne* is based on Marie-Justine-Benoîte and Charles Simon Favart's satire of Jean-Jacques Rousseau's musical play *Le Devin du village*. The light opera was commissioned by Dr. Anton Mesmer (who "invented" mesmerism, or hypnosis, to treat disease) for an autumn garden party, and it premiered in Vienna, most likely in September 1768. Despite Mozart's later acclaim and fame, the opera was not performed again for almost a century.

Bastienne, a shepherdess, is in love with Bastien, a shepherd. Bastienne complains to Colas, a magician, that she thinks her beloved is fond of another girl instead of her. Colas suggests that Bastienne pretend both to be unconcerned and to court other beaus. While Bastienne hides, Colas tells Bastien of the shepherdess's "true feelings"; the shepherd, proclaiming his love for Bastienne only, asks for the magician's help in restoring his sweetheart's affection. Colas reads aloud from his GRIMOIRE, chanting ludicrous INCANTATIONs full of gibberish words such as *diggi-daggi* and *schurry-murry*. The lovers meet, have a silly argument and then make up. The three characters sing a final aria celebrating the weather and Colas's wizardry.

Belle et la Bête, La See BEAUTY AND THE BEAST.

Carmen One of the most popular operas ever written, *Carmen* is the tragic tale of a young and flirtatious GYPSY girl. Its primary interest to the occultist is a fortune-telling scene in the third act. Also, *carmen*, Latin for "song," is the root of the modern English word CHARM.

Composed in four acts by Georges Bizet with a French libretto by Henri Meilhac and Ludovic Halévy, *Carmen* is based on a novel by Prosper Mérimée. Its first performance was at the Opéra Comique in Paris on March 3, 1875.

Carmen is set in Seville, Spain around 1820. Throughout the first two acts of the opera, Carmen plays Corporal Don José against the toreador Escamillo.

Act Three opens in a smuggler's mountain hideaway. Two gypsies, Frasquita and Mercédès, begin to tell their own fortunes with cards. One foresees a fiery lover, a vagabond prince; the other will marry a rich, elderly man who will die and leave her a fortune. Carmen joins in the reading and turns over the death card, the ace of spades. She solemnly accepts the prophetic prediction of the cards, saying "It is useless to try to escape one's fate." Indeed, in the final scene, set outside the bullring, Carmen is fatally stabbed by the jealous Don José.

Carmen served as the inspiration for a 1949 BALLET choreographed by Roland Petit.

Carmen Jones, a musical based on *Carmen*, appeared on Broadway (see MUSICAL THEATER), opening at the Broadway Theater on December 2, 1943, and running for 502 performances. With a libretto featuring all African-American characters and new lyrics (to Bizet's music) by Oscar Hammerstein II, the Billy Rose production of *Carmen Jones* updated the opera to World War II. A 1954, 20th Century Fox FILM version of *Carmen Jones* followed.

Cenerentola, La See CINDERELLA.

Consul, The Gian-Carlo Menotti composed his first full-length opera, *The Consul*, to his own English libretto. It premiered in Philadelphia on March 1, 1950, and opened on Broadway at the Barrymore Theatre 14 days later. *The Consul* won the Pulitzer Prize for musical composition as well as the New York Drama Critics Circle award and the Donaldson Award for best musical play of 1950.

Set in Europe sometime after World War II, *The Consul* tells a story of Magda, the wife of John Sorel, who does undercover antigovernment work for an unnamed association. Most of the opera is taken up with Magda's attempts to meet with the consul to receive an visa to exit the country. At the end of the opera, John is captured and Magda commits suicide by gas.

Nika Magadoff, a conjuror, is seen in the first two acts. In the second scene of Act One, he entertains the consul's secretary with magic tricks, hoping that it will prompt her to expedite his visa application. His efforts, however, are in vain. Magadoff reappears in the second scene of Act Two, back in the outer office of the consul. This time, he hypnotizes all of the people who are waiting. They break into dance, so the secretary makes him bring them out of the trance.

Coq d'or, Le Originally titled *Zolotoy Pyetushok* in Russian, *Le Coq d'or* (*The Golden Cockerel*) was composed in three acts, with a prologue and epilogue, by Nikolay Andreyevich Rimsky-Korsakov. The Russian libretto was by Vladimir Ivanovich Byelsky, based on a fairy tale written by Aleksandr Sergeyevich Pushkin, as told to the poet by his nurse. The opera's first performance was in Moscow, October 7, 1909.

In the Prologue, the Astrologer, accompanied by the music of a xylophone, promises to conjure up a fairy tale for the audience.

In Act One, King Dodon, his sons Guidon and Afron and General Polkan worry about the prospect of war and the defense of the country. The astrologer appears and offers the king a golden cockerel that will only crow when the kingdom is in danger of attack. The king gladly receives the enchanted creature and offers the astrologer anything he wishes in exchange for it. The astrologer demurs, postponing payment and disappears. Two crows of the cock send the king and his army to war.

As Act Two opens, it is clear that the king has lost the most recent battle. The queen of Shemakha, a BEWITCHing beauty, seduces the king into taking her as his consort and sharing his kingdom. In the final act, King Dodon arrives back home with his new bride. The astrologer materializes and asks for his payment for the cockerel: he wants the queen for himself. The king offers him half the kingdom instead, but astrologer is adamant. Angered, Dodon kills the astrologer with his sword.

Suddenly, the golden cock swoops down and pecks the king to death. Everything goes black. The queen's cackling laugh is heard. When the lights return, the queen and the astrologer have vanished.

In an Epilogue, the astrologer informs the audience that only he and the queen were real. All of the other characters were imaginary.

Damnation of Faust, The Subtitled "Dramatic Legend (in Four Parts), op. 24," *The Damnation of Faust* (*La Damnation Le Faust*) by Hector Berlioz is based in general on the FAUST legend and specifically on Goethe's *Faust*.

Berlioz became obsessed with Gérard de Nerval's French translation of the poem at an early age. In 1827, he wrote *Eight Scenes from Faust*, based on parts of the poem which indicated musicalization: the Easter hymn, the Peasant's Chorus, the Sylphs' Chorus, the "Song of the Rat," two melodies for Marguerite and two songs for Mephistopheles (the "Song of the Flea" and his "Serenade"). Berlioz paid to have the numbers published at his own expense, numbering them "Opus 1." Impetuously, he sent a copy to Goethe. He received word from a friend that Goethe had received the manuscript, but Berlioz never received a direct reply from the poet himself.

The Damnation of Faust was not Berlioz's only work based on a supernatural theme. Often inspired by SHAKESPEARE, Berlioz composed one of his most brilliant works, *Fantasie sur la Tempête*, based on *The TEMPEST*, in 1830. Two years later, the music was incorporated into his score for *Lélio ou le Retour à la Vie*.

Almost 20 years passed before the composer began work on an full orchestral and choral version of *The Damnation of Faust*. Starting with the already completed eight pieces, Berlioz added music to his own text and scenes fashioned from an Almire Gandonnière translation of Goethe. He dedicated the completed score to Franz Liszt, who later reciprocated by dedicating his 1854 *Faust Symphony* to Berlioz.

On December 6, 1846, *The Damnation of Faust* premiered at the Opéra Comique in Paris. Received with mixed reviews, only two more performances of sections of *The Damnation of Faust* were given in Paris during Berlioz's lifetime. It wasn't until February 1877 that the work was once again performed complete. The first full production of *The Damnation of Faust* staged as an opera took place in Monte Carlo on February 18, 1893.

In Part One, a melancholy Faust is seen alone in the fields of Hungary at sunrise. Part Two opens with Faust in his den in northern Germany, about to drink poison, but he pauses when he hear a nearby choir singing an Easter hymn. Suddenly, Mephistopheles appears in the room and offers Faust anything his heart desires. Faust asks to, first, behold some of the devil's wonders.

They are instantly transported to Auerbach's Cellar in Leipzig, where Brander, one of a chorus of revelers, is singing a comic tale about a rat. Mephistopheles tops the song with one of his own, the story of a royal flea, and produces endless streams of beer. Faust, bored with the proceedings, asks for quiet. They fly on Faust's cloak to the woods on the banks of the River Elbe. Mephistopheles calls up the "SPIRITs of earth and air" to sing Faust to sleep. They place the image of the beautiful virgin Margarita into Faust's dreams. Faust awakens. He demands to meet Margarita, and Mephistopheles agrees to take him to her.

Part Three begins with Faust and his infernal companion in Marguerite's bedroom. The Devil departs, but Faust hides behind a curtain and overhears the girl declaring that, in a dream, she has seen her future lover. Marguerite discovers Faust and recognizes him as the man of her dreams. Their love duet awakens the entire household, so Faust flees.

The final section of *The Damnation of Faust*, Mephistopheles appears to Faust in the forest and tells him that Marguerite is in prison, charged with murder. Faust had given Marguerite a sleeping potion (which he acquired from Mephistopheles) to administer to her mother so that the lovers could meet. A mild poison, it eventually killed the old woman.

Faust insists that Marguerite be saved. Mephistopheles agrees to do so; but, in exchange, he requires something from Faust:

> Nothing but a signature / On this old parchment.
> I can save Marguerite on the instant
> If you swear and sign a pledge /
> To serve me tomorrow.

Faust agrees to the pact and signs. Mephistopheles immediately sweeps up Faust; on they ride to the Abyss on two black steeds, Vortex and Giaour. Once in the Abyss, the Prince of Darkness confirms with Mephistopheles that Faust has freely signed. As a jubilant chorus of demons breaks into song and dance, the scene moves heavenward to show that Mephistopheles has fulfilled his part of the bargain with Faust. Marguerite, repentant, is welcomed by the Seraphim into Paradise.

Dido and Aeneas Composed in three acts by Henry Purcell to an English libretto by Nahum Tate based on Book IV of Virgil's *Aeneid*, *Dido and Aeneas* premiered in Chelsea (London) in 1689. The opera was specifically written for a girls' school run by Josias Priest, a dance master.

In Act One, Queen Dido of Carthage, urged on by Belinda, her lady-in-waiting, falls in love with Aeneas, a hero from the Trojan War who has recently arrived on her country's shore. Meanwhile, a sorceress, two witches and their assistants plot and conjure a tempest to separate the lovers.

In the second act, the storm interrupts a royal hunt, and the queen with her entourage flee indoors. Aeneas is held behind by a SPIRIT who has assumed the shape of Mercury, messenger of the gods (see HERMES). The phantom tells Aeneas he must leave Carthage immediately for he is destined to found a great city (Rome). Reluctantly, Aeneas agrees to go, and the witches celebrate their victory.

In the final act, Aeneas and his crew are preparing their boat. The sorceress and the witches are still triumphantly rejoicing. Queen Dido arrives. Aeneas offers to disregard the gods and stay on in Carthage, but the queen insists that he must go.

Don Carlos Originally composed in five acts by Giuseppe Verdi to a French libretto by François Joseph Méry and Camille du Locle based on a play by Johann Christoph Friedrich von Schiller, *Don Carlos* had is premiere in Paris on March 11, 1867. The opera was revised in 1882 into four acts with an Italian libretto by Antonio Ghislanzoni. Today, the five-act version of *Don Carlos* is performed equally as or more often than the four-act version, and it is usually sung in Italian.

The story is set in Madrid, Spain, in 1559 and focuses, in part, on the power of the INQUISITION. In fact, Act Three ends with the fire being lit beneath heretics tied to the stake. As the crowd celebrates the auto-da-fe, a heavenly voice sings pardon for the martyrs.

Don Carlos, grandson of Charles V, the former emperor of the Holy Roman Empire, is in love with Elizabeth of Valois. Although the woman reciprocates his love, she has been married, for political reasons, to Don Carlos's father, King Philip II.

Following an argument with his son, Philip feels threatened and bargains with the Grand Inquisitor, a somber, severe and blind old man, to arrest Don Carlos for insolence and insurrection. The Inquisition finally assents.

In the final act, Don Carlos meets Elizabeth. Again, they exchange their vows of love, but Don Carlos must leave for Flanders, where he has promised to lead the rebellion against the crown. King Philip and the Grand Inquisitor unexpectedly arrive, see the couple and pronounce a death sentence upon them. Suddenly, a ghost of a priest appears near the sepulcher of Charles V and pulls Don Carlos with him back into the tomb.

Don Giovanni Composed in two acts by Wolfgang Amadeus Mozart with an Italian libretto by Lorenzo Da Ponte, *Don Giovanni* (*Don Juan*) is based in part on the opera *The Stone Guest* (Giuseppe Gazzaniga, composer; Giovanni Bertati, libretto). Its first performance was in Prague on October 29, 1787.

Although no wizard or sorcerer character appears in this tale of the scandalous libertine and womanizer, a diabolic SPIRIT is central to the denouement of the piece. In the third scene of the second act, set in a cemetery at two o'clock in the morning, Don Giovanni and Leporello, his servant, are laughing about the Don's conquests and infidelities. Suddenly, the statue in front of which they are standing intones, "Before dawn your joking will end." Leporello, frightened by the ghostly voice, reads the inscription on the tombstone: "Here I await vengeance on the impious man who killed me." It is the grave of the Commendatore of Seville, whom Don Giovanni had killed in a duel. Unshaken, Don Giovanni twice invites the statue to dinner; it accepts both times, first by nodding its head and then by verbally affirming "Yes."

In the final scene of the opera (Act Two, Scene Five), Don Giovanni and his friends are having a party. There is a knock at the door. The statue of stone, somehow animated, has arrived for dinner. The phantom gives Don Giovanni a chance to repent his wicked ways, but the boastful wanton refuses. The statue grabs Don Giovanni's arm, and the entire chateau along with its inhabitants vanish in infernal hellfire.

Elixir of Love, The Composed in two acts by Gaetano Donizetti to an Italian libretto by Felice Romani, *The Elixir of Love (L'Elisir d'amore)* tells a story of herbal magic in which a fraudulent doctor offers a love potion for sale. Set in 19th-century Italy, the opera had its premiere in Milan on May 12, 1832.

Adina, a young well-to-do lady, reads to her friends the story of Tristan and Isolde, how drinking a magic ELIXIR brought the two lovers together. Nemorino, a peasant in love with Adina, wishes that he, too, had such a concoction. He approaches Doctor Dulcamara, who claims that his elixir of love, when drunk, will make one irresistible within 24 hours. Nemorino pays extra to receive the famous love potion of Isolde, but the crafty Doctor Dulcamara gives him the same Bordeaux wine that he has dispensed to his other customers. Nemorino drinks heavily and, Adina, appalled by his intoxicated state, agrees to marry a rival suitor.

After drinking more elixir, Nemorino finds his confidence, and Adina *now* becomes interested in *him*. Doctor Dulcamara offers her some of his elixir, but she tells him that she has the best elixir of all: feminine cunning.

Adina confesses to Nemorino that she loves him. More happy news arrives: Nemorino is rich, having received an inheritance from a distant uncle. The lovers unite, and when Doctor Dulcamara proclaims that it was his philtre that brought the couple together, all of the townspeople line up to buy more of the doctor's elixir of love.

Faust Composed in four acts by Charles François Gounod to a French libretto by Jules Barbier and Michel Carré, the opera is based on Part I of Goethe's poetic FAUST. Set in 16th-century Wittenberg and Leipzig, Germany, as well as in the Harz Mountains, Gounod's *Faust* was first performed at the Théâtre Lyrique in Paris on March 19, 1859.

After a musical prelude by the orchestra, Act One opens to Faust's study in Wittenberg. The old and weary doctor, frustrated with life, is about to poison himself. Faust pleads to the Devil for release from his woes, and Mephistopheles enters. The demon offers Faust youth and tempts him with a vision of Marguerite. Faust signs a pact, drinks an ELIXIR of youth and flies away with the Devil.

The pair alight at a fair in Leipzig. The student Wagner sings about a rat, and Mephistopheles counters with his own song, "The Calf of Gold." The Devil magically produces wine for the crowd and offers a toast to the beautiful Marguerite. Valentine, her brother, challenges the stranger to a duel for his effrontery. Mephistopheles snaps Valentine's sword by merely gesturing at it, and the townsfolk suddenly discern the true identity of the interloper. Terrified, they form the Sign of the Cross with their swords as they flee, and Mephistopheles falls to the ground in agony. Faust arrives, anxious to meet Marguerite. The Devil conjures her up, but despite a bewitching waltz, Marguerite refuses to dance with the entranced Faust.

In Act Two, Faust climbs Marguerite's balcony and falls into her welcoming arms as Mephistopheles sings of his success.

Originally, the first scene of the third act, cut from most modern productions, showed Marguerite at her spinning wheel lamenting her desertion by Faust. The second scene is in the church, where Marguerite has gone to pray for heavenly pardon for her carnal sin. In a final scene, Valentine and his fellow soldiers return from war and, hearing of his sister's downfall, challenges Faust to a duel. With mystical aid from Mephistopheles, Faust mortally wounds Valentine. With his last breath, Valentine CURSES his sister.

The first scene of the final act, a BALLET, is also usually deleted in modern productions. The scene takes place at a SABBAT on the Brocken in Harz Mountain on Walpurgis Night. (Legend has it that the Devil holds court and revelry with witches, ghosts, demons and SPIRITS on the eve of May 1, St. Walpurgis Day, named after an 8th-century English canonized nun.) (See FILMS, FANTASIA.) Mephistopheles conjures up beauties out of antiquity for Faust's pleasure, including Lais of Sicily and Cleopatra. Suddenly, Faust sees a vision of Marguerite with a bloodline around her neck, and the scholar commands the Devil to take him to her.

Marguerite is in prison, nearly insane and about to be executed for killing her own baby! Mephistopheles and Faust appear in her cell. While the Devil seeks horses for their escape, Faust and Marguerite reminisce and swear their love. When the demon returns, Marguerite at last recognizes him and falls to her knees in prayer. Seeking salvation, she steadfastly refuses to leave with the pair. Mephistopheles damns her, but a heavenly choir sings her redemption as the curtain falls.

Der Freischütz Composed in three acts by Carl Maria von Weber to a German libretto by Johann Friedrich Kind based on a tale by Johann August Apel, *Der Freischütz (The Free-Shooter)*, premiered in Berlin on June 18, 1821.

In mid-1600s Bohemia, a shooting match is set before Prince Ottokar. The champion will win the hand of Agathe, the daughter of Cuno, the head forester.

Cuno reminds everyone of the contest's origin. Cuno's great-great-grandfather had saved a man's life with an incredible shot, and legend grew that he had used a free or magic bullet, that is, one that could not miss its mark because it had been enchanted by the Devil. (According to the legend, the Devil gives the shooter seven bullets. The first six hit wherever the marksman aims; the seventh is controlled by the Devil.) To prove their competence, each year the foresters must forswear infernal assistance during a shooting match before their prince.

Caspar, who has already sold his soul to the Devil, is revealed in the demonic Wolf's Glen. He conjures up Samiel and begs for three more years of life in exchange for providing Max's soul. The new pact is formed: Caspar is to convince Max to accept seven free bullets, but Samiel may direct the seventh toward Agathe if he wishes.

Max accepts the bargain. Caspar boils a magic potion, and the bullets are cast. The pair call upon Samiel. When the Devil appears, Max takes his hand (actually a dead tree branch). The contract has been signed.

The contest begins in Act Three. The prince orders Max to fire at a white dove. Max aims, but Agathe, who has dreamed that she was shot while in the guise of a dove, begs him not to fire. The gun goes off, and Agathe drops, but Caspar has also fallen. Realizing he has been tricked by the demon, Caspar curses Samiel and then dies.

Agathe has only fainted. Max confesses his sin, and the prince prepares to send him into exile. Suddenly, a wizened hermit appears and suggests that Max be given a year to prove his righteousness and be allowed to marry Agathe at the end of that time. To the delight of all, he also recommends that the annual shooting matches be forever discontinued; the Prince agrees.

Hänsel und Gretel   Composed in three acts by Engelbert Humperdinck to a German libretto by his sister Adelheid Wette, based on the popular fairy tale by Jakob and Wilhelm Grimm (the BROTHERS GRIMM), *Hänsel und Gretel*, conducted by composer Richard Strauss, premiered in Weimar, Germany, on December 23, 1893.

Hänsel and Gretel's mother Gertrude sends them out to pick berries for dinner. Their father, Peter, a broommaker, returns home and is horrified to learn that the children may have wandered to Ilsenstein mountain. It is haunted, he claims, by a witch who flies on a BROOMSTICK and bakes boys and girls into gingerbread. The parents rush out to find their children.

Hänsel and Gretel become lost in the woods. The Little Sandman spreads his sleep dust over them, and 14 GUARDIAN ANGELs surround them in their sleep.

The Dew Man softly awakened the children, and they find themselves in front of a cottage decorated with life-size children made of gingerbread. As Hänsel eats a bit of gingerbread, an offstage voice sings, "Who's nibbling at my house?"

The wicked witch appears. She throws a lasso around Hänsel's neck, but he escapes. She invites the children into her house, but they decline. For her third attempt, she waves her magic WAND, made out of a piece of juniper wood, and intones, "Hocus-pocus Hexenschuss!" (See HEX; HOCUS POCUS.) The children are immediately frozen in place. Hänsel is placed in a large cage; as the witch fires up her oven and takes a ride on her broomstick, Gretel is forced to clean the cottage.

The witch decides to taste Hänsel to see if he is ready to bake into gingerbread. He sticks a twig rather than his finger out of the cage, and the witch concludes he is too bony. Gretel finds the magic wand and uses it to help her brother escape. Then, when the witch bends into the oven to show Gretel how to check its readiness, the girl pushes the wicked enchantress inside. The oven and house explode, ending the witch's magic, and all the bewitched gingerbread children start to come back to life. With a wave of the wand by Hänsel, the children are completed restored. As Peter and Gertrude finally arrive, the children pull the witch, baked into a giant gingerbread cake, from the shattered oven.

Love for Three Oranges, The   Composed in Russian in four acts with a prologue as *Lyubov k tryom apelsinam* by Sergei Prokofiev to his own libretto, *The Love for Three Oranges* was based on an 18th-century comic play by Carlo Gozzi and an even earlier story. The opera was commissioned in 1919 by Cleofonte Campanini, musical director and conductor of the Chicago Opera Company; Prokofiev himself conducted its debut (with a French libretto) in Chicago on December 30, 1921.

The critics were especially unkind, and the opera was not produced again in the United States until 1949—and then only after changes in the libretto by Theodore Komisarjevsky and Vladimir Rosing and an English translation by Victor Seroff.

The son of the King of Clubs is unable to laugh. The monarch worries aloud about who will inherit the throne: he feels that there is hope for his son yet if the boy can be made to laugh.

The next scene introduces the forces for good and evil, of WHITE MAGIC and BLACK MAGIC. Fata Morgana, an evil enchantress, appears in a flash of lightning. She plays three rounds of cards with Celio, a kind and pure wizard. Fata Morgana wins all three matches to the delight of a choir of demons.

At a festival, the jester sees Fata Morgana and tries to eject her. During the struggle, the witch is flipped over in a somersault, and the prince laughs.

Embarrassed, the witch lays a CURSE on the prince: he will fall in love with three oranges and will follow them throughout the world. The young man informs his father that he must go in search of the fruit; Farfarello, a demon, uses a blacksmith's bellows to blow the prince and Truffaldino on their way.

In the third act, the prince and the jester are near the palace of Creonte, the witch who possesses the oranges. Celio is unable to break the SPELL and stop Farfarello because of his loss of a card game with Fata Morgana. He does manage, however, to warn the travelers that the oranges are actually held by Creonte's cook, who is strong enough to kill them with a swipe of her copper ladle. He gives them a ribbon to take as a gift.

As the cook tries the ribbon on, the prince and the jester steal the oranges. While they cross a desert, the oranges grow to an enormous size. Hoping to quench his thirst, Truffaldino opens two of the oranges. A princess emerges from each one, but they both quickly die of thirst.

The prince cuts open the remaining orange to reveal Princess Ninetta, sister to the deceased girls, and they declare their love for each other.

Once Ninetta is alone, Fata Morgana appears. The witch stabs the princess in the head with a hat pin and transforms her into a rat (or, in some productions, a pigeon). Smeraldina, Morgana's attendant in blackface—a common theatrical device of the period to denote a demon—disguises herself to take the princess's place. The prince immediately realizes that Smeraldina is not the true princess and refuses to marry her, but the King of Clubs says he must fulfill his pledge.

The final act opens with an argument between Fata Morgana and Celio, ending with the sorceress being locked up in a box. The royal party arrives back in the palace, and they are surprised to see a gigantic rat on the king's throne. Celio, his magic rejuvenated, changes the creature back into the Princess Ninetta. Smeraldina is accused of treason along with Clarissa, the king's niece, and Leandro, her consort. Just as the conspirators are about to be led off to be hanged, Fata Morgana appears to rescue them. All four drop through a trapdoor, apparently escaping to hell. The opera ends happily as the king toasts the prince and princess.

Macbeth   Composed during the winter of 1846–1847 in four acts by Giuseppe Verdi to an Italian libretto by Francesco Maria Piave based on the play by William SHAKESPEARE, the opera tells the tragic tale of MACBETH, a general in the Scottish army who murders his king to assume power. Set in Scotland and England around A.D. 1040, the story is permeated with BLACK MAGIC and sorcery. Among the fiendish characters called for in the *dramatis personae* are "HECATE, the goddess of witchcraft," plus "witches, . . . aerial SPIRITS [and] apparitions."

Macbeth, Verdi's tenth and reportedly favorite opera, premiered at the Teatro della Pergola in Florence, Italy, on March 14, 1847. A revised version debuted at the Théâtre Lyrique in Paris on April 21, 1865.

The opera closely follows the Shakespearean text, including Macbeth's early encounter with the three weird sisters. Act Three begins in the witches' cave. They dance around their CAULDRON, chanting INCANTATIONs as they prepare a nefarious brew. In some productions, a ballet (first introduced for the 1865 Paris production) follows, featuring Hecate, who tells the witches how to complete Macbeth's downfall.

The king arrives and demands to know his future. They conjure up "unknown powers" to provide his fate: a disembodied head tells Macbeth to beware Macduff. A blood-soaked child promises that "none born of woman" can harm the king. Another child, this one wearing a crown and bearing a small tree branch foresees that Macbeth will reign "until / Great Birnam wood to high Dunsinane hill / Shall come against him." After this last set of predictions, the witches fade forever from Macbeth.

Macbeth's lust for power ends in tragedy for both him and his wife; before dying, he rues the day he listened to the three witches. He admits that by pursuing their prophecies, he brought about his own doom.

Masked Ball, A Composed as *Un Ballo in maschera* in three acts by Giuseppe Verdi to an Italian libretto by Antonio Somma, *A Masked Ball* is based on Augustin Eugène Scribe's script for Daniel Auber's *Gustave III ou Le bal masqué.* The opera premiered at the Apollo Theater in Rome on February 17, 1859.

Riccardo, the governor of Boston, is planning a masked ball. Among the invited guests is Amelia, whom he loves, but she is the wife of Renato, his best friend, secretary and confidant. A panel of judges requests that Riccardo exile a fortune-teller named Ulrica. To determine the extent of her crimes, if any, the governor decides to disguise himself as a sailor and visit the seer himself.

He discovers Ulrica concocting a philtre in a CAULDRON and chanting INCANTATIONs. Silvano, a sailor, asks the crone about a possible promotion. As she answers in the affirmative, Riccardo secretly slips money and papers for the promotion into the young man's pocket. The entire group is impressed with Ulrica's powers when Silvano discovers the items.

Amelia has a private session with the soothsayer, asking what she can do to end her love for Riccardo. The witch tells her that she must go alone in the dead of night and collect magic herbs that grow beneath the gallows outside the city walls. Riccardo overhears the remarks and secretly swears to meet Amelia there.

The crowd returns to the fortune-teller, and Riccardo, still dressed as the sailor, asks his fate. She gives him a dire prophecy: he will be murdered by the next man who shakes his hand. Suddenly, Renato bursts into the hut and greets his friend by warmly shaking his hand. Riccardo reveals that he

is actually the governor. Entertained and convinced of the absurdity of her predictions, he allows Ulrica to stay in the country and continue with her divination.

Although this is the last the audience sees of Ulrica, her revelations do come to fruition. Riccardo and Amelia meet at the gallows, swear their love but agree that it must never be consummated. Renato discovers that they had been together and, jealously assuming the worst, mortally wounds the governor. As he dies, Riccardo pardons Renato and gives orders to allow him to travel to England with Amelia.

Medium, The After a New York City debut on May 8, 1946, *The Medium* had a commercial run of 212 performances on Broadway at the Barrymore Theatre, beginning on May 1, 1947. The chamber opera, composed in two acts to his own English libretto by Gian Carlo Menotti, opened on a double-bill with another short, though unrelated operatic piece, the curtain-raiser *The Telephone.*

Madame Flora, or Baba for short (a role originated by Marie Powers) is a fraudulent medium. The somewhat shabby parlor in which she conducts her seances has a puppet booth in the corner (through which the SPIRITs appear).

During a seance, the medium is touched in the dark. Later she hears voices. The medium suspects her secret assistant Toby, but he swears he not been playing tricks on her.

Over the next several days, Madame Flora becomes convinced that her powers are real and that she is being haunted. The opera culminates in her insane shooting of the ghost—in actuality Toby, who had hidden himself behind a curtain.

Mefistofele Composed in four acts with a prologue and epilogue by Arrigo Boito to his own Italian libretto based on both Parts I *and* II of Johann Wolfgang von Goethe's FAUST. *Mefistofele* (*Mephistopheles*) premiered in Milan on March 5, 1868, and lasted six hours in performance. Boito spent seven years editing the libretto and another year to ready it for a new production.

In the Prologue, Mephistopheles claims that he can corrupt Johann FAUSTUS and cause his downfall. In Act One, Faust is followed home from an Easter Sunday festival in Frankfort am Main by a Gray Friar who, once in the old scholar's study, reveals himself to be Mephistopheles. Before long, Faust has signed his soul over to the Devil. He will serve the demon in death if he is shown perfect beauty in life.

The opening of Act Two takes place in Margherite's garden. Faust, now transformed into a young, handsome man, seduces the innocent girl even as Mephistopheles ravishes her mother Martha. The scene shifts to Brocken Peak in the Harz Mountains where Mephistopheles is wildly celebrating Walpurgis Night with his witches. A vision of Margherite, with a bloody throat and bound in chains, appears to Faust, but he is unable to escape the revelry of the BLACK MASS.

By the time they return, Margherite is mad and imprisoned, having poisoned her mother and drowned her bastard child. Mephistopheles and Faust offer to help her escape her execution, but she refuses. Suddenly, she recognizes Mephistopheles as the Devil. She utters a final prayer and dies. A heavenly chorus sings her salvation.

The last act transports Faust and the Devil back to ancient Greece where the scholar is wooed by Helen of Troy. Faust's search for beauty seems to be fulfilled. The Epilogue places Faust, again an old man, back in his study in medieval Germany. Mephistopheles has come to claim his soul, but Faust has repented. He realizes that true beauty can only be found in the glory of God. He dies, rescued from Mephistopheles's grasp by the angels.

Mignon Composed in three acts by Ambroise Thomas to a French libretto by Michel Carré and Jules Barbier based on Goethe's *Wilhelm Meister*, *Mignon* had its premiere in Paris on November 17, 1866.

Occult references serve as a background to the story of the love triangle between Wilhelm Meister (a student), Philine (an actress) and Mignon. The title character, living as a GYPSY, had actually been stolen in infancy by the nomads, a fact not revealed until the final scene of the opera. Also, an acting troupe, led by Philine as Titania, performs one of SHAKE-SPEARE's most supernatural-oriented plays, A MIDSUMMER NIGHT'S DREAM. In the end, Mignon is shown to be of noble birth, and she and Wilhelm Meister, having fallen in love, live together happily ever after.

Norma The opera *Norma* was composed in two acts with four scenes (although now usually seen in four acts) by Vincenzo Bellini to an Italian libretto by Felice Romani adapted from *Norma*, the French drama by Louis Alexandre Soumet. The story may be based on the life of Gaius Asinius Pollio (or *Pollione*, in French), a young poet and politician appointed proconsul to Gaul around 50 B.C. by Mark Antony. During his commission, Pollio did stay among the DRUIDS, but he returned to Rome, was made a consul a decade later and lived to the age of 81.

As the first act opens, Druid priests are assembled in a hallowed grove around the holy tree of their god Irminsul. The High Priest Oroveso prepares them for an imminent revolt against Roman domination. When the conflict is to begin, his daughter, Norma, the high priestess, will cut a sprig of sacred mistletoe as a sign.

Meanwhile, it is learned that Pollione, the Roman proconsul, is secretly the father of Norma's two children, but he is now in love with Adalgisa, a vestal virgin of the Druids.

Norma, back with the Druids, explains that they will not have to cause an uprising. Rome, she feels, will destroy itself through its own sins. In an INCANTATION to the moon, Norma sings of peace and her love for Pollione. Adalgisa approaches Norma and asks to be released from her vows so that she may follow Pollione back to Rome.

With war imminent, Pollione is discovered and captured among the vestal virgins; death is proscribed by the Druids for this transgression. Left alone with Pollione to interrogate him, Norma offers him his life if he will leave Gaul without Adalgisa.

Norma realizes that she has lost Pollione's love, so she reveals to the Druids that one of the priestesses has broken her vows of celibacy and must die: it is she! Her children are left to her father. As Norma ascends the funeral pyre, she is joined by Pollione, who finally realizes the depth and nobility of her love.

Rusalka Composed in three acts by Antonín Dvořák to a Czech libretto by Jaroslav Kvapil based primarily on the French story of Melusine (Undine) as adapted by La Motte-Fouqué (*nom de plume* of the German baron Friedrich Heinrich Karl) in his book *Undine*, *Rusalka* tells the story of a sea nymph's love for a human prince.

Rusalka (variously translated as "mermaid," "naiad" or "water nymph") follows in the long tradition of Undine tales, in which an underwater creature becomes mortal, often with catastrophic consequences. An example of the myth is "The Little Mermaid" by Hans Christian Andersen, which served as the basis for the contemporary Disney FILM of the same name.

Rusalka, Dvořák's eighth opera, premiered at the National Theater in Prague on March 31, 1901. Its debut in the United States took place in Chicago on March 10, 1935.

Act One opens at a lake by the cottage of the witch Ježibaba. Rusalka confesses to her father, the Watersprite, that she has fallen in love with a mortal. The mysterious man often visits her, jumping naked into the lake to be with her, but in her supernatural state, Rusalka cannot be touched. The Watersprite warns her that loving a human will cause her ruin, but also that if her mind is set, she should ask the witch for help.

Rusalka asks Ježibaba for a philter to allow her to walk on land, and the witch obliges. When the nymph, now transformed into a woman, asks for a potion that will give her a human soul, Ježibaba strikes a bargain: Rusalka must relinquish her naiad's veil, and on land, she will lose her ability to speak. Also, if the object of her affection abandons or betrays her, they both are doomed to die.

Rusalka agrees to the terms of the pact, and they begin to brew the magic ELIXIR in the witch's CAULDRON. While reciting ancient INCANTATION, Ježibaba adds such ingredient to the pot as dragon's blood, bile, a bird's heart and a tomcat. Rusalka

Carter Scott sings the role of the witch, Ježibaba, in the San Diego Opera's 1995 production of Dvořák's *Rusalka*. (Photo by Ken Howard. Courtesy of the San Diego Opera)

Petitioners were awed when the massive doors to the oracles' temples opened without assistance. Lighting the altar fires produced the effect through pneumatics. (From a manuscript by Hero of Alexandria)

drinks. The next morning, the prince appears by the lake, discovers Rusalka, is instantly enraptured and leads her back to his palace.

As Act Two opens, the prince, who wanders about the castle as though bewitched, has declared his intention to marry the mysterious, silent girl. Nevertheless, he has recently shown interest in a visiting foreign princess.

Standing by a pond outside the palace, Rusalka begs her father to help her return to her underwater home. When the prince finally rejects her, the Watersprite leaps from the water, claims his daughter and vanishes with her beneath the waves. Terrified, the prince pleads with the princess to save him from this unnatural phantom, but the princess, sensing that the prince will always be under Rusalka's SPELL, tells him to follow the SPIRIT to hell.

In the final act, Ježibaba offers Rusalka a cure to the CURSE and her heartbreak: she hands Rusalka a knife and demands the blood of her lover, but Rusalka throws the blade into the lake.

The gamekeeper and the kitchen boy arrive at the witch's hut to ask her to heal the prince. He seems to be mad or haunted, babbling only about his lost love, a water nymph. Ježibaba ignores their plea but wonders aloud whether the young boy, once fattened up, would make a good meal.

That night, the prince emerges from the forest and calls out over the water for Rusalka to come to him. The half-woman, half-nymph kisses him, and the prince dies.

Tristan und Isolde *Tristan und Isolde* was composed in three acts by Richard Wagner to his own libretto in German based on ancient legends. The opera, set in Britain during the time of King ARTHUR, debuted in Munich on June 10, 1865.

Isolde is an Irish princess and a witch's daughter; an enchantress, she is familiar with herbal cures, potions and poisons. She is being taken by ship and under duress to marry King Marke of Cornwall. The ship's captain, Tristan, is the king's nephew.

During battle, Tristan had killed Morold, Isolde's fiancé. Tristan was wounded, however, and, disguised, he was healed by the mystical cures of Isolde. Although she discovered his true identity, Isolde fell in love with Tristan.

On board the ship, she decides to die with Tristan rather than marry King Marke. She commands Brangaene, her servant, to prepare a cup of poison. Isolde offers Tristan the chalice, and they share a drink. Brangaene had filled the cup with a love potion instead of poison, however, and the pair are immediately overwhelmed with passion.

King Marke is informed of Isolde's unfaithfulness and his nephew's betrayal by Melot. Melot and Tristan duel, and Tristan, remorseful, allows himself to be struck by Melot's sword.

Wounded and feverish, Tristan is taken to his castle in Brittany. Isolde arrives too late to heal him, and Tristan dies in her arms. King Marke enters to see Isolde cradling Tristan. She sings of her never-ending love and then dies.

oracle The word *oracle* comes from the Latin word *oraculum*, derived from *ovave*, and technically means "to speak" or "to pray." *Oracle* can refer to either the person giving the psychic utterances, the enigmatic response itself, the deity consulted or the location where the prophetess was installed.

Over the years, the word has generically come to mean anyone whose words are considered wise, deep or unerring. A slang phrase has evolved from the oracle's practices of receiving monetary tokens and of remaining hidden out of sight: "to work the oracle" means to raise money secretly or to manipulate others into joining a plan of action.

In the time of the pharaohs, the land of Egypt was well known for its oracles. The most remarkable was located at Amphiarus, near Thebes. A person wishing to consult the oracle would sacrifice his most prized ram at the temple and then sleep on the hide of the slaughtered animal. In the morning, the priests would interpret the visitor's dream from the night before. After the completed prophecy, the caller was expected to drop a golden coin into the temple's holy spring.

To maintain power, the ancient oracular priests often used the methods of wizards and magicians to astonish and therefore influence their supplicants. One particularly awe-inspiring marvel was the massive temple doors opening by themselves. The secret technique is particularly intriguing and was revealed in a manuscript discourse on pneumatics by Hero of Alexandria: a fire built on the temple altar heated the air in a bladderlike bag hidden below. The bag was attached to weights and ropes which, by a series of pulleys, opened the temple doors as the concealed bag inflated.

The most famous and celebrated oracles in ancient times were located in Greece. The revered prophetesses, conduits to the gods, sat throughout the country at significant temples, each dedicated to a particular god or goddess. From far and wide, patrons would travel to these holy spots, seeking solutions to their current problems or entreating a glimpse into the future.

An oracle was a *prophet* in the truest sense of the word. The Greek word *prophetes* was a combination of the roots *pro* ("for") and *phemi* ("speak"). Therefore, the prophet (or prophetess) would be claiming literally to "speak for" a particular god.

Although there were dozens of oracles throughout the kingdoms, these were the most important seers:

Oracle of Apollo at DELPHI

Oracle of Apollo at Delos (where the priestess bathed and fasted in seclusion for three days before responding to an inquiry)

Oracle of Apollo at Claros (also seen as Clarus), near Colophon (where the priestess received her visions after drinking from a holy spring)

Oracle of Diana at COLCHIS

Oracles of Esculapius at Epidaurus and in Rome

Oracles of Hercules at Athens and at Gades

Oracle of Mars in Thrace

Oracle of Minerva in Mycenae

Oracle of Pan in Arcadia

Oracles of Venus at Paphos and at Aphaca

Oracle of Jupiter at Crete

Oracle of Jupiter at Dodona (the most important of Jupiter's seers, where the revelations emanated from a tree, variously identified as an oak or a beech)

Oracle of Jupiter at Ammon, probably in Libya (most fully described by the Roman poet Lucan, A.D. 39–65. Prophecies were given by the silent nodding statue of the god, carried by priests)

Oracle of Jupiter Triphonius in Boeotia (where, according to most scholars, the oracle was always male. The historian Pausanias states that the prophecies, which emanated from a cave either verbally or as a vision, began when Triphonius, a master architect, sank and disappeared into the ground on the site during an earthquake).

Oracle of the Holy Bottle, The   Mentioned in Rabelais's epic work *Pantagruel* (Books IV and V), the story of the

Ruins of the temple of the oracle of Apollo at Didyma (Turkey), one of the most important sites for prophecy in the Hellenistic world. The oracle spoke from an inner chamber, now destroyed, within the temple walls. Cult worship had originally grown around a sacred well, which was later enclosed within the temple courtyard.   (Photo by author)

Oracle of the Holy Bottle is a satirical look at the consultation of ORACLEs in the ancient world.

Early in the tale, Panurge and his companions consult a sibyl, a poet, a monk, a fool, a philosopher, a witch and a judge to see if Panurge will ever marry. They then travel to Bacbuc, "near Cathay in Upper Egypt" to consult the Oracle of the Holy Bottle.

The bottle itself sits in an alabaster fount. The temple priestess throws some secret item into the fount, and it begins to bubble furiously. Soon, a voice comes out of the bottle, saying "Drink." Rather than disobey the oracle, Panurge and his party obligingly consume vast quantities of Falernian wine until, full of drink, nonsensical but clairvoyant gibberish issues from their own lips.

Order of the Golden Dawn

Also seen as the Hermetic Order of the Golden Dawn, this occult society was founded in England in the mid-19th century. The order, at its strongest, had lodges in London, Edinburgh, Bradford and Weston-super-mare.

Among its most notable members were Algernon Blackwood, W.B. YEATS, Arthur Machen (the astronomer royal of Scotland) and Allan Bennett (who had abandoned Catholicism when he learned the secrets of childbirth). One of the order's early leaders was William Wynn Wescott, an expert on the KABALLAH, who headed the society as the "Visible Head" of the Order of the Golden Dawn.

In 1884, a member of the order unearthed a rare occult manuscript in a London bookstore. It soon become the order's most valuable holding, and it was translated into English by S.L. MacGregor MATHERS, who had succeeded Wescott.

Demonologist Aleister CROWLEY was the cause of many of the disputes among his fellow members. According to Crowley's biographer, John Symonds, Mathers dispatched a vampire to kill the satanist in an attempt to prevent his taking over the order. Crowley "smote her with her own current of evil," and in the battle all of Crowley's infernal bloodhounds died defending their master. In revenge, Crowley conjured up Beelzebub and 49 fellow demons to assault Mathers.

The original society came to an end shortly after World War II.

Orlando Furioso

Written by Ludovico Ariosto (1474–1533) and published in 40 cantos in 1516 and then in 46 cantos in 1532, *Orlando Furioso* was intended to be both a continuation of and sequel to ORLANDO INNAMORATO. It told the story of the mythic Rogero (also seen as Ruggiero) and the founding of his lineage, the house of Este. Both works are examples of ROMANCE LITERATURE and are permeated with enchantment, although *Orlando Furioso* contains far more mystic creatures and supernatural events.

As the poem begins, the Saracens, led by Agramant, king of Africa, are attempting to conquer Europe. With the assistance of Marsilio, the Moorish king of Spain, and the great soldiers Rodomont and Mandricardo, the Saracens have trapped the Christian knights, led by Charlemagne, in Paris. Angelica, made the ward of Namo in *Orlando Furioso*, flees Bavaria. Orlando, who is otherwise a true and faithful knight to Charlemagne, is obsessed in his love for Angelica and chases her rather than remain with the Paladin legion, which he heads.

On her flight, Angelica chances upon Medoro, a handsome Moorish boy who was wounded in battle. They fall in love and wed. Orlando catches up to her and, learning of her marriage, goes insane (i.e., becomes *Orlando furioso*). He runs naked, rampant through the woods, finally ending up at his camp. His sanity is returned by Astolfo, and Orlando, having ridded himself of his obsession for Angelica, personally kills Agramant in the climactic clash of the war.

Concurrent with Orlando's story is that of the poem's other major hero, Rogero. The son of a Saracen princess and a Christian knight, Rogero was raised in Africa and joins Agramant's battle against Charlemagne. There he meets and seeks the hand of Bradamante, a female warrior, who reciprocates his love. Rogero is beset by two evil sorceresses ALCINA and Morgana, and, though imprisoned, he is kept from harm by their sister, Logistilla, also an enchantress. He is finally freed from Alcina by the good witch Melissa. Rogero promptly rides the hippogriff (a mythical monster with the hindquarters of a horse, body of a lion and the head and talons of a griffin or eagle) to free Angelica, who has been captured by the legendary Orc.

First mentioned in *Orlando Innamorato*, Marfisa is another female soldier, fighting for the Moors; for a time, she is also in love with Rogero. Raised by an African wizard, Marfisa is crowned queen of India before leading her army to Albracca to help free Angelica. By the end of *Orlando Furioso*, Marfisa learns that her true parents were Christians. She converts to Christianity, becomes baptized and unites her forces with Charlemagne's army. In the process, she discovers that she is Rogero's sister.

Rogero also becomes a Catholic and joins Charlemagne. Bradamante's parents disapprove of her union with Rogero despite his religious and military conversion, so she announces, to her parent's satisfaction, that any man she marries has to be her equal in combat for an entire day. Only Rogero meets the challenge, and they are married.

Rinaldo's story also continues from *Orlando Innamorato*. In *Orlando Furioso*, among his other adventures, Rinaldo captures the magical golden helmet owned by Mambrino, a pagan king. (See DON QUIXOTE.)

Elsewhere in *Orlando Furioso*, Alcina imprisons Astolfo, a cultivated British knight and a suitor for Angelica in *Orlando Innamorato*. Astolfo is released by Logistilla, who gives him a magic horn (whose blast fills listeners with fright) and an enchanted book (which will answer any question posed to it). Borrowing Rogero's mythical beast, the hippogriff, Astolfo flies around the world. On his travels, he defeats the Harpies (hideous winged monsters out of Greek mythology, each having the head and trunk of a woman and the tail, legs and talons of a bird) who are pestering Prester John. On a visit to Paradise, Astolfo meets St. John, who carries him to the moon. There, they find everything that has ever been lost on Earth. Astolfo locates the lost sanity of Orlando and returns it to him.

The first complete translation of *Orlando Furioso* into English was by Sir J. Harrington in 1591. The narrative epic work had a large impact on Edmund Spenser (c. 1552–99) who, with *The FAERIE QUEENE*, hoped to "overgo" Ariosto and his masterpiece.

Orlando Innamorato Published in 1487, this narrative poem by Matteo Maria Boiardo (1441?–1494) tells the story of "Orlando in love" with Angelica, the daughter of Galafron, the king of Cathay. At the time of Boiardo's death the poem was incomplete, but it was finished by Francesco Berni (1496 or 1497–1535) and first translated into English in 1823 by W.S. Rose. Common to epic literature of its time, the poem is full of supernatural SPELLS and events.

Angelica and her brother Argalia sneak into France to recruit Charlemagne's Christian Cathay knights. She is wooed by several of the men, including Astolfo, Rinaldo and Orlando (the Italian name for *Roland*, the protagonist of related French ROMANCE LITERATURE involving Charlemagne). During a fight, Argalia is killed, so Angelica quickly leaves the court for home.

On the way, she drinks from an enchanted fountain and instantly falls in love with Rinaldo. Rinaldo, drinking from a different BEWITCHed fountain immediately develops a loathing for Angelica and flees, chased by Angelica, to Cathay.

A subplot involves Malagigi who, having discovered Angelica's plot to capture Charlemagne's men, tries to kill her.

He is caught and dragged to Cathay, where he is jailed. Angelica learns of Malagigi's arcane knowledge of magic and agrees to free him if he makes his cousin, Rinaldo, fall in love with her.

Meanwhile, Agrican, king of Tartary, places Albracca, the capital city of Cathay, under siege and demands that Angelica, who has been pledged to him in marriage, be given up. Orlando appears, defeats Agrican, frees Angelica and carries her away to France where he is to join Charlemagne's forces against Agramant, king of the Moors.

The passions of Angelica and Rinaldo switch when they drink again from the enchanted waters: Angelica now abhors Rinaldo as much as he adores her. This leads to a battle between Rinaldo and Orlando. To prevent bloodshed between two of his best knights, Charlemagne stops the duel and sends Angelica to Bavaria to stay with Namo, the duke.

Orniscopy See AUGURY.

Oz See WIZARD OF OZ, THE.

Palmer, Annie (d. 1831) Known as the White Witch, Annie Palmer was the second mistress of Rose Hall Great House in Jamaica. She is alleged to have murdered three husbands and numerous lovers, including the plantation keeper, and she was notorious for torturing her slaves.

Rose Hall Plantation is located on 6,600 acres about nine miles east of Montego Bay, Jamaica. Palmer lived in the Great House, which was built in the late 1700s and, for its time, was one of the grandest in all of the West Indies. The Great House fell into disrepair, however, after Palmer's mysterious murder because her reputation for evil scared off prospective buyers and residents. It was also said that her ghost haunts the mansion.

Rose Hall Great House, restored in the mid-1900s by John and Michele Rollins, is now a major Jamaican tourist attraction. While it remains a splendid example of period architecture and furnishing, it is primarily the Annie Palmer tale that brings so many of the curious to Rose Hall.

The saga of Annie Palmer forms the basis for two novels, *The White Witch of Rose Hall* and *Jamaica White*.

Palmerin of England Like most ROMANCE LITERATURE of the 16th century, *Palmerin of England* (*Palmeirim de Inglaterra*) is a heroic tale filled with royal characters and supernatural creatures (in this case, the wicked sorcerer Eutropa). The work

A palmist in Bombay, India, sets up shop as a sidewalk psychic. (Photo by author)

was written in Portuguese, most probably by Francisco de Moraes (c.1500–72). It is the sixth in a series of eight books concerning Palmerin d'Oliva, emperor of Constantinople, and his extended family. Between 1581 and 1595, the works were translated into English from a French source by Anthony Munday (1560–1633) and were very popular with Elizabethan readers.

Flerida, the daughter of the emperor, marries Don Duardos, the son of Fadrique, the king of England. The prince is captured by the sorcerer Eutropa and is locked in the castle of Dramusiando, a giant.

The two infant sons of Flerida and Duardos, Palmerin of England and Floriano of the Desert, are abducted by a barbarian and turned into slaves. As young men, Palmerin is sent to Constantinople to attend on his distant cousin Polinarda, and Floriano becomes his mother's page.

Palmerin and Floriano join the continuing quest to find Don Duardos, still under Eutropa's power, and eventually Palmerin of England rescues the prince. The brothers discover their lineage, and Palmerin marries Polinarda, with whom he has fallen in love.

The remainder of the book tells of the Turkish battles against the Christians and Constantinople.

The Great House on the Rose Hall Plantation of Annie Palmer, the White Witch of Barbados. (Photo by author)

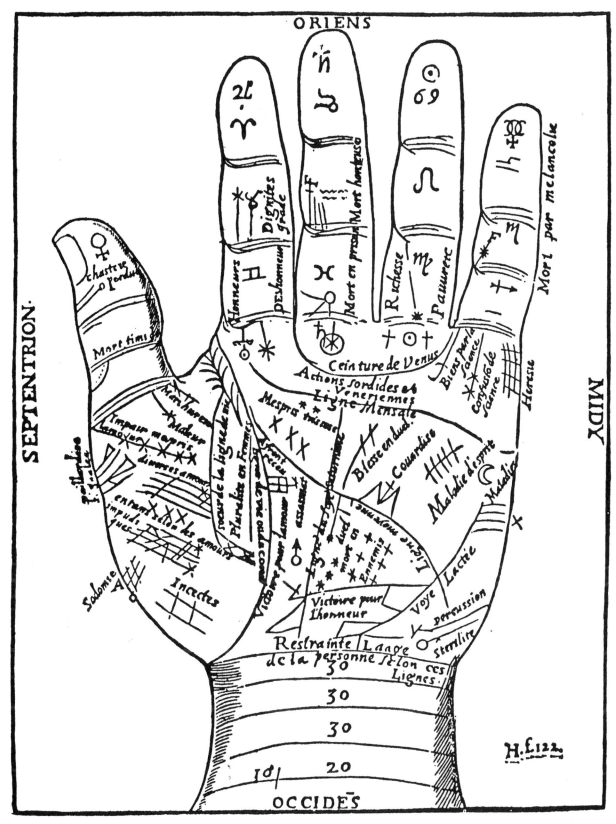

The principal lines and mounts on the hand, some identified with the zodiac and other astral influences, which are examined in palmistry. (Jean-Baptiste Belot, *Oeuvres*, 1640)

palmistry One of the oldest forms of DIVINATION, palmistry is technically known as chiromancy (from the Greek *cheiro*, meaning "hand"). Chiromancy also involves the reading of the length and shape of the entire hand, its fingers and nails. Most probably palmistry was devised in India, and the technique moved on to Asia and then into Mesopotamia.

Occultists claim that there is biblical sanction for palmistry, although the claim is certainly open to interpretation. Job 37:7 of the Old Testament of the Bible (King James Authorized Version) reads "He sealeth up the hand of every man; that all men may know his work," but the verse has been variously translated by cabalists as "God has placed signs in the hands of all the sons of men, that all the sons of men may know His work" and "God Who sets, as it were, a seal in the hand of all men that they may discover their works" (Maistre de Sacy).

More definitively, palmists quote Proverbs 3:16: "Length of the day *is* in her right hand; *and* in her left hand riches and honour" (KJV) and "Long life is in her right hand; in her left hand are riches and honor" (Revised Standard Version).

Palmistry reached Greece around 500 B.C. It was promoted by Aristotle, who taught it to Alexander the Great, and Hippocrates. In Rome, Augustus Caesar was a firm believer in its validity.

Although banned by the church in parts of Europe by A.D. 1000, the tradition continued, especially in GYPSY camps. The first printed book on the subject, *Die Kunst Ciromantia* (*The Chiromantic Art*) by Johan Hartlieb, appeared in 1475.

In the Middle Ages, laws were passed against palmistry in Paris (1427) and in London (1530, by King Henry VIII), but it continued to be practiced secretly by occultists.

By the 1800s, palmistry was once again practiced openly in Paris (Napoleon was an adherent), and in 1889 the English Chirological Society was founded. Noted mentalist Max Maven explains that the 20th-century acceptance of palmistry—the belief that a person's past, present and future is engraved on the palm—is no doubt tied to the 1885 discovery by England's Sir Francis Galton that each individual's fingerprints is unique.

Hundreds of book have been written on the art of palmistry and it is a complete study in itself. Basically, for a right-handed person, a reading using begins with the left hand, which is thought to show the innate characteristics of the individual. The right hand shows how those tendencies have developed and where they will lead.

The raised, fleshy mounds of the palm, called mounts, are examined first, followed by the three major lines crossing the palm: the Life Line (curving from between the index finger and thumb to the center of the wrist), the Head Line (a semihorizontal line crossing mid-palm) and the Heart Line (a semihorizontal line between the Head Line and the base of fingers). Eight other secondary lines are also scrutinized, as are other geometric patterns found on the palm, such as circles, stars, forks or triangles.

papacy, the In the beginning, magic and religion were one as people sought to understand the universe.

Their quest to comprehend the cosmos and to discover ways to control it led to the development of magic. They made supplications to the SPIRITS believed to exist within all things, both animate and inanimate.

It has been suggested that religion was born when humanity began to invoke deities and spectral creators that were separate from the world, yet capable of controlling it. Later, when prayers started to be diverted from angelic (or Good) powers and directed to demonic (or Evil) forces, the quest for the supernatural was further split, colloquially, into the practice of WHITE MAGIC and BLACK MAGIC.

The modern Western belief in true magic (i.e., the ability to use natural means and forces to effect change in the physical laws of the universe) can trace a direct line from the earliest EGYPTIAN MAGIC to many of today's Judeo-Christian traditions. Few of the world's great modern religions retain as many vestiges of magic ritual (including the use of symbolic paraphernalia) as Christianity, particularly the Catholic Church.

Occultists could not help but compare the rituals of the church and the rites of the cabalists: the priest wearing robe and mitre, carrying a staff, making prayers during procession to the altar; the wizard wearing a long-flowing gown and pointed hat, holding a WAND and uttering INCANTATIONS while drawing a MAGIC CIRCLE.

The Bible is full of tales of sorcery, WITCHCRAFT, DIVINATION and spirits. Purportedly, many popes of the early Catholic Church, many of whom were elected from the ranks of the laity for political and social stability, openly practiced (or, perhaps secretly performed) sorcery and/or NECROMANCY. Astrologers (see ASTROLOGY) informed at least two popes that they would ascend to the throne: Leo X (by seer Louis Gauric) and Marcellus II (who, as Mervel Cervin, received the prophecy from his own father and was elected 1555).

Among the most notorious practitioners of wizardry were Benedict XIII (who reigned as an antipope A.D. 1394–1417 and was said to have had "continuous traffic with spirits . . . [possessed] two demons . . . and [searched] everywhere for books on magic"; he was deposed by the Councils of Pisa and Constance in 1409 and 1413, respectively, but he refused to acknowledge them); Gregory VI; Gregory VII (who reigned as Pope for three years as A.D. 1081–84 even though he had been branded a sorcerer by the Synod of Bressanone on June 25, 1080); Gregory VIII; Hildebrand; Pope Honorius III (who reigned 1216–1227 and was credited with writing the magical manuscript *Le Grimoire*, or the *Black Book*); John XXIII (who reigned as antipope A.D. 1410–1415 and purportedly consulted Abramelin for assistance after being dethroned by the Council of Constance; see *The Book of the SACRED MAGIC OF ABRAMELIN THE MAGE*); Leo I (also known as Leo the Great, who reigned A.D. 440–461); Leo III (who reigned A.D. 795–816 and was the purported author of the GRIMOIRE *Enchiridion*); John XX and John XXII.

Three more "sorcerer popes" are of particular interest. The Holy Father most frequently accused of practicing witchcraft was Pope Sylvester II, but his mentor and teacher was Pope Benedict IX, born Theophylactus, also seen as Teofilatto. Benedict was elected as "The Boy Pope," most probably at the age of 12. It was popularly believed that Benedict IX worshipped demons and invoked them to help in his seduction of women.

Pope Sylvester II (né Gerbert) held office from A.D. 999 to 1003. He was noted for his great wisdom, but his enemies proclaimed that he could only have gained such knowledge and understanding—and been elected pope—through necromancy. He reputedly kept a demon mistress named Meridiana and, according to Williams of Malmesbury, received a bronze head able to speak prophecies in exchange for his soul. Legend has it that bronze head predicted that equivocal Sylvester would die in Jerusalem: fulfilling the prediction of the ORACLE, he did so—but at the church known as the Holy Cross of Jerusalem located in Rome. The pope was buried in the Lateran in the Vatican, and his tomb is said to "sweat" immediately before the death of a notable person. Just before the death of a pope, the tomb purportedly produces streams of water.

Pope Sixtus V reigned from A.D. 1585 to 1590. Born Felice Peretti in 1520, he became a Franciscan in 1533. He was named an inquisitor general in 1557 and in 1565 he investigated the alleged heresy of the archbishop of Toledo (a city in Spain known as a center for sorcery and necromancy). The Franciscan was made a bishop in 1566 and a cardinal in 1570. After Sixtus V was named pope, the vengeful and influential Spaniards claimed that he had made a pact with Satan in order to be elected. It was during Sixtus's time at the Vatican, and on his order, that the Spanish Armada sailed. Rumor had it that the destructive storms that helped the British during the battle had been created by English witches. Legend also says that, although Sixtus had agreed to sell his soul in exchange for a six-year reign, the Devil collected after only five because the Pope had ordered the execution of a boy one year too young to legally be put to death.

Many Catholic clerics were also infamously involved in magical interests:

Bocal, a French priest during the reign of Henry IV, was put to death for leading a BLACK MASS

Roger BACON, a friar who was a scientist, philosopher and occultist

Augustin Calmet (1672–1756), a French Benedictine monk and author of a book on demons and witchcraft

Joseph Glanvil (1636–80), an English minister, sorcerer and author of a 1668 book on witchcraft

Francesco Maria Guazzo, an 17th-century Italian priest and sorcerer, author of COMPENDIUM MALEFICARUM (*Witches' Manual*)

Guibourg, an 18th-century French abbé, executed for his involvement in Madame de Montespan's alledged demonic rites to enslave the heart of her lover, King Louis XIV

Cardinal RICHELIEU, a statesman as well as a sorcerer

Johannes TRITHEMIUS, an abbot of Spanheim, Germany.

Although witchcraft was named as a specific offense against the Catholic Church in the Canon Episcopi of A.D. 906, it was not addressed by the papacy until 1233. Almost every successive pope through the 17th century issued a bull condemning sorcery. In 1317, Pope John XXII extended his condemnation to ALCHEMY, proclaiming that its practitioners were evil because "they present a false metal for gold and silver." It was not until Pope Innocent VIII's bull of 1484, however, that the INQUISITION was, in effect, given free rein to ferret out witchcraft, magic, sorcery and heresy. Thus began two centuries of merciless persecution of almost certainly innocent crones, miscreants and enemies of the state for the supposedly practice of black magic.

Pope Innocent VIII (whose Papacy dated 1484–1492), was born Giovanni Battista Cibò (1432–1492) in Genoa. He was elected a bishop by the age of 35 and a cardinal within six years later. A brief 11 years later he was pope. He kept a mistress, who bore him two children: his son was wed into the Medici dynasty, and his daughter married the Vatican treasurer. As his life ebbed, he was kept alive by supping breast milk. He also received constant blood transfusions; the necessarily "pure" blood was taken from three young boys, who died in the process. (See also JESUS; SOLOMON.)

Paracelsus (1493–1541) Born Theophrastus Bombast von Hohenheim in Switzerland, Paracelsus began his career as a doctor and lecturer on medicine. Despite his scientific training, he was drawn to the occult fields of ASTROLOGY and DIVINATION. He owned a speculum, or magic mirror used for prophecy, and he wrote detailed directions on how to manufacture one.

Paracelsus was especially preoccupied with ALCHEMY. During his travels throughout the last 13 years of his life, Paracelsus performed incredible healings, perhaps effected by his own advancements in pharmacy. This, coupled with his unorthodox beliefs, led others to brand him as something between a wizard and a practitioner of simple FOLK MEDICINE, between a charlatan and a heretic.

Paracelsus was accused of having a demon FAMILIAR named Azoth, which he kept in a CRYSTAL BALL at the end of his sword hilt. Paracelsus was pictured holding the engraved sword in a famous Augustin Hirschvogal woodcut which appeared in the occultist's book *Astronomica et astrologica opuscula.* Azoth was actually the word Paracelsus used to denote

Paracelsus. (Paracelsus, *Astronomica et astrologica opuscula,* Cologne, 1567)

Vital Mercury, which he believed to be one of the most important substances in alchemy.

His alchemic convictions postulated a God (the Divine Artificer) who, at Creation, divided matter into the four Aristotelian ELEMENTS (Earth, Air, Fire and Water). These Elements were each occupied and controlled by specific supernatural SPIRITS: Earth (gnomes), Air (sylphs), Fire (salamanders) and Water (nymphs). To this notion, Paracelsus brought his own reliance on three principles: mercury, sulfur and salt.

In 1536 he published much of his occult thinking in his most famous work, *Die grosse Wundartzney*. Despite his radical views, Paracelsus was offered a medical/lecture position in Salzburg in 1541, but he died soon after. His thinking and writings, which include *Liber Azoth* and *Archidoxa*, continued to influence occultists, alchemists and mystic philosophers. His spiritual ideas were incorporated by Alexander Pope (1688–1744) into *The Rape of the Lock*. In 1835 Robert Browning (1812–89) published *Paracelsus*, a poem that metaphorically followed the life of the notorious doctor/alchemist as a means to examine the metaphysical world.

Parsis (Parsees)   See MAGI; ZOROASTER.

patter   A jargon term to mean the story or words used by a modern stage magician, the word *patter* has its origins in religious INCANTATIONS.

Until the middle of the 20th century, almost all Catholic services were conducted in Latin. Unfortunately, most people, especially the uneducated peasants in the Middle Ages, did not comprehend, nor could they speak, the language.

Thus, when worshipers were directed to recite the Pater Noster (the "Our Father" prayer) they usually had no choice but to quickly mumble out nonsensical syllables in the same rhythm as the priest's invocation. This form of incomprehensible speech came to be known as pattering, from which the abbreviated form *patter* received its current connotation.

pentacle   In occult literature, a pentacle is any consecrated seal or symbol used in magic. One or more pentacles were often engraved on an AMULET to ward off evil or placed on a TALISMAN to conjure SPIRITS (angelic or demonic). A pentacle was also frequently used to decorate magical objects, such as RINGS, or was included in the design of a MAGIC CIRCLE.

The most famous pentacle, representing perfection and the divine forces, is the pentagram, a five-pointed, or perfect, star with its single point upward. Although *pentacle* and *pentagram* are frequently used interchangeably, the former word probably comes a French word meaning "to hang," and the latter, technically, means "drawn with five points." Thus, not all pentacles are pentagrams; in fact, most are not. Pentacles in such shapes as circles, squares and crosses abound in cabalistic books.

Most magical GRIMOIREs are illustrated with pentacles. *The KEY OF SOLOMON*, for example, gives precise instructions how to make, sanctify and use a pentacle. The *LEMEGETON: THE LESSER KEY OF SOLOMON* advises the sorcerer or wizard to decorate his robes with pentacles. Further, in order to prepare for his rituals, the sorcerer should inscribe a parchment with an inverted star, drawn inside a circle. The TETRAGRAMMATON should also be written inside the circle, and one of the holy

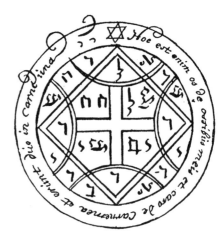

A pentacle drawn to induce love, its Latin inscription of Genesis 2:23 from the Bible translates "For his is now bone of my bones, and flesh of my flesh and they shall be one flesh." The French subscript promises that the pentacle "has great virtue because it compels the Spirits of Venus to obey and to force any woman whatever to come instantly." (*The Key of Solomon*)

names of power (Hallya, Ballater, Soluzen, Bellony, Hally) should be written inside each of the legs of the star. This paper must then be carried by the sorcerer in his hand at all times during his magical rite.

The Pentacle of Solomon, also called the Magician's Pentacle, is a circle (or two concentric rings) or a disk with a pentagram star inscribed inside of it. Ritually symbolic in magic, the five points of the Magician's Pentacle have been variously identified as representing God (or Man) and the four ELEMENTS; the five wounds endured by JESUS on the cross; the five known senses; or the five points of Man when standing arms and legs outstretched.

The pentagram is also the single most important symbol in WITCHCRAFT. In *Transcendental Magic*, Eliphas LEVI wrote "The pentagram, which in GNOSTIC schools is called the blazing star, is the sign of intellectual omnipotence and autocracy. It is the star of the MAGI; it is the sign of the Word made flesh."

The inverted five-pointed star, with its single point downward, originally had no demonic meaning, but over the centuries it has mistakenly come to represent evil. It seemed logical that, if the unright pentacle represented divinity and God, then the inverted pentacle must represent the diabolic and Satan.

In his book *Keys of the Mysteries*, Levi compared the "legs" of an inverted pentacle to the horns of the Devil (who supposedly appears at witches' SABBATs in the form of a goat): "It is the goat of lust attacking the Heavens with its horns. It is a sign execrated by initiates of a superior rank, even at the

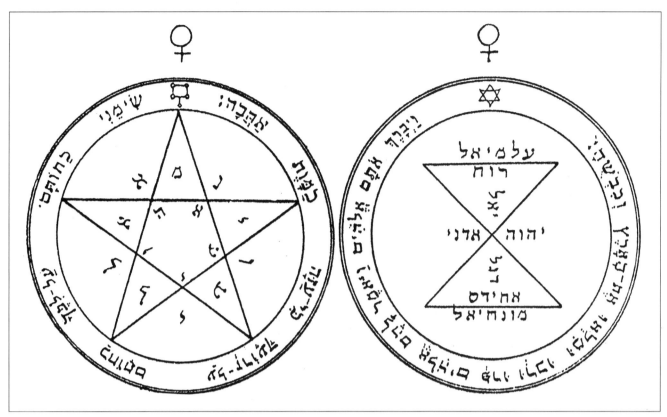

Two versions of the pentagram. The Second Pentacle of Venus (left) is the standard five-pointed star, and it is drawn for the purpose of "obtaining grace and honour, and for all things which belong unto Venus." The pentagram variation (right) is the Third Pentacle of Venus. "This, if it be only shown unto any person, serveth to attract love." (*The Key of Solomon*)

Sabbath." The ORDER OF THE GOLDEN DAWN warned that the inverted pentacle should only be drawn "if there may arise an absolute necessity for working or conversing with a Spirit of an evil nature."

Unfortunately, in America the inverted pentacle was forever linked with Satanism when Anton LeVay made it part of the symbol of his Church of Satan in 1966.

pentagram   See PENTACLE.

Perceforest   An anonymous 14th-century example of French prose ROMANCE LITERATURE, *Perceforest* combines elements of the legends surrounding King ARTHUR and Alexander the Great. Mysticism plays a role in the story, too, as the title character receives his name because he had killed a sorcerer in a dark, impregnable wood.

After successfully invading India, Alexander is shipwrecked on the British coast during a tempest. Before leaving, he crowns one of his warriors, Perceforest, the king of England. During the reign of Perceforest's grandson, the quest for the Holy Grail is realized, and the chalice is carried to England.

Perkins, William (1558–1602)   A Puritan thinker at Christ's College, Cambridge, England, William Perkins was a forceful and vocal opponent of occult practices. Along with *MALLEUS MALEFICARUM* and *DEMONOLOGIE*, Perkins's book, *A Discourse of the Damned Art of Witchcraft*, was one of the most frequently consulted books by WITCHCRAFT investigators of the late 16th and early 17th centuries. Its fire-and-brimstone approach was especially effective in striking terror into the hearts of its religious readers.

Perrault, Charles (1628–1703)   A French wit and storyteller, Perrault wrote a series of fairy tales entitled *Histoires et contes du temps passé* and subtitled *Contes de ma mère l'Oye*. Published in 1697 under the name of his son Pierre, the collection was translated into English by Robert Samber in 1729 as *Mother Goose Tales*. The storyteller character of Mother Goose was purportedly inspired by Queen Goosefoot, the mother of Charlemagne. *CINDERELLA* and *The SLEEPING BEAUTY* are two of the most famous fairy tales in the collection, but many of the other stories also contain supernatural creatures or characters with magic powers.

Peter of Abano (c.1250–c.1310)   Although an Italian physician, Pietro d'Abano (Peter of Abano) was intrigued with the world of the supernatural. After being trained by an unnamed wizard in the mysteries of the occult, Peter authored *The Elements of Magic* (or *The Heptameron*).

Peter set out on tour of Europe, where his demonstrations of WHITE MAGIC drew the attention of the INQUISITION. Among other accusations, it was claimed that Peter had learned the "seven black arts," the *trivium* and the *quadrivium*, from seven tiny demons that he carried with him in a jar. The holy body branded him a devil's disciple, and Peter of Abano died while imprisoned.

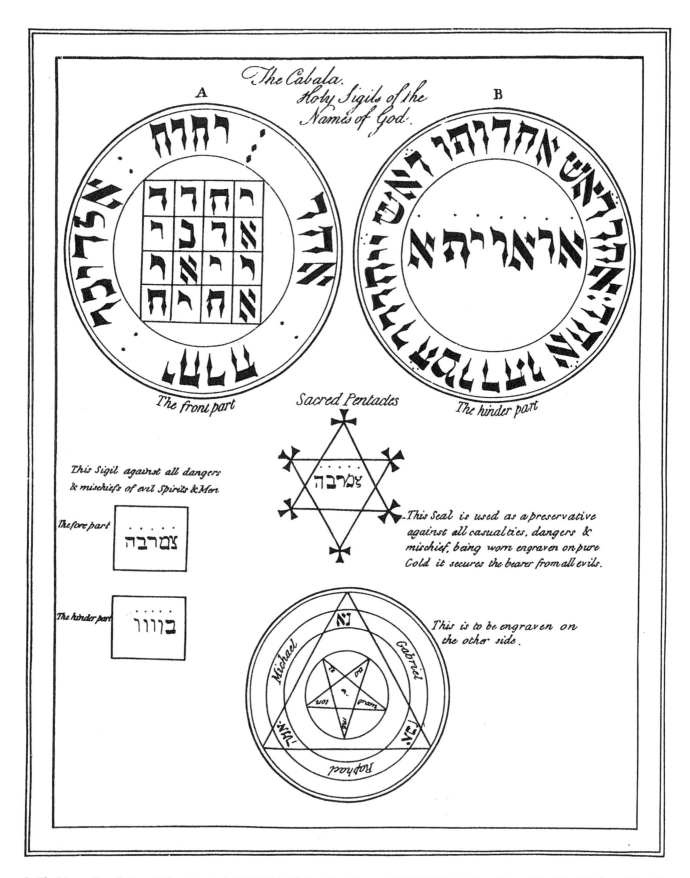

In *The Magus*, Francis Barrett illustrated cabalistic "Holy Sigils of the Names of God." Note that the obtuse side of the The Sacred Pentacle (bottom) acts as "a preservative against all casualties, dangers & mischief"; although the pentacle has no demonic association, its reverse side bears an inverted Abano.

Petrushka   See BALLET.

philosopher's stone   Pursued by alchemists, the philosopher's stone (also seen as philosophers' stone or Philosopher's/s' stone) was an object thought to have the power to transmute base metals, such as lead, into the purest of metals, gold. The quest to discover or synthesize this catalyst was one of the major goals of ALCHEMY. The common consensus was that even a small bit of the stone, in any form (powder, rock or liquid), when mixed with other materials (usually chemicals or another metal) could produce the transformation or transmutation.

Because alchemic textbooks were deliberately cryptic, there is no single, simple description of the stone. It has been described as being made of one of the basic ELEMENTS such as Fire or Water. Some manuscripts referred to it as a gift of God received after prayer and study, as being worthless in itself and yet priceless.

Over the centuries, many alchemists claimed to have produced the philosopher's stone. In the 15th century, Paracelsus supposedly added the stone (in the form of a red powder) to hot, liquid mercury to create gold. Wenceslaus von Reinburg reportedly produced alchemical gold for Emperor Leopold I in 1677.

Skeptics point out that no discovery of the philosopher's stone has ever been validated. As for those who professed to have discovered it, they suggest that the release of mercury vapors, a popular ingredient in the chemical process, could have caused the alchemist to experience hallucinations. Also, there is no record of any alchemist experiencing sudden wealth as a result of his ability to change lead into gold.

The financial benefits of claiming to be able to transmute metals were enormous, usually in the form of royal patronage. At first, any yellowish metal produced, such as the common by-product brass, might have been mistaken for gold. True gold was quite common in 14th- and 15th-century Europe, however, and any reliable jeweler was able to test the alchemist's gold for authenticity.

Mystics have proposed that, rather than being a physical object, the philosopher's stone was a kind of psychokinetic ability, acquired by the alchemist after years of study, training and prayer to God. In essence, the alchemist would be able to will the metal to change. These parachemical processes, as they have been termed, would have been infrequent indeed—which would have explained their rarity, the difficulty in documentation and the lack of wealth of the alchemist. Because such intense psychic flashes, if they occurred, would undoubtedly have seemed miraculous—or diabolic—their production would have added to the ever-present danger of the alchemist being charged with sorcery.

Pico, count of Mirandola (1463–1494)   Born near Modena, Pico became interested in the occult at an early age. He was a true believer in CHALDEAN magic as well as DIVINATION in the form of augury, oneiromancy and hepatoscopy (reading entrails).

At only 24, Pico traveled to Rome, the heart of the Catholic Church, and circulated 900 unorthodox postulates for debate. Pico hoped to reconcile the church-endorsed Aristotelian thinking with Plato's "unacceptable" views. Also of concern to the church, Pico wished to use the KABBALAH and other magical writings as proof that JESUS was divine.

Pope Innocent VIII was wary and asked a clerical committee to investigate the proposals. Of these, six theses were condemned outright; four were found to be rash and heretical, three were judged false and heretical.   (See also INQUISITION; PAPACY, THE.)

"Pied Piper of Hamelin, The"   Subtitled "A Child's Story," "The Pied Piper of Hamelin" by Robert Browning (1812–1889) was first published in 1842 as part of his collection of poetry, *Dramatic Lyrics*.

The poem tells the story of the Pied Piper, who accepts the mayor of Hamelin's challenge to rid the town of rats in exchange for a sack of gold. Although the source and exact nature of his powers are never revealed, the Pied Piper is certainly magical, if not in fact a wizard. Playing his pipe (i.e., flute), he BEWITCHes the rats and leads them out of town.

The mayor refuses to "pay the Piper," giving him only a single gold coin. The Piper blames the entire town for the insult and wrong done to him, and he swears that the children of Hamelin will not grow up to be as deceitful and hardhearted as their elders. The boys and girls follow the Piper and his entrancing music out of Hamelin and up into the mountains, where they die.

Early in his FILM career, Walt Disney produced two animated shorts which featured the Pied Piper character: *Old King Cole* and *The Pied Piper* (July and September 1933, respectively). Made much more magical by Disney than in the original Browning poem, the Piper hypnotizes the rats into thinking they have eaten their way into a huge wheel of cheese; then he causes the cheese—along with the rats—to vanish. Disney felt it necessary to amend the ending: Rather than leading the children to their doom, the Pied Piper takes them to the Garden of Happiness, where they can stay young and play forever. A feature film version was also produced in Great Britain in 1971.

Pisces   See ASTROLOGY; HOROSCOPE; ZODIAC.

Pope Sylvester II   See PAPACY, THE.

Porta, Giovanni Battista della (1538–1615)   Like many other Italian physicians of his era, Porta (whose given name is also seen as Giambattista) was also interested in the *meta*physical. He founded his own research and learning center, the Academy of the Secrets of Nature, in Naples (c.1578). His investigations into the occult led to his writing a 20-volume work, *Natural Magic*, which detailed the results of his analysis of ALCHEMY.

Postel, Guillaume de (1510–1581)   Professionally, Guillaume de Postel was a professor of mathematics and Asian languages in Paris. A fervent follower of the KABBALAH as well, he spoke internationally about his belief in ASTROLOGY. He was convinced that hidden knowledge was being imparted to him through his careful study of the stars. His lectures and his book, *The Key of Things Kept Secret from the Foundation of the World*, brought him to the attention of the INQUISITION, which jailed him for heresy and WITCHCRAFT.

Postel managed to escape prison, and he was temporarily reinstated in his teaching position. He was unable to escape the eye of the Inquisition, however. Constantly in fear for his life, one day he "vanished." Ironically, Postel was hidden by the sisters in a convent, where he remained for the rest of his life.

power doctor   See POWWOW.

Power Rangers   See *MIGHTY MORPHIN POWER RANGERS*.

powwow   In the southeastern and south-central counties of Pennsylvania, the community of German settlers known as the Pennsylvania Dutch has accepted the existence of WHITE MAGIC, also known as *braucherei*, since the immigration of their ancestors in the 17th century. Its practice is commonly referred to as powwowing, and it is performed by a powwow doctor or powwower.

The word *powwow* was adopted from the vernacular term used by the colonists to describe NATIVE AMERICAN MAGIC and rituals. Although the Native American gods differed from their own, the pioneers saw that their tribal rites were obvi-

Mrs. Anna Furst, a 70-year-old powwow doctor from York, Pennsylvania, who cured a patient of a stomach ailment by "trying for him": While chanting prayers, she placed her right hand against his cheek, then patted the top of his head three times, patted his stomach three times, made a few magical gestures in the air and finally patted his stomach three more times.   (Photo courtesy of author)

ously directed toward a higher SPIRIT. Both groups believed that diseases could be caused by demons, and the Native Americans helped the Germans identify medicinal roots and plants that were effective in healing.

The powwow doctor tends to specialize in cures, and the powwowing ceremony over a patient involves INCANTATIONs and ceremonial magic. Usually, powwowers are only visited for small ailments, such as removing a wart or minor arthritis. Powwow doctors have been consulted, however, to provide treatment for more serious diseases, such as cancer.

Because it is believed that the power to heal comes from God through JESUS Christ, the afflicted person must believe in the Trinity. Thus, the powwow doctor is as much faith healer as herbalist or a dispenser of FOLK MEDICINE, and his methods are thought to be a force for good.

BLACK MAGIC, known as *hexerei*, is only performed by a witch, called a HEX, and never by a powwow doctor. If a victim truly believes he or she is *ferhext*, or BEWITCHed, the only recourse is to seek out a hex doctor to remove the CURSE. Frequently a powwow doctor is consulted instead for the simple reason that their numbers in the Pennsylvania Dutch country have always exceeded those of the hex doctors, so a hex doctor may not be known or available. Plus, the client knows that a hex doctor uses black magic to counteract SPELLs; the client may, therefore, be fearful of approaching one.

Powwow doctors can be of either sex, and the arcane wisdom of the craft (some of which can be found in magical GRIMOIREs) is often passed down from one generation to the next. The novice is usually introduced to the art at a young age and is always taught by a family member of the opposite sex. Healing methods include the laying on of hands, making signs in the air, administering potions and philtres or chanting incantations.

Because powwowing as a form of performing medicine is technically illegal in Pennsylvania, its practice is kept quiet, and the powwow doctor receives his clients through word-of-mouth. Fees are not charged, but donations or offerings are accepted (and expected).

In the Ozark Mountains region of the United States, the power doctor has the same role as of the powwow doctor in the Pennsylvania Dutch country. They have similar methods, but rather than consulting occult books for their secrets, power doctors only pass down their craft orally from master to apprentice, though never through blood relatives.

pricking   During the WITCHCRAFT hysteria of the Middle Ages, DEVIL'S MARKs (i.e., skin blemishes of any type) were considered to be proof that a person was a witch. The spots were thought to be immune to pain, so if no visible marks existed on the body of the accused, the witch hunter might resort to the alternate method of pricking to discover invisible Devil's marks. During pricking, the skin of an accused witch was stuck with a long pin or other sharpened objects to test for sensitivity.

Discovering witchcraft in 14th- to 16th-century Europe was a very profitable profession, so it was in the witch-hunter's best interest to locate a definite sign of bewitchment (such as a Devil's mark) as quickly as possible. This often led to the witch-hunter pretending to find an insensitive spot on the body by using a trick knife with a retractable blades, such as

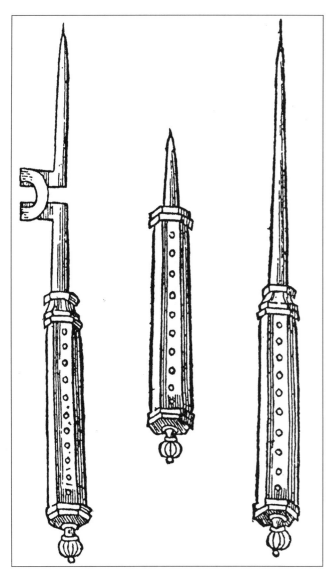

False "bodkins" used by witch hunters for pricking and by conjurers. The knife to the right is the "plaine bodkin serving for shew." The blade of the center knife, however, pushes back into the handle, or "holow haft"; and the gimmicked blade to the left can be used to create the illusion of thrusting the bodkin "through your toong, &c." (Scot, *The Discoverie of Witchcraft*)

those illustrated in Reginald Scot's 1584 DISCOVERIE OF WITCH-CRAFT. Father Frederich von Spee (1591–1635), a German theologian who actively sought to end the witchcraft mania in Europe, debunked witch-hunters by warning lawyers and judges in his 1631 book *Cautio Criminalis* (*Precautions for Prosecutors*) to be on the lookout for "cheating pricks" and gaffed knives that were "*so made* that at pleasure they enter and wound or only seem to do so *by sliding back into themselves.*"

No prohibition on the use of torture to extract confessions existed in Europe, but its use was technically forbidden in England. Even though the act was often painful enough to elicit a confession of witchcraft from the victim, pricking was not considered to be (or defined as) torture. Thus, pricking was much more common in Britain than on the Continent.

Matthew HOPKINS, an infamous English witch-hunter working in 1645–1647, was particularly notorious as a pricker.

Prophecies of Merlin, The See GEOFFREY OF MONMOUTH.

Prospero The most famous sorcerer in Shakespearean literature, Prospero, aided by a SPIRIT named ARIEL, rules over an enchanted island in the play *The TEMPEST*. A wizard practicing WHITE MAGIC, Prospero is able to raise storms, control the sun and resurrect the dead. At the end of the drama, with his work finished and his enemies forgiven, he repents his powers of enchantment, breaks his magic WAND and casts his book of SPELLS into the sea.

Although supernatural creatures appear in many plays in the SHAKESPEARE canon, *The Tempest* is the most clearly magical, both in terms of characters and deeds. The very discussion of magic was risky during the reign of James I (see DEMONOLOGIE) when *The Tempest* was written. Prospero, therefore, is portrayed as a benign wizard, practicing WHITE MAGIC.

Normally, Prospero's acts, such as raising the dead and creating tempests, would have been considered the work of sorcerers, who dealt in BLACK MAGIC. Prospero's storm, however, does not even wet the clothing of the shipwreck survivors. Plus, it allows Prospero to bring all the characters together on an enchanted island to work the wonders of forgiveness and transformation. Perhaps most significantly, at the end of the play, with his enterprise complete, Prospero gives up magic.

Some scholars have suggested that the character of Prospero can be viewed as an older and more mature Oberon (See MIDSUMMER NIGHT'S DREAM, A.) Another interpretation suggests that Prospero is really an autobiographical rendering of Shakespeare. Like a playwright, Prospero creates situations and manipulates people for his own devices. In other analogies, Ariel's grace represents the poet's genius while CALIBAN is his desire, and Prospero's mastery over Ariel and Caliban signifies the playwright's control over his characters. Also, just as Shakespeare retired to Stratford-upon-Avon around 1611 shortly after finishing *The Tempest*, Prospero's final speech in which he gives up magic may represent Shakespeare's farewell to his craft.

Puck See MIDSUMMER NIGHT'S DREAM, A.

Puss in Boots Seen in different variations throughout Europe, *Puss in Boots* tells the classic fairy tale of an enchanted prince who is transformed into a CAT by an wicked sorceress.

The hero of the story receives the cat as his only inheritance and is greatly disheartened until the feline begins to speak. Dressed in court attire, Puss in Boots, as the cat has come to be known, tells the king that his owner is a young nobleman. Puss supplies his master with riches, splendid wardrobe and a castle. In the process, he helps the young man win the hand of the princess in marriage.

To repay Puss in Boots, the new prince promises to grant any wish to the cat. The entire court is shocked when Puss asks to be beheaded, but the prince must unwillingly agree to his feline friend's demand. As soon as the deed is done, the evil SPELL is broken and Puss visibly transforms from a cat back into a handsome prince.

Pythagoras (fl. 2nd half of 6th century B.C.) One of the most influential occultists in ancient history, the Greek philosopher and mathematician Pythagoras is best remembered for his proof of the "Pythagorean theorem": The square of the hypotenuse of a right-angled triangle is equal to the sum of the squares of the other two sides.

A native of Samos, Pythagoras moved to Cortona, Italy, where he established a reclusive commune of mystics to study mathematics and its relationship to the cosmos. Through deduction, Pythagoras discovered the rotation of the Earth on its axis and, therefore, the true cause of day and night. His analysis of music led him to assert that the planets were spaced apart according to harmonic intervals.

Pythagoras's cabalistic training is said to have come from Abaris, a Scythian wizard. A mythic character, Abaris purportedly could live without eating and could fly through the air on an arrow made of gold.

A basic tenet of Pythagoras's occult thinking was the belief in metempsychosis, or the transmigration of souls. An underlying doctrine in reincarnation, metempsychosis asserts that souls move from person to person, human to animal or animal to human in a continual process of castigation or cleansing toward perfection.

None of the original manuscripts written by Pythagoras are extant, but his ideas influenced scientists, mystics and philosophers (most noticeably Plato) for centuries.

Indeed, Pythagoras is invoked by MARLOWE's *DOCTOR FAUSTUS* in his final moments on earth (scene XIV, 116–121):

Ah, Pythagoras' *metempsychosis*—were that true,
This soul should fly from me, and I be changed
Unto some brutish beast.
All beasts are happy, for when they die
Their souls are soon dissolved in ELEMENTS,
But mine must live still to be plagued in hell.

qabbalah See KABBALAH.

Queen of Cornwall, the Famous Tragedy of the A verse play written by Thomas Hardy (1840–1928) and first produced (by the Hardy Players in Dorchester) and published in 1923, *Queen of Cornwall* recounts the tragic legend of Tris-tram and Iseult. MERLIN, a character throughout the play, introduces the drama and magically conjures up the action.

After several difficult attempts, Queen Iseult, who is married to King Mark, meets her lover Tristram, who is also married (to another Iseult, of Brittany). King Mark finds the lovers together and murders Tristram. To avenge his death, the queen stabs the king; then, unable to live without Tristram, she jumps over a precipice. (See also OPERA, *TRISTAN UND ISOLDE*.)

Radagast See *HOBBIT, THE*; *LORD OF THE RINGS, THE*; TOLKIEN, J.R.R.

rainmaker In any agrarian society, rain is a matter of life and death. In African tribal societies, it was believed that all catastrophes such as droughts were caused by wicked SPIRITS and/or WITCHCRAFT. It was the duty of the WITCH DOCTOR to either discover the witch who was causing the calamity or to produce rain by ceremonially dancing and chanting away the evil spirits causing the drought. Failing to do so could result in the witch doctor himself being accused of witchcraft.

In the l9th and 20th centuries, where parts of the Midwest and the western United States were beset by drought, con men calling themselves rainmakers claimed that they could produce thundershowers. *The Rainmaker*, a 1954 play and 1956 FILM written by N. Richard Nash, examined this phenomenon. Darren McGavin originated the stage role, and Burt Lancaster starred in the movie. In 1963, Nash further adapted his story (with Harvey Schmidt, music; Tom Jones, lyrics) into a musical entitled *110 in the Shade* with Robert Horton in the lead role. A 1993 New York City Opera revival featured Brian Sutherland as Starbuck, the rainmaker. (See also MUSICAL THEATER, *RAINMAKER OF SYRIA, THE*.)

Rais, Gilles de (1404–1440) The Baron de Rais (also seen as Rays, Rayx and Retz) Gilles de Laval was both sorcerer and alchemist, invoking demons to learn the secret of transmutation of base metals in gold. He was formally charged and executed for heresy.

Already the most wealthy man in Europe, Gilles de Rais married a rich heiress, Catherine de Thouars, in 1420. He lived so lavishly on his estates that in 1436 Gilles de Rais's heirs successfully petitioned King Charles VII to prevent his selling his properties to support his costly lifestyle. As a result, Gilles de Rais turned to ALCHEMY as a possible means to produce gold.

In his quest for the PHILOSOPHER'S STONE, the baron consulted a series of supposed alchemists, all charlatans, including the priest Gilles de Sillé, magicians such as Jean de la Rivière, Antoine de Palerme and Du Mesnil, and Father Francesco Prelati of Florence. Prelati, it was said, used the sacrificial blood and powdered bones of young children in his conjurations.

In Brittany, Duke John V; his chancellor, Bishop Malestroit; and his treasurer, Geoffroi le Ferron all wished to obtain Gilles

One of the great powers of a witch—and a necessary skill for an African shaman—was the ability to raise a storm or make rain. (Molitor, *De Lamiis*, 1489)

de Rais's land. Geoffroi actually purchased one of the baron's castles, St. Etienne de Malemore, but when Geoffroi's brother, the priest Jean le Ferron, arrived, he was denied entrance and was beaten and imprisoned. The bishop pressed the INQUISITION to charge Gilles de Rais with heresy, knowing that he, the duke and the inquisitor would then be able to legally expropriate the baron's property.

The subsequent 47 charges called Gilles de Rais "a heretic, apostate, conjurer of demons . . . accused of the crime and vices against nature, sodomy, sacrilege, and violation of the immunities of the Church." Thus, the charges against him can be divided into three categories: (1) trafficking with SPIRITS, (2) physical abuse and sexual perversions with both young boys and young girls, including their murder, decapitation, dismemberment, burning, torture and ritual sacrifice, as well as masturbation onto and sodomy of children (either when the victims were alive, dead or dying), and (3) offense to and mistreatment of the clergy.

The first of these charges was based on Gilles de Rais's dealings with Prelati and the other sorcerer/alchemists. It was asserted that Gilles de Rais "adored and sacrificed to spirits, conjured them and made others conjure them, and wished to make a pact with the said evil spirits, and by their means to have and receive, if he could, knowledge, power and riches." The second charge, by far the most heinous, was also the most spurious and all but certainly groundless. The last of these charges, of course, resulted from Gilles de Rais's handling of Jean le Ferron.

Hearings began on September 28, 1440; starting 17 days later, Gilles de Rais was tried in the episcopal courts of the bishop of Nantes. Gilles de Rais was tried concurrently in civil court, with proceedings having begun on September 17. In all, 110 witnesses (some after torture) spoke against him.

On October 19, torture was begun on Gilles de Rais to exact a confession, and two days later he admitted all charges raised against him. Six days later, he was excommunicated from the church; on October 26, 1440 he was granted the mercy of strangulation before being burned. Although his body was raised onto the pyre, Gilles de Rais's heirs were allowed to retrieve the unburnt corpse.

A few months later, the duke of Anjou dropped all charges against Father Francesco Prelati, who had also been jailed, and released him.

Rangda

In the Indonesian myths, Rangda is a witch-goddess who terrorizes villagers with her vast magical powers. Rangda is always depicted as having a large, extended tongue, long straggly hair, eyeteeth sharpened into curved fangs and protracted, pointed fingernails. The *jalon arang*, also known as the *barong* dance, is a popular entertainment in Bali; it portrays the battle between Rangda (the force for evil) and a priest. The barong, a fabled animal with an elongated body and looking somewhat like a Chinese dragon, appears to aid the priest in his fight. His attendants also enter the fray. Putting themselves into a trance, the warriors show that they are invulnerable by attempting to stab themselves with sharp, wavy-bladed knives known as KRIS. Eventually, the powers of good win the fight against Rangda, and the village enjoys newfound peace, prosperity and happiness.

relic

As opposed to an AMULET, CHARM or TALISMAN, a relic does not receive its supernatural powers from an outside human source. The life-changing force is inherent in the object because of its connection with a particular person or event. Usually significant in the religious or cultural belief systems of its civilization, a relic is often unable to be substantiated, but belief in its origin nevertheless continues.

An example of a Christian relic, claimed to be owned by many churches and cathedrals in the Dark and Middle Ages, was a piece or splinter of the actual cross upon which JESUS was crucified. Although there is no biblical mention of the cross having been saved, one Christian tradition states that the cross was removed from Golgotha and then later cut up to be distributed among the early Christian churches and groups of converts. Scholars have ironically noted, however, that if all the pieces of wood that were purported to have come from the

crucifix were ever reassembled, it would created a cross many, many times larger than the original must have been.

During the days of serfdom in Europe, peasants were allowed to leave their servitude only for the purpose of holy pilgrimage. For a cathedral to draw large numbers of pilgrims (and, therefore, their tithes), it became necessary for the church to come up with a "genuine," and preferably unusual, relic. Rome, for instance, is full of such relics: the 28 steps that Jesus supposedly climbed to receive his death sentence from Pilate were brought from Jerusalem to Rome by St. Helena and are housed in the Piazza San Giovanni in Laterano; the church known as St. Peter in Chains houses the chains purportedly worn by St. Peter during his imprisonment in Rome.

Remy, Nicholas (c.1530–1612)

A French demonologist and witch-hunter, Nicholas Remy wrote the influential *Demonolatreiae*, published in Lyons in 1595.

Remy was born at Charmes, Département des Vosges in Lorraine, France. Descended from a family of lawyers, Remy entered the profession, first studying at the University of Toulouse, then practicing law in Paris from 1563 to1570. He succeeded his uncle as lieutenant general of Vosges in 1575.

Remy had seen WITCHCRAFT trials as a youth and prosecuted his first case in 1582 (against a woman accused of using a CURSE to kill her son). By 1591 Remy had risen to attorney

A Balinese mask of the sorceress-goddess Rangda. (Photo by author)

general of Lorraine, and, as such, he was a harsh prosecutor of witchcraft, often overturning the acquittals of lower judges. Between 1582 and 1591, he was said to have personally condemned 900 people to burn as witches.

He married Anne Marchand, had at least seven children and died while still in office.

Demonolatreiae was hastily written in 1592 and was printed without much revision or organization. Nevertheless, it quoted 800 authorities on demonology and is divided into three books, detailing

1. Satanism,
2. Witchcraft and the lives of witches, with emphasis on their the sexual activities, plus
3. Case histories and the author's opinions.

In France, *Demonolatreiae* replaced the MALLEUS MALEFI-CARUM, to a large degree, as the book of authority on witchcraft. It was also one of the main books consulted and referenced by Guazzo when writing his encyclopedic COMPENDIUM MALEFICARUM.

Repulsa, Rita See MIGHTY MORPHIN POWER RANGERS.

rhabdomancy See DIVINATION; DIVINING ROD; DOWSING.

Richelieu, Armand Jean du Plessis, Cardinal and Duc de (1585–1642) First renowned as the bishop of Luçon, France, Richelieu was named prime minister by King Louis XIII in 1624. An outstanding statesman, Richelieu successfully fought the political influence of the Protestants and built the Palais-Cardinal (today the Palais-Royal) in Paris. As a man of letters, he established the Académie française.

Behind his public facade, however, Richelieu had a deep, secret interest in cabalism (see KABBALAH) and the occult. He reputedly practiced sorcery in private, and he retained a noted French wizard, Jacques Gafferel (1601–81), as his official librarian.

ring Throughout fantasy legend and literature, many inanimate objects are seen to be AMULETs or to possess magic powers of their own. These powers are often transferred to the owner or wearer.

One of those most frequently seen is a magic ring. Perhaps the belief in the magic properties of a ring are associated with the cabalistic use of a MAGIC CIRCLE, whether drawn or human, in ritual ceremonies.

In "The Squire's Tale" of Chaucer, found in *The CANTERBURY TALES*, Canacee possesses a magic ring. In a reworked version of the tale seen in *The FAERIE QUEENE* by Edmund Spenser, the ring has the power to heal.

In *Floris and Blancheflour*, an anonymous 13th-century 1,083-verse ode in Middle English based on a 12th-century French original, Floris, the son of a Saracen king, seeks his beloved but nonroyal Blanchflour with the aid of a magic ring. This same story is presented by Giovanni Boccaccio (1315–1375) in his romantic prose work *Filocolo*.

Horn Childe, a 1,136-1ine verse produced in northern Britain between 1290 and 1340 tells the story of Horn, a prince from the north of England who falls in love with Rimnild, a

king's daughter in the south. When Horn's forbidden love is divulged by two of his comrades, he travels to Wales and Ireland, wearing Rimnild's magic ring for protection. Horn kills the religious pagans in Ireland and then returns to England to slay his betrayers and claim the hand of Rimnild.

In Germanic myths, DRAUPNIR is the magic ring owned by Odin. A ring is also central to the plots of the four OPERAs of Richard Wagner's *Der RING DES NIEBELUNGEN*. One of the most famous magical rings in modern fantasy literature is the ring of invisibility found in J.R.R. TOLKIEN's *The HOBBIT* and *The LORD OF THE RINGS* trilogy.

The mystic belief in magical rings still exists. As an emblem to their craft, many Western magicians wear a traditional "wishbone" ring," so-called because breaking the ring in half will produce a metal *W* or *M* (for *Magic*). Some historians of the occult have suggested that ring was originally designed as a piece of jewelry for African SHAMANs and WITCH DOCTORs. Early explorers brought the lucky CHARM back to Europe, where it was adopted by magicians and their secret societies.

Ring des Nibelungen, Der A cycle of four operas by Richard Wagner (1813–1883), *Der Ring des Nibelungen* was composed between 1853 and 1870 and first produced between 1869 and 1876. The complete program of four musical dramas, often referred to by aficionados as the Ring Cycle or simply the Ring, were staged together for the first time in 1876 at Wagner's own Bayreuth Festival Theater in Germany. The cycle takes up to 18 hours to perform in its entirety. The festival is produced annually in July and August, having been suspended only during the world wars. (Richard Wagner Festival, Postfach 100262, D-95402, Bayreuth, Germany.)

As a basis for his libretti, Wagner utilized *Nibelungenlied*, a Germanic epic poem written by an anonymous Austrian around 1200. In the *Nibelungenlied*, Siegfried, a Burgundian prince, falls in love with Kriemhild, a Burgundian princess who lives further up the Rhine River. Kriemhild's brother, King Gunther, is in love with Brunhild, an Amazon queen who has agreed to marry the first man who can equal her in combat. (A similar subplot is found in *ORLANDO FURIOSO*.) Siegfried agrees to fight in disguise as Gunther if the king allows him to marry Kriemhild should he be victorious. Siegfried prevails, and the respective couples are married. Brunhild finds out the truth and assists in the assassination of Siegfried, which leads to a climactic funeral. The second half of the ode tells of Kriemhild's revenge and slaughter using Siegfried's sword.

While the *Nibelungenlied* and *Der Ring des Nibelungen* (also known as the *Nibelungenlied*) share some characters and events, Wagner's series adds mystical elements not seen in its source. The additions also afforded Wagner an opportunity to employ immense, magnificent sets and costumes.

In *Das Rheingold*, the first of the four operas, Alberich, king of the Nibelungs, steals the gold of the Rhine maidens. It is used to form a magic RING, which is stolen by Wotan. The ring allows its wearer to rule the world but CURSEs anyone who owns it.

Die Walküre (*The Valkyries*) concerns Wotan's placing Brunnhilde, a goddess Valkyrie, into a deep sleep and encircling her with flames. In a concurrent story, Seiglinde and Siegmund declare their love.

Siegfried, the son of Seiglinde and Siegmund, sees Brunnhilde and falls in love. He steals the ring from Wotan, walks through the ring of fire, wakes Brunnhilde and gives her the ring (which makes her a mortal).

In *Die Gotterdämmerung* (*The Twilight of the Gods*), Siegfried drinks an enchanted potion which makes him desert Brunnhilde for Gutrune. While Siegfried is boating on the Rhine, the betrayed Brunnhilde plans her lover's death. At his funeral, she places the ring once more on her finger and rides her horse into his pyre. In the spectacular finale, the flames destroy Valhalla, the realm of the gods. The Rhine overflows, putting out the holocaust, and the Rhine maidens regain their gold from the magic ring.

Rocail   Although not mentioned in the Bible, according to legend Rocail was a son of Adam, a younger brother of Seth. He was one of the world's first wizards, and he used his powers to produce a mighty palace. His courtiers and attendants were, in actuality, living statues.

romance literature   Although the term *romance novels* was used briefly in the 18th century and today is used to describe overly sentimental and mawkish writing, the phrase actually comes from the Latin word *romanice*, meaning "in the Roman language." In France, the word *roman* was used to mean the verse tales with heroic subjects, such as those dealing with legends of King ARTHUR, Charlemagne and others nobles.

The earliest English romance literature was in translation, starting after A.D. 1200. The stories often involved the use of magic (either by a person, CHARM or AMULET) and gave moral (i.e., ethical) instruction.

English romantic literature in prose appeared around the 15th century. Emulation of these writings by such authors as Sir Walter Scott (1771–1832) and John Keats (1795–1821) ushered in the age of romanticism in literature in the 19th century.

Roman de Brut   A version of the legend of King ARTHUR, the *Roman de Brut* (or *Geste des Bretons*) was completed by the French (Norman) writer Wace in A.D. 1155. Appearing in 15,000 rhyming couplets, the complete epic survives today in 22 manuscripts.

Based on GEOFFREY OF MONMOUTH's *The History of the Kings of Britain*, which was translated into French by Wace, *Roman de Brut* added significant components to the Arthurian legend. Perhaps the two most important were the promise that Arthur would one day return to lead the Britons and the king's use of a Round Table, around which disputes were settled.

Rose and the Ring, The   Subtitled a "Fireside Pantomime for Great and Small Children," *The Rose and the Ring* is a farcical fairy tale written and illustrated by William Makepeace Thackeray (1811–1863) and published in 1855.

For merriment, the fairy Blackstick removes Prince Giglio and Princess Rosalba from their noble surroundings. Two magic AMULETS, a rose and a RING, cause humorous consequences by their ability to make those who own them overpoweringly alluring.

Rosicrucians   A mystical order and secret society, the order of Rosicrucians can trace its roots back to the 15th century, although it did not become active until the second decade of the 17th century. It was believed that its members held arcane wisdom and magical powers. The society takes its name from Christian Rosenkreuz (1378–1484), a legendary character who purportedly traveled throughout Europe, the Middle East and Africa in search of occult knowledge.

Rosenkreuz returned to Germany and, with three monks, started the Fraternity of the Rosy Cross, which was dedicated to preserving the secret philosophies he had learned on his journeys. He translated a now-unknown work, *Liber M*, which is said also to have been known to PARACELSUS, and wrote extensively on occult matters. His most important original works are considered to be the *Axiomata*, the *Rotae Mundi* and the *Proteus*. The Fraternity of the Rosy Cross continued after its founder's death. Rosenkreuz's body was discovered at the monastery in a perfect state of preservation 120 years after its burial.

Interest in the Rosicrucian legend was revitalized in the second decade of the 17th century with the appearance of three booklets, published anonymously between 1614 and 1616: *Fama Fraternitatais* (Kassel, Germany, 1614), *Confession Fraternitatis R.C.* (Kassel, 1615) and *Chymische Hochzeit Christiani Rosenkreutz* (Strasburg, 1616). The small tracts contained the alleged history of Rosenkreuz, his fraternity and their cabalistic philosophy. It has since been discovered that the author of the third volume was Johann Valentin Andreae (1586–1654); it is probable that he authored the other two books as well.

The first modern organized society of Rosicrucians established itself in Germany in the late l9th century, and as of 1972, there were four separate sects in the United States.

Ruggieri, Cosmo (fl. 16th century A.D.)   Also seen as Cosme Ruggier, this infamous Florentine astrologer to the French court was accused of "having made a waxen image with hostile intent against the King, Charles IX, in 1574." Ironically, the charge was made by Queen Catherine de Médicis, who was herself suspected of sorcery by many people.

According to the queen, "Cosmo has made a wax figure and dealt it blows on the head. . . . Cosmo inquired whether the King was vomiting and whether he was yet bleeding and if he had pains in his head." Her informant was Monsieur le Procurer Général of the Paris Parliament.

Whether or not the hearsay was the result of political intrigue, it was enough to arrest Ruggieri and make him a "ward with the Provost of the Palace." On May 31, 1574, Charles IX died, most likely of consumption (tuberculosis). It was said that the king's final death blows were dealt by Protestant sorcerers who melted waxen images to kill the king through SYMPATHETIC MAGIC. (See also ASTROLOGY; VOODOO DOLL.)

runes   A form of early Germanic ALPHABET, runes were used by the Anglo-Saxons of northern Europe and in Scandinavia in the first centuries after Christ. The first runes, modeled after Greek and Roman letters, appeared around the third century A.D.. The word *rune* means "mystery" or "secret." *Futhorc*, the word for the entire Anglo-Saxon runic alphabet, derives its name from its first six letters.

Runes were carved in wood totems, stone, tombstones, armor and swords. Because the power of written communication seemed so awesome to the uninitiated (i.e., the illiterate), the runes themselves probably seemed to possess magical properties. While an oral SPELL or CURSE might be effective, inscribing the message onto an AMULET or other object allowed the wearer or bearer to carry the protective magic with him.

As Christianity spread north from Rome, Catholic priests equated the runes with the pagan religion, rites and rituals and actively worked to eradicate the use of runes.

Today, there is an international organization, the Association for Rune Research, that is dedicated to locating, preserving and deciphering ancient runes worldwide.

sabbat The term *sabbat* (also seen as *sabbath*) came into common usage in Europe during the 14th to 16th centuries to mean a gathering of witches. It was believed that they assembled to meet with the Devil and renew their devotion and allegiance through arcane rituals and debauchery.

The Oxford English Dictionary states that *sabbat* comes from the Hebrew word for "sabbath," though Dr. Margaret Murray claims that the word derives from the French *s'ébattre*, meaning "to revel or frolic." In his book *Materials Towards a History of Witchcraft*, H.C. Lea states that the phrase *witches' sabbat* was first used during the INQUISITION. The first mention of *sabbat* in extant trial records occurred in Toulouse, France, in 1335.

Sabbats were held in remote locations, far from human view and often deep in the forest, in caves or on mountaintops. According to German myth, witches met their master on Walpurgis Night (April 30) on the Brocken in the Harz Mountains (see FAUST; OPERA, FAUST). In Russian folklore, it was believed that witches met on Bald Mountain on St. John's Eve (June 23) (see FANTASIA). Mount Atlas was a popular sabbat meeting place in North Africa, and the Bructeri, also known as Meliboeus, in the Duchy of Brunswick was a legendary site of witches' sabbats in Britain.

To reach the sabbats, witches, accompanied by their FAMILIARS, flew on their BROOMSTICKS or rode on the backs of demons. The Devil appeared, often in the form of a goat. Naked, the witches paid him homage by kissing him on the backside (the Kiss of Shame). As the devil sat on his throne, new witches were initiated; unbaptized babies were sacrificed; feasting, dancing and sex continued throughout the night, with the witches flying home just before dawn.

Sabbats are important festivals in wicca, the actual religion of WITCHCRAFT, and today, sabbats are held as Neo-Pagan celebrations. Although there are many other observances in wicca, including the nights of the full moon on which COVENS meet, there are eight major sabbats:

Candlemas (February 2, a "fire" festival)
Spring equinox (March 21, celebrating fertility and the arrival of spring)
Rudemas (May 1, a fertility festival)

Beltane (June 21, also seen as Beltaine, celebrating the arrival of summer)
Lammas (August 1, celebrating prosperity and love)
Autumn Equinox (September 21, celebrating harvest)
Hallowmas (October 31, more commonly known as HALLOWEEN, honoring the dead. Rites include the invocation of their SPIRITS.)
Yule (December 21, a celebration promising the passage through death, [i.e., winter] and into the resurrection [i.e., the return of the sun and life and the beginning of spring].)

Sacrapant See *OLD WIVE'S TALE, THE*

Sacred Magic of Abramelin the Mage, The Book of the
Supposedly first appearing as a 1458 French translation of an even earlier magic GRIMOIRE written in Hebrew, *The Sacred Magic of Abramelin the Mage* was actually written anonymously in the 18th century. The purported author was Abraham the Jew, a German alchemist and wizard born in Mayence in 1362. Writing the book as a message to his son Lamech, Abraham gives an accounting of his worldwide travels and the arcane wisdom he accumulated along the way, especially the secrets of the Egyptian occultist, Abramelin (or Abra-Melin) the Mage. *The Sacred Magic of Abramelin the Mage* was first translated into English by S.L. MacGregor MATHERS.

The pseudohistorical grimoire states that the universe is filled with both angels and demons, with Man being the entity between their two stations. Every person has an angel and a demon assigned to him or her. The demons are subject to the angels' command, but if the occultist is an adept or practiced in the ways of wizardry, he can subjugate the demon to do his bidding as well.

The work is comprised of three books, subdivided into 62 chapters, plus prologues and concluding remarks. [NOTE: The use of capital letters, where at odds with current usage, are repeated as used by Mathers and are taken directly from the text.]

In the first book, Abraham relates how he studied the KABBALAH with Rabbin [sic] Moses of Mayence. Beginning on February 13, 1397, and accompanied by a Bohemian Jew named Samuel, Abraham travels across Europe to Constantinople, where Samuel dies. Abraham visits Egypt for four years and then stays in the Holy Lands for an additional year. He returns by way of the Arabian Desert to Egypt, where Aaron, a Jew living in Arachi on the banks of the Nile, tells him of Abra-Melin, a devout Mage and Great Adept in Magic.

Abraham visits Abra-Melin and studies with him. The Mage gives Abraham two arcane manuscripts to master and to copy. (They form the foundation for Books Two and Three of *The Sacred Magic of Abramelin*.) The Egyptian wizard tells Abraham that this esoteric wisdom will remain solely in the hands of the Jews for only 72 more years. Abraham departs for Constantinople and then home.

The next two chapters describes the occult magic utilized in various countries and details the work of several wizards and sorcerers, including Antony of Prague in Bohemia (later called Antony the Bohemian of Prague, who performs BLACK MAGIC), Simon and Rabbin of Constantinople, Joseph of Paris, the Sorceress of Lintz and the Egyptian magicians Horay, Abimech, Alacaon, Orilach and Abimelec.

After receiving guidance from his GUARDIAN ANGEL, Abraham the Jew practices Magic from 1409 to 1458. Chapter Eight recounts many of his great feats, including healings, his loan of a FAMILIAR to the Emperor Sigismund of Germany, the production of a 200-horseman army for Count Frederick, the magical release of the Count of Varvich (Warwick) from an English jail, the safe passage of Pope John XXIII from the Council of Constance, prophecies to the Greek Emperor Constantine Palæologos, the resurrection of two people from the dead (one in Saxonia, the other in the Marquisate of Magdeburgh) and, finally, how he used magic to obtain wealth.

The remainder of the first book is taken up with advice on the Kabbalah, warnings against evil SPIRITs and demons, counsel regarding contact with a Guardian Angel and "the use of a Child as Clairvoyant in the Invocation."

The Second Book enumerates the types of Sacred (or Veritable) Magic and their uses. Abraham explains the need to consult ASTROLOGY to determine the correct day, time and planetary influence before undertaking an Operation and how and where the Operations should be carried out. He

Demons serve witches and their consorts a ritual meal as part of a sabbat. (Guazzo, *Compendium Maleficarum*)

warns of the types of spirits (divided into three Troops) that might be invoked and what the sorcerer is able to demand of them.

The Third Book is a collection of MAGIC SQUARES, each one designed for a specific magical purpose, such as the ones enabling the wizard to do any of the following:

Become clairvoyant
Achieve wisdom in all the "doubtful sciences"
Evoke a spirit and transform it into other shapes
Procure Visions
Keep Familiar Spirits
Locate gold mines
Perform alchemical operations
Raise Tempests
Transform animals into men or stone, and vice versa
Ward off NECROMANCY and other magic
Obtain any book (including those lost or stolen)
Be telepathic
Resurrect the Dead (for seven years at a time)
Become invisible
Command Spirits to serve food, drink and "everything which we can think of"
Locate and obtain Treasure unprotected by Magic
Fly and travel anywhere desired
Heal "divers Maladies"
Acquire Affection and Love
Cause "all kinds of Hatred, Enmity, Discord, Quarrels, Contests, Combats, Battles, Loss, and Damage"
Transform oneself into any shape or form
Work Evil (with the admonishment that "We should not avail ourselves hereof")
Destroy Buildings and Castles
Discover Theft
Walk on and function under water
Secretly open any lock without a Key and without detection
Evoke Visions
Obtain "as much gold and silver as one may wish"
Materialize Armed Men
Cause "Comedies, OPERAS, and all kinds of Music and Dances to appear"

In the conclusion to the third book of *The Book of the Sacred Maqic of Abramelin the Mage*, Abraham the Jew insists that the magic squares and PENTACLES must be used for WHITE MAGIC only. The wizard/Mage planning to perform the magic must be properly prepared for the rites through purification and fasting before the Operations can begin. As for attendants taking part in a magical ceremony, any Children assisting in the rites should be six or seven years old, must have been born legitimate, have "clear speech and pronounce well," plus be "vivacious, and witty . . . well-behaved" and innocent. Also, an adult woman should never be used in any magical Operations, especially in lieu of a young girl.

Finally, The Third Book details Three Hierarchies of Spirits:

The Order of the First Hierarchy, comprised of the Seraphim, the Cherubim and the Thrones, which "serve to make [the wizard] respected and loved for works of Charity."

The comte de Saint-Germain.

The Order of the Second Hierarchy, comprised of the Dominions (who dominate enemies, conquer foes and gain liberty for the wizard, plus give him "command over Princes and Ecclesiastics"), the Virtues (giving "strength and force" and good health) and the Powers (who rule over all Inferior Spirits, both good and evil), and

The Order of the Third Hierarchy, comprised of Princes (which are "capable of giving Treasures and Riches"), Archangels (which reveal all Occult matters, Theology and Law) and the Angels, of which there are an infinite number.

Sagittarius See ASTROLOGY; HOROSCOPE; ZODIAC.

Saint-Germain (1707?–1784 A.D.) Little is known about the early and private life of Saint-Germain. He was nondescript, being of average height and appearance with dark hair. He was, however, an elegant dresser, and his clothes were often adorned with gems and semiprecious stones.

A Renaissance man, Saint-Germain was a skilled violinist, harpsichordist and painter. The mystic was fluent in a dozen languages, including Arabic, Chinese, English, French, German, Greek, Italian, Latin, Portuguese, Sanskrit and Spanish.

His best remembered cabalistic treatise was *La Très Sainte Trinosophie* (*The Most Holy Triple Philosophy*).

Although Saint-Germain himself later tried to destroy all copies of the manuscript, one miraculously escaped ruin. The volume had been acquired by CAGLIOSTRO on a visit to Saint-Germain in Holstein. The book was then confiscated from Cagliostro's library when the INQUISITION arrested him in Rome in late 1789 and somehow made its way into the hands of a private collector named Masséna. Today the lushly illuminated manuscript resides in the Bibliothèque de Troyes (MSS No. 2400).

For a time, Saint-Germain was a court wizard of King Louis XV, supposedly being able to render himself invisible. Through his studies of ALCHEMY, Saint-Germain claimed to possess the PHILOSOPHER'S STONE and to have discovered the ELIXIR OF LIFE. As proof of the latter, Saint-Germain asserted that he was over 2,000 years old (although he always looked to be about 40). Frederick the Great agreed that Saint-German was "the man who would not die."

Contemporaries at court said that he spoke with ease about events that had happened centuries earlier, including generations-old "family secrets" of the members at court. When questioned as to the source of his information, Saint-Germain calmly explained that he had been there when it had happened. Even after the occultist's death, several members of the French court are said to have communicated with him. (See KABALLAH.)

Salem

The most notorious WITCHCRAFT trials in America took place in Salem Village, Massachusetts Bay Colony, in 1692.

The psychological climate in the New England colonies at the time was rife with a belief in diabolic interference in their community. In 1623, King James I (the author of *DEMONOLOGIE*) granted the charter to the Puritans to own land at the Massachusetts Bay Colony. In 1684, the edict was revoked, reverting the land to England. Five years later, the Puritans ousted the king's governor and reinstated the old charter, but by the events of 1692 the community knew that the ownership of their own land was tenuous. As had been the case in Europe, land claims were undoubtedly at the bottom of many of the witchcraft accusations of neighbor against neighbor.

In addition, the Puritans founded Salem on the basis of their religion. While they themselves wished to avoid religious persecution in England, they were uncompromising in their own convictions. They believed in the literalness of the Bible, that witches, as the Devil's servants, roamed the earth. The Old Testament (Exodus 22:18) gave them the authority to seek out and destroy them: "Thou shalt not suffer a witch to live."

One more component must be added to the equation: the strictness of Puritan doctrine resulted in severe discipline for breaking the laws of the church. Even simple frivolity was frowned upon, and there was constant stress in maintaining the essential outward appearance of goodness. Therefore, when allegations of true sin were made—and nothing could be more sinful than being in league with the Devil—the instinct for self-preservation often caused those who were accused to prove their innocence, or at least transfer the charge, by blaming or naming others.

The immediate impetus for the witchcraft hysteria in Salem came from a group of girls, who listened to tales of occult folklore told by Tituba, the black slave of the Reverend Samuel Parris. His daughter, 9-year old Elizabeth, and her cousin, 12-year old Abigail, who lived with them, fell into frenzied delirium, perhaps due to emotional distress. Witchcraft was suspected, and outside experts, such as Cotton MATHER in nearby Boston, soon confirmed their fears. Before long, other young women, ranging in age from 12 to 20, also fell into fits. They began to name names—who had BEWITCHed them and who they had seen with the Devil.

Tituba was arrested. In short order, three village outcasts were charged: Sarah Good (a beggar who smoked a pipe, on February 29), Sarah Osborne (a cripple who had been married three times) and Martha Corey (who had a bastard son of mixed blood). Others followed, including John Proctor, who had been publicly scornful of the arrests, and the 71-year-old bedridden Rebecca Warren.

In court, the girls gave convincing testimony, at times shrieking in fear as they were supposedly attacked by invisible SPIRITS. This "spectral evidence" was, perhaps, the most damning in the whole trial.

Almost 150 people were arrested, but because of the manner and length of testimony in each case, only 31 (of which six were men) actually went to trial in 1692. All were found guilty of witchcraft and sentenced to death. Beginning June 10 through September 22, 19 were hanged. Two (Sarah Osborne and Ann Foster) died in jail. On September 19, hoping to force a confession, executioners pressed Giles Corey to death, a particularly heinous torture in which large slabs of stone are stacked, one at a time, on top of the body until the victim is crushed. Tituba was jailed indefinitely: her eventual fate is still unknown. One, Mary Bradbury, escaped from prison. Five confessed and were reprieved. Two women, Abigail Faulkner and John Proctor's wife, Elizabeth, claimed to be pregnant; their execution was postponed long enough for them to be reprieved.

By October 1692, religious, judicial and political authorities were already questioning the admissibility of the dubious spectral evidence. Although such testimony was soon proclaimed unacceptable, in January 1693 more than 100 people were still in prison awaiting trial. Eventually, only 52 were formally accused, and only three of them (all mentally handicapped and who had confessed) were found guilty. Chief Judge Stoughton ordered them to be hanged along with five prisoners remaining from 1692 (including Elizabeth Proctor), but Governor Phips reprieved all eight of them.

In 1702, Samuel Sewall, who had been one of the presiding judges at the Salem trials, begged forgiveness for the court's actions, asking "to take the blame and shame of it, asking pardon of men." Although the courts reversed the attainders (which deprived the convicted witches of their of civil rights and property) and awarded some financial recompense to survivors or descendants, it wasn't until two centuries later, in 1957, that the State of Massachusetts formally removed the last of the attainders, in essence officially acknowledging the errors of the court during the Salem witchcraft trials.

Still considered to be the authoritative literary work on the trials is Charles Wentworth Starkey's 1867 book *SALEM WITCHCRAFT*. Also worthy of significant note is *The CRUCIBLE*, the 1953 play by Arthur Miller based on events that took place in Salem in 1692.

sangoma   See WITCH DOCTOR.

Saruman the White See HOBBIT, THE; LORD OF THE RINGS, THE; TOLKIEN, J.R.R.

scarab   With the possible exception of the EYE OF HORUS, the scarab was most common and most powerful AMULET in ancient EGYPTIAN MAGIC. Oval in shape, flat-bottomed and rounded on the top, scarabs were carved to resemble a beetle. Prayers or supplications were often engraved on the underside of the scarab. Scarabs were carved from all sorts of materials, including precious and semiprecious gemstones, alabaster (frequently covered with blue glazing) and gold. They were carried, kept in homes, used as ornaments on jewelry and placed in the tombs of the deceased. Used as a TALISMAN, the scarab's life-giving magic offered vitality, good health, potency and protection from evil.

The word *scarab* comes from the Latin *scarabaeus*, the insect from the genus *Lamellicorn*, commonly known as the dung beetle. Its Egyptian name *kheprer(i)* related to the words *kheper* (meaning "to believe" or "to come into existence"), *kheperu* (meaning "stages of development") and *Khepri*, another name for Ra (or Re), the sun god. The scarab, or dung beetle, feeds on a ball of ANIMAL feces that it has stored in the ground. The scarab stays buried with the dung until the feces is completely consumed, then tunnels its way out and emerges from the ground. Newborn beetles spring from the shell of the dung ball.

The scarab's unique life cycle was described by Horapollo, an Egyptian writer of the Greco-Roman period: The dung beetle supposedly "rolls the ball from east to west, looking himself toward the east. Having dug a hole, he buries it for twenty-eight days; on the twenty-ninth day he opens the ball, and throws it into the water, and from it the scarabeaei come forth."

To many, the beetle's (purported) practice of balling the dung from east to west made its task analogous to that of Ra, who was believed to start each day anew, bringing it back into existence by resurrecting the sun and rolling it across the sky from east to west.

Also, the rebirth of the beetle, after almost a month underground, was certainly seen as analogous to resurrection after mummification and burial. In fact, the most magical of all scarab amulets was the royal heart scarab, which was placed on the chest of the pharaoh's mummy in the tomb. The amulet was inscribed with relevant verses from *The Egyptian* BOOK OF THE DEAD, imploring the heart not to censure the deceased when the heart is weighed on the scales of truth on the day of judgment.

Schlemihl, Peter   The hero of an allegorical tale, *Peter Schlemihls wundersame Geschichte*, by Adelbert von Chamisso (1781–1838), Peter Schlemihl begins the story as a poverty-stricken young man. In what seems an excellent bargain, he trades his seemingly useless shadow to the Devil (described as an old, thin man in a grey coat) for the fortune of the wealthy

Fortunatus. Schlemihl becomes rich, but people find it so odd that his shadow is missing that, repulsed and appalled, they banish him.   (See FAUST, JOHANNES.)

School of Night   Although experts now debate whether such a society ever existed, the School of Night was a group of 16th-century British mystics, most of them poets, playwrights or novelists, who purportedly flirted with ALCHEMY, occult writings, cabalism (see KABBALAH) and other arcane practices. Supposedly among their numbers were Thomas HARRIOT (or Hariot) (1560–1621), Sir Walter Ralegh (1554–1618), Christopher Marlowe (1564–1593) and the "Wizard Earl" Northumberland.

The name *School of Night* was first assigned to the group by Arthur Acheson in his 1903 book *Shakespeare and the Rival Poet*. The phrase comes from SHAKESPEARE's *Love's Labour's Lost* (IV. iii. 214), which, according to Acheson and other scholars, was intended by the playwright as a satirical criticism of the literary clique.

Schröpfer, Johann Georg (1730–1774)   A notorious German sorcerer and necromancer of the mid-18th century, Schröpfer trained many disciples in the art of BLACK MAGIC. He was also notorious for using his nefarious forces to punish or attack his many foes. Broken in spirit while still a young man, Schröpfer committed suicide at the age of 44.   (See also NECROMANCY.)

Scorpio   See ASTROLOGY; HOROSCOPE; ZODIAC.

Scot (or Scott), Michael (c.1175–c.1235)   The occultist Michael Scot was born in Balwaearie, Scotland, and studied astronomy at Oxford as well as in Bologna and Paris. He became a court wizard (and probably the astrologer) of Emperor Frederick II at Palermo, Italy.

Scot was a prolific author and translator, writing books on ALCHEMY, astronomy, DIVINATION, dream interpretation, INCANTATIONS and NECROMANCY, many still extant in manuscript. Among his translations were works of Aristotle (384–322 B.C.) from Arabic into Latin, including (at some point before 1220) the Greek philosopher's *De Anima*. Scot also began, and possibly completed, a translation of the noted "Aristotelian Commentary" of Averroës (née Ibn Rushd) (A.D. 1126–1198).

His fame, coupled with his interest in mysticism, led to thinly veiled references to him in other authors' works, most notably in Dante's masterpiece, *The DIVINE COMEDY* (Inferno, xx. 116).

Michael Scot is probably buried in the Cistercian abbey, which he called Kennaquhair. The cloister's church is also the purported resting place of Alexander II and the heart of Robert Bruce. The location of Scot's tomb is uncertain because the abbey, which had been famous for its perpendicular windows, was severely damaged by Edward II in 1322 and by Richard II in 1385. It was totally destroyed during an incursion by Lord Hereford in 1545.

Founded around 1136 by David I, the abbey is situated about 35 miles southeast of Edinburgh, Scotland and five miles from Abbotsford, the home of Sir Walter Scott, who mentioned Michael Scot in his first notable poem, *The LAY OF THE LAST MINSTREL* (1805).

scrying   See DEE, JOHN; DIVINATION; NOSTRADAMUS.

Seal of Solomon   The Seal of Solomon (or Solomon's Seal) is one of the oldest PENTACLEs known and is considered to be one of most powerful in all of magic and sorcery. It draws its name from an Arabic legend that states that King SOLOMON had the figure engraved, along with the true name of God, on his magic RING.

The design is one equilateral triangle (with the point upward) drawn on top of a second equilateral triangle (with the point downward) to produce a six-sided star. Often, the figure is drawn within a circle.

The Seal of Solomon dates back to at least to the Bronze Age, and according to occultist/author Robert Graves the design was a fertility symbol in Babylonian magic, representing the sexual union of the god Tammuz and the goddess Ashtaroth.

The Seal of Solomon was adopted into ancient Hebraic magic and, as such, became known as the Shield of David or, more commonly, the Star of David. In Judaic symbolism, it has variously been said to represent the union of male and female, body and soul, fire and water, and the reciprocal love between God and humans.

The Seal of Solomon figures prominently in cabalistic teachings and writings. As an AMULET, it was thought to be particularly effective in protecting against the EVIL EYE, LILITH

An artistic rendering of the Double Triangle of Solomon, in which "the God of Light and the God of Reflections, mercy and vengeance, the white Jehovah and the black Jehovah" appear as mirror images. (Eliphas Levi, *Transcendental Magic*)

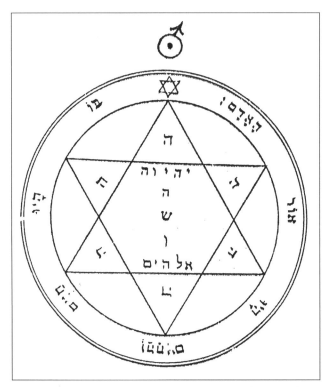

The Seal of Solomon, drawn as part of the Second Pentacle of Mars. "This Pentacle serveth with great success against all kinds of diseases, if it be applied unto the afflicted part." (*The Key of Solomon*)

and (beginning in the Middle Ages) fire. For use as a TALISMAN against evil SPIRITS and demons, sorcerers drew the Seal of Solomon within and/or surrounding their MAGIC CIRCLES. As an added precaution, the TETRAGRAMMATION was often written in the hexagonal center of the pentacle. The Seal of Solomon was also frequently used as a decoration on the breast of wizards' and sorcerers' ceremonial robes.

Occultists also use the Seal of Solomon as a sign of the macrocosm, where each of the points of the six-rayed star represents a different emanation from God. Each of the points is also associated with one of the planets, with the center of the seal aligned with the sun. The points also represent the six days of Creation, along with their respective ruling houses from the ZODIAC (in order, Cancer, Pisces, Scorpio, Capricorn, Virgo and Taurus).

In *The MAGUS*, Francis Barrett gives specific instructions on how to draw the Seal of Solomon. The pentacle was to be drawn at a date and time under the influence of Mercury, in gold letters on a kidskin parchment or white paper. Finally, the seal was to sanctified with holy water.

Although the Seal of Solomon is the most common hexagram pentacle used in ritual magic, three other pentacles formed by two triangles are also seen. In the first, the triangles point in opposite directions (up and down), either sharing a common base or with bases slightly separated but parallel.

The second design has the two triangles meeting point-to-point. The third alternate configuration has both triangles pointing upward, superimposed one on the top of the other, but with one slightly elevated.

Finally, the Seal of Solomon is perhaps second only to the pentagram as the penultimate symbol of demonology. It has been adopted by Satanists, who use it to symbolize a sorcerer's power and control over all hellish forces. (See also KABALLAH.)

seventh son of a seventh son　According to the folklore of many cultures, the seventh son of a seventh son is considered to be born with innate magical abilities, including DIVINATION and the power to heal (especially by laying on of hands). Among the Pennsylvania Dutch, it is believed that the seventh son of a seventh son will be a particularly powerful and formidable witch (or HEX) or, if he chooses, a potent POWWOW doctor.

Among GYPSY clans, the seventh daughter of a seventh daughter is also thought to have a special gift for fortune-telling and prophecy.

Shakespeare, William (1564–1616)　The premier playwright of Elizabethan England, William Shakespeare is believed by many to be the greatest playwright in the English language. His plays were divided at the time of the publication of the First Folio edition (1623) into comedies, tragedies and histories. Many of the plays incorporated fantasy and illusion and were populated with such supernatural creatures as sorcerers, fairies, ghosts and SPIRITS.

Shakespeare was born in Stratford-upon-Avon around April 23, 1564, to a merchant and town-councilman father, probably of upper-middle class. William's early, and possibly only, education would have been the local public school. In 1582 he married Ann Hathaway, eight years his senior; their first child Susanna was born only six months later. Twins Hamnet and Judith followed three years later. Around 1587 he left Stratford for London, but his family stayed behind in Stratford. By 1592 he was well enough known to be denounced in print as an "upstart crowe" by a fellow playwright, identified as Robert Greene (1558?–92) or possibly Henry Chettle (c.1560–c.1607). For approximately two decades he worked with a company of actors at the Globe theater, at first under the noble patronage of the Earl of Southampton. When James I became the royal patron in 1603, the troupe's name was changed from the Chamberlain's Men to the King's Men. In 1597, Shakespeare bought a large house, New Place, in Stratford. By 1611, Shakespeare seems to have been retired from the theater; he was living in Stratford, when he died on April 23, 1616.

Scholars have assumed that Shakespeare took advantage of several published sources for his plots and themes, notably including Ovid's *Metamorphoses* among others, but it is mostly conjecture as to the basis for his knowledge of the occult. However, Shakespeare lived and wrote primarily during the reign of Elizabeth I (who held the throne from 1558 to 1603), when interest in the metaphysical sciences openly flourished.

By the time James I (who reigned from 1603 to 1625) came to power, the public was well aware of the WITCHCRAFT hysteria that was sweeping Europe and much of the British Isles.

In fact, while still reigning as James VI, king of Scotland, James I had written the antiwitchcraft tome *DEMONOLOGIE* (1597). Shakespeare was therefore no doubt sensitive to the intense, sometimes maniacal fear of witchcraft, so he had to be careful of its mention in his writing.

Many of Shakespeare's plays that did not deal with magic or witchcraft still had allusions to the supernatural. For example, in *Othello* (which is recorded as having played at court in November 1604 but was not published until 1622), Barbantio accuses the Moor of using "foul CHARMS" or "drugs or minerals" to seduce his daughter Desdemona. Barbantio brands Othello a sorcerer, claiming that it is the only way Desdemona would have chosen the black man over the Venician youths he deems more suitable and handsome. Othello counters that

> She loved me for the dangers I had passed,
> And I loved her that she did pity them.
> This only is the witchcraft I have used.
> (I, iii, 158)

In *Richard III* (probably dating from 1595), Clarence is imprisoned by the impressionable Edward IV, who had been told by a wizard that someone whose name begins with a *G* will prevent his heirs from assuming the throne. Clarence tells Richard, who is behind the scheme, that he was christened George but he has committed no treason.

Pericles, often attributed to Shakespeare, makes use of "healing magic" in its story line. The play was first published with an imperfect text in 1609, although it was probably written at least a year prior. It was not printed in a corrected form until the second issue of the third edition of the First Folio in 1664.

The major actions of MACBETH are set into motion by the prophecies of the three "weird sisters." A MIDSUMMER NIGHT'S DREAM is set almost entirely in a forest inhabited by fairies, and, of course, Shakespeare's final work, *The TEMPEST*, has a wizard, PROSPERO, as its main character.

Even in death, William Shakespeare's legend involves a touch of mysticism. His tombstone is engraved with a famous epitaph, a CURSE ascribed to the poet himself:

> Blest be the man that spares these stones,
> And curst be he that moves my bones.

Shakūntalā　An ancient Sanskrit play by Kālidāsa (prob. third century A.D.) and first translated into English by Sir William Jones (1746–94), the plot centers around King Dushyanta and the young Shakuntala. While hunting in the forest, the king sees the girl and pledges his love. To prove his worthy intentions of marriage, he gives his RING to her. Unfortunately, she loses the ring while bathing.

Durvasas, a wicked wizard, CURSEs Shakūntalā because he felt that she had been discourteous to him. According to his secret SPELL, the king will not remember Shakūntalā, until he sees the ring. Pregnant with the king's child, the maiden goes to the palace, but she is not recognized and is turned away. Cast out, she goes back to the woods and delivers the baby Bharata.

A fisherman discovers the enchanted ring inside a fish. Tragedy turns to joy, and the wizard is foiled when King Dushyanta sees the ring. He remembers Shakūntalā, goes on a quest to find her and, once reunited, they marry.

shaman Wrongly perceived by nonoccultists as a sorcerer or necromancer, a shaman holds the door open between the physical, rational world and the invisible, unseen world, acting as a conduit or mediator between the two dimensions.

In order to receive the other-world messages, or at least to sensitize one's self to them, a shaman will often enter trance states. In the trance state, the shaman is actually in both worlds, totally oblivious to the external world around him and yet still operating within it. Physical reactions during the state of possession might include frantic gestures, dancing or contortions. In addition, entranced shamans often seem to be invulnerable to pain, demonstrated by their ability to walk on fire. They experience rapid healing of wounds, and they are unable to pierce themselves with ritual knives (see KRIS). A frequent phenomenon manifested by the shaman while in a trance is speaking in a different voice or language. This curiosity, commonly referred to as speaking in tongues, has been produced by such varied figures as the ancient ORACLE of Apollo at DELPHI and modern Pentecostal Christians.

Although shamans deal with the beyond, they need not be religious figures. The *dalang*, the shadow puppeteer of Indonesia, for example, also acts a shaman when he performs. Entranced, he can perform at fever pitch often for eight hours at a time; his plays enact the great legends of the community. During the course of the play, he introduces up to 125 different characters in his mythic pageant, each puppet figure having a different voice. At the same time, the *dalang* conducts the orchestra!

The shaman was also an important figure in Western tribal societies. Among some of the NATIVE AMERICAN tribes, the shaman was colloquially called a MEDICINE MAN by European settlers.

Shamans often developed a particular talent or field of magical influence, such as a being able to control the weather (a RAINMAKER) or ferret out BLACK MAGIC, and they relied on each other's assistance and abilities in times of need.

The mystic never was elected as chief, however. While his powers were considered strong, the erratic shaman himself was not considered the type of warrior/leader that was necessary to head the tribe.

Shaving of Shagpat, The Subtitled *An Arabian Entertainment,* this group of comic whimsical stories written by George Meredith (1828–1909) was published in 1856. Shagpat, a bearded wizard, has but one hair on his head, "The Identical," which he uses to magically control a king and his realm. It has been prophesied, however, that Shibli Bagarag, a humble barber and story-teller, will shave Shagpat, break the SPELL and be named "Master of the Event." With his fiancée, Noorna bin Noorka, Bagarag eventually succeeds.

Shipton, Mother (1488–1561) Ursula Sontheil, known as Mother Shipton, was born at Dropping Well Estate in Knaresborough, Yorkshire, England. Her mother, an orphan

Three witches (one holding a wand and standing within a magic circle), their familiars and impish demons, as depicted in the 17th-century book *The Strange and Wonderful History of Old Mother Shipton.*

girl, claimed that Ursula's father was actually a SPIRIT. She was accused of WITCHCRAFT, tried and acquitted.

Ursula was considered to be quite unattractive, and she was apparently also a hunchback. Despite her physical handicaps, she attended school, learning to read and write. About the same time, she began to cast SPELLS and conjure. In 1512, she married Toby Shipton. Her reputation as a fortune-teller grew, and her clients included much of the British nobility.

The story of Mother Shipton was chronicled in a series of pamphlets. The first, appearing in 1641, placed her during the reign of King Henry VIII and credited her with predicting the deaths of Oliver Cromwell, Lord Percy and Cardinal Wolsey (along with his arrest at York). In 1677 Richard Head published his *Life and Death of Mother Shipton*. In Charles Hindley's 1862 edition, Mother Shipton was said to have predicted the Apocalypse (in 1891) and the invention of the telegraph and the steam engine. Around 1900, Dropping Well Estate published its own tract entitled *The Life and Prophecies of Ursula Sontheil, Better Known as MOTHER SHIPTON*, crediting the seer with having prophesied major world events, both contemporary to her time and of the distant future.

Among her many other predictions were Henry VIII's marriage to Anne Boleyn, the reigns of Elizabeth and "Bloody Mary," Edward VI's caesarian birth, the rein of James I, the civil war and violent death of Charles I, the Restoration, Sir Walter Ralegh's bringing tobacco and potatoes to Great Britain, iron boats, the Crystal Palace and Francis Drake's defeat of the Spanish Armada. Like the temple priests who phrased the barely coherent utterances of the ORACLE of Apollo at DELPHI into rhymes, Mother Shipton often gave her prophecies in verse. Modern believers claim that the following lines are prophecies of cars, scuba diving, submarines and airplanes:

Through hills men shall ride
And no horse or ass be by their side,
Under water, men shall walk,
Shall ride, shall sleep, and talk;
In the air men shall be seen,
In white, in black, and in green.

In the end, Mother Shipton apparently did correctly prophecy the exact day and time of her own death.

Sibly, Ebenezer (fl. late 18th century)

Ebenezer Sibly, a noted English physician, was a firm believer in the strength of the KABALLAH and the intervention of demons in worldly affairs. He shared these convictions in his book of mysticism, *New and Complete Illustration of the Occult Sciences*.

sigil

Seen in the books of the KABALLAH and other Western occult writings, sigils are symbolic signs or illustrations upon which wizards and sorcerers would focus to invoke deities and demons.

From the Latin *sigillum*, meaning "seal," the sigil was usually in one or a combination of geometric shapes, such as stars, circles or triangles. It might also be drawn within a MAGIC SQUARE. The PENTACLE and the pentagram were among the configurations most frequently seen, especially in the many arcane GRIMOIRES, such as *The KEY OF SOLOMON, LEMEGETON: THE LESSER KEY OF SOLOMON* and *The MAGUS*. The most famous sigil in all of occult literature is the so-called SEAL OF SOLOMON.

To be most effective, the design of the sigil had to include the secret name of the SPIRIT or deity that the necromancer wished to summon. Properly inscribed sigils could also be used to represent almost any concept, such as the planets, the supposed layers of the heavens, the hierarchy of the angels or the days of the week. They could be also prepared to work as (or on) AMULETs and TALISMANS.   (See also ANGELIC ALPHABET; DEE, JOHN; MAGIC CIRCLE.)

Simon (fl. 20–40)

Usually seen as Simon Magus (i.e., Simon the Magician or Wise Man), Simon was a renowned wizard living during the time of JESUS. He is notable, in large part, because his performances convinced some observers that Jesus was also nothing more than a wizard; other believed that Simon himself was the Messiah.

Simon was purported to have been the apprentice of a wizard named Dosithesus. Simon became the center of an Eastern-style religious cult, and his followers variously referred to him as the First Aeon, the Emanation, the First Manifestation of the Primal Deity, the Word, the Paraclete and the Almighty.

Simon's greatest claim to fame was his ability to fly. Today it is believed that, if he achieved the feat at all, it was done through some form of mass hypnosis. Simon Magus's end is alleged to have come during a final, unsuccessful demonstration of flight. He fell to his death, and his enemies quickly claimed that this was proof of the sorcerer's association with demons and his eternal damnation.

According to some versions of the legend, Simon Magus moved to Rome, where he became a trusted advisor to Nero. The magician purportedly challenged the disciples Peter and Paul to a series of trials, but the wizard could not resurrect the dead like the Apostles. Perhaps to prove his powers before the emperor, Magus threw himself from a high tower, "flying" by the support of devils. Peter prayed for the demons to abandon him. The infernal fiends departed, and Simon fell to his death. (Supplication to heavenly forces to control demons was a common practice, as described in the writings of the KABBALAH and ALCHEMY.) The apocryphal meeting of the wizard and Peter and Paul before Nero is pictured in "The Dispute of Simon Magus," a fresco painted by Filippino Lippi in the Brancacci Chapel in the church of Santa Maria del Carmine in Florence, Italy.

The same or another wizard Simon is mentioned in the Acts of the Apostles in the New Testament of the Bible:

. . . there was man named Simon who had previously practiced magic in the city and amazed the nation of Samaria, saying that he himself was someone great. They all gave heed to him, from the least to the greatest, saying, "This man is that power of God which is called Great.

And they gave heed to him, because for a long time he had amazed them with his magic. But when they believed Philip as he preached good news about the kingdom of God and the name of Jesus Christ, they were baptized, both men and women. Even Simon himself believed, and after being baptized he continued with Philip. And seeing signs and great miracles performed, he was amazed. (Acts 8:9–13)

Later, when Jesus's disciples Paul and John visited Samaria, they bestowed the Holy Spirit on converts with the laying on of hands. Simon, saying "Give me also this power," offered the disciples money but was rebuked by the Apostle Peter.

Before his conversion to Christianity, Simon was said to have had a disciple-companion named Helena. Remaining under demonic control, she purportedly "possessed" a succession of temptresses, most notably Helen of Troy.

Simon Magus is an apocryphal figure because it appears that many different magicians of his and later eras were also referred to by the name *Simon*.

Justin the Martyr (A.D. 105–165), for example, mentions "a certain Simon, a Samaritan of Gitton, who in the reign of Claudius Caesar performed works by the magic arts of demons." Irenaeus, author of *Refutation of the Gnostics*, and Hippolytus claimed that Simon Magus was an early (or possibly the *first*) GNOSTIC. More recent Irish lore refers to him as Simon the DRUID. He is most often identified, however, as the wizard Simon of the Bible.

Sinclair, George (1654–1696)

Sinclair, a Scottish professor of philosopher and mathematics, was also a confirmed occultist. His book, *Satan's Invisible World Discovered*, states his conviction that demonic forces are active on Earth.

Sinistrari, Ludovico Maria D'Ameno (1622–1701)

An Italian follower of BLACK MAGIC and dark forces, Sinistrari was the author of a study on WITCHCRAFT, *De La Démonalité et des animaux incubes et succubes*. In 1876, the work, which told of the demonic life of the INCUBUS and the SUCCUBUS, was translated into French.

Sirens

Found in Homer's *The ODYSSEY*, the Sirens were two enchantresses, half-woman and half-bird, who BEWITCHed sailors by their beautiful voices. Sitting on an open meadow on their island in the sea, the Sirens sent their songs out across the waves. The men, mesmerized by the melodious sounds, steered their ships to crash onto the shore. All around the Sirens lay the remains of the men who had been lured to their deaths—"bones of dead men rotting in a pile beside them and flayed skins shrivel around the spot."

Ulysses, having been told by CIRCE that his vessel would have to pass the Sirens on his homeward voyage, put wax into the ears of his crew. So that he could hear the temptresses's song, however, he had himself bound to the mast. Although Odysseus screamed to be set free, his men refused to release their leader until long after they had safely passed the Sirens.

In a separate mythological tale, Jason and his Argonauts were saved from the Sirens' calls by Orpheus. The god's enchanting music overpowered the sounds of the Sirens, allowing the Argonauts to pass by safely.

Scholars have suggested several possible locations for the island of the Sirens. The site most often mentioned in connection with the Odysseus story is the Greek island of Santorini. Based on evidence from the mythological tales, Jason ventured into the Black Sea; scholars conjecture that, if they were real, the Sirens who tempted him must have been found in or near Hellespont (today the Dardenelles) in Turkey.

The word *siren* has lost its mythological meaning but is still in common usage to refer to a woman who is mysteriously and perhaps dangerously alluring.

"The Siren of the Philosophers." (Basile Valentin, *L'Azoth des philosophes*)

6th and 7th Books of Moses, The See HEX.

"Sleeping Beauty, The"

Written by the French wit and story-teller Charles PERRAULT (1628–1703), "The Sleeping Beauty" is literally a fairy tale, one of a series of fantasy stories found in *Histoires et contes du temps passé*, subtitled *Contes de ma mère l'Oye* (1697).

In "The Sleeping Beauty," seven fairies appear at the baptism of a king's daughter. Six of them deliver their benedictions upon the baby, but an evil, old fairy, angry and vengeful because she had not been invited, arrives to pronounce a CURSE: In her youth, the princess will fatally prick herself with the needle of a spindle. The seventh fairy, having expected such a HEX from the crone, amends it with a counter-SPELL. Instead, the princess will merely fall asleep for a hundred years, to be awakened by the kiss of a prince.

The monarch orders all of the spinning wheels destroyed in the kingdom. For years, the princess is unharmed. One day, while exploring a high tower, she meets an old crone at a spinning wheel that the hag had kept hidden. Curious at the strange device, the princess reaches out and accidentally pricks her finger on the needle.

The princess falls into a deep sleep. The benevolent fairy returns to place everyone else in the royal palace into a trance so that they will wake up at the same time as the princess. She encircles the castle with thick thorns and trees. A hundred years later, the handsome prince arrives and kisses the "sleeping beauty." She awakens along with all of the castle residents, and they all lived happily ever after.

In 1959, Walt Disney Studios released a now-classic animated FILM version of the story. *Sleeping Beauty*, composed by Peter Ilich Tchaikovsky, is also one of the most romantic BALLETs ever written.

Solomon

The historical tale of Solomon, king of the Hebrew tribes for 40 years, is told in I Kings 1–11 in the Old Testament of the Bible. He is justly remembered as a great and wise judge, for the notable visit from the Queen of Sheba, for building the first great temple in Jerusalem and for his dedication to the God of Israel. Occultists, however, focus on his alleged association with and belief in the powers of wizards, seers and sorcerers. In fact, in mystic circles he is often referred to as the Arch Magician.

The son of King David and Bathsheba, Solomon was chosen by his father to succeed him on the throne. After David's death, Solomon quickly vanquished his rivals to secure his position as king. Solomon showed sincere humility before God, wishing only to be given "an understanding mind to govern" and to be able to "discern between good and evil." The Lord was so pleased that He rewarded him not only with great wisdom, but also "that which thou hast not asked, riches and glory; in such wise that none shall have been like unto thee in times gone by."

Only a few incidents in the Bible illustrate Solomon's wisdom as a judge, but his management skills and artistic talents are well documented. For administrative purposes, he divided Judea into 12 districts with overseers. He assembled a huge standing army of 1,400 chariots, 40,000 chariot horses and 20,000 infantry horses which gave him enormous military might over his foreign enemies. He drank from cups of gold. He built an immense palace from the cedars of Lebanon, which he called Iahar-Halibranon ("Forest of Lebanon") and constructed a duplicate palace for the Egyptian pharaoh's daughter. His penned 3,000 *mashal*, or proverbs, and composed 5,000 *shirim*, or canticles (many of which appear in the Proverbs, Ecclesiastes and The Song of Solomon in the Bible). His reception of the queen of Sheba proved that Solomon was internationally revered and famous far beyond the borders of Israel. Beginning in the fourth year of his reign, Solomon erected his magnificent holy temple to honor the Lord.

As he grew old, Solomon failed to heed the Lord's warning not to marry outside the faith. As God had foreseen, Solomon was tempted to worship the false gods of his foreign wives (including the daughter of the pharaoh) and mistresses: "For Solomon went after Ashtoreth the goddess of the Sidonians, and after Milcom the abomination of the Ammonites . . . for Chemosh the abomination of Moab, and for Molech the abomination of the Ammonites." (1 Kings 11:5,7)

Solomon fell out of favor with the Lord, but, in deference to his love for King David, God allowed Solomon to rule throughout the remainder of his life. As punishment, however, after his death the Hebrew nation would once again split—into 11 tribes, each with its own leader and territory. Solomon's son would rule over only one region, the area which included the city of Jerusalem.

No details are given of Solomon's last years. Despite Solomon's 40 years of rule over the nations of Israel, his end merits only one brief verse in the Bible: "And Solomon slept with his fathers, and was buried in the city of David his father [i.e., Jerusalem]." (I Kings 11:45)

Although Solomon is mentioned elsewhere in the Old Testament, most of the remainder of his biblical story is told in II Chronicles. There is a tantalizing suggestion, however, that there were apocryphal writings which augmented his

deeds mentioned in the Bible: "And the rest of the acts of Solomon, and all that he did, and his wisdom, *are* they not written in the book of the acts of Solomon?" (I Kings 11:41).

Throughout the centuries, occult scholars have identified all sorts of mystic Hebraic and other ancient writings as legacies from Solomon's era. Some are poets' descriptions of Solomon's dominion over the angels and demons. Other manuscripts claim to reveal the secret knowledge that Solomon obtained from his direct communication with the god of the Israelites and the heathen deities. Still others purport to have actually been written by Solomon himself.

Among the Eurasian poets and writers on Solomonic mythology were Saas-ed-din, Ishag-ibn-Ibrahim, Ahmed-el-Kermani, Shems-eddin-Siwasi, Jalal-ud-Din, Firdausi (the Persian poet, whose life of Solomon was entitled *Suleimen Nameh*, or *Nameb*), the Jewish historian Flavius Josephus (A.D. 37–c.98), plus many Talmudic writers and commentators. The apocryphal writings, legend and fact are hard to separate.

In the first century A.D., Josephus wrote in *Antiquities of the Jews* that Solomon, an exorcist and demonologist, could control the heavens and the forces of nature.

King Solomon receiving Belial and infernal demons at his throne. (Jacobus de Teramo, *Das Buch Belial*, 1473)

Calling him Suleiman-ibn-Dauod ("Solomon, son of David"), various authors declared that Solomon reigned over all the SPIRITS of the heavens, earth and damnation. The Arabic book *Tarikh-mon-Te-Kheb*, for example, says soon after Solomon ascended the throne (at the age of 12), the Lord presented him with the birds, the wind and the JINN (good and evil spirits). Thus, Solomon, was given dominion over the angelic, the earthly and the demonic regions.

Solomon's minions were supernatural elves, salamanders, pygmies and gnomes. According to the Koran, the jinn labored to build Solomon's palaces and personal possessions, and they carried him on their back during his travels.

Daily, Solomon's entire entourage, human and supernatural, would dine with him, seated at tables appropriate to their respective stations. The jinn were placed at a separate iron table. Although Solomon was the jinn's master, he was always wary and drank from glass cups: if his vision was blocked by raising an opaque cup, the jinn would stick their tongues out at him!

Through the persuasion of Asmoedeus, the king of the demons, the jinn were convinced to capture the Shamir for Solomon. The Shamir, a tiny worm, was created by God at twilight on the world's first Friday, the week of the Creation. Only as large as a speck of barley corn, the Shamir was a powerful, magical creature, and its aid in building the temple (without tools) was invaluable.

One of Solomon's most unusual examples of judicial wisdom occurred when, for the king's pleasure, Asmoedeus reached into the bowels of the earth and produced a two-headed beast, a distant descendant of Cain. The creature was the seventh of seven sons (see SEVENTH SON OF A SEVENTH SON); but after its father's death, the monstrosity demanded two parts of the birthright because he had two heads. Encouraged by the demon, Solomon sought a solution. He blinded both heads and poured scalding water over one. When both heads screamed, Solomon declared that they / it was really only one son and due only one-seventh of the inheritance.

During his lifetime, Solomon used several pieces of magical paraphernalia to maintain his control over the jinn and the demons. Most notable among the mystic items were his RING (possibly inscribed with the talismatic SEAL OF SOLOMON), a magic lamp, a CAULDRON, a magic mirror (actually a polished plate used for DIVINATION), the PHILOSOPHER'S STONE and a flying carpet. (Similar items of enchantment appeared in the Arabic tales of Aladdin and the *ARABIAN NIGHTS*.)

Mythology abounds with the power found in magic rings. Some stories said that Solomon used his ring to control and command the jinn. Arabic writers said it was the true source of Solomon's wisdom. Others said the king used it to brand the demons as his slaves.

Similar to the tale of SHĀKUNTALĀ, one story tells how Solomon's ring once slipped off his finger while he was bathing in the Jordan River. It was swallowed by a fish, but the ring was later recovered and returned by a fisherman. Another tale tells that it was stolen by a jinn, who used the ring's power to usurp Solomon. The king roamed the deserts as a peasant until the Lord forced the jinn to toss the ring into the ocean.

By using his magic lamp, Solomon was able to call up demonic spirits, such as Abigor, Alastor, Baalzephon, Lucifuge, Rofocale and Zapan. Then, by raising his ring, Solomon

held sway over them all. Once, just to prove his power, he chained Sachra Elmarid, one of the strongest devils, to the side of a mountain.

The story of Solomon's magic carpet provided poets the opportunity for endless exaggeration. The carpet supposedly covered 60 square miles and was woven with green silk and threads of gold. The carpet would swoop down from the sky at Solomon's quietest call; the king's entire retinue—army, kitchen, stables—could fit aboard. Once Solomon was seated, he was surrounded by Ramirat (Prince of Demons), the Lion (Prince of Beasts) and the Eagle (Prince of Birds); flocks of birds acted as Solomon's sun screen. Upon the king's command, the carpet would fly anywhere requested of it.

Many miraculous stories were written of Solomon's aerial adventures. On his travels, he found deserted palaces, whose statuary shouted out their fear and loathing of his supremacy. He saw talking birds and gorillas dressed as men.

The king's throne is an important part of the Solomon myth because it reportedly became the depository of Solomon's occult writings. The Bible describes Solomon's throne as a marvel, with its six steps bordered by statues of lions, but Muslim writers claimed that it was made, in part, of the most expensive sandalwood and that the lion and eagle statuary framing the stairs came to life upon Solomon's approach. The Arabic author Jalal-ud-Din described the throne as being made of gold and silver and encrusted with rubies and emeralds.

Some Talmudists wrote that when Solomon sat on the throne, a dove emerged, flew to the Ark of the Covenant and returned the Torah to Solomon's hands, while the 12 decorative, golden lions roared. The Koran claims that the throne originally belonged to Blakis, the queen of Sheba, and that the jinn Ifrit, on instructions from the king, stole it. Finally, Arabic religious scholars thought that Solomon, with the assistance of demons, buried his infernal manuscripts (which contained his magical methods of controlling the jinn) under the throne.

The poetic biographies also offer some accounts of Solomon's life after his fall from the grace of God. *De penitentia Adæ* says that Solomon and the Lord were never reconciled, and that the king died in damnation. Juvenal des Ursins, the medieval court historian of Charles VI, repeated the long-standing story that Solomon was condemned to be devoured by a thousand ravens every day until the end of time.

A fascinating Talmudic study claims that Solomon attempted to appease the Lord, asking only that God conceal his death from the jinn until they had completed work on his temple. The Lord complied, and Solomon died on his knees in prayer, supported by his wooden staff. The Koran comments that a reptile chewed away the staff, allowing Solomon's body to fall. The jinn, discovering the deceit, immediately stopped their labors and disappeared.

The rumor of hidden occult books written by Solomon persisted long after Solomon's death and into the Christian era. At least one book of SPELLS purportedly written by Solomon was in existence during the first century: Josephus claimed to have seen the Jewish wizard Eleazar use it to perform an exorcism. The healer read from the book while touching the nose of the possessed person with a magic ring (inscribed with a seal specially designed by Solomon).

Michael Psellus, a Greek author of the 11th century, writes about a Solomonic manuscript about demons and stones. Nicetas Choniates, a 13th-century Byzantine-era biographer, claimed that Aaron Isaac, the royal interpreter in the court of Emperor Manual Comnenus owned a book that, if read, "could cause legions of demons to appear."

This latter book was, most probably, an early version of *The Clavicle, or The* KEY OF SOLOMON. Besides this, the most important apocryphal Solomonic work is a collection of manuscripts from different sources, assembled under the title LEMEGETON: *THE LESSER KEY OF SOLOMON*. While *The Key of Solomon* indicates ways to summon angelic forces, the *Lemegeton* (in the section known as the *Goetia*) lists 72 demons, their hierarchy and ways to invoke them.

Other archaic writings credited to, and almost certainly not written by, Solomon include *Le Livre de Salomon* (destroyed by papal order around 1350) and the TESTAMENT OF SOLOMON. Most probably written sometime between the 2nd and 5th centuries, this is supposedly an autobiography, with each chapter beginning "I, Solomon. . . ." In it, "Solomon" reveals the mysteries of demonology along with a list of demons, his invocational methods and the secret source of his great wisdom. He gives details of his visit by the sorceress named the Queen of Sheba and the receipt of his magic ring (which could control demons) from an angel of the Lord.

Prehistoric aboriginal rock paintings depict spirits from the Dreamtime creation legends. Namarrgon, the lightning man (top right), produces thunder and lightning by striking *garramalg*, or stone axes, against the clouds or the earth. (From the Anbangbang Gallery at the Nourlangie site in Kakadu National Park, Northern Territory, Australia. Photo by author)

Regardless of the veracity of the poets' verses or the authenticity of the GRIMOIRES' authorship, Solomon will remain in occult legend as the Arch Magician, whose unequaled wisdom rivaled only God's and whose cabalistic keys opened the doors of magic to his mystic successors.

Sorcerer, The   See MUSICAL THEATRE, *SORCERER, THE*.

Sorcerer's Apprentice, The   See FANTASIA.

sortilege   From the Latin words *sortis* ("lot" or "piece") and *legere* ("to choose"), sortilege is a method of fortune-telling that involves the interpretation of objects randomly selected from a larger set of ritual items.

The most common form of sortilege involves reading the symbols on the objects or the patterns formed when the items are tossed or placed onto the ground or a level surface. Examples would be the use of the HAKATA, EKWELE and BAO among the WITCH DOCTORS of various African tribes. Shells, leaves,

At a *corroboree* celebration, an Australian aboriginal musician plays the didjeridu for ritual dancing to honor ancestral spirits. (Photo by author)

colored beans and many other objects have also been used in different cultures.

The pointed arrow is a natural symbol for aiming toward the future and its use in sortilege was so common that the practice developed its own name: *belomancy,* from the Greek *belos* ("arrow") and *tikos* ("prophecy"). The ancient Babylonians were among the civilizations that practiced belomancy; the two-arrow form unique to Tibet was known as *Dahmo.*

Perhaps the most famous system of sortilege—and one still practiced internationally—is the *I-Ching,* which originated an estimated 7,000 years ago in China.

spell   A spell is a word or phrase that, when uttered, will bewitch or enchant another person or object. A spell, in and of itself, is not considered evil; it is the purpose or application of the spell which assigns it to WHITE MAGIC or BLACK MAGIC.

The intent of many spells is to have a continuing domination or power over the captivated subject. In this sense, a spell differs from a CURSE or HEX whose purpose is to damn or destroy its recipient.

A spell can be cast in a single utterance, although it more often involves an elaborate ritual or a series of INCANTATIONS

Fragile and worn by the weather, rock paintings were frequently restored or replaced by successive aboriginal artists. Though already damaged and faded, many of the current mythological figures found at Nourlangie date only to 1964, when they were painted by artisan Nayombolmi.   (Photo by author)

to effect the magic. It is the slow repetition of phrases and actions that gave rise to the metaphorical expression "to weave a spell."

spirit   A spirit is a disembodied, ethereal essence or life force. Animistic societies believed that all animate and inanimate objects had a spirit within them, many of which could be consulted for wisdom and guidance. Other spirits were believed to be the noncorporeal entity of deities or demons.

The soul of a deceased person that returns to interact with the realm of the living is commonly referred to as a ghost. Ancestor worship, however, holds a much higher regard for the spirits of the dead. The Mexican Day of the Dead, for example, is a celebration aimed at honoring and placating the deceased.

Most, but not all, tribal cultures are to some degree animistic.

In the animated FILM *Pocahontas,* the character of Grandmother Willow, herself a familial spirit dwelling in a giant tree, gives the Native American princess a simplified explanation of animism: "All around you are spirits, they live in the earth, the water, the sky. If you listen, they will guide you. (See also MUSICAL THEATER, *INTO THE WOODS.*)

Steganographia   Written by Johannes TRITHEMIUS in 1500, the *Steganographia* was one of the most revered occult manuscripts of the 16th century. It was also, almost certainly, AGRIPPA's inspiration for writing his *Occult Philosophy* (*DE OCCULTA PHILOSOPHIA*).

The fact that the *Steganographia* purportedly hid a secret code or cipher within the four books of its text fascinated John DEE, an expert on cryptograms; he was ecstatic when he found a copy of the work in Antwerp in 1562. In an February 16, 1563, letter to Sir William Cecil, he wrote

> I have purchased on boke, for which a Thowsand Crownes have ben by others offered, and yet could not be obteyned. A boke for which many a lerned man has long sowght, and dayly yet doth seeke: Whose use is greater than the fame thereof is spread: The title is on this wise, Steganographia Joannis Tritemij . . . Of this Boke the one half (with contynuall Labor and watch, the most part of X days) have I copyed oute. [sic]

The book, considered vital to the true understanding of ENOCHIAN MAGIC was just as important to Dee's fellow-Elizabeth wizard, Simon FORMAN. He was not as fortunate as Dee: He noted in his journal that he was not able to make a copy of the four books of the *Steganographia* until 1600.

The manuscript is actually made up of three books plus a *Clavis Steganographia* (*Special Key*) to interpret the signs, symbols and rituals found in the first sections. The four parts were collected at some point and circulated privately throughout the 16th century. The work was finally published in Frankfurt in 1606.

In the introduction to his 1656 translation to PARACELSUS's *Of the Supreme Mysteries of Nature,* Robert TURNER announced that he one day hoped to translate the entire *Steganographia.* Unfortunately, he died before doing so.

The first book of the *Steganographia* was completed on March 27, 1500. This part, later reworked anonymously and named the *Theurgia-Goetia,* was made the second section of the infamous *LEMEGETON: THE LESSER KEY OF SOLOMON.*

Wooden effigies known as tau-tau adorn balconies in front of tombs of the wealthy, carved into the wall of a cliff outside the village of Lemo in the Toraja Highlands (known as Tanatoraja, "Land of the Toraja People," or, more colloquially, "Torajaland"), Sulawesi, Indonesia. Each tau-tau represents the spirit of a deceased ancestor, and it is thought that the totem watches over and protects the grave. (Photo by author)

No copy of the 1606 Frankfurt edition nor any full manuscript is known to exist. Today, the second book and the final key found in the original *Steganographia* are considered to be lost.

Subtle   See ALCHEMIST, THE.

succubus   In medieval times, it was believed that a female demon SPIRIT known as a succubus (plural, *succubi*; from the Latin *succumbo*, meaning "lie beneath") could fly into a human male's bed and engage him in sex as he slept.

Certainly no man could be held responsible for acts performed in his sleep; so if a jealous woman were to catch her husband or lover in bed with a young vixen, who then seemed to fly magically out the window, the man could explain away the witch as having been a succubus. A visit by a succubus was also used to justify away daytime drowsiness or fatigue and rationalize such temporary sexual incidents as impotence or nocturnal emissions.

Although the word is only infrequently heard today, *succubus* has maintained its original meaning, minus its occult connotations, of a harlot or fallen woman.

Superman   Created by Jerry Siegel and Joe Shuster, Superman first appeared in DC's *Action Comics* (#1, June 1938). His history was radically revised and modernized in *Man of Steel* (#1, June 1986) and again following his celebrated death and rebirth in 1993. Today, Superman is arguably the most famous COMIC BOOK character in the world.

Sent to Earth just before his native Krypton exploded, the baby Kal-El is discovered by Jonathan and Martha Kent, who raise the infant as their son, Clark. As he grows under Earth's stronger yellow sun (Krypton's was a cooler red), Clark develops powers such as near-limitless strength, supervision, superhearing and the ability to fly. He leaves Smallville for Metropolis, where he takes up the dual identity of a reporter for the *Daily Planet* newspaper and Superman.

Only three things are known to be able to weaken Superman: Kryptonite (fragments from Krypton meteorites), some psychic powers and magic. In "The Curse of Magic!" (*Superman*, August 1964), the Man of Steel laments, "Too bad my invulnerability can't protect me from magic or a sorcerer's SPELL!" It is his susceptibility to magic that has resulted in his being taunted by such pranksters as the fifth-dimensional pixie Mr. Mxyzptlk.

In additional to the many DC Comics titles in which Superman (and Superboy) have appeared, the character has appeared on TELEVISION, in FILMS and in the MUSICAL THEATER. Outside of the comics, Superman's vulnerability to magic is seldom, if ever, mentioned.

The first film Superman was Kirk Alyn, who played the man of steel in two black-and-white serials in 1948. *The Adventures of Superman* was produced for television syndication from July 1951 through November 1957 and starred George Reeves as Clark Kent/Superman. *"It's A Bird It's A Plane It's Superman,"* a Broadway musical (music by Charles Strouse; lyrics by Lee Adams) based on the superhero, opened at the Alvin Theatre on March 29, 1966, with Bob Holiday as Clark Kent/Superman. Several animated cartoon versions of Superman have been produced for television, beginning in 1966. Christopher Reeve starred as Superman in a series of four major films between 1978 and 1987.

A syndicated half-hour *Superboy* (renamed *The Adventures of Superboy* for its last season) was produced for television from 1988 to 1991. John Haymes Newton portrayed Superboy/Clark Kent for the first season, and he was replaced by Gerard Christopher for the last two years. Significantly, besides human criminals, Superboy had to battle supernatural foes, including witches and Mr. Mxyzptlk.

A new television version, *Lois and Clark: The New Adventures of Superman*, premiered on ABC in 1993. The show, starring Dean Cain (Superman/Clark) and Teri Hatcher (Lois), portrays Lois and Clark/Superman as young, modern romantic leads.

On September 7, 1996, an animated series *Superman* debuted on Kids' WB! network, with Tim Daly voicing Superman/Clark Kent and Dana Delany voicing Lois Lane.

First appearing in DC Comics's *Superman* (in "The Mysterious Mr. Mxyztplk," September/October 1944), Mr. Mxyzptlk (pronounced "Mix-yez-pitel-ick") and his magic have been a recurring bane to Superman. Details about Mxyzptlk changed over the years as his character evolved, including the spelling of his name, his costume and physical appearance.

Mxyzptlk comes from the Land of Zrfff, which (since the March/April 1948 issue of *Superman*) has always been classified as being located in the fifth dimension. Zrfff is a monarchy, ruled over the King Brpxz, and it has been insinuated that in the fifth dimension, Mxyzptlk is a sort of court jester.

When visiting our dimension, the prankster seems to have unlimited magical abilities. In fact, the only way in which it possible to return the sprite to his own dimension against his

The tau-tau often stand 3 feet or taller. They are painted and colorful costumed; due to exposure to the elements, the paint is touched up and the clothing is changed periodically. Some Torajas believe that the spirit of the individual actually inhabits the tau-tau, so the figure's wardrobe will often include a traveling sack for the voyage to the Land of Souls. (Photo by author)

The swimming of accused witch Mary Sutton in 1612.
(From anonymous pamphlet *Witches Apprehended, Examined, and Executed*, London, 1613)

will is by tricking him into saying or spelling his name backwards! (Kltpzyxm is pronounced "Kel-tipz-yex-im.") Fortunately, when he disappears back to the fifth dimension, his magic and Spells in this world also vanish. As of the May/June 1953 *Superman* issue, Mr. Mxyzptlk must remain in his own dimension for at least 90 days before being able to return to earth.

Not really a villain, Mxyzptlk is more aptly described as puckish and whimsical. Mxyzptlk has been known to fly, animate objects, turn invisible, read minds and hypnotize people. Among his more unusual tricks have been elasticizing his body, bringing movie characters to life and causing rivers to run upstream. He has also emulated Earth legends: In the May/June 1946 *Superman* issue, Mxyzptlk floated an entire theatrical production of *FAUST* high into the sky; in November 1946, he transformed himself into a genie (see JINN), emerging from his lamp to grant wishes.

The exact nature and source of Mxyzptlk's mystic powers have never been definitively identified, but they have been variously described as "magical," "supernatural," "extra-dimensional," "dimensional magic," "fifth-dimensional legerdemain," "5th dimensional magic," "weird magic" and "magical mischief." In the March 1955 *Superman* issue, Mr. Mxyzptlk explained that "a fifth dimensional brain in a three dimensional world can do anything!"

swimming   Proving guilt or innocence by immersion in water dates back at least to the third century B.C.'s Babylonian Code of Hammurabi, which decreed

> If a man charges another with BLACK MAGIC and has not made his case good, the one who is thus taxed shall go to the river and plunge into water. If the river overcometh him, then shall his accuser possess his property. If, however, the river prove him innocent and he be not drowned, his accuser shall surely

be put to death, and the dead man's property shall become the portion of him who underwent the ordeal.

This ordeal was adopted into the examination of accused witches during the WITCHCRAFT hysteria of the 14th through the 16th centuries in Europe. The witch was bound, sometimes sealed in a porous bag, and thrown into a lake or river. The theory was that pure water refused to accept those who denounced baptism. Thus, if the accused sank, the person was declared innocent. If the victim floated, the person was declared guilty and was prosecuted as a witch. This type of accusation was a popular way of eliminating enemies: the person either drowned while swimming or was later burned or hanged for witchcraft.

Swimming was popular in England as well. Second only to searching for DEVIL's MARKs and PRICKING, it was the favorite method of proving witchcraft. British witch-hunter Matthew HOPKINS was especially noted for his use of swimming.

The terms *dunking* (or ducking) are sometimes used interchangeably with *swimming*; but they are more often used to denote a related ordeal, also designed to exact confessions of sorcery. In dunking, the accused person is tied securely to a chair and by means of a pulley or lever is repeatedly dipped into the water. With each immersion, the time that the victim is left underwater is increased until a confession is finally received. This form of examination, too, had its share of casualties because it was hard to determine exactly how long a witch could remain underwater before drowning.

Sword in the Stone, The   See FILMS, *SWORD IN THE STONE, THE*; *ONCE AND FUTURE KING, THE*.

Sycorax   Mentioned (but not appearing) in William SHAKE-SPEARE's play *The TEMPEST*, Sycorax was a witch and the mother of an illegitimate son, CALIBAN. Sycorax practiced BLACK MAGIC and worshiped Setebos, a demonic god of the Patagonians. She conceived Caliban during a sexual liaison with the Devil.

Even Prospero, himself a sorcerer, was impressed with her magical powers, commenting that she was "one so strong / That could control the moon, make flows and ebbs."

sympathetic magic   Under the "Law of Sympathy," a wizard is able to affect a person through sympathetic magic, the magical manipulation of some object that is similar to or has sympathy with the victim. The term *sympathetic magic* was coined by Sir James George Frazer in his landmark study on myth and magic, *The GOLDEN BOUGH*.

Frazer identified two types of sympathetic magic: homeopathic magic (also known as IMITATIVE MAGIC) and CONTAGIOUS MAGIC. The best-known example of the former would be a sorcerer inflicting pain by melting a waxen image or sticking pins in a VOODOO DOLL that represents the victim. Contagious magic requires an article that has been touched by the victim. The sorcerer incorporates the token (such as a lock of hair, a tooth, nail clippings or a piece of the victim's clothing) into the object over which the sympathetic SPELL will be cast.

talisman The use of talismans is common to every known civilization and culture throughout history.

Colloquially, the words CHARM, AMULET and *talisman* are often used interchangeably to mean some object, carried or displayed, that protects the bearer from harm or evil or brings good fortune.

Many occultists, however, make a great distinction between a talisman and the other mystic items. The object used to create a talisman, they contend, has no magic properties in and of itself. Its power must be given or infused by some outside person or force. In fact, the word *talisman* comes from the Greek root *teleo*, meaning "to consecrate."

Thus, the talisman is also representative of some supernatural SPIRIT behind it. That unseen power, therefore, can also be called on to aid or intercede on behalf of the talisman's owner.

According to *The Golden Dawn*, the handbook of the ORDER OF THE GOLDEN DAWN, a talisman is "a magical figure charged with the Force which it is intended to represent. In the construction of a talisman, care should be taken to make it, as far as possible, so to represent the universal Forces, that it should be in exact harmony with those you wish to attract, and the more exact the symbolism, the easier it is to attract the Force—other things coinciding, such as consecration at the right time, etc."

In EGYPTIAN MAGIC, there was an entire cosmos of deities and Forces from which to choose. The most common talismans left in tombs were in the form of the sacred SCARAB.

The St. Christopher's medal and rosary beads, two common objects recognized by the Catholic Church, are by definition talismans. These religious items do not have supernatural power within them; yet they invoke the aid of a holy saint and the Virgin Mary, respectively.

Most of the Greek and Roman talismans drew their powers from astrological figures. For best results, the talisman was magnetized during the most auspicious time, possibly according to one's HOROSCOPE or as set forth in a GRIMOIRE. It was considered most advantageous for the wizard to enchant a talisman while it was under the influence of its correct astronomical planet or day. The talisman was crafted from one of the seven metals associated with the seven known heavenly spheres as well as with one of the seven days. Most gemstones were likewise aligned.

Talismans have been devised for both good and evil purposes, although far more of the former exist. The PENTACLES and MAGIC SQUARES illustrated in the cabalistic works attributed to SOLOMON were considered to be particularly powerful talismans. It was a simple task to draw the appropriate pentacle on a piece of virgin parchment and carry it along or hide it on one's own property for protection. Conversely, a talisman for harm might easily be secreted among an enemy's possessions. (See also ASTROLOGY; CURSE TABLET; KABBALAH; *KEY OF SOLOMON, THE*; *LEMEGETON: THE LESSER KEY OF SOLOMON*.)

Talisman, The A novel by Sir Walter Scott (1771–1832), published in 1825, *The Talisman* is a story of various heroic acts and treacheries among the Crusaders led by Richard I of England. Saladin, head of the Turks, disguises himself as a doctor to cure an ailing Richard with the aid of the magical talisman. At the end of the story, Richard awards the talisman to Sir Kenneth, a victorious knight, who is in fact Prince David of Scotland.

Inspiration for the book came, in part, from the tales surrounding the Lee-penny, an ancient AMULET which was acquired by Sir Simon Lockhart during the Crusades and was long held (and purportedly still is) by his heirs in Lanarkshire, Great Britain.

Tam o' Shanter A poem by Robert Burns (1759–1796), published in 1791, *Tam o' Shanter* tells the story of Tam who, after an evening of drink at the local pub, heads home to his farm. On the way, he spies eerie lights in the Kirk of Alloway and, peering inside the church, sees a SABBAT of witches and WARLOCKS dancing to the bagpipe music of Old Nick, the Devil. Having had a bit too much ale and feeling a bit frisky, Tam calls out to the most beautiful of the witches. Discovered, the witches immediately chase the horrified Tam o' Shanter, who gallops on his mare Meg over the River Doon. Halfway across the bridge he escapes their grasp, but the poor grey mare's tail, having not yet reached the midway point, is snatched off by the witch who was the object of Tam's desire.

tarot cards First seen in their current form in Italy in the 14th century, tarot cards are a set of playing cards, usually 72 per deck, which are used to foretell the future. The name is derived from *tarocchi*, itself a word with an obscure origin.

While the use of tarot cards for DIVINATION is a complete field of study in itself, a working understanding of the deck was essential knowledge for wizards of the Middle Ages.

Unfortunately, there is very little written that tells how the earliest tarot decks were used in fortune-telling. One monograph by Marcolino da Forlì, *Le Sorti di Francesco Marcolino da Forlì, intitolate Giardino di pensieri* was published in Venice in 1540, but no other books on the subject appeared (or, at least, are extant) until the 18th century.

The oldest known tarot deck is housed in the Cabinet des Estampes in the Bibliothèque Nationale in Paris. It is believed to be one of the decks hand-painted by Jacquemin Gringonneur for King Charles VI of France.

The tarot is actually made up of two separate decks called the Major Arcana (22 cards) and the Minor Arcana (usually 56 cards, but only 52 according to some occultists). If mixed or used together in fortune-telling, they are known as the Great Pack.

The Major Arcana contains the figures usually thought of as tarot cards. Tradition has placed the 22 classic characters in a specific order, as follows: The Juggler (or the Magician), the High Priestess, the Empress, the Emperor, the Pope, the Lovers (also known as Marriage), the Chariot, Justice, the Hermit (or Sage), the Wheel of Fortune, Strength, the Hanged Man, Death, Temperance, the Devil, House of God (or Hospital, or Lightning-Struck Tower), the Star, the Moon, the Sun, the Judgment, the World and the Fool. (The order of the World and the Fool is reversed in some decks.)

The Minor Arcana is comparable to a regular deck with the addition of four knight-court cards. Until the end of the 18th century, the suits today known as clubs, hearts, spades and diamonds were called WANDS, cups, swords and shekels (or money), respectively. The original suits represented four classes or occupations in the Dark and Middle Ages.

During a reading, each of the Major Arcana has a specific meaning. Some, like Death, were obvious; other, like the Empress (night, darkness), less so. Different combinations of cards from the Minor Arcana and in which direction they are laid out also have different interpretations. The best fortune-tellers, however, are not usually those who make their predictions by the book. Rather, they use the cards merely as a guide or stimulus to arouse their own prophetic powers.

In an attempt to establish a link to the KABALLAH, some occultists have tried to make a connection between the 22 cards of the tarot deck and the 22 letters of the Hebrew alphabet, but no correlation has ever been proven to exist.

Taurus See ASTROLOGY; HOROSCOPE; ZODIAC.

Telemos A great wizard and soothsayer, Telemos is mentioned in Homer's *The ODYSSEY*. The son of Eurymos, Telemos lived among the dreaded Cyclops. He predicted the coming of Odysseus to the gigantic Polyphemos, whose eye was put out by the wandering hero.

television Since television's infancy, wizard, witch and sorcerer characters have regularly appeared on dozens of regular prime-time series. Even more have appeared in episodes of anthology series such as *Playhouse 90*, *The Twilight Zone* and *Tales from the Crypt*. Indeed, literally thousands of magicians and mystic characters have been seen since the medium began. Some of the best examples of regularly broadcast television series and specials that featured wizard and sorcerer characters follow.

Addams Family, The Broadcast on ABC from September 18, 1964, through September 2, 1966, *The Addams Family* of kooky and ooky characters was based on comic panels created by Charles Addams for *The New Yorker* magazine. The enchantress characters were Morticia Frump Addams (Carolyn Jones), who dressed in tight, black gowns, looking like a cross between a witch and a vampire; and Grandmama Addams (Blossom Rock), who indeed *was* an old crone witch, with stringy silver hair. Others regulars included wide-eyed, mustachioed Gomez Addams (John Astin); bald-pated, electrically charged Uncle Fester Frump (Jackie Coogan); the 7-feet tall, Frankensteinlike monotoned butler Lurch (Ted Cassidy, who doubled as the disembodied hand, Thing); the children Pugsley (Ken Weatherwax) and Wednesday Thursday (Lisa Loring) Addams; and the pint-sized hairy Cousin Itt (Felix Silla).

An animated version of the show was seen on NBC's Saturday morning cartoon lineup from September 1973 to August 1975.

In 1991 a FILM version of *The Addams Family* appeared, and a sequel, *Addams Family Values*, appeared two years later.

Adventures of Sir Lancelot, The Telecast on NBC for one season, from September 24, 1956, through June 24, 1957, this series was filmed in England. Oxford University provided the necessary research for art direction and to find authentic sixth- and seventh-century Arthurian sites. The regular characters included Sir Lancelot (William Russell), King ARTHUR (Ronald Leigh-Hunt), Queen Guinevere (Jane Hylton) and the wizard MERLIN (Cyril Smith).

Bewitched Telecast on ABC from September 17, 1964, through July 1, 1972, *Bewitched* followed the attempts of Samantha (Elizabeth Montgomery), a young witch newly married to Darrin Stephens (Dick York, 1964 to 1969; Dick Sargent, 1969 to 1972), to curb her magic powers and act like a mortal. Her use of WITCHCRAFT often led to comic misadventures, and she cast her SPELLS by a mere twitch of the nose. (A similar premise—a woman with magic abilities trying to lead a traditional domestic life—was seen on the competing show, *I Dream of Jeannie*, see below.)

Making matters difficult for Darrin was the huge clan of witches who regularly descended upon the Stephens household over the years. They included Samantha's mother Endora (Agnes Moorehead), debonair father Maurice (Maurice Evans), the batty and befuddled Aunt Clara (Marion Lorne, 1964–68), cynical and wise-cracking Uncle Arthur (Paul Lynde, 1965–72), sarcastically pessimistic Esmerelda (Alice Ghostly, 1969–72) and the WITCH DOCTOR Dr. Bombay (Bernard Fox, 1967–72). Occasionally, Samantha's impishly wicked and slightly saucy sister Serena, also portrayed by Montgomery, would turn up.

Samantha's first baby was introduced on the January 13, 1966, telecast. Tabitha was born with magic powers, wiggling her nose with a finger to cast a spell. Due to labor laws restricting the number of hours a minor can work on the set, Tabitha was portrayed by a succession of identical twins: Heidi and Laura Gentry, Tamar and Julie Young, Erin and

Diane Murphy (1966–72) and, eventually, by Erin Murphy alone. (See *Tabitha* below.)

The Stephens later had a son Adam, introduced on October 16, 1969, but the boy, portrayed by David and Greg Lawrence, was not seen regularly until the final season.

Produced and directed by William Asher (Montgomery's then-husband), the well-written comedy and fine acting earned the show and its participants several Emmys over its eight-year run.

Although Elizabeth Montgomery would forever be lovingly remembered as Samantha, she was a versatile actress on television and on stage both before and after the series. She was born in 1933 or 1938, the daughter of actors Robert Montgomery and Elizabeth Allen and made her television debut on *Robert Montgomery Presents* in 1951. Following *Bewitched*, Montgomery starred in a wide range of made-for-television movies as well as in several feature films. Elizabeth Montgomery died on May 18, 1995, following a long battle with cancer.

Blacke's Magic Telecast from January 5, 1986, through September 9, 1988, this NBC detective program starred Hal Linden as Alexander Blacke, a retired stage-magician-turned-crime-buster, and Harry Morgan as Leonard Blacke, his father, a con artist and master of disguise. All of the magic was actually performed by Linden, who was trained by illusionist Mark Wilson.

Charmings, The This novel fantasy/situation comedy aired on ABC from March 20, 1987, through February 11, 1988. According to the show's premise, after Prince Charming awakened Snow White with a kiss, the Witch Queen was thrown down a well which was thought to be bottomless. The royal mother-in-law clambered out, however. Furious, she cast a SPELL that was *so* strong that it put *everyone* in the kingdom, including herself, to sleep for centuries.

They all wake up in suburban Van Oaks, California, in 1987 and must cope with the 20th century. Prince Eric Charming (Christopher Rich), still in tights, writes children's books. Snow White (Caitlin O'Hearney, spring 1987; Carol Huston, summer 1987–1988) designs dresses. Their sons Thomas (Brandon Call) and Cory (Garette Ratliffe) go to school. Their court dwarf Luther (Cork Hubbert) does windows. Queen Lillian White (Judy Parfitt), still an enchantress (though now more crabby than evil), lives in an upstairs bedroom causing problems for the family, especially when her spells just don't seem to work right. (See FILMS, *SNOW WHITE AND THE SEVEN DWARFT*)

Cinderella Telecast live on March 31, 1957, *Cinderella* was the only musical Richard Rodgers and Oscar Hammerstein II wrote specifically for television. The show, with Julie Andrews as CINDERELLA and Edith (later, Edie) Adams as the Fairy Godmother, was viewed by an estimated 107 million people, the largest television audience for any program up to that time.

A new production of *Cinderella*, aired in 1965, cast Leslie Ann Warren in the title role and Pat Carroll as the Fairy Godmother. For many years, it was an annual television event, and it has since been released on home video and laser disc.

Rights for a stage adaptation were eventually granted, and the Rodgers and Hammerstein *Cinderella* has become a staple of American community theater.

Elvira See FILMS, *ELVIRA, MISTRESS OF THE DARK*.

Free Spirit Telecast by ABC from September 22, 1989, through January 14, 1990, *Free Spirit* was a cross between *Bewitched* (see above) and *Mary Poppins* (see FILMS). Thomas J. Harper (Franc Luz) is a divorced father of three children: Robb, 16 (Paul Scherrer), Jessie, 13 (Alyson Hannigan) and Gene, 10 (Edan Gross). The hard-working attorney dad doesn't have near enough time to spend with his family, especially Gene, whose wish for a friend conjures up Winnie Goodwin (Corinne Bohrer), a witch. Sent by her WARLOCK leader, Winnie immediately sets out to make things right in the household, with just a spoonful of magic thrown in.

Friday the 13th Unrelated to the movies series of the same name, 78 episodes of *Friday the 13th* were produced for syndication between 1987 and 1990. The premise was based on the FAUST legend. Lewis Vendredi, an antiques dealer, had agreed to sell cursed curios provided by Satan in exchange for riches. Vendredi died, and without knowing the history of the shop she inherited, his niece Micki Foster (Louise Robey) reopened the store as Curious Goods. She discovered the horrible secret about her uncle—also that the relics always caused death. Foster confided in her cousin Ryan Dallion (John D. Le May) and a retired illusionist Jack Marshak (Chris Wiggins); together they began the task of retrieving all of the antiques that had already been sold to unsuspecting patrons in order to lock the demonic relics away forever. For the third and final year of production, Dallion's place on the team was filled by one of Micki's friends, Johnny Ventura (Steven Monarque).

Highway to Heaven See GUARDIAN ANGEL.

I Dream of Jeannie Telecast on NBC from September 18, 1965, through September 1, 1970, *I Dream of Jeannie* told the story of a genie (see JINN) in modern America. Tony Nelson (Larry Hagman), an astronaut, parachuted onto a deserted island during a failed space mission. He found an antique bottle, opened it and out popped a 2,000-year-old genie: a beautiful young woman in a harem outfit (but, due to television censorship rules, with no navel showing!). Jeannie (Barbara Eden) immediately accepted Nelson as her new master.

Instead of the "Samantha twitch" (see *Bewitched* above), Jeannie performed her magic by crossing her arms, closing her eyes and making a quick nod of the head.

Once back in Cocoa Beach, Florida, Captain Nelson was unable to convince anyone he had a genie, especially because Jeannie refused to materialize or work magic for anyone else. This began an ongoing suspicion of Nelson's mental health by staff psychiatrist Dr. Alfred Bellows (Hayden Rorke).

Capt. Nelson's buddy, fellow astronaut and skirt-chaser Capt. Roger Healey (Bill Daily) was introduced in the show's second season. Healey, however, learned of Jeannie and her powers and was constantly disappointed that she would not provide him with a little magical help now and then. By season's end, Nelson and Healey were both promoted to Majors.

Major Nelson had long stopped mentioning his genie. In fact, to avoid trouble, he tried to hide the mystical powers of his girlfriend Jeannie from Bellows and NASA. Although their love was obvious from the start, Jeannie and Tony Nelson were not married until their fourth season, on December 2, 1969.

Jeannie, an animated version of the program, aired on CBS's Saturday morning cartoon lineup from September 1973 through August 1975.

Jim Henson Hour, The   Telecast on NBC from April 14 through July 30, 1989, *The Jim Henson Hour* was an hour of puppetry, song and story hosted by Henson, the creator of the Muppets. The first half of each program was usually a variety-format show, with major roles taken by Muppet characters and human guest stars. (On *The Muppet Show,* another Henson production, one of regular Muppet characters, Gonzo, often appeared as the Great Gonzo, a turbaned magician whose secret words were *Ala Peanut Butter Sandwiches!* rather than ABRACADABRA.)

The second half of *The Jim Henson Hour* was modeled after an earlier series of NBC specials. The segment opened on the storyteller (John Hurt), sitting with his talking dog by the fireplace in his cozy cottage, weaving a fairy tale of wizardry and wonder. The story would be enacted by actors (frequently children) as well as puppet characters from the Henson stable.

Just Our Luck   Telecast on ABC from September 20 through December 27, 1983, this cross between *I Dream of Jeannie* and *WKRP in Cincinnati* featured Shabu (T.J. Carter), a trendy black genie (JINN) with a milquetoast television reporter named Keith Barrow (Richard Gilliland) for a master. Neither was happy with the arrangement: Shabu wanted a famous, dynamic master; Barrow had enough trouble at work at KPOX-TV without having to endure the genie's gags and pranks. Still, they were reluctant partners, and Shabu proved to be a miraculous problem-solver on more than one occasion.

Magician, The   Airing on NBC from October 2, 1973, through May 20, 1974, this short-lived series starred Bill Bixby as Anthony Blake, an internationally known illusionist. Though innocent, he had served a prison term, so after his release he used his special skills to fight crime. In January, midseason, Blake moved into the Magic Castle as his headquarters.

Though fictionalized for the television series, the Magic Castle is a real private club in Hollywood, California, created by and for magicians and their friends. Although a restaurant and bar with several showrooms, there are no living quarters as seen on *The Magician*—not even for an Anthony Blake. Bill Bixby, an amateur magician and member of the castle, performed his own tricks for the series. His instructor and consultant for *The Magician* was television illusionist and current president of the Magic Castle Board of Directors Mark Wilson.

Mr. Merlin   Telecast on CBS from October 7, 1981, through August 18, 1982, *Mr. Merlin* brought *the* MERLIN from the days of CAMELOT into the 20th century where, as Max Merlin (Bernard Hughes), he owned and operated a garage in San Francisco. He took on 15-year-old Zachary Rogers (Clark Brandon) as an apprentice wizard, but the mischievous boy seemed to always have problems with his SPELLS. Among the other regular characters was Alexandra (Elaine Joyce), an ethereal intermediary between Max and his sorcerer superiors.

Monsters   These 52 half-hour episodes produced for syndication between 1988 and 1990 were created by the producers of *Tales of the Darkside* and were similarly themed. The occult stories included yarns of sorcery, wizardry, WITCHCRAFT, ZOMBIES and SPIRITS.

Odyssey, The   In May 1997, NBC aired a $40 million four-part mini-series adaptation of The ODYSSEY, produced by Robert Halmi, Sr. and directed by the Andrei Konchalovsky. The international cast included Armante Assante (Odysseus), Irene Papas (his mother, Anticlea), Greta Scacchi (his wife, Penelope), Geraldine Chaplin (Penelope's maid), Eric Roberts (a suitor to Penelope), Richard Trewett (Achilles), Isabella Rossellini (the goddess Athena), Vanessa Williams (the SIREN Calypso) and Bernadette Peters (the sorceress CIRCE).

Off to See the Wizard   Aired between September 8, 1967, and September 20, 1968, *Off to See the Wizard* was a series of children's movies; some were made specifically for television, and others were edited and telecast in two parts from theatrical films (e.g., *Clarence, the Cross-eyed Lion* and *Flipper*). Introducing the segments were animated characters from *The Wizard of Oz* (see WIZARD OF OZ, THE), including the Wicked Witch of the West and the Wizard himself.

Paradise   *Paradise* was telecast from October 27, 1988, through June 14, 1991. During its final season, the show was retitled *Guns of Paradise.* Lee Horsely starred as Ethan Allen Cord, a gunfighter-turned-adoptive-parent in the 1890s gold-mining town of Paradise, California. The show is perhaps the only western ever to portray a Native American MEDICINE MAN as a regular character (John Taylor, played by Dehl Berti).

Sabrina, the Teenage Witch   Debuting on ABC in September 1996, *Sabrina, the Teenage Witch,* based on characters that originally appeared in Archie Comics, stars Melissa Joan Hart as Sabrina, who discovers on her 16th birthday that she is a witch. Other than having magical powers, she is a normal high school girl. She lives with her two aunts, Hilda (Caroline Rhea) and Zelda (Beth Broderick), who are also witches. Joel Hodgson is the program's magic consultant.

Tabitha   From November 12, 1977, to August 25, 1978, *Tabitha* told the adventures of Samantha and Darrin Stephens's daughter (see *Bewitched* above) as an adult. Still a witch, Tabitha (Lisa Hartman) has taken a normal mortal's job, a production assistant at KLXA-TV, where her younger brother Adam (David Ankrum) was also employed. Regular characters included their interfering enchantress Aunt Minerva (Karen Morrow).

A Saturday-morning cartoon series based on the Tabitha character also aired.

Through the Crystal Ball   Telecast on CBS in television's infancy, from April 18 through July 4, 1949, this unusual show interpreted popular fairy tales and fables through dance. For the first few weeks, Jimmy Savo, a mime, was host and narrator. Different choreographers and dancers told such well-known stories as "Cinderella" (see FILMS, CINDERELLA) and "Ali Baba and the 40 Thieves" (see ARABIAN NIGHTS).

Touched By An Angel   See GUARDIAN ANGEL.

Tucker's Witch   Telecast on CBS from October 6, 1982, to August 8, 1983, *Tucker's Witch* was a detective series featuring crime solvers Rick Tucker (Tim Matheson) and his wife Amanda (Catherine Hicks), who also happened to be a witch. While he plied the normal gumshoe route, she used intuition and SPELLS, although her magic was not infallible. She was sometimes assisted by Dickens, her Siamese cat FAMILIAR, and her mother Ellen Hobbes (Barbara Barrie) who was a witch as well.

Wizards and Warriors   Telecast on CBS from February 26 through May 14, 1983, *Wizards and Warriors* was set in the mythical time of King ARTHUR but not at CAMELOT. Instead, the show told the tales of the mythical kingdom of Camarand. Princess Ariel (Julia Duffy), the daughter of good King Baaldorf (Tom Hill) and Queen Lattinia (Julie Payne), is betrothed to Prince Erik Greystone (Jeff Conaway). Greystone is occasionally assisted by the ancient Wizard Tranquil (Ian Wolfe) in his fight against the malevolent Prince Dirk Blackpool (Duncan Regehr), whose attempts to usurp the throne are aided by the sorcery and BLACK MAGIC of the enticing Witch Bethel (Randi Rooks) and Wizard Vector (Clive Revill).

Year at the Top, A   A summer replacement series on CBS, *A Year at the Top* aired from August 5 through September 4, 1977. Greg (Greg Evigan) and Paul (Paul Shaffer), two young rock-and-roll musicians from Boise, Idaho, move to Hollywood to get a record contract. Frederick J. Hanover (Gabriel Dell), famous for discovering new talent, offers them the titular "year at the top." There is only one catch: Hanover is the son of Satan and wants their souls at the end of the tour. (See FAUST.)

Tempest, The   Penned during the reign of James I (the author of DEMONOLOGIE), *The Tempest* was the last play written, at least in its entirety, by William SHAKESPEARE. It was first presented at the king's court in Whitehall on November 11, 1611. It was given another royal performance at the wedding festivities of Princess Elizabeth. The play remained unpublished, however, until 1623 when it appeared as the first play in the First Folio.

Although there are several possible inspirations for the play, including the actual shipwreck of the *Sea-Venture* in the Bermuda islands, there is no single source for the drama. The play is composed in a classical five-act structure, although little or no time passes between the fourth and final acts.

The Tempest tells the story of PROSPERO, the duke of Milan, who was usurped by his brother Antonio and cast afloat with his daughter Miranda. They finally washed up on a remote island which was once the refuge of SYCORAX, a witch, but was then inhabited only by her deformed son CALIBAN. Prospero, a sorcerer, used his magic to make Caliban his attendant. Prospero also freed ARIEL and other SPIRITS from Sycorax's captive SPELL, and he forced them to become his servants as well.

As the play opens, Prospero and Miranda have been stranded on the enchanted island for 12 years. Prospero produces a mighty sea storm (the tempest) to crash the ship of Antonio and members of the court onto his island; all survive the shipwreck. Among those onboard with Antonio are Alonso (the king of Naples and Antonio's accomplice), Sebastian (Alonso's brother), Ferdinand (Alonso's son), Gonzalo (a court counsellor to Antonio), Stephano (a servant and sot) and Trinculo (the court jester or fool). Ferdinand is washed up on shore away from the others, and each party assumes the other to be dead.

Prospero arranges the meeting of Ferdinand and Miranda, who, according to his wishes, fall in love and pledge their vows to marry. The sorcerer conjures up spirits to "bestow upon the eyes of this young couple / Some vanity of mine art." When the visions later evaporate, Prospero explains to Ferdinand

> Our revels now are ended. These our actors,
> As I foretold you, were all spirits, and
> Are melted into air, into thin air;
>   . . . We are such stuff
> As dreams are made on.
>   (IV, i, 148–150; 156–157)

Meanwhile, Sebastian and Antonio conspire to kill Alonso and Gonzalo, both of whom had aided Prospero during his initial exile. Caliban, however, urges Stephano and Trinculo to assassinate Prospero instead. Prospero, of course, prevails and banishes Caliban, Stephano and Trinculo.

As the play draws to an end, Prospero has BEWITCHed Alonso, Antonio and Sebastian, turning them into madmen. Ariel pleads on their behalf. He tells his master that, although as a spirit *he* has no feelings, the sorcerer would be saddened if he saw them in their reduced state. Prospero agrees to forgive the men and remove the CURSE—not because he *wants* to but because, as a noble man, he knows that he *should*.

Prospero delivers a soliloquy in which he renounces the art of magic. Generally divided by Shakespearean scholars into three sections, the first eight lines (V, i, 33–40) speak to his enchanted assistants, such as the fairies and the elves.

In the second section (V, i, 41–50), Prospero describes the magic he has performed. In addition to his creation of the tempest, Prospero has (with the aid of his supernatural servants) eclipsed the sun at noon, caused thunder, lightning and earthquakes, uprooted trees and resurrected the dead.

In the last eight lines of the speech (V, i, 50–57), Prospero actually disowns his sorcery, saying that after he removes his CHARMs and spells he will break and bury his staff (see WAND) and throw his GRIMOIRE of magical INCANTATIONS into the sea:

> But this rough magic
> I here abjure, and, when I have requir'd
> Some heavenly music, which even now I do,
> To work mine end upon their senses that
> This airy charm is for, I'll break my staff,
> Bury it certain fathoms in the earth,
> And deeper than did ever plummet sound
> I'll drown my book.

Ariel delivers Antonio, Alonso and Sebastian to his master. Prospero draws them into his MAGIC CIRCLE and ends their insanity. He greets Gonzalo warmly, pardons Antonio, then reunites Alonso and Ferdinand. Alonso, in turn, apologizes and offers to atone for his actions. Antonio and Sebastian also acquiesce but remain distant. Finally, Prospero blesses the union of Ferdinand and Miranda.

The master carpenter (boatswain) and captain of the ship arrive, following Ariel, to announce that the ship has been repaired as if by magic. Stephano and Trinculo and Caliban are brought in. Prospero commends the first two to their masters, then, as a final gesture before sailing home for Italy, Prospero releases Ariel and his fellow spirits. Caliban is freed, to be once again left alone on his deserted island.

The Tempest has been the basis for many stories, novels, FILMS, MUSICAL THEATER and plays. Among these are the movies *Forbidden Planet* (1954), *The Tempest* (1980) and *Tempest*

One of the many mysterious coves along the coastline of Corfu, which is traditionally believed to be the island that Shakespeare used as a model for his isle of enchantment in *The Tempest.* (Photo by author)

(1982); the 1989 musical comedy *Return to the Forbidden Planet* by Bob Carlton; an unfinished opera by Wolfgang Amadeus Mozart (1756–1791) utilizing a libretto, *Die Geisterinsel*, by F.H. von Einsiedel with revisions by F.W. Gotter (the libretto finally being used in 1798 to produce four separate operas by different composers); a proposed opera by Felix Mendelssohn (1809–1847), who rejected a libretto in 1831 and another in 1846 by two different librettists, Romani in Italy and Scribe in France; *The Tempest*, a play by John Dryden (1631–1700) and Sir William D'Avenant, (also seen as Davenant) (1606–1668), adapted in 1674 by Thomas Shadwell (1642?–1692) as *The Enchanted Island*, with incidental music by Henry Purcell (1659–1695); a musical composition by Hector Berlioz (1803–1869); the 1873 Symphonic Fantasia on *The Tempest* by Peter Ilich Tchaikovsky (1840–1893); and a prelude and 17 other incidental pieces, considerable both in amount of musical selections and required instrumentation, by Jean Sibelius (1865–1957), all composed to accompany a 1925 Finnish production of the play; *Comus*, a court masque by John Milton (1608–1674), written in 1634, first performed that same year at Ludlow Castle in England and published anonymously in 1637; the poem "Ariel to Miranda" by Percy Shelley (1792–1822), the poetic collection *The Sea and the Mirror* by W.H. Auden (1907–1973); and the poem *Caliban upon Setebos* by Robert Browning (1812–1889), in which Caliban deduces why Setebos created the earth. In the summer of 1995, a celebrated production of *The Tempest* starring Patrick Stewart as Prospero appeared at the Delacorte Theatre in Central Park as part of the New York Shakespeare Festival and then re-opened for a limited run on Broadway at the Broadhurst Theatre from October 10 through December 31, 1995.

tetragrammaton   IHVH (also seen as YHWH and JHVH), called the tetragrammaton, was used first by ancient Jewish priests and then by the laity when speaking of the Lord of the Old Testament of the Bible. The actual name, *Jehovah* or *Yahweh*, was considered too sacred to be written or uttered aloud.

Other appellations, also of Hebraic origin, were Adonai, Elōai, Elohim, IAŌ and JAH.

Like many mysterious signs and symbols of archaic times, the tetragrammaton was adopted centuries later by wizards as an occult aid in angelic INVOCATION. The tetragrammaton is also frequently seen throughout the KABALLAH and other GRIMOIREs.

Thalaba the Destroyer   Written by the British poet Robert Southey (1774–1843) and published in 1801, *Thalaba the Destroyer* tells of the Muslim warrior Thalaba's quest to annihilate Domdaniel, an empire of sorcerers under the ocean. His success is due in part to a magic RING, but he dies in the process of achieving victory. After death, he meets his wife in Paradise.

Theophilus (fl. early sixth century A.D.) Theophilus, the bursar of his church in Adana, in north Cilicia or Trachyn was the first recorded person to have sold his soul to the Devil. The bishop removed Theophilus around A.D. 538, so to regain his holy position Theophilus turned to demonic forces. He contacted the sorcerer Salatin, who conjured Satan for him. The bursar sealed a pact, exchanging his eternal soul for earthly reward and revenge.

The legend became infamous throughout Europe. Eutychianus, Theophilus's apprentice, recorded the tragic tale in Greek, and Paul the Deacon translated it into Latin. Hrotswitha, a nun in Gandersheim, was inspired by the story to write a series of dialogues in poetry about the incident. In the 13th century, Gautier de Coinsy used it as the basis for a French poem.

Ruteboeuf used the story of Theophilus as the plot for his play *Le Miracle de Théophile*. He clearly dramatized the consummation of the pact between the Devil and Theophilus:

> **The Devil**: Now join thy hands and so become my man; I will help thee to the uttermost.
> **Theophilus**: Behold, I do thee homage, fair lord, but I shall have my punishment hereafter.

The pact with the devil read in full:

> To all who shall read this open letter I, Satan, let know that the fortune of Theophilus is changed indeed, and that he has done me homage, so might he have once more his lordship, and that with the RING of his finger he has sealed this letter and with his blood written it, and no other ink has used therein.

The story was also memorialized on a celebrated set of church-door engravings at the Abbey of Souillac, France. (See also *FAUST*; FAUSTUS, JOHANNES.)

Thoth The Egyptian god of magic, ASTROLOGY, learning and mathematics, Thoth was believed to have created all of the occult wisdom of the universe. Thoth was also believed to be a great healer, and he restored Horus's sight after he was blinded by Set. Because of his mystic powers, Thoth's name is part of many of the SPELLS and INCANTATIONS found in *The Egyptian BOOK OF THE DEAD*.

Thoth most frequently appears in hieroglyphs as an ibis-headed man, although he is sometimes portrayed with the head of a baboon and holding the crescent moon. Also the god of writing, Thoth was also often depicted carrying a receptacle for pen and ink; he was known as the Scribe of the Company of Gods and The Lord of the Divine Books.

In occult literature, Thoth is often associated with HERMES, the Greek messenger god and patron god of magic. Over centuries, these gods merged together in the minds of occultists and they became identified with the mystic HERMES TRISMEGISTUS.

Legend has it that Thoth produced several arcane papyruses, now lost, teaching ALCHEMY, astrology and imparting the secrets of EGYPTIAN MAGIC. The most famous of these manuscripts was *The Book of Thoth*, which revealed the path to the gods. Originally kept in a golden box and housed within a temple, the book was hidden by Thoth's priests in antiquity. (See also EYE OF HORUS.)

Tinkerbell See FILMS, *PETER PAN*.

Tiresias In ancient Greek mythology, Tiresias was blinded by the gods, but, in exchange, he was gifted with the powers of prophecy and DIVINATION. He was also able to communicate with birds, and he was an "adept" (i.e., a master) at calling up SPIRITS through NECROMANCY.

When mentioned in Homer's *The ODYSSEY*, Tiresias was an elderly sage and soothsayer residing in the Underworld. The enchantress CIRCE told Odysseus that he would find Tiresias there and that the seer would tell the wanderer how to finally find his way home.

Soon after his arrival in the Kingdom of the Dead, Odysseus was met by the old man bearing a golden staff. The stranger prophesied that on Ulysses's journey the hero's ship would land on the island where Apollo's cattle grazed. Odysseus was warned not to touch the cattle lest all be lost. He further prophesied that it would be a long, long time before Odysseus would reach Ithaca. Once there, Tiresias warned, Odysseus's troubles would still not be over. He would discover many suitors courting his faithful wife. Tiresias admonished that after he justly slays the men, Odysseus must escape the city and make sacrifice to Poseidon. Finally, the soothsayer predicted that Ulysses would live to a "rich old age" and have a gentle death at sea.

Titania See *MIDSUMMER NIGHT'S DREAM, A*.

Thoth, the Egyptian deity (right), stands before the goddess Isis (seated, left). (Modern rendering on papyrus of ancient tomb painting and hieroglyph. Photo by author)

Tolkien, J(ohn) R(onald) R(euel) (1892–1973) Best known for his fantasy novel *The HOBBIT* and its sequel, *The LORD OF THE RINGS* trilogy (1954–1955) Tolkien was born January 3, 1892, in Blomfontein, South Africa. After his father's early death, the boy returned to Birmingham, England, to be with his mother. She died when Tolkien was 12, and he became the ward of a Catholic priest.

Tolkien studied at Oxford University. During World War I he served as a member of the Lancashire Fusiliers, married during the war, and returned to university after the armistice. He received his M.A. in 1919.

A specialist in Middle English, Tolkien was a professor of Anglo-Saxon language and literature at Pembroke College at Oxford for 20 years. He was named a Fellow of the College and received an Honorary Fellowship from Exeter College.

Tolkien was 45 years old when he published what he considered to be a children's book, *The Hobbit*. The first volume of *The Lord of the Rings* trilogy was published in 1954; the others followed within two years.

Tolkien died in 1973, leaving behind numerous manuscripts on the creation, history, mythologies and languages of Middle-Earth. Foremost among these is *The Silmarillion*, a prequel of sorts to *The Hobbit*, which was published posthumously in 1977. Tolkien's other writings included philosophical essays and literary critiques.

Tragicall History of the Life and Death of Doctor Faustus, The See DOCTOR FAUSTUS.

transmutation See ALCHEMY.

transvection See BROOMSTICK; WITCHCRAFT.

Trithemius, Johannes (1462–1516) The abbot of Sponheim (near Mainz), Germany, Johannes Trithemius was a contemporary, friend and, purportedly, teacher of Cornelius AGRIPPA and PARACELSUS. Their combined philosophies and manuscripts influenced generations of occultists.

Following his education in Heidelberg, Trithemius returned to his native Sponheim. There, he took shelter in a Benedictine monastery and soon entered the clerical life. Trithemius was said to have exorcised the Devil out of Mary of Burgundy, wife of Emperor Maximilian.

Like many clerics of his day, Trithemius was also interested in all matters of the supernatural. Under the guise of ecclesiastical articles, Trithemius wrote on ALCHEMY, a subject that was to be a lifelong passion. Wary that the church might disapprove of his thinking, Trithemius designed secret codes to hide his occult thoughts within his texts. Unfortunately, he never disclosed the secrets to his ciphers. When read in translation, all arcane meanings in his texts are lost; even read in the original Latin, the manuscripts pose enigmas for modern occultists.

Trithemius wrote several books on magic and sorcery, including *Liber Octo Quaestionum*, in which he categorized different types of demons, and *Antipalus maleficiorum*, in which he refuted the belief that SOLOMON had actually written *The Clavicle* attributed to him.

Perhaps the best known work of Trithemius is his 1500 occult manuscript *STEGANOGRAPHIA*, one of the most important and influential books ever written on Angelic magic. (See also DEE, JOHN; ENOCHIAN MAGIC; FORMAN, SIMON; *KEY OF SOLOMON*; LEMEGETON: *THE LESSER KEY OF SOLOMON*; TURNER, ROBERT.)

Turner, Robert (c.1620–1665) Living a half-century after the era of mysticism that pervaded the reign of Queen Elizabeth I, Turner was the first (and to this day, the best) translator into English of several of the most important early texts on ALCHEMY and other occult matters.

Little is known about Turner's early life due to the loss of records during the Great London Fire of 1666. Definitive genealogy is also difficult because Turner was a very common name of the period, and the author provided few autobiographical notes. The fact that the translator refers to himself in four of his works as "Robert Turner of Holshott" has given scholars the best clue to his identity.

Turner's father lived in the Holshott manor, near a bog and the Grove Copse, located in the southern region of Heckfield parish, North Hampshire, England. The first record of Robert Turner is his admission on June 17, 1636, to Christ's College, Cambridge. In addition to his regular studies, he was tutored by a Mr. Brearley. Turner moved to Middle Temple on October 9, 1637, and he received his bachelor of arts degree two years later. In November 1639, Turner entered Lincoln's Inn (one of the Inns of Court, a "finishing school" for sons of the wealthy), where he studied law. He did, in fact, practice law after graduation, but not until the mid-to-late 1650s.

There is no certain record of Turner's life between 1640 and 1654. A note exists that he lived for a time in Workingham. He later wrote that he was already interested in FOLK MEDICINE by this time, having cured "the Itch" by means of water gathered from a hollow beech tree in 1644. Oddly, signs point to the possibility of his having worked, at least for a time, as a domestic servant or valet to Sir John Thorowgood during this period. By the mid-1650s, Turner was living in London. He moved into Carpenter's Yard and then settled into Christopher Alley, possibly in a section of Christ's Hospital that was opened to lodgers.

With the civil war and commonwealth rule (1642–1660), church control over affairs of state waned. Books on occult themes were no longer subject to immediate censorship, and authors were not automatically charged with heresy or WITCHCRAFT.

Turner's fame began in 1654 with the publishing of his first book, *Mikrokosmos: A Description of the Little World, Being a Discovery of the Body of Man . . . Hereunto is added . . . the cure of wounds . . . the sicknesses attributed to the twelve Signes and Planets, with their Natures*. His only other wholly original work of the decade was the 1657(?) *Woman's Counsellor, or the Feminine Physician modestly treating of such occult accidents and secret diseases incident to that sex*. *Woman's Counsellor . . .*, reprinted in 1686, was unusual, if not unique, for its day in that it addressed medical problems specific to women.

These two works both displayed Turner's interest in mystic thinking. Most of Turner's books, however, were translations of early occult writings, and it is for these translations that Turner is justly remembered. Following is a list of Turner's translations, along with their first publication dates, plus other relevant information:

Fourth Book of Occult Philosophy. (1655; attributed to Heinrich Cornelius AGRIPPA)

Arbatel of Magick, de Magia Veterum. (1655; published anonymously in Basel, 1575; bound with the *Fourth Book . . .*)

Astrologicall Opticks. Wherein are represented the Faces of every Signe, with the Images of each Degree in the Zodiack. (1655; first published as *Astrolabium Planum* in Augsburg in 1488 by author Johannes Angelus [also seen as Johann Engel], 1472–1512; second edition published in Venice in 1494)

Astronomical Geomancy. (1655; attributed to Gerard of Cremona, 1114–1187; bound with the *Fourth Book . . .*)

Heptameron: or, Magical Elements. (1655; Peter de Abano, 1250–1317; bound with the *Fourth Book . . .* ; provides methods to summon angels)

Isagoge . . . Of the Nature of Spirits (1655; published in Basil, 1563, by author Georg Pictorius von Villingen, c.1500–1569; bound with *Fourth Book . . .*)

Of Geomancy (1655; Agrippa; bound with *Fourth Book . . .*)

Compleat Bone-Setter: Being the Method of Curing Broken Bones, Dislocated Joynts, and Ruptures, commonly called Broken Bellies. (1656, reprinted 1665; written by Thomas Moulton, fl. 1540?, a self-proclaimed "Doctor of Divinity of the Order of Friar Preachers")

Of the Supreme Mysteries of Nature (1656; part of the *Archidoxes Magicae* by PARACELSUS; first published in Latin in Cracow in 1569)

Ars Notoria: The Notary Art of Solomon; shewing the Cabalistic key of magical operations, the liberal sciences, divine revelation, and the art of memory. Whereunto is added an Astrological Catechism, fully demonstrating the art of Judicial Astrology. (1657; written in Latin by APOLLONIUS, Leovitius and others)

An Astrological Catechisme. (1657; Leovitius; bound with *Ars Notoria*)

Enchiridion Medicum. (1657; written in Latin as *Praxis Medicorum* by Dr. John Sadler, d. 1595)

Of the Chymical Transmutation, Genealogy, and Generation of Metals and Minerals. (1657; Paracelsus; originally published in Latin in 1576)

Philosophical and Chymical Experiments of that famous Philosopher Raymond Lully; containing the right and due Composition of both Elixirs; the admirable and perfect way of making the great Stone of the Philosophers. (1657; written in High German and Latin by LULLY; cotranslation with an otherwise-unidentified "W. W., student in the Celestial Sciences"; bound with *Of the Chymical Transmutation . . .*)

Sal, Lumen et Spiritus Mundi Philosophici: or, the dawning of the Day, discovered by the beams of light: shewing, the true salt and secrets of the philosophers, the first and universal Spirit of the World. (1657; written in French around 1600 by Clovis Hesteau, Sieur de Nuysement. Turner worked from a 1651 Latin translation by Dr. Lodovicus Combachius, also known as Ludwig Combach of Hesse, 1590–1657. The book deals with the Salt of the Philosophers which, along with Mercury and Sulpher, make up

the three "Alchemical Principles of Nature" necessary for manifestation. Turner felt enough material was already available in print on the latter two Principles)

The church reestablished its power over the state and its citizens beginning with the monarchic Restoration in 1660. Philosophic thought was discouraged, and passage of the Licensing Act of 1663 allowed the church or state to censor any work that it considered to promote heresy. Turner wisely turned his attention away from translating occult tracts and concentrated on his interest in medicine, especially herbal cures.

In March 1663, Turner finished his masterpiece, *Botanologia. The Brittish Physician; or, the Nature and Vertues of English Plants* [sic]; and it was published the following year. The book held to the DOCTRINE OF SIGNATURES, a metaphysical belief that each plant carried a signature, or clue, as to its possible medicinal uses. Perhaps it was the prevailing conservative religious mood that led Turner to warn that the herbs should only be used for good and simple curative purposes, not like "Cacochymists, Medean Hags and Sorcerers now adays; who . . . out of some Diabolical intention search after the more Magical and Occult Vertues of Herbs and Plants to accomplish some wickedness." Frequently mentioned throughout the book was Turner's offer to sell ready-made herbal medicines, including a "Sovereign Antidote against the Plague, and all infectious Diseases," either directly from his home or through his booksellers (especially his main distributor, Thomas Rooks.)

Unfortunately, Turner's work was inevitably compared to the earlier 1653 home-cure book of Nicholas Culpeper (d. 1654), *The English Physician Enlarged, with 369 Medicines made of English Herbs.* Culpeper's famous book also subscribed to the Doctrine of Signatures, but, written in layman's language, it was always more popular than Turner's guide (although *Botanologia* did have a second edition in 1687).

In 1665, Robert Turner rereleased his *Compleat Bone-Setter.* Supposedly just a revision and enlargement of his original translation of the Moulton book, this second edition, dated June 25, 1665, was almost entirely new material, including the timely chapter "Treating the Pestilence." Perhaps influenced by the unfavorable comparison of his earlier writing style to Culpeper's, Turner stated in his preface that he had written in "plain English" so that "people who are able, may easily make medicines for themselves."

Another decimating bout of the plague hit London beginning the first week of June 1665. Almost 1,200 died in a single week in September! Because no record of Turner appears (except for reprints of earlier works) after June 1665, it is presumed that Robert Turner died of the plague and was buried anonymously, as were so many hundreds of others.

Announced for publication by Turner but untranslated at the time of his death were the STEGANOGRAPHIA (TRITHEMIUS) and the other sections of *Archidoxes Magicae* (Paracelsus) and *Occult Philosophy* (Agrippa).

Four of Turner's translations have had modern reprint editions: *Arabatel of Magick* [sic] (1979), *Archidoxes of Magic* (1975, reprint title for *Of the Supreme Mysteries . . .*), *Fourth Book of Occult Philosophy* (1978) and *Compleat Bone-Setter* (1981). (See also ARS NOTORIA; LILLY, WILLIAM.)

Ursula See FILMS, *THE LITTLE MERMAID*.

Utchat See EYE OF HORUS.

Vathek, an Arabian Tale *Vathek* was written in French by William Beckford (1759–1844) and, after translation by Samuel Henley and the author, was first published in English in 1786. Over the years, Beckford added three more "Episodes" to the book (the last being incomplete) and incorporated them into the 1815 French edition.

Caliph Vathek is a cold and ruthless ruler, whose eyes have the power to kill (see EVIL EYE). His mother, a wicked enchantress, convinces Vathek to make a pact with the devil Eblis. Vathek slaughters 50 innocent children in exchange for a mere glance of a legendary treasure amassed by ancient sultans and hidden in the ruined city of Istakar. When he finally reaches the underground realm of Eblis, the caliph finds the hoard to be worthless. For his transgressions, Vathek's heart explodes into flames while he is still alive.

Virgo See ASTROLOGY; HOROSCOPE; ZODIAC.

Vivien In the Arthurian legends, *Vivien* is one of the most commonly known names accorded to the LADY OF THE LAKE. According to some Arthurian scholars, however, the name is actually a corruption, perhaps due to a clerical misreading or improper transcription, of the less-known name *Nymus*. (See also ARTHUR, KING; MERLIN; NIMUË.)

voodoo Also seen as *vo-dou, vo-du, vodou* and *vodun*, voodoo is a religion, permeated with magical beliefs, that was first practiced by tribal nations in Africa. It shares mystical ritual traditions with the Catholic church and occult European societies such as the ROSICRUCIANS and the Freemasons. One early legend even suggests that MOSES practiced voodoo at one point, having been converted by the black Midian priest Râ-Gu-El Pethro (Jethro).

The origin of the name *voodoo* is uncertain. Most occult scholars suggest that the word means "SPIRIT" or "god." Other authorities contend that the name *voodoo* comes from two smaller words of the Fons, a Western African tribal group from what is today Benin (formerly Dahomey): *vo*, meaning "introspection" and *du*, meaning "into the unknown."

Many of the modern terms used in the practice of voodoo are a combination of the original African Fon and Kongo cultures and French, the language of many of the New World colonies where voodoo flourished. For instance, *mambo*, the Haitian word for a voodoo priestess is a mixture of the Fon *nanbo* (meaning "Mother of magic CHARMS") and the Kongo *mambu* (meaning "healer").

Voodoo worships a supreme god called *Bondye* and numerous gods known as *Iwa* (also seen as *loa* or *loas*.) There are three types of spirits: ancestral, the souls of twins and the mysteries, which are human emotions or forces of nature in divine form. The *Iwa* are separated into different "families" of gods, the two largest being the benign *Rada* spirits of Western Africa and the fiery *Petwo* spirits of Central Africa and the Americas.

An example of *Rada* spirits are the *Gede*, which represent the dead and sexual regeneration. They dress in black and adorn themselves with graveyard images, and they are known as tricksters and healers. The foremost *Gede* is the Baron (Baron Samedi, or Baron Saturday). The *Ogou* are warrior spirits, found in both the *Rada* and *Petwo* families. They are hot-tempered, have power over iron and are known as healers and magicians.

The *loa* spirits are found in all things: plants, animals, man and the ancestral dead. Thus, voodoo, asserts that there *is* life after death and the ancestral spirits are able to return to and interact with the mortal world, for good or evil.

As is common with other religions, the rites, ceremonies and customs of voodoo evolved slowly over the centuries, changing from their original rituals. In Africa, for instance, each tribe had a set of *loas*, who required specific invocational rites to contact them. The rituals of each individual tribe varied greatly, according to the environment of the tribe and its members' personal experiences (both awake and in dreams). Different loas provided different answers when confronted with a challenge.

During the slave trade, voodoo was brought to the New World, flourishing in the Caribbean, Brazil and what would become the southeastern and south-coastal United States. Voodoo took particular hold in the West Indies, especially Haiti, Cuba and the bayou region of Louisiana. During the process of relocation, sects observed the worship, songs and dance of each other, and the sharing of rituals and beliefs occurred.

Today, the voodoo temple or church structure is known as the *oum'phor* or *ounfò*. It consists of a large, usually circular room, called the peristyle, where most of the rituals are performed. The area may be opened, or, if enclosed, have a conical ceiling, thatched or made of corrugated iron. The floor is always of stamped earth, and the walls are only 4 or 5 feet high. Benches surround the interior perimeter of the walls. One large central wooden pole called the *poteau-mitan* or *poto mitan* stands at the room's center. The *poteau-mitan* is said to act as a form of lightning rod for divine energy.

Attached to the peristyle are one (or more) room(s) acting as an altar room or sanctuary. Some voodoo practitioners reserve the word *oum'phor* or *ounfò* to mean the actual altar room, or the holy of holies. The altar, or altar stone, is known as the *pé*, from the Dahomey word *kpé*, meaning "stone." About four feet high, the pé contains ceremonial implements and several clay pots, such as the *pots-de-tête*, into which part of a worshiper's spirit mystically travels while he or she prays, and the *govis*, which is where the spirits of the voodoo gods dwell when summoned.

In addition to the altar room, a special room called a *djévo* is also sometimes present. Shaped like a tomb, the area is used to question and initiate newcomers, who metaphorically die and are born again or resurrected into the voodoo faith.

As the world turns on its solar axis, so the *poteau-mitan* acts as an axis for the peristyle. The post represents *Legba Ati-Bon* (meaning "wood of justice"), the chief voodoo god, and it is usually painted or carved with spiral bands representing two serpent gods, *Danbhalah Wédo Yé-H-we* and *Aida Wédo*. The top of the post represents the sky, and the bottom represents hell. Suspended from the ceiling near the *poteau-mitan* is a small model boat. This vessel represents the moon goddess, Erzulie, on her nightly flight.

If such a sturdy structure is not available for worship, an open space will do, with a lighted candle substituting for the *poteau-mitan* and a bowl of holy water for the boat. Even if the temple does not have an actual wooden *poteau-mitan*, the magic post is, nevertheless, believed to hold there, but invisible.

Even the trees in the area of the *oum'phor* have mystical importance. Called *reposoirs* or *arbres-reposoirs*, they are the tabernacles, the homes, of the voodoo gods, and the trees themselves are considered to be holy spirits.

Voodoo paraphernalia is full of symbolism. Similar to the PENTACLES of Western wizardry, mystic, geometric drawings called *vèvès* (from the Fon *veve*, meaning ritual ground marking) are inscribed on such ritualistic surfaces as the floor of the *oum'phor*, the peristyle and food offerings. The illustrations represent astral forces located on three different astral planes within the voodoo cosmology. Voodoo priests often carry notebooks filled with *vèvès* and cosmographs (also seen as cosmograms).

Ritual flags (*drapo*) are often used to decorate the peristyle, and they are often paraded around the *ounfò* at the beginning of a voodoo ritual. A ceremonial sword, known as a *ku-bhs-sah*, is at hand, representing the ability of the gods to vanquish all foes. The *assen*, an iron rod used to assist in intercession to the gods, is always found in a temple, but a voodoo practitioner also receives a personal *assen* for his home upon being initiated into the faith. Personal *oangas* (AMULETs) and *bakas* (TALISMANs) are also thought to hold magical power against harm and enemies.

Any object can be dedicated to an *lwa* and set on a voodoo altar, either at the temple or in one's own home. Once dedicated to the spirit, the item is believed to contain magic powers. There are four basic types:

Signifiers, such as *mirwa* (mirrors) and crosses (representing crossroads, thought to be sacred spots)
Summoning objects, such as drums and bells
Spirit repositories, such as *pakèt kongo* (*kongo* packets, which hold herbs), *govi* (said to hold the spirit of the deceased), *potèt* (head pots, which hold hair and nail clippings) and *wanga* (or charms). A popular *wanga* is the sorcerer's bottle which holds the spirits of the dead known as *zonbi*.
Offerings, including ceremonial calabashes or dishes known as *kwi*, sequin-covered bottles and small, cloth dolls. These dolls are thought to be able to carry messages to the spirits. They are left in cemeteries or in crossroads, often with notes pinned to them.

Although the voodoo religion does not have a hierarchy of clergy like most Western organized faiths, there are ritualistic positions for a voodoo ceremony. A male leader of the services is called a *houn'gan*; a female leader is known as a *mam'bo*. (If male, a future *houn'gan* is called a *confiance*; a novice female is a *mam'bo caille*.) The leadership capacity of the *houn'gan* or *mam'bo* goes far beyond the time of the actual ceremony. He or she is thought to be in direct contact with the *loa* and their opinions extend, therefore, to all aspects of life, religious and secular.

The ceremony itself has ritual procedures, beginning with the recitation of special prayers, the drawing of *vèvè*, the lighting of magical lamps and ritual bathing (for cleansing and purification). ANIMAL blood sacrifices might also performed. Although human sacrifice, known as *cabrit thomazos*, is now taboo, the practice is said to covertly continue among the red, or criminal, voodoo sects. (Ironically, the red cults justify their acts by referring to the crucifixion of JESUS as a human sacrifice.)

Music is an important part of all rituals, and there are three types of drummers known as *manmanier*, *secondier* and *boulahier*; collectively they are called the *houn'tôrguiers*. Other musical performers are the *ogantier*, playing an *ogan*, a sort of flattened bell without a clapper, and the *trianglier*, playing a triangle. The voodoo leader brandishes a magical/bell called an *asson*. A chorus called the *houn'sihs*, led by a *houn'guénicon* peristyle, chants and prays. Of course, no ritual would be complete without ecstatic dancing.

It is believed that during a voodoo ceremony, one of the spirits can "mount" a person, called a "horse" while possessed, to take command of his or her physical body. The god might do so to protect the human, to implant temporarily a special skill or power, such as the ability to heal, advise, punish or give warnings.

Perhaps the most prevalent misconception of voodoo is the practice of sticking pins into a wax or cloth VOODOO DOLL to CURSE, wound or kill an enemy. Another is the idea that voodoo masters control undead slaves known as ZOMBIES. Both voodoo dolls and zombies, however, are the product of creative writers and Hollywood fantasy—or, if they exist, they are not part of the voodoo religion.

voodoo doll   The term *voodoo doll* has become generic for any doll-like figure which is used for casting SPELLs by SYMPATHETIC MAGIC. *Voodoo doll* is actually a misnomer because in the religion of VOODOO, practitioners do not use dolls or *popets* to lay CURSES on their enemies. The depiction of a cloth doll stuck with pins is a fantasy of writers and FILMmakers, but the image is difficult, if not impossible, to erase.

Ancient Greek and Roman sorcerers, however, *did* utilize miniature figurines in their cursing. European sorcerers during the Middle Ages most often fashioned their images out of wax, adorning them, if possible, with pieces of hair, nails clippings or clothing of intended victim. If these items were unavailable, the next best option was to use an object that had come in contact with or touched the victim.

After the appropriate INCANTATIONS, any harm or wound that was inflicted on the doll would magically afflict the intended party, even over long distances and even if the victim were unaware of the HEX. Popular methods to cause pain included melting or breaking the limbs of the doll.

In some necromantic circles it was believed that, in lieu of a doll, a human heart or skull could be used. In their absence, an object resembling a person, such as a MANDRAKE might be employed.

The connection of this type of BLACK MAGIC with voodoo probably began during the years of the slave trade to the colonial Americas. The unusual religious ceremonies of the Africans, coupled with fear of and prejudice against their race, must have led to wild speculations about their strange pagan ceremonies.

In *The CRUCIBLE,* Arthur Miller's 1953 play examining the SALEM witchcraft trials, Tituba, a slave from Barbados, confesses to having led several of the girls of the village in WITCHCRAFT rituals. One of the girls, Abigail Williams (who is secretly in love with John Proctor, the husband of Goody Elizabeth Proctor), is later seemingly BEWITCHed by the use of a voodoo doll. During dinner with the Reverend Paris, she suddenly screams and falls to the floor. The preacher "goes to save her, and stuck two inches in the flesh of her belly he draw [sic] a needle out."

Upon questioning, Abigail claims she was stabbed by the FAMILIAR SPIRIT of Elizabeth Proctor. When Ezekiel Cheever and John Willard, two court officials, deliver an arrest warrant to the Proctor house, they find "a poppet Goody Proctor keeps . . . And in the belly of the poppet a needle stuck."

Modern Satanist Anton La Vey, the self-proclaimed high priest and doctor of Satanic theology who founded the Church of Satan in San Francisco in 1966, wrote that, when trying to curse an enemy, a photo or a wax or clay model *can* be quite effective, but a "handmade doll, similar in construction to those used in . . . voodoo" is preferable. He also suggested that the evildoer construct the doll personally because "the creative energy you expend fashioning the doll will definitely add to the effectiveness of your ritual," adding that a flesh-colored figure (or as close as possible to "the basic color of the victim's skin") is always better than the clichéd straw doll, and the face should resemble the intended victim as much as possible. Most importantly, none of the materials used in the production of the doll should have been worn by the sorcerer or "anyone for whom you care."

After waiting 24 hours, according to La Vey, the doll is ready. He recommends that "it is best to perform this ritual in complete privacy." Finally, "the use of nails rather than pins is recommended," trying to aim for the part of the body where the victim is most vulnerable.

Vulgate Cycle, The   The Vulgate Cycle is a collection of French prose writings on the legends of King ARTHUR, most probably written between 1215 and 1230. Written between those of GEOFFREY OF MONMOUTH and Sir Thomas MALORY, it was the most significant version of the Arthurian myths in its time. Among its most important contributions was the significantly expanded role given to MERLIN.

The cycle consists of three sections. The first, called *Lancelot,* contains three stories: "Lancelot," "Queste del Saint Graal" ("Quest for the Holy Grail") and "Mort Artu" ("The Death of Arthur"). The second piece is entitled *Estoire del Saint Graal* (*History of the Holy Grail*). Only part of the remaining piece, a variant of Robert de BORON's *Merlin,* survives.

There are several firsts for the Arthurian legend found in the Vulgate Cycle. The "Mort Artu" was probably the origin of the myth that EXCALIBUR vanished back into the enchanted lake when King ARTHUR was swept off to Avalon. De Boron's *Merlin* agrees with Geoffrey's tale of Merlin's role in Arthur's conception, but it seems to be the earliest mention that Arthur was raised by Sir Ector (Sir Kay's father). More importantly, the Vulgate Cycle (and de Boron's *Merlin*) originated a key part of the legend: that Arthur proved his worthiness and was proclaimed the king of England by pulling a sword from a stone. (See also *ARTHOUR AND OF MERLIN, OF.*)

Waite, A(rthur) E(dward) (1857–after 1910) A.E. Waite was the author of several books on the occult, including *Devil-Worship in France* and his masterpiece, *The Book of Black Magic*. Profusely illustrated with PENTACLES and SIGILS, the modern GRIMOIRE purports to teach "the rites and mysteries of Goëtic Theurgy, Sorcery, and Infernal NECROMANCY." Its first American edition was published in 1972.

A.E. Waite was born in Brooklyn, New York, but shortly thereafter he moved with his mother to England. She converted to Roman Catholicism, and her young son was strongly influenced by the church's penchant for ritual and mysticism.

Self-critical, he claimed in his later years that he didn't enter "intellectual puberty" until the age of 21. His first foray into the occult field was a brief but disappointing exploration of Spiritualism.

In 1881, Waite was introduced to the works of the French cabalist Eliphas LEVI. Just four years later, Waite published his first book, an index and summary of Levi's writings. Then, after reading A.P. Sinnett's *Occult World*, Waite became intrigued with the supernatural phenomena claimed to have been produced by Mme Blavatsky (1831–1891).

In 1875, Blavatsky had established Theosophy (a mystic study named from Greek words meaning "knowledge of God" or "divine wisdom") and had founded the Theosophic Society. Blavatsky disclosed these arcane truths, many of which she claimed were revealed to her by the goddess ISIS herself, in her book *Isis Unveiled* (1877, New York). Waite joined the Theosophic Society to investigate both its claims and Blavatsky's manifestations, but he was soon disappointed.

Instead, Waite threw his lot in with the newly formed ORDER OF THE GOLDEN DAWN, then under the direction of the so-called Visible Head S.L. MacGregor MATHERS and Wynn Wescott. He attempted to follow their rules for ritual magic but was not terribly successful. After advancing through the ranks of the First Order, he resigned in protest of, what he felt, were questionable legal procedures by the association. He did return to the order during the struggle for power between Mathers and Aleister CROWLEY. For a time, he gained control of the Isis-Urania Temple (the main lodge, located in London) and modified many of the order's ceremonies and its canon to be more in line with those of the Catholic church.

Gradually, he became more and more disenchanted with the teachings of the KABBALAH, hastened by escalating personality conflicts and a general disillusionment with

Mathers. Before long, Waite turned to Freemasonry, a secret society grounded in Christian mysticism.

Waite hoped to combine the various teachings of ALCHEMY, Freemasonry, Catholicism and the Kabbalah into one unified approach to comprehending the universe. He was convinced that a secret society called the Hidden Church of the Holy Grail held the true answers to the mysteries of Life and of the godhead.

Nevertheless, he had certainly matured, or at least become more conservative, since his proclamation in 1891 that only magic could find the ideas to life's eternal questions, and by 1910, he had reembraced the Catholic church.

wand The wand has been a traditional mark of authority and power for wizards, sorcerers and other occult figures since prehistory. Tracing the origins of the magic wand, then, depends on its definition, delineated by its shape and usage. William R. Akins, a former executive administrator of the Parapsychology Foundation classified three types of wands:

1. the baton or staff, thick and about the height of the carrier
2. the heavy walking stick, cane or rod, and
3. the modern magician's wand.

When the club evolved in prehistory into a weapon, it undoubtedly also became recognized as a symbol of power. It could be conjectured that the club might also been construed as the first physical means to control the environment. Although burial mounds of the Neanderthal man (160,000–40,000 B.C.) suggest a belief in life after death and a combined religious/magic view of nature, there is no hard evidence to suggest that the club embodied understanding and magical control, and therefore power, over the elements.

Perhaps the earliest drawing of a wand is an Egyptian hieroglyph of a priest holding a small rod over the head of a bull.

In other representations, the pharaoh's scepter, clearly a wand of power, was seen as a shepherd's crook.

HERMES, the messenger to the Greek gods, is a mythological figure quite probably derived from THOTH, an early Egyptian deity. Hermes carried a style of wand now called a CADUCEUS, and it is usually pictured as a rod encircled by two intertwining cords (or, often, snakes) and topped by wings. The caduceus, signifying both wisdom and the ability to heal, was subsequently adopted as the emblem of the physician.

One of the oldest recorded uses of a staff or rod as a form of magic wand is in the Old Testament of the Bible. In the book of Exodus, Moses is given the ability to perform miracles with his staff, known today as AARON'S ROD, to prove the power of his Lord.

Religious figures were often perceived as actually (or also) being wizards. According to *Man, Myth & Magic*, JESUS is portrayed in a third-century painting holding a magic wand while nailed to the cross. The staff of Joseph of Arimathea, who was connected with the legend of King ARTHUR, supposedly bloomed into the Glastonbury Thorn after it was planted near the saint's burial spot at Glastonbury Abbey.

Wands of one sort or another are also present in both oral and written traditions of the Hindu, Buddhist, Tao and other Chinese religions.

Mystic literature abounds with the use of magic wands by sorcerers and enchantresses. Two famous Celtic legends tell of using a wand for transformations. In the tale of Diarmaid and Grainne, a wizard uses a wand to turn a boy into a pig; in another story, one fairy turns another into a wolfhound by the touch of a wand.

The most famous literary descriptions of a magic wand being used to change a human into an ANIMAL occurs in Homer's *The ODYSSEY*. CIRCE, the wicked enchantress, turns Odysseus's men into swine by striking them with her rod.

The early DRUIDS's wands were produced with great rituals, including chanting and prayers to their Supreme Beings to endow the wand with extra power. Various Celtic tribes preferred different woods, including hazel, yew, and hawthorne. The Druidic priesthood was separated into seven degrees, or levels; each priest carried a ceremonial wand made of a metal specially designated to his level. (Similarly, unique wands accompanied each of the seven to nine degrees of enlightenment in early Hindu and Chinese religious practices.)

In other cultures with fertility-based religions, magic wands were sometimes carved from wood from the elder tree.

A 17th-century mountebank using a wand in his performance of the cups-and-balls trick. (Author's collection)

In folklore and superstition, the elder tree was considered to be a powerful and magical plant. Forest SPIRITs were said to live within elder trees, and witches were able to transform themselves into elders. The tree's flowers were used for herbal medicines, and its berries were used to make medicinal wine.

In later times, the alchemists often capped their wands with ornamental metal tips. Symbolically, the tips trapped the occult powers in the wand, preventing it from bleeding out the ends; practically, the tips, if magnetized, could be used for a variety of magical effects.

Sorcerers, especially those dabbling in the black arts, also made use of wands. Because cypress was known as the tree of death, its wood was fashioned into wands used to help converse with the Devil. The wand was used to draw the pentagram (see PENTACLE) or MAGIC CIRCLE in ceremonies, and touching a corpse of suicide nine times with the wand would allow the wizard to talk to the departed soul. (See NECROMANCY.)

In the 15th century, *Errores Gazariorum* told of a witch receiving a wand at the time of her initiation rite. In 1564, Lambert Daneau claimed in *Les Sorciers* that this stick could be used to fly, a variation on the legend of riding BROOMSTICKs. Writing in the 17th century, Henri Boguet agreed that witches flew by mounting white sticks.

The wand's phallic shape has long made it a symbol of virility. Its sexual strength was shown in the *Mabinogion*, a medieval collection of 11 Welsh legends, when a sorcerer named Math tested Lady Arianrhod for virginity. In the Welsh counterpart to the American custom of carrying a bride over a threshold, the couple steps over a broomstick. (Some GYPSIES follow this same custom, with an added wrinkle; the couple can divorce at any time within a year by simply stepping backwards over the same broomstick.)

Rods have been used throughout history for divining (see DIVINING ROD), one of the most popular types being the DOWSING rod used to locate water. Similar staffs have been employed to locate ore deposits, wild game or secret treasures. A section of a 1651 Sheppard epigram reads:

> Some sorcerers do boast they have a rod
> Gathered with Vowes and Sacrifices
> And (borne about) will strangely nod
> To hidden treasure where it lies.

Medieval doctors were referred to as wand carriers, and as late as the 18th century, rural doctors walked the back roads with the aid of their healing staffs.

The magic wand is still used today by some neo-Pagan witches as the instrument through which they call up spirits. In the neo-Pagan (or modern) WITCHCRAFT tradition, all ritual or ceremonial tools are associated with one of the four ELEMENTS of Earth, Wind, Water or Fire. To the witch, the wand usually symbolizes fire (or occasionally air) as well as the practitioner's own life-force.

Today, variations of the wand are seen as the symbols of many professions, such as the royal scepter, the staff carried by NATIVE AMERICAN chiefs and emissaries of the kings of Europe, the physician's caduceus, the batons of the symphony conductor and the drum major, the swagger sticks of the army general and the movie director, the witch's broomstick (although some early British witches were also known to carry swords) and the shepherd's crook of the Catholic bishop.

Even though it has lost much of its supernatural overtones, the wand remains the traditional symbol of the stage magician. The magic wand used by the average magician today is a lightweight rod of wood, about 12 to 15 inches long and three-quarters of an inch in diameter.

In addition to its innate symbolism, the wand can also be used by the magician to assist in performing many of his illusions. For instance, as the "wizard" picks up the wand, anything that is hidden in the hand can be discarded. Conversely, objects to be produced can be secretly picked up along with the wand. Magicians have also crafted a large assortment of gimmicked wands that enable them to perform a number of unusual effects.

The wand has remained such a classic symbol of the wizard and his powers that fraternal magic societies such as the International Brotherhood of Magicians and the Society of American Magicians often perform special wand-breaking ceremonies at the funerals of their members.

warlock   A term most often used in Britain and North America to denote a male witch, *warlock* comes from the Old English *wer loga*, meaning a traitor, enemy, deceiver or liar. Because these characteristics are all considered to be attributes of Satan, the word *warlock* came to also mean any male (especially a wizard or sorcerer) who had made a pact with the Devil.

Men who practice WITCHCRAFT as a religion generally prefer to refer to themselves with the gender-neutral words *witch* or *wiccan*.

wax image   See VOODOO DOLL.

white magic   White magic calls on natural forces or appeals to angelic SPIRITs in order to provide benevolent results. White magic is benign, the sort of power usually associated with the rural grandmotherly "witch" who offers cures with FOLK MEDICINE.

White magic cannot employ the evocation of diabolic powers (even for good cause). Nor does white magic involve demon worship (Satanism), making pacts with Satan (WITCHCRAFT) or contacting the spirits of the dead (NECROMANCY).

White magic is distinguished not only by its source and method but also by its purpose. Ideally, the enchantment should not cause any physical or emotional harm. The cliché of using their powers "only for good" characterizes the magic of such literary figures as Glinda, the Good Witch in *The WIZARD OF OZ* and the wizard Gandalf in *The HOBBIT* and *The LORD OF THE RINGS*.

Wicked Witch of the West   See WIZARD OF OZ, THE.

widdershins   Also seen as *withershins*, the term *widdershins* comes from the Anglo-Saxon *with sith*, meaning "to walk against." Widdershins is an anti- or counterclockwise motion of the hand(s) or arm(s), sometimes used by a wizard in removing SPELLS, CURSES or adverse circumstances.

VINCE TE IPSVM.

EFFIGIES IOANNIS WIERI ANNO
ÆTATIS LX SALVTIS M D LXXVI

John Wierus. (16th-century engraving)

The movement is associated with the path of the sun across the heavens; thus, walking widdershins would be against the sun, an unnatural act creating negative powers or forces. Thus, sorcerers or witches dealing in BLACK MAGIC use widdershins gestures to HEX their victims. A MAGIC CIRCLE created for diabolic purposes might also be drawn in a widdershins direction. (See also DEOSIL.)

Wierus, Johannes (1515–1588) The 16th-century German occultist and author Johannes (also seen as Johan, Jean and John) Wierus (also seen as Wier and Weyer) was one of the first eminent thinkers to decry the persecution of innocent people accused of WITCHCRAFT and sorcery.

Wierus was born into nobility at Grave, in Brabant, and became a noted student of the mystic Cornelius AGRIPPA. He moved to Paris, where he matriculated in medicine. There he was tutor to the two sons and a nephew of King Francis I and accompanied them throughout their kingdom and on their travels to Africa and Crete. Leaving the king's service, Wierus accepted an appointment as personal physician to Duke William of the Duchy of Cleves and Juliersberg.

A learned demonologist, Wierus was considered an authority on the evocation of infernal SPIRITs through the use of potions and satanic prayers. His book, *De Praestigiis Daemonium et incantationibus ac veneficiis* (*On Magic*), which he published in Latin in Basel in 1563, served as a practical guide on the subject as well as methodically inventorying all the infernal demons of Hell. It was also used by witch-hunters, judges and consultants (such as John DEE) to help identify and prosecute those possessed by Lucifer.

Wierus believed that Satan could and did intervene in the everyday life of man. He felt that witchcraft did exist, that the Devil did procure women for his purposes and that sorcerers such as FAUST deserved to spend Eternity in Hell.

Nevertheless, he contended that many of the extraordinary deeds credited to magic were the product of fancy, hallucination and invention. As a doctor, Wierus argued that many of those accused of sorcery were merely lunatics and thus did not deserve torture or death. In the 16th century, almost any unexplainable disease was rumored to have been effected by witchcraft, and, although he did not know the true cause of many ailments, he was certain they were not a result of SPELLs. Wierus was a devout Protestant, so he was particularly upset by the prevalent practice of Catholic priests diagnosing almost any illness to be demon possession so that they might earn money through conducting exorcisms.

Wierus also maintained that there was a huge difference between the old crone hags who worked WHITE MAGIC and FOLK MEDICINE and those who were actually in league with the Devil. Even witches deserved pity, he declared, because it was really Satan, and not his servants, who had the true power to perform the evil.

Wierus continued these arguments in *Cinq livres de l'imposture et tromperie des diables*, published in Paris in 1569. In 1577, Wierus, sensing a reawakening of witchcraft hysteria, republished *De Praestigiis* in a shorted version and titled it *De Lamiis* (*On Witches*).

The *Pseudomonarchia Daemonum* portion of *De Praestigiis Daemonium* seemingly was a source for the *Goetia* (which, in turn, formed part of the LEMEGETON: THE LESSER KEY OF SOLOMON). In 1570, the *Pseudomarchia* was translated into English by a T.R., and it was subsequently included by Reginald Scot in his DISCOVERIE OF WITCHCRAFT (1584).

Witch, The *The Witch*, a drama written by Thomas Middleton (1580–1627), was published in 1778 but was written around 1627 and, according to some sources, before 1616. *The Witch* tells of Rosamond, a duchess of Lombardy, who exacts revenge on her husband Alboin after he forces her to drink a toast from a cup fashioned out of her father's skull. Her human aide is Almachides, but she also has supernatural assistance from HECATE, the witch, who also takes part in the play's subplot.

Elizabethan scholars, such as Charles Lamb (1775–1834) in his treatise *Specimens*, often compare and contrast the Hecate of Middleton with the three weird sisters in MACBETH, written by Middleton's contemporary, William SHAKESPEARE. The Shakespearean commentator George Steevens [sic] (1736–1800) points out that Hecate and the weird sisters perform an identical incantation in their respective plays:

Black spirits and white, red spirits and gray, [sic]
Mingle, mingle, mingle, you that mingle may.
The Witch (V, ii)
Macbeth (IV, i)

Steevens suggests that "the song was, in all probability, a traditional one."

witch doctor   The common Western or European image of the African witch doctor, sometimes called a *sangoma* (Zulu) or *maganga* (Kenyan Masai), is that of a masked charlatan, dressed in feathers and bones, doling out mumbo jumbo to a gullible following. In truth, the witch doctor is an essential part of the fabric of the tribal community who works as an agent against evil.

In a pagan society where it is believed that SPIRITS, both deities and ancestral, roam the earth and interfere with daily life, the witch doctor has the crucial duty of working for good against wicked spirits and their human agents, witches. Because it is believed that no deity or good spirit would cause harm, logically it must be a witch who causes unexplainable, devastating events such as sudden deaths (especially of chieftains), unnatural weather or plagues.

It is the job of a witch doctor to use his powers to ferret out the evildoer, usually by some trial by ordeal. Torture is a particularly direct method to obtain a confession; another effective means consists of secretly administering poisons to the subject, his family or animals, the resultant illness being seen as proof of guilt. Once the witch doctor has pronounced his sentence, the witch is killed. If circumstances do not imme-

diately improve for the community, another witch might be sought until the catastrophes subside.

Because it is believed that droughts are also caused by BLACK MAGIC, another important function of the witch doctor is that of RAINMAKER.

Needless to say, the job of witch doctor is a precarious one. He knows that much of his success in discovering witches depends upon the fear instilled by his power and position and his understanding of human nature. The only weapon he has as a rainmaker is prayer. If he fails, villagers might begin to suspect that the witch doctor is himself a witch in disguise—in which case, the penalty would be death.

Among many African tribes, the position of witch doctor is often an inherited one, dependent upon the acceptance of the applicant's petition to his ancestral spirits. As part of his initiation, the apprentice must live apart from the tribe for up to two years, during which time he is taught the sacred and arcane arts of magic. Among his many trials, the candidate sometimes must kill a python with his bare hands and eat its meat raw. His final tests are marked by ritual dances and mystic ceremonies. Among the Zulus, the *abathakathi*, or wizard/enchanters, play a less active role today than in previous years. The witch doctors are still an important part of their culture, however, especially in nonurban districts. The village or territorial witch doctor

An African witch doctor in his thatched, dirt-floored hut near Victoria Falls, Zimbabwe. The shaman prophesies by geomancy, a form of divination in which the pattern of bits of bone, rocks or sticks tossed to the ground are interpreted. (Photo by author)

Witches pay tribute to Satan as heinous fiendish creatures (possibly familiars) fly overhead. Demonologists debate exactly what this well-known illustration depicts: The witches may be receiving images or dolls for use in their curses or they may be furnishing the Devil with babies. (John Ashton, *Chap-Books of the Eighteenth Century*, London, 1882)

continues to be consulted for advice and assistance in childbirth, DIVINATION, rainmaking, sickness and protection against harmful spirits. Much of his medical diagnosis and soothsaying is still done through SORTILEGE, or "casting the bones." See also MEDICINE MAN; VOODOO; WITCHCRAFT.)

witchcraft   Witchcraft, or *wicca*, is one of the world's oldest religions. It is a pagan faith, non-Christian rather than anti-Christian, based on the belief that it is possible to control nature and the universe through magic and the invocation of divine SPIRITS.

The word *witch* comes from the Old English *wicce* (feminine form, pronounced "wiche") and *wicca* (masculine form), both of which are derived from the root *wikk-* (OE)(meaning, in essence, a "witch"). *Wicce* is further derived from the German root word *wic* (meaning "to turn or bend"), and the word *wiccian* (OE) (meaning "to bewitch" or "to use sorcery"). The word *witch* may also be related to the Old English words *wita* (meaning "councillor") or *wis* (meaning "wise").

Before the 12th century, sorcery and magic were generally overlooked by the church; according to the CANON EPISCOPI, witchcraft and its manifestations, such as transvection (flying) and the ability to conjure up spirits of the dead (NECROMANCY), were considered to be the result of mere mischief or hallucinations. By 1300, however, witchcraft was equated with sorcery in the minds of most Europeans, and it was soon labeled heresy by the PAPACY. Pope Innocent VIII's antiwitchcraft bull of 1484, attached to the influential *MALLEUS MALEFICARUM*, ushered in the age of the INQUISITION.

The image of an old, eccentric woman who practices FOLK MEDICINE and cures was transformed into an evil hag who worships the Devil. Where once COVENs gathered in simple celebrations of the harvest and the seasons, the connotation

changed to a circle of 13 naked infidels, frolicking in a moonlit forest clearing.

It was thought that the meetings, or SABBATs, were attended by Satan himself, sometimes disguised in the form of an ANIMAL. Ritual dancing and sexual relations with the Devil were part of the ceremony, and the witches often showed their allegiance to Satan by kissing his buttocks (the *osculum infame*, or Kiss of Shame).

Books denouncing witchcraft began to appear about five centuries ago. One of the first major works, the *Malleus Maleficarum*, or *The Witch's Hammer*, was published in 1486. *DEMONOLOGIE* by King James VI of Scotland (who later became James I of England) appeared in 1597, and Guazzo's *COMPENDIUM MALEFICARUM*, was first printed nine years later.

Alternatively, such books as Reginald Scot's The *DISCOVERIE OF WITCHCRAFT* (1584) attempted to end the witchcraft mania by showing that most, if not all, of the supernatural feats were simple legerdemain and trickery, not devil inspired. Indeed, it was one of the first books to make a distinction between the BLACK MAGIC of sorcerers and witches and the innocent magic of entertainers and herbalist doctors.

Despite such efforts, witchcraft hysteria raged in Europe and England throughout the 13th to 16th centuries, resulting in waves of persecution. Professional witch-hunters began to assist the Inquisition and secular judges.

Witches, it was believed, could be detected by many methods. A rash, a patch of discolored skin or even a wart could be declared a "DEVIL'S MARK," an identifying spot on the body supposedly placed by Satan. Especially damning was an extra breast or nipple because it was purportedly used by the Devil to suckle. It was thought that invisible Devil's marks could be discovered by PRICKING. Repeatedly dunking the victim in water to obtain a confession was also quite effective. Perhaps the most creative test was SWIMMING, a test of purity by total immersion in water.

Once proclaimed guilty, witches were executed in a variety of ways, varying by custom and country. The most common method in Europe was by burning at the stake; in England,

A witch pays homage to Satan by applying the *osculum infame*, or "Kiss of Shame," to the Devil's rear. (Guazzo, *Compendium Maleficarum*)

hanging was the preferred method. Other means included strangling, stoning and pressing (covering the prone body first with a flat rock and then piling on boulders until the skeleton was crushed).

Because it was almost impossible for the victim to survive the torture inflicted during the inquisition preceding a hearing or to be found innocent during the trial itself, many accusations of witchcraft were no doubt motivated by the envy and greed of those in a position to inherit or otherwise obtain the victim's goods.

Just as often, however, the allegations were made out of suspicion and fear or a true belief that the accused really was somehow causing malevolence in the community, such as cattle dying, stillborn children or drought. After all, it was reasoned, if God is omnipotent and good, then only Satan could cause evil, and his ministers on earth, enacting the evil, had to be witches and sorcerers.

In the 1950s, the Neo-Pagan religion of witchcraft, based on benign WHITE MAGIC and the worship of a nature goddess (and her mate, the Horned God), began to enjoy a new popularity. Its resurgence is credited to Gerald B(rosseau) Gardner (1884–1964), a British cabalist. The next two decades showed the greatest growth in the movement, paralleling a general rise in interest in the occult. To avoid negative connotations, many modern witches prefer to be called *wicca* or *wiccans*.

In many modern societies, however, especially those of tribal Africa, its nearby islands and Southeast Asia (especially Papua New Guinea and Borneo in Indonesia), the belief in witchcraft, demonic spirits, black magic and sorcery is still quite strong. In much of Western Africa, the Caribbean, parts of Latin America and the bayou regions of south-central United States, the practice of VOODOO continues. Even the most underground of cults—Satanists and devil worshipers—are occasionally exposed in civilized suburbia.

Nor has the practice of witch hunts disappeared. In 1994 alone, 73 people are known to have been accused of witchcraft and murdered by neighbors in the former homeland Lebowa in South Africa. Patriarchs of the village acknowledge the reality of witchcraft: "In the old days, the victim of the witch would go and hire a *nyanga*, a witch doctor, to reverse the spell," said Abram Mharala, himself suspected of witchcraft by his village of Bayswater. "Everyone knows you cannot smell out a witch. Only a *myanga* can do that."

This resurgence of witchcraft is worldwide. In late October 1994, for example, the World Society for the Protection of Animals announced that body parts of gorillas slaughtered in central Africa were appearing on the "fetish market" for use in witchcraft rites. Although actual numbers are impossible to ascertain, according to a CNN International report in September 1994 there were at least 12,000 self-professed sorcerers, witches and fortune-tellers in Italy.

As long as humans continue their quest to control the universe around them and to know God and his divine wisdom, magic, wizardry, sorcery and witchcraft will continue to flourish.

Witches of Morva, The (Orddu, Orgoch and Orwen)
See FILMS, *THE BLACK CAULDRON*.

Witch Hazel See FILMS, *TRICK OR TREAT*.

Witch of Atlas, The A 78-stanza poem, *The Witch of Atlas*, was written in three days by Percy Bysshe Shelley (1792–1822) in 1820 and published four years later. The story concerns a ravishing and playful witch, the daughter of Apollo, who travels around the world with her friend, Hermaphrodite, casting SPELLS over one and all. The poem is filled with magical allusions and may have been inspired by Shelley's meeting a supposed enchantress on a visit to Italy in 1820.

Witch of Edmonton, The Written by Thomas Dekker (1570?–1632), John Ford (1586-post 1639), William Rowley (1585?–1626) and possibly John Webster (1578?–c.1632), the play *The Witch of Edmonton* was probably first performed in 1621, although it remained unpublished until 1658. The drama's two separate plots both deal with the subject of vengeance.

Frank Thorney secretly marries Winifred, but his father, horrified that he has not married into a better station, forces him (with the threat of disinheritance) that he *also* marry Susan Carter, the father's choice for his son. Humiliated that his father had so successfully controlled him, Thorney kills his second wife and tries to implicate her two former beaus. The truth is discovered, and Thorney is executed.

A concurrent plot is based on an event contemporary with the writing of the play: the 1621 hanging of Elizabeth Sawyer as a witch. In the play, an aged hag is wrongly suspected of WITCHCRAFT, as were so many innocents in the 17th century. Merely because she is feeble, poor, ugly and defenseless, the old woman is abused and branded a pariah by her neighbors. Angry and vindictive, she decides to make the actual satanic pact of which she is being accused. She excuses her imminent damnation by her sad explanation

> Some call me witch;
> And being ignorant of my self, they go
> About to teach me how to be one.

Satan approaches her in the guise of a dog, and the deal is done.

Witch of Endor, The
Among ancient Middle Eastern civilizations, the belief in magic and the use of NECROMANCY for DIVINATION was almost universal. Only the early Jewish faith had any proscriptions against the nefarious art.

The Old Testament of the Bible gave the first written, and perhaps the most influential, invective against WITCHCRAFT: "Thou shalt not suffer a witch to live." (Exodus 22:18) Nevertheless, soon after the banishment of "those that have FAMILIAR SPIRITS, and the wizards" by Saul, king of the Israelites, the ruler himself consulted a witch.

When the Lord anointed David as Saul's successor, David collected an army against the ruling monarch. In I Samuel 28:7–16, Saul disguised himself and sought out a medium, the Witch of Endor, to call up the spirit of Samuel to seek advice. The deceased king was infuriated at being disquieted and refused to help or counsel Saul.

Current scholarship suggests that the Witch of Endor might have been neither a witch nor a medium in the modern sense of the word. Most probably, she functioned much like the ancient Grecian ORACLES.

The Witch of Endor conjures up the prophet Samuel at the request of Saul. (Joseph Glanvil, *Saducismus Triumphatus*, 1681 edition)

In the original Hebrew of the biblical texts, the woman is identified by the phrase, "There is at Endor a woman *Behabalth-Ob*." Like the words of the oracles themselves, this phrase can be translated several ways. In some translations, *Ob* means "python," which could refer to a literal serpent or an evil spirit. Therefore, *Behabalth-Oh* could mean that the woman "owns" a python or is "owned by" (i.e., possessed by) a python. Indeed, the Latin Vulgate calls the Witch of Endor a *pythonissa* or *mulier pythonem habens*, meaning a women who tells fortunes by consulting a python or conjured spirits. (The python was often associated with prophecy in ancient times: Predating the oracle of Apollo at DELPHI, for example, the original prophetess at the temple served Gaia and her python, which was purportedly born at the site.)

The Greek Septuagint translated the Hebrew *'ôbh* differently, into *heggastramythos*. Modern biblical scholars have suggested that this translation, which means "belly-talker" rather than "witch," might be taken literally. This would indicate that the Witch of Endor created the voices herself and was actually practicing gastromancy, the art of lowering one's voice in tone and volume to make it appear as if coming from underground. If this is true, the Witch of Endor was not an enchantress but one of the world's first ventriloquists!

In his *Discoverie of Witchcraft* (1584), Reginald Scot was one of the first authors to point out the differences in the Hebrew and Greek words:

> Samuel was not raised from the dead, but . . . it was an illusion. . . . . Augustine [concludes] that the devil was fetched up in his likeness. From whose opinions, with deference, I hope I may dissent.

In 1604, however, King James I, who was a fervent enemy of sorcery and the author of DEMONOLOGIE, convened a conference at Hampton Court to prepare the Authorized Version of the Bible in English. It seems likely that, given the king's bias, the 47 revisers working on the new edition would have been much more likely to translate the Hebrew *'ôbh* as "witch" rather than as "oracle" or "ventriloquist."

witch's mark See DEVIL'S MARK.

Wizard of Id, The Created by Johnny Hart (1931–) in collaboration with Brant Parker (1920–), the comic strip "The Wizard of Id" first appeared through Herald-Tribune Syndicate in about 50 newspapers on November 8, 1964. The strip was later transferred to North America Syndicate and currently appears in more than 1,000 newspapers. More than 20 collections of the comics have been reprinted in paperback by Fawcett Books.

An award-winning cartoon, "The Wizard of Id" was named Best Humor Strip by the National Cartoonist Society in 1971, 1976, 1980, 1982 and 1983; in 1984 Parker and Hart (the order in which the strip is by-lined) were corecipients of the society's top honor, the Reuben award. Today the cartoon strip is still written by Hart with the assistance of Jack Caprio and Dick Boland and is illustrated by Parker.

Johnny (John Lewis) Hart was born in Endicott, New York, on February 18, 1931 and graduated from Union-Endicott High School in 1949. While stationed with the Air Force in Korea, he drew cartoons for the *Pacific Stars & Stripes*; in 1954, Hart sold his first cartoon to the *Saturday Evening Post*. His first comic-strip sensation was the still-popular *B.C.*, which was accepted by Herald-Tribune Syndicate and first appeared on February 17, 1958. In 1963, Hart began work on an idea for a new strip set in the Middle Ages. For his artist, Hart approached his longtime friend, Brant Parker.

Parker was born in Los Angeles on August 26, 1920. Following his graduation from public school, Parker attended Otis Art Institute (his only formal art training). He worked in the animation department of Walt Disney Studios and had two stints in the Navy before becoming a technical illustrator for IBM. He met Hart while judging an art show by the students of Hart's alma mater, Union-Endicott High School in Binghamton, New York, the hometown of Parker's wife.

The strip is set in the mythical kingdom of Id in medieval times. In addition to a pint-sized monarch who is vain, greedy and cruel, regular characters include the cowardly knight Rodney, the drunken court-jester Bung and the perpetual prisoner Spook.

Also featured in the strip, of course, is the Wizard of Id himself. Dressed in a pointed cap and flowing star-studded robe, the bearded wizard does his best, but his SPELLS often fail or backfire. Perhaps his power is greater than it appears: he is the only character who can criticize or poke fun at the king without fear of retribution. The Wizard of Id, however, *is* always under the watchful eye of his shrewish wife and of the SPIRIT that rises from the brew in his CAULDRON.

Wizard of Oz, The   The Wizard of Oz was created by L. Frank Baum as the title character of his 1900 book *The Wizard of Oz*. In early editions, the work was entitled *The Wonderful Wizard of Oz*, a phrase later immortalized in a song lyric for the 1939 MGM film version. Original working titles for the book had been *The Emerald City* and *From Kansas to Fairyland*.

Born on May 15, 1856, in Chittenango, New York, L(yman) Frank Baum was a newspaper writer and editor before he conceived the tale of Oz. In his classic book, Dorothy, a farm girl from Kansas, is hurled "over the rainbow" by a cyclone. She lands in the Land of Oz, a bizarre kingdom populated by such strange beings as the Hammerheads (armless creatures with domelike heads), the Kalidahs (combination bear-tiger ANIMALS) and the lilliputian Munchkins, not to mention the Scarecrow, the Tin Woodman and the Cowardly Lion. Various parts of the country are dominated by witches, including the Wicked Witch of the West and Glinda, the Good Witch of the North. The capital city of Oz, Emerald City, is ruled over by the Wizard of Oz, who throughout the book appears to Dorothy and other visitors variously as a disembodied voice, a floating head, a lady, a beast or a ball of fire. In the end, the wizard is revealed to be human, a tired, old humbug.

The wizard was, in fact, born Oscar Zoroaster Phadrig Isaac Norman Henkle Emmanuel Ambroise Diggs. Despite the objections of his politician father, young Oscar became a ventriloquist and joined a circus. He realized that his full name would not fit on his trunks, so he painted just his initials. Diggs had no problem with the first two letters, but he felt the rest of them—*PINHEAD*—might be viewed as a reflection on his intelligence. Thus, he merely stencilled *OZ* on his props, baggage and hot-air balloon. While aloft, sudden winds carried him "somewhere over the rainbow," and when he landed in a magical city named Oz, the local denizens, seeing the letters *OZ* painted on his balloon, naturally assumed the stranger to be their missing leader.

Part of the wizard's story may have been inspired by a real-life incident: a well-publicized spectacle with great hoopla that ended with a mysterious disappearance. In the latter part of the 19th century, hot-air-balloon ascensions were popular attractions on the midways of many American circuses. On July 15, 1875, in Chicago, "Professor" Washington H. Donaldson along with a reporter, Newton S. Grimwood of the Chicago *Journal*, rose in the *P.T. Barnum* from the circus grounds of P.T. Barnum's Great Roman Hippodrome. The balloon was swept out over Lake Michigan, where it disappeared. A month later, on August 18, the reporter's body came ashore at Stony Creek, Michigan, on the east shore of the lake, but no trace of "Professor" Donaldson or his balloon was ever seen again.

The Wonderful Wizard of Oz was an immediate success, and it spawned numerous theatrical treatments and 13 Baum book sequels—eight of which were also staged. (After Baum's death, other authors continued the Oz series for a total of 40 books by 1963.)

The first Broadway MUSICAL THEATER version, with book and lyrics by Baum himself, opened on January 20 or 21, 1903, as the first production at the original Majestic Theatre on Columbus Circle in New York City. Baum freely adapted his own text while creating a vehicle for the already-established comedy team of Montgomery and Stone, who were making their Broadway musical debut. Before the play begins, an earthling traveled to Oz by balloon, overthrew King Pastoria II and exiled him to Earth. At the show's opening, a cyclone blows the king and his girlfriend Tryxie Tryfle all the way to Oz. The same tornado sweeps up Dorothy Gale and her pet *cow* Imogene. The king enlists his old friend General Riskitt to help him regain the throne. At the same time, Dorothy, with the assistance of a witch and a former court poet named Sir Dashemoff Daily, sets out to find the Wizard—the only one who would be able to transport her back to Kansas. Along the way, the two groups meet the Scarecrow (Fred A. Stone), the Tin Man (David C. Montgomery) and, in a very minor role, the Cowardly Lion. Eventually, the king captures the balloonist, who has assumed the title of wizard. Once back on the throne, the king denies Dorothy permission to leave Oz. Finally, the witch intervenes, telling the king to let Dorothy return to Earth or she will create an even bigger whirlwind than before.

The first *film* of *The Wizard of Oz* was produced in 1908, with others appearing in 1910, 1914 and 1925. Baum personally toured an unusual production in which he read excerpts from *The Wizard of Oz* live on stage while portions of the 1910 Selig Company silent-film version was projected beside him. Baum became infatuated with the movie industry and moved to Hollywood in 1911, living in a small frame home he named Ozcot. Two years later he set up the Oz Film Company which produced, among other features, three silent movies with an Oz theme—*The Patchwork Girl of Oz*, *The Magic Cloak of Oz* and *His Majesty, the Scarecrow of Oz* (retitled for distribution as *The New Wizard of Oz*). Baum and his wife had four sons, and he died in his Hollywood home on May 6, 1919.

An animated cartoon short of *The Wizard of Oz* was shown theatrically in 1933, and a radio program based on the stories hit the air in 1933 and 1934.

Better known today than the plot of the book or the early theatrical or movie productions is the lavish 1939 Metro-Goldwyn-Mayer musical film version of the story. The character of the wizard was substantially changed in the screenplay adaptation by Noel Langley, Florence Ryerson and Edgar Allan Wolfe. The film received Academy Award nominations for Best Picture and Art Direction, and the Oscar was won for Best Song ("Over the Rainbow," Harold Arlen, music; E.Y. "Yip" Harburg, lyrics) and Musical Direction (Herbert Stothart).

The film was produced by Mervyn LeRoy and directed by Victor Fleming, with King Vidor directing the Kansas sequences. The phenomenal cast included Judy Garland (Dorothy Gale), Frank Morgan (the Wizard of Oz/Professor Marvel), Ray Bolger (the Scarecrow/Hunk), Jack Haley (the Tin Woodman/Hickory), Bert Lahr (the Cowardly Lion/Zeke), Margaret Hamilton (the Wicked Witch of the West/Miss Elvira Gulch) and Billie Burke (Glinda, the Good Witch of the North).

Today, the cast seems so perfect that any other actors would be inconceivable in the roles. Many, however, won their "roles of a lifetime" by default. It is well known that Lowes, Inc., M-G-M's parent company, wanted Shirley Temple to play Dorothy (a choice that would have made *The Wizard of Oz* a much different picture!). Twentieth Century Fox would not loan out their major star to another studio.

Producer LeRoy offered the Wizard role to Ed Wynn, but the actor purportedly turned it down because, in the early draft of the screenplay he received, the role wasn't large enough. W.C. Fields opted out to star in *You Can't Cheat an Honest Man*; and Wallace Beery, Robert Benchley, Hugh Herbert, Victor Moore and Charles Winninger were apparently seriously considered. Eventually, the title role went to the reliable M-G-M contract player Frank Morgan, who had been associate producer Freed's first choice all along.

Although few actresses have become so identified with a single role as Margaret Hamilton has for her portrayal of the Wicked Witch, Edna May Oliver was almost cast to play her as a semicomic villain. Gale Sondergaard actually made a screen test for the Wicked Witch as a beautiful, black-sequin-gowned enchantress. Before Billie Burke, Fanny Brice and Beatrice Lillie were considered for the role of Glinda.

Buddy Ebsen was originally cast to play the Scarecrow, but Ray Bolger, who was set to be the Tin Man, convinced the studio to switch their roles. Early into production, Ebsen was hospitalized with blood poisoning from the aluminum paint that was being used for his Tin Man makeup. Because a delay in shooting was impossible, Ebsen was replaced by Jack Haley.

Among the film's creative staff was the famous costume designer Adrian. There is an apocryphal story surrounding Frank Morgan's wardrobe as Professor Marvel and the Wizard. To create the old, dusty look of an itinerant showman's wardrobe, one of the costumers supposedly scrounged through second-hand-clothing and rummage stores for an authentic period jacket. When a perfect round-winged tailcoat was discovered and subsequently tried on by actor Morgan, it fit perfectly. It was only then that they noticed a label sewn onto the inside lining: the jacket had originally been hand-tailored for, worn and later discarded by L. Frank Baum.

Among the many changes from the book to the screen is the expansion of the wrap-around Kansas segments of the story. At the beginning of the movie, as Dorothy flees from home she happens upon the encampment of Professor Marvel. Although the traveling clairvoyant is a fraud, Marvel realizes that the young girl is in trouble and greets Dorothy kindly, welcoming her for dinner. He invites her into his wagon for protection from the weather and offers to peer into her future. Employing a CRYSTAL BALL, Marvel begins awkwardly and then "divines" only the obvious: that she is a runaway. Because Dorothy's eyes are closed, Marvel is able to dig through her hand basket for more information. He finds a faded photograph and uses its clues to convince Dorothy to return home.

Later, in Oz, Dorothy discovers that belief in the Wizard's powers is strong. Even the magical Glinda recommends that Dorothy seek out the Wizard for help and advice. Along with her companions, Dorothy eventually gains an audience with the Wizard, a terrifying, disembodied head wafting in flames and speaking with a booming voice. The heroes are sent on a quest for the BROOMSTICK of the Wicked Witch of the West.

On the way, they are attacked by the Winged Monkeys, led by Nikko, the Wicked Witch's "FAMILIAR." The savage creatures capture the girl and Toto and fly them to the witch's castle, leaving behind the broken bodies of Dorothy's friends. Toto escapes and leads the rejuvenated trio to rescue Dorothy.

After the witch is melted by water, Dorothy, Toto and her companions return her scorched broomstick to Oz. The Wizard is revealed not to be "great and powerful" but to be a mere mortal, a balloon ascensionist who drifted off course while giving an exhibition.

Although exposed as a fake with no real magical powers, the Wizard convinces the Scarecrow, the Tin Woodman and the Cowardly Lion that they do have brains, a heart and courage, respectively. He offers to take Dorothy home personally in his giant balloon that he has been saving for just such an occasion.

On a day of great celebration, all the residents of Emerald City meet around the inflated balloon to see their Wizard and say good-bye. Suddenly, his humorously pompous speech is interrupted by the untimely release of the mooring. As Dorothy pleads for him to return to take her along, the Wizard displays his total impotence as he floats away without her.

Glinda comes to Dorothy's aid, telling her that she has had the power to return home all along: she just had to find it for herself. Dorothy clicks her heels together while chanting "There's no place like home. There's no place like home. . ."; and she awakens in her bed back in Kansas. In the last scene of the film, we see the concerned Professor Marvel one last time.

On January 5, 1975, a new all-black musical stage version of *The Wizard of Oz*, entitled simply *The Wiz*, made its debut at the current Majestic Theatre on 44th Street in New York City. Directed by Geoffrey Holder, *The Wiz* featured Stephanie Mills (Dorothy), Hinton Battle (Scarecrow), Tiger Haynes (the Tinman), Ted Ross (Lion), Dee Dee Bridgewater (Glinda) and André, De Shields (The Wiz) in the cast. *The Wiz* received seven Tony Awards: Musical (Ken Harper, producer); Actor, Supporting or featured, Musical (Ted Ross); Actress, Supporting or Featured, Musical (Dee Dee Bridgewater); Director, (Geoffrey Holder); Score (Charlie Smalls, music and lyrics); Costume Designer (Geoffrey Holder); and Choreographer (George Faison). The show received an additional Tony nomination for Book of a Musical (William F. Brown).

The cast of the 1978 Sidney Lumet-directed film version of *The Wiz* included Diana Ross (Dorothy), Michael Jackson (Scarecrow), Nipsey Russell (the Tinman), Ted Ross (Lion), Lena Horne (Glinda), Richard Pryor (The Wiz) and Mabel King (Wicked Witch). Academy Award nominations were received by Quincy Jones (Musical Score Adaptation and Musical Direction) and Oswald Morris (Cinematography).

The Wiz was briefly revived at the Lunt-Fontanne Theatre in 1984 and then again off-Broadway (starring Stephanie Mills) in 1993.

In 1985, Disney Studios released *Return to Oz*, in which Dorothy is given shock treatments to cure her recurring psychological problems due to her trip to Oz.

The New York premiere of a British stage version of the MGM film, adapted by John Kane but utilizing the Arlen-Harburg songs, opened on May 12, 1997, at the Theater at Madison Square Garden. Cast members included *television's* Roseanne (Wicked Witch of the West/Miss Gulch), Judith

McCauley (Glinda, the Good Witch of the North), Gerry Vichi (Wizard), Jessica Grove (Dorothy), Ken Page (Lion), Lara Teeter (Scarecrow) and Michael Gruber (Tinman).

If there be a moral to *The Wizard of Oz*, perhaps it is this: Wizardry, and magic, may take many forms. Sometimes it is only illusionary, sometimes downright dishonest, and our belief in it and the reliance on its ability to solve our problems is misguided. The true magic in the world must be found within ourselves, and the real quest in life is self-discovery.

Wizard's Funeral, The   A short piece by British poet Richard Watson Dixon (1833–1900), *The Wizard's Funeral* was most widely circulated in a 1909 edition.

Wonderful Wizard of Oz, The   See WIZARD OF OZ, THE.

World Bewitched, The   Published in Dutch as *Die Betooverde Wereld*, this philosophical and theological work was written in 1691 by Balthazar Bekker (1634–1698). Born in Friesland in the Netherlands, Bekker was educated at Groningen and Franeker, where he became a Dutch Protestant pastor. After 1679, he moved to a congregation in Amsterdam.

His best-known book, *The World Bewitched*, was a treatise on comparative religion. In it, Bekker suggested that true magic, SORCERY and even Satan were nonexistent. His views were considered radical, if not heretical, and as a result Bekker was expelled from the ministry.

Yeats, William Butler (1865–1939) While studying art (the profession of his father and uncle) at the School of Art in Dublin, Yeats acquired a fascination with mysticism and the supernatural. He shared his interest with fellow student, friend and mystic George William Russell (1867–1935). Russell would go on to write such magic-themed poetry as *Homeward* (1894), *The Divine Vision* (1904) and, based on Celtic mythology, *The House of the Titans* (1934).

A preoccupation in the occult was to influence much of Yeats's writing, a career he followed full force after 1886. Two of his earliest assignments, editing both *The Poems of William Blake* (1893) and the three-volume *The Works of William Blake* (with F.J. Ellis, 1893), dealt with material by one of England's greatest literary mystics.

Yeats was particularly interested in the legends and myths of his native Ireland, and three of his own works grew out of his obsession with the local lore: *Fairy and Folk Tales of the Irish Peasantry* (1888), *The CELTIC TWILIGHT* (1893) and *The Secret Rose* (1897).

Yeats passionately believed in the need for a national Irish theater. To further this cause, his play *The COUNTESS KATHLEEN* (1892) was first acted in Dublin in 1899 under the auspices of the Irish Literary Society, which Yeats had helped to found. This dramatic production eventually led to the creation of the Irish National Theatre Company, which Russell helped to organize. The National Theatre subsequently evolved into the Abbey Theatre.

In 1917 Yeats married Georgie Hyde-Lees. On a whim, during their honeymoon she experimented with automatic writing, a technique by which a SPIRIT moves a pen held against paper by an entranced medium. Its apparent success reawakened Yeat's passion for the transcendental that had lain dormant for over a decade.

Some of Yeats's later works which showed nuances of metaphysical thinking and symbolism include the following poems and collections: *Michael Robartes and the Dancer* (1922), *Seven Poems and a Fragment* (1922), *The Cat and the Moon and Certain Poems* (1924), *A Vision* (1925), *October Blast* (1927), *The Tower* (1928), *The Winding Stair* (1928), *Words for Music Perhaps and Other Poems* (1932), *Wheels and Butterflies* (1934), *The King of the Great Clock Tower* (1934), *A Full Moon in March* (1935), *New Poems* (1938) and *Last Poems and Two Plays* (1939).

Yeats was an early member of the ORDER OF THE GOLDEN DAWN, where his mystic name was Daemon est Deus ("The Devil is God Reversed"). He was a particularly close friend and frequent guest of S.L. and Moina MATHERS.

In 1923 Yeats received the Nobel Prize for literature. He died in France but was reinterred at Drumcliff in Sligo, Ireland, in 1948.

Yen Sid See FILMS, *FANTASIA*.

Ywain and Gawain An anonymous medieval British romantic ode of 4,032 lines dating from the early 14th century, *Ywain and Gawain* was inspired by the Welsh poem *Owein* and a translation of the 6,818-line epic *Yvain* by Chrétien DE TROYES. Abbreviated and more eloquent than either of its sources, *Ywain and Gawain* primarily tells the adventures of Ywain.

Ywain slays a knight who, by wizardry, has the ability to control the weather. He marries the magical knight's widow, Alundyne, but almost immediately he deserts her to follow more quests at the urging of his fellow knight Gawain. During a masked joust, Ywain discovers his combatant to be Gawain, from whose company he had separated. The friends reunite, and Ywain returns to his wife.

zemi Carved wood or stone idols kept by the Arawak tribes of the Caribbean, zemi were discovered in Jamaica by the Europeans as early as 1791. Zemi were believed by the Arawaks to protect them, their families and homes from SPIRITS of the dead. The AMULETs take their name from Zemi, the Arawak deity of death.

According to Arawak theology, in the beginning, the god Jocchu lived in the sky along with the sun and moon. The celestial orbs had originally emerged from caves, just like the ancient Arawak ancestors, and the first Arawaks to leave the caves were turned into ANIMALS, trees and rock by the sun. Thus, the Arawaks believed that all living things (including trees) and many inanimate objects, such as stones, contained a spiritual essence or force.

It was also commonly thought that when a human died, the spirit traveled to a beautiful valley, located in what was later called Hispaniola. The spirits, however, could come back at night to the villages to look for a particular fruit they especially enjoyed eating. The Arawaks feared the spirits and sought protection against them.

Large zemi were kept by the Arawaks in their houses to keep out the spirits. Smaller versions might be strung and worn as amulets or carried as TALISMANs against harm.

Zend-Avesta See ZOROASTER.

Zlito (fl. 14th century A.D.) The sorcerer Zlito was the court wizard of King Wenceslas of Bohemia. Among his occult powers, Zlito was said to have been able to levitate and fly.

zodiac In the study of ASTROLOGY, the zodiac is made up of 12 imaginary divisions in the sky through which the sun appears to travel on its path around the Earth. Each section of the zodiac, a 30-degree wedge of that circle, has been assigned a representative sign bearing specific qualities.

Zodiac comes from the Greek word *zodion*, meaning "little animal"; indeed, most of the astrological signs (made up of star configurations) are meant to represent ANIMALS, although some of the signs are human or mythological in nature. In ancient times, this imaginary band of creatures was actually thought to travel the heavens, ruling over all Mankind.

The construct of the zodiac was devised, possibly by the MAGI, during the zenith of the ancient Babylonian empire. The stargazers discovered that people born under a particular sign appeared to share common characteristics; supposedly, they also shared traits with the symbol of the zodiac symbol as well. A knowledge of the idiosyncrasies (and probable actions) of a person based on his or her zodiac sign could be a powerful tool in the hands of a wizard or a sorcerer.

Zodiac signs are assigned to a person according to where the sun, the most influential and important "planet," was located at the time of birth. The position of the sun in the zodiac at the time of birth was also thought to link a person to the influence of one of the classic four ELEMENTS.

The order of the zodiac sun signs do not adhere to the modern Gregorian calendar. In fact, the first sign of the zodiac, whose influence begins in late March, is Aries, followed in order by Taurus, Gemini, Cancer, Leo, Virgo, Libra, Scorpio, Sagittarius, Capricorn, Aquarius and Pisces.

Some modern astrologers have adjusted the traditional dates given for the zodiac signs due to a phenomenon known as the precession (or falling back) of the equinoxes. Since the time that astrology was originally devised, the dates of the spring and autumn equinoxes (when the amount of day and night are equal) have changed due to a shifting of the Earth's rotation. Thus, if astrology were based solely on the sun's procession across the sky, all HOROSCOPES cast since the third century A.D., technically, should have to be adjusted one horoscope sign backwards.

Astrologers disagree on the exact dates that separate the horoscope signs, but the acceptable dates never vary by more than one day. A brief listing of the most traditional dates (according to modern astrologer and newspaper columnist Sydney Omarr), along with some of the qualities, good and bad, generally assigned to each of the 12 zodiac signs follows.

Aries (March 21–April 19). The Ram. Impetuous; energetic; natural leader. Some early Romans, including the poet Virgil, considered Taurus the first sun sign, and Babylonians employed the symbol Hireling, a paid laborer, in the place of Aries. In early EGYPTIAN MAGIC, the star sign was Amun, the ram-headed ruler of their northern territory. The Greeks called the zodiac sign *eras*, meaning "lamb," which transferred to Latin as *aries*, or "ram."

Taurus (April 20–May 20). The Bull. Patient; persistent; dependable. The Latin word *taurus* means "bull." The Sumerians felt the bull was created by Anu, their sun god; the Egyptians thought it was the sacred bull of Osiris, god of the Underworld.

Gemini (May 21–June 20). The Twins. Clever; flexible; moody. The Israelites saw the Gemini as Jachin and Boaz, the twin pillars at the entry to SOLOMON's Temple; the Arabs thought them to be peacocks; the Indians, horsemen. The Greeks called them the *Dioskuri* or "sons of god," and today they are associated with Castor and Pollux, the twin sons of Zeus.

Cancer (June 21–July 22). The Crab. Imaginative; humorous; sensitive. The word *cancer* is from the Greek *karkinos,* meaning "crab," which was Latinized as *cancer,* with the same meaning. Ancient CHALDEANS saw the constellation as a portal between the heavens and earth. The Egyptians saw it as the SCARAB, but the Arabs first identified it as a crab, naming the strongest star in the cluster *Al-Zubayan* ("the claws"). Many modern astrologers call the sign Moonchild to avoid any association with the unrelated disease cancer.

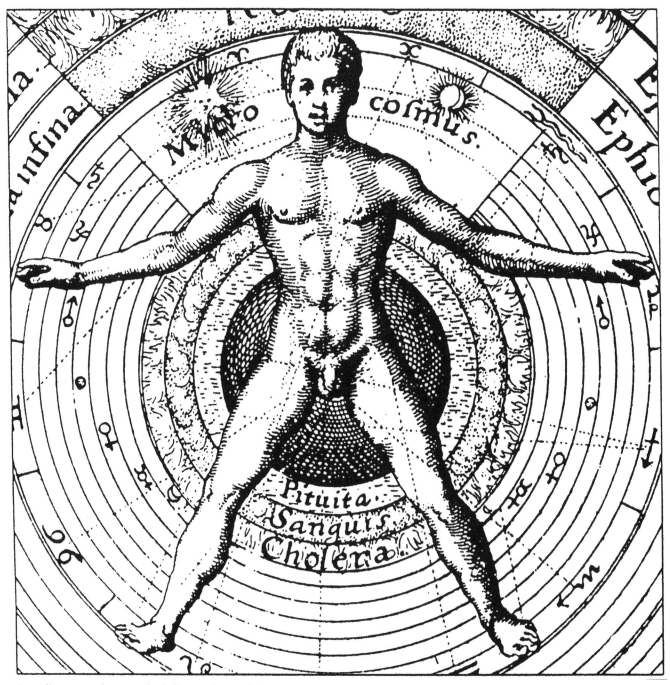

According to astrologers and cabalists, each part of the human body was ruled, or controlled, by a specific planet and sign of the zodiac. Occultists' opinions differed on which heavenly spheres ruled over which organs. Note that the drawing depicts the man as standing in the shape of a pentagram. (Robert Fludd, *Ultriusque cosmi historia*)

Leo (July 23–August 22). The Lion. Powerful; dignified; sense of humor. From the Greek *leon* and Latin *leonis*, meaning "lion," the constellation has been identified as a lion for more than 6,000 years.

Virgo (August 23–September 22). The Virgin. Logical; contemplative; stable. From the Latin *virginis*, meaning "maiden," the Babylonians saw the stars as Belit, the wife of Bel, their supreme god. Each culture identified the figure with one of their own female deities, usually the harvest goddess; among the Egyptians, ISIS; the Greeks, Ceres; the Romans, Demeter.

Libra (September 23–October 22). The Scales. Intuitive; innovative; artistic. The Latin *libra* means scales. The ancient Mesopotamians thought the constellation resembled an altar. Astrologers from Alexandria, Egypt changed the symbol to Julius Caesar holding a set of scales, indicating justice, when the emperor designed the Julian Calendar. After Caesar's assassination, his image was removed, but the scales remained.

Scorpio (October 23–November 21). The Scorpion. Domineering; self-assured; moody. The constellation has always been associated with the scorpion. In Greek, it is *skorpios*; in Latin, *scorpius*. Akkadians called it *girtab* (meaning "stinger"), and the Egyptians personified it as Selk, a sun goddess with the tail of a scorpion.

Sagittarius (November 22–December 21). The Archer. Energetic; forceful; industrious. The name is from the Latin *sagitta*, meaning "arrow," but it was the Greeks who portrayed the constellation as a mythological centaur (with the trunk and head of a man and the body of a horse) holding a bow and arrow.

Capricorn (December 22–January 19). The Sea Goat. Tenacious; practical; reliable. The sea goat is a fictional creature, with the upper body of a goat and the tail of a fish. Some scholars suggest that the beast is descended from Ea, the Babylonian god who was ruler of "the waters under the earth." The Greeks associated the constellation with their pastoral god Pan, which had the *lower* body of a goat. Its name comes from both Latin (*caper*, meaning "goat") and Greek (*cornus*, meaning "horn").

Aquarius (January 20–February 18). The Water Bearer. Spiritual; gentle; generous. The constellation has always been associated with water. Before being named from the Latin *aqua* ("water"), the Babylonians called the constellation *Gu* ("water jug"). The Greeks added Ganymede, the gods' servant, to the constellation.

Pisces (February 19–March 20). The Fish. Trustful; cooperative; compassionate. In ASSYRIAN MAGIC, astrologers called the constellation *Nanu* (meaning "fish"); and the Phoenicians identified it as Dagon, their fish-tailed agriculture god. In GRECO-ROMAN MAGIC, occultists perceived the stars as a fish, and the sign received its name from the Latin *pisces*, plural of *piscis*, meaning "fish."

Those born near a juncture of two signs (i.e., usually from a day or two before the end of one sign and up to a week into a new sign) are said to have been born on the cusp. Often they exhibit some of the personality traits of each zodiac sign.

The stereotypical wardrobe of the medieval wizard or sorcerer. (18th-century French print, drawn by Gillot and engraved by Toullain)

These characteristics are, of course, very broad generalizations. For an astrological reading to be accurate, it must take many more details into account than just the zodiac sign. Precise time of day, date (month, day, year), place of birth and so on are required to calculate a precise, complete horoscope.

Eastern astrology does not make use of the same zodiac signs as the West. The Chinese, who have certainly been charting the stars for more than the recorded 3,300 years, run their astrological calendar in 12-year cycles. In other words, a full year is represented by one zodiac sign, which symbolizes certain traits and attributes. A different zodiac sign follows the next year, and so on, until the original sign reappears on the thirteenth year of the cycle. The zodiac names (in Chinese and English) with some sample years and characteristics follow:

TZU—The Rat (1900, 1912 . . .) Diligent, industrious
CHOU–The Ox (1901 . . .) Strong, patient
YIN—The Tiger (1902 . . .) Forceful, quick
MAO—The Rabbit (1903 . . .) Flexible, social
CH'EN—The Dragon (1904 . . .) Ambitious, committed
SSU—The Snake (1905 . . .) Independent, self-reliant
WU—The Horse (1906 . . .) Striking, showy
WEI—The Sheep (1907 . . .) Unassertive, group oriented
SHEN—The Monkey (1908 . . .) Creative, capricious
YU—The Rooster (1909 . . .) Confident, adventurous
SHU—The Dog (1910 . . .) Loyal, trustworthy
HAI—The Boar (1911, 1923 . . .) Courageous, generous.

Colloquially, Westerners usually refer to each zodiac year of the Chinese calendar by referring to its animal representative, such as "The Year of the Cat" or "The Year of the Tiger."

The search for truth in the study of the zodiac, horoscopes and astrology is a lifelong inquiry. A solid understanding is required, however, for any wizard or sorcerer who wishes to practice DIVINATION, discern the inner secrets of ALCHEMY or comprehend such mystic writings as the KABBALAH.

Zohar, The   See KABBALAH.

zombie   A term with occult origins in VOODOO worship in Africa, the word *zombie* traveled to the West Indies during the slave trade of the 1700s. In Haitian tradition, a zombie is one of the living dead, a corpse that has been reanimated by a voodoo master and is held under his or her command. Because the zombie, having no will of its own, completely and *only* follows the bidding of its master, the creature cannot truly be described as being alive or having been brought back to life. Once the master releases hold of its cadaverous slave, the corpse will return to the world of the dead.

Certainly there are no zombies such as those seen in some grade-B horror films, but some noted cultural anthropologists contend that zombies do exist. They may in fact be people who have been poisoned into a comatose state by a voodoo practitioner, buried alive while seemingly dead and then secretly exhumed. Drugged into a vegetative state, the zombie can remain under the complete control of its master indefinitely.

Sociologists suggest that such a zombie really does not have to actually *do* anything to be effective: its mere existence and appearance is proof of the magic power of its owner. The master's reputation as a skilled sorcerer would only be magnified as accounts of the walking dead spread among his superstitious neighbors.

Zoroaster (fl. sixth century B.C.?)   Although many myths surround this early religious figure, Zoroaster (the

Greek name for Zarathustra) was undoubtedly a true historical personage. Some scholars have placed him as living around 1500 B.C., others as late as 628 B.C., but the Zend-Avesta, the holy book detailing Zorastrian principles, positions him even earlier. According to one legend, Zoroaster was trained in WITCHCRAFT by the sorcerer Agonaces, who lived around 7000 B.C. Most probably, Zoroaster was a Persian living at some period during the sixth century B.C.

Zoroastrianism, sometimes called the Magian religion, shares many of the polytheistic beliefs prevalent in the Middle East at the time of the faith's beginnings. The main distinction is that Zoroastrians recognize two main SPIRITS: Ahura-Mazda (or Ormazd), who represents good and light (and whose earthly symbol is fire); and Ahriman, who embodies evil and darkness. There is continuous warring between the two godlike forces, often fought on Earth, and a corresponding emotional conflict is, therefore, always present in Man, to whom Ormazd gave freedom of choice. It was believed that Good is eternal and will eventually triumph over Evil.

Zoroaster's teachings were carried on by a group of priests known as the MAGI, who were at the peak of their power at the time of the founding of the Persian Empire by Cyrus. Their cosmic beliefs and practices led to the Magi's fame as wizards, stargazers and astrologers. (See ASTROLOGY.) The Magi were also very influential in secular affairs, and their ever-increasing political power eventually led to their persecution around 500 B.C.

Today, the last remaining religious community that follows the teachings of Zoroaster are the Parsis (also seen as Parsees) of India. The Parsi (literally meaning "from the city of Pars") moved from Fars, Persia (modern-day Iran) to India between 1,300 and 1,400 years ago to escape suppression by the Muslims. Legend says that when they arrived in Gujarat, India, the rajah sent them a full jar of milk, suggesting that his city was too full to accommodate them. One Parsi carefully added a coin to the jug, proving that the new immigrants would not displace the residents. Today, almost 70% of the world's Parsis live in Bombay.

The Parsi / Zoroaster creed states that the rich and poor will unite in death; yet they oppose cremation and burial: the four ELEMENTS of Earth, Air, Water and Fire must not be polluted. The Towers of Silence in Bombay, where the Parsi dead are laid to rest, stand as tacit testimony to this tenet of the Zoroastrian religion. Only followers of the faith may enter the two towers, and only the dead reach the innermost sanctums. The deceased body is placed uncovered atop one of the tall chimneylike columns, exposed to the elements and vultures. After several days, the remaining skeleton is dropped down the tower's well to return to ashes. Because strict Zoroastrians must marry within their faith and conversion is not recognized, it is estimated that only 36,000 Parsis will remain by the year 2021.

BIBLIOGRAPHY

Books

Advanced Dungeons & Dragons (2nd ed.): The Complete Wizard's Handbook. Lake Geneva, Wisc.: TSR, 1990.

Aldington, Richard, and Delano Ames, trans. *New Larousse Encyclopedia of Mythology*. New York: The Hamlyn Publishing Group, 1978.

Allen, Steve. *Curses! or . . . How Never To Be Foiled Again*. Los Angeles: J.P. Tarcher, 1973.

Atkinson, R.J.C. *Stonehenge and neighbouring monuments*. London: Her Majesty's Stationery Office, 1978.

Bali. Berlitz Guidebook. Lausanne, Switzerland: JPM Publications, 1992.

Bartlett, John. *Familiar Quotations*. 15th ed. Edited by Emily Morison Beck. Boston: Little, Brown and Company, 1980.

Baskin, Wade. *Dictionary of Satanism*. New York: Philosophical Library, 1972.

Baum, L. Frank. *The Wonderful Wizard of Oz*. (The Pennyroyal Press Edition; Illustrated by Barry Moser) Berkeley, Calif.: University of California Press, 1986.

Bayhan, Suzan. *Priene • Miletus • Didyma* Translated by Anita Gillett. Istanbul: Keskin Color Kartpostalcilik, 1989.

Benét, William Rose, ed. *The Reader's Encyclopedia: An Encyclopedia of World Literature and the Arts*. New York: Thomas Y. Crowell, 1948.

Billy, Christopher, ed. *Fodor's 91: Europe*. New York: Fodor's Travel Publications, 1991.

Blair, Lawrence, with Lorne Blair. *Ring of Fire*. New York: Bantam Books, 1988.

Bloom, Ken. *Hollywood Song: The Complete Film & Musical Companion*. New York: Facts On File, 1995.

Bordman, Gerald. *American Musical Theatre: A Chronicle*. New York: Oxford University Press, 1986.

Bradley, Marion. *The Mists of Avalon*. London: Sphere Books Lts., 1983.

Brooks, Tim, and Earle Marsh. *The Complete Directory to Prime Time Network TV Shows 1946–Present*. 5th ed. New York: Ballantine, 1992.

Brown, Dale M., series ed. *Mesopotamia: The Mighty Kings*. (Part of the *Lost Civilizations* series.) New York: Time-Life Books, 1995.

Budge, E.A. Wallis, trans. *The Egyptian Book of the Dead*. (Unabridged reprint of 1895 edition, authorized by the Trustees of the British Museum) New York: Dover Books, 1967.

Burger, Eugene. *Spirit Theater*. New York: Richard Kaufman and Alan Greenberg, publishers, 1986.

———. *The Experience of Magic*. New York: Richard Kaufman and Alan Greenberg, publishers, 1989.

———. *Strange Ceremonies*. New York: Richard Kaufman and Alan Greenberg, publishers, 1990.

Burger, Eugene, and Robert E. Neale. *Magic & Meaning*. Seattle: Hermetic Press, 1995.

Cavendish, Richard, ed. *Man, Myth & Magic: An Illustrated History of the Supernatural*. 24 vols. New York: Marshall Cavendish Corporation, 1970.

Christopher, Milbourne. *Panorama of Magic*. New York: Dover Publications, 1962.

———. *ESP, Seers & Psychics*. New York: Thomas Y. Crowell Co., 1970.

———. *The Illustrated History of Magic*. New York: Thomas Y. Crowell Co., 1973.

Claiborne, Robert. *Loose Cannons and Red Herrings*. New York: Ballantine Books, 1988.

Clarke, Mary, and Clement Crisp. *The Ballet Goer's Guide*. New York: Alfred A. Knopf, 1981.

Cosentino, Donald J., ed. *Sacred Arts of Haitian Vodou*. Fowler Museum of Cultural History. Los Angeles: 1995.

Cross, Milton, and Karl Kohrs. *The New Milton Cross' More Stories of the Great Operas*. Garden City, N.Y.: Doubleday & Co., 1980.

Crowley, Aleister. *Magick in Theory and Practice*. (Unabridged reprint of 1929 London edition.) New York: Dover Publications, 1976.

Dannhorn, Robin J., ed. *Fodor's Southeast Asia 1985*. New York: Fodor's Travel Guides, 1984, p. 360.

Davidson, Gladys. *The Barnes Book of the Opera*. New York: A.S. Barnes & Co., 1962.

DC Comics. *Who's Who in the DC Universe*. (Also known as *DC Universe*.) Edited by Jenette Kahn. Vols. 10–14. New York: DC Comics, 1991.

———. *Who's Who in the DC Universe*. Edited by Jenette Kahn. Vols. 15–16. New York: DC Comics, 1992.

———. *Who's Who in the DC Universe*. Edited by Jenette Kahn. Update 1993. Vol. 1. New York: DC Comics, 1992.

———. *Who's Who in the !Impact! Universe*. Vols. 1 and 2. New York: Archie Comic Publications, 1991.

———. *Who's Who in the !Impact! Universe*. Vol. 3. New York: Archie Comic Publications, 1992.

DeGivry, Grillot. *Witchcraft, Magic & Alchemy*. Translated by J. Courtenary Locke. New York: Bonanza Books, n.d.

Drabble, Margaret, ed. *The Oxford Companion to English Literature*. 5th ed. Oxford, Great Britain: Oxford University Press, 1985.

Ebon, Martin. *The Satan Trap: Dangers of the Occult*. Garden City, N.Y.: Doubleday & Co., 1976.

Elworthy, Frederick. *The Evil Eye*. New York: Collier Books, 1970.

Ewen, David. *The New Encyclopedia of the Opera*. New York: Hill and Wang, 1971.

Faulkner, Raymond, Ph.D., trans. *The Egyptian Book of the Dead*. San Francisco: Chronicle Books, 1994.

Fleisher, Michael L. *The Great Superman Book: vol. 3*. New York: Harmony Books, 1978.

Franklin, Joe. *Classics of the Silent Screen*. New York: Cadillac Publishing Co., 1959.

Frazer, James George, Sir. *The Golden Bough: A Study in Magic & Religion*. New York: Macmillan Co., 1940.

Fricke, John. *The Wizard of Oz: An Appreciation and Brief History of the Film and an Annotated Guide to the Original Motion Picture Soundtrack*. Book accompanying double-CD "Deluxe Edition" release, produced by Marilee Bradford and Bradley Flanagan. Los Angeles: Rhino Records, 1995.

Funk, Wilfred. *Word Origins and Their Romantic Stories*. New York: Grosset & Dunlap, 1950.

Gänzl, Kurt, and Andrew Lamb. *Gänzl's Book of the Musical Theatre*. New York: Schirmer Books (Macmillan, Inc.), 1988.

Garfield, Richard. *The Magic: The Gathering Pocket Players' Guide*. Renton, Wash.: Wizards of the Coast, 1994.

Gibson, Walter B., and Litzka R. Gibson. *The Complete Illustrated Book of the Psychic Sciences*. Garden City, N.Y.: Doubleday & Co., 1966.

Goethe, Johann Wolfgang von. *Faust, I & II*. Translated by Charles E. Passage. Indianapolis: Bobbs-Merrill Educational Publishing, 1965.

González-Wippler, Migene. *The Complete Book of Amulets & Talismans*. St. Paul, Minn.: Llewellyn Publications, 1993.

Grant, John. *Encyclopedia of Walt Disney's Animated Characters: From Mickey Mouse to Aladdin*. New York: Hyperion, 1993.

Green, Stanley. *Encyclopedia of the Musical Theatre*. New York: Da Capo Press, 1976.

Guiley, Rosemary Ellen. *The Encyclopedia of Witches and Witchcraft*. New York: Facts On File, 1989.

———. *The Encyclopedia of Ghosts and Spirits*. New York: Facts On File, 1992.

Haining, Peter. *Witchcraft and Black Magic*. New York: Bantam Books, 1973.

Haining, Peter, ed. *The Necromancers*. Essays. New York: William Morrow & Co., 1972.

Halliwell, Leslie. *Halliwell's Film Guide*. 7th Ed. New York: Harper and Row, 1989.

———. *Halliwell's Film Guide*. 8th Ed. Edited by John Walker. New York: HarperPerennial, 1991.

Hansel, C.E.M. *ESP and Parapsychology: A Critical Re-evaluation*. Buffalo, N.Y.: Prometheus Books, 1980.

Hansen, Chadwick. *Witchcraft at Salem*. New York: George Braziller, 1969.

Hay, Henry. *Cyclopedia of Magic*. (Unabridged copy of 1949 David McKay Company ed.) New York: Dover Publications, 1975.

Highwater, Jamake. *Myth & Sexuality*. New York: Meridian/Penguin Books, 1990.

Hill, Douglas. *Magic and Superstition*. London: Hamlyn Publishing Group, 1968.

Holy Bible, The. Revised Standard Version. Cleveland, Ohio: The World Publishing Company, 1962.

Holy Bible, The. King James Ed. New York: Oxford University Press, n.d.

Homer. *The Odyssey*. Translated by Robert Fitzgerald. New York: Alfred A. Knopf, 1992.

———. *The Iliad and the Odyssey*. Adapted by Jane Werner Watson. New York: Golden Press, 1956.

Horn, Maurice. "Johnny Hart" and "Wizard of Id." In *World Encyclopedia of Comics, The*. Ed. by Maurice Horn. New York: Chelsea House Publishers, 1976.

Hugo, Victor. *The Hunchback of Notre Dame*. New York: TOR (Tom Doherty Associates), 1996.

Insight Guides: Bali. Created and directed by Hans Höfer. Hong Kong: Houghton Mifflin Co. (APA Publications), 1994.

Jurkowitz, Deborah, ed. *Fodor's India*. New York: Fodor's Travel Guides, 1985.

Kramer, Heinrich, and James Sprenger. *The Malleus Maleficarum*. Translated by the Rev. Montague Summers. (Unabridged reproduction of 1928 edition published by John Rodker, London, with the Summers introduction from the 1948 reprint.) New York: Dover Publications, 1971.

Kunitz, Stanley J. and Howard Haycraft, eds. *Twentieth Century Authors: A Biographical Dictionary of Modern Literature*. New York: H.W. Wilson Co., 1942.

Lehane, Brendan. *Wizards and Witches*. From *The Enchanted World* series. Alexandria, Va.: Time-Life Books, 1984.

Lerner, Alan Jay. *Camelot*. New York: Dell Publications, 1967.

Levinson, Richard, and William Link. *Merlin*. Unpublished draft/working script of Broadway production. November 24, 1981, p. 75.

Lewis, C.S. *The Magician's Nephew*. New York: HarperCollins (Harper Trophy), 1994.

———. *The Lion, The Witch and the Wardrobe*. New York: HarperCollins (Harper Trophy), 1994.

———. *The Silver Chair*. New York: HarperCollins (Harper Trophy), 1994.

———. *The Voyage of the Dawn Treader*. New York: HarperCollins (Harper Trophy), 1994.

Lewis, H. Spencer. *The Symbolic Prophecy of the Great Pyramid*. San Jose, Calif.: The Rosicrucian Press, 1953.

Loewenberg, Alfred, comp. *Annals of Opera: 1597–1940*. Geneva: Societas Bibliographica, 1955.

Lorie, Peter. *Superstitions*. New York: Simon and Schuster, 1992.

Malory, Sir Thomas. *Le Morte D'Arthur*. Prose rendition by Keith Baines. New York: Mentor Books (Dutton Signet/Penguin), 1962.

Maple, Eric. *Superstition and the Superstitious*. Cranbury, N.J.: A.S. Barnes and Co., 1972.

Marlowe, Christopher. *The Tragedy of Doctor Faustus*. New York: Washington Square Press, 1963.

Marschall, Richard. "Brant Parker." In *The World Encyclopedia of Comics*. Ed. by Maurice Horn. New York: Chelsea House Publishers, 1976.

Marvel Comics. *The Official Handbook of the Marvel Universe*. (Also known as *Marvel Universe*). Tom DeFalco, ed. Master Editions, vol. 3, nos. 34 and 35. New York: Marvel Entertainment Group, 1993.

Mason, Anita. *The Illusionist*. New York: Holt, Rinehart and Winston, 1983.

Mathers, S. Liddell MacGregor, trans. *The Key of Solomon the King (Clavicula Salomonis)*. York Beach, Me.: Samuel Weiser, 1972.

———. [as S.L. MacGregor Mathers, trans.] *The Book of the Sacred Magic of Abramelin the Mage*. (Unabridged reprint of 2nd ed., as published by John M. Watkins, London, 1900.) New York: Dover Publications, 1975.

Maven, Max. *Max Maven's Book of Fortunetelling.* New York: Prentice Hall, 1992.

McClelland, Doug. *Down the Yellow Brick Road: The Making of The Wizard of Oz.* New York: Pyramid Publications (Harcourt Brace Javonovich), 1976.

Miller, Arthur. *The Crucible.* (1952) Reprinted with permission in *Arthur Miller, The Crucible: Text and Criticism.* Gerald Weales, ed. New York: The Viking Press, 1971.

Minch, Stephen. *From Witchcraft to Card Tricks.* Seattle: Hermetic Press, 1991.

Moore, Frank Ledlie, comp. *Crowell's Handbook of World Opera.* New York: Thomas Y. Crowell Co., 1961.

Nash, N. Richard. *The Rainmaker.* New York: Samuel French, 1955.

Nostradamus. *Prophecies on World Events.* Translated and interpreted by Stewart Robb. New York: Liveright Publishing Corporation, 1961.

Petsas, Photios. *Delphi: Monuments and Museum.* Athens: Krene Editions, 1981.

Phillips—the Egyptian. *Tutankhamen's Victims in America.* Los Angeles: Egyptian Antiques, 1977.

Pucci, Eugenio. *All Rome and the Vatican.* Translated by Nancy Wolfers Mazzoni. Firenze (Florence): Collano Italia Artistic, 1967.

Ramsland, Katherine. *Prism of the Night: A Biography of Anne Rice.* New York: Dutton, 1991.

———. *The Witches' Companion: The Official Guide to Anne Rice's "Lives of the Mayfair Witches."* New York: Ballantine, 1994.

Rigaud, Milo. *Secrets of Voodoo.* San Francisco: City Lights Books, 1985.

Riva, Anna. *Spellcraft, Hexcraft and Witchcraft.* Los Angeles: International Imports, 1977. (1995 reprint.)

Robbins, Rossell Hope. *The Encyclopedia of Witchcraft & Demonology.* New York: Bonanza Books, 1959.

Rohmer, Sax. *The Romance of Sorcery.* New York: Causeway Books, 1973.

Russell, Jacqueline, and Christopher Billy and Vernon Nahrgang, eds. *Fodor's 90 Caribbean.* New York: Fodor's Travel Publications, 1989, pp. 297–298.

Russell, Jeffrey Burton. *The Devil: Perceptions of Evil from Antiquity to Primitive Christianity.* Ithaca, N.Y.: Cornell University Press, 1977.

Schueler, Gerald and Betty. *Egyptian Magick.* St. Paul, Minn.: Llewellyn Publications, 1994.

Scot, Reginald. *The Discoverie of Witchcraft.* (First published 1584. Unabridged reprint of the John Rodker 1930 London printing.) New York: Dover Publications, 1972.

Shakespeare, William. *The Complete Plays and Poems of William Shakespeare.* Ed. by William Allan Neilson and Charles Jarvis Hill. Cambridge, Mass.: The Riverside Press (Houghton Mifflin Co.), 1942.

Shaner, Richard H. *Hexerei: A Practice of Witchcraft Among the Pennsylvania Dutch.* Indiana, Pa: A.G. Halldin, 1973.

Simon, Henry W. *100 Great Operas and Their Stories.* New York: Anchor Books, 1989. (Originally published by Doubleday as *Festival of Opera,* 1957).

Sinyard, Neil. *Silent Movies.* New York: Gallery Books (W.H. Smith Publications), 1990.

Sladek, John. *The New Aprocrypha: A Guide to Strange Science and Occult Beliefs.* New York: Stein and Day, 1974.

Smith, Morton. *Jesus the Magician.* New York: Barnes & Noble, 1978.

Smith, Willard S. "S.A.M. Funeral Ceremony." In *The Ritual Manual of The Society of American Magicians,* revised by Leo Rullman, Leslie P. Guest and Gerald L. Kaufman, 30–32. New York: Society of American Magicians, 1946. Additional short-form edition by the Society of American Magicians Parent Assembly #1, New York, 1985.

Steele, John H. *Dr. Gardner's Museum of Witchcraft & Magic.* Souvenir booklet. Gatlinburg, Tenn.: Ripley Museum, 1974.

Steinbeck, John. *The Acts of King Arthur and His Noble Knights.* New York: Ballantine Books, 1976.

Stevenson, Burton. *The Home Book of Quotations.* Philadelphia: Blakiston Co., 1944, p. 11. (Distributed by Dodd, Mead & Co., New York.)

Stevenson, Isabelle, ed. *The Tony Award.* New York: Crown Publishing, 1984.

Stewart, Mary. *The Crystal Cave.* New York: Fawcett Crest Books, 1970.

———. *The Hollow Hills.* New York: Fawcett Crest Books, 1973.

———. *The Last Enchantment.* New York: Fawcett Crest Books, 1979.

———. *The Wicked Day.* New York: William Morrow & Co., 1983.

Tennyson, Alfred Lord. *Idylls of the King.* (Selections) New York: Dell Publishing, 1967.

Thompson, C.J.S. *The Mysteries and Secrets of Magic.* New York: Barnes & Noble, 1993.

Turner, Robert. *Elizabethan Magic: The Art and the Magus.* Longmead (also Shaftesbury, Dorset), England: Element Books, 1989.

Twain, Mark. *The Adventures of Tom Sawyer.* In *The Unabridged Mark Twain,* ed. by Lawrence Teacher, pp. 437–586. Philadelphia: Running Press, 1976.

———. *The Works of Mark Twain: Vol. 9. A Connecticut Yankee in King Arthur's Court.* Ed. by Bernard L. Stein. Berkeley, Calif.: University of California Press for The Iowa Center for Textual Studies, 1979.

———. *A Connecticut Yankee in King Arthur's Court.* In *The Unabridged Mark Twain,* ed. by Lawrence Teacher, pp. 957–1192. Philadelphia: Running Press, 1976.

———. *A Connecticut Yankee in King Arthur's Court.* New York: Signet Classics, n.d.

Visions and Prophecies. Mysteries of the Unknown series. Alexandria, Va.: Time-Life Books, 1988.

Waite, Arthur Edward. *The Book of Black Magic.* York Beach, Me.: Samuel Weiser, 1972.

Waldman, Carl. *Word Dance: The Language of Native American Studies.* New York: Facts On File, n.d.

Walsh, Roger, M.D. *The Spirit of Shamanism.* Los Angeles: Jeffrey Tarcher, 1990.

Ward, Charles A. *Oracles of Nostradamus.* New York: The Modern Library (Random House), 1940.

Waters, T.A. *The Encyclopedia of Magic and Magicians.* New York: Facts On File, 1988.

Wedeck, Harry E. *A Treasury of Witchcraft: A Source Book of the Magic Arts.* New York: Bonanza Books, 1990. (Originally published by the Philosophical Library, 1961.)

Wedeck, H.E., and Wade Baskin. *Dictionary of Pagan Religions.* New York: Philosophical Library, 1971.

Wepman, Dennis. "Wizard of Id." In *The Encyclopedia of American Comics: From 1897 to the Present.* Ed. by Ron Goulart. New York: Facts On File, 1990.

White, T.H. *The Book of Merlyn.* New York: Berkley Medallion Books, 1978.

———. *The Sword in the Stone.* London: Fontana Lions (William Collins Sons & Co.), 1979.

———. *The Once and Future King.* Canada: Fontana Books (William Collins Sons & Co.), 1979.

Willis, John. *Theatre World.* Vol. 44, 1987–1988. New York: Crown Publishers, 1989.

Winstedt, Richard. *The Malay Magician.* Oxford: Oxford University Press, 1993.

Zolar. *The Encyclopedia of Ancient and Forbidden Knowledge.* Los Angeles: Nash Publishing, 1970.

Periodicals, Pamphlets, Small Publications

Achenbach, Joel. "Why?" *Sky Magazine.* (Delta Air Lines's In-flight magazine.) Ft. Lauderdale, Fla.: Halsey Publishing Co., April 1995, p. 144.

Albright, William. "Disney puts might behind 'Beauty.'" *The Houston Post.* April 14, 1994, pp. D–1 and D–8.

Atalay, Özcan. Ephesus, map with text and commentary. Translated by Sevin Okyay. Izmir, Turkey: Güney Books, 1994.

Bash, Alan. "Edgy Scandinavia unplugs 'Rangers.'" *USA Today International Edition.* LIFE section. October 20, 1994.

Crisafulli, Chuck. "Bytes . . . Camera . . . Action!" *Los Angeles Times.* Calendar. June 25, 1995, pp. 4–5, 32–35.

Damn Yankees. Playbill Magazine. New York: Playbill, May 1994, pp. 23–43.

Disney's Beauty and the Beast: A New Musical. Souvenir brochure to the Broadway production. Produced by Roundtable Press for Walt Disney Productions. New York: Hyperion, 1994.

"The Evil Eye." *Seabourn Herald.* August 26, 1994, p. 3.

Folkart, Burt A. "Elizabeth Montgomery Dies of Cancer" *Los Angeles Times.* May 19, 1995, pp. B1, B3.

Gilman, Donald. Commentary and critique of *Merlin in German Literature* by Adelaide Marie Weiss, which first appeared in *Studies in German, Vol. III.* Washington, D.C.: Catholic University of America Press and reprinted, New York: AMS Press, 1970. Article appears in *The Journal of Magic History.* Steven S. Tigner, ed. Toledo, Ohio: November 1979, pp. 189–191.

Goodstein, Laurie. "Fright for Christian Right: Halloween Vilified as Pagan Holiday." *International Herald Tribune* (from *Washington Post Service*). Paris. November 1, 1994, pp. 1, 8.

Hochman, Steve, and Don Shirley. "Jackson to Produce New Musical." *Los Angeles Times.* July 26, 1995, pp. F1, F3.

Houston Chronicle, "Funky Facts: Aladdin, the sequel," April 7, 1994, p. 7.

"It's Magic." *The New York Times Magazine. The New York Times.* March 20, 1994, p. 17.

Kaplan, James. "It's Morphin Time!" *TV Guide.* Radnor, Penn.: News America Publications, June 24–30, 1995, pp. 14–20.

Keller, Bill. "A Liberation Legacy: South Africa's Witch Murders." *International Herald Tribune* (from *The New York Times* Service). Rome. September 19, 1994, pp. 1, 5.

"Kusadasi/Ephesus." Pamphlet excerpt from Berlitz Guide for Turkey. Switzerland: Berlitz Publishing, 1990.

Logan, William Bryant. "Searching for Hidden Water the Intuitive Way." *The New York Times.* June 26, 1994. "Pastimes" section.

"Magic: The Gathering." Instructional booklet accompanying Deckmaster game cards. Darla A. Willis, ed. Renton, Wash.: Wizards of the Coast, 1995.

Malnic, Eric. "Museum Too Weird, County Says." *Los Angeles Times.* Los Angeles, Calif. June 9, 1995, pp. B1, B3.

Manheim, Michael. Commentary and critique of *Majesty and Magic in Shakespeare* by Frances A. Yates, Boulder, Colo.: Shambhala Press, 1978. Article appears in *The Journal of Magic History.* Steven S. Tigner, editor. Toledo, Ohio: November 1979, pp. 191–192.

Medea. Playbill Magazine. New York: Playbill, May 1994, pp. 23, 38.

Mitchell, Sean. "Give 'em Hell, Randy." *Los Angeles Times.* Calendar section. September 17, 1995, pp. 5, 88–89.

Osbourne, Charles. "*Macbeth*: The Earliest of Verdi's Masterpieces." *Performing Arts* magazine. March 1995, pp. P7–9.

Rauscher, William V. "The Wand: In Story and Symbol." *The Illusionist.* Part 2, p. 22. Part 4, p. 57, n.d.

Reif, Robin. "Making Broadway Magic." *Playbill* Magazine. New York: American Theatre Press, December 1982, pp. 6, 8, 10.

"Report: Apes killed to feed loggers." *Seabourn Herald.* October 26, 1994, p. 5.

Richards, David. "Tony Kushner Adapts a French Classic by Corneille." *The New York Times.* January 20, 1994, pp. B1, B4.

Sagal, Peter. Program notes for Los Angeles Theatre Center 1990 production of Tony Kushner's adaptation of *The Illusion* (1639) by Pierre Corneille.

Sayer, George. "The Background to *Shadowlands.*" *Theatreprint* magazine. Volume V, Number 7. (Program to London production of *Shadowlands*). London: Theatreprint, 1989.

Shirley, Don. "Is Michael Pasadena's Prince?" *Los Angeles Times.* Calendar section. July 30, 1995, p. 42.

Sider, Sandra. Commentary and critique of *The Occult in Art* by Fred Gettings. (First published by Cassell Ltd.) New York: Rizzoli International Publications, 1979. Article appears in *The Journal of Magic History.* Steven S. Tigner, ed. Toledo, Ohio: November 1979, pp. 195–196.

"Siegfried Saga, The." *Travel Holiday* (TWA In-flight Magazine). September 1994, p. 57.

Smith, Leo. "Magic in the Air." *Los Angeles Times.* May 30, 1995, pp. E1, E4.

Teen Dream's Power Heroes and Villains (no. 92). Paramus, New Jersey: Starline Publications, 1994.

Thomas, Kevin. "A Dazzling Leap From TV to Big Screen for 'Rangers'." *Los Angeles Times.* June 30, 1995, pp. F1, F18.

Tigner, Steven S. Commentary and critique of *Robert Fludd: Hermetic Philosopher* by Joscelyn Godwin. Boulder, Colo.: Shambhala, 1979. Article appears in *The Journal of Magic History*. Steven S. Tigner, ed. Toledo, Ohio: November 1979, pp. 193–194.

Wallstin, Brian. "Aggie Alchemy." *Houston Press*. April 7–13, 1994, pp. 6–15.

Which Witch. Program, original London production, Piccadilly Theatre. Libretto based on incidents suggested by the *Malleus Maleficarum*. London: Dewynters, 1992.

Wilford, John Noble. "Tomb of Ramses II's Many Sons Is Found in Egypt." *The New York Times*. International Edition. May 16, 1995, pp. A1, A7.

Winerip, Michael. "Making Peace with the Power Rangers." *Parenting* Magazine. San Francisco: Time Publishing Ventures, February 1995.

Recordings

Amahl and the Night Visitors. Original television cast. Music and libretto by Gian Carlo Menotti. LP. New York: RCA, 1952.

Beauty and the Beast. Original Motion Picture Soundtrack. Music, Alan Menken; lyrics, Howard Ashman. CD. Burbank, Calif.: Walt Disney Records, 1991.

Berlioz, Hector. *The Damnation of Faust.* Boston Symphony Orchestra, Charles Munch, Conductor. LP. Notes and translation of libretto by John N. Burk. New York: RCA Victor, 1954.

———. *The Damnation of Faust.* Boston Symphony Orchestra, Seiji Ozawa, Conductor. LP. Translation of libretto by David Cairns. Notes by Wolfgang Dömling, English translation by Jane Wiebel. Hamburg, Germany: Deutsche Grammophon, 1974.

Camelot. Original Broadway cast recording. LP. Music, Frederick Loewe; lyrics, Alan Jay Lerner. New York: Columbia (Masterworks).

Carnival. Original Broadway cast recording. LP. Music and lyrics by Michael Stewart. MGM Records.

———. Original Broadway cast recording, plus "bonus tracks" by additional artists. CD. New York: PolyGram Records, 1989.

Damn Yankees. Original Broadway cast recording. LP. Music and lyrics by Richard Adler and Jerry Ross. New York: RCA Victor, 1955.

———. 1994 Original Broadway cast recording. CD. New York: PolyGram Records, 1994.

Faust. Studio cast CD. Randy Newman, composer/lyricist. Reprise Records, 1995.

Godspell. Original cast recording. LP. Music and lyrics by Stephen Schwartz. New York: Bell Records.

Into the Woods. Original Broadway cast recording. LP. Music and lyrics by Stephen Sondheim. New York: RCA Victor, 1987.

"It's A Bird It's A Plane It's SUPERMAN." Original Broadway cast recording. LP. New York: Columbia Records (CBS Records).

Jesus Christ Superstar. Original "concept album" studio cast. Double LP. Music, Andrew Lloyd Webber; lyrics, Tim Rice. London: MCA Records, 1970.

Joseph and the Amazing Technicolor Dreamcoat. Studio cast. Music, Andrew Lloyd Webber; lyrics, Tim Rice. LP, "London" label. New York: PolyGram Records (Decca Records), 1969.

———. Original Broadway cast recording. LP. Los Angeles: Chrysalis Records, 1982.

Kismet. Original Broadway cast recording. Music, Alexander Borodin; lyrics by Robert Wright and George Forrest. LP. Reissue under "The Columbia Treasury of the American Musical Theatre" series. New York: CBS Records, 1973.

Magic Show, The. Original Broadway cast recording. Music and lyrics by Stephen Schwartz. LP. New York: Bell Records, 1974.

Man of la Mancha. Original Broadway cast recording. Music, Mitch Leigh; lyrics, Joe Darion. LP. Universal City, Calif.: MCA Records, 1973.

———. Original London cast recording. Complete musical play, including full Dale Wasserman libretto, on two LPs. London: Decca Records.

Man of Magic. Original London cast recording. Music, Wilfred Wylam; lyrics, John Morley and Aubrey Cash. London: CBS.

Mussorgsky. *Pictures at an Exhibition / A Night on Bald Mountain.* New York Philharmonic; Leonard Bernstein, conducting. "Great Performances" series, produced by John McClure. Jacket notes. New York: CBS Records, 1981.

110 in the Shade. Original Broadway cast recording. LP. Music, Harvey Schmidt; lyrics, Tom Jones. New York: RCA Victor, 1963.

———. Original Broadway cast recording, plus previously unreleased material from score. CD. New York: BMG, 1963.

Pippin. Original Broadway cast recording. Music and lyrics by Stephen Schwartz. LP. Hollywood, Calif.: Motown, 1972.

Which Witch. Original studio album. Music, Benedicte Adrian and Ingrid Bjornov; lyrics, Helen Hampton, Benedicte Adrian and Ingrid Bjornov. CD (pressed in Sweden). Oslo: Notabene Records, 1987.

Witchcraft. Music and lyrics by Coven. Chicago: Dunwich Production for Mercury Records.

The Wizard of Oz. Original Motion Picture Soundtrack. LP. Culver City, Calif.: Metro-Goldwyn-Mayer, 1956.

Videotapes

Aladdin. Walt Disney. Burbank, Calif.: Buena Vista Home Video.

Bankler-Jukes, Stephen, and Lee Fulkerson. "Pocahontas: Ambassador of the New World." *A&E Biography.* New York, Arts & Entertainment Network, 1995. (Perpetual Motion Films/Non-Fiction Films; produced and directed by Monte Markam and Adam Friedman)

Beauty and the Beast. Walt Disney. Burbank, Calif.: Buena Vista Home Video.

Bedknobs and Broomsticks. Walt Disney. Burbank, Calif.: Buena Vista Home Video.

Caplan, Michael, and Eugene Burger. *Eugene Goes Biazarre.* Chicago: 1990.

Fantasia. Walt Disney. Burbank, Calif.: Buena Vista Home Video.

The Hobbit. Made-for-TV Animated Movie. Rankin/Bass Productions: 1977.

Lion King, The. Walt Disney. Burbank, Calif.: Buena Vista Home Video.

Little Mermaid, The. Walt Disney. Burbank, Calif.: Buena Vista Home Video.

Mary Poppins. Walt Disney. Burbank, Calif.: Buena Vista Home Video.

Pinocchio. Walt Disney. Burbank, Calif.: Buena Vista Home Video.

Return of Jafar, The. Walt Disney. Direct-to-video. Burbank, Calif.: Buena Vista Home Video.

Snow White and the Seven Dwarfs. Walt Disney. Burbank, Calif.: Buena Vista Home Video.

Sword in the Stone, The. Walt Disney. Burbank, CA: Buena Vista Home Video.

Press Kits

Disney's Beauty and the Beast: A New Musical. Broadway production kit prepared by Boneau/Bryan-Brown, New York, March 1994.

EFX. Warren Cowan & Associates, 1995.

Excalibur Hotel/Casino, 1995.

Faust. Randy Newman's musical. La Jolla Playhouse, 1995.

MGM Grand Hotel, Casino & Theme Park, 1995.

Mighty Morphin Power Rangers. Saban Entertainment

Theses on Compuserve

Harris, Elree Irene, Ph.D. *"The Wounded Angel": The Lilith Myth in Nineteenth and Twentieth-Century British Literature.* 1986. The University of Utah. From *Dissertation Abstracts International. Volume 47/08-A, p. 3047.* As described on CompuServe, copyright University Microfilms International.

America Online

"The Tempest"
"Gulliver's Travels: Glossary"
"Gulliver's Travels: Chapter VII"
"William Shakespeare: The Author and His Times"
"Macbeth: Glossary"
"Richard III"
"The Tempest"

"The Tempest: Lines 58–215"
"Othello"
"Don Quixote" (excerpts, "The Plot," "Dulcinea" and "Chapters 30–41")
"Old Testament: David"
"Doctor Faustus: The Faust Legend and Marlowe"
"The Hobbit & The Lord of the Rings: Gandalf"
"The Lord of the Rings: Book II, Chapters 1–5"
"Arthur Miller: The Author and His Times"
"The Crucible"
"Divine Comedy: The Inferno: Wall of Dis"
"Divine Comedy: The Inferno: An Overview of Events"
"Divine Comedy: The Inferno: Canto XX"

Everyman's Encyclopedia
(copyright 1978 J.M. Dent & Sons, Ltd.)

"Bekker, Balthazar."
"Caduceus."
"Circaea."
"Colchis."
"Dobu."
"Druid."
"Enchanter's Nightshade."
Jarman, A.O.H. *The Legend of Merlin.* 1960.
Loomis, R.S. *Arthurian Literature in the Middle Ages.* 1959.
"Melrose."
"Merlin."
"Nightshade."
"Pemba."
Piggott, *The Druids.* 1975.
Spence, L. *The Origins and History of Druidism.* 1971.
Wright, D. *Druidism, the Ancient Faith of Britain.* 1974.

Lectures, Exhibitions and Interviews

Blair, Lawrence, Ph.D. "The Mysticism, Magic and Creativity of Indonesia." At sea onboard the *Seabourn Spirit,* Seabourn Cruise Lines, in Makassar Strait, February 9, 1994.

Blair, Lorne. "Java, Land of Strange Powers." At sea onboard the SS *Rotterdam,* Holland America Line, in Java Sea, February 28, 1995.

Luck, Adrian. Private consultation/interview with Indonesian expert on board Seabourn Spirit, January 26, 1994.

Sacred Arts of Haitian Vodou. Exhibition at UCLA Fowler Museum of Cultural History. Donald J. Cosentino and Marilyn Houlberg, curators. October 15, 1995–June 16, 1996.

INDEX

The main A–to–Z entries are indicated by **boldface** page references.
Illustrations are indicated by *italic* page references.

A

Aaron's rod **1**, 7, 216, *See also* divining rod; wand
Abaris (wizard) 178
Abba, Rabbi 116
Abimech (magician) 186
Abimelec (magician) 186
ablanathanalba 1
Abognazar, Rabbi (Aben Ezra) 118
aboriginal rock paintings *197, 198*
abracadabra **1–2**, *See also* hocus pocus
Abraham the Jew 185–187
Abra-Melin the Mage (or Abramelin) 185–187
Abraxas (Gnostic god) **2–3**, *2*
"Acrasia" (enchantress in *Faerie Queen*) **3**
Addams Family, The (television) 203
Adventures of Sir Galahad (film) 73
Adventures of Sir Lancelot, The (television) 203
Ady, Thomas 103
African magic *180*
    medicine men and 84, 137
    voodoo in 212–213, 221
    witch doctors and 219–220
    zombies in 230
AGLA (cabalist word) **3**
Agonaces (sorcerer) 230
Agricola, Georg 53
Agrippa, Heinrich Cornelius **3–4**, *3*, 69
    De Occulta Philosophia 49
    followers and teachers of 46, 209, 218
agrippa (grimoire style) **3**
"Ahmed, Prince" (*Arabian Nights* character) **4**
Aix–en–Provence nuns 88
Akasa *See* alchemy; alkahest
Alacaon (magician) 186
Aladdin (film) 73
Aladdin, Jr. (musical) 144
"Aladdin and the Wonderful Lamp" (Oriental tale) **4**, *See also Arabian Nights; Chin-Chin; Chris and the Wonderful Lamp*
Alceste (opera) 157
Alchemist, The (film) 73
Alchemist, The (play by Jonson) **4**, 26
alchemy **4–6**, *See also* philosopher's stone
    alkahest in 6
    caduceus in 24
    Elements of 63
    Elixir of Life quest 63–64

homunculus in 91, 103
Inquisition and 171
practioners of 24–25, 84–85, 98–99, 127, 187–188, 189
"Alcina" (fictional enchantress) **6**
Alexander IV, Pope (r. 1258) 108
Alexander V, Pope (r. 1409–10) 109
Alexander VI, Pope 40, 109
Alexander the Great 29, 56, 173
    grimoires and 95
    palmistry and 170
Alexander the Paphlagonian **6**
Alias Nick Beal (film) 73
Alibeck the Egyptian 95
"Alice Brand" (Scott) **6**
alkahest **6**, *See also* alchemy
Allen, Thomas 116
Alleyn, Edward 54–55
All Hallow's Eve 97, 185
All That Money Can Buy (film) 73
alphabets **6–7**, *7*, *See also* angelic alphabet; Enochian magic, alphabet of; hieroglyphics
    correspondences of 40, 116
    magic squares and 130
    numerology and 155
    runes 183–184
Alrunes (mythical sorceress) **7**
Amahl and the Night Visitors (opera) 157
American Society of Dowsers 57
Ammon, oracle of Jupiter at 165
amulets **7–8**, *See also* charms; relics; talismans
    against evil eyes 66, 67
    in Greco-Roman magic 93
    inscriptions on 1–3, 172
    Lee-penny 202
    mummies and 60
    plants used for 58, 133
    scarabs 189
    Seal of Solomon 190
    voodoo and 213
    zemi 227
"Ancient One " (*Strange Tales* wizard) 35–36
Andreae, Johann Valentin 183
Androclos (Greek prince) 64
Angel Heart (film) 73
angelic alphabet **8–9**, 47, 116–117, *See also* Enochian magic
Ani, "Royal Scribe of Thebes" 20
animals **9**, *See also* cats; familiars
    Devil as a goat 19, *122*
    Druid magic and 58
    voodoo and 212, 213
    witchcraft and 221
    in zodiac 227
Anjou, Duke of 181

Ank-f-n-Knonsu (wizard-priest) 40
Anthony, Francis 5
Antony of Prague (later Antony the Bohemian) 186
Apollo, oracles of 165, *See also* Delphi, oracle of Apollo at
Apollonius Niger 9
Apollonius of Tyana **9**, *9*, 99
Apostles of Jesus 112–113, *See also* Bible
    exorcism by 115
    Simon Magus and 193–194
    sons of Sceva and 64–65
Apuleius, Lucius **9–10**
Aquarius, sign of 229, *See also* astrology; horoscope
Aquila, Gaius Julius 65
Aquinas, St. Thomas **10**
    Ars Notoria and 11
    Canon Episcopi and 26
    Lemegeton: The Lesser Key of Solomon and 122
    ligature belief of 123
Arabian Adventure (film) 73
Arabian Knight (film) 73
Arabian Nights (Persian tales) **10**, 95, *See also* "Aladdin and the Wonderful Lamp"
Arawak tribe of Jamaica 21, 227
"Archimago" (*Faerie Queen* wizard) **10**, 68
Argenson, Antoine René de Voyer d', marquis de Palmy 117
"Ariel" (*Tempest* spirit) **10**
Aries, sign of 227, *See also* astrology; horoscope
Arioso, Ludovico 166
Aristotle 10, 104, 170, 189
Arneson, Dave 58
Arnold of Villanova 5, 103
Arnuphis (Egyptian wizard) 61
Ars Notoria (occult book) 9, **11**, 124
Artemidorus (A.D. 2nd c.) 93
Artephius (sorcerer) **11**
arthame (mystical knife) 129, *See also* kris
Arthour and of Merlin, Of (poem) **11**
Arthur, King **11–12**, *12, 13, See also* Arthurian legend
Arthurian legend
    in books 20, 37–39, 42–43, 68, 88–90, 156–157, 173
    Camelot in 25
    characters in 11–13, 30, 120–121, 138–139, 153, 212
    in comic books 36–37
    Dolorous Stroke in 56

Excalibur in 66
    in films 73, 75, 76, 77–78, 80
    in musicals 114, 144–145, 146, 149
    in operas 161–162
    in plays 179
    in poems 11, 21, 23, 49, 106, 141–143, 183
    in television 203, 205
    Vulgate Cycle 214
Artorius (Briton general) 11
Ascletarion (sorcerer) 94–95
Ashmole, Elias 5, 9
Ashurbanipal, King of Nineveh 12
Asmeodeus, King 196
Assyrian magic **12–13**, *See also* Chaldeans; Cham-Zoroaster
    astrology and 229
    Lilith in 124
astrology **13–14**, *13*, *See also* horoscope; zodiac
    animals in 9, 227–229
    Doctrine of Signatures and 56
    Kabalah and 116
    magical operations and 186–187
    magic circles and squares in 130–131
    medicine's use of 85, 86
    practitioners of 99, 124, 153–155, 175, 183
augury 9, 51, 58
Augustine, St. 99
Autumn Equinox (festival) 58, 185
Avalon *See* Arthurian legend; Camelot
Avalon, Queen of *See* Arthurian legend; le Fay, Morgan
Aymar of Dauphiné, Jacques 53

B

"Baba Yaga" (Russian folklore witch) **15**
Babylonia, magic of *See* Assyrian magic; Chaldeans
Bacis (sage of Boeotia) 92
Bacon, Francis **15**, 39
Bacon, Roger **15**, 171
    Key of Solomon and 117
    tales based on 87
Balaam (Jewish wizard) 115
ballets **15–18**, *See also specific ballets*
bao **18**, *197*, *See also* ekwele; hakata
Baphomet (Goat of Mendes) *122*
Barchusen, Johann Conrad 5
Bar-jesus (sorcerer) 115